The Myth of American Individualism

The Myth of
American Individualism

THE PROTESTANT ORIGINS
OF AMERICAN POLITICAL
THOUGHT

• *BARRY ALAN SHAIN* •

PRINCETON UNIVERSITY PRESS

PRINCETON, NEW JERSEY

Library of Congress Cataloging-in-Publication Data

Shain, Barry Alan, 1950–
The myth of American individualism : the Protestant origins of American political thought /
Barry Alan Shain.
p. cm.
Includes bibliographical references and index.
ISBN 0-691-03382-X
ISBN 0-691-02912-1 (pbk.)
1. Political science—United States—History—18th century.   2. Individualism—
United States—History—18th century.   3. Common good—History—18th century.
4. Community—History—18th century.
I. Title.
JA84.U5S46   1994
320.5'12'097309033—dc20   94-158265

This book has been composed in Sabon

Princeton University Press books are printed on acid-free paper and meet the guidelines for
permanence and durability of the Commitee on Production Guidelines for Book
Longevity of the Council on Library Resources

Third printing, and first paperback printing, with corrections, 1996

Printed in the United States of America by Princeton Academic Press

3 5 7 9 10 8 6 4

• FOR MY MOTHER AND FATHER •

WITH LOVE AND GRATITUDE FOR ALL

THEY HAVE SACRIFICED FOR ME

• CONTENTS •

• *A C K N O W L E D G M E N T S* •

THE FRUITS of most scholarly endeavors belong only partly to the author, while their faults are entirely his or hers alone. This book is no different. In writing it, I have been aided, guided, and supported by so many unselfish friends, family members, and colleagues that, unquestionably, this final product is not fair value for all they have given me.

Most especially, I give heartfelt thanks to my wife, Carolyn Nagase Shain, who, even when attending to her own academic career and the demands of raising our daughter, Susan, has always given freely of herself. To the extent that this book is written in comprehensible English, it is the result of her labors. But most of all, it is because of her enormous patience and moral support that I owe her my thanks and love.

I extend my gratitude to Joseph Hamburger who, because of his deep and keen understanding of Western political philosophy, has forced me to think and write more crisply about early American political thought. Not only has he always been available to discuss my work with me and offer his insights but, possibly more importantly, he has provided encouragement and guidance on a wide range of concerns. In effect, he has nurtured me in a fatherly way, and for that I must publicly thank him.

Rogers Smith read and copiously marked up (with much-appreciated illustrations) various incarnations of the manuscript. His clear and incisive ideas helped shape the project and guided me away from polemics that only would have distracted the reader. And in spite of sharp differences in our normative commitments, he has always been a loyal friend.

David Mayhew provided seminal guidance in the development of this book. It was he who initially encouraged me to take on a project this broad in scope. All political theorists should have a scholar of empirical politics read their manuscripts because of the demanding scrutiny that will be brought to bear. This especially was the case with Professor Mayhew, who never failed to provide lucid and trenchant criticisms that always proved telling.

Thanks are similarly due to Philip Siegelman. He introduced me to political theory, to the life of a scholar and teacher, and served as an exemplar whose equal I rarely have met. Most importantly, he helped me focus my intellectual energies while constantly reminding me to challenge myself.

Two men I met only after several years of correspondence must be acknowledged for their assistance. In phone conversations and letters, Forrest McDonald and Donald Lutz made available to me their rich understanding of 18th-century America. If I have captured correctly its spirit, that is in no small part due to their repeated instruction. Additionally, I wish to recognize the work of Ronald Peters and John P. Roche; their forceful defense of the majoritarian character of 18th-century American political thought helped condition my initial thinking. Indeed, much of what I have argued they intimated years ago.

There are still others whom I wish to acknowledge for their unselfish assistance in helping me develop the arguments advanced in this book. I thank Peter Berkowitz, a most trusted friend, incisive critic, and partner in many a heated discussion where I have tried (unsuccessfully, I might add) to educate him concerning the deeper truths of political philosophy. I still have much to learn from this truly unusual individual. I also want to thank Laura Scalia for her friendship, our long and edifying debates, and her thoughtful criticism of my written work. Both are fellow students of modern political thought and faithful friends whose judgment I value highly. More recently, Joseph Wagner, Robert Kraynak, Douglas Macdonald, and Stanley Brubaker, in frequent and useful conversations, have helped me clarify my thinking on numerous points addressed in this book.

Thanks are due to others who read my manuscript, or some portion of it, and offered needed criticism. Each possesses expertise of a singular caliber. They are David Brion Davis, Harry Stout, John Demos, Steven Skowronek, Pauline Maier, Akhil Amar, Bill Pencak, Jon Butler, James Ceaser, Bruce Kuklick, Jeremy Rabkin, Steve Macedo, Chris Grasso, and particularly, Steven B. Smith and William C. Dennis, who, during frequent conversations and readings of the text, each gave much more than I am able to acknowledge here. I also wish to thank two anonymous reviewers of this manuscript, and Edward Countryman and Peter Onuf, for their insightful criticism. I have attempted to respond to their concerns and I am confident that the book is stronger as a result.

I am grateful to my department chair, Michael Johnston, for having arranged release time from teaching, and the administration at Colgate University for having granted it and for supplying me with two research assistants, John Holzworth and Brenda Johnson, whose aid I appreciate. Thanks are certainly due to my editors, Ann Himmelberger Wald, whose every suggestion has noticeably improved "our" book, and Jane Lincoln Taylor, for her remarkable patience, care, verbal grace, and perseverance.

Several individuals and organizations have supported the writing of this book. I am grateful to the Institute of Humane Studies, under the direction of Leonard Liggio, which provided financial support for my exploratory work on American thought. The bulk of my research was generously and patiently supported by the Lynn and Harry Bradley Foundation. I greatly appreciate the freedom allowed me and the assistance offered by the Board of Directors and the principal officers of that foundation, Michael S. Joyce and Hillel Fradkin, as well as that of Irving Kristol, who, in spite of our disagreements, encouraged me and most graciously intervened on my behalf. In addition, I am grateful to Antony T. Sullivan, the Board of Directors of the Earhart Foundation, and the Research Council of Colgate University for their summer grants, which made it feasible for me to conduct part of my research at the British Museum Library.

Above all, I wish to recognize the generous support of the National Endowment for the Humanities, and the Board of Directors and the Executive Director, James Piereson, of the John M. Olin Foundation. Their assistance made possible extensive and lengthy revisions of the manuscript and its timely completion. I thank all these organizations for their generous support and hope that my work, at least in part, merits it.

Finally, I thank my parents, to whom I dedicate this book, for having stood by me all these years and given me the confidence with which to finish it. I am indeed humbled by all to whom I owe so much.

Colonial historians during the past twenty years have demonstrated that America was not born free, rich, and modern. By looking closely at the details of ordinary life, they have transformed our conception of the American past and made salient the strength of traditional mores among the common people.

—Joyce Appleby, *Capitalism and a New Social Order*

FOR THOSE unfamiliar with the heated scholarly debates surrounding the era of the American Founding, let me provide a brief synopsis; without such a map, little of the following will make sense. The most contentious debate concerns which of two political philosophies, liberalism or republicanism, best describes the political thinking, moral precepts, political institutions, and long-term aspirations of the Revolutionary and Founding generations (sometimes treated together and at other times separately).[1] This question is the source of an acrimonious debate because the answer is widely believed to have contemporary political implications. As the colonial historian Gordon Wood has noted, "the stakes in these historical arguments about eighteenth-century political culture are very high—they are nothing less than the kind of society we have been, or ought to become."[2] A journalist further explains that at the heart of the raging cultural war between contemporary conservatives and liberals "are competing moral visions of what the Founding Fathers meant by 'ordered liberty': how to

---

[1] The Revolutionary era can conveniently be described as the years 1765–1785, or more inclusively as the years 1760–1790, with the founding of the national institutions having been planned and executed in the years 1786–1790. I will usually use "the Revolutionary era" to describe 1765–1785 and "the late 18th century" or "the Founding era" to descibe the longer period of 1760–1790. I treat the last decade of the century, the beginning of the early national period and of the "greater 19th century," as part of a quite different transitional world. For a similar chronology, see Wiebe, *Segmented Society*, pp. ix–x. Republicanism is generally associated with the years surrounding the Revolution, and most historians now relate the emergence of liberalism to the early national period, 1790–1820. This seems to be a fair assessment.

[2] Wood, "Virtues and Interests," p. 32; see also "Fundamentalists and the Constitution," p. 35, and "Hellfire Politics," p. 29; and Matthews, "Liberalism," p. 1152. Wood's collapse of past and preferred future is a curious commonplace among students of American political thought.

balance individual rights with the social responsibilities on which families and communities depend."[3] As one might expect, each of the two foundational philosophies understood this balance differently and awarded contrasting legitimacies to the immediate needs of the individual and those of the community.[4]

Thus, much of the importance attached to America's foundational vision results from contemporary Americans being, or being thought to be, influenced by the political thinking of the late 18th century.[5] The philosophy believed to have been dominant in shaping the thinking of the earlier era, therefore, has significance as a cultural icon. In some ways, it defines how Americans understand themselves as a historical people, as well as constraining what they might become.

Until the last two decades, there was no such debate—not because the political thought of the late 18th century was without influence in 1950s (and earlier) America,[6] but because there was only one claimant to the role of reigning 18th-century political philosophy: the still-vibrant philosophy of liberal individualism. The proponents of this traditional interpretation argued (and continue to argue) that late 18th-century Americans were advocates of political individualism and thus defended something like the modern concept of individual freedom—freedom to do what one wishes.

The upstart alternative, some historic form of republicanism, was not widely understood as such until it was recently pressed into service by the revisionist scholarship of intellectual and social historians.[7] Those who embrace this newly prominent view of the Founding era hold that America's Revolutionary-era aspirations and commitments were those of a secular leadership and a nominally Christian people who sought fulfillment in overcoming the self, in corporate membership, and in an active political life. More critically, this new historiography has greatly benefited those who wish to legitimate an alternative portrait of America. As one observer recently remarked:

> Over the past twenty years a number of distinguished historians of early America have built up an impressive scholarly edifice designed to house the seductive idea that, once upon a time, Americans were not the materialistic, self-centered seekers of profit and pleasure that we seem to have become in the late twentieth century. . . . perhaps it was inevitable that historians would

---

[3]K. L. Woodward, "Elite, and How to Avoid It"; see also Hunter, *Culture Wars*, p. 50; Rischin, "New York Savants," pp. 289–92; and Lasch, *True and Only Heaven*.

[4]I too will take a side in this debate, but will do so by defending the prominence of an alternative political theory, a reformed-Protestant and communal one.

[5]See Sandoz, *Government of Laws*, p. 106; and Ackerman, *We the People*, p. 5.

[6]For example, see Butterfield, *Whig Interpretation of History*; Hofstadter, *Progressive Historians*; and Shaffer, *Politics of History*.

[7]See Rodgers, "Republicanism," for his incisive account of the development of this school of thought.

discover the roots of another America, where authority was located outside the individual and . . . socialism enjoyed important precedents.[8]

The political implications are obvious, for by destroying the idea of an America of innate individualism, exploitative market relations, and materialism, other political options become imaginable.[9]

After having been introduced in the early 1980s to the revisionist historiography of republicanism, I experienced something approaching an epiphany and began to conduct my research. I expected that republicanism, with its particular intellectual contours, would prove congenial to someone like me, since I had been deeply influenced by the activist democratic aspirations of 1960s radical politics. Republican historiography is a product of the 1960s and 1970s, and projects a bold democratic vision of the Revolutionary era. Thus, after reading the appropriate canon of secondary historical works, I set out to demonstrate that republicanism best describes and explains the aspirations and goals of the Revolutionary and Founding generations.

I did so expecting to recover from the years surrounding the American Revolution a well-articulated public philosophy that emphasized the need for individual sacrifice and the active participation of all citizens in the life of the polity. These ideas are most attractive to secular scholars who are not satisfied with the moral depth of liberal individualism. On a practical level, I believed that modern America's individualistic and materialistic public philosophy lacked the conceptual resources required to confront a broad range of contemporary social, economic, and political problems. I hoped, therefore, that by drawing attention to what I expected to be the republican and communitarian character of our past, truly American alternatives to the present set of individualistic options would become available—not in order that atavistic, two-hundred-year-old, communal political practices and attitudes appropriate for a preindustrial, slave-tolerant society be adopted, but that Americans might remember what they had been as a people and might think more openly about what they could become.[10]

Although I was not disappointed in my search for a communal American past, my endeavor to discover a noble and powerful secular republican one was fruitless. The Revolutionary-era intellectual foundations that I uncovered proved to be less classical or Renaissance republican and more Calvinist (or reformed Protestant) than I had anticipated.[11] Late 18th-cen-

---

[8] J. J. Ellis, review of *The Lost Soul of American Politics*, p. 133.

[9] See Hanson, *Democratic Imagination in America*, pp. 18, 48; and Kloppenberg, "Virtues of Liberalism," p. 33.

[10] See Kirby, "Early American Politics," pp. 837–38.

[11] See Ahlstrom, *Religious History of the American People*, pp. 79–81, for his description of the reformed tradition. Simply put, the reformed tradition is a broad grouping of Calvinist-inspired denominations.

tury Americans proved not to be the idealized, politically active citizens so eloquently defended by Hannah Arendt and her followers.[12] Thus, in spite of the contemporary need for appropriately secular foundational myths, Americans proved to have little interest in forming dialogic communities where life's meaning was gained through political activity. Most were more interested in possessing everlasting life through Christ's freely given grace by serving their religious and geographical communities and their families, and by attending to agricultural matters.

My investigations, however, have not been altogether disappointing. More striking than the absence of a meaningful republican past was the abundant evidence that, in the years 1760–1790, when Americans defined themselves as a separate nation, they truly were not yet dominated by an individualist ideology. This, it turns out, the 1960s and 1970s republican revisionists got exactly right. Contrary to beliefs widely held by the general public and by many scholars (most prominently, political scientists), Americans had demonstrably not founded a new nation "around a pervasive, indeed, almost monolithic commitment to classic liberal ideas" such as individualism.[13] Nor was it true, as David Greenstone claimed in 1987 (and again in 1993), that Revolutionary-era Americans wished to "pursue their individual goals and aspirations in a society dominated by the norm of 'atomistic social freedom.'"[14] Indeed, to the limited degree that such idiosyncratic attitudes existed, they are descriptive of a dozen or so elite nationalists, mostly in the early national period (after 1790). They do not capture the aspirations and goals of most Revolutionary-era Americans as expressed in political sermons and pamphlets, newspaper editorials, magazine articles, diaries, and public documents.

It appears that, based on lived testimony as well, most 18th-century Americans cannot be accurately characterized as predominantly individualistic or, for that matter, classically republican. The vast majority of Americans lived voluntarily in morally demanding agricultural communities shaped by reformed-Protestant social and moral norms. These communities were defined by overlapping circles of family- and community-assisted self-regulation and even self-denial, rather than by individual autonomy or self-defining political activity. (For those who have lived in America's small towns, I imagine this is not an altogether surprising finding.)

I have come to believe that the apologists for each of the dominant explanatory models of late 18th-century American political thought, republicanism and individualism, have exaggerated those models' impor-

---

[12]See Arendt, *On Revolution*, pp. 275–81; Ackerman, *We the People*, p. 206; and for his critical commentary, Pangle, *Spirit of Modern Republicanism*, pp. 28–30, 48–49.

[13]E. C. Ladd, "205 and Going Strong," p. 11.

[14]Greenstone, "Political Culture and American Political Development," pp. 2, 4, 17, and see also *Lincoln Persuasion*; for additional references, see the introduction below.

tance, coherence, hegemony, and institutional strength. Each of these accounts purports to represent too fully late 18th-century American political and social thought.[15] Regrettably, the exaggerated attention shown them by contemporary commentators speaks more to our needs for a usable secular or individualistic past than to the historical needs of a communal, rural, and Protestant people.[16]

In short, the Protestant-inspired character of the primary materials I have consulted and the town histories (written by social historians) I have examined have led me to abandon my hope of showing that 18th-century American political thought was predominantly republican. These same sources, however, have done nothing to weaken my opposition to the claim that individualism, as a body of thought, played an active role in shaping the aspirations of Revolutionary-era Americans. I have become confident that more-powerful influences (though more atavistic and thus less politically useful) on the speech, writing, and practices of the majority of European Americans have been underemphasized. This, I intend to show, is most true of the reformed-Protestant foundation of American social and political thought.[17] As Philip Schaff explained to his distinguished Berlin audience, America was "a land thoroughly Protestant, almost to an extreme, since Protestantism embraces not merely the large majority of the population, but is the source, at the same time, of all its social and political principles."[18] And the 18th-century Americans I have come to know were indeed preponderantly reformed Protestants (either in practice or attitudinally). They were a varied group of rural farmers, highly educated ministers, and judges who held a strained and eclectic Protestant communal vision of the good that defies facile characterization.

More disconcerting, however, than my realization that we are a people enjoying a limited republican inheritance and a more questionable liberal foundation has been my recognition that we are a people without a past. As a people, we have consistently re-created our past. Apparently, we have collectively wished to avoid the acknowledgment of failure. The Revolution is only one example of what I believe may be a more widespread pattern of cultural prevarication.[19] Eighteenth-century American history is not a story of ordered change, but rather a tale of unmet expectations and

---

[15]See Wood, "Hellfire Politics," p. 30; McDonald, *Novus Ordo Seclorum*, p. viii; and Banning, "Quid Transit?" p. 199.

[16]See Appleby, *Liberalism and Republicanism*, p. 15; and Herzog, "Some Questions for Republicans," pp. 487–88.

[17]See Pahl, *Free Will and Political Liberty*, pp. 170–72, who recently has come to comparable conclusions.

[18]Schaff, *America*, p. 214.

[19]There is almost certainly a strong relationship between our unwillingness to recognize that the Revolution in many ways was a failure and the continued obfuscation of the period. How this has occurred and what the consequences of destroying foundational myths might be, however, are much more difficult to know. These concerns are touched on in the afterword.

unplanned transformation. In other instances, I surmise, Americans as a people have failed to adhere to the particular goals of extrapersonal service they have set for themselves. This is surely the case when the vision is the evolving one of the 17th and 18th centuries of serving God and achieving freedom from sin through Christ,[20] and the more secular but short-lived, late 18th-century, elite Revolutionary vision of moral regeneration through political service to the public. It is likely true also of the 19th-century notion of overcoming oneself and nature through service to family, to work, and to community that has only come to be abandoned by prominent contemporary elites in the second half of the 20th century. If what I have discovered of the 18th century holds true for the 19th and 20th centuries, political individualism is not a goal toward which Americans intentionally strove in those centuries, but instead is the unintended end product of multiple failures.

Such creative historical accounting is troubling not only because it has falsely reified individualism into America's chosen political ideology, but because, as a consequence, a long and rich tradition of American political thought has been ignored. What has been largely overlooked is a normative theory of the good political life that is enduring, democratic, and communal. American history has been constantly revised so that it appears that this earlier political vision, with its self-overcoming intentions, never existed, or that as a people we gladly and willingly relinquished it for more individualist alternatives. As Josh Miller has pointed out, the history of American liberalism is not the same as that of American democracy, and it is the latter that has been largely ignored.[21] I suggest that Americans have been misled concerning their democratic and communal inheritance by those who have sought to shape a history that meets the needs of America's more progressive citizens.

America's Protestant, democratic, and communal localism, however, is its most enduring political tradition. To understand American politics and history better, one must explore its role in shaping and limiting the range of political options that were available to political actors in the 19th and 20th centuries.[22] This tradition is not the politically noble and existentially self-creating secular past that I had sought and that continues to be pursued by many republican revisionists. Neither, however, is it illusory. And this authentic and powerful inheritance still resonates with the religious and social beliefs of many working-class Christian Americans. The living

---

[20]See Carden, *Puritan Christianity in America,* p. 221.

[21]See J. Miller, *Rise and Fall of Democracy,* pp. 10–11.

[22]See R. M. Smith, "Beyond Tocqueville, Myrdal, and Hartz," pp. 554–62; and Banning, "Jeffersonian Ideology Revisited," p. 13, who argues that "the Revolutionaries left to their successors a lasting and profound commitment to values and ideas that were not part of a liberal consensus, transmitting to their heirs a more complex political tradition whose rediscovery permits important reinterpretations of American developments and conflicts from the War of 1812 to Watergate."

communal tradition still has something to offer, therefore, to those who are striving to solve some of America's most nagging social and political problems.[23] From various scholarly, practical, and normative vantage points, then, it is a tradition that is worth investigating.

[23]See Wolin, *Presence of the Past,* pp. 81, 191; Ignatieff, *Needs of Strangers,* p. 138; Lienesch, *New Order of the Ages,* p. 214; and Nicgorski, "Significance of the Non-Lockean Heritage," p. 177. In the afterword, I will return to this theme and will discuss the dangers that could accompany a renewed legitimacy and efficacy being attached to our purer democratic and communal traditions.

The Myth of American Individualism

We're not going to understand Puritans, or lynch-mobs, or
fundamentalist anti-textbook movements, or anti-busing
protestors, or American Revolutionary crowds . . . [until
we] move beyond politics, to culture, and values and ideas
. . . [and the often moving Christian] realities of the lives of
ordinary people in early America.

—Jesse Lemisch, "Bailyn Beseiged in His Bunker"

AT THE HEART of my argument is a conceptual mapping; that is, an exploration of the meanings late 18th-century Americans attached to their most
significant political concepts. In the first part of this book, the exploration
is framed by an investigation into the standing enjoyed by one of the most
central of these concepts, the public good. In the second part, my effort to
reconstruct the thought of late 18th-century America is organized around
its most cherished political ideal, liberty. From these investigations of the
meanings of and the relationships among these and other ideas, such as the
self, sin, and slavery, the dominant reformed-Protestant communalism of
late 18th-century Americans slowly emerges.[1]

For Revolutionary-era Americans, the common or public good enjoyed
preeminence over the immediate interests of individuals. Amid the overlapping traditions of discourse that can be teased out of American sermons
and pamphlets, public-centered limitations on the individual's autonomy
or individuality are discoverable. Although each of the traditions of discourse valued the "true" interests of the individual, none can be described
fairly as individualistic in anything like the modern sense of the word.

I discuss the communalist aspects of American local political culture as
chronicled by contemporary social historians, and explore the late 18th-
century American understanding of the self. In both instances, I offer further evidence that Americans awarded the public's needs preeminence over
the immediate ones of discrete individuals. Local communities catered little
to the particular wants of individuals, and the autonomous self was
thought to be at the core of human sinfulness. For Revolutionary-era

---

[1] See D. Miller, "Resurgence of Political Theory," p. 426; and Herzog, review of *Transforming Political Discourse*, p. 143, in which he asks if there are "any takers" to Ball's
challenge to create a theoretically informed conceptual history.

Americans, that self was neither an ultimate ethical category nor a center of moral worth.

The American concept of liberty, which I explore in depth in the second section, did not describe autonomous individual freedom or self-expression as these terms are generally understood today. There were as many as eight kinds of liberty—natural, familial, prescriptive, political, spiritual, civil, philosophical, and individualistic. In all but the last of these various senses, liberty characterized a voluntary submission to a life of righteousness that accorded with objective moral standards as understood by family, by congregation, and by local communal institutions. Only the last sense of liberty, then, looked forward to 19th-century individualism.

I also discuss the 18th-century American understanding of slavery, which, because it was then understood to be liberty's antipode, helped shape the contours of the American conception of liberty. Surprisingly, however, slavery understood as chattel enslavement was not among those meanings most frequently encountered in Revolutionary-era political sermons and pamphlets. In them, the inability or unwillingness to be strictly self-governing is what defined a slave. By closely examining Americans' printed thoughts and surveying current research on their social lives, one comes to know an America whose vision of the good—its core understanding of human flourishing and how it is socially and politically best achieved—was reformed Protestant and communal, rather than secular and individualistic.

ON STUDYING 18TH-CENTURY AMERICAN POLITICAL THEORY

Even if I am successful in persuading the reader that late 18th-century Americans (like some of their rural descendants) really did defend a reformed-Protestant, communal theory of the good, and were not individualists, a cynic might still ask, "Who cares?"[2] My answer would be that in carrying out this study, my assumption has been that what a people understands the good life to be is formative in shaping its ethical and political horizons, institutions, and culture.[3] Moreover, in a nation where contending conceptions of its foundational thought are used to provide legitimacy for present-day political alternatives,[4] getting the late 18th-century story right should be a necessity.

[2]This was a response offered by one of the readers of the manuscript of this book.

[3]See Tocqueville, *Democracy in America* (1835), 1:13, who claimed that in all nations "the circumstances which accompanied their birth and contributed to their rise affect the whole term of their being."

[4]See E. S. Morgan, "Popular Fiction," p. 27, who writes that "the American past impinges on the present in a way that can scarcely be matched in countries where the government is not obliged to justify its actions by reference to a document two centuries old." And at least as important to contemporary debates as correctly representing foundational thought on political institutions is determining if the foundational vision was essentially Protestant, or secular and Enlightenment. The terms of contemporary debate on a range of contentious social

Take, for example, a recent attempt by a prominent thinker to use the political thought of late 18th-century Americans for contemporary political or cultural ends, which fails to get the story right. In *We the People: Foundations,* in spite of his claim that he has constructed a narrative that is true to the historical facts,[5] Bruce Ackerman says that the federal Constitution was established with the broad support of the great majority of Americans.[6] He makes this assertion without providing historical substantiation; it is unlikely that any could be provided.[7] I suspect that his willingness to force his argument in this manner stems from his desire to provide a legitimating foundation for his republican vision of an America in which citizens are self-defining members of a dialogic community. His political goals apparently necessitated that he overlook certain inconvenient historical conditions.[8] Only works that treat the historical record with respect can hinder such political proselytizing from being given an overly generous public hearing. If for no other reason, then, works that provide persuasive evidence that they do in fact get the story right are of value.[9] They demand that all who wish to defend contemporary political visions either forgo legitimating them through appeals to foundational history, or pursue political ends that are consistent with the established historical record.

Even in a work committed to historical accuracy the whole story cannot be told; the author must, by necessity, be selective. I expect that some readers, especially professional historians, will be dissatisfied with my historiography, for I offer here a static intellectual portrait or mapping of selected late 18th-century American political concepts. Instead of trying to

---

and political issues might well be affected by a depiction of the Founding different from that provided by the two dominant secular paradigms. In particular, the recent turn of liberal theorists to historical legitimation accentuates this debate. See Neal and Paris, "Liberalism," p. 432; and cf. Herzog, "Some Questions," p. 475.

[5] See Ackerman, *We the People,* pp. 5, 22, 46–49, 91–92.

[6] See ibid., pp. 10, 41, 74, 88, 211, 242.

[7] See McDonald, *E Pluribus Unum,* p. 319, who estimates that in a nation of 4,000,000 "some 480,000 of the roughly 640,000 adult males in the country would not participate [in sending delegates to the ratifying conventions]—some of them because of being disenfranchised by law, the vast majority because it was simply too much trouble"; and consider "The Address and Reasons of the Dissent of the Minority of the Convention of Pennsylvania," in *Anti-Federalist,* p. 206, where it is reported that "we find that of upwards of *seventy thousand* freemen who are intitled to vote in Pennsylvania, the whole convention has been elected by about *thirteen thousand* voters." See also E. S. Morgan, "Popular Fiction," p. 26, and "Power to the People," p. 28, where he describes that in the one instance where the Constitution was put to a popular referendum, it was defeated 2,711 to 239; and J. J. Ellis, "Persistence of Antifederalism after 1789," p. 297, who writes that "it is undeniable that the Constitution was not very popular."

[8] See the reviews by Berkowitz and Holt of *We the People;* Holt finds that "facts that get in the way are discarded [and] often not even sought out."

[9] See Pocock, "Virtue and Commerce," p. 134, who additionally argues that "the eighteenth-century quarrel between virtue and commerce, citizen and government, republic and empire was still going on in the twentieth century, and that historiography and political philosophy were still much involved in it. For this reason, it may be important to get the historical story straight."

describe and understand fully the dynamics of change effecting them, I use them to highlight Americans' vision of human flourishing and how it was to be achieved in group life rather than individually. Keeping in mind present-day debates whereby foundational authenticity is used to legitimate various political and social alternatives, I focus more on discovering the essence or ground of Revolutionary-era American political thought than on detailing all of its complexity. This demands, however, that I emphasize the distinctiveness of particular streams of thought that are treated singularly today but were not necessarily treated thus in Revolutionary America, and that I do not stress their changing character as they move across the late 18th-century intellectual and social landscape.

I am not seeking to avoid historical complexity. Indeed, when my subject demands specificity I do not hesitate to offer it, as, for example, in my exploration of the varying meanings of liberty available to Revolutionary-era Americans. But in other instances, the question I most want to answer—what did and did not form the essential core of Americans' understanding of the good—precludes a full exploration of the evolution of all aspects of late 18th-century thought. This is most evident in my treatment of American Protestantism; my interest here is instrumental. I explore it not for its intrinsic importance, but in order to demonstrate that Revolutionary-era American political thought was, above all, Protestant inspired. I do not demean the importance of American Protestantism as a subject of inquiry in its own right; rather, I leave the exploration of it and its contentious and evolving character to others.

Additionally, I have not intended to provide an all-encompassing historical narrative of the Revolutionary era, nor to explain how America changed from being relatively communal in the 18th century to being far more individualistic in the 19th century. Both these projects are important ones, but they are not mine. I offer my intellectual map with its Protestant essence, fully cognizant that many of the Revolutionary-era positions I describe would in a short time be transformed and would then contribute to the weakening of Americans' Protestant communalism. Indeed, I devote a chapter to exploring these often perverse transformations. But again, I happily leave it to others to detail and systematically explain these developments. Finally, since my research depends on printed materials, my sample necessarily has a Northern bias. The textual evidence I have gathered from the Middle and Southern colonies suggests, however, that this should not be seen as a significant distortion. In works from these other regions, the concepts used and the meanings assigned differ little from those present in New England materials.

The primary sources I consulted include "occasional" sermons (primarily from New England, but from other colonies and states as well), civic orations and college commencement addresses, newspaper editorials, political pamphlets, formal European works in political philosophy (in order to provide the intellectual setting in which 18th-century Americans wrote, thought, prayed, and lived), British dictionaries, and various local, state, and national public statements and documents, such as the national Proc-lamations for Days of Humiliation and Fasting and the Declaration of Independence.

Most important among the occasional sermons,[10] and the ones on which I have drawn heavily, are the election sermons of New England. These sermons were delivered before a state's legislature (the Massachusetts Gen-eral Court, the Connecticut General Assembly) at the opening of each year's legislative session. Usually in attendance were the governor, the members of the upper and lower legislative houses, and various notables and dignitaries. Being asked to deliver one was a great honor because of those in attendance, and because the sermons were nearly always pub-lished and widely distributed and read. A presenter became part of a pub-lic ceremony with a rich tradition; for example, in Massachusetts, the state with the longest continuous practice, these annual sermons were delivered from 1634 to 1884.[11]

That these sermons were prestigious, were given with great pomp and circumstance, were printed and widely distributed, and were sometimes even reprinted is important. The minister delivering one became (if he was not already) "a leading actor in a major event of the colony's social, politi-cal, and religious life."[12] But what makes these sermons so valuable to a political theorist derives from the unusually rich content of the sermons themselves. Unlike the dry and legalistic concerns of most political pam-phlets, the questions these sermons usually addressed were those of "the role of God in men's affairs, the nature of man, the origin and purposes of government"—in short, the nature of the good.[13] Along with other occa-sional sermons, some commencement lectures, and numerous newspaper editorials, they offer us a rare look at the ethical, social, and normative views of late 18th-century Americans. Political pamphlets, with their more pragmatic concerns, tend to provide much sparser fare. In fact, the election sermons collectively offer us something close to an 18th-century American political-theory text.

My intention has been to capture, as best I can, commonly held Ameri-can understandings of the political good, and Americans' ancillary beliefs about the nature of man and the appropriate goals of a polity. Therefore my focus has not been on the true elite, but rather on the group that wrote most of these materials. Donald Lutz characterizes this population as the

[10]These sermons were not preached in observance of the Sabbath. Instead, most were deliv-ered on a regular basis on an occasion such as the seating of a legislature, days of thanksgiv-ing or contrition, or the gathering of the militia, events that usually invited a political focus.

[11]Connecticut's were delivered between 1674 and 1830, New Hampshire's between 1784 and 1861, and Vermont's between 1777 and 1858. There was no tradition of delivering election sermons in either Rhode Island or Maine.

[12]Kerr, "Character of Political Sermons," p. 38.

[13]Counts, "Political Views," p. 1.

political class. I have focused on it rather than on the true elite for the reasons that he and Michael Lienesch thoughtfully outline.[14]

They suggest that this relatively large population of articulate Americans offers us a window not only on the minds of the true elite, but also on those of more common Americans with whom the political class intimately lived. In effect, they formed a social, religious, and political bridge between the true elite who populate our history books and the obscure farmer-citizens of 18th-century America. The orations and written works of the political class can help inform our understanding of the critically important language of seminal public documents like the Declaration of Independence and the constitutions, which were penned by the great elite. The writings of this broad political class, rather than those of the great elite, are likely to reflect more accurately the thoughts of the common men and women of America.[15] The norms and sensibilities of the political class are most likely our closest approximation to a public sounding capable of clarifying the political thought of most late 18th-century Americans.

This political class includes state and local public officials, college presidents, the majority of those attending important political conventions and congresses, members of state legislatures and various national ones, prominent lawyers, state and local jurists, and the most eminent ministers (e.g., those invited to give election sermons, those chosen to be the chaplain for Congress, or those with well-respected ministries). These men were almost certainly among the best-educated Americans, even if not the most politically powerful. (The only other group of Americans that contained men of comparable educational and intellectual achievement were the handful of truly elite. On this list, one would certainly wish to see Jefferson, Adams, Jay, Rush, Hamilton, Madison, Washington, Franklin, and others with established national and international reputations.) Although I have considered numerous other sources, many of which were anonymously written, authors from this population form the core constituency of what I take to be Lutz's political class, and it is on them and their sermons and essays that I ground much of my argument.

By relying on the works of men in this relatively large but still not fully representative political class, I cannot be certain that I have successfully grasped the most widely held normative political beliefs of the Revolution-

[14]See Lutz, *Preface to American Political Theory*, p. 106; and Lienesch, *New Order of the Ages*, pp. 9–11, for his graceful defense of situating the study of political theory in "public discussion and debate."

[15]Chief Justice John Marshall held that "the intention of the instrument must prevail; that this intention must be collected from its words; [and] that its words are to be understood in that sense in which they are generally used by those for whom the instrument was intended." Cited by Hutson, "Creation of the Constitution," p. 3. See also Blackstone, *Commentaries*, 1:59–60, who writes that "words are generally to be understood in their usual and most known signification; not so much regarding the propriety of grammar, as their general and popular use."

ary and Founding eras. I can, however, be confident that I have portrayed a powerful but often ignored current of Protestant communal thought in late 18th-century America.[16] Admittedly, though, there were other divergent streams of thought present in 18th-century America. Researchers may legitimately question whether the communal political theory described below was a common possession of most Americans. Some may even argue that the reformed-Protestant and communal vision of the good I have described was the idiosyncratic possession of a small, self-selected population of religious zealots. Furthermore, they might maintain that, in reality, a liberal or individualistic theory of the good more accurately describes the political thought of most late 18th-century Americans. If this can be demonstrated, then the political theory explored below must be understood to be an important (rather than the principal) late 18th-century understanding of the good.

But to make their case persuasively, these scholars must do more than provide evidence extracted from private letters exchanged among a few members of the national elite, some of whom had been in America for a very short time. They must do more than note that the communal portrait painted below is unable to provide apodictic certainty of its having been overwhelmingly accepted. For an individualistic portrait to be considered the dominant understanding of the period, critics must demonstrate that it was more widely embraced than the communal one presented below. But far too often the claim that Revolutionary America was a land of individualism has been accepted on faith or on its normative appeal, not on the strength of persuasive evidence. A change would be most welcome.

THE MYTH OF AMERICAN INDIVIDUALISM: A STRAW MAN?

Let me aid such challengers by clarifying why I have chosen to draw attention in the book's title to the myth of American individualism rather than what might seem a more obvious choice, the myth of liberalism. In part, it is because liberalism is a more highly contested term and much more difficult to pin down. Here, I follow George Kateb. He explains that he has used individualism to name the common adversary to communal theories of the good because it "is more accurate, and also because 'liberalism' is by now so frequently and variously used that we cannot be sure what it means in any given case."[17] It is also out of deference to liberal theorists such as Charles Larmore, who defend a "neutral" version of liberalism that does not take sides in the conflict between individualism and communalism.[18] I do so, however, without accepting their contention (I am unper-

---

[16] See Botein, "Religious Dimensions," p. 315.
[17] Kateb, "Democratic Individuality," p. 184.
[18] See Larmore, "Political Liberalism," p. 346; MacIntyre, "Privatization of Good," p. 346;

suaded both historically and analytically) or preferring their version of liberalism over the more robust versions defended by the likes of Rogers Smith, Stephen Macedo, and William Galston.[19] Additionally, I find liberal institutionalism in America far more defensible, both normatively and historically, than I do individualism. My argument has been framed against individualism rather than liberalism, then, because I believe it yields a more telling and far stronger case.

This raises the specter, however, that by arguing against American individualism I have gone after the weak link of American liberalism and have created a straw man to attack. Indeed, there are historians who believe that a defense of Revolutionary-era individualism is so untenable that they have accused me of having fabricated it so that I might easily vanquish it. This charge is unfounded, for there are well-regarded scholars who argue that 18th-century America was individualistic. (I will return to this question.) But such a charge, even if it were true, would fail to acknowledge the critical impact of public opinion on political processes, and thus the important role public history serves in a nation like the United States.[20] Widely accepted historical misperceptions, even if not advanced by professional historians, demand scrutiny. And almost all public commentators in contemporary America regularly maintain that "the animating idea of the American Founding was individual liberty," or that "this country's originating ideas were . . . notions of individual autonomy," or that "individualism lies at the very core of American culture."[21] In fact, I am not sure that outside a small group of political theorists, a larger group of historians, and a few republican-inspired law professors one can find a public figure who entertains the possibility that America was not foundationally individualistic. Clearly, that it was not is a message that has not yet been effectively aired by the historians and theorists who have enunciated it.[22]

Political scientists almost uniformly believe that in 1955 Louis Hartz offered the final word on the individualistic nature of American founda-

---

Sandel, *Liberalism and the Limits of Justice*, p. 1; and Sinopoli, "Liberalism and Contested Conceptions of the Good."

[19] See R. M. Smith, *Liberalism and American Constitutional Law*; Macedo, *Liberal Virtues*; and Galston, *Liberal Purposes*. I am convinced that a "neutral" liberalism is not in fact neutral, for it is by necessity destructive of corporate-based theories of the good (as Mill and others well understood), and necessarily evolves into some form of individualism.

[20] See Lacey and Haakonssen, "Introduction," p. 6, and Becker, "What Are Historical Facts?" pp. 338–39, who writes that "whether the general run of people read history books or not, they inevitably picture the past in some fashion of other, and this picture . . . helps to determine their ideas about politics and society."

[21] D. Himmelfarb, "Freedom, Virtue, and the Founding Fathers," p. 117; Jehlen, *American Incarnation*, pp. 3–5; and Bellah et al., *Habits of the Heart*, p. 142; see also Ignatieff, "Strange Attachments," p. 42; and Whitehead, "Dan Quayle Was Right," p. 84, who cites in support of her contention William Galston, a prominent political theorist and domestic-policy advisor to President Bill Clinton.

[22] For reasons discussed in the afterword this could be by intention, and defensibly so.

tional political thought and culture.[23] This body of scholars is the second-largest group studying late 18th-century American political thought, and through teaching and scholarship, it is also able to shape public opinion. For example, Mark Roelofs and his former student Richard Sinopoli continue to praise Hartz for having identified individualism "as the rock upon which all else in American politics was built."[24] Nor is it only less-visible political scientists who continue to tout the virtues of the Hartzian understanding of America's foundational individualism. As Rogers Smith observes, "most political analysts who have directly addressed the topic of American political culture in recent years, such as [Samuel] Huntington, Sacvan Bercovitch, and David Greenstone, have strongly endorsed Hartz's basic view." He adds that many other members of the profession have "been even more emphatic in endorsing Hartz's theory."[25]

If one leaves aside the avowed Hartzian connection, and simply seeks political scientists writing on the Founding era who claim that its residents were enthusiastic individualists, or that at the core of American values is an overarching dedication to individualism, the supply is more abundant.[26] One student of the period explains that the commitment to individualism, to the belief that "government exists for the purpose of permitting that individual to serve his or her own needs and attain personal fulfillment," has "remained essentially constant from the earliest days of the republic to the present." Another concludes that "the goal of the Revolution was [more] to secure [a] people's right to be vicious" than it was to secure the public good.[27] I doubt that many historians understand how widespread

---

[23]See Hartz, *Liberal Tradition in America*, and Rodgers, "Republicanism," pp. 42–43 (draft version), who observes from the perspective of an accomplished historian that "the Hartzian idea of a consensual liberalism was never more than a debating point which hardened into a myth." It is one, however, that is happily alive in most departments of political science. See also R. M. Smith, "Beyond Tocqueville, Myrdal, and Hartz," p. 555, for his long list of prominent political scientists who continue to treat Hartz as authoritative.

[24]Roelofs, "American Political System," p. 326; see also Sinopoli, *Foundations of American Citizenship*, pp. 3–5, and "Liberalism, Republicanism, and the Constitution." Sinopoli was lauded by his peers and was awarded the American Political Science Association's Leo Strauss Award for the best dissertation in political philosophy for 1985–1986.

[25]R. M. Smith, "Embedded Oligarchies," pp. 28–29. However, not all who subscribe to the Hartzian doctrine also defend individualism in the comprehensive sense employed here. For example, Huntington understands individualism to be economic opportunity and he does not argue for the broader sense of the term, either historically or normatively.

[26]See for example, Abbott, *Political Thought in America*, p. 6; Greenstone, "Political Culture and American Political Development," pp. 2–4, 17, and *Lincoln Persuasion;* Kramnick, "Republican Revisionism Revisited," p. 664, and *Republicanism and Bourgeois Radicalism,* pp. 17, 40, 179, 190, 254; Lukes, "Meanings of 'Individualism,'" pp. 60–63; Pangle, *Spirit of Modern Republicanism;* Skidmore, *American Political Thought,* p. 68; Schmitt and Webking, "Revolutionaries, Antifederalists, and Federalists," pp. 210–13; and Vetterli and Bryner, *In Search of the Republic,* p. 79.

[27]Dolbeare, *American Political Thought,* pp. 5–9; and Webking, *American Revolution,* p. 150; see also pp. 125–26.

this perspective is among political scientists, who continue to support the individualistic historiography of Hartz.[28]

Even among historians, there are learned scholars who claim that 18th-century America was individualistic. Some, such as Vernon Parrington, Max Lerner, and Ralph Perry, are retired or deceased.[29] There are many contemporary historians, some of whom are not primarily students of the period, who also find political individualism foundational in America—for example, Yehoshua Arieli, Patrice Higonnet, James Kloppenberg, and James Ward.[30] More significant, however, is the research of several specialists who argue that 18th-century America was individualistic.[31] At least one of them, well read in both intellectual and social history, has recently defended the pervasive existence of 18th-century American individualism.

This highly regarded colonial historian, Jack P. Greene, argues that all the colonies other than Massachusetts and Connecticut were bastions of "social atomism." Their citizens, he finds, were primarily shaped by materialism and individualism and were emerging "liberated individual[s]" concerned with "their own private pursuits of personal and individual happiness." By the middle of the 18th century in New England, its citizens were attending to "the authority of self rather than of the community," and had rejected self-denial as an acceptable standard of personal behavior. They were defending the "capacity of the individual to direct his own existence rather than" insisting on the individual's need for corporate guidance and

---

[28]The lack of communication between them, I believe, helps explain why many historians treat Revolutionary-era individualism as a straw man, while political scientists just as often respond to an attack on it as if it were blasphemous. Satisfying both populations may prove difficult.

[29]See Lerner, *America as a Civilization*, p. 49; R. B. Perry, *Puritanism and Democracy*, p. 146; and Parrington, *Main Currents in American Thought*.

[30]See Arieli, *Individualism and Nationalism in American Ideology*, pp. 106, 241, 319; Curry and Goodheart, "Individualism in Trans-National Context," p. 1; Higonnet, *Sister Republics*, pp. 37, 46; and Kloppenberg, review of *Sister Republics*, p. 195. Ward, *Red, White, and Blue*, p. 231, explains that the individualism he ascribed to Americans "meant the primacy of the individual person, the denial of social restraint, [and] freedom from involvement with others"; see also pp. 257–59. In regard to Higonnet, it should be noted that his remarks are not without equivocation (or confusion). For example, in *Sister Republics*, Higonnet claims that Americans' practice was individualistic but their theory communal (pp. 107–8), while earlier he came to the opposite conclusion (pp. 81–82).

[31]For example, see Bushman, *From Puritan to Yankee*; Grant, *Democracy*; J. P. Greene, *Pursuits of Happiness*; Lemon, *Best Poor Man's Country*, and more recently, "Spatial Order"; and Wolf, *Urban Village*. See also Wall, *Fierce Communion*, pp. 126–52, who, after defending the communal and familial foundations of early 18th-century America, suggests in her afterword that in the second half of the 18th century, individualism replaced communalism. Here, she relies less on her own work, and instead follows the lead of several other well-known historians: Philip Greven, Jay Fliegelman, Jan Lewis, Linda Kerber, and Mary Beth Norton. The historian most prominent on this list by her absence is Joyce Appleby. Although widely taken by political scientists to be a wholesale defender of Hartz, she is in fact far too judicious. Her claims regarding 19th-century American individualism are usually preceded by a warning that such conditions little obtained in pre-1790 America.

oversight. (For evidence of this last allegation, Greene turns to the work of two social psychologists who were describing, in a Weberian ideal fashion, a fantasy of the oppressed, not the actual thought of 18th-century New Englanders.) In New York and New Jersey, citizens were strongly committed "to the tenets of possessive individualism."[32] Greene's view of 18th-century America is unabashedly individualistic.[33]

I do not mean to suggest that individuals in 18th-century America were without important political, social, and economic influence. Surely they possessed such power. Nor am I claiming that Americans evidenced a lack of interest in the true welfare of the individual. To the contrary, I argue that their concern with the "true" needs of the individual urged them to reject a liberal, neutral theory as well as a more aggressive, individualistic theory of the good political life. It is the latter understanding of human flourishing that usually holds that human development is best pursued by freeing the individual from restrictive and intrusive familial, social, religious, and local political intervention.[34] Central governmental officials should, accordingly, actively seek to free the individual from such restrictive intervention while helping, when needed, provide the means to pursue autonomous self-development.[35]

Most Revolutionary-era Americans, however, believed it was the legitimate and necessary role of local religious, familial, social, and governmental forces to limit, reform, and shape the sinful individual. Moreover, it was assumed that these intermediate institutions would have to act restrictively and intrusively (if not coercively), for in no other way would the recalcitrant and naturally deformed human being take on a godly and publicly useful shape.

The important question in describing late 18th-century American political theory, then, is not whether Americans were interested in seeing that

[32]J. P. Greene, *Pursuits of Happiness*, pp. 55, 125, 76, 140; see also pp. 53, 195–96. The vision of America he defends here has little in common with that portrayed in earlier works of his, *All Men Are Created Equal* and *Landon Carter* (pp. 22, 25, 33, 41–43). But in other early essays, such as his 1973 "Uneasy Connection," pp. 56–57, Greene defended individualism's centrality. In the same essay collection, Bernard Bailyn also argued in defense of Revolutionary-era individualism. In the lead essay, "The Central Themes of the American Revolution," p. 28, he finds that "everywhere in America the principle prevailed that in a free community the purpose of institutions is to liberate men, not to confine them."

[33]My intention in highlighting Greene's views is not to challenge his portrait of late 18th-century America; I will address that below. Rather, it is to show that one respected specialist, like many other prominent historians, other well-educated commentators, and the larger public, continues to defend foundational American individualism.

[34]See Abbott, *Political Thought in America*, pp. 3–4; Schapiro, *Liberalism*, pp. 9–10; and Dewey, *Reconstruction in Philosophy*, p. 186.

[35]For a sampling of contemporary theorists who defend an individualist understanding of human flourishing, see Ackerman, *Social Justice in the Liberal State*, pp. 152–55; Gutmann, *Democratic Education*, pp. 30–31; Herzog, *Happy Slaves*, p. 242; R. M. Smith, *Liberalism and American Constitutional Law*, p. 223; Kateb, "Democratic Individuality," p. 188; and Macedo, *Liberal Virtues*, p. 205.

the true needs of the individual were met. Of course they were. Rather, it concerns what kind of relationship between the individual and his or her community was favored and sought. Was it individualistic, believing that human flourishing was best promoted by freeing the individual from the restrictive confines of familial, communal, and religiously imposed traditional limits? Or was it some form of inchoate reformed-Protestant communalism that understood that both individual and communal good can only be obtained by embracing the culture-laden barriers to individual autonomy that are Edmund Burke's beloved little platoons? It was the latter.

On Reading 18th-Century American Political Theory

Most present-day (and many 19th-century) commentators have found that 18th-century Americans were adherents of some kind of liberal or individualistic political philosophy rather than a communal one. But why have well-intentioned scholars, reading much the same materials that I (and other scholars who see America as communalistic) have read, come to such different conclusions?[36] I believe the problem largely results from the way in which what passes for American political-theory texts have been read, misread, and not read.[37] Consider a provocative statement of Donald Lutz. He recently suggested that late 18th-century Americans produced no great texts of political thought, nor any great political theorists.[38] But in arguing this, he may not have gone far enough. In truth, late 18th-century Americans produced no texts dedicated to ethical political theory and no systematic theorists concerned with defending a particular vision of the good.[39] Even their most renowned political work, *The Federalist*, only addressed ethical questions elliptically and surreptitiously.

But in fairness to Lutz, it must be admitted that from Aristotle onward, Western political theory has been concerned with more than what a well-lived human life is to look like when viewed from a collective perspective—that is, theories of the political good. Its practitioners have also addressed questions that are more narrowly political, involving the shape of regimes, their goals, and the political institutions necessary for achieving the regimes' desired ends. In this second sense of political theory, one

[36]It seems inescapable that the history of the Founding period and its historiography must be considered together, if only because authors try to make sense of the seemingly indefensible positions taken by those who defend a different history.

[37]I return to this question in chapter 3.

[38]See Lutz, *Preface to American Political Theory*, pp. 27–34.

[39]See Boorstin, *Genius of American Politics*, p. 66, who is correct in arguing that the Revolutionary era "did not produce in America a single important treatise on political theory," and yet wrong when he concludes from this that it was not a "great age of American political thought." In spite of the lack of any true American texts or authors, important and often unintended changes in Western political thought did emanate from the Revolution and the Founding.

much closer to what we usually think of as political science, Americans in the late 18th century wrote copious (and often tedious) tracts,[40] particularly on their legal disputes with the Crown, which, except for the light they shed on the development of the concept of rights, are without normative theoretical importance. Americans' most important theoretical works moved rapidly from theology to jurisprudence and political science.[41]

This absence of works in late 18th-century America that directly treat ethical political theory helps explain why so many political scientists and public commentators on early America have mischaracterized the political thought of the time as liberal.[42] Two errors in particular have facilitated this outcome. First, some students of the period may have equated an absence of texts defending a particular understanding of the good with a lack of interest in the subject, and this putative void has been then identified, not altogether unfairly, with liberalism.[43] Second, it appears that Americans' readily discoverable interest in regimes and political institutions has been conflated with their much less visible understanding of the good.

The first error, I surmise, results from investigators having embraced exegetical approaches that are inappropriate for 18th-century America. Many political theorists and older intellectual historians were trained to approach their subject principally by reading texts that are considered canonical. When they found little that passes as ethical political theory and nothing at all of stature, they (not surprisingly) declared that America lacked a substantive political theory of the good. Because of liberalism's putative neutrality concerning the good, Americans as psychological hedonists were then described as liberal, either by intention or default.

For comparable reasons, other political theorists may have been compelled to turn to works such as *The Federalist* and to transform them into works of normative political theory.[44] This is not to say that *The Federal-*

---

[40]See ibid., p. 75. Boorstin follows Moses Coit Tyler in describing these works as "a vast morass of technical discussion."

[41]The great exception was the somewhat earlier but towering presence of Jonathan Edwards in philosophy and theology. See Jenson, *America's Theologian.*

[42]This generalization does not apply to all political scientists, many of whom (such as Don Lutz, Rogers Smith, Michael Lienesch, Ronald Peters, and John Roche) have a sophisticated understanding of early American political thought. Nor is it meant to apply to most historians, who, in the last few decades, have more often defended the preeminence of republican theorizing in late 18th-century America.

[43]See Boorstin, *Genius of American Politics,* who defends this proposition tenaciously.

[44]This is most descriptive of some of the followers of the late Leo Strauss. See Wood, "Fundamentalists of the Constitution"; Onuf, "Historians and the Bicentennial"; and Bromwich, "Un-American Mind," p. 30, who in reviewing the posthumously published essays of the late Allan Bloom, one of Strauss's most gifted students, is sharply critical of him. He writes that Bloom, in spite of his willingness to write on American subjects, was curiously uninterested in "American history, American political theory, and American writing generally. He may scorn it, or he may not know it: the effect is the same. Two American sources are mentioned in these essays with some regularity. The first is Tocqueville's book on democ-

ist, for example, is without an ethical teaching (even if it is concealed). Rather, it is to point out that its primary authors were immediately concerned with explaining and defending in these essays a particular set of governmental institutions. As they themselves said, their efforts were those of political scientists, not of philosophers. Yet this work, above all, promulgated a theory of the good. Indeed, it was a revolutionary new theory that informed their support of various political structures.[45]

However, to extract the ethical teaching embedded in *The Federalist* and most other late 18th-century texts, one must be prepared to hunt, uncover, and reconstruct their theory of the good.[46] It effectively is a different activity than the exegesis of focused works of political philosophy, which may demand even greater patience and effort to unlock their far richer teachings. For example, those who criticize Gordon Wood for not having explicated whole texts in his *Creation of the American Republic* demonstrate their lack of understanding of the environment within which students of American political thought work. For the 18th century in particular, studying theoretical works that are not primarily concerned with political institutions is more akin to archaeology than histology—one must sift through large quantities of extraneous matter to find the residues of their normative writings.[47] And when this archaeological path is followed, one finds that a Protestant communal understanding of the good is usually present in normative theoretical works from the period.

But 18th-century Americans were more likely to discuss in print subjects that are best described as political science; scholars have followed suit and

racy, the second is a composite entity called the Founding Fathers. With the latter one can never be sure whether Bloom has in mind the Constitution, the Declaration of Independence, the *Federalist Papers,* or the powerful interpretation of all these documents by Abraham Lincoln. Anyway we are left with two American texts: one of them written by a French intellectual after a visit, the other scarcely meeting the common understanding of a 'text.' " Although this might apply to some "Straussians," many others have added greatly to our understanding of early American political thought. Such men as Martin Diamond, Herbert Storing, and Ralph Lerner readily come to mind.

[45]See Howe, "Political Psychology of *The Federalist,*" pp. 506–7, who disagrees and finds them only to be "masterpieces of special pleading. Accordingly, it is a mistake to try to extract from them a complete political theory."

[46]See Lutz, *Preface to American Political Theory,* for his instructive thoughts on this matter; and Matthews, *Radical Politics of Thomas Jefferson,* pp. 16–17.

[47]More generally, the study of American political thought must be recognized as a field of inquiry that demands specialized knowledge that cannot be acquired by reading in isolation *The Federalist.* And if political theorists are to take an active role in the systematic examination of the essays, speeches, and public documents from which American political thought is drawn, they must work within the limits imposed by the diffuse character of this material. Additionally, they and their colleagues in political science must make a more focused and disciplined commitment to the study of American political thought. See Lutz, *Preface to American Political Theory;* and Abbott, review of *Preface to American Political Theory,* who usefully criticizes Lutz's overly narrow understanding of this area of study while applauding him for demanding that American political theory be researched with the same degree of professionalism found in other areas of political science.

have examined in detail the political pamphlets concerned with such mat-ters.[48] The ethical views of Revolutionary-era America that concern things political, therefore, remain underresearched. And this situation, I suggest, has led to the second problem noted above: the conflation of highly visible liberal theories about regimes and political institutions with much less visible American views of the good. I fear that Americans' salutary and abundant concerns about governmental abuse of power, and how best to provide needed limits on it, has been taken as evidence that they similarly embraced a liberal theory of the good.

Such an association is likely mistaken in two ways. First, it would be wrong to assume that such institutional concerns are only correctly associated with liberal constitutionalism when, in fact, they are issues confronted by ancient and medieval theorists as well.[49] The contested essence of liberalism does not necessarily lie in its strictures regarding institutional arrangements. Rather, it may exist in the normative or ethical belief that "reasonable people tend to differ and disagree about the nature of the good life," and therefore the public must play a limited role in determining the ends to be pursued by individuals.[50]

Second, assuming that the particular institutional arrangements embraced by Americans were truly liberal, it would be wrong to conclude that their theory of the good must likewise be. Americans could have adhered to liberal theories on how to limit central governmental power vis-à-vis the people while continuing to believe that the government, especially at the state and local levels, had been empowered by the people to protect and foster their respective communal visions of human flourishing. It is conceivable that both those who describe America's constitutional (or more precisely, its institutional) arrangements as liberal and those of us who find that their theory of the good was communal are correct.[51] But if this proves true, theories of the good and those of regimes, Plato notwithstanding, may be less tightly linked than is often assumed.

This confusion between political theories of regimes and those of the good, I suspect, is not particular to America, but rather broadly descriptive of contemporary theorizing about the 17th and 18th centuries. Although we have immediate access to typologies of different regimes (for example,

---

[48]See Stourzh, *Alexander Hamilton;* W. P. Adams, *First American Constitutions;* and Sandoz, *Government of Laws,* who represent exceptions to this claim.

[49]See Larmore, "Political Liberalism," p. 340.

[50]Ibid., pp. 339–40. This is a much-debated understanding of liberalism's essence. Others prefer to associate liberalism more strongly with what I call individualism, a particular rather than a neutral understanding of the good, while still others claim that liberalism is only appropriately linked to particular modern governmental institutions. For example, see Dees, "Liberalism in Context," pp. 571–77.

[51]However, as Lutz has persuasively shown in *Popular Consent and Popular Control* and *Origins of American Constitutionalism,* American political institutions are also predominantly derived from Protestant foundations.

monarchy versus republic), we have no vocabulary for describing early modern social and political theories of the good that is comparable to that describing republicanism, Catholic organicism, or liberalism. Is it true, as suggested by Pocock, that Protestant thinkers and peoples produced no social and political theories to fill the void that existed between the efflorescence of Renaissance republicanism in the 16th century and the self-conscious emergence of individualism in the 19th century?[52] It is clear that in the 17th and 18th centuries at least one nation did defend a communal and reformed-Protestant theory of the good. But whether competing visions of the good life from Greece in the fourth century BCE, 13th-century continental Europe, 16th-century Italian city-states, or 19th-century England accurately describe the thought of other Protestant nations in the early modern period is a question I leave for others to answer.

[52]See Pocock, *Machiavellian Moment,* p. 507, who holds that there was no tradition of political discourse available to Americans other than that of "neoclassical politics." See also Mitchell, *Not By Reason Alone,* p. 156, who suggests that much of early modern political theory remained "enchanted within Protestant thought."

PART ONE

Standing: The Public Good, the Individual, and the Community

CONTRARY to popular belief, Americans in the years surrounding the Revolution were not adherents of political individualism; they were opposed to political theories that gave priority to "the liberty, rights, or independent action of the individual." And "the liberation of individuals so that realization of their capacities may be the law of their life" was not their goal. They would have rejected those theories that held that human development and the political good life are fostered by individual freedom and self-direction. For them, "the pursuit of individual rather than common or collective interests" was not valued "over that of public interest."[1] They were not, however, collectivists in the way that fascists are commonly portrayed. For Americans, the public good was not an ultimate end, but an intermediate and aggregate one that was valued ahead of the short-term and particular ends of the community's constituent members. The 18th-century mind assumed that the preeminent standing awarded the public's rational and aggregate needs reflected the natural hierarchy of ends formed by an ordered and purposeful universe.[2]

Yet foreign travelers, historians, and the authors of present-day political, sociological, and journalistic accounts describe Americans as an individualistic people. Louis Hartz influenced many when he argued that "the master assumption of American political thought, the assumption from which all of the American attitudes" flowed, was "the reality of atomistic social freedom."[3] Although such characterizations are perhaps true of modern-day Americans, they are not true of late 18th-century ones. Indeed, this account is so fundamentally flawed that it distorts the national memory of the Revolutionary and Founding years, and this creates an inheritance that limits and corrupts contemporary American political thinking.[4] Therefore, in exploring the political vocabulary of 18th-century Americans and their normative political theory, this description of them as valuing private over public good must be corrected.

Chapter 1 confronts this problem and shows American writers and public spokesmen as regularly having valued public over private good. Their

---

[1]*Random House Dictionary of the English Language,* s.v. "individualism"; Dewey, *Liberalism and Social Action,* pp. 56–57; and Henretta, "Families and Farms," p. 3; see also Sabine, *History of Political Theory,* pp. 439, 608; Lukes, "Types of Individualism," pp. 597–601; Manuel and Manuel, *Utopian Thought in the Western World,* p. 452; and Damico, "Problem with Liberalism," p. 549.

[2]See A. O. Lovejoy, *Great Chain of Being,* pp. 205–7; Pocock, "Virtues, Rights, and Manners," p. 353; Lakoff, "Autonomy and Liberal Democracy," pp. 388–89; and Pahl, *Free Will and Political Liberty,* pp. 154–55.

[3]Hartz, *Liberal Tradition in America,* p. 62.

[4]See Sullivan, *Reconstructing Public Philosophy,* p. 159, who similarly holds that "those who read the American spirit as so dominantly individualistic . . . are both dangerously distorting our past and threatening our future."

lack of concern with the rights of individuals or minorities is also noted. Chapter 2 relies on the recent research of contemporary social historians and advances the bolder claim that 18th-century American political culture was localist and communal. Even historians such as Jack Greene, who found that this culture had changed in individualistic ways, recognize that Americans' normative communal beliefs lagged behind more individualistic material changes. Chapter 3 considers Revolutionary Americans' understanding of a key aspect of their political theory: the morally sanctioned relationships among the individual, the public good, and the community. It also explores their near-universal condemnation of the aspirations of the liberated self. Their understanding of the concepts of self and family are in tension with the ethical and political claims of modern individualism.

Chapter 4 focuses on late 18th-century Americans' views of the individual as filtered through three overlapping traditions of normative discourse. Collectively, they advanced what were understood to be the true rather than the temporary needs of the individual. The chapter also discusses an emerging fourth strand of political thought, an individualistic one. Americans were committed, in multiple and sometimes competing ways, to serving the true needs of the individual. Yet it was the community's immediate and aggregate good that most frequently concerned them. Most Americans were committed to serving aggregate public and true private ends without, however, embracing a normative theory of the good that might be described as individualistic (or for that matter, liberal or republican). It was instead through the intrusive and delimiting intervention of various intermediate social institutions that limits were to be inculcated and human flourishing was to be advanced.[5]

[5]See Skinner, "Paradoxes of Political Liberty," p. 232, for the history of this understanding of what once was widely considered liberty.

Three Discourses in Defense of the Public Good

To recognize the true boundaries between the individual
and the community is the highest problem that thoughtful
consideration of human society has to solve.

—Georg Jellinek, *Declaration of the Rights of
Man and of Citizens*

REVOLUTIONARY-ERA Americans believed that the needs and good of the
public must be awarded priority over those of the individual. But this is
not equivalent to what is described as a communal theory of the good.
Such a theory of the good, or communalism (as opposed to both collectivism and individualism), is a commitment to a particular moral vision
wherein human flourishing is to be pursued through familial and communal shaping of the individual. This sanctioned formation of the individual
by intermediate social institutions is guided by an underlying moral, usually religious, conception of a good human life.[1] (Such institutions might
include the family, the neighborhood, a religious congregation, fraternal
organizations, and locally controlled schools and governments.) There is
nothing inherently communalist, therefore, in a widely accepted social
standard that values the aggregate good of the public over that of the
individual. Communalism and an overarching preference for the public
good are reinforcing but nevertheless distinct social ideals.

Imagine a society of moderate individualists in which serving the public
and the collective good first is the precondition for the subsequent exercise
of a measured amount of autonomous individual freedom. In such a society, there would be limited public intervention in the moral formation of
the individual. This possibility is, I believe, familiar to most Americans
who grew to maturity at the time of the Korean War. Serving the public
good demands no concomitant devotion to communalism or a world of
gemeinschaft in which this would occur.[2] Therefore, the priority that Rev-

---

[1]For a preview of the American commitment to communalism, see the Preceptor, "Social
Duties of the Political Kind" (1772), p. 177; see also Nisbet, review of *Conservatism*, p. 104,
who describes this sense of communalism as the essence of the conservative theory of freedom.

[2]See Bender, *Community and Social Change in America*, pp. 15–44.

olutionary-era Americans awarded the public, its rights, and its good need not have demanded that the individual be seen as radically incomplete living outside an enveloping and ethically intrusive community (as was in fact the case).

Awarding high value to serving first the common or public good is also not necessarily communal in a secondary sense. That is, it need not be localist. And a dedication to serving the common good does not demand that appropriate corporate decisions be made by the smallest possible viable polity in an extended political system.[3] In fact, awarding priority to the public's needs is compatible with localism as well as with various forms of nationalism, and possibly even internationalism. Defense of the public's welfare is often claimed by each system of aggregation and sovereignty to be its particular preserve, as it alone best understands the needs of the people. There are sound analytical reasons, therefore, for distinguishing between the preeminence Americans awarded to the public good and their supplemental embrace of a communal rather than an individualistic approach to a good human life.[4]

The communalist character of American thought will be examined below. Here, my concern is with Americans' valuation of the rights and aggregate needs of public bodies over those of individuals. This position was not idiosyncratic to them, but instead reflected the received Western wisdom of their age. The Dillys, 18th-century British publicists widely read in America,[5] noted in their legal handbook that "the ultimate end of government, in its original institution certainly was, as it still ought to be, the *good* of the *whole society*." They continued: "if the authority of *Locke, Montesquieu* and *Natural Reason* are not sufficient to prove this position, and any one desires further satisfaction . . . we would refer them to *Pufendorf*." Finally, they turned to Sir William Temple (volume 3 of his *Works*), who had written that "the public safety or good is the end of all public institutes as it was of the *Roman* laws; *Salus populi suprema*."[6]

But the Dillys need not have stopped with these prominent authors. They could have included such additional luminaries of 18th-century political thought as Bolingbroke, Blackstone, Burke, Burgh, Rousseau, and Burlamaqui.[7] Montesquieu, the most cited and authoritative author in late

---

[3]See Drengson, "Toward a Philosophy of Community," p. 107, who writes that a community "is the smallest unit capable of bearing and sharing a cultural heredity and common meaning."

[4]In addition, their emphasis on the common or public good and their adherence to a reformed-Protestant variant of communalism, when first viewed separately and then in combination, makes more evident their antipathy toward an aggressive individualism.

[5]The Dillys' *British Liberties* is argued by Hudson, in "William Penn's *English Liberties*," p. 585, to have been one of the most popular political "texts" in the American colonies, as evidenced by its numerous editions.

[6]Dilly and Dilly, *British Liberties* (1766), p. xli.

[7]See, for example, Handlin and Handlin, "James Burgh and American Revolutionary Theory," p. 46.

18th-century America,[8] for example, had cautioned that "the independence of individuals is the end aimed at by the laws of Poland, [and] thence results the oppression of the whole."[9] Serving the public or common good in the 18th century was thus an almost unimpeachable social and political shibboleth.

This was the dominant mode of thought circulating in Revolutionary America as well. And the three most widely held patterns of late 18th-century political discourse in America did argue for such a hierarchy of values. I hesitate, however, to discriminate between these traditions of political understanding; the clarity one can ascribe to these positions post hoc certainly did not exist during the historical period itself.[10] In addition, they had much in common.[11] For example, they all valued the public good in ways that we would today describe as illiberal. Nevertheless, such groupings, when not absolutized or reified into something more than heuristic organizing principles, can be employed in analytically useful ways.[12]

With this caveat in mind, three sets of mutually reinforcing and overlapping theoretical positions can be teased out of late 18th-century ethical, religious, legal, and political literature. They are: classical, Renaissance, or Whig republicanism;[13] reformed-Protestant-derived social and political theory; and early modern (moderate Enlightenment) rationalism.[14] This three-way characterization is not original. It follows Herbert Schneider's 1946

---

[8]See Lutz, *Origins of American Constitutionalism*, p. 142.

[9]Montesquieu, *Spirit of the Laws* (1748), 1:150–52; see also Neumann's, introduction thereto, p. l.

[10]See Kramnick, "Great National Discussion," pp. 4–5; and Banning, "Jeffersonian Ideology Revisited," p. 12.

[11]See May, *Enlightenment in America*, p. 196, who notes that "up to 1795, Protestantism, republicanism, and the [moderate] Enlightenment seemed to most New Englanders to belong together."

[12]Cf. Wood, "Virtues and Interests," p. 34, who criticizes political theorists for having "anachronistically invented too many 'paradigms' and forced too much material into them. Perhaps this is in part because the leading contestants were trained as political theorists and not as historians." Conversely, see M. Weber, *Methodology of the Social Sciences*, pp. 89–104, for his defense of the utility of such categorization in the social sciences.

[13]In spite of the tendency to conflate these three traditions, numerous and substantial differences exist among classical political theory, its Renaissance civic-humanist interpreters (or in Machiavelli's case, transformer), and the British radical Whigs. I will often speak of this family of authors and discourse as though they were one. This is common in the literature, even if inaccurate. For example, see Diggins, *Lost Soul of American Politics*, p. 9, who writes that "classical republicanism, which has been variously referred to as civic humanism, republican ideology, classical politics, the commonwealth tradition, dissent and opposition, and radical Whig thought is perhaps the dominant theme in contemporary scholarship on early American political ideas and culture."

[14]A fourth pattern of "thought" that was a major influence in late 18th-century America, English "lived" agrarianism, was also more communal than individualistic, but will not be discussed here because it is not a theoretical tradition that is accessible through texts and public records. Nevertheless, see Fischer, *Albion's Seed*, for his defense of the centrality of such influences in the formation of the American political culture, and the highly critical forum considering his work, with a rejoinder in "*Albion's Seed.*"

typology. He argued that "in the Revolutionary generation three distinct systems of thought, three historically separate faiths, were flourishing; for want of better terms I shall call them rationalism, pietism, and republicanism."[15]

Additionally, these three traditions are not to be taken as a comprehensive list of all significant 18th-century bodies of thought.[16] This is especially true in regard to the Scottish moral-sense philosophy and the creation of Anglo-American political and legal institutions in which common-law jurisprudence and legal precedents played dominant roles. Any exploration of Revolutionary-era thought, however, is necessarily incapable of illuminating all aspects of American constitutional, legal, and political history or theory.[17] My exploration concentrates on these three traditions of social and political discourse because they help most in explicating 18th-century Americans' assessment of the just relationship to be had between the community and the individual, and other essential aspects of their normative political theory.

THE PUBLIC-CENTERED REVOLUTIONARY YEARS

The writings of the men who brought about the American Revolution offer striking testimony of the pervasiveness of the high value Americans attached to the public good. Throughout the 18th century, claims defending the good of the whole took precedence over the particular concerns of private individuals.[18] For example, an anonymous author in a 1753 *New-York Mercury* editorial held that "in all Communities, as it is the highest Reason, that private Convenience should give place to publick Emolument,

[15]Schneider, *History of American Philosophy*, p. 61; see also May, *Enlightenment in America*, p. 196. Noll, *Princeton and the Republic*, p. 294, argues that Witherspoon "made his reputation by linking" these three bodies of thought, but on p. 141 he argues for four: classical republicanism, the Didactic Enlightenment, liberal republicanism, and Protestantism.

[16]Those dissatisfied with this tripartite division should see Murrin, "Religion and Politics in America," pp. 26–27, who offers a typology of six different value systems, which even then did not "exhaust the possibilities."

[17]This is not to say that such histories are not needed. See in particular Lutz, "Relative Influence of European Writers," pp. 195–96, who concludes that "the prominence of Blackstone would come as a surprise to many, and he is the prime candidate for the writer most likely to be left out in any list of influential thinkers," and that "such a respected writer deserves a much closer look by those studying American political thought." See also Lutz, *Origins of American Constitutionalism*, p. 62. This is a theme that Pocock has been arguing for years. See K. Thomas, "Politics as Language," p. 39, who in a review of *Virtue, Commerce, and History* notes that Pocock finds that common-law jurisprudence offered a quite separate political tradition in competition with civic humanism.

[18]See Gross, *Minutemen and Their World*, p. 66; Gillespie, "Ratification of the Constitution," p. 7; and Wall, *Fierce Communion*, p. ix. Cf. Schmitt and Webking, "Revolutionaries, Antifederalists, and Federalists," pp. 210–13; and J. P. Greene, "Uneasy Connection," pp. 56–57, who claims that it was the norm "to subordinate the welfare of the community to the pursuit of self-interest."

so 'tis the Business of the Legislature, in providing for the publick Good, to prescribe to all the Members of the Community, Limits and Restrictions of their Enjoyments and Conduct."[19] In 1773, the radical Baptist preacher and activist John Allen held that "the body politic can only be in health, and prosper, when every member unites regularly, and ardently, to preserve the privileges of the whole."[20] The representatives of Berkshire County, Massachusetts, expressed in 1778 the common feeling of Americans when they stated that "the larger Number (Caeteris paribus) is of more worth than the lesser, and the common happiness is to be preferred to that of Individuals."[21]

By this, however, I am not suggesting that the agricultural majority's outlook on the public and its good was different from that of the various elites. In fact, until almost the end of the 18th century, the elite and the common folk shared the idea that the public good demanded priority. Consider the respected Levi Hart, pastor of the Congregational Church in Preston, Connecticut, for forty-six years and an early antislavery activist. He took a position comparable to that of the presumably less educated men cited above. Preaching to his congregation in 1775, he affirmed that in a well-ordered society "each individual gives up all private interest that is not consistent with the general good . . . and every individual is to seek and find his happiness in the welfare of the whole."[22] The fiery architects of the Revolution James Otis and Sam Adams went further and noted that "the only principles of public conduct, that are worthy of a gentleman or a man, are to sacrifice estate, ease, health, and applause, and even life to the sacred calls of his country."[23]

On the other side of the Revolutionary ledger, a highly regarded British author, John Brown,[24] observed that "the first Foundation of civil [society was that] the Habits of the youthful Heart [should be formed in] *Coincidence* with the *general Welfare*" and that this is accomplished by "checking every rising Appetite that is contrary to This, and in forwarding every Passion that may promote the Happiness of the Community."[25] Likewise, the Loyalist Jonathan Sewell urged that "man in society [should no longer consider] 'himself as an *individual,* absolutely unaccountable and uncontroulable, but as one of a community, every member of which is bound to

[19]*New-York Mercury,* 17 September 1753, p. 1; see also the *Newport Mercury,* 22 August 1763, p. 2.

[20][J. Allen], *American Alarm* (1773), p. 21.

[21]"Statement of Berkshire County Representatives" (1778), in Handlin and Handlin, *Popular Sources of Political Authority,* p. 375.

[22]L. Hart, "Liberty Described and Recommended" (1775), pp. 309–11.

[23]Otis, "Speech of 1761," p. 524; see also S. Adams, "Letter to John Scollay" (20 March 1777), in *Writings of Samuel Adams,* 3:365.

[24]See Bailyn, *Ideological Origins of the American Revolution,* p. 87, who notes that in 1758, Brown was of sufficient stature to write a flattering introduction for an English-language edition of Montesquieu.

[25]Brown, *Thoughts on Civil Liberty* (1765), p. 28.

consult and promote the general good.' "²⁶ Finally, to round out this diversified sampler of 18th-century public spokesmen, we might take into account the remarks of one of the most aggressive defenders of chattel slavery, Richard Nisbet. In 1773 he defended its continuation by reminding his readers "that private considerations must always give way to the publick good."²⁷ All agreed, then, on the priority of the common or public good over the good of particular individuals.

Late 18th-century American social and political thought allowed—even demanded—that the public, in pursuit of its collective good, require in a sometimes illiberal fashion the subordination and possibly even the sacrifice of immediate individual rights.²⁸ Pronouncements in support of the common good thus were often not neutral (as they might have been) regarding the immediate wants of particular individuals. Many of them had a certain collectivist coloration that was in tension with the overall high worth they attached to the individual. Public and private needs were often seen as potentially competitive demands, with a definite hierarchy of value that placed corporate needs ahead of subjective individual ones.

James Lockwood in 1759 counseled that "our petty, personal Interests ought to be subordinated to the Good of the Public."²⁹ In his sermon before the Massachusetts legislature, Andrew Eliot declared that it was certainly better that "a particular person, yea many individuals should suffer," than that the public be disturbed.³⁰ And an anonymous author writing in the *Boston Evening Post* in 1771 recommended that man, upon entering society, should "no longer consider himself as an *individual* . . . but as one of a community, every member of which is bound to consult and promote the *general good*."³¹ A year later "The Preceptor," in the radical Whig newspaper *Massachusetts Spy*, added that political duties included "love of our country, resignation and obedience to the laws, public spirit," and "*sacrifice of life and all to the public*."³² These remarks suggest not only that the public's good was preferred but that it was normal to disparage the needs of the individual. Some 18th-century authors did equivocate on this point; they, however, were in the minority.

The quintessential American patriot, physician, statesman, minister, and future justice and congressman Nathaniel Niles was unequivocal in 1774

²⁶Cited by Potter, *Liberty We Seek*, p. 47; see also W. H. Nelson, *American Tory*, pp. 187–88.

²⁷[Richard Nisbet], *Slavery Not Forbidden by Scripture* (1773), pp. 14–15.

²⁸See Maier, *Old Revolutionaries*, pp. xiv, 32, and "Good Show," p. 196; and Wood, *Radicalism of the American Revolution*, p. 204.

²⁹Lockwood, *Worth and Excellence* (1759), p. 30.

³⁰Eliot, *Massachusetts Election Sermon* (1765), pp. 43–44; see also Fobes, "Election Sermon" (1795 Massachusetts election sermon), p. 995, who writes that "the good of the whole" cannot be achieved "without injury or inconvenience to some individuals."

³¹*Boston Evening Post*, 14 January 1771.

³²The Preceptor, "Social Duties of the Political Kind" (1772), p. 177.

when he insisted that everyone "be required to do all he can that tends to the highest good of the state: For the whole of this is due to the state, from the individuals of which it is composed. Everything, however trifling, that tends, even in the lowest degree, to disserve the interest of the state must also be forbidden."[33] Some ten years later the highly regarded, theologically liberal, and politically active pastor Henry Cumings urged that "every one ought to consider that he was born, not for himself alone, but for others, for society, for his country."[34] And the next year, near the end of the Revolutionary era, the theologically more liberal pastor Moses Hemmenway, standing before the Massachusetts legislature, declared that "no individual ought to hold his natural right of independence, if it stands in opposition to the general interest—it would seem that men's entering into civil society was a matter of duty as well as right; and that they may be justly compelled to it, when the general interest so requires."[35] This language seems more reminiscent of polities we consider totalitarian than it does of contemporary liberal ones.

These ideas were not entertained only by Northern Congregational ministers supportive of the Patriot cause. The great Virginian planter Landon Carter wrote that "'one or a few' could never 'be better Judges of' the public 'Good than was the multitude,' and if that good required the suspension of 'Private Justice' or the suppression of the individual liberty of the minority that opposed it, then it was . . . 'a Thing absolutely necessary to be done' and 'therefore just in itself.'"[36] One of the most articulate of the Loyalists, Ambrose Serle, while attacking the Patriots in 1776, agreed that "indeed, there is no person, and perhaps, in strictness of speaking, there never was one, born OUT of *society*. . . . When we talk of states and communities, the notion of *individuals* is absorbed: *their* rights and privileges are not merely their own, but the rights and privileges of the state to which they belong. There is nothing for a man's own, in an enlarged political view, as to be abstracted and independent of his community."[37] And the Philadelphia Committee of Trade declared in 1779 that society "requires that every right or power claimed or exercised by any man or set of men should be in subordination to the common good, and that whatever is incompatible therewith, must by some rule or regulation, be brought into

[33]N. Niles, "[First of] Two Discourses on Liberty" (1774), p. 260.
[34]Cumings, *Massachusetts Election Sermon* (1783), p. 8.
[35]Hemmenway, *Massachusetts Election Sermon* (1784), p. 17.
[36]Cited by J. P. Greene, introduction to *Diary of Colonel Landon Carter*, p. 31; see also *Landon Carter*, pp. 42–43.
[37][Serle], *Americans against Liberty* (1776), p. 14. *Civil Liberty Asserted* (1776), pp. 32–33, notes that "it is just to say, that it is essentially necessary to Government, that Individuals should give up all right of being guided by their own wills, in perfect submission to the guidance of the will of the State of which they are Members." See also the radical Priestley, "Essay" (1771), pp. 32–33, who holds that "all claims of individuals inconsistent with the public good, are absolutely null and void."

subjection thereto."[38] Even an elite nationalist such as James Wilson was willing to appeal to this widely held view. In 1790, addressing a Philadelphia audience, he reminded them that according to "the will and by the interest of the community, every private will and private interest must be bound and overruled."[39]

Most Americans in the 18th century had little patience with those who might claim that the rights of individuals (except religious conscience) were inviolable and capable of trumping public needs. As America's first ordained black minister, Lemuel Haynes, observed, the public good must be the end sought by human laws. In the event of majoritarian injustice, the individual or minority could legitimately either depart or submit, unless it was "the real rights of conscience" that had been invaded. To respond otherwise would be to attack "the rights of men, and the principle of true liberty."[40] American sensibilities were thus not yet supportive of the demanding claims of political individualism. Quite to the contrary: the rights, aggregate interests, and good of the public enjoyed preferential standing vis-à-vis those of the individual. And during and after their war for independence from Britain, while Americans were developing new political institutions, this public-spirited understanding of the collective interests of the people found its way into their public documents as well.

Donald Lutz has shown that the first state constitutions "assumed the rights of the community to be generally superior to the rights of the individual," allowing them to affect nearly every "right we today consider inalienable."[41] For example, the Vermont Declaration of Rights states that "the people of this State have the sole, exclusive and inherent right of governing and regulating the internal police of the same" and that this same aggregate "community hath an indubitable, unalienable and indefeasible right to reform, alter, or abolish, government in such a manner as shall be, by that community, judged most conducive to the public weal."[42] Delaware put it more succinctly: all legitimate governments are popular and majoritarian, "and instituted solely for the good of the whole."[43] These very public statements of rights left no ground on which to defend the individual against state encroachments on what we today would call

---

[38]Cited by E. Foner, *Tom Paine and Revolutionary America*, pp. 169–70, from the *Pennsylvania Packet,* 10 September 1779.

[39]J. Wilson, *Works of James Wilson,* ed. McCloskey, 2:577; see also 1:242, where he notes that man is free up to the point where "more public interests do not demand his labours." On this point, one might also consider Franklin's life of public service after his early retirement and his remarks on this subject. See *Autobiography,* p. 111, where he describes how the public "laid hold of me for their purposes" without his "ever asking any elector for his vote."

[40]Haynes, "Nature and Importance of True Republicanism" (1801), pp. 79–80.

[41]Lutz, *Popular Consent and Popular Control,* p. 50, and *Origins of American Constitutionalism,* p. 71.

[42]Reproduced in B. Schwartz, *Roots of the Bill of Rights,* pp. 322–23; for comparable language see the "Virginia Declaration of Rights" (1776), in ibid., p. 234.

[43]"Delaware Declaration of Rights" (1776), in ibid., p. 277.

individual civil rights. The majority was to set moral standards and to judge the behavior of individuals.

Instead of protecting the inalienable rights of individuals, as one might have expected, these Revolutionary-era documents defended the absolute rights of the majority and the common good. Thus, even in the most carefully crafted state constitution of arguably the most important state, Massachusetts, Ron Peters finds that "the political theory of the Massachusetts Constitution of 1780 subordinates the individual to society."[44] In the most radical of the state constitutions, that of Pennsylvania, individual rights were again subservient to the needs and will of a "majoritarian government completely capable of legitimately qualifying all individual liberties."[45] It held that to the state alone belongs the right to regulate the morals of its citizens, that government must serve the community, not "any single man, family, or set of men, who are part only of that community," and that the majority has the right to determine what the appropriate ends to be served are.[46]

Knowledgeable students argue that even the 1787 federal Constitution (in spite of the efforts of an influential circle of the Framers, who had hoped to imbue it with a moderately individualistic political philosophy) was predominantly concerned with guarding the public's, not the individual's, welfare and interests. John Roche, for example, holds that "the freedom which the Constitution was intended to guarantee was corporate rather than individual."[47] Robert Palmer would have us believe that even the relatively individualistic elements of the Constitution were put in place by the majority at the convention with a view to protecting not individual rights but the public good and the corporate character of the individual states.[48]

The legal historian William Nelson makes the same point, but more broadly. He contends that some of the most sacrosanct of 18th-century private rights had not been granted for the benefit of the individual. He suggests that, on the contrary, such rights received legal protection only because they were believed to be consistent with the good of the community.[49] John Jay, one of the authors of *The Federalist* and the first chief justice of the United States, said as much. Speaking before the First Circuit

---

[44]Peters, *Massachusetts Constitution of 1780,* p. 193.

[45]Palmer, "Liberties as Constitutional Provisions," pp. 66–68.

[46]"Pennsylvania Declaration of Rights" (1776), reproduced in B. Schwartz, *Roots of the Bill of Rights,* pp. 264–65.

[47]Roche, "American Liberty," p. 145; and Amar, "Consent of the Governed," p. 492. See also Epstein, *Political Theory of the Federalist,* p. 86, who is more equivocal.

[48]See Palmer, "Liberties as Constitutional Provisions," p. 146; Howe, "Political Psychology of *The Federalist*," pp. 491–92; and Hutson, "Bill of Rights," p. 84. For an opposing view, see E. S. Morgan, *Inventing the People,* pp. 275–77.

[49]See W. E. Nelson, *Americanization of the Common Law,* pp. 51–52; and Lutz, *Popular Consent and Popular Control,* pp. 34–35.

Court on 4 April 1790, he reminded his auditors that "civil liberty consists, not in a right to every man to do just what he pleases," but only to do that which "the equal and constitutional laws of the country admit to be consistent with the public good."[50] And an Old Federalist at the turn of the century, Noah Webster, who was not known for majoritarian sympathies, continued to appeal to the priority of the public will. On the anniversary of the Declaration of Independence, he argued that "it is needless to discuss questions of natural right as distinct from a social state, for all rights are social, and subordinate to the supreme will of the whole society."[51] The common or public good was a standard that no one in the 18th century could comfortably attack.

In the early years of the 19th century, prominent public figures still lectured that "the whole powers, moral and physical, of society" are to make "the public will and the public good, the great rule of her conduct, and the object of all her proceedings."[52] If Daniel Rodgers is correct, such a preference for public over private rights continued to guide the lives of most Americans for yet another century.[53]

PUBLIC RATHER THAN PRIVATE GOOD—REPUBLICANISM

Republicanism, in its many guises, was particularly concerned with the standing of the public good and the priority it was to enjoy. Yet its shifting political and social prescriptions are difficult to capture across the centuries. It is clear, however, that the teachings of the ancients were taken to be uncompromising in their insistence that the common or public good be valued over that of private individuals. This was believed to be the essence of their concept of virtue. In the early 19th century, the liberal French statesman and essayist Benjamin Constant described classical and Renaissance republicanism as demanding "the complete subjection of the individual to the authority of the community"; as a consequence "the individual, almost always sovereign in public affairs, was a slave in all his private relations."[54]

Scholars today largely agree with this earlier assessment and hold that even in the most liberal of the Greek city-states, Athens, individual rights had little or no standing when opposed to the public's good.[55] "Athenian

---

[50]Cited by C. Warren, *Supreme Court in United States History*, p. 60.

[51]Webster, "Oration" (1802), p. 1228.

[52]A. Wilson, *Oration* (1801), pp. 16–17.

[53]See Rodgers, *Contested Truths*, pp. 117, 159–61. For example, in 1907, prominent writers held that the citizen "has not the right to demand anything of the community . . . [rather he] must do what the community determines it is best for him to do."

[54]Constant, "Liberty of the Ancients" (1819), p. 311.

[55]See Patterson, *Freedom*, p. 55, for his partial dissent, in that this generalization did not hold for women; and Lindsay, "Individualism," p. 675, who places the beginning of individualism in Greece in the fifth century B.C.E.

liberty was not based on any clear notion of individual rights, or on the sanctity of individual autonomy . . . [and] ostracism symbolized the ultimate power of the community over the individual and the individual's relative lack of rights against the community."[56] As the even less compromising Numa Denis Fustel de Coulanges held, "individual liberty could not exist" in the ancient city-states, for even the free "citizen was subordinate in everything, and without reserve to the city; he belonged to it body and soul. [For] the ancients, especially the Greeks, always exaggerated the importance, and above all, the rights of society."[57]

Educated Americans inherited this long tradition of political thought from ancient histories and philosophies, Renaissance political tracts, and writings by English republicans of the 17th century. It taught them, as did the other traditions of political and social thought to which they had access, that the immediate rights of the public were paramount.[58] It has lately become accepted that educated Americans, particularly during the 1770s, were influenced by some variant of this tradition of political thought.[59] After reviewing the relevant literature in 1982, Robert Shalhope (following Robert Kelley) suggested that "republicanism offered Americans a universe of discourse [that] established a framework for discussion, certain generally accepted ideas," and a shared language.[60] More recently, Paul Rahe affirmed that the study of the ancients did much to inform American thinking. In particular, he believes that Ancient writers were able to provide "the 'logic' and 'grammar' of the thinking that animated the revolutionary generation."[61] Prominent 18th-century American political actors were, it is known, students of classical Greek and Roman sources. Many of the best educated, in fact, continued to read them in the original languages throughout their lives.[62]

Even more popular than the political teachings advanced by Greek and Roman authors were their Renaissance interpreters and their 17th-century

[56]Mulgan, "Liberty in Ancient Greece," p. 14.

[57]Coulanges, *Ancient City,* pp. 211–12, 215.

[58]See MacIntyre, *After Virtue,* pp. 158–59.

[59]Those loosely associated with this school (or these schools) of thought include an earlier generation of scholars: Fink, *Classical Republicans* and Rossiter, *Seedtime of the Republic;* and a later generation, including Bailyn, *Ideological Origins of the American Revolution* (who actually never characterized the thought he was describing as republican or civic humanist); Wood, *Creation of the American Republic;* Pocock, *Machiavellian Moment;* Banning, *Jeffersonian Persuasion;* Murrin, "Great Inversion"; and McCoy, *Elusive Republic.* Of late, historians have become skeptical regarding the depth of influence exercised by republican thought in the 18th century. Many professors of law, however, have become newly influenced by this literature. See Ackerman, *We the People,* pp. 325–28, for his references.

[60]Shalhope, "Republicanism and Early American Historiography," p. 342.

[61]In partial disagreement with other students of "republicanism," see Rahe, *Republics Ancient and Modern,* pp. 570ff. (quotation from p. 570). Cf. Pangle, *Spirit of Modern Republicanism,* p. 35, in which he argues that classical republicanism shares no traits with American political thought.

[62]See Gummere, "Heritage of the Classics," pp. 75–76; and Zvesper, "American Founders and Classical Political Thought," pp. 701–3.

English Whig adherents.[63] The English, Shelley Burtt argues, insisted more strongly on the need for private sacrifice than had the original Greek and Roman defenders of the republican vision of the good life.[64] And it is the limited standing awarded to the rights of the individual that makes this traditional Western alternative to the monarchical understanding of the best ordering of social and political life of interest here. Americans using republican-inspired language appeared to view comfortably its preference for the rights of the public over those of the individual.

In this tradition of political thought, the common good was sacrificed when the people became corrupt. Corruption was understood as "a failure to devote one's energies to the common good, and a corresponding tendency to place one's own interests above those of the community."[65] It was seen as invidious, for it "separates the Particles, or Individuals from their attachments to the Whole," and, like "*Rottenness* to a Piece of Timber," it must be prevented if a polity's health is to be preserved.[66] Political health, particularly in a republic, demanded that the converse of corruption, public virtue, be fostered. In fact, *virtu* or public virtue was one of the most revered political concepts of the 18th century, and it demanded "self-government and, above all, the citizen's willing subordination of his personal interest to the communal good."[67] Educated Americans took this quality to be the essence of the republican theory they had studied in their grammar schools.

By considering the marked hostility shown by liberal and monarchist critics to the 17th and 18th centuries' renewed interest in republicanism, one can discover indirect but persuasive evidence of republicanism's early modern appeal. And it is apparent from the character of these criticisms that republicanism's adherents must have understood its anti-individualist precepts.

Among the most strident 17th-century critics was the early liberal theorist Thomas Hobbes. Excoriating the preeminence of the public realm in the ancient city-states, Hobbes lavishly details republicanism's lack of interest in the immediate needs of the individual. His readers could not have misunderstood him.

---

[63]See McDonald, *Novus Ordo Seclorum,* p. xi; Pocock, "Virtue and Commerce," p. 119; Banning, *Jeffersonian Persuasion,* p. 72; and Bailyn, *Ideological Origins of the American Revolution,* pp. 34–35.

[64]See Burtt, "Good Citizen's Psyche," p. 35.

[65]Skinner, *Foundations of Modern Political Thought,* 1:164, and "Paradoxes of Political Liberty," p. 243; Maier, *Old Revolutionaries,* pp. 209–10; and Lutz, *Origins of American Constitutionalism,* p. 29. For example, see one of America's Latin favorites, Sallust's "Conspiracy of Catiline," in Sallust, *Jugurthine War and The Conspiracy of Catiline,* p. 223.

[66][Brooke?], *Liberty and Common-Sense* (1760), letter 3, p. 14.

[67]Hampson, *Enlightenment,* p. 209; see also E. Foner, *Tom Paine and Revolutionary America,* pp. 158–59; Pocock, *Machiavellian Moment,* pp. 88, 201; Henretta, "Slow Triumph of Liberal Individualism," p. 90; and Wood, *Radicalism of the American Revolution,* pp. 103–4.

The *Athenians,* and *Romanes* were free; that is, free Common-wealths: not that any particular men had the Libertie to resist their own Representative; but that their Representative had the Libertie to resist, or invade other people. There is written on the Turrets of the city of *Luca* in great characters at this day, the word *LIBERTAS;* yet no man can thence inferre, that a particular man has more Libertie, or Immunitie from the service of the Commonwealth there, than in *Constantinople.* Whether a Commonwealth be Monarchicall, or Popular, the Freedome is still the same. But it is an easy thing, for men to be deceived, by the specious name of Libertie; and for want of Judgement to distinguish, mistake that for their Private Inheritance, and Birth right, which is the right of the Publique only.

He continued by denouncing "*Aristotle, Cicero,* and other men, Greeks and Romanes," for (among other failings) having recommended a republican form of government as the only one consistent with true liberty. Individuals, he reminded his readers, are most truly free under a monarchy.[68] His understanding of the just relation between the individual and the polity, however, was rejected by 18th-century Americans.[69]

Writing a century later, the progressive Genevan jurist J. L. de Lolme condemned in *The Constitution of England* "writers of the present age, misled by their inconsiderate admiration of the Governments of ancient times, and perhaps also by their desire of presenting striking contrasts to what they call degenerate manners of our modern times, [who] have cried up the governments of Sparta and Rome, as the only ones fit for us to imitate."[70] Like Hobbes before him and David Hume, his famous Scottish contemporary,[71] Lolme found little to admire in these "tyrannies," which allowed their citizens no individual rights,[72] but provided so copiously for the public's immediate corporate needs.

The Baron de Montesquieu, neither an unambiguous liberal nor a republican apologist, characterized the great difficulty of maintaining a republican form of government. In so doing, he drew attention to the republican authors' strenuous demand that the public good be awarded

[68]Hobbes, *Leviathan* (1651), pp. 266–67. See also Weintraub, "Virtue," p. 112, for his numerous references to this recurrent theme in Hobbes's work.

[69]See Bailyn, *Ideological Origins of the American Revolution,* p. 28. Skinner, "Context of Hobbes's Theory," p. 125, writes that "it seems likely, moreover, that even amongst those writers who might have felt Hobbes worthy of citation as an authority, the number may have been further diminished by considerations about Hobbes's dangerous reputation."

[70]Lolme, *Constitution of England* (1775), pp. 221–22.

[71]Regarding England, see also Hey, *Observations* (1776).

[72]Contemporary liberals continue to be concerned. See, for example, Shklar, "Gone with the Wind," p. 41, who warns that "republicanism now is a threat to personal freedom and justice," and R. M. Smith, "'American Creed' and American Identity," p. 245, who cautions that "despite republicanism's attractions for contemporary theorists, any honest assessment of it as an actual American communal tradition must recognize that in legal and political debate it has usually and quite naturally served to assist the repressive side of American ethnocentrism."

unconditional preference over immediate individual interests. He warned that in a republican government "virtue is a self-renunciation which is ever arduous and painful . . . [and] requires a constant preference of public to private interest."[73] In a rather ironic vein, David Hume in a letter to his son highlighted republicanism's indifference to individual rights when he wrote that a great advantage of its prescriptions being adopted "over our mixt Monarchy is, that it [would consid]erably abridge our Liberty, which is growing to such an Extreme, as to be incom[patible wi]th all Government. Such Fools are they, who perpetually cry out Liberty: [and think to] augment it, by shaking off the Monarchy."[74] Yet such criticism, even by the likes of Hume, was unable to convince many late 18th-century Americans to reject their republican-inspired embrace of the public good,[75] or not to seek their independence from the British Crown.

Americans did so, then, not out of ignorance of the likely anti-individualist consequences of adopting republican-inspired institutions. The admonitions of Montesquieu, Hume, Hobbes, Lolme, and the progressives among American Loyalists (who argued that a rejection of monarchy and an adoption of republican institutions in America would result in a loss of individual liberty) ensured that educated Americans understood the likely effects of the policies that many of them promoted during the war years.[76] Americans must have fully appreciated that a necessary consequence of their success would be that "the liberty of the individual [would be] subsumed in the freedom or independence of his political community."[77] They must have recognized that, in the language of the 20th century, republicanism was "in a word, totalitarian. No exercise of liberty, or at least none fraught with any moral significance, could be legitimate unless it contributed to public virtue."[78] Numerous and highly visible critics of republicanism ensured that its hostility to the claims of what would become political and social individualism were widely known. (In a perverse fashion, discussed below, republicanism can be said to have also facilitated this unsought transformation.)

Thus, the presence of those who spoke against republicanism's (to borrow from Stephen Holmes) antiliberal features are of considerable importance; they clarify what Americans meant when they spoke or wrote in

[73]Montesquieu, *Spirit of the Laws* (1748), 1:34.

[74]Hume, *Letters of David Hume*, 2:306.

[75]See Ketcham, *Presidents above Party*, p. 83, who describes 18th-century individualistic public statements as "rare and decidedly eccentric."

[76]Strikingly, Loyalists opposed the Revolution from several points of view. One, described here, was a progressive individualistic outlook; a second was nearly the opposite and took a reactionary High Anglican monarchical perspective. A third outlook shared with the Patriots their infatuation with republicanism but was skeptical of Americans' ability to meet their shared understanding of its severe demands of selflessness. According to the latter, Americans were already too corrupt for such an experiment to prove successful.

[77]McDonald, *Novus Ordo Seclorum*, p. 71.

[78]Eastland, "Use and Abuse of Liberty," p. 28.

ways that appear today hostile to the rights or wants of the individual. One is better able to accept, because of the powerful hue and cry raised by critics, that Americans understood republicanism's almost collectivist implications. Foreign theorists widely read in America and soon-to-be marginalized Americans (Loyalists) drew repeated and specific attention to the repercussions of embracing various planks of the republican theory of government. It would have been extremely difficult for educated American adherents of republicanism to have been ignorant of the antiliberal consequences of the commitments they were enthusiastically making in the 1770s.

By the 1780s, however, some of the previously enthusiastic elite had come to reject their earlier embrace of republican-inspired doctrines. This change of heart mirrored their loss of control of their experiment in moderate republicanism to more popular political forces.[79] This does not exempt them, though, from having earlier made uncompromising and illiberal commitments to the needs and good of the public. It only implies that they might have been naive or even wrong in their estimation of their ability to control the consequences of the republican-inspired language they had invoked. It does not show that they had been confused or uninformed regarding its anti-individualistic character.

In practice, Americans' republican-inspired aspirations were almost never achieved. Further evidence of the appeal of republican discourse is found in the lament of those who believed that most Americans were unwilling to live up to the demanding standards that some had set. An obviously pained army officer complained that "while we are pleasing and amusing ourselves with Spartan constitutions on paper, a very contrary spirit reigns triumphant in all ranks [of society]. . . . Our political constitutions and manners do not agree. . . . Spartan constitutions and Roman manners, peculiar to her declining state, never will accord."[80] But Americans were neither so Spartan in their political thought nor so licentious in their behavior as this dissatisfied officer might lead one to believe. However, his description of a people caught between communal normative aspirations and more materialist and individualist practices has much to recommend it. Indeed, it captures the essential tension in late 18th-century America between communal political thought and changing economic and social practices.

The republican-influenced writings of late 18th-century Americans offer evidence that the individual's immediate interests were to be surrendered when needed to those of the public. According to Gordon Wood,[81] this

---

[79]See Wood, *Creation of the American Republic*, pp. 391–468; see also Wood, "Freedom and the Constitution," pp. 49–50; and Greven, *Protestant Temperament*, p. 359.

[80]*Independent Chronicle*, 3 June 1779.

[81]See the editor's remarks in *"Creation of the American Republic,"* p. 549, in which he states that Wood remains one of the most authoritative colonial historians.

"sacrifice of individual interests to the greater good of the whole formed the essence of republicanism and comprehended for Americans the idealistic goal of their Revolution."[82] But republicanism was not unique. Late 18th-century Americans embraced multiple public philosophies that denigrated the satisfaction of individual needs in favor of those of the public. Republicanism was only one of several traditions that led to the same public-centered goal.

PUBLIC RATHER THAN PRIVATE GOOD—REFORMED PROTESTANTISM

Americans also embraced other traditions of social and political thought that were at least as diffuse as republicanism. For lack of a better name, I call the one that was derived from reformed-Protestant roots reformed-Protestant communalism.[83] It too held that the public or common good should be valued over the secular wants of particular individuals. Such a finding is not unexpected given that a "Christian Sparta" was what some of the Revolutionary generation, such as Sam Adams, were committed to creating.[84] Nor was such a choice adventitious: republican Sparta symbolized a morally intrusive and public-centered polity of the kind that American Revolutionaries influenced by reformed-Protestant and republican thought hoped to forge.[85] [The tradition of valuing the welfare of the whole over that of the individual had deep roots in American reformed-Protestant social and political thought](such as was found in Puritan, Particular Baptist, and Scottish, German, and Dutch Reformed teachings).

Consider Rev. John Barnard, whom Perry Miller describes as "one of the finest examples of the eighteenth-century New England parson."[86] Approaching the mid-18th century, he wrote that the first of "the great ends of government" is "that God in all things may be glorified"; the second, "as it respects man, is the common good of the society, state, or kingdom." "No man," he counseled, "was born for himself, but for mankind." Additionally, he advised his legislative auditors that "tho' the law should prove injurious, as possibly it may, to a particular person when it designs the good of all, yet it is to be submitted to; because everyone has so far

---

[82]Wood, *Creation of the American Republic*, pp. 53–54. But I will argue (as does Pocock) that this overstates republican severity. As noted above, Shelley Burtt has pointed out that this insistence on absolute sacrifice was more characteristic of the English republicans of the 17th century than of classical or Renaissance ones. This is not surprising when one remembers that Englishmen were reformed Protestants.

[83]See my discussion in the introduction regarding our lack of an appropriate vocabulary to describe the Protestant-inspired political theory of the early modern era.

[84]See S. Adams, "Letter to John Scollay" (30 December 1780), in *Writings of Samuel Adams*, 4:238.

[85]See Greven, *Protestant Temperament*, p. 358. Pocock, *Machiavellian Moment*, p. 74, argues that for much of modern Europe, Sparta was the model to emulate.

[86]Miller and Johnson, *Puritans*, 1:270.

resigned up his private thoughts of right and wrong in civil matters to the public judgement."[87]

Others, such as President Samuel Davies of Princeton, were just as direct and succinct. Davies directed his students to "live not for yourselves, but the Publick . . . [and] let your own Ease, your own Pleasure, your own private Interests, yield to the common Good."[88] Marblehead's Congregational pastor, Isaac Story, instructed his auditors that "if we are to love a neighbor *as* ourselves, we are to love the public *better*."[89] Samuel Sherwood of Weston, Connecticut, agreed. In clear and unequivocal language, he found that "the welfare and happiness of such a community, or body, is to be valued above, and preferred to the happiness of an individual."[90] Even the theologically liberal pastor of the West Church in Boston, Simeon Howard, when preaching before the Massachusetts legislature, held that "the people may and ought to give up every right and power to the magistrate which will enable him to more effectually promote the common good."[91] This consistency among American pastors is not surprising, because the traditional Christian view of the just relation between the individual and the community is not individualistic in any modern sense; it is better described as communal, public-centered, and morally restrictive.[92]

Particularly important in spreading this teaching in America were the still-popular 17th-century English pietists: for example, Lewis Bayly, Richard Steel, Richard Allestree, Richard Brathwaite, and Richard Baxter, who taught that the source of all of man's unhappiness was his selfishness. Reformed teachers attacked this innate (post-Fall) reluctance to value the public good over the good of the individual. The 18th-century American audience was receptive to the message that immediate private wants and needs must be relegated to an inferior status. True "fulfillment of the self came from its regulation in accordance with rational social needs. . . . [For] to live life according to one's own impulses and in reference to a personal scale of importance was equivalent to 'alienating the life from [God's] service, to this present world, and the service of the flesh.'"[93] The influential Presbyterian pastor and teacher Gilbert Tennent put it thus: "brethren, we were born not merely for ourselves, but the Publick Good!

[87]Barnard, "Throne Established" (1734 Massachusetts election sermon), pp. 244, 268–70; see also Colman, *Government the Pillar of the Earth* (1730), p. 8.

[88]Davies, *Religion and Public Spirit* (1761), pp. 4–7.

[89]I. Story, *Love of Our Country* (1775), p. 7.

[90]Sherwood, "Scriptural Instructions to Civil Rulers" (1774), p. 391.

[91]S. Howard, "Massachusetts Election Sermon" (1780), pp. 373–74.

[92]See Pocock, *Machiavellian Moment*, pp. 106–7; see also two of the preeminent students of the subject: Troeltsch, *Protestantism and Progress*, p. 150; and M. Weber, *Protestant Ethic*, pp. 265–66.

[93]Cited by Crowley, *This Sheba, Self*, p. 17. The material is from a frequently cited and well-respected English Puritan divine, Richard Baxter, *A Christian Directory; or, A Sum of Practical Theology, and Cases of Conscience.*

which as Members of Society we are obliged *pro virili* to promote."[94] Thus, for the committed reformed Protestant, living without public spirit was equivalent to living without God.

Americans, inspired by reformed Protestantism, equivocated little in their denigration of sinful private needs in favor of God-serving public ones.[95] Man, they held, "was born, not for himself alone, but for others, for society, for his country." Benevolence for the public good was "the prime virtue and self-interestedness . . . the root vice." Indeed, "benevolence meant placing the welfare and rights of others above the welfare of self."[96] As Samuel Davies, an advocate of religious liberty, observed, "unless you conscientiously observe the duties of social life, you cannot enter the kingdom of heaven."[97] The African American pastor Lemuel Haynes reminded his Rutland, Vermont audience on the twenty-fifth anniversary of the Declaration of Independence that public-spiritedness was still demanded of Christians. He noted that "when a man distinguishes himself by a proper regard for the general good, he is then worthy . . . [of] that true dignity the blessed Jesus taught among men."[98] Public virtue was understood by Protestant America to be a form of individual disinterestedness that insisted on private interests giving way before the public good.[99]

Among the most orthodox and committed reformed Protestants, however, true virtue demanded more: the total denial and suppression of the self in subservience to God and the public good. As two of the Puritan fathers had observed, "the very Habit and gift of Faith is of an Emptying Nature, emptying the soule of all confidence in it self and in the Creature, and so leaving and constituting the soule as an empty vessel, empty of its own worth."[100] Throughout New England, "only the offender who failed to confess stood outside that social order; only he truly sinned, because he asserted his own inclinations and impulses, his own will, against the standards of the community. Confession was a curbing of such pride, a denial of the individual will, and an affirmation of the primacy of public values over any possible private ones."[101] Reformed-Protestant orthodoxy was uncompromising in its hostility to the demands of the self.

Yet for many 18th-century Protestants the language of self-denial was more muted. Their understanding of the demand to serve the public good

[94]Cited by Trinterud, *Forming of an American Tradition*, p. 194.

[95]See Hamden, "On Patriotism" (29 November 1773); Hurt, "Love of Country" (1777), p. 147; and [Lathrop], "Politician" (December 1789), p. 446.

[96]Cumings, *Massachusetts Election Sermon* (1783), p. 8; and Valeri, "New Divinity and the American Revolution," pp. 748–49.

[97]Cited by Trinterud, *Forming of an American Tradition*, p. 194.

[98]Haynes, "Nature and Importance of True Republicanism" (1801), p. 78.

[99]See Hatch, *Sacred Cause of Liberty*, p. 105; Heimert, *Religion and the American Mind*, p. 254; Baldwin, *New England Clergy*, pp. 22–23, 171; and Kerr, "Character of Political Sermons," p. 50.

[100]Bulkeley and Cotton, "On Union with Christ" (1637), p. 40.

[101]Zuckerman, *Peaceable Kingdoms*, p. 62; see also pp. 70, 76, and 256.

was largely indistinguishable from that associated with more secular adherents of republicanism. (It is not surprising that reformed Protestantism and republicanism were linked in this fashion, since American republicanism drew heavily on reformed-Protestant norms and culture.)[102] There was, however, a third way of viewing these matters: early modern rationalism.

PUBLIC RATHER THAN PRIVATE GOOD—MODERN RATIONALISM

Early modern rationalism, the third major influence on social and political thought in Revolutionary America, also emphasized that virtuous individuals were to sacrifice short-term or irrational interests to benefit the common good.[103] Although Enlightenment thought, in its many guises, was of limited interest to America's agrarian majority, its rationalistic perspective was not without influence. It helped shape the thought of the more progressive elite in an America where reformed Protestantism and Enlightenment rationalism were not yet competing worldviews. Before the debacle of the French Revolution at the end of the century, most well-educated Americans were confident that there was no conflict between the dictates of true reason and biblical revelation.[104]

Rationalism, which defended the needs of the individual, but only those that were rationally justifiable, was not simple. Defensible interests, for example, were sharply contrasted with licentious ones, which were closely associated with the idiosyncratic wants of particular individuals.[105] Isaiah Berlin finds that for adherents of 18th-century rationalism, "a law which forbids me to do what I could not, as a sane being, conceivably wish to do is not a restraint on my freedom,"[106] but rather true freedom. Rational

---

[102]See Shalhope, "Republicanism and Early American Historiography," pp. 350–51; Wood, *Creation of the American Republic*, pp. 418–19; and Pocock, *Machiavellian Moment*, pp. 403, 462–63, and "Between Gog and Magog," p. 337. Pocock writes that American history is "largely a history of the mutations of Protestantism into civil religion."

[103]See Wood, *Creation of the American Republic*, p. 60.

[104]See May, *Enlightenment in America*, pp. xiv–xv, xviii; Bloch, *Visionary Republic*, p. 188; and Fliegelman, *Prodigals and Pilgrims*, pp. 183–84. For a striking example of overlapping currents of thought in Britain, see A. Sidney, *Discourses Concerning Government* (1698), p. 38; Blackstone, *Commentaries*, 1:40–42; and Dworetz, *Unvarnished Doctrine*, p. 124, who argues that Locke believed that "revelation, not reason (though not in opposition to reason), constituted the original and only source of a complete ethical doctrine." Not all Americans, however, were so sanguine. An early critic of deism and theories of natural religion and natural law divorced from revelation was Clap, *Nature and Foundation of Moral Virtue* (1765). See pp. 47–50 for his caustic denunciation of rationalist pretensions; see also H. S. Smith, *Changing Conceptions of Original Sin*, pp. 42–45, who draws attention to Peter Clark's even earlier condemnation (1758) of human beings' depraved reason.

[105]See R. M. Smith, "Constitution and Autonomy," p. 177; and Haakonssen, "Natural Law," pp. 52–53.

[106]Berlin, "Two Concepts of Liberty," p. 149.

freedom was thus akin to self-imposed restraint, and was to be guided by the higher and more rational needs of both the individual and the public. Consider, then, an anonymous pamphleteer's notice that "man, as a reasonable Creature, is a sociable one [who] so long as he keeps within the Rules of Reason and Society . . . must of Course desire and seek the Welfare of the whole Community." Conversely, he who "endeavors to obstruct or defeat the Happiness of his Fellow Creatures [is] an enemy to Reason, a Slave to Ill nature, and a Substitute of the Devil."[107] The particular wants of the individual, so cherished by 19th-century Romantic individualists, were not among those protected by the dictates of 18th-century rationalism.

Another anonymous author, arguing for the subordination of the individual's irrational wants to the public's rational needs, captured rationalism's understanding of the borders that separate private from public good. "True liberty," he writes, "is not the being able to do *what we will*, but the being able to do *what we ought to will*." To do otherwise is to behave "like a savage or wild beast," and

> man is a rational being; intended by his Creator to lead a rational life; and therefore he must consent to submit to the rules and laws of reason. He is intended likewise to live in society; and in order to be useful in society he must frequently resign his own will and inclinations, and follow those of others. He must curb his appetites, and restrain his inordinate desires; indulging them no farther than is consistent with the good of those among whom he lives.[108]

To the degree, then, that individual good, public good, and individual reason converged, the public good was to serve as the benchmark for each of the others.

Instances of the rationalist outlook, and the priority it awarded the public's needs, are observable throughout the late 18th century. One might begin early in the century with the radical Whig polemics of John Trenchard and Thomas Gordon (otherwise known as Cato), two of the most extensively, though selectively, read English authors in America.[109] This is not to say, however, that Cato was solely influenced by rationalist thought. Their most famous collaboration, *Cato's Letters*, was an eclectic work of disparate, and even inconsistent, parts.[110] Yet notwithstanding their uneven character, these essays held before the American public the idea that the higher good of the public could only be preserved if individ-

---

[107]The Monitor, "On Good Nature" (28 January 1736).

[108]*Liberty: Civil and Religious* (1815), pp. 4–5.

[109]Although neither *The Independent Whig* nor *Cato's Letters* was in its entirety reprinted in the colonies, particular numbers of each were widely cited in newspaper editorials. For a listing of the numbers that were frequently cited or reprinted, see Rossiter, *Seedtime of the Republic*, p. 492, nn.120–21.

[110]See Pangle, *Spirit of Modern Republicanism*, p. 33; cf. Burtt, "Good Citizen's Psyche," p. 31.

uals, through reason, surrendered their arbitrary needs and wants to it. Subjects, and presumably citizens as well, were to maintain "a Passion to promote universal Good, with personal Pain, Loss, and Peril. . . . every Man has a Right and a Call to provide for himself, to attend upon his own Affairs, and to study his own Happiness. All that I contend for is, that this Duty of a Man to himself be performed subsequently to the general Welfare, and consistently with it. The affairs of All should be minded preferably to the Affairs of One."[111] This was a position, then, espoused both by radicals and by conservatives.

On the other side of the Atlantic, a socially prominent Quaker, Chief Justice Samuel Chew of Delaware, maintained at midcentury that "in all governments the private ought to yield to the public good whenever they come in competition with each other."[112] A progressive polemicist, highly respected lawyer, governor of New Jersey, and future delegate to the Constitutional Convention who was influenced by early modern rationalist thought, William Livingston, made even bolder claims on behalf of the public good. He wrote in 1753 that "to exemplify our Love for the Public, as far as our Ability and Sphere of Action will extend, is true Patriotism" and "whoever, from Indolence or Lukewarmness, neglects to advance the common Weal, when it is in his Power, is not only a bad Citizen, but a real Enemy to his Country."[113]

Nevertheless, early modern rationalism was more equivocal in its devaluing of the individual's wants than were the other dominant traditions of political thinking. That is, it did not demand that one discriminate in a zero-sum fashion between the true good of the individual and that of the public. Its adherents assumed that truly rational needs and interests, both public and private, were compatible.[114] Somewhat like its ancient predecessor, rationalism in the 18th century held that the individual and the larger public were both part of a distant god's rationally formed and purposeful universe. As described by an anonymous author in 1776, when God endowed man with free will, he conveniently "laid down certain immutable rules or laws to regulate that free will, and in his infinite goodness has so connected the laws of eternal justice with the happiness of each

---

[111]Trenchard and Gordon, *Cato's Letters* (1733), no. 35, "Of Publick Spirit," in Jacobson, *English Libertarian Heritage*, p. 89. In contrast, see ibid., no. 62, "An Enquiry into the Nature and Extent of Liberty," pp. 127–28, where Trenchard and Gordon write that every man has the "right to enjoy the Fruit of his Labour, Art, and Industry, as far as by it he hurts not the Society, or any Members of it. . . . thus, with the above Limitations, every Man is sole Lord and Arbiter of his own private Actions and Property."

[112]Chew, *Speech* (1742), pp. 2–3.

[113]Livingston, "Of Patriotism" (1753), in Livingston et al., *Independent Reflector*, p. 217.

[114]See Arieli, *Individualism and Nationalism in American Ideology*, pp. 96, 115; W. P. Adams, *First American Constitutions*, p. 223; Burtt, "Good Citizen's Psyche," p. 37; D. Miller, *Philosophy and Ideology*, p. 194; and Friedman, "Shaping of the Radical Consciousness," pp. 789–90.

individual, that the one cannot be attained without the other."[115] If each individual, then, were to order his existence in accord with God's perfect plan, there need not be any deleterious trade-offs between the true rational needs of the individual and those of the public.

Yet this rationalistic world can only be understood in terms of the assumptions of the age, ones that "conceived of nature as harmony and of human society as part of the natural order."[116] Only then were the needs of the individual and those of the public reconcilable, and those of the individual to be countenanced. As Berlin observes, "if the universe is governed by reason, then there will be no need for coercion; a correctly planned life for all will coincide with full freedom—the freedom of rational self-direction—for all."[117] But the rationalist linkage of individual and public good was only possible when each acted in accord with universal norms. One anonymous American author explains that "men, who are endowed with rational and moral powers, act then and then only, with *true liberty* . . . when their reason, freed from ignorance, error, lust, passion, and every false bias, and corrupt inclination, is made their guide. . . . the more they are able to choose and act under the guidance of reason, free and unconfined reason, the more enlarged is the liberty they are possessed of."[118] The author's understanding of individual freedom depicts early modern rationalism's still limited (in comparison to modern-day norms) concession to the standing of the individual.

Each individual had the privilege of doing that which was just and right in the eyes of nature's God. However, that which was just and right was not to be left to individual discretion; it was to be guided by the public. John Dickinson, a prominent Pennsylvania lawyer and future Constitutional Convention delegate and member of Congress, in the most popular Revolutionary series of essays before *Common Sense,* agreed that "a *people* is traveling fast to destruction, when *individuals* consider *their* interests as distinct from *those of the public*. Such notions are fatal to their country, and to themselves."[119] As Richard Bushman reluctantly concludes, "in 1765 confidence in the natural harmonies of the universe were not well enough established to permit the belief that unfettered self-interest could work for the good of the whole. The rationalists always tempered their position by acknowledging that the public good must take precedence."[120] And it was usually the good of the public and its will, rather than the particular wants of the individual, that were most closely associated with reason and God's will. (James Madison would cleverly transform this hallowed truism.)

[115]*Licentiousness Unmask'd* (1776), pp. 8–9.
[116]Hampson, *Enlightenment,* p. 216.
[117]Berlin, "Two Concepts of Liberty," p. 147.
[118]S. M., "Letter to the Printer" (6 April 1778), p. 2.
[119][J. Dickinson], "Letters of a Farmer in Pennsylvania" (1768), p. 397.
[120]Bushman, *From Puritan to Yankee,* pp. 279–80.

Although this valuation of the common good was all but universally accepted in 18th-century America, a few people held that such a public philosophy could never actually be put in practice. In addition to the well-known figures who energetically defended the federal Constitution at the end of the century, three other Revolutionary-era public figures stand out for having taken issue with the need for private sacrifice for the public good.

Arthur Lee, living, studying, and being radicalized in England,[121] argued that the "individual who best promotes the interest of the public with his own, is most laudable." He skeptically noted, however, "the nature of man admits not of such disinterested action, and the nature of society seldom demands it; for the good of the whole is rarely to be separated from that of the individual."[122] We recognize that when Lee wrote of the identity between the individual's and the public's good, he was following a well-worn rationalist line of thinking in which the ordered character of the cosmos ensured their compatibility. Before the late 1780s, however, this limited concession to man's selfishness, grounded in a certain optimism in the providential ordering of the universe, is as close as one usually would get to a public defense of the immediate needs of the individual.[123]

Two other figures, Carter Braxton and William Vans Murray, were still more skeptical, both of people's ability to act unselfishly and of any assumed identity between individual and corporate needs. Braxton argued with considerable cynicism that a republican government in America would doom the experiment in popular government to failure. Americans, he noted, were too wealthy a people for such a demanding system of government. Braxton charged that most Americans mistakenly believed that "a man, therefore, to qualify himself for a member of such a community, must divest himself of all interested motives, and engage in no pursuits which do not ultimately redound to the benefit of society." But, according to Braxton, American popular government would fail if such a public outlook were truly necessary. It would fail because the required public virtue demanded "a disinterested attachment to the public good, exclusive and independent of all private and selfish interest," which he was confident

---

[121]See Maier, *Old Revolutionaries*, pp. 179, 197; Maier notes that Arthur's brother, William, was the "first American alderman of the City of London." Arthur's having spent so long in England is significant because greater sensitivity to the needs of the individual was already to be found there in the early 18th century, though it was hotly contested by more numerous and traditional public-centered thinkers.

[122][Lee], *Essay in Vindication* (1764), p. 19.

[123]For the argument that such positions were taken, but not dominant, see W. P. Adams, *First American Constitutions*, pp. 161–62, who cites from a speech of Gouverneur Morris of uncertain date that was published by Adams in *Amerikanstudien* in 1976. For a position even less in agreement with my characterization, see J. P. Greene, *Pursuits of Happiness*, pp. 138–39; and in full opposition, see Webking, *American Revolution*, p. 130.

"never characterized the mass of the people in any state," Revolutionary Americans included.[124]

It was not the ethics of private sacrifice that he challenged, but rather the utility and public need for it. In opposition to Montesquieu and the wisdom of the ancients, he argued that popular government did not depend on a virtuous citizenry for its success. Without attacking the priority of the public good, he suggested that a certain measure of self-interested behavior was fully compatible with it. This was a position that Madison would make famous ten years later. Braxton, in his stronger (than Lee's) but still lukewarm embrace of selfishness, was at least ten years ahead of his time.

A decade later, William Vans Murray was more timely in explaining that if popular commitment to the public good were truly necessary for the success of democracy, then "it certainly is a principle of too whimsical a nature to be relied on." Moreover, he believed that Sparta had failed because its political institutions had been based on a faulty understanding of human nature. This led the Spartans "to force the human character into distorted shapes," instead of giving it the "easy play and exercise, in which alone its development and vigour will be found to consist."[125] Such public-centered errors, he advised, could and must be avoided if the American experiment in self-government were to succeed. By this time, his view was more likely to be well received, because elite confidence in the virtues of the public had quickly eroded.

In a manner comparable to that of Publius, though possibly even more emphatically, Murray concluded that previously accepted notions of public virtue were not necessary to the maintenance of a popular form of government. Popular governments could only flourish if they accommodated themselves to the long-reviled self-interested nature of man. But while flirting with individualistic notions, he too was unwilling to defend the principle that the needs of the individual had a protected status that the corporate good could not preempt.

Braxton and Murray (and to a lesser degree Lee) did not share their fellow citizens' faith in their ability to adhere to such a public-spirited existence. But they expressed skepticism concerning the peoples' ability to do so without defending the rights of the individual against those of the public or, except for Murray, even anticipating the individualist understanding of human flourishing. And their criticism of their contemporaries powerfully confirms that the dominant social and political thought of the time did value the rights of the public over those of the individual. Braxton's commonsense remark was at the time dismissed (though later embraced) by John Adams as being unable to make any progress "in the

---

124[Braxton], "Address to the Convention" (1776), p. 334.
125W. V. Murray, "Political Sketches" (1785), pp. 231–33.

world [for] it is too absurd to be considered twice."[126] The contention that the rights and immediate needs of the individual were superior to those of the public was not discussed in late 18th-century America, let alone embraced publicly.[127] It was enough to hold that in a truly rational world they were both capable of being satisfied. The priority of the public good was a value that late 18th-century Americans did not question—not even Murray or Publius.

A shared understanding of virtue was held by almost all 18th-century Americans who have left some record of their beliefs. It bridged the differences among those most clearly influenced by early modern rationalism, those who favored Protestant communalism, and elite admirers of republicanism. As Gordon Wood has shown, "virtue—that is, the willingness of the people to sacrifice their private desires for the good of the whole . . . represented all that men of the eighteenth century, from Benjamin Franklin to Jonathan Edwards, sought in social behavior."[128] Available evidence leaves little doubt that the dominant traditions of political and social thought demanded that the public good be valued over the rights (except one) of individuals.

[126]J. Adams, "Letter to Patrick Henry" (3 June 1776), in *Works,* 9:387.

[127]See C. M. Kenyon, "Alexander Hamilton," p. 172. See also Morris, "Political Enquiries" (n.d.), p. 329. That the unusually liberal sentiments expressed by Morris are found only in an undated, unpublished, and apparently never circulated fragment of an essay further supports this contention. Individualistic sympathies, if they existed, must be kept private.

[128]Wood, introduction to *Rising Glory of America,* pp. 5–6; see also Bloch, *Visionary Republic,* p. 109; Kloppenberg, "Virtues of Liberalism," p. 19; Maier, *Old Revolutionaries,* p. 164; Noll, "American Revolution and Protestant Evangelicalism," p. 631; Peters, *Massachusetts Constitution of 1780,* pp. 116, 121–22; Selby, *Concept of Liberty,* p. 122; Stourzh, *Alexander Hamilton,* pp. 63–64; and Vetterli and Bryner, *In Search of the Republic,* p. 1. For an opposing view, see Pangle, "Civic Virtue," pp. 114–15, who nevertheless finds the Christian and republican concepts to have been compatible.

CHAPTER TWO

A Sketch of 18th-Century American Communalism

Following Geertz's suggestions, I would argue that public,
readily observable scenes of social activity best enable the
anthropologist and the historian to grasp the norms and
values that order the lives of a particular people.

—Richard R. Beeman, "The New Social History and the
Search for 'Community' in Colonial America"

REVOLUTIONARY-ERA AMERICANS awarded preeminence to the public's
needs. But more was expected from each of them than this, for they were a
communal people. They believed that local intermediate (familial, social,
religious, and governmental) institutions must play a prominent and intrusive role in defining the ethical life of individuals by placing limits on individual autonomy.[1] Without such barriers, a well-lived life was believed
impossible.

Recent research by social historians has done much to reconstruct the
social, economic, and political lives of 18th-century Americans.[2] These historians have had to go beyond the normal resources of intellectual history.
From their empirically based portraits of 18th-century American life one
can gain an understanding of otherwise undiscoverable lived American
political and social norms. Here, their political thought is "inferred from
ordinary daily behavior, rather than formal ideas."[3] What has been revealed is that the less-articulate agrarian majority adhered to an understanding of the political good that was public centered and communal.
Americans were local communalists who "did not espouse the ethic of
individualism" but instead backed a localism in which freedom "was possible only within a community of like-minded men."[4] The research findings
of most social historians largely corroborate this characterization of the
political thought of the articulate political class of Americans.

[1] See Will, *Statecraft as Soulcraft*, pp. 77, 164.
[2] See Hays, "Theoretical Implications of Recent Work," p. 16, for his defense of political
scientists using the work of historians as "primary" source material.
[3] Berthoff, "Peasants and Artisans, Puritans and Republicans," p. 590.
[4] Henretta, "Morphology of New England Society," p. 394.

AMERICAN COMMUNALISM'S TWIN FEATURES

There has been a general failure among historians to agree on a definition of community.[5] As it had for centuries,[6] communal political theory in America described two interconnected features of social thought and life. First, most Americans were dedicated, in theory and practice, to local rather than central and national political, religious, and economic organization. Second, they insisted that it was the responsibility of these local institutions to shape and make possible their members' ethical existences.[7] Aristotle taught that a political community "must devote itself to the end of encouraging goodness"; otherwise it sinks into being "a mere alliance."[8] Edmund Burke reminded his readers that the political community was more than "a partnership agreement in a trade of pepper and coffee." Instead, it is "to be looked on with other reverence, because it is not a partnership in things subservient only to the gross animal existence of a temporary and perishable nature."[9] In such an understanding of the good life, individual ethical ends were publicly defined that could only be satisfied in a local communal existence. And these two facets of communalism, localism and corporately shaped moral existence, supported each other in 18th-century America.

The sense of communalism used above is not idiosyncratic.[10] The *Oxford English Dictionary* states that communalism is "the principle of the communal organization of society: a theory of government which advocates the widest extension of local autonomy for each locally definable community."[11] In America, "the pressure of the community [was] much more the pressure of the small community than that of the state, or of the nation as a whole."[12] Elsewhere, communalism has been described as "a theory or system of government in which communes or local communities, sometimes on an ethnic or religious basis, have virtual autonomy within a federated state."[13] Communalism, then, is appropriately understood as comprising localist elements. Corporate ethical elements are also important to a complete understanding of communalism. The anthropologist

[5]See Beeman, "New Social History," p. 427.

[6]See Skinner, *Foundations of Modern Political Thought,* 1:6–7.

[7]See Lutz, *Origins of American Constitutionalism,* p. 76; and J. Miller, *Rise and Fall of Democracy,* pp. 10–11.

[8]Aristotle, *Politics* 1280b; see also Bryan and McClaughry, *Vermont Papers,* p. 63.

[9]Burke, *Reflections on the Revolution in France* (1790), p. 85.

[10]See Hillery, "Definitions of Community," for his list of ninety-four definitions of community. See also Bender, *Community and Social Change in America,* pp. 3–11 (in particular, see the works cited in his n. 4); and D. L. Phillips, *Looking Backward,* pp. 10–18, for his selective distillation of the contemporary communitarian understanding of community.

[11]*Compact Edition of the Oxford English Dictionary,* s.v. "communalism."

[12]Pekelis, *Law and Social Action,* p. 75; see also Pole, *Political Representation in England,* pp. 52–53.

[13]*Webster's New World Dictionary,* s.v. "communalism."

Robert Redfield explained that at the core of community lie "conceptions the people have as to the good." These shared norms must include standards that define "relations between one's self and other people and between one's self and God."[14]

American communalism joined these two elements. Americans assumed that each segment of the population from the larger whole would enjoy "autonomy in its domain . . . homogeneity of its membership, and . . . the right to fulfill its destiny without interference" from external elites.[15] In America, both the localist geographical aspect and the commitment to corporately shaped ethical lives (usually associated with a particular ethnic and Protestant dispensation) were essential parts of communalism. The latter element demanded that an individual's ethical existence be corporately envisioned, defined, and enforced. Individual autonomy, as it is understood today, would have been viewed as inconsistent with human flourishing—in fact, it would have been seen as a form of sinful degeneration.

American localism is a matter of little controversy. The geographical isolation of 18th-century American villages almost demanded it. Ninety-five percent of Americans lived in rural, largely agricultural communities. And most Americans were proud that they lived in such communities and that their communal standards were often parochial and idiosyncratic.[16] Often their central corporate aspiration was to be left alone in their secluded villages to shape their lives as they collectively saw fit.[17] Indeed, rural Americans were hostile to any superordinate governmental intrusion (whether of a county, state, or imperial government).[18] In the most rural areas, the settlers "were so local-minded . . . that to get them to become loyal to the state and conscious of its problems would have constituted a vast broadening of their horizons."[19] This is further evidenced by the ability of local governments to function unaffected whenever the provincial or imperial governments were rendered inoperative (most notably in New En-

---

[14]Redfield, *Little Community*, p. 80. See also Hine, *Community on the American Frontier*, p. 25, who argues that communities must fail "without commonly assumed values"; Bellah et al., *Habits of the Heart*, pp. 139–40, 333; and Nisbet, *Quest for Community*, p. xxix. For an opposing view, see J. Ladd, "Idea of Community," p. 29, who argues against such criteria for the existence of community; and Arensberg, "American Communities," p. 1143. See also Bender, *Community and Social Change in America*, who recognizes that a commitment to shared ethical norms is a traditional feature of healthy communal life, but also contends that it should not be constitutive of contemporary communities.

[15]Wiebe, *Segmented Society*, pp. 42, 48–49, 50; see also Wiebe, *Opening of American Society*, p. 124.

[16]See Bender, *Community and Social Change in America*, p. 89; and Elkins and McKitrick, "Founding Fathers," p. 381.

[17]See Rossiter, *First American Revolution*, p. 113.

[18]See Handlin and Handlin, *Popular Sources of Political Authority*, pp. 63–64; J. Madison, "Federalist No. 46," in Hamilton, Jay, and Madison, *Federalist*, p. 309; Elazar, *American Federalism*, pp. 92–93; and Hatch, *Democratization of American Christianity*, p. 108.

[19]McDonald, *E Pluribus Unum*, pp. 201, 221.

gland in 1689, and more generally in 1774).[20] Yet, even when operating normally, state governments were forced to act "for local and provisional interests and seldom for any" larger centralized, imperialistic, or nationalistic interest.[21] Localism was an inescapable and enduring feature of American political life.

Thomas Jefferson was a witness to the strength of American localism. In later life, he stood in awe of the democratic power of the New England villages' local autonomy. He claimed that these little hamlets had shaken the very foundations of government under his feet during his administration's embargo, and thereby "overrule[d] the Union." Jefferson, however, defended such localism and argued that "generalizing and concentrating all cares and powers" in the central state was always the death knell of liberty.[22] He added that "these wards, called townships in New England, are the vital principle of their governments, and have proved themselves the wisest invention ever devised by the wit of man for the perfect exercise of self-government, and for its preservation."[23] Localism had been and continued to be so central to the American experience that it might well be the essence of the American political tradition.[24]

With some disappointment, then, Jefferson acknowledged in a letter to John Taylor that with the adoption of the Constitution, Americans had failed to preserve their local democratic inheritance and that they had retained "less regular control over their agents, than their rights and their interests require."[25] Hannah Arendt, a passionate defender of democratic freedom, would later lament that the Constitution's "failure to incorporate the townships and the town-hall meetings, the original springs of all political activity in the country," had resulted in "a death sentence for them."[26] But such observations were premature.[27] The power of local communities to shape their own lives and those of their individual citizens—to some a frightening power—is a peculiarly American tradition.[28]

American local communalism found great support in the thought and

[20]For example, see Sly, *Town Government in Massachusetts*, pp. 99–100, and Carr, "Foundations of Social Order," p. 90.

[21]Bridenbaugh, *Spirit of '76*, p. 68.

[22]Jefferson, "Letter to Joseph C. Cabell" (1816), in *Writings*, ed. Peterson, pp. 1380–81.

[23]Jefferson, "Letter to Samuel Kercheval" (1816), in ibid., p. 1399.

[24]See Lutz, *Popular Consent and Popular Control*, p. 75.

[25]Jefferson, "Letter to John Taylor" (1816), in *Writings*, ed. Peterson, p. 1394; see also Countryman, "Very Spirit of Liberty," p. 24 (draft version); and Arendt, *On Revolution*, p. 255.

[26]Arendt, *On Revolution*, p. 239.

[27]See Somkin, *Unquiet Eagle*, p. 1, and Pole, *Political Representation in England*, p. 248, who notes that it would not be until 1857 that the constituencies of the Massachusetts legislature would finally cease to be the towns of that state.

[28]See Barber, "Where We Learn Democracy," p. 15, who writes that "community appears to prosper only when parochialism and exclusivity are championed."

practices of reformed Protestantism,[29] for it demanded local autonomy to support and foster individual salvation and godly service.[30] From the reformed-Protestant perspective, only "local resistance to social hierarchy and to religious and political centralization" allowed the community to remain free to effect moral discipline and thus aid the individual in honoring God and living a godly life.[31] As was true in Europe, "the town even considered itself as a kind of intermediary through which the individual found his salvation."[32] Only within the compass of a small community could the visible saints be known—those principally responsible for subjecting "the damned to the divine supervision of the Church" in a manner "consistent with the glory of God."[33] From the reformed-Protestant perspective, then, any loss of corporate autonomy to extralocal religious, social, or governmental power made these divine functions difficult to fulfill.

Americans derived from their reformed-Protestant roots, a marked distrust of elites who were not locally situated. They believed that it was the responsibility of a local population or congregation, not distant authorities, to define the ethical ends to be pursued by its members. Commenting on the unequaled local control exercised by village and congregation in America, a British minister, after a fourteen-month visit to the United States in 1807, observed that "whether Anglican or separatist, we [the English] have a notion of Church and nation. In the American states, even Anglicans speak only of village and congregation."[34] An absence of nationalism, however, did not foster individualism, but instead a restrictive localism that offered little protection to its deviant individual members and ethnic minorities. The exclusive right to enact and enforce moral legislation was reserved for the states at most.[35]

Another reflection of Americans' insistence on local control, and their hostility to the centralization of authority,[36] was their embrace of federalism. Americans believed that a confederated form of government would allow them to benefit from the collective military and economic strength of a large number of small republics while preserving local communal control. It would also permit them to maintain control over "police powers," which allowed a communal shaping of the ethical lives of individuals, in-

---

[29]See Ahlstrom, *Religious History of the American People*, p. 124; and Lynd, *Intellectual Origins of American Radicalism*, pp. 164–65, who finds that the foundations of the American vision of the "good society were English and American local institutions combining sacred and secular functions: the parish, the congregation, the town meeting."

[30]See Baron, "Calvinist Republicanism and Its Historical Roots."

[31]Lockridge, "Afterword," in *New England Town*, pp. 184–85.

[32]Moeller, *Imperial Cities and the Reformation*, p. 73.

[33]M. Weber, *Protestant Ethic*, p. 242.

[34]Samuel Benninger, cited by Singleton, "Protestant Voluntary Organizations," p. 551.

[35]See, for example, "Maryland Declaration of Rights" (1776), in B. Schwartz, *Roots of the Bill of Rights*, p. 280.

[36]See S. Huntington, *Political Order in Changing Societies*, pp. 93–139.

cluding "the rules for daily life; rules concerning the production and distribution of wealth, personal conduct, the worship of God."[37] If such powers
were not retained, the seven-term governor of New York, George Clinton,
feared, the citizens of different states would lose any sense of themselves as
particular peoples.[38] Revolutionary-era Americans envisioned as their preferred polity a confederation in which the needs and ethical ends of the
locality (elsewhere despised as particularistic) would dominate.[39]

One anonymous opponent of the Constitution, in defending local communalism and federalism, observed that the people should "convene in
their local assemblies, for local purposes, and for managing their internal
concerns," and that "the essential characteristic of a confederated republic" is "that this head be dependent on, and kept within limited bounds by
the local governments."[40] As the 20th-century progressive nationalist Herbert Croly later described it, "behind the opposition to a centralized government were the interests and the prejudices of the mass of the American
people."[41] Here, then, was the ground on which federalism, in contrast to
centralization and nationalization, had been initially supported: localism.[42]
In the tradition of his great predecessor Publius, Croly found nothing of
value in either authentic federalism or its localist-preserving foundations.

Localism, however, was not without 18th-century elite support. It had
been defended by many of the European political theorists most respected
in America. For example, the frequently cited Baron de Montesquieu was
best known for his defense of the multiple benefits enjoyed by confederations.[43] He had written that there is "a kind of constitution that has all the
internal advantages of a republican, together with the external force of a
monarchical, government. I mean a confederate republic."[44] Americans'
beloved Dr. Richard Price had also urged,[45] "every state, with respect to all
its internal concerns, be continued independent of all the rest" while "a
general confederacy be formed" which is to "possess the power of manag-

---

[37]Bailyn, *Ideological Origins of the American Revolution*, p. 204; see also McDonald, *Novus Ordo Seclorum*, p. 288.

[38]See Clinton, "Letter III of Cato" (25 October 1787), p. 259.

[39]See The Federal Farmer, "Letter XVII" (23 January 1788), p. 92; Agrippa, "Letter IV of Agrippa" (3 December 1787), p. 235; Lynd, *Intellectual Origins of American Radicalism,* pp. 164–65; and W. P. Adams, *First American Constitutions*, pp. 129–229.

[40]The Federal Farmer, "Letter XVII" (1788), p. 92.

[41]Croly, *Promise of American Life*, p. 31.

[42]See Lienesch, *New Order of the Ages*, pp. 105–6.

[43]See Spurlin, *Montesquieu in America*, pp. 220–21.

[44]Montesquieu, *Spirit of the Laws* (1748), 1:126.

[45]See W. Morgan, *Life of the Rev. Richard Price*, pp. 62–63, 105, who writes that "in the course of a few months, by means of the cheap edition, near 60,000 copies had been disposed of. . . . On the western side of the Atlantic it so far prevailed, that these observations . . . were believed to have had no inconsiderable effect in determining the Americans to declare their independence." The same widespread popularity and influence is reported by Peach, *Richard Price*, pp. 9–11.

ing all the *common* concerns of the united states, and of judging and deciding between them."[46]

Thomas Jefferson's defense of localism was as compelling as that of any
European. He argued that "generalizing and concentrating all cares and
powers into one body" had destroyed liberty in every government. Therefore, he urged that each level of government be entrusted with only those
concerns most appropriate to it.[47] Comparable views were expressed by
other Revolutionary members of the elite as well.[48] Americans believed that
authentic federalism, not the purloined version marketed by nationalists,[49]
would offer them the benefits of political stability and local corporate self-
government.

This position was rejected shortly after the Revolution, however, by
other emergent national elites. Luther Martin, a member of the convention
who refused to sign or support the Constitution, angrily observed of his
peers that "a majority of the convention hastily and inconsiderably [had]
. . . decided that a kind of government, which a Montesquieu and a Price
have declared the best calculated of any to preserve internal liberty, and
to enjoy external strength," was for America "totally impracticable; and
they acted accordingly."[50] They did so because nationalist supporters of
the Constitution sought an end to American local communalism.[51] Many
sought the demise or weakening of traditional American localist institutions in order to promote more modern economic, social, and political
practices.[52] Like the imperial elite before them, they zealously opposed
America's rich tradition of local communalism that, in the words of
Gouverneur Morris, was "one of our greatest misfortunes" because "the

---

[46]Price, *Observations* (1776), pp. 8–9; see also Rousseau, *Social Contract* (1762), p. 96,
for his praise of confederations.

[47]Jefferson, "Letter to Joseph Cabell" (2 February 1816), in *Writings*, ed. Peterson, p.
1380.

[48]See S. Adams, *Writings of Samuel Adams*, 4:325; Ramsay, "Oration of 1778," p. 190;
and Henry, "Speech Against the Federal Constitution" (1788), pp. 7–8.

[49]See Melancton Smith, "Speeches before the New York Ratifying Convention" (June
1788), p. 334, who asks that those who wish to reduce the states to a unified national
government "exchange names with those who disliked the Constitution," for the latter were
the true Federalists, whereas "those who advocated it [were] Anti-Federalists"; and A
Farmer, "Essay III" (1788), p. 29.

[50]Martin, "Genuine Information" (29 November 1787), in Farrand, *Records of the Federal
Convention*, 3:197.

[51]See The Federal Farmer, "Letter I," pp. 35–37, who states that the Constitution was
"clearly designed to make us one consolidated government. . . . This consolidation of the
states has been the object of several men in this country for some time past"; Brutus, "Essay
XII," p. 170; and "The Address and Reasons of Dissent of the Minority of the Convention of
Pennsylvania to Their Constituents," in *Anti-Federalist*, pp. 209–10, 213.

[52]See Countryman, *American Revolution*, p. 212; Stourzh, *Alexander Hamilton*, p. 40;
Crowley, *This Sheba, Self*, p. 123; Yazawa, *From Colonies to Commonwealth*, p. 177;
Wiebe, *Opening of American Society*, pp. 24–25; and Banning, "Jeffersonian Ideology Re-
visited," p. 13.

great objects of the nation had been sacrificed constantly to local views." And as Hamilton noted, "the small good ought never to oppose the great one."[53] The dozen or so modernizing state-builders who are celebrated in contemporary history books and in the commentaries of conservative students of the period were resolutely opposed to "those who preferred local" political advantages.[54]

These new men, however, would prove no more successful in immediately transforming American local communalism than various English monarchs and their bureaucracies had been before them.[55] In defense of nationalism, moderate individualism, and the protection of a victimized minority, it would be Abraham Lincoln, not James Madison, who would lead an army of millions and be the first to prevail against American local communalism. Most in the victorious army, communalists themselves, little understood the long-term consequences of their actions. Only in the 20th century, with its wrenching economic transformations, impressive technologies of communication and organization, and a national elite committed to ridding America of its racist institutions, would a final defeat of American localism seem at hand.[56] With its demise, however, historic America with its overwhelming commitment to local communalism would also be transformed.

Their contempt for parochialism was not the only factor that led the nationalizing elite to oppose localism. Another was the corporate ethical aspect of American communalism, the vision of human flourishing guided by family and community, which so troubled some of the nationalists at the end of the 18th century.[57] As Forrest McDonald points out, the local community had traditionally exercised nearly absolute power over the lives of its members.[58] But from the perspective of localists, the local community needed such controls because it served as the front line of defense against the presence of undesirable individuals and minorities.[59]

[53]Morris, in Farrand, *Records of the Federal Convention,* 1:551–53; Hamilton, "Remarks and Speeches at the New York Ratifying Convention," p. 219; and see Hamilton, Jay, and Madison, *Federalist,* pp. 3–4, 59, 91–93, 307–8, and 339; J. Madison, *Mind of the Founder,* pp. 57, 96, 206, 221, and 524; McWilliams, *Idea of Fraternity in America,* pp. 188–93; Yarbrough, "Republicanism Reconsidered," pp. 86–87; and J. Miller, "Ghostly Body Politic," p. 114.

[54]George Bryan, cited by Storing, *What the Anti-Federalists Were For,* p. 9.

[55]See Palmer, "Liberties as Constitutional Provisions," pp. 88, 101.

[56]The prosecution of three great wars and the need to protect minorities, especially African Americans, from intolerant majorities have been the most important vehicles in the elite's legitimation of their dismantling of American localism.

[57]See Brutus, "Essay XII," p. 169, who argued that the nationalists sought to take control away from states and localities of "the administration of private justice," so they could regulate "the internal and local affairs of the different parts."

[58]See McDonald, *Novus Ordo Seclorum,* p. 289.

[59]See Hatch, *Sacred Cause of Liberty,* p. 111, and P. Miller, *Errand into the Wilderness,* pp. 142–43.

With something like a spiritual *cordon sanitaire,* local and county officials guarded against physical, social, and religious pathologies, internal as well as external, that might guide the weak away from their God-appointed duties. Local communities were, therefore, little concerned about a loss of freedom for nonresident individuals with "communicable" diseases. Public officials and their constituencies did not doubt that it was their legitimate responsibility to prevent the spread of all manner of disease. For example, they believed that stopping the spread of "smallpox was more important than the right of victims to wander" into their midst.[60] But it was not physical diseases alone that they sought to isolate. The Handlins note that "the corporate community bred intolerance of every form of deviant behavior," primarily "out of fear that wrong behavior by some would destroy the health of all."[61] Most 18th-century Americans accepted that the public had an intrusive role, both ethically and physically, to play in fostering human development and flourishing while recognizing that the ultimate ends served were nonetheless individual ones.

In the 17th century, Americans had believed that the community was not "an aggregation of individuals," but instead "an organism, functioning for a definite purpose, with all parts subordinate to the whole."[62] Individual sacrifice, to the point of self-abnegation, was for them therefore not a heroic act but a moral obligation. In the 18th century, such corporatist, almost collectivist, thinking was still present in America, although in a more nuanced form. For example, Abraham Williams, preaching before the Massachusetts legislature, held that "the natural Body consists of various Members, connected and subservient one to the other, each serving some valuable purpose and the most perfect and happy State of the Body results from all the Members regularly performing their natural Offices; so collective Bodies, or Societies, are composed of various Individuals connected together, related and subservient to each other."[63] This corporatist view of society continued to be defended in Revolutionary America. Also before the Massachusetts legislature, a respected pastor held that "as in the body natural, all the parts and members are necessary; and in their places severally concur to the health, strength and beauty of the whole: So in the body politick. . . . When the parts are disadjusted, the body is out of health."[64] Society was thus seen, at least by prominent New Englanders, as an organic whole, a community, within which each member found meaning and ultimately the means to achieve his or her true, everlasting welfare.

---

[60]Countryman, *American Revolution,* p. 78.

[61]Handlin and Handlin, *Liberty and Power,* p. 91; see also Lockridge and Kreider, "Evolution of Massachusetts Town Government," p. 555.

[62]P. Miller, "The Puritan State and Puritan Society," in *Errand into the Wilderness,* p. 143.

[63]Williams, "Massachusetts Election Sermon" (1762), pp. 3–4.

[64]J. Clark, *Massachusetts Election Sermon* (1781), pp. 29–30.

And the corporate body was enjoined to do that which was necessary to maintain its health and that of its parts.[65]

More generally, the sermon literature of New England commonly rehearsed and defended the ethical intrusiveness of communal life. On one such occasion, the future Vermont Supreme Court judge and United States congressman Nathaniel Niles excoriated materialism and the foundations of individualism. In a lengthy note, Niles explains what he meant in his sermon when he argued that "originally, there were no private interests." From a common 18th-century perspective,[66] he writes that "a compact formed with a particular design to secure and advance the private interests of those by whom the compact was made" is indeed "the maxim on which pirates and gangs of robbers live in a kind of unity." After denouncing materialist and contractual foundations for civil society, he argues in favor of an ethically demanding communal one in which "every individual is to have his part assigned him . . . but he is not to have any separate interest consigned to him, for this would tend to detach him from the community. . . . Thus each individual is to take care of the community, and the community in its turn, is to make provision for the individuals."[67] The individual in this communal view is not without ethical standing, but rather is radically incomplete outside a defining, nurturing, and morally intrusive communal environment.

A close student of early modern political thought, Father Francis Canavan, describes this communal aspect of the 18th-century mind and its critical role in ethics and political thought. He finds that for these people,

> man is designed by God and nature for life in civil society, without which he cannot arrive at the full development of which his nature is capable. The potential for that development sets the goals of human life. The goals of human life, in turn, are the source of moral obligation, both individual and political, because man is morally obliged to consent to his nature's goals and to the necessary means of achieving them. Obligation is thus prior to consent and commands consent.[68]

Only within a communal habitat could the individual develop his or her life to its fullest potential. As the prominent 18th-century author John Brown noted, the "solitary and wretched State is strictly *unnatural;* be-

---

[65]See J. Huntington, *Discourse* (1781), p. 14; Westminster Assembly, "Westminster Confession of Faith" (1646), p. 220; and Haskins, *Law and Authority in Early Massachusetts*, p. 79.

[66]See W. E. Nelson, *Americanization of the Common Law*, p. 47; Rossiter, *First American Revolution*, p. 31; E. Foner, *Tom Paine and Revolutionary America*, pp. 145–82; and Heimert, *Religion and the American Mind*, p. 514, who believes that Niles's *Two Discourses* provides the key to the social and political theory of Revolutionary America.

[67]N. Niles, "[First of] Two Discourses on Liberty" (1774), pp. 260–63.

[68]Canavan, "Relevance of the Burke-Paine Controversy," p. 166.

cause it prevents the Exertion of those Powers, which his *Nature* is *capable* of *attaining:* But those *Powers Society* alone can *call forth* into *Action.* Man is therefore formed for Society."[69] Community life was foremost a shared moral life that by necessity demanded restrictive, not liberating, corporate intrusion into the lives of its members.

For most colonial Americans, serving God and leading a fulfilled human life depended on membership in a locally controlled community. In turn, each community was to be guided by appropriate substantive ethics (usually a particular understanding of Protestant Christianity) that, in effect, defined it as a community. One anonymous author drew attention to the centrality of such a shared ethical vision; he noted that "in the solitary state of nature" the most elevated motive that man is able to produce is a "*natural affection* towards one's offspring." But it is only in an environment of shared morality, "supported with the joint advice and affections of his fellow creatures," that man is able to reach his highest development by sustaining "a common relation to the same moral system or community."[70] For this author, Americans' inherited English and Protestant ethical and legal systems defined them as a people. He continued: "*love of our country* does not import an attachment to any particular soil, climate, or spot of earth, where perhaps we first drew our breath," but rather "it imports an affection to that *moral system,* or *community which is governed by the same laws.*"[71] Morality and community were for him not separable.

In most cases, the community's ethics was an uncompromising commitment to some variant of reformed Protestantism. At the end of the Revolutionary years, the considered opinion of the politically active, much-published, and respected liberal pastor of the Congregational Church in West Springfield, Massachusetts, Joseph Lathrop, was still that "government is a combination of the whole community against the vices of each particular member" so that it might "exercise a controul over each member, to restrain him from wrong and compel him to right."[72] Michael Zuckerman observes that "the community they desired was an enclave of common believers, and to the best of their ability they secured such a society, rooted not only in ethnic and cultural homogeneity but also in common moral and economic ideas and practices."[73] Even in Pennsylvania, in many ways the most progressive state, only the right of religious conscience is protected in its Declaration of Rights. Outside this protected sphere, the state was to enact "laws for the encouragement of virtue, and prevention of vice and immorality." Such laws were to be "constantly kept in force, and

[69]J. Brown, *Thoughts on Civil Liberty* (1765), pp. 12–13.
[70]The Preceptor, "Social Duties of the Political Kind" (1772), p. 176.
[71]Ibid., p. 177.
[72]Lathrop, "Miscellaneous Collection of Original Pieces" (1786), pp. 670–71.
[73]Zuckerman, "Social Context of Democracy in Massachusetts," pp. 538–39.

provision shall be made for their due execution."[74] Only when so guided and within a restricted enclave of unified believers was a good human life, a life of moral limits guided by tradition and custom, possible.[75]

This vision demanded that little protection be awarded the potential source of discord—the nonconforming individual. In such communities, "narrow but consensual norms might be necessary for any clear sense of communal purpose and unity."[76] Their shared commitment to a fixed (and objective) telos for individual members demanded intolerance, for toleration "led neither to improvement nor to regeneration."[77] The British social historian Keith Thomas observes of a still closely connected Anglo-American world that the single most powerful impression of 18th-century village life was "of the tyranny of local opinion and the lack of tolerance displayed towards nonconformity or social deviance." This was a world in which "a man's most personal affairs were the legitimate concern of the whole community."[78] Men and women standing outside the circle of agreed-upon ethical precepts were without antecedent fully inalienable individual rights (except that of religious conscience).[79]

Moral pariahs either reconciled themselves with the community,[80] or they were expelled by villages that "had efficient ways of driving out strangers and disciplining and humbling individual deviants within its own fold."[81] Although "individual dissidents were always free to pull up stakes and depart to other places,"[82] during the Revolutionary years and the 150 years of American history preceding them, what they could not choose was self-defined, individualistic freedom.[83]

The early 19th century was not much different in this regard, at least at the level of public opinion.[84] As Alexis de Tocqueville wrote of early 19th-century America, "the multitude requires no laws to coerce those who do not think like themselves: public disapprobation is enough; a sense of their loneliness and impotence overtakes them and drives them to despair."[85] At the midpoint of the 19th century, American communalism was still strident. Consider the words of Senator Stephen Douglas, employing political language that would have been equally familiar in the late 18th century.

---

[74]"Pennsylvania Declaration of Rights" (1776), in B. Schwartz, *Roots of the Bill of Rights,* p. 274.

[75]See Grasso, "Between Awakenings," p. 94.

[76]Conkin, "Freedom," p. 209.

[77]Haskins, *Law and Authority in Early Massachusetts,* p. 224.

[78]K. Thomas, *Religion and the Decline of Magic,* p. 527.

[79]See Lockridge, *Settlement and Unsettlement in Early America,* p. 118.

[80]See Zuckerman, *Peaceable Kingdoms,* p. 258.

[81]Hofstadter, *America at 1750,* p. 281.

[82]W. E. Nelson, "Eighteenth Century Constitution," p. 28.

[83]See Bailyn, *Ideological Origins of the American Revolution,* pp. 204–5.

[84]Cf. W. E. Nelson, *Americanization of the Common Law,* pp. 109–10, who describes in the late 1780s the "virtual cessation of criminal prosecution for various sorts of immorality."

[85]Tocqueville, *Democracy in America* (1840), 2:275.

He writes that "if there is any one principle dearer and more sacred than all others in free governments . . . it is that which asserts the exclusive right of a free people to form and adopt their own fundamental law, and to manage and regulate their own internal affairs and domestic institutions." Daniel Rodgers clarifies that "Douglas's people was a patchwork of local peoples, each clutching to its vested rights, its fraternal exclusion."[86] Nevertheless, American communalism in the 19th century, like almost everything else in American cultural, social, economic, and religious life, had changed from what it had been in the 18th, to say nothing of the 17th century.

The change in the character of communalism was not precipitated, as one might expect, by the rapid spread of tolerance of individual deviance among American communities or by a desire for enlightened individualism.[87] Rather, toward the end of the 18th century, American communalism increasingly began to lose some of its ethical dimension as village self-direction and order "without reference to the saving of souls or the building of God's kingdom on earth" became increasingly the goal of communal life.[88] It was localism, the deeply traditional Anglo-American desire of a people "to be left alone in their villages,"[89] that began to emerge, stripped of some of its ethical moorings, from the 18th century. Although deference to the common good would long remain, something of the legitimating moral force supporting the corporate shaping of ethical lives had already been lost.

American dedication to the precepts of localism, defended so vociferously by Anti-Federalist authors,[90] remained vibrant. But communalism, with its more attenuated moral vision, attracted fewer elite adherents. Kenneth Lockridge perceptively argues that "although deeply descriptive of the conditions of American life, localism failed to express itself as a creative ideology. It was too visceral, too much in the realm of the uneducated."[91] As regularly pointed out by Anglicans and orthodox Lutherans (members of state-administered denominations), localism without outside elite supervision was susceptible to uncontrolled degeneration, particularly toward what Edward Banfield later described as "amoral familism."[92] By the early national period, rural Americans with increasingly less articulate leader-

[86]Cited by Rodgers, *Contested Truths*, p. 110.

[87]See Conkin, "Freedom," pp. 206–7.

[88]Flaherty, "Law and the Enforcement of Morals," p. 248, and see W. E. Nelson, *Americanization of the Common Law*, p. 120.

[89]Lockridge, *Settlement and Unsettlement in Early America*, pp. 46–47.

[90]Above all see Storing's almost poignant comment, *What the Anti-Federalists Were For*, p. 83, n. 7; Ketcham, *Presidents above Party*, p. 79; Main, *Anti-federalists*, p. 7; McDonald, *E Pluribus Unum*, pp. 317–18; Wood, *Creation of the American Republic*, pp. 192, 194–95; Shalhope, "Republicanism and Early American Historiography," pp. 352–53; Roche, "Founding Fathers," p. 438; and Bridenbaugh, *Spirit of '76*, p. 68.

[91]Lockridge, *Settlement and Unsettlement in Early America*, p. 51.

[92]Discussed by Skerry, "Individualist America and Today's Immigrants," p. 116.

ship opposed centralization, incipient individualism, and nationalism a little less admirably.

SOCIAL HISTORIANS' PORTRAIT OF A COMMUNAL PEOPLE

Recent intensive research into the lives of colonial Americans has caused many previously well regarded beliefs about American social and political practices to be rejected as untrue.[93] The scholarship of social historians during this period has produced a portrait of Revolutionary America that because of its diversity almost defies generalization.[94] Nonetheless, in this growing body of research on American life,[95] one feature continues to emerge: the reality of American local communalism. The previously accepted norm of individualism is now seen as rather exceptional.[96]

As early as 1953, political scientist Clinton Rossiter described Americans as intensely self-reliant and distrustful of "centralized government." He wrote, for example, that "the central governments of the colonies exercised even less control over local institutions than did the mother country over the colonies."[97] His observations are now supported by the research of numerous social historians and historical sociologists.[98] Social historian Christine Heyrman captures the essence of their findings when she describes the norms of a challenging test case, an 18th-century commercial

[93]See Murrin, "Review Essay," pp. 227–33, and Waters, "From Democracy to Demography."

[94]See Beeman, "New Social History," p. 426.

[95]See ibid., pp. 423–25, for his bibliography of research that was current as of 1977; Lockridge, "New Afterword" and "Updated Bibliography" in *New England Town*, current as of 1985; and J. P. Greene, *Pursuits of Happiness*, for his 1988 encyclopedic survey of the literature.

[96]See Appleby, "Value and Society," pp. 304–5.

[97]Rossiter, *Seedtime of the Republic*, p. 119.

[98]A partial listing must include: F. Anderson, *People's Army*; Barron, *Those Who Stayed Behind*; Bender, *Community and Social Change in America*; Bonomi, *Under the Cope of Heaven*; Breen, "Persistent Localism"; Bridenbaugh, *Myths and Realities*; Cook, *Fathers of the Towns*; Countryman, *American Revolution*; Daniels, *Connecticut Town* and *Town and County*; Demos, *Little Commonwealth*; Ditz, *Property and Kinship*; Dunn, "Social History of Early New England"; Greven, *Four Generations*; Gross, *Minutemen and Their World*; Hahn and Prude, introduction to *Countryside*; D. D. Hall, "Religion and Society"; Haskins, *Law and Authority in Early Massachusetts*; Henretta, "Morphology of New England Society"; Heyrman, *Commerce and Culture*; Hine, *Community on the American Frontier*; Isaac, *Transformation of Virginia*; Jedrey, *World of John Cleaveland*; Kross, *Evolution of an American Town*; Lingeman, *Small Town America*; Lockridge, *New England Town*; McDonald and McDonald, *Requiem*; Murrin, "Myths of Colonial Democracy"; Nobles, *Divisions throughout the Whole*; S. C. Powell, *Puritan Village*; Rutman and Rutman, *Place in Time*; Slaughter, *Whiskey Rebellion*; Sly, *Town Government in Massachusetts*; Szatmary, *Shays' Rebellion*; A. Taylor, *Liberty Men and Great Proprietors*; Tracy, *Jonathan Edwards, Pastor*; Waters, "From Democracy to Demography"; Whitlock, *Parish of Amity*; Winslow, *Meeting House Hill*; and Zuckerman, *Peaceable Kingdoms*.

center. She finds that even the men and women engaged in modern economic activities such as international maritime trade were communalists committed to "localism, insularity, [and] intolerance towards outsiders," and had "an aversion to risk and an attachment to tradition."[99] Only a minority of social historians today question whether most of late colonial American society was communalistic in this sense.[100]

Other historians have also contributed to this portrait of Americans as communal. Intellectual historians Oscar and Lilian Handlin find that communal institutions and aspirations "endured through the eighteenth century."[101] Colonial historian Gordon Wood has drawn attention to the use by patriots such as Sam Adams of communal, if not collectivist, language. For example, Wood draws attention to Adams's insistence that "the state was 'a moral person, having an interest and will of its own.'"[102] John Crowley, an economic historian, also offers a convincing case for the predominance of a communalistic outlook among Americans. For them, "the important tension in values applied to work was not that between individualistic and communitarian impulses," because everyone accepted the communal position and "granted the appropriateness of the regulation of social and economic life."[103] Drawing together the sacred and secular dimensions of American communalism, legal historian William Nelson notes that in late 18th-century Massachusetts, "all members of society shared common ethical values and imposed those values on the occasional individual who refused to abide by them voluntarily."[104] Historians thus largely accept the communal description. (They are more intent on understanding exactly when, how, and in what ways American norms and practices changed during the 19th century,[105] particularly regarding the advance and further penetration into rural areas of a capitalist market in labor and goods.)[106]

Some historians have even argued that before English settlers were "Americans," they were already committed local communalists. Timothy Breen writes that "having to resist Stuart centralization, a resistance that pitted small congregations against meddling bishops," English settlers in America were "determined to maintain their local attachments against outside interference, and to a large extent the Congregational churches and

[99]Heyrman, *Commerce and Culture*, p. 143.

[100]Among those in full or partial disagreement are: Bushman, *From Puritan to Yankee*; Grant, *Democracy*; J. P. Greene, *Pursuits of Happiness*; Lemon, *Best Poor Man's Country*; and Wolf, *Urban Village*. See also D. L. Phillips, *Looking Backward*, pp. 24–60, whose overview of the historical scholarship has led him to conclusions diametrically opposite to mine.

[101]Handlin and Handlin, *Liberty and Power*, pp. 85, 89.

[102]Cited by Wood, *Creation of the American Republic*, p. 58.

[103]Crowley, *This Sheba, Self*, p. 6.

[104]W. E. Nelson, *Americanization of the Common Law*, p. 4.

[105]See Matthews, "Liberalism," pp. 1132–33, and Banning, "Quid Transit?" pp. 199–200.

[106]I thank Peter Onuf and Ed Countryman for forcefully drawing this to my attention.

self-contained towns of Massachusetts" were demonstrable evidence of their success.[107] Kenneth Lockridge finds that "long before the migration to New England, Puritanism had begun to serve as a weapon in the hands of men and women who resented the erosion of local customs and local power by the evolving central state" and that, in particular, their "Puritanism was characterized by a passionate devotion to the authority of the local congregation."[108]

This incipient American communalism occurred when dedication to parochial political control had already begun to become anachronistic in Europe. By the mid-17th century, Western Europe was starting to witness the development of the modern nation-state. This structural transformation was reflected in the abstract theories of prominent political theorists, who had begun to argue that sovereignty was, in essence, absolute and indivisible.[109] Local communalism and other forms of subnationalism were therefore condemned by avant-garde theorists (such as Thomas Hobbes and, even earlier, Jean Bodin) as feudal remnants to be abandoned in the quest for the higher unity of the leviathan monarchical state. This state would join in a great union atomistic individuals, freed from the reactionary intermediate institutions of family, local congregation, and local community.[110] But in New England and somewhat less successfully in the Chesapeake region, Englishmen reestablished a tradition of local communalism that was so reactionary that it sometimes embarrassed supporters of the colonies still in England.[111]

As one of the more able foreign observers of American life noted, with regard to the localist character of the 17th-century colonies, "at the time of the settlement of the North American colonies, municipal liberty had already penetrated into the laws as well as the customs of the English, and the immigrants adopted," benefited from, and "knew how to appreciate" it.[112] In acting thus, Americans were able to realize traditional European communal ideals in their locally autonomous, consensual, and unusually democratic peasantlike villages.[113] From the moment of settlement, in an almost reactionary stance, the village, township, or county community sought to be the center of Americans' self-directing communal lives.

Throughout the colonies in the 17th century, American communities

[107]Breen, "Persistent Localism," p. 4; see also Greven, *Four Generations*, pp. 267–68.

[108]Lockridge, *Settlement and Unsettlement in Early America*, pp. 36–37.

[109]See Sabine, *History of Political Theory*, pp. 372–440, and Krieger, *Kings and Philosophers*, p. 6.

[110]See Krieger, *Kings and Philosophers*, pp. 115–36; Bendix, *Nation-Building and Citizenship*, pp. 39–66; and P. Anderson, *Lineages of the Absolutist State*, p. 51.

[111]See Kupperman, "Definitions of Liberty," p. 26.

[112]Tocqueville, *Democracy in America* (1835), 1:434.

[113]See Waters, "Traditional World," p. 21; Lockridge, *New England Town*, pp. 18–19; Murrin, "Review Essay," p. 231; Appleby, *Liberalism and Republicanism*, p. 15; and Main, "Agenda for Research," pp. 592–93, who finds local communalism, congregationalism, and the physical environment responsible for America's early democratic development.

guarded their ability to be largely autonomous, as they "did not want the individualistic, competitive, commercialized, ruthlessly hierarchical social world or the centralized state characteristic of the Renaissance England whence they fled."[114] The freedom they sought reflected a deep and rich reformed-Protestant communalism, described in possibly exaggerated fashion by Lockridge as a "Christian Utopian Closed Corporate Community,"[115] which the early colonists hoped would flourish in America.[116]

This was true beyond the Northern plantations; as David Hackett Fischer shows, "the founders of Virginia shared the religious obsessions of their age," so much so that in Virginia each individual was also expected to join in common religious practices.[117] Darrett and Anita Rutman, after years of studying and writing about New England, found that a communal form of life was similarly sought in Virginia. They noted that the scattered entry of initial immigrants into the region was more a response to the riverine geography than the result of any larger individualist political vision. Once installed, Virginians, like their neighbors to the north, structured their lives around families, neighborhoods, and counties, and regarded anything else as "anathema, even sinful."[118] John Waters concludes that the collective portrait emerging from town studies displays a conservative and communal people who "lived in nucleated villages just as they had in the old country."[119] According to the research of the majority of social historians, then, the 17th century must be understood as the foundation on which an American commitment to local communalism was built. Ethnic and religious solidarity and attendant intolerance, rather than enlightened individualism, provided the atmosphere in which this localism flourished.[120]

Colonial historian John Murrin holds that for too long, scholars in search of individualism have ignored the communal character of 18th-century American life and politics. (This, he believes, has resulted in our limited ability to explain later phenomena such as states' rights and "that last of the medieval rebellions, the American Civil War."[121] This insight applies to the politics and culture of the 19th and 20th centuries as well.) Other historians have demonstrated that in the Northern colonies, political, so-

---

[114]Lockridge, *Settlement and Unsettlement in Early America*, p. 7.

[115]Lockridge, *New England Town*, p. 16.

[116]See Fischer, *Albion's Seed*, p. 18.

[117]See ibid., pp. 232–33, and P. Miller, "Religion and Society in the Early Literature of Virginia," in *Errand into the Wilderness;* Miller had earlier demonstrated that the religiosity and ethical intrusiveness of the Southern planters was almost on par with their more zealous neighbors to the north.

[118]Rutman and Rutman, *Place in Time*, pp. 59–60.

[119]Waters, "From Democracy to Demography," p. 248.

[120]For an exception, see Innes, *Labor in a New Land*. See also Menard, "Yankee Puritans," pp. 385–86, who describes the "'communitarian' interpretation of early New England" as "the reigning consensus [that was now] breaking apart."

[121]Murrin, "Myths of Colonial Democracy," p. 55.

cial, and religious existence continued along largely local communal lines. American lives were still lived at the local level with as much power being retained there as possible.[122] Communities sought to shape, in ethically intrusive ways, the "souls" of their residents. Gregory Nobles, in his innovative work on Hampshire County, Massachusetts, finds that "by the middle of the eighteenth century the desire for local autonomy seemed generally to be much more compelling."[123]

Most men and women continued to live within overlapping and concentric circles of family, congregation, neighborhood, parish, town, and county. This formed a thick communal network that made possible a good life. Throughout the 18th century, more and more towns founded two or three generations earlier were, as their populations grew and their familial bonding increased, developing the richly layered texture typical of highly communal societies.[124] The good life demanded local corporate closure regarding essential ethical and religious issues, often along ethnic lines.

Intense localism should be expected, for as Alfred Chandler reminds us, America in 1790 was overwhelmingly rural. It was a country in which only "202,000 out of 3,930,000 Americans lived in towns and villages of more than 2,500."[125] Among the relatively urbanized areas, there were twelve with about forty-five hundred people, seven towns of about seven thousand, three of about sixteen thousand (Boston, Albany, and Charlestown in South Carolina), and two (New York and Philadelphia) with about twenty-five thousand inhabitants each.[126] The modal population for the villages where the other 95 percent of the population lived was five hundred to a thousand residents.[127] So the vast majority of Americans lived in rural environments, including those living in the even more sparsely populated frontier regions of the larger states. It is often forgotten that as late as 1870, "fewer than one-in-four Americans lived in places of twenty-five hundred or more."[128]

The portrait that most social historians provide of Northern colonials living in developed communities is one in which citizens surrounded their meetinghouses (though by European standards very loosely). Some historians even contend that Americans lived in environments more like those of (and also acted more like) European peasants "than the mobilized, activated,

---

[122]See the essays in Daniels, *Town and County.*

[123]Nobles, *Divisions throughout the Whole,* pp. 143–44.

[124]See Greven, *Four Generations,* pp. 141, 269; Wood, *Radicalism of the American Revolution,* p. 46; and Lemon, "Spatial Order," p. 87.

[125]Chandler, *Visible Hand,* p. 17. Not until 1920 would more than 50 percent of Americans live in cities or towns of more than 2,500 people.

[126]See United States Bureau of the Census, *Historical Statistics of the United States, Colonial Times to 1957.*

[127]See Murrin, "Review Essay," pp. 248, 256.

[128]Bender, *Community and Social Change in America,* p. 12.

entrepreneurial individualistic man read back into colonial history."[129] One can at least agree with the findings of most historians that deviation from village standards was met with communal censure. At town meetings, a man was expected to "set the needs of the group before his own and strive to think as his neighbors thought."[130] Although social historians find that this hoped-for ideal was not always met, they nevertheless report abundant evidence that this was the goal that most Americans, even in the 18th century, strove to achieve.

Ironically, the pervasiveness of the communal character of life in the North is perhaps most convincingly displayed where one least expects to find such evidence. Heyrman does just that as she demonstrates that not even exposure to the modernizing effects of commercialization eroded the communal character of Northern town life. She writes that searching in the late 18th century for "stereotypical 'Yankees' of boundless initiative and ambition, restive under the restraints of established institutions and inherited values, turns up instead Puritan traditionalists." In the trading center of Gloucester, she finds that its residents throughout the century, despite their cosmopolitan connections, "remained committed to corporatism" and "to localism and conservative Calvinist orthodoxy."[131]

Her evidence challenges the conclusions of Richard Bushman in *From Puritan to Yankee*. Yet even his findings, sometimes taken as evidence that Revolutionary New England had already become powerfully individualistic, are generally supportive of the position argued here. He too finds that late in the century, prominent residents continued to warn that "indulgence of self-interest [w]as a dangerous and un-Christian attempt to reconcile egotistical impulses with the good of the whole. Religious experiences committed them to a total subjection of the human will to God. The retention of prideful desires in any form was a devilish scheme to prevent the abasement that had to precede rebirth."[132] These residents of New England certainly seem to have been reformed Protestants of a traditional vintage rather than adherents of a secular brand of political individualism.

Americans' commitment to local communalism is also ironically evident in cases where goodwill and comity had broken down. Those who argue that the numerous town divisions experienced in the Northern colonies in the late 18th century evidence an increased individualism among the inhabitants have, I believe, misinterpreted this phenomenon. The communalist assumptions of American political thinking were most conspicuous precisely when an older town in one of the Northern states was torn by religious strife and when ill feelings ran highest. For common American farmers, a town was to be ethically, religiously, and preferably ethnically

[129]Lockridge, "Social Change," pp. 420–22.
[130]Gross, *Minutemen and Their World*, p. 14; and see Grant, *Democracy*, p. 167.
[131]Heyrman, *Commerce and Culture*, pp. 203–4.
[132]Bushman, *From Puritan to Yankee*, pp. 279–80.

one people. When significant ethical or religious differences developed between divergent groups, "separation was often seen as the only solution. The communities of the province simply could not conceive of successfully maintaining structural diversity. Harmony required homogeneity."[133] It was not individual freedom, then, that these wreckers of corporate harmony were seeking, but instead traditional local communalism with its attendant ethnic, ethical, and religious homogeneity and intolerance. With political and religious culture as their main conduit to morality, the promise of eternal life and the ability to lead a good life on earth demanded no less.

Admittedly, this portrait relies heavily on research conducted on the covenanted communities of New England, about which we know, according to Zuckerman, far more than any sane human being should want to know.[134] This imbalance, however, is more a reflection of the greater ease of conducting research on these townships than it is an attempt to skew our view of colonial history. Current research on the Southern colonies has begun to show that local communalism was not unique to the North. Historians of the Southern colonies have noted that "politically the attitude of the Southern planters was neither national or imperial, but intensely local, dominated by a fierce suspicion of any active central government."[135] Rossiter finds that autonomous county self-government in the South was "as typically colonial as the towns of New England."[136] Charles Sydnor charges that Southern county governments were almost beyond colonial (and later state) control.[137]

More adamantly, Don Lutz holds that these governments were not just communal in the localist sense, but were intrusive ethically, for "in Virginia, the Carolinas, Georgia, and Maryland, local government was centered in the county due to the absence of population concentrations. . . . they involved themselves in every aspect of economic, social, and political life. . . . If a government today were to have such complete powers, it would be termed totalitarian."[138] Carl Bridenbaugh adds that, in the back settlements of the South, these intrusive communities were organized along overlapping ethnic and religious lines. And "the toleration born of the Enlightenment and voiced by some liberal Tidewater Anglican gentlemen had no interior echoes before 1775."[139] As social historical research on local communities in the colonial South proceeds,[140] it should continue to

[133]Zuckerman, *Peaceable Kingdoms*, p. 140.

[134]See Zuckerman, "Michael Zuckerman's Reply," appended to D. G. Allen, "Zuckerman Thesis," p. 466.

[135]W. H. Nelson, *American Tory*, p. 53.

[136]Rossiter, *First American Revolution*, p. 121.

[137]See Sydnor, *American Revolutionaries in the Making*, p. 111.

[138]Lutz, *Popular Consent and Popular Control*, pp. 159–60.

[139]Bridenbaugh, *Myths and Realities*, pp. 184–85.

[140]See Isaac, *Transformation of Virginia* and "Evangelical Revolt"; Munford, "Candi-

yield a communalistic portrait of 18th-century American life, one that was communal in both the localistic and the corporate ethical senses, even though geographically centered on the county rather than the more intimate Northern village.

Largely because of their internal diversity, it is the Middle colonies, unlike the more ethnically homogeneous colonies to the north and the south, that are often seen as being the birthplace and repository of American individualism.[141] Their social and political arrangements are often presented as challenging the depiction of Americans as communal people. For instance, Zuckerman argues that "almost all the lineaments of American liberalism were normative in the valleys of the Delaware and the Hudson before they were even broached along the James or the Charles."[142] This may be true. But if what he has in mind is the lack of provincewide norms, this tells us little about the social and political goals found in villages and towns—that is, the degree of their internal communalism. No one doubts that the Middle colonies and states lacked the religious and ethnic homogeneity and other communal characteristics often found at the provincial level in the colonies to the north and south. Statewide commitments to particular ethical systems (beyond a vague Christianity) are not expected. But one need not find such broad commitments in order to argue that 18th-century Americans, including those living in the Middle states, were local and ethical communalists.

There is good reason to expect that communalism was as descriptive of villages or towns in the Middle states as elsewhere in America—with the anomalous exception of the chartered corporate city of Philadelphia, whose urban government, "in striking contrast to the New England town," was closed "to full or even meaningful citizen participation."[143] Thomas Bender has it right, then, when he argues that Revolutionary-era Americans sorted themselves ethnically and religiously and that "the same thing occurred, in more obvious ways, in the middle colonies, where the differences among towns were sharper. Men and women sharing particular cultural values came together to form the small, intensely parochial, local units of life that made up the kaleidoscopic American social landscape."[144] Bender's (and John Roche's) analogy to a sea of tolerance dotted with large and small islands of intolerance seems particularly apt, especially in the Middle states.

This might be the essence of America's particular political genius. Patricia Bonomi suggests that in New York State, it may well have been its

dates"; McDonald, *E Pluribus Unum*, pp. 137–39, and McDonald and McWhiney, "South from Self-Sufficiency to Peonage"; Bridenbaugh, *Myths and Realities*; and the essays in Daniels, *Town and County*, especially Wheeler, "County Court in Colonial Virginia."

[141]See Fischer, *Albion's Seed*, pp. 595–603, for his contrasting claim.
[142]Zuckerman, "Introduction," in *Friends and Neighbors*, p. 5.
[143]Diamondstone, "Government of Eighteenth-Century Philadelphia," pp. 243–44.
[144]Bender, *Community and Social Change in America*, p. 68.

"very parochialism—its very narrowness of view, its suspiciousness, its jealous attachment to local prerogatives—that furnished the vital ingredient" of its political institutions.[145] If one does not think only of New York City, her conclusions seem difficult to dispute. One-fourth of New York's population comprised deeply religious New Englanders living on Long Island; another large percentage was made up of Dutch members of their reformed church, which was until the 1780s highly suspicious of English intrusion;[146] and the even more religiously conservative Congregational East Jersey was one of New York's nearest neighbors.

The diverse character of life in most of the Middle colonies and states, unlike that in the other states to the north and south (at least along their Atlantic seaboards), does make its statewide politics more like that of the 19th and 20th centuries than like the colonial experience of Tidewater Virginia or Massachusetts. But given my normative focus, I am principally interested in the patterns of political and social life of Americans within villages and towns, not between them. And the existence of pluralism on the province level does not truly speak to the issue of the communalism or individualism present in the social, political, or religious life of each separate village or town.

Much of the confusion regarding the Middle colonies and states apparently stems from a conflation of two kinds of pluralism. One takes a group of individuals in competition with other such groups in a common political body as the basic unit, whereas another sees a homogeneous and self-governing community as the core component. The former is consistent with a system of pluralism that accommodates populations of diverse peoples living together in a specific geographical area; it is most often associated with liberal or individualistic political philosophies.[147] The latter creates a plural system that exists between divergent local populations and allows for the maintenance of communal visions of the good human life. They are distinct, and one must not assume that when one is present, the other is as well. In truth, they are closer to being antithetical than not. In Pennsylvania and the other Middle colonies, especially in the backcountry, the form of pluralism most often found was the corporate variety that defined itself through ethnic and religious exclusivity. Fundamental forms of corporate identity such as ethnicity and religion were not weakened by this form of pluralism; indeed, they may have been strengthened.[148]

Evidence that addresses how various ethnically homogenous communities coexisted in the Middle states shows that each group adhered to traditional European patterns of local intolerance in separating itself from

[145]Bonomi, "Local Government in Colonial New York," p. 50.
[146]See Hackett, "Social Origins of Nationalism," pp. 664–65.
[147]See Chapman, "Voluntary Association."
[148]See D. D. Hall, "Religion and Society," p. 339; and Bridenbaugh, *Myths and Realities,* p. 134.

its ethnically or religiously distinct provincial neighbors. This was partic-
ularly true in New York and Pennsylvania, with large minority enclaves of
traditionally communalistic Dutch, reformed Protestant Swiss, separatist
German Pietists (a third of Pennsylvania's population), and Quakers.[149]
Even according to one of the most powerful defenders of an individualistic
America, the geographer James Lemon, the Pennsylvania countryside was
filled with separatist settlements of Welsh, Scotch-Irish, Quakers, and
Mennonites that were both ethnically and religiously exclusive.[150]

John Waters, in detailing the ways of the reformed-Protestant Scotch-
Irish (a second third of Pennsylvania's population, and far more numerous
than Quakers), writes that they had not come to America "either to compromise or to assimilate." Instead, as they had in Ulster, "these Scotch-
Irish 'did not intermarry to any extent with the other settlers who came
from the English settlements' . . . [and they retained] Old Country ethnic-
cultural and religious values. . . . When they assembled with blackened
faces . . . and rode on a rail a wife beater, it was to enforce collectively by
this 'rough music' the mores of their community."[151] Bonomi adds that
New York's towns were comparably parochial. When challenged by outside cultural or political forces, like "a thousand similar places in the
1770's, they would make a special point of insisting on their competence"
to handle their own affairs, as they had in the past.[152] The residents of the
Middle colonies and states seem, in fact, to have had much more in common with the highly polarized, ethnically exclusive, lower-middle-class
neighborhoods of contemporary Brooklyn and the Bronx than with the
integrated elite sections of Manhattan. At stake in these 18th-century ethnically and religiously exclusive enclaves was a vision of human flourishing
that rested on local self-control and corporate shaping of the individual.

Michael Zuckerman is correct, however, regarding the progressive character of Middle-state politics. Indeed, to understand the evolution of the
plural political and social structures that characterize most of America in
the 20th century, one would do well to study the politics of 18th-century
New York or Pennsylvania rather than of Massachusetts or Virginia.[153]
Perhaps better still, one might explore the politics of Rhode Island, whose
citizens were reported to have been "cunning, deceitful, and selfish."[154]

---

[149]See Hackett, "Social Origins of Nationalism," p. 668; Bridenbaugh, *Myths and Realities*,
pp. 131–32; Simler, "Township," p. 64; Varga, "Development and Structure of Local Government"; and Bockelman, "Local Government in Colonial Pennsylvania."

[150]See Lemon, *Best Poor Man's Country*, pp. 43–49, 99–109, 115–17; Snydacker, "Kinship and Community in Rural Pennsylvania," p. 43; and Bender, *Community and Social
Change in America*, p. 69.

[151]Waters, "From Democracy to Demography," pp. 225–26.

[152]Bonomi, "Local Government in Colonial New York," p. 49.

[153]See Zuckerman, "Introduction," pp. 9–11; and Murrin, "Roof without Walls," pp.
346–47.

[154]Burnaby, *Travels Through the Middle Settlements* (1775), p. 127.

Such a concession, however, in no way compromises the local and ethical communalist portrait of late 18th-century American life offered here. In fact, the history of 19th-century America suggests that the ethnic and political rivalries in the Middle states were not to be short-lived phenomena.[155] Province-level diversity in the Middle colonies and states may have led to the erosion of confidence in local communal values, but as the Amish communities in Pennsylvania and the ethnic neighborhoods of the New York boroughs continue to demonstrate, it need not do so.

In sum, one might consider James Henretta's observation that "ethnic, linguistic, or religious ties did not reflect a coherent ideological system," nor a self-consciously organized communal culture, but that nonetheless, these community-oriented patterns of social interaction "circumscribed the range of individual action among the inhabitants."[156] Many inarticulate Americans may well have been adherents of a communal political theory of which they were not consciously aware. This is one of the benefits of having access to records of lived values in addition to the more self-conscious accounts of the articulate political class. This widespread lack of self-consciousness among less-articulate Americans may help explain the distorted image such Americans have of their social and political foundations.

The exception to the rule in the Middle colonies, however, might be the Quakers. An important minority religious group predominantly located in Delaware, West Jersey, and Pennsylvania,[157] its members saw themselves as "an organized segment of the population which kept morality and good order in its own ranks, expected no special favor from the government, and thought other elements should do likewise."[158] Their religious exclusivity, therefore, did not demand, as it did for most other religious or ethnic communities, geographical separation, corporate homogeneity, or political autonomy. Because of their religious, social, and political views, they were content to live as a morally closed cell in close proximity with others. In spite of their own corporate exclusivity and communally imposed moral strictures, they played a critical role in introducing into Philadelphia benevolent, voluntaristic, and individualistic social and political arrangements.[159]

---

[155]See Ireland, "Crux of Politics," and Jaenicke, "American Ideas of Political Party," p. 131.

[156]Henretta, "Families and Farms," pp. 4–5.

[157]See Stark and Finke, "American Religion in 1776," p. 46, who note that in 1776 "there were twice as many Presbyterians as Quakers in Pennsylvania," and that even the German Reformed church outnumbered the Quakers in Pennsylvania. A large population of Quakers who resided on the island of Nantucket has received considerable attention of late because of their precocious individualism. See Byers, "Nation of Nantucket," and Crèvecoeur, *Letters from an American Farmer* (1782), pp. 83–153.

[158]James, *People among Peoples*, pp. 332–33.

[159]See Fischer, *Albion's Seed*, pp. 193–215.

The key to these innovations was the Quakers' embrace of social and political voluntarism. Yet if they were directly or indirectly responsible for these progressive social or political changes, this was largely unintentional. Such changes occurred in spite of their richly fraternal organization, the public spirit they encouraged in Philadelphia, their intrusive regulation of their members' personal lives at quarterly meetings, their extreme sexual repressiveness, and the morally severe laws they helped enact in Pennsylvania.[160]

Quakers were committed to voluntarism and a certain kind of individualism. But it was for reasons religious rather than secular, and reactionary rather than modern, that they fostered a precocious hostility toward corporate organicism or political communalism wherever they were politically important. Their devout religious sectarianism, when conjoined to secular political power and promulgated as political doctrine, was destructive to communities dedicated to a publicly directed shaping of individual virtue. Yet it was not until the 19th century that others began to join the Quakers in viewing morality as primarily a private rather than a social or local governmental concern, even though, as with the Quakers, it was both a voluntary and a corporate one. A perverse result of these innovations when they were adopted was that seemingly public-directed and communal activities such as voluntary and fraternal associations "served to set neighbors off from one another, [and] to nurture attachments separate from the whole community." The result was that the community "lost a certain moral unity."[161] Robert Hine, a historian of American communalism, explains that some public-spirited activities championed by Quakers, such as charity, are in truth "individualistic, and [their] arena may more realistically be called the neighborhood than the community."[162]

Judith Diamondstone has written of Quaker-dominated Philadelphia that its residents "may have been satisfied by the sense that many of the voluntary associations were responsive to them, hence they were deflected from any popular assault on the elitist character of the city government." It is possible that Philadelphian politics showed how concerns for "economic growth of the town and . . . pursuit of personal property" could displace those regarding the community's direction of the ethical development of its citizens.[163] In the Quaker mind, these were preeminently private, or fraternal, rather than public and political concerns. Rousseau, however, understood all too well the corrosive character of such partial associations to communal public life.[164]

Quakers were translocalists (as well as transnationalists), with little

[160]See ibid., p. 587.
[161]Gross, *Minutemen and Their World*, pp. 174–75.
[162]Hine, *Community on the American Frontier*, p. 118.
[163]Diamondstone, "Government of Eighteenth-Century Philadelphia," pp. 259–60.
[164]See Rousseau, *Social Contract* (1762), p. 27.

commitment to a local community (or a nation) and its corporate values, concerns, and constraints. It was this particular Quaker trait that the majority of Americans found so repugnant (as some people in central Europe found separatist Jews threatening). Regarding the Quakers, David Hackett Fischer is even less charitable. He writes that almost the only thing that all other 18th-century Americans could agree on was their genuine hatred of the Quakers "as dangerous radicals" and "pious frauds and hypocrites."[165] For too many Americans, a cosmopolitan sectarianism smacked of conspiracy and bordered on treason.[166] The Quakers, then, might be justly seen as having championed values and having been the creators of social structures that eventually proved to be effective solvents of American local communalism. Yet in recognizing the anomalous nature of the Society of Friends and its hostility to communal political mores, and Americans' reciprocal loathing of the Quakers, one indirectly confirms the overall communalist nature of late 18th-century America.

TWO DISPUTES AND ONE CONCERN: MUCH ADO ABOUT NOTHING

Few students of the 17th century disagree with the characterization of the colonies as morally intrusive and coercively communalistic in both the North and the South.[167] The consensus regarding the 18th century, however, is not nearly so solid, and the field is not without controversy. Social historians are motivated by different ideological, methodological, and research agendas. Furthermore, some commentators have suggested that social history, in particular, is a body of research that was fueled by "an ideological push from the New Left of the late 1960s." Others have argued that social historians have suffered from "a nostalgic pining for a heroic, communitarian ancestry" that would "help justify and encourage a moral rebellion" against "'bourgeois' liberalism."[168] But political intentions and scholarly disagreements are of limited relevance here.

History is either persuasively argued or it is not, and the communal position that social historians have produced has been powerfully presented. Therefore, ad hominem criticisms of the possible "left-wing" (whether communal or socialist) political intentions of those who have added so greatly to our understanding of American social life will not detain me here. Also, historians are frequently interested in understanding

---

[165]Fischer, *Albion's Seed,* p. 821.

[166]See Heyrman, *Commerce and Culture,* p. 143.

[167]See Henretta, "Slow Triumph of Liberal Individualism," p. 89, who writes that "few historians would now [1991] argue that America in 1700 was, in any fundamental sense, a liberal society."

[168]Beeman, "New Social History," p. 435; Pangle, *Spirit of Modern Republicanism,* p. 43; and see Waters, "From Democracy to Demography," pp. 231–32, 247–48. See the preface for my mea culpa.

change, and at the end of the 18th century there is much to explain. My interest, however, is more static: it is with recovering the essential character of 18th-century Americans' underresearched political theory. Without diminishing the importance of concerns more often pursued by historians than by theorists, certain issues must be recognized as of limited relevance to this investigation. Two such matters of controversy, however, demand consideration.

One is whether or not rural Americans were commercial farmers enmeshed in a largely cash economy.[169] On one side of the debate are those who emphasize that white Americans were involved in agricultural pursuits, worked privately owned tracts of land, and aggressively pursued profits in selling a sizable part of their produce. Thus, they contend, Americans should be seen as commercial farmers. They further insist that because these Americans maintained such an economic posture, they must have held individualistic and materialistic values. Charles Grant suggests as much concerning the Connecticut frontier town of Kent. He writes that "one is impressed not so much with the contented, subsistence way of life as with the drive for profits. This drive is reflected in the large number of farms that produced saleable surpluses."[170]

On the other side are those who hold that, outside the Tidewater South, most white Americans were part of a "family-based, community-oriented culture" of subsistence-plus farmers. They were opposed by a tiny urban and landlord minority committed to "an acquisitive, individualistic way of life" that was "dominated by merchants, professionals, speculators, and commercial farmers."[171] In New England, these peasantlike farmers are said to have sought "a fruitful wife, and oxen and sons to till the soil and thus to place a man's name upon the land."[172] Even in the Middle colonies, most farmers, James Henretta finds, participated in the cash market economy only in a limited fashion.

Bettye Pruitt, in usefully reviewing this literature, writes that there are, thus, "two competing personae. On the one hand is a portrait of the farmer as an entrepreneurial type—competitive, profit-conscious, and motivated by the desire for wealth." On the other, Americans are pictured as being "community-oriented rather than individualistic, and motivated

---

[169]See McCusker and Menard, *Economy of British America*, pp. 298–99; and Kulikoff, *Agrarian Origins of American Capitalism*, pp. 264–65.

[170]Grant, *Democracy*, pp. 31–32, and see Lemon, *Best Poor Man's Country*, which is among the most important and persuasive works emanating from this school of thought.

[171]Szatmary, *Shays' Rebellion*, p. xiv; see also p. 6, where he defines his understanding of this controversy and notes that "'the peasant,' wrote Eric Wolf, 'does not operate an enterprise in the economic sense; he runs a household, and not a business concern.' In contrast Wolf equated an agricultural entrepreneur with a producer of chiefly marketable commodities. . . . In relation to these commonly used definitions, New England farmers would appear to have been peasants rather than rural businessmen."

[172]Waters, "Traditional World," p. 5.

more modestly—toward a decent standard of living and family security."[173] In substantial agreement with the latter position, she finds that 18th-century family farmers understood subsistence-plus farming (with local networks of exchange) and cash farming to be complementary goals.[174] Such cash farming, however, never included a willingness to participate in the labor market, which is one of the key elements of a capitalist economy in which all market inputs become priced commodities. And the need for an adult male to sell his labor, with a consequent loss in independence, was a fate that 18th-century family farmers avoided at all costs.[175] Pruitt prudently concludes that there existed in Revolutionary-era America "a more complex relationship between economic behavior and cultural values than we are accustomed to imagine."[176]

It seems, therefore, that some of the proponents on each side of this issue helped create an overly stark contrast "between subsistence and commercial farming." But as Edward Countryman explains, out of these debates, something close to a consensus has recently emerged. As he describes it, historians recognize that from the earliest settlements there was a sizable number of Americans who were full economic participants in a complex transatlantic market that was clearly capitalistic. Nonetheless, most colonials were enmeshed in "local patterns of exchange and reciprocity that did not operate strictly or even loosely according to profit-and-loss individualism exercised over a long distance." These local communal patterns of exchange operated differently in various regions, but "did operate in all of them." The communal norms that structured these local patterns of exchange almost always placed great emphasis on reciprocity. And Countryman reports that it is now widely accepted that "these norms and the day-to-day lived experience that they framed provided the overwhelming majority of colonials with a strong sense that the community ought to take primacy in every day life."[177]

But because "exchange transactions" cannot simply be equated with "market social relations,"[178] this otherwise important set of concerns has limited relevance here. Did Americans hold to a political theory that allowed for intolerance, and defend local autonomy and the communal

[173]Pruitt, "Self-Sufficiency," p. 334. See also Vickers, Lemon, and Pruitt, "Communication"; "Toward a History of the Standard of Living"; and Main, *Social Structure of Revolutionary America*, pp. 150–51.

[174]See also F. Anderson, *People's Army*, p. 28; Ditz, *Property and Kinship*, p. 172; C. Clark, "Household Economy," pp. 181–83; and Mutch, "Yeoman and Merchant," pp. 280–87.

[175]See A. Taylor, *Liberty Men and Great Proprietors*, p. 8, and Merrill, "Cash Is Good to Eat," pp. 57–61.

[176]Vickers, Lemon, and Pruitt, "Communication," p. 561. See also Pruitt, "Self-Sufficiency," p. 34; and Vickers, "Competency and Competition," p. 7.

[177]Communication from Edward Countryman, November 1992; see also Merrill, "Cash Is Good to Eat," p. 65, and McCusker and Menard, *Economy of British America*, p. 300.

[178]Hahn, "'Unmaking' of the Southern Yeomanry," pp. 196–97.

shaping of the ethical lives of a community's residents? Or were they adherents of a political vision that sought to end the multiple forms of intolerance then current in their local villages and to free the individual from the intrusive and restrictive management of patriarchal family, congregation, neighborhood, and local government? A family's ability to grow surplus grain for other local residents or extralocal markets is not dispositive here, for it cannot demonstrate that because of such modern economic relationships, America's agrarian majority abandoned its belief in or lived commitment to local communalism. For most Americans, economic advancement was important, but it was not an overarching goal to which traditional familial and social values were sacrificed.[179] Common sense and the nature of agrarian rural life as late as the early 20th century, where subsistence and cash economies coexisted, suggest as much.[180]

Christine Heyrman, the author of *Commerce and Culture,* and Hal Barron, who wrote *Those Who Stayed Behind,* are not direct participants in this debate. Nevertheless, their 1984 research severs the necessary link between commercialization and individualistic and hedonistic values, even for those living in urban environments. (Nothing is, however, being claimed regarding the absence of long-term consequences of commercialization.) Their findings should be particularly disconcerting to those who too easily associate commercial activity with high levels of wealth, Unitarianism, Quakerism, Deism, self-indulgence, and individualism. Not all commercial towns in Revolutionary America, they show, were little Bostons or Philadelphias.

Heyrman studied 18th-century towns in Massachusetts and Barron researched 19th-century Vermont. They found that these states' residents, though economically tied to national and worldwide commercial markets, nevertheless remained committed to communalist values. Of 18th-century Massachusetts maritime ports, Heyrman writes that in spite of successful commercialization "Gloucester residents still resembled the inhabitants of a small, rural village. . . . the emergence of a communal order in Marblehead involved no repudiation of the market. On the contrary . . . localistic and communitarian impulses exhibited a totally unexpected resilience among all classes and groups in town."[181] Barron writes of early 19th-century rural Vermont, "farmers there were at once tied to larger national markets and also entwined in a face-to-face local life that remained central. . . . Whereas the transitions from feudal to bourgeois, from traditional to modern, or from *Gemeinschaft* to *Gesellschaft* may characterize the broad path traveled by nation-states, they do not reflect

---

[179]See Henretta, "Families and Farms," pp. 17–19; C. Clark, "Household Economy," p. 175; and Mutch, "Yeoman and Merchant," p. 286. Cf. McCusker and Menard, *Economy of British America,* pp. 305–8.

[180]West [Withers], *Plainville, U.S.A.,* p. 40. His superb account of just such a community in 1939 offers powerful testimony to the continuity of communal values, at least until that date.

[181]Heyrman, *Commerce and Culture,* pp. 95, 404–5.

accurately changes in smaller rural communities."[182] The necessary link between commercialism and individualism does not seem to be sustainable—at least not in the short term.

In deference to those who argue that Americans were an especially commercial or modern people, it must be admitted that 18th-century Americans were already mobile (though reportedly less so than their rural contemporaries in England). It is also true that they were becoming increasingly litigious.[183] And they had always been concerned with their economic well-being, if for no other reason than the responsibility of providing for their many children. Some Americans, as Countryman noted, were not involved in subsistence-plus farming, but were instead involved in relatively advanced market economic relationships. Yet the portrait much recent scholarship offers us of Revolutionary America is nevertheless one of extreme localism, moderately patriarchal familism, racism, xenophobia, sexism, and clear intolerance for individual moral and religious deviance. The obstacles to autonomous individual development that these communal traits present do not need further elaboration. (The benefits, though, are much more difficult to uncover and defend.)

There remains a second controversy among social historians: whether the towns of Massachusetts (and indirectly those of other colonies, and counties in the South) were becoming more or less autonomous during the 18th century. This matter is of consequence because the justices of the peace of each county, their officers, and the courts on which they sat were, to varying degrees, agents of the Crown. Thus, these county officials by increasing their power over local communities might have been able to return political and religious control to the Crown—that is, to the central imperial government. If so, they were making Massachusetts (and other Crown colonies where similar changes would have been occurring) less communal in the localist sense. This is obviously a challenge to my thesis, and it demands consideration.

Historians have staked out three positions. Each has something to recommend it. First, and least complicated, is the contrary claim that American towns during the 18th century were becoming more, not less, autonomous and self-governing. According to Michael Zuckerman, in 18th-century Massachusetts this increase in local autonomy occurred in response to the 1691 charter, which promoted provincewide religious tolerance. In order to maintain Congregational orthodoxy in opposition to the more religiously liberal aspirations of the Crown, Massachusetts's provincial officials limited their own control over the lives of rural citizens.[184] Heightened localism was engineered by the provincial center to overcome the centralizing efforts of London.

[182]Barron, *Those Who Stayed Behind*, p. 136.
[183]See Mann, *Neighbors and Strangers*.
[184]See Zuckerman, *Peaceable Kingdoms*, pp. 18ff.

Zuckerman's reading is supported by others, such as David Konig, who reports that in Essex County, Massachusetts, the towns were indeed becoming more autonomous. Students of other colonies report the same. Robert Wheeler describes how the counties in the South were gaining new power and becoming less the creatures of the Crown. Nicholas Varga offers similar reports for New York boroughs and towns. Wayne Bockelman provides similar findings for Pennsylvania, with the notable exception of Philadelphia.[185] And Kenneth Lockridge claims that one of the aftershocks of the Great Awakening was that "New England, with its special traditions of covenanted localism, was joined by New York, Pennsylvania, and Virginia in manifesting the early stages of an inchoate" populist political movement demanding greater local control.[186]

Second is the claim that is most interesting. Its defenders argue that from the middle of the 18th century, the towns, at least in Massachusetts, were becoming less autonomous. As David Allen and John Murrin argue, "the founders had been unable to import" strong county governments "from England in the 1630s, and a strong county community took a century to create out of local demographic materials." But, Allen and Murrin contend, centralizing political institutions, such as powerful justices of the peace, had come into being near midcentury, and they were able to effect a shift in the balance of power away from local communities to the imperial center. The result was "a serious challenge to the autonomy of the towns."[187]

Third is a position that seemingly joins the other two. Gregory Nobles argues that in 18th-century Massachusetts there were two different levels of parochialism in conflict. During the first half of the century, he contends, the county elite did successfully wrest power from the towns. But this would later be contested by a resurgent reactionary wave of local communalism that challenged the county elite's usurpation of power. As Nobles envisions it, there was an active struggle in Hampshire County, Massachusetts (his case study), between the citizenry of towns and the county elite. By midcentury, in opposition to county elites, "there emerged a widespread movement among common people to maintain—or regain—local control of their political and religious affairs," and "a growing number of people sought to establish their own independent churches and towns, to recreate the traditional patterns of town life, and in the end to separate themselves from the dominance of the county leadership. This second sort of conservatism, with its emphasis on localism and in many cases on strict religious practices, was almost reactionary in nature, looking back to stan-

---

[185]See Konig, "English Legal Change," pp. 29–30, 37; Daniels, "Political Structure of Local Government," pp. 48–49; Wheeler, "County Court in Colonial Virginia," p. 130; Varga, "Development and Structure of Local Government," pp. 189, 211; and Bockelman, "Local Government in Colonial Pennsylvania," pp. 226, 228.

[186]Lockridge, *New England Town*, p. 188.

[187]Murrin, "Review Essay," p. 268; and see D. G. Allen, *In English Ways* and "Zuckerman Thesis."

dards of an idealized past."[188] Yet, he contends, both groups were in fact localists of different sorts who were unwilling to cede power to more centralized provincial or imperial authority.

Heyrman also claims that late in the century, it was the "backcountry farmers of all classes" who resisted the "eastern-sponsored" elite as they claimed "the traditional rights of local autonomy and self-determination" against the pretensions of cosmopolitan adversaries.[189] Even Murrin concedes that by the 1760s, the county elite in Massachusetts, due to their relatively close ties to the Crown, had come under fresh attack, particularly in the western counties.[190]

Regardless of how historians ultimately resolve this issue, local communalism, whether in contention with county-level regionalism, or increasing or decreasing in strength, emerges as one of the most pervasive forces in 18th-century American social, political, and religious life. The overwhelming response of the towns of Massachusetts to the Government Act of 20 May 1774 lends great support to such a conclusion.[191] When deprived of their traditional right of local self-government, Americans formed, in Massachusetts and throughout America, local extralegal committees.[192] David Hacket Fischer recounts a conversation between George Bancroft and an aged veteran that is particularly telling. In it, the old man was asked whether it was the writings of Locke and Paine that had moved him and his friends to revolt. He answered that he had never heard of Locke and had to admit that he had not read Paine. But then he explained that "New Englanders had always managed their own affairs, and Britain tried to stop them, and so the war began."[193] Local autonomy was evidently still alive and well in late 18th-century America.

---

[188]Nobles, *Divisions throughout the Whole*, pp. 10–11; see also pp. 185–86.

[189]Heyrman, *Commerce and Culture*, p. 322.

[190]See Murrin, "Myths of Colonial Democracy," p. 66.

[191]See Gordon, "Discourse Preached December 15th, 1774," p. 202. The editor, John Thornton, comments that "the towns were so many commonwealths, petty democracies, and the British ministers could not have adopted any device which would more keenly touch the people than this interference with their wonted assemblies."

[192]See Simmons, *American Colonies*, pp. 340–57; and Hunt, *Provincial Committees of Safety*.

[193]Fischer, *Albion's Seed*, p. 827; see also C. M. Kenyon, "Republicanism and Radicalism," p. 304. Morison, *Oxford History of the American People*, pp. 212–13, tells of a young man interviewing in 1842 a Captain Preston, who was then an aged veteran of the battle at Concord. The twenty-one-year-old began by asking whether it had been oppression or taxes that had led Americans to revolt. The old man responded that he had neither felt oppressed nor ever seen any evidence of the stamp or tea taxes. The young man continued, "Then I suppose you had been reading Harrington or Sidney and Locke about the eternal principles of liberty?" The veteran responded, "Never heard of 'em. We read only the Bible, the Catechism, Watts' Psalms and Hymns, and the Almanac." The interviewer followed up: "Well, then, what was the matter? And what did you mean in going to the fight?" The ninety-one-year-old man retorted, "Young man, what we meant in going for those redcoats was this: *We always had governed ourselves, and we always meant to. They didn't mean we should.*"

The image of a communalist people interested primarily in local control of their lives agrees with articulate Americans' arguments in print and from the pulpit. Social historians have thus helped us recognize that American communalism was not uniquely a product of elite concerns. The near-congruence of the communal values of the political class, those of most of the true elite, and those of popular forces during the Revolutionary period was less the result of shared secular texts, and more the result of a shared religion and lived experiences. Especially important was the common experience of growing to maturity in a reformed-Protestant communal environment of local political and social institutions that had blossomed in the luxurious American soil.

Edward Everett, the famous 19th-century orator, Unitarian pastor, and Harvard professor of classics, argued as much in 1828. He reminded his auditors that "it was no refinement of philosophical statesmen to which we are indebted for our republican institutions of government. They grew up, as it were, by accident, on the . . . simple foundation" of ordinary English communal practices.[194] Bernard Bailyn agrees that "most of what these [Revolutionary] leaders considered to be their greatest achievements" were "matters of fact before they were matters of theory."[195] And another modern historian argues, Revolutionary political thought was not a product of "alien ideologies [that] were often borrowed as rationales." It was instead primarily a reflection of Anglo-American lived political reality—one of relative parochial isolation and communal autonomy, "of indigenous folkways which were deeply rooted in the inherited culture of the English-speaking world."[196]

Regardless of which source—lived or intellectual, common or elite—was the foundation of their political norms, in the late 18th century, "the town, not the individual, was the basic unit of political representation," and the "family, church and town provided overlapping [homogeneous] contexts of life."[197] Social history thus offers confirmation that Revolutionary-era America was a land shaped by hallowed traditions and learned theories that taught that the good life was to be found in a life of local communalism.

Nevertheless, America at the end of the 18th century had begun to change. There is persuasive evidence that preceding the Revolution, economic and social practices had already begun to conflict with most Americans' communal normative precepts. Americans were beginning to be torn between dynamic demographic, economic, religious, and social material forces and their static ideational communal norms and expectations.[198] In

---

[194]Everett, "History of Liberty" (1850), pp. 161–62.
[195]Bailyn, "Political Experience and Enlightenment Ideas," p. 20.
[196]Fischer, *Albion's Seed*, p. 897.
[197]Bender, *Community and Social Change in America*, p. 67.
[198]See Countryman, *American Revolution*, p. 167; Isaac, *Transformation of Virginia*, pp.

many ways Americans, in resisting their changing material conditions and in trying to preserve their traditional patterns of thought, were replicating the wrenching changes that had begun two centuries earlier in England.[199] Of special interest, then, is Keith Thomas's claim that the rising number of witchcraft accusations at the beginning of the 17th century in England had resulted from "an unresolved conflict between the neighborly conduct required by the ethical code of the old village community, and the increasingly individualistic forms of behaviour which accompanied" the beginnings of modern economic relationships.[200] In each instance, a conservative communal people was trying to resist disruptive social, religious, and economic changes while integrating them into an unyielding communalistic public philosophy.[201]

Yet even those historians who have emphasized the individualistic character of the new social and economic forces insist on the communalism of late 18th-century political thought. For example, Jack Greene, one of the most aggressive defenders of an individualistic 18th-century America, admits that "the revolution in behavior suggested by growing evidence of increasing individuation had not yet been accompanied by a revolution in values." Most importantly, new social and economic patterns were unable to challenge "the old system of values that deplored" individualistic behavior. Thus, in the Revolutionary era, "the fear that excessively atomistic behavior would lead to social chaos and loss of control and the belief that man could not tolerate freedom without strong societal restraints were still too deeply embedded in cultural consciousness and too easily activated to permit the development of an alternative morality that would more accurately reflect the modes of behavior."[202] As Joyce Appleby suggested, the very persistence of increasingly dysfunctional communal norms, in the face of social and economic change, attests to their continued, if waning, power to shape the American consciousness.[203]

Without conceding that the overall landscape of social practices had given up its communal character, this emerging disjunction between com-

---

239–40; Gross, *Minutemen and Their World*, pp. 105–7; Pocock, *Machiavellian Moment*, p. 467; and Wood, *Creation of the American Republic*, p. 15.

[199]See Somkin, *Unquiet Eagle*, p. 7.

[200]K. Thomas, *Religion and the Decline of Magic*, pp. 561–63.

[201]See May, *Enlightenment in America*, pp. 180–81, and McDonald, *Novus Ordo Seclorum*, pp. 291–92.

[202]J. P. Greene, *Pursuits of Happiness*, p. 77; see also Yazawa, *From Colonies to Commonwealth*, p. 111, who describes a lag that produced "an ever-widening gap between the way men were and the way they thought"; and Higonnet, *Sister Republics*, pp. 81–82, 107–8, who finds that "this cleavage between social reality and political ideology is the key to the unfolding of American history at the end of the eighteenth century." However, as noted above, Higonnet's account is somewhat confusing, for he also writes that in their social practices (the supposedly individualistic side of the tension), Americans demonstrated a sense of community that exceeded that in "the more traditional parts of rural France."

[203]See Appleby, "American Heritage," pp. 216–17, and "Modernization Theory," p. 116.

munal norms and evolving individualistic practices evidences in still another way the desperate attempt mounted by Revolutionary-era Americans to preserve their traditional norms. In the face of unplanned and little-understood destabilizing institutional and structural changes, they were trying to preserve, both in practice and in thought, Western ethical injunctions against what would come in the 19th century to be called individualism. As Heyrman concludes, Americans "clung to the past, relinquished their hold on it reluctantly, tried to recapture it, and gave no thanks to those who would wrest it from them."[204] In some ways, then, the War of Independence itself might be seen as an oddly reactionary communalist effort to resolve the tension between new structural demands and old ideational goals confronting 18th-century Americans. They sought to delay secular changes that could not be reversed or readily stopped in American cultural, economic, and political life. As Robert Gross puts it, "in 1774 the townspeople had set out only to protect their traditional community life against outside attack. But in the course of the resistance to Britain their goal had become a revival of the community itself. Concordians sought not revolution but regeneration: an end to the bickering and fighting . . . and a rebirth of the virtue and public-mindedness that infused the ideal New England town."[205] But, to the extent that these goals were widely shared, as most evidence suggests, the Revolution clearly was a perverse failure that only exacerbated the problems it was meant to solve.[206]

These changes, whose roots were already solidly planted in the prewar period, came fully to fruition neither during the Revolution nor its immediate aftermath, but only some years later, in the early 19th century.[207] As Robert Wiebe observes, "the immediate effects of the war were decentralization and diffusion [as] liberty for most Americans remained a local matter."[208] Thomas Bender and Henry May find that "for two decades following the ratification of the Constitution, American society seems to have regressed into a stolid communalism."[209] Thus, it might be said that the commitment of Americans to local communalism led them both into and out of the Revolutionary War, even if the war itself did so much to undermine the lived and theoretical foundations on which this communalism had flourished for over a century in much of British America.

The death of communalism, however, must have been slow. As Alexis de Tocqueville observed, American towns in 1835 continued to "regulate

[204]Heyrman, *Commerce and Culture*, p. 414.

[205]Gross, *Minutemen and Their World*, p. 153; see also Berthoff and Murrin, "Federalism, Communalism, and the Yeoman Freeholder," p. 263.

[206]See Crowley, *This Sheba, Self*, p. 124.

[207]See Lockridge, *New England Town*, pp. 162–63.

[208]Wiebe, *Opening of American Society*, p. 3.

[209]Bender, *Community and Social Change in America*, p. 86; see also May, *Enlightenment in America*, p. 307; E. S. Morgan, "Government by Fiction," p. 338; and Watts, *Republic Reborn*.

the minor details of social life [and] to promulgate such orders as concern the health of the community and the peace as well as the morality of the citizens."[210] Even in the early 20th century, America's rural inhabitants continued to be primarily concerned with local farm life, and their morals were shaped by their local churches and affected by "gossip and the fear of gossip." The local community thus continued to exercise great control over each individual's behavior.[211] And far more irksome to many, the values "of community autonomy and states rights" continue to survive in modern America.[212] Without the support of cultural elites and most of the national political leadership,[213] traditional communal values are still those of "the lower levels of 20th-century society." Indeed, according to Wiebe, most Americans are "still going somewhere, often still going to heaven or hell."[214] American local communalism, like its reformed-Protestant foundations, apparently has been unexpectedly slow to die, at least among America's working and lower-middle classes.

[210]Tocqueville, *Democracy in America* (1835), 1:44; see also Griffin, *Their Brothers' Keepers*, who describes an increase in morally regulatory legislation.

[211]West [Withers], *Plainville, U.S.A.*, p. 162.

[212]Wiebe, *Opening of American Society*, pp. 383–84.

[213]This, however, is changing. Of late, political theorists dissatisfied with certain features of contemporary liberalism have shown a renewed interest in communalism. See Galston, *Liberal Purposes*; Larmore, "Political Liberalism"; Macedo, *Liberal Virtues*; Etzioni, *Spirit of Community*; and Sandel, *Liberalism and the Limits of Justice*. For example, Kamenka, in his introduction to *Community as a Social Ideal*, p. viii, writes that "in the last two decades, the concept of community has become even more central to a wide-spread atmosphere and movement in Western society—a revolt against progress and modernization, a rejection of individualism and of economic growth as alienating, a longing for the warmth, comfort and humanity of a *real* community."

[214]Wiebe, *Opening of American Society*, pp. 383–84; see also Lasch, *True and Only Heaven*.

Localism and the Myth of American Individualism

The process of anti-authoritarian revolt cannot be stopped
within the person himself. The individual who has set up
his conscience in rivalry to the God-given law of the church
discovers that conscience, subject to no sovereign, becomes
prey to rebellious desires within him.

—H. R. Niebuhr, "The Protestant Movement and
Democracy in the United States"

THE LOCALIST and communal character of 18th-century America, explored
above, suggests that individualism would be one of the least useful ways of
describing America. Yet since at least 1839, when the term first made its
way into English, America has been regularly so characterized, and America's founding period continues to be so described.[1] But if late 18th-century
America was not in fact individualistic, why has this occurred?

There is good reason to believe that America's highly localist communalism (religious, social, and political) must have appeared in the late 18th
and early 19th centuries as bordering on anarchical or atomistic when
compared to centrally administered European religious establishments and
nation-states. Many of the most prominent commentators, those who initially labeled America individualistic, were Europeans. In other words,
America's powerful localism probably fostered illusions that came to be
described, largely pejoratively, as individualistic. Bereft of an appropriate
vocabulary to describe that which was little understood and was usually
disapproved of for being localistic, irrational, particularistic, or peasantlike, foreign observers in the early 19th century described American
local communalism as individualistic. Over time, what begins as a misper-
ception can become a myth, especially if it accords with the political interests of dominant elites.

The dismissive attitude of (European) Western culture toward cultural
and epistemic particularism contributed to this misconception. Particular-

---

[1] For example, see Kramnick, *Republicanism and Bourgeois Radicalism*, pp. 17, 40, 179,
190, 254; and Pangle, *Spirit of Modern Republicanism*, pp. 25–48, 288. For additional references, see the introduction.

ism describes a propensity to elevate to the level of truth that which is locally believed, culturally conditioned, or traditionally accepted.[2] It is a form of chauvinism that is at once conservative, populist, ascriptive, and ethnically or religiously exclusive. Furthermore, particularism projected a confidence in one's own corporate (ethnic, religious, or racial) way of seeing and doing that was in tension with Americans' Christian universalism (as nativism would continue in the 19th century to be in tension with liberal universalism). Reformed Protestantism, however, proved more easily assimilated to particularism than was the more hierarchical Catholicism. In America, this was especially true of the Congregational and Baptist variants of Protestantism, with their insistence on local ecclesiastical control. When joined to high degrees of local political autonomy, reformed Protestantism's particularistic propensities were even further accentuated.

Cultural and epistemic particularism was one of the banes of the Enlightenment. As Gordon Wood explains, "too intense a local attachment was a symptom of narrow-mindedness, and indeed of disease."[3] Localism was thus associated with peasants and backward peoples. Oddly enough, it was also paired with the Catholic church by apologists for Enlightenment thought as a most entrenched and pernicious foe. Progressive thinkers, therefore, associated particularism (as they did Catholicism) with error, superstition, and degeneracy.

But in spite of the Enlightenment's hostility to the church, it still saw ethical truth as a universal norm that was linked in a hierarchical chain of increasing purity to the truths of nature (or, for the less enlightened, the mind of God). Centralization of reason and power has been demanded by progressive thinkers during much of the last two centuries. Such thinking was especially likely to shape the minds of those raised in areas dominated by Catholic religious and social thought. One can begin to see how extreme localism in society, church, and state might be misunderstood by foreign observers, particularly Enlightenment ones, better acquainted with monarchical, Catholic, or (later) statist centralized institutions. Indeed, the supposed primordial "individualism" that foreign observers found so rampant in America may not have been applicable at all to atomistic individuals, but rather to America's exotically autonomous local communities and their constituent families.

The term *individualism* was not invented until the 19th century. Yet by the end of the 18th century, much of what it would come to mean was already embodied in an emergent autonomous sense of the individual and, in an older concept, the self. One can indirectly gain a purchase on individualism's 18th-century valuation by exploring Americans' view of the self. Contrary to America's putative innate individualism, the liberation of those elements of the individual that truly define the uniqueness of a sepa-

[2]*Compact Edition of the Oxford English Dictionary,* s.v. "particularism."
[3]Wood, *Radicalism of the American Revolution,* p. 221.

rate being was met with widespread disapprobation. In the late 18th century, the self continued to be understood as the center of human sinfulness. In the language of rationalism, it was the embodiment of human estrangement from nature's perfect ordering of the universe.

This sinfulness or estrangement was believed to be reflected in individual selfishness, an aspect of one's being that was especially deplored. As Lemuel Haynes noted, "selfishness enervates every social bond and endearment, sets men at variance, and is the source of every evil."[4] From the perspectives of the three dominant 18th-century traditions of social and political thought, the self-serving parts of one's being were to be socially controlled, not accommodated. In opposition to individualism, which seeks to liberate the self from restrictive social, familial, religious, and political controls, Americans' communal understanding of human flourishing demanded the opposite—communal intrusion. As David Daggett, chief justice of the Connecticut Supreme Court and United States senator, explained, nothing was so absurd as the then-new French theories that held that children are to be free to perfect themselves and therefore "all reproof, restraint and correction, tend directly to extinguish the fire of genius, to cripple the faculties and enslave the understanding."[5] This fostering of the autonomous and self-directing individual, the ideal of individualism, described for most Americans a terminus that perversely elevated the base aspects of the fallen sinner.[6] Later claims to the contrary notwithstanding, individualism could not have been 18th-century America's guiding vision of the good and of human flourishing.

LOCALISM MISPERCEIVED: THE GENESIS OF THE INDIVIDUALIST ILLUSION

Like a voice in the wilderness that went unheard, the legal theorist Alexander H. Pekelis argued in the 1940s that his contemporaries had indeed mischaracterized American local religious and political communalism. In particular, they had confused America's communal jury system and its parochial hostility toward individual autonomy with their antithesis, political individualism. He surmised (as I have) that local communal hostility toward the provincial or the imperial (later national) center, "the government," had been systematically conflated with a common 20th-century hostility toward all authority. He believed that his contemporaries had mistakenly identified "individualism with intolerance of a *central* authority." "As a matter of fact," what others call "individualism seems to be in reality collectivism within a smaller group"—that is, one of individualism's principal adversaries, local communalism. He further observed that

---

[4]Haynes, "Nature and Importance of True Republicanism" (1801), p. 85; see also Rodgers, *Contested Truths*, p. 32.

[5]Daggett, "Sunbeams May Be Extracted from Cucumbers" (1799), pp. 39–40.

[6]See Kuklick, "Self and Selflessness in Franklin and Edwards," p. 12.

"what is typical for the English and American way of life is not the lack of social control but its decentralized character," and concluded that "the use of the term individualism greatly beclouds the issue."[7] In sum, localism with its consensually supported corporate intolerance had been confused with individualism and a later Romantic hostility to all authority. Unlike localism, individualism is suspicious of societal, congregational, local governmental, and possibly even familial intrusion into the private realm of the individual, and usually condemns communal oversight and restrictions as illegitimately invasive.

Earlier in the 20th century, like another lost voice, the respected colonialist Charles Andrews, though even willing to describe American local communalism as "individualism," came to similar conclusions. He noted that each local community, and above them the states, "looked on each other as 'foreigners,' in the medieval sense of the word, that is, as men of other communities. . . . generally speaking, the colonists were opposed to any federal scheme that involved a sacrifice of local power or autonomy; and to the end of the period the colonies remained a group of separatistic individualistic communities."[8] As Lord Bolingbroke noted, true "individuality belongs to communities, not to persons. Families might be conceived as individuals, though not men, in the state of nature; and civil societies much more so in the political state."[9] Such remarks suggest how self-government in these highly particularistic towns, the true "individuals" of the 18th century, might be confused with an ideology that awards merit to the particularism of individuals.

Michael Zuckerman, however, contends that part of the fault for the creation of this continuing confusion actually lies in the 18th century. He argues that even then, Americans lacked an adequate vocabulary with which to describe their local autonomy and highly communal political culture. Often, "they would speak of 'the people' or 'individualism' when they meant merely the people or individuals aggregated on different principles than those of the centralized state, when what they really meant was sovereignty in severalty, the sovereignty of local groups and localities."[10] Localism and its inherent particularism with its cultural shaping of ethical practices and norms was even then without an adequate language of explanation and defense. And the Enlightenment's demand for universal reason and uniformity and centralization in governmental function could only have further restricted Americans' positive assessment and understanding of their own condition.[11]

---

[7]Pekelis, *Law and Social Action*, p. 67.
[8]Andrews, *Colonial Background of the American Revolution*, p. 27.
[9]Bolingbroke, "From Philosophical Fragments" (1754), in *Viscount Bolingbroke*, p. 6.
[10]Zuckerman, *Peaceable Kingdoms*, pp. 46–47.
[11]See Wolin, *Presence of the Past*, pp. 132, 136, who says it is difficult to defend localism because "those who would theorize it are put in the paradoxical position of seeking to gener-

The core of the descriptive problem is, then, the unusually sovereign character of America's local communities. And "what is generally considered as and taken for the individualistic aspect of American life is simply the existence and coexistence of a plurality of communities." Pekelis holds that through an "optical error this phenomenon of decentralization of collectivistic pressure, which by its very decentralization only *increases* power, has sometimes been taken for individualism."[12] The irony is, as Pekelis recognized, that the autonomy of the locality is historically inversely related to that of the individual.

John Murrin also finds that the corporate and localistic character of 18th-century life is frequently and mistakenly viewed through contemporary individualistic filters. For example, he finds that voting was generally valued not because it represented an individual's right per se, but rather because it was part of a community's corporate right to self-direction. He states that "individuals functioned in society through their membership in counties and other corporate bodies. One man might not mean one vote, but one county did mean two representatives."[13] In their express concerns, the representatives of Lincoln, Massachusetts, supported this understanding. They wrote that the state was not made up of atomistic individuals, but was instead "constituted of a great number of Distinct and very unequal Corporations [in] which Corporations are the Immediate Constituent parts of the State and the Individuals are only the Remote parts."[14]

In the late 18th century, autonomous individual freedom was only beginning to be found in a dozen or so nascent cities and, in stark contrast, in the absolute wilderness. Elsewhere, individual freedom amounted at best to the limited ability of the dissatisfied individual or aberrant minority to enter and to leave intrusive communities. As Paul Conkin notes, "minorities excluded from local communities had one consolation—they could usually find their own fulfilling niche somewhere in the vast expanse of America."[15] Regarding this particular individual freedom, America's communities even compare unfavorably with the repressive polities of classical Greece. In 17th-century New England, citizens and church members had to get permission to relocate,[16] and even late in the 18th century, movement into some established communities was controlled by public officials.

---

alize about difference, of trying to make a theory about exceptions, local idiosyncrasies, regional differences."

[12]Pekelis, *Law and Social Action*, pp. 66–67.

[13]Murrin, "Myths of Colonial Democracy," p. 55.

[14]Handlin and Handlin, *Popular Sources of Political Authority*, p. 45; see also W. P. Adams, *First American Constitutions*, p. 237, who reports that Northampton, for example, "wanted to see the 'principle of corporate equality' prevail over the 'principle of personal equality.'"

[15]Conkin, "Freedom," p. 210.

[16]See Handlin and Handlin, *Liberty and Power*, p. 218.

As Oscar Handlin and Lilian Handlin have noted, "once in, each surrendered individual choice. A cooperative community required subordination of the person to the collectivity. The contrast between the freedom to enter a group and that to make [autonomous] individual decisions intruded into every aspect of colonial experience. All settlements aimed at the same communal objectives."[17] Not even in the corporate city-states of Greece was this freedom abridged. Unlike in American villages, "the one individual freedom which seems never to have been compromised [in ancient Greece] was that of leaving the community altogether." But this freedom has traditionally offered little to the autonomy-seeking individual, as it "underlines rather than limits the importance of the community and its power over its members. So long as the individual remains a member of the community, the extent of his submission to it may be unlimited and unconditional."[18]

Even those who opted to depart from a particular village, or jointly to seek separation from an older town, those one might expect to be pursuing their own autonomy, did not usually possess individualistic aspirations. Although town divisions that led to "hiving off" may have weakened corporate control, that was not the end sought by those separating. The motivation behind such splits "was not because some townsmen had fought to reduce a degree of local authority they considered in principle excessive, but because their attempt to create new foci of that same authority in the form of new towns had led to disputes."[19] Those involved were often families that were relatively poor, had young heads of household, or lived on the geographical edge of town life. They were in one sense or another marginal. Nevertheless, their desire to separate or "hive off" usually indicated that they were as committed to local communalism as the wealthier or better-situated families they left behind.

Such separatist families late in the century were in fact seeking the communal intimacy of earlier 18th-century villages, the world of their fathers, which they believed would allow them to become fully independent householders (in the agrarian sense) and communally self-governing. As in the Great Awakening, when group religious independence and greater corporate control over the dissolute individual, rather than individual liberation, was sought,[20] towns most often divided so that separating religious communities might "rule themselves . . . with the strictest moral discipline." These moments of town divisiveness, then, reflected Americans' commitment to communal ethical solidarity, rather than the desire of dissatisfied "rugged individualists" in search of autonomous freedom. In fact, in most of these new communities the moral authority of the group "was absolute

[17] Ibid., p. 51.

[18] Mulgan, "Liberty in Ancient Greece," p. 15.

[19] Lockridge, *New England Town*, p. 175.

[20] See H. S. Smith, *Changing Conceptions of Original Sin*, p. 10; Butler, "Enthusiasm Described and Decried," p. 323; A. S. Brown, "Visions of Community," p. 262; and Hatch, *Democratization of American Christianity*, p. 77.

over every individual."[21] One must thus avoid conflating political individualism, the logical terminus of extreme particularism, and America's long-enduring local communalism. In America, the local and communal midpoint between tyranny and license proved to be unexpectedly stable.

Even late in the 18th century, the goal of village separation continued to be "a new communal identity with the creation—indeed, the recreation—of a town," not increased individual autonomy. "Their actions bespoke a fundamentally conservative impulse to recreate for themselves the traditions of localism and communal autonomy."[22] These families were not escaping from communal oppression, but rather searching for their own local center of political liberty and ethical orthodoxy. And when frontier villages confronted the centralizing aspirations of county elites, they defensively and stridently demanded corporate, not individual, "freedom." A desire for individual emancipation from corporate intrusion had no role in the demands, for example, of separatist Congregational and Baptist congregations seeking corporate independence.[23] Migrations were often a means of preserving communities and families when communal ways of life "were threatened by land scarcity in the original town. The form migration took was in itself an expression of community."[24] Yet some commentators, such as Richard Bushman, have pointed to this as evidence of emerging individualism.[25]

The local communalism of reformed-Protestant America, because of its extreme character, has proved difficult for commentators to assess correctly. Too often, that which is only an expression of their powerful parochialism has been understood to be its opposite. Even the most perspicacious of visitors has mischaracterized American localism. This problem is exemplified in the widely countenanced reports of two prominent French visitors in the early 19th century, Alexis de Tocqueville and Michael Chevalier.[26] Both men applied French, Catholic, monarchical, and universalistic standards to the politics, religions, and peoples of the states they visited. They were not intellectually prepared to confront small self-governing polities that were stable, communal, reformed-Protestant, and still able to enjoy ordered liberty. In particular, it was Protestantism that Perry Miller believed Tocqueville could not understand. Miller found Tocqueville's pages on religion in *Democracy in America* to be "the least perceptive he

[21]Lockridge, *Settlement and Unsettlement in Early America*, pp. 44, 100.

[22]Nobles, *Divisions throughout the Whole*, pp. 148, 161–62.

[23]See Nobles, "Breaking Into the Backcountry," p. 670.

[24]Bender, *Community and Social Change in America*, pp. 72–73; see also Nobles, *Divisions throughout the Whole*, pp. 161–62.

[25]See Bushman, *From Puritan to Yankee*, pp. 235–90.

[26]See Arieli, *Individualism and Nationalism in American Ideology*, p. 200, who notes that "Chevalier's *Lettres sur l'Amérique du Nord* were hardly less famous or less celebrated in France than Tocqueville's *Democracy in America*."

ever wrote." Miller also sensed that "this would not be the last time that Gallic logic failed to encompass the spectacle of American irrationality."[27]

After their visits, these two French men of letters each independently used a recently coined French word, *individualisme,* to describe 19th-century America. Since their translated accounts were among the first to call Americans individualistic, they demand our attention. But these narratives seem to suffer from the same kind of reporting errors that continue to be found in accounts of 18th-century individualism. These two talented authors had confused America's localism, communalism, and particularism with social and political individualism. By conflating these localist attributes with individualism, they greatly added to, if they did not originate, the semantic chaos that surrounds this subject. Either way, 18th-century America became burdened with an inappropriate characterization.

Important segments of the postrevolutionary French intellectual world were hostile toward federalism and the defense of parochial interests, which were even taken by some to be counterrevolutionary crimes.[28] Yet both federalism and parochialism were essential aspects of American political culture. It would not be surprising, then, if American localism could not gain an accurate or fair hearing from men intellectually formed in an Enlightenment environment. (Those more influenced by Romanticism were under quite different influences.) Even today, in France, individualism is associated with a theory that "pushes towards the negation of the state." It is also teamed with anarchism, which is defined as a political theory that "eliminates from society all power to dispose of the right of constraint over the individual."[29] The strident French understanding of individualism (in comparison to the English one) is suggestive of how a French mind might have confused American localism with individualism. Localism, like individualism, must have appeared anarchical to those accustomed to hierarchy and centralization of power. They shared an aversion to the centrist, statist, and rationalistic characteristics of French political life and non-Romantic French thought.

The translation of *individualisme,* used by the two French authors to describe American social and political life, was its first use in English. (It had appeared in French thirteen or fourteen years earlier.) Henry Reeve, in his 1840 translation of Tocqueville's second volume of *Democracy in America,*[30] noted, "I adopt the expression of the original [individualism],

---

[27]P. Miller, "From the Covenant to the Revival," p. 365; in partial defense of Tocqueville, see Kessler, "Tocqueville's Puritans," pp. 778–79, 790–91.

[28]See May, *Enlightenment in America,* pp. 108, 228–29.

[29]*Petit Robert: Dictionnaire de la Langue Française,* s.v. "anarchisme," "individualisme"; see also Lukes, "Types of Individualism," pp. 594–95. The translation is mine.

[30]See *Compact Edition of the Oxford English Dictionary,* s.v. "individualism." In a rather confusing fashion the date given is 1835, which is the publication date for volume one, but the language in question only appeared in volume two, published in 1840. This fact is also noted by Ward, *Red, White, and Blue,* p. 232, and by Arieli, *Individualism and Nationalism*

however strange it may seem to an English ear . . . because I know of no English word exactly equivalent to the expression."[31] If not then, individualism had made its first appearance in English a year earlier in 1839 "in the English as well as the German language translations of Chevalier's *Lettres sur l'Amérique du Nord.*" Here, Chevalier "made the statement, so widely repeated after him, that the Americans, especially the Yankees, were individualistic *par excellence.*"[32] Yet it is likely that what he meant by individualism was far different from what it came to mean in English. In defining individualism, Tocqueville had noted that it described a "novel expression, to which a novel idea has given birth." In France, too, this was a concept that was incomprehensible to the generation preceding his own.[33] But he later claimed that this earlier generation would have described this phenomenon as "égoïsme (selfishness),"[34] the condition to which he believed individualism inevitably led.[35] What was most novel about the concept of individualism, then, was the relatively positive light in which it was viewed (especially when compared with the wholly derogatory status heretofore assigned to selfishness).

Tocqueville also seemingly conflated localism (and familism) with aspects of political individualism without clarifying that these are distinct and frequently adversarial principles. He had written that "individualism is a mature and calm feeling, which disposes each member of the community to sever himself from the mass of his fellows and to draw apart with his family and his friends . . . [leaving national] society at large to itself." Is he not in fact describing familism or localism rather than individualism? Are these forms of particularism indistinguishable to him? He notes that these feelings result less from an individual's depravity and more "from erroneous judgment." Nevertheless, like selfishness, individualism first "saps the virtues of public life," before "all virtue."[36] Is a public and virtuous life for Tocqueville not equivalent to national life? If so, there would be little separation between local communal and private egoistic life in his mind. By having conflated local communalism with true individualism, he

---

in *American Ideology*, p. 388, who attributes this error to Charles and Mary Beard. In the 1989 second edition of the *O.E.D.*, an 1827 English use of *individualism* is listed. However, it is not clear that individualism was being used in the social or political sense discussed here.

[31] Reeve, cited by Phillips Bradley in his "Note to the Reader," in Tocqueville, *Democracy in America*, 1:vi.

[32] Swart, "'Individualism' in the Mid-Nineteenth Century," p. 86; see also Arieli, *Individualism and Nationalism in American Ideology*, pp. 190, 388, 400, who reports that in 1841 the term made its appearance in both a translation of Friedrich List's *National System of Political Economy* and in Robert Owen's *Development of the Principles and Plans on which to Establish Self-supporting Home Colonies*.

[33] Tocqueville, *Democracy in America* (1840), 2:104.

[34] See ibid., 2:3–13, for his less satisfying discussion of individualistic epistemology, Puritanism, and the tyranny of public opinion.

[35] See ibid., 2:104.

[36] Ibid.

was moved to attribute to American communalism those very ills against which it had successfully fought, in some cases, for two centuries (as he had recognized in much of the first volume).

In a fashion reminiscent of Edmund Burke, Tocqueville also disapprovingly discriminated between individualism and an aristocratic sense of transgenerational virtue. He argued that men living in an age of democracy and equality suffer from individualism and an attendant impoverishment of the spirit.[37] Thus, they are unlike those superior "men living in aristocratic ages" who are "always closely attached to something placed out of their own sphere," an edifying condition that "often disposed [them] to forget themselves."[38] The comparable demand of American local communalism that people be guided to live beyond their most narrow selfish selves distinguished it from the modern ills Tocqueville condemned.[39] But the difference between aristocratic self-overcoming (whose loss he laments) and that of Americans is that his version was nationalistic, elitist, Catholic, and sharply defined by notions of hierarchy.[40] Theirs was not.

Tocqueville, the product of an aristocratic, French, and Catholic world, had trouble fully understanding (or defending) in the second volume the idea that the genius of America was its autonomous local communities.[41] As a consequence of the imprecise language then available to him and his failure to distinguish between two forms of particularism, individualism and localism, a localist people came to be mischaracterized. Americans were transformed in volume 2 of Tocqueville's *Democracy in America* into an individualistic people, a depiction that his own descriptive account shows not to have been accurate, even in 1840.

Chevalier too described America using the term *individualism* in a manner different from that in which it would come to be used in English. Again, what he meant by individualism was not autonomous individual behavior protected from the narrow constraints of family and community, but extreme localism. Unlike Tocqueville, however, Chevalier correctly associated localism with intolerance of self-expression, and for that, faulted it. He described a Yankee as "individualism incarnate; in him the spirit of locality and division is carried to the utmost. . . . In Massachusetts, with a population of 610,000 souls, the House of Representatives consists of 600 members; the most petty village must have its representative."[42]

Chevalier later noted that healthy political authority must rest on two

[37]See Sullivan, *Reconstructing Public Philosophy*, pp. 215–16.

[38]Tocqueville, *Democracy in America* (1840), 2:105.

[39]See I. Story, *Love of Our Country* (1775), p. 8.

[40]See Ward, *Red, White, and Blue*, p. 234.

[41]See Tocqueville, *Democracy in America* (1835), 1:61–101. In volume 1, Tocqueville's central concern seems to have been democratic tyranny, and in that light, localism appeared relatively attractive. In volume 2, with a different set of concerns, however, localism is portrayed much less favorably.

[42]Chevalier, *Society Manners and Politics* (1839), p. 116.

bases: "unity or centralization, and the distinction of ranks." He found Americans, however, devoid of both, especially in New England, which he described as the "incarnation of the spirit of division and individualism." More to his taste, he found the Southern states to "have more of the spirit of centralization." To his French mind, it was centralization that was rational and defensible. Localism—his individualism—was flawed by its irrationality and its lack of centralization, and in comparison to the grand scale of French nationalist aspirations, it was narrow-minded, selfish, and petty.

Without sensing the contradiction, he further described how American localism or centripetal power (read individualism) set limits, "sometimes narrow ones, to the independence of personal action whether exercised by individuals or collectively by [commercial] companies." To his dismay, "the private transactions of individuals" were interfered with in America. Fortunately, however, "the germ of a vigorous central authority" that was attempting to extirpate parochialism was found in all sections of the country "with the exception [again] of New England, which is held back by its spirit of subdivision."[43] When he described Americans as being individualistic, then, he could not have meant that they were individualistic in the modern sense of the word. Instead, he used the term to describe a polity that is markedly parochial, localistic, and (contrary to popular myth) opposed to uncontrolled commercial freedom and autonomous individualism. He applauded the latter two characteristics and took "individualism" to task for opposing them; he correctly suggested that commercialism and authentic individualism were more consistent with monarchical governments than with intrusive and demanding local communal ones. It is ironic, then, that the 19th-century American governments and communities, which he faulted for a lack of liberal tolerance and individual freedom, he mistakenly described as individualistic.

It appears that Chevalier's use of the term *individualism* to characterize Americans, like Tocqueville's, was the result of analytical confusion as well as of a particularly Enlightenment French inability to describe accurately a reformed-Protestant and local communal people who possessed sovereignty and self control over their corporate religious and political life. Chevalier, in fact, described Americans pejoratively as extreme localists rather than as protectors of individual rights and the autonomous self, which protection he approvingly associated with centralized monarchical governments. Americans thus came to be known as individualists, although their behavior, even as reported by those describing them as such, did not offer corroboration. And if these authors were wrong about the 19th century, they were even more in error concerning the late 18th century. In short, 18th-century American localism or particularism must not

43Ibid., pp. 116, 407–8.

be confused with individualism, which was, to the degree it was visible, deplored by most Americans.

FAMILISM, NOT INDIVIDUALISM

America in the late 18th century, in which the most basic political unit was the individual community, is perhaps best captured by a historian of the American city, Thomas Bender. He finds that "colonial America was a heterogeneous culture made up of homogeneous and largely isolated individual units."[44] But because of the overwhelming sense of openness between communities, it has often been easier for observers to view the heterogeneous forest rather than the particularism, exclusivity, and intolerance normally associated with the communal trees. Yet in this America, autonomy and self-government were goals most appropriate to communities, or at the very minimum, to the family. They were clearly not appropriate goals for individuals. Each self-governing village, therefore, sought to create a regime of local orthodoxy, and by necessity a measured level of intolerance; in some instances they continued to do so for another century.

However, from the interstices between this system of marked and intentional local communal intolerance, a certain degree of unintended freedom for the individual paradoxically grew. This was not the result of "an overall ideology of freedom—but of the existence of many communities within the society each with its own canons of orthodoxy."[45] In other words, a diversity of intolerance created an 18th-century form of pluralism. Again, this arose from America's intense local communalism rather than from adherence to an ideology that encouraged such dispensations. American localism thus often appeared to be what it resisted, or in unexpected and unintended ways actually gave ground to that which it opposed. In either case, autonomous individual freedom was an unintended by-product.

The elevated standing of the family unit in American political and social thought is even more likely to be mischaracterized as individualistic. The family's relative autonomy in American social and political life and its small size compared to all other social groups has led to this confusion. But a belief in the heightened value of the family, or familism, is distinct from individualism.[46] The family is often taken by individualists to represent "the corrupt past, an institution guilty of the abuse of power and the suppression of individual freedom." It is only when "liberated from the bonds of the family [that] the individual can achieve independence and

---

[44]Bender, *Community and Social Change in America*, p. 69.

[45]Roche, "American Liberty," p. 134; see also Sowell, *Ethnic America*, p. 10.

[46]Familism, according to *The Unabridged Random House Dictionary of the English Language*, is "the subordination of the personal interests and prerogatives of an individual to the values and demands of the family," and is associated by the editors with the patriarchal family.

experience a new beginning."[47] As modern feminists have made still clearer,[48] a doctrine that subordinates an individual's immediate interests to a corporate body, even a small one such as the family, cannot be equated with the tenets or goals of authentic individualism.

The distinction between family and self was recognized in 1620 in the first use in English of the word individual to denote "a single human being, as opposed to Society, the Family, etc."[49] And in the world of the 18th century, "man owed his first duty to God, the next to his country, and his third to his family."[50] "The whole edifice of ethics" rested on "a grand descending staircase from one's duties to God, to the nation, to family," and only then "to one's self."[51] Anyone who altered "the gradation of these duties, breaks upon the order of nature established by God."[52] Thus, the true end of government was that it "inforce the Observance of the Laws of Virtue or Nature, according to the Subordination" of the individual's happiness to that of family and community, society, and humankind.[53] All corporate bodies, even ones as small as families, stood as barriers to heightened senses of the self and served to control the sinful and irrational wants of individuals.

Service to the family was therefore a calling that was valued over that to the individual, and service to the larger public good was deemed superior to both.[54] For example, William, a member of the talented and politically influential Livingston family, held that "family affection and private Friendship, if they so engross our Hearts as to render us insensible of the general Welfare, are not only mean and unworthy Passions, but naturally hurry us into the basest, the vilest, and most immoral Conduct."[55] And the highly respected physician, statesman, and signer of the Declaration of Independence Dr. Benjamin Rush, whose values comfortably drew on the three dominant languages of 18th-century American moral thought, held the family to even stricter public standards. He noted that "next to the duty which young men owe to their Creator, I wish to see a SUPREME REGARD TO THEIR COUNTRY inculcated in them." Young men were to be converted "into republican machines" and each man was to be taught to forget his own needs for "he does not belong to himself, but that he is

---

[47]Whitehead, "Dan Quayle Was Right," pp. 83–84. The author is attempting to explain why family breakup has been greeted by such a "triumphant rhetoric of renewal" in America. See also Eastland, "Attorney General and Social Worker," p. A15; and Douglas, "Dissent from *Wisconsin v. Yoder*," p. 1122, who clearly distinguishes between the needs of the family and those of the individual members, especially children.

[48]For example, see the pathbreaking work of Okin, *Justice, Gender, and the Family*, p. 15.

[49]*Compact Edition of the Oxford English Dictionary*, s.v. "individual."

[50]See Sidney, "Maxims for Republics" (July 1787), p. 81.

[51]Cited by Rodgers, *Contested Truths*, p. 120.

[52]Sidney, "Maxims for Republics" (July 1787), p. 81; see also A. Smith, *Theory of Moral Sentiments*, p. 384.

[53]"Virtue" (16 November 1747).

[54]See Wall, *Fierce Communion*, p. 83.

[55]Livingston, "Of Patriotism" (1753), in Livingston et al., *Independent Reflector*, p. 216.

public property. Let him be taught to love his family, but let him be taught at the same time that he must forsake and even forget them when the welfare of his country requires it. . . . he must be taught that his life 'is not his own.' "[56]

Such sentiments were especially common during the heady days of the Revolution. Even as sober a character as John Adams, a man known for his close attachment to his family, wrote at the beginning of the Revolution that

> men must be ready, they must pride themselves, and be happy to sacrifice their private Pleasures, Passions and Interests, nay, their private Friendships and dearest Connections, when they stand in Competition with the Rights of Society. . . . Every man must seriously set himself to root out his Passions, Prejudices and Attachments, and to get the better of his private Interest. The only reputable Principle and Doctrine must be that all Things must give Way to the public.[57]

The powerful public sympathies of many Americans during the Revolutionary period not only continued to undercut any commitments to the rights of particular individuals, but also demanded that, when needed, commitments to the family should be sacrificed.[58] The family and individual were thus both inferior to the public good.

Americans understood the family, even with its natural propensity for self-absorption, self-direction, and unacceptable narrowness, as preferable to the individual for serving the higher ethical demands of God and the public. In the words of James Henretta, "the lineal family—not the conjugal unit and certainly not the unattached individual—thus stood at the center of economic and social existence."[59] Americans believed that the family, not the free individual, should be viewed as the basic building block of all larger religious, social, economic, and political aggregations.[60] They thus followed Lord Bolingbroke who, in dissent from Locke, had concluded that "civil governments were formed not by the concurrence of individuals, but by the association of families."[61]

In America, this position was reinforced by the distrust of an individual unburdened by the self-overcoming demands of even the smallest aggregate body, a family. Marriage was essential to human flourishing. Americans felt that "marriage did not obliterate the self, but it did mute its force." It was recognized that in marriage, "the need for mutual spiritual

[56]Rush, "Thoughts upon the Mode of Education" (1786), pp. 684–87.

[57]J. Adams, "Letter to Mercy Warren" (16 April 1776), in Adams, Adams, and Warren, *Warren-Adams Letters*, 1:222–23.

[58]See Wood, *Creation of the American Republic*, p. 61.

[59]Henretta, "Families and Farms," p. 32; see also Countryman, *American Revolution*, p. 229.

[60]See Ditz, *Property and Kinship*, pp. 159–60; Demos, *Little Commonwealth*, p. 186; and Bender, *Community and Social Change in America*, p. 131.

[61]Bolingbroke, "Philosophical Fragments" (1754), in *Viscount Bolingbroke*, p. 10.

aid and the inhibiting of the self, that ominous repository of worldly inclinations,"[62] could best be met. The presence of intimate others contained and controlled the individual; this is what corporate bodies, even ones as small as the nuclear family, most importantly had to offer.[63]

From the familist perspective, an individual male enjoyed his status as a full citizen not because he was a rights-bearing individual human being, nor even because he was an adult white male in a patriarchal and racist society,[64] but because he was a landed head of a household. American social and political norms were not dedicated to serving the interests of adult white males at the expense of women and children in their ethnic communities. Above all, God, the family, and the community were to be served. The adult white male was awarded his preferred position, with all the responsibilities that were entailed, only when he stood at the head of a household.[65] From the perspective of Americans' English cousins as well, a man without a family "was not a householder[;] he was outside civil society, [and was] classed as a cottager. Marriage we must insist . . . was the entry to full membership" in public life.[66] Thus, as in many traditional societies (observant Jews, for example), living a life without wife and children was not socially sanctioned. The life of the free individual, like that of the tyrant, was a form of rootlessness, immaturity, or sacrilege that was viewed, at least, with suspicion.[67] Living alone, or even without children,[68] frequently made one unworthy of acceptance as a full member of society.

The individual in America was initially subject to such social and legal pressures and familial discipline that "no one was allowed to live alone or keep a bachelor residence" and "all single people had to live with a family."[69] Some modern defenders of traditional morality who look back fondly on historic America might find this pleasing. However, they might find it disconcerting to discover that the family, although enjoying a standing superior to that of the selfish and sinful individual, was not the haven of bourgeois privacy that it reportedly became in the 19th century. Instead,

---

[62]Saum, *Popular Mood*, pp. 117–18.

[63]See Patten, *Discourse Delivered at Hallifax* (1766), pp. 9–10.

[64]Females and nonwhites were frequently unable to achieve this privileged status based on their gender and race. My point is that being white and male were not sufficient, even though they were usually necessary, conditions.

[65]See F. Anderson, *People's Army*, p. 35, and J. P. Greene, *All Men Are Created Equal*, p. 17.

[66]Laslett, *World We Have Lost*, p. 12.

[67]See Rossiter, *First American Revolution*, p. 150.

[68]See West [Withers], *Plainville, U.S.A.*, pp. 203–4, whose description of a rural community in the early 20th century is instructive. He reports that status declined as children were married and parents had no further need to remain fully engaged in matters of church and school. Moreover, he reports that "their diminishing importance as heads of functioning families is quickly reflected in the respect which they themselves, their activities, and their opinions enjoy in the eyes of neighbors."

[69]Daniels, "Political Structure of Local Government," p. 52; see also Flaherty, *Privacy in Colonial New England*, pp. 175–78.

the family had more in common with a collectivist or totalitarian environment than it did with a contemporary liberal one.[70] In Revolutionary America, the family was subject to invasive community control just as individual family members were to the head of the household (usually a man).[71]

The close supervision of the family was in keeping with reformed Protestants' distrust of all people—even fathers, pastors, and kings—as hopelessly sinful. "The sin of the first Adam had so vitiated human nature that," in particular, "family governors could not be trusted to maintain the order that God had commanded."[72] Most communities did not recognize the border between local community and family as sacrosanct—with an important exception. In the novel familial practices of the Quakers, such patterns of local governmental and societal intrusion were rejected. The Quakers were "the very first group in all the Western world to maintain the modern sentimental family, predicated on privacy."[73] Only among the Quakers would familism lose its link to broader forms of communalism— one more reason Quaker religious, social, and political practices alienated their fellow Americans.

Usually even the parent-child relationship was subject to communal intervention.[74] In Virginia, for example, churchwardens under an act of 1727, renewed in 1748, were to remove children from poor parents "to prevent the evil consequences attending the neglect or inability of poor people to bring up their children in an honest and orderly course of life."[75] As argued by a Southern author, if parents could not properly educate their children, then "it certainly would be just and expedient, to take them out of their hands, and have them brought up in such a way, as might afford some rational prospect of their being useful to society."[76] In the North, a prominent minister noted that "that sentiment of *Lycurgus*, that 'children belong to the State more than to their parents' ought to be deeply engraved on the heart of every person who is concerned in making or

[70]See Hareven, "Divorce, Chinese Style," p. 76, who writes that "like the Puritan elders, the rulers of the People's Republic consciously use the family as an agent of reform and morality. They endorse public intervention in family affairs and they subordinate, to the extent they can, the individual to the larger community."

[71]See Flaherty, *Privacy in Colonial New England*, pp. 85–112; Wall, *Fierce Communion*, pp. 8–9; and Demos, *Past, Present, and Personal*, p. 82.

[72]E. S. Morgan, *Puritan Family*, p. 142.

[73]Zuckerman, "Introduction," pp. 11–13; see also Fischer, *Albion's Seed*, pp. 481, 595, 898.

[74]See Yazawa, *From Colonies to Commonwealth*, p. 46.

[75]Cited by Seiler, "Anglican Church," pp. 148–49; see also Kramnick, *Republicanism and Bourgeois Radicalism*, pp. 193, 214–23, for his description of the similarly repressive character (by current standards) of John Locke's thought on this matter, as well as that of later 18th-century British dissenters, such as James Burgh. For example, both men proposed that children of the poor were to be removed from them to prevent idleness and disorderly behavior.

[76]Reese, *Essay on the Influence of Religion* (1788), p. 75, and see similar remarks from an earlier editorial in the *New-York Weekly Journal*, 16 June 1735.

executing laws."[77] It was the community's or public's interest (and only in the long term, the interests of God and his saved) that must be served, and not the idiosyncratic ones of parents or children qua individuals.

In 18th-century moral and political thought, the family and the local community represented sources of collective selfishness and self-indulgence to be overcome in the quest to serve God (and truth, reason, justice, and so forth). But what made Americans so different from others in the Western world was the degree to which familial and local communal concerns were sanctioned and not overawed by those of larger political, social, and religious aggregations. American society (and, by intention or default, the central government as well) was surprisingly indulgent of traditional peasant-level concerns and often hostile to those of higher levels of integration. Yet Americans defended their local religious and political autonomy, to the confusion of European visitors, without supporting the next, more atomistic, level of particularism, individual autonomy. The family, then, was an intermediate institution between the infinitely sinful and untrustworthy individual and the larger, more acceptable collectivities of congregation, neighborhood, and village. Americans, a people shaped by reformed Protestantism, rejected coercive aggregations much larger than the local community or smaller than the family. Only in the last decade of the 18th century would some Americans learn to speak the entwined languages of nationalism and individualism.

The Hated, Sinful Self: Surrogate for Individualism

Revolutionary-era Americans' distrust of the socially unbounded individual is further evidenced in their attitude toward the self. As a surrogate for their infrequently discussed views of the autonomous individual (and indirectly for their views toward the emerging theory of individualism), it provides a useful window through which to view them. Simply stated, Americans denounced personal attributes associated with the self (such as self-interest, selfishness, self-centeredness, and self-love) as common forms of personal pathology.[78] Most, in fact, held that the self was the penultimate source of personal confusion, "intestine" turmoil, or evil.[79]

The South Carolinian Presbyterian pastor and schoolmaster Thomas

---

[77]Belknap, *Election Sermon* (1785), pp. 12–14. This was the first regular New Hampshire election sermon.

[78]See Masur, "Age of the First Person Singular," p. 197; Bercovitch, *Puritan Origins of the American Self,* p. 17; Isaac, *Transformation of Virginia,* p. 72; Heimert, *Religion and the American Mind,* p. 55; and J. P. Greene, *Landon Carter,* p. 22. But see also J. P. Greene, *Pursuits of Happiness,* pp. 75–76, who now finds that the self was to be served, not tamed; and Friedman, "Shaping of Radical Consciousness," pp. 789–92, who holds that radicalism promoted a new positive valuation of the self.

[79]See Pahl, *Free Will and Political Liberty,* pp. 107–9; and Carden, *Puritan Christianity in America,* pp. 47, 51.

Reese, in an often reprinted series of essays, was not unique in arguing that "the love of self is almost always inordinate in the pursuit of the present good, and frequently, by a blind and furious impulse to present gratification, breaks thro' all the fences of law, and leads men to all manner of violence and injustice. Indeed, to counteract and restrain the excess of this passion, and correct the evils which arise from it, is the very design of the civil compact."[80] On one of the national days of humiliation and fasting declared by the Continental Congress, Jacob Green, vice president of Princeton and chair of the committee that drafted the New Jersey Constitution, took much the same position. He too argued that selfishness was "really the root of all the vices in the world," in particular because "a selfish person will promote his own private interest at the expence of the public."[81] For one anonymous commentator, the principal end of government was to curb selfishness and keep "it within those bounds, which common good requires."[82] Many American Christians went even further and held that the self must die again and again. Indeed, for the reformed Protestant, "life remained an unceasing war with the self and an unending quest, fulfilled only by death itself, for selflessness. Only then could the monster self be slain at last, and the self become truly one with Christ."[83]

That Americans held such views is not surprising. Only at the end of the 18th century, "under the sails of philosophy, religion, politics, and the arts," did the modern understanding of the self begin to gain acceptance.[84] (The modern view has been fairly described as positing a "series of theses about total self-actualization," as seeing "the human individual as uniquely the source of value," and assigning "unconditional trust in and love of the self.")[85] Michel Foucault even believes that until the end of the 18th century, the individual self as we know it did not exist. The modern concept of the individual with its glorification of the self was, he says, "a quite recent creature" that was invented "less than two hundred years ago."[86] Louis Dumont finds that members of traditional societies little understand the Western view of the individual and "have basically a collective idea of man."[87] And among such people even today there is little "valuation of each as unique, and, in truth, of the 'very concept of an established self.' "[88] Thus, the modern sense of the individual as embodying

[80]Reese, *Essay on the Influence of Religion*, p. 16.
[81]Green, *Sermon Delivered at Hanover* (1779), pp. 9–10.
[82]"Remarks on a Passage" (April 1791), p. 184.
[83]Greven, *Protestant Temperament*, pp. 84–86.
[84]Lyons, *Invention of the Self*, p. 16.
[85]Manuel and Manuel, *Utopian Thought in the Western World*, p. 446; Sabine, *History of Political Theory*, p. 673; and Vitz, "Secular Personality Theories," p. 91; see also D. Bell, "Resolving the Contradictions."
[86]Foucault, *Order of Things*, p. 308.
[87]Dumont, *Homo Hierarchicus*, p. 8.
[88]Zuckerman, "Fabrication of Identity in Early America," pp. 186–87.

an autonomous center that demands public accommodation and nurturing of his or her uniqueness is a recent product of Western culture.[89]

It was 19th-century opponents of this new vision of the self or the individual with heightened moral standing who coined the term *individualism*. For them, it was "to designate the disintegration of society, which French reactionaries believed had resulted from the French Revolution and the doctrine of the individual rights of man." Joseph de Maistre in the 1820s made explicit his dissatisfaction and "originated the term individualism to characterize this atomization of society" and the "excessive fragmentation of all philosophical and political doctrines." Maistre described these new currents of thought "as a form of 'political protestantism carried to the most absolute individualism.'"[90] To his French Catholic mind, individualism was an extreme form of particularism that was only a step away from absolute anarchism. Other leading European thinkers were also "convinced that 'individualism' constituted a serious evil undermining the political and social order of their times." The adherents of movements so stigmatized, "Romanticism, political and economic liberalism, Protestantism—either rejected the new word as a meaningless term of abuse" or employed it as a pejorative label.[91]

Most Americans at the very end of the 18th century, to the degree they were aware of it, also opposed Revolutionary French individualism and its valuation of the self. For example, the frequently published Congregational minister Joseph Lyman lamented the changing character of the world around him and reminded his listeners that among the most important purposes of government ordained by heaven was "to extirpate vice, to avenge public and individual wrongs; [and] to curb the excesses of selfish avarice and ambition." Jeremiah Atwater, Middlebury College's future first president, speaking before the Vermont legislature, also argued that government had its origins "in the vices of man. . . . But such is man's nature . . . that he needs restraint: The selfish passions need curbing and regulating."[92] Thomas Jefferson captured best the common sense of Americans when in the early 19th century he wrote that "self-love . . . is the sole antagonist of virtue, leading us constantly by our propensities to self-gratification in violation of our moral duties to others. Accordingly, it is

[89]The earliest positive use of the concept of self that approaches in meaning the idea that the individual is a unique center to be valued as such, rather than as a being that finds meaning by partaking in something universal and superpersonal, is reported by the *Oxford English Dictionary* to have been in the late 17th century.

[90]Swart, "'Individualism' in the Mid-Nineteenth Century," p. 78; see also Hampson, *Enlightenment*, pp. 282–83.

[91]Swart, "'Individualism' in the Mid-Nineteenth Century," pp. 77–78, 84; see also Lyons, *Invention of the Self*, p. 3; Lukes, *Individualism*, pp. 77–78; and Arieli, *Individualism and Nationalism in American Ideology*, pp. 217, 288, 398, 400. Arieli reports, however, that individualism was first used not by de Maistre, but in 1826 by Saint-Simon in *Le producteur*.

[92]Lyman, *A Sermon* (1787 Massachusetts election sermon), pp. 15–16, and Atwater, "Vermont Election Sermon" (1802), pp. 1171–72.

against this enemy that are erected the batteries of moralists and religionists, as the only obstacle to the practice of morality. Take from man his selfish propensities, and he can have nothing to seduce him from the practice of virtue."[93] Still later in the 19th century, a former Dartmouth professor of chemistry and the president of Hobart College, Benjamin Hale, before an audience in Geneva, New York, held that Americans must not let "a selfish regard to their private interest . . . govern them" nor give in to "the present promptings of self-indulgence, the present impulses of passion."[94]

Americans believed, then, that the passions of the self must be constrained within a social framework and that little freedom was needed beyond that required in the service of familial, societal, divine, or rational ends. But within this general outlook, Philip Greven has identified three separate attitudes toward the self. One of them was held by the prerevolutionary group whom he describes as the "genteel" class. He associates them with the imperial administrators populating a handful of "urban" centers, and finds that they had a relatively relaxed and cosmopolitan understanding of the self. They were "far more at ease with themselves, their desires, and their pleasures than were the others," and they viewed themselves with less of a sense of debasement than did most other Americans.[95] They made up, however, only a minute fraction of the population before the Revolution, and after it, partly as a result of emigration, both voluntary and coerced,[96] they ceased to exist as such. Thus, their more benign attitude toward the self did little to shape American perspectives.[97]

Those who were to replace them as politically dominant, whom Greven calls "moderates," also constituted a small percentage of the population. But by framing the first Revolutionary-era charters and political institutions and later in 1789 the national ones, they became a significant minority (our true elite). Most of this Revolutionary ruling class was made up of men drawn from the upper-middle ranks of politics and commerce,[98] and interestingly "were either foreign born or educated abroad." It is significant that they frequently were engaged in businesses that were intercolonial or international in nature or provided the leadership of the inter-

---

[93]Jefferson, "Letter to Thomas Law, 13 June 1814," in *Writings,* ed. Peterson, pp. 1336–37.

[94]Hale, *Liberty and Law* (1838), p. 10.

[95]Greven, *Protestant Temperament,* p. 14.

[96]See W. Brown, *Good Americans;* and for his estimate of the number of loyalists who were forced into exile, see Van Tyne, *Loyalists in the American Revolution,* pp. 286–307.

[97]Pitkin, "Are Freedom and Liberty Twins?" p. 29 (draft version), reminds us that even for these gentlemen and ladies, when "freedom threatens to engulf the self, to release uncontrollable and dangerous forces out of the social underclass or the psychic underworld," then these forces must be controlled by "external laws and regulations or the genteel self-control of the liberal gentlemen."

[98]Greven, *Protestant Temperament,* p. 12.

colonial political institutions, such as the Continental Congress and the army.[99]

During the Revolutionary crisis, these men, who otherwise were adherents of Henry May's moderate Enlightenment, defended passionate love of country and advocated extreme forms of corporate oversight. This Revolutionary elite "did not intend to lay the basis for the revolutionary individualism, one may even say the philosophic anarchism, that inheres in the interpretation of the Declaration as an assertion of absolute immanent individual rights."[100] The Revolutionary years were marked, therefore, by a more extreme hostility toward the demands of the self than was true of the century as a whole. In part this was because the members of the Revolutionary elite, unlike the other two populations Greven describes (genteel and Christian), were transformed by their Revolutionary commitments. They embraced self-abrogating ideals that they had previously held in more nuanced versions. And within a generation after the Revolution, many subsequently rejected these self-denying values and returned to a more equivocal stance.[101] Yet, both before and after the Revolution, "they too believed in the need for self-denial." They did so without, however, accepting the reformed-Protestant "insistence upon the virtual annihilation of the corrupted and sinful self."[102]

Many in the Revolutionary leadership found the language of classical or Whig republicanism congenial to their enlightened sensibilities. But in embracing this discourse during the Revolutionary years, their former (as well as future) equivocation regarding the acceptable nature of the self was overcome. Republican theorists who were read in the colonies, like traditional Protestant apologists, excoriated the selfish individual as a potential source of corruption and the ultimate cause of a people's destruction.[103] Whig republicanism, in particular, is said to have ideally required that "the citizen must cancel the man, the patriot must collectivize his love for himself, and the individual must give himself to the whole; he dies as a particular and is reborn."[104] Outspoken Whig patriots claimed that Americans should strive to reach this self-denying ideal. They wrote that "it was the duty of a republic to control 'the selfishness of mankind,'" for "ideally

[99]See McDonald, *E Pluribus Unum*, p. 187; Maier, *Old Revolutionaries*, p. 280; and Kramnick, "Great National Discussion," p. 25.

[100]Wishy, "John Locke," p. 421.

[101]See Melancton Smith, "Speeches before the New York Ratifying Convention" (June 1788), p. 344, who asks in dismay, "who would have thought ten years ago, that the very men who risqued their lives and fortunes in support of republican principles, would now treat them as the fictions of fancy."

[102]Greven, *Protestant Temperament*, p. 13.

[103]See Pocock, *Machiavellian Moment*, pp. 506–53; Bailyn, *Ideological Origins of the American Revolution*, pp. 22–54; Banning, *Jeffersonian Persuasion*, pp. 21–91; and McDonald, *Novus Ordo Seclorum*, pp. 57–96.

[104]Sartori, "Liberty and Law," p. 280.

republicanism obliterated the individual."[105] It was frequently argued that in a healthy polity, "each individual gives up all private interest that is not consistent with the general good, and interest of the whole body."[106]

Gordon Wood explains that the Revolution was an effort "to reform American society and to realize once and for all the moral values intellectuals had espoused for centuries." Especially "in 1776, this republicanism represented an eighteenth-century secularized version of Puritanism, an updated reactionary effort to bring under control the selfish and individualistic impulses."[107] Robert Bell, following Rousseau, explained that "good social institutions are those which conduce the best to civilize man, take from him his absolute existence, to give him a relative one and transport *self* into the common whole: so that each particular, no longer thinking of himself as one, but as part of the whole."[108] From such a vantage point, one defined by a desperate desire to live beyond the self in an enlarged community, the birth of the national republic must be viewed as a substantial failure. Harvard's Samuel Huntington, in fact, looking over the expanse of American history, finds that "new beginnings and flawed outcomes, promise and disillusion,"[109] are patterns that would be repeated.

The common men and women of America whom Greven describes as predominantly reformed Protestant and who today would be characterized as lower-middle class were even more hostile to the demands of the self than the republican-influenced elite.[110] Greven describes them as "engaged in a constant battle not only against the flesh but even more encompassingly against everything within themselves that gave them a sense of self and self-worth. Self-denial meant nothing less than the denial of the *self.*" For them, he continues, "life was nothing less than a constant battle with pride and self, and a constant seeking after humility, abasement, and impotency."[111]

Greven's understanding of the hostility felt by Protestant Americans toward the autonomous individual is accepted by historians of diverse outlooks and areas of interest. For example, the intellectual historian Joyce Appleby writes that "when the humble white folk of Southern society rebelled," it was not by heeding the words of John Locke, "but rather by embracing the fellowship offered by Baptist congregations." Their preeminent belief was that one should make a profound commitment to God, "above all to reject those telltale signs of creeping secularism—absorption

---

[105]Wood, *Creation of the American Republic*, pp. 60–61.
[106]L. Hart, "Liberty Described and Recommended" (1775), p. 309.
[107]Wood, introduction to *Rising Glory of America*, p. 5.
[108]R. Bell, *Illuminations for Legislators, and for Sentimentalists* (1784), p. 23.
[109]S. Huntington, *American Politics*, p. 11.
[110]See Appleby, "Introduction," p. 471; Bercovitch, *Puritan Origins of the American Self*, pp. 11–14; and Calhoon, "Religion and Individualism in Early America," p. 53.
[111]Greven, *Protestant Temperament*, p. 74.

with material well-being, and justifications for self-interest."[112] Christine Heyrman also finds that the earlier religious revivals of the mid-18th century, for all their social disruptiveness and effusive support of religious freedom, did not alter the American discomfort with self-serving behavior. "On the contrary," she writes, these newly reborn Christians "wished to strengthen the hold of the old order over the lives of the individuals, especially those who deviated from the norms" of reformed orthodoxy.[113]

The economic historian J. E. Crowley draws attention to their hostility toward the self as evidenced in the Protestant idea of the calling (divine sanction for one's employment). He argues that it is predicated on an unflattering view of the self that demanded that the individual be aided in restraining the demands of the self. For most Americans, the correct answer to the rhetorical question "What is the vilest creation upon Earth?" was "Mine owne self, by reason of my sins." For them, the self was sinful and dangerous and "work was the chief way to discipline it."[114]

As interpreted by American reformed Protestants, Christianity stands in adamant opposition to the wants, the siren calls, of the sinful self. For them "salvation comes from putting down the very self—the old man or the old woman—that the gnostics think can be repaired and made whole. The very will, the very desire, which drives people to find wholeness of self is the same self-will that is at the center of our sin."[115] For America's greatest philosopher and theologian, Jonathan Edwards, the first president of Princeton, man's self-denial consisted "in being emptied of himself; so that he does freely and from his heart, as it were renounce himself, and annihilate himself."[116] Protestant sources throughout the 18th century argued that the "self is undeniably the greatest Bias," and that "the religion of Jesus enlarges the mind" and "makes us willing to deny ourselves, to sacrifice our worldly ease, our temporal interest, to the honor of God and the good of men."[117]

President Witherspoon of Princeton inculcated in his students, many of them future Southern patriot leaders, the precept that the most fundamental teaching of Christianity was "self-denial." This, he advised, "should extend to your whole deportment."[118] President Clap of Yale, although insisting that Christianity did not demand complete annihilation of the self, also taught his students about the error of self-love in his ethics course, the capstone experience of their college education. He reminded

---

[112]Appleby, *Capitalism and a New Social Order*, p. 8.

[113]Heyrman, *Commerce and Culture*, p. 197.

[114]Crowley, *This Sheba, Self*, p. 17.

[115]Vitz, "Secular Personality Theories," p. 73.

[116]Cited by Greven, *Protestant Temperament*, p. 78.

[117]S. Hall, *Legislature's Right, Charge and Duty* (1746 Connecticut election sermon); and Eliot, *Massachusetts Election Sermon* (1765), pp. 26–27; see also Atwater, "Vermont Election Sermon" (1802), p. 1172.

[118]Witherspoon, *Dominion of Providence* (1776), pp. 58–59.

them that "for a Man to make the *sole, supreme,* or *ultimate End* of all Being and Action to be for *himself alone* or his *own* Happiness, as the *summum Bonum;* and to regard God and all other Beings, only so far as they may *serve himself* or be subservient to his own Happiness, or to *gratify* his *Principle of Self-Love* is the most absolute Inversion of the *Order, Dignity* and *Perfection* of Beings: and one of the worst Principles that can be in human Nature."[119] Similarly, Yale's president from 1777 to 1795, Ezra Stiles, believed that his rebirth in Christ demanded that he "annihilate himself in an intire Submission to the infinitely holy will of God."[120] The view of Greven's "evangelicals" was so widespread that, as exemplified by the highly educated Witherspoon, Clap, Stiles, and their elite students, hostility to the demands of the self cannot be tied to an uneducated parochial class.

Americans, in their hostility to self-centered activity, maintained a particular aversion to a driven pursuit of wealth.[121] Wealth, it was commonly understood, "corrupts a whole neighborhood" and poisons "the morals of a whole community." The Reverend Phillips Payson, a member of the American Academy of Sciences and a celebrated combatant during the Revolutionary War, speaking before the Massachusetts legislature in 1778, noted that the "sovereign power of interest seems to have been much the source of modern politics abroad, and had given birth to such maxims of policy as these, viz., that 'the wealth of a people is their truest honor.'" He found America different, for its people were virtuous and would be able to show the world that "such maxims are base and ill-founded."[122] A few years earlier, however, John Adams had claimed that the spirit of commerce was "as rampant in New England as in any Part of the World." But this was a spirit that he believed was invidious and incompatible with the "greatness of soul which is necessary for an happy Republic." Instead, Adams counseled that everyone must "get the better of his private Interest. The only reputable Principle and Doctrine must be that all things must give Way to the public."[123] And Jefferson a few years later was even less sanguine as he predicted that Americans would become corrupt and careless as they forgot "themselves, but in the sole faculty of making money."[124]

Also prominent on the list of self-serving ills that Americans hoped to

[119]Clap, *Nature and Foundation of Moral Virtue* (1765), pp. 16–17.

[120]Cited by Grasso, "Between Awakenings," p. 283.

[121]See E. Foner, *Tom Paine and Revolutionary America,* p. 169.

[122]Payson, "Massachusetts Election Sermon" (1778), pp. 528–29.

[123]J. Adams, "Letter to Mercy Warren" (16 April 1776), in Adams, Adams, and Warren, *Warren-Adams Letters,* 1:222–23; see also "Oration" (4 July 1787), p. 421; and Main, *Social Structure of Revolutionary America,* pp. 207–8.

[124]Jefferson, "Notes on the State of Virginia" (1787), in *Portable Thomas Jefferson,* p. 213; and see Fobes, "An Election Sermon" (1795 Massachusetts election sermon), pp. 1001–2, who finds that "national wealth, especially when carefully accumulated in the hands of a few individuals, is dangerous in the extreme to human liberty."

avoid contracting were those associated with the more cosmopolitan British. As a result of the Revolution, however, they believed they would be able to avoid Britain's embrace of what would come to be called modernity,[125] that is, "infidelity, selfishness, luxury, and dissipation" and "irreligion . . . drunkenness, lewdness, excessive gaming, clandestine marriages, [and] breach of matrimonial vows." They wished, above all, to escape the contagion of "*vain, luxurious,* and *selfish* EFFEMINACY."[126] The behavior most derided was the pursuit of luxury, which consisted of "dull, selfish, criminal enjoyments in minds stupefied and bodies enervated by wallowing forever in one continual puddle of voluptuousness."[127]

Such descriptions and heightened concerns testify both to the changing economic and social opportunities of the late 18th-century Anglo-American world and to the principled resistance such changes encountered in America. Church historian Harry Stout notes that for Revolutionary-era Americans,

> Success was cause for grave alarm because it gave rise to pride and inordinate attachment to "the world." . . . Too many farmers, tradesmen, and land speculators were caught in what Samuel Danforth, Jr.'s brother John termed "This *Sheba,* SELF"—the all-out pursuit of self-aggrandizement that came at the expense of corporate loyalty and mutual commitment. Material aspirations were insidious; they were like a deafening "Trumpet of Rebellion" in which *Self* is the *Idol.*[128]

To insist too strenuously on the uniqueness of the reformed-Protestant component in American hostility to the self, as Greven at times does, is to argue in an anachronistic fashion for nonexistent demarcations between complementary early modern communalistic patterns of social and political thought.

A potent example of the broad appeal enjoyed by hostility to the claims of self is provided by an obscure New England farmer, William Manning. This man lacked Christian piety and scandalously (for rural New England) sympathized with the French revolutionaries and their suspect Jeffersonian supporters.[129] He was neither reactionary in his politics nor devout in his religion. In fact, he was a rabble-rouser trying to organize an early national populist alliance of farmers and artisans—that is, men who performed honest manual labor.[130] Yet even for this otherwise progressive au-

---

[125]See Pocock, *Machiavellian Moment,* p. 546.

[126]S. Howard, "Massachusetts Election Sermon" (1780), p. 395. The citations from James Burgh (1746) and John Brown (1758) are from Bailyn, *Ideological Origins of the American Revolution,* pp. 86–87. See also Liddle, "'Virtue and Liberty'"; and Kerber, *Women of the Republic,* p. 31.

[127]W. M. Smith, "On the Fall of Empire" (28 May 1775).

[128]Stout, *New England Soul,* p. 143.

[129]See Morison, notes and foreword to Manning, *Key of Libberty* (1798), pp. vi–viii; and Jefferson, "Letter to Short" (1793), in *Writings,* ed. Peterson, p. 1004.

[130]Morison, notes and foreword to Manning, *Key of Libberty* (1798), pp. viii–ix.

thor the self is sinful and greatly in need of social control.[131] In his hand-written manuscript, *The Key of Libberty,* Manning wrote:

> Men . . . have strongly implanted within them numerous pashons & lusts continually urging them to fraud violence & acts of injustis toards one an-other. . . . He is sentanced by the just decrees of heaven to hard Labour for a Living in this world, & has so strongly implanted in him a desire for Selfe Seporte, Selfe Defense, Selfe Love, Selfe Conceit, Selfe Importance, & Selfe agrandisement, that it Ingrosses all his care and attention so that he can see nothing beyond Selfe—for Selfe (as once described by a Divine) is like an object plased before the eye that hinders the sight of every thing beyond. This Selfishness may be deserned in all persons, let their conditions in life be what they will.

From these philosophical reflections, he draws common 18th-century po-litical implications:

> Man is a being made up of Selfe Love seeking his own hapiness to the misery of all around him, who would Damne a world to save him selfe from temporal or other punishment, & he who denyes this to be his real carrictor is ignorant of him selfe, or else is more than a man. . . . From this disposition of Man or the depravity of the human hart, arises not ondly the advantage but the abso-lute nesecaty of Sivil government—without it Mankind would be continually at war on their own spetia.[132]

In sum, even for a progressive author like Manning, the wants or needs of the self were not to be condoned, let alone accommodated.

This was not yet a world, then, of individualism or of glorification of the autonomous individual. Rather, it was one in which most available theories of the good continued to teach self-overcoming, public shaping of the individual, and sacrifice for the public good. And for many, even Jeffersonians like Manning, this remained true as late as 1798.[133]

AMERICAN COMMUNALISM: LIMITS AND THE LOSS OF CONSENSUS

If the communal account offered here is true, another quandary presents itself (in addition to the one regarding how America came to be described as individualistic). Why did something like a modern authoritarian or col-

---

[131]See Merrill and Wilentz, *Key of Liberty,* pp. 135–36, who argue that there exists a great similarity between Manning's ideas on sin and the self and those of Samuel Hopkins, one of the leading students of Jonathan Edwards.

[132]Manning, *Key of Libberty* (1798), pp. 8–9; see also J. Madison, "Federalist No. 51," in Hamilton, Jay, and Madison, *Federalist,* p. 337, where he remarks "but what is government itself, but the greatest of all reflections on human nature? If men were angels, no government would be necessary."

[133]Cf. Friedman, "Shaping of Radical Consciousness," p. 792, who argues that it was radi-cals like Manning who first defended the propriety of self-centered behavior.

lectivist regime fail to arise in Revolutionary or early-national America? In other words, why did no incipient forms of fascism arise?

America initially failed to develop in a recognizably authoritarian way because of the localism of its communities, the particularism of its religious denominations, and the parochialism of its states. Each was unwilling to cede power to a national government for almost any reason, but they were especially opposed to allowing the development of some kind of nationwide solidarity based on a specific ethnicity, ethical framework, or religious dispensation. Americans may well have been bigoted, xenophobic, and highly intolerant of any kind of "deviancy," but significantly, except on few issues, their ideas differed widely. Where agreement did exist, such as in regard to sexual orientation, race, and gender, their intolerance was capable of supporting a broad ethical solidarity. But crosscutting cleavages, along with enormous local diversity and the animosities among differing groups of ethnic or religious intolerants, did much to prevent a nationwide intolerance from developing much beyond racism and sexism (not trivial matters in themselves).[134]

Because of both the overarching strength of American localism and the particular restraints on it, the individual was partly, though unintentionally, freed from having to experience some of the most restrictive forms of corporate limitation. In particular, four readily identifiable factors muted American localist intolerance. First, each local town's or county's autonomy was, at the highest level of sovereignty, limited by its subordinate relationship to both the provincial (later state) and imperial (later national) governments. These governmental centers were usually populated by relatively enlightened men and women sensitive to the 18th century's continuing loss of a Christian-based ethical consensus.[135] They therefore did not subscribe with equal fervor to the communal ethical goals pursued by the residents of rural communities. But because of this, each village or town in the colonies often sought to protect its local autonomy from elite intrusion. Over time, however, the pressure for greater toleration exercised by governing elites, and the inability of those of different faiths or ethnic backgrounds to combine in a common cause of oppression,

[134]Consider that religious Americans, in the late 18th century and thereafter, have regularly elected people who cannot be considered deeply religious. Part of the explanation for this must be sought in the religious particularism of Americans. In the 18th century, fervently religious Baptists preferred to vote for a Deist like Jefferson rather than someone else who might reimpose an establishment on them. And today, it seems probable that two of the largest and fastest-growing Protestant denominations, Pentecostals and Southern Baptists, each of whom reportedly believes the other to be influenced by the devil, would rather vote for a weakly religious person for president than for a fervently religious person of the wrong denomination.

[135]See Brinton, *Shaping of the Modern Mind,* pp. 106–11; and Baumer, *Modern European Thought,* pp. 302–30, 439–55.

did provide some relief for individuals. (This was, however, little consolation for African Americans, many women, and known homosexuals.)

A second factor, one that made the American experience of local community different from that in much of Europe, was the availability of land.[136] Except immediately before and during the Revolution when the frontier was effectively closed,[137] persecuted minorities or individuals could depart from inappropriate communal environments. In effect, a person had the freedom to go and "settle in with his co-believers in safety and comfort and exercise the right of oppression."[138] A further consequence of abundant land was a labor shortage throughout many of the Northern and Middle colonies. In a land-rich wilderness, prudence rather than principle often demanded that communities come to terms with inhabitants who might possess critical skills and might otherwise leave to form their own villages. Even the author of the most influential liberal account of early American political thought, Louis Hartz, agrees. He finds that "the abundance of land in America, as well as the need for a lure to settlers, entered so subtly into the shaping of America's liberal tradition, touched it so completely at every point, that William Graham Sumner was actually ready to say, 'We have not made America, America had made us.' "[139]

A third factor blunting the oppressiveness of American local communalism was the paucity of powerful coercive mechanisms. Because of the absence of professional armies and police forces (which had not yet been developed), majorities could only enforce their moral codes by developing a broad consensus.[140] In particular, local majorities were prevented from imposing their moral vision on those committed to legitimate ethical alternatives (for example, fellow Protestants of a different denomination) or across a geographical expanse marked by ethnic or religious diversity. These limiting characteristics were especially present in the Middle colonies. But after a broad but not all-inclusive consensus was reached, those who were dependent or socially marginal could either be "dispensed with" or "excluded, often emphatically."[141] Limitations on public coercive means did not imply a positive regard for individual or minority rights.

[136]William Dennis forcefully made this point in several unpublished papers that he kindly made available to me. See also Handlin and Handlin, *Liberty and Power*, p. 50; Crèvecoeur, *Letters from an American Farmer* (1782), pp. 20–21, 38, 184; and Boorstin, *Genius of American Politics*.

[137]See Lockridge, "Land," pp. 75, 77–78, 80. That land pressures had begun to develop in mid-18th-century New England is a common theme in the social histories of the period. See for example Grant, *Democracy*; Gross, *Minutemen and Their World*; Greven, *Four Generations*; and Jedrey, *World of John Cleaveland*.

[138]Roche, "American Liberty," p. 137.

[139]Hartz, "American Political Thought," p. 341.

[140]See W. E. Nelson, "Eighteenth Century Constitution," p. 28; and Zuckerman, *Peaceable Kingdoms*, p. 85.

[141]Zuckerman, "Social Context of Democracy in Massachusetts," p. 531.

A fourth factor limiting the oppressiveness of American communalism was America's inheritance of the norms and precedents of English common law. This legacy reduced the frequency of arbitrary communal actions and the oppression of individuals by other individuals not communally authorized to act. Yet here too the value of this limitation on the power of American local institutions to shape the moral lives of their members should not be exaggerated. The rights embodied in various English legal precedents or statutes, whether characterized as historical or natural, had been traditionally directed against the English central government. As Lord Bryce noted early in the twentieth century, "the Civil liberties of those older days were extorted from arbitrary monarchs, whereas what we call individual liberty to-day had to be defended . . . against the constitutional action of a self-governing community."[142]

The common law had not been crafted to be applicable in local contexts, especially in ethically unified communities. This body of precedents was designed to redress not the grievances of one villager against the combined power of his peers, but rather grievances against extralocal government. Indeed, "rights in the eighteenth century were thought of as restraining arbitrary government rather than as liberating the individual."[143] Police powers (concerned primarily with morality) were both local and Crown (and later, state) responsibilities. In all cases, prescriptive or civil rights as they were then understood offered scant protection to deviant individuals. The common-law tradition was concerned more with the transfer and protection of property than with the right of individuals to make autonomous moral choices. By current standards, the common law suffered from an inability to protect an individual when confronted by a unified people. What was little understood in Revolutionary America, and less protected against, was a phenomenon that would soon come to be called the "tyranny of the majority."[144]

The capacity of 18th-century Americans to intrude into the moral lives of their neighbors was nevertheless limited by these various constraints. Yet an individual in opposition to a consensually committed people had little legal or ethical recourse. One could either accept the community's moral norms or depart. This was the situation in which Loyalists eventually found themselves. According to Wallace Brown, "the idea of the 'sovereignty of the people' gave an ideological and philosophical justification and an awesome dignity to the brutal physical abuse or killing of men that tarring and

---

[142]Bryce, *Modern Democracies,* p. 56; see also Reid, *Constitutional History of the American Revolution: The Authority of Rights,* p. 73.

[143]Roche, "Curbing of the Militant Majority," pp. 35–36; see also Peters, *Massachusetts Constitution of 1780,* pp. 155–56; and Haakonssen, "Natural Law."

[144]See Roche, "Strange Case of the 'Revolutionary' Establishment," p. 179; Handlin and Handlin, *Liberty in Expansion,* p. 339; and J. Madison, "Speech before the Virginia Ratifying Convention" (1788), p. 23.

feathering, vigilantism, and lynching came to embody."[145] The Loyalists' pleas for freedom of the press, conscience, and speech were cavalierly ignored by intolerant majorities (or those who claimed to be acting in their behalf). The newly inalienable right of popular sovereignty, an early consequence of the Revolution, thus resulted in an immediate loss, not a gain, in individual freedom.

Shortly after the War of Independence (which ended in 1783), however, some of the nationalist elite began to turn away from communal ethical goals. First to be rejected by the likes of Murray and Madison were political goals that demanded too much self-sacrificing behavior.[146] It might seem that the national leadership had finally embraced the individualist project, but this is at best a partial truth. The nationalist elite was unwilling to accept that the public good could be left to fend for itself. Public officials were therefore to defend and protect it and "correctly" educate future citizens to do the same. Nor would most have accepted that an individual could, without recourse to public mediation, be the final arbiter of value in a universe devoid of meaning. Instead, the individual was to be taught to respect and serve a simplified set of secularized Christian-like ethical principles that were believed to be self-evidently true. Voltaire and his brand of radical skepticism found few adherents in America.[147]

Through the Holy Spirit, reason, or an innate moral sense,[148] all except the entirely reprobate were believed able to recognize true moral principles. And each of these paths to morality demanded a measured amount of self-sacrifice for the public good in order to serve long-term interests, both public and private. Progressive Americans seem to have believed that these moral principles could be readily agreed on, and that the proper kind of civic education could then be consensually devised. But the goal of education was rather traditional. Children were to be armed "with moral principles as a security against the seductions of a country, rapidly increasing in the means of dissipation and voluptuousness." More particularly, students were to be prepared so that they could better "repel the assaults of infidelity and libertinism."[149]

In the early 19th century, however, a small group of exceptional Americans envisioned the self in a manner compatible with the new European social and political theory of individualism. For them, the traditional condemnation of the individual and idiosyncratic inwardness was to be stood

---

[145]W. Brown, *Good Americans*, p. 103; see also Potter, *Liberty We Seek*.

[146]See Countryman, *American Revolution*, p. 147.

[147]See May, *Enlightenment in America*, p. 353.

[148]See Jefferson, "Letter to Thomas Law" (13 June 1814), *Writings*, ed. Peterson, pp. 1335–37, for his defense of the theory of moral sense.

[149]Bancroft, *Massachusetts Election Sermon* (1801), p. 22; see also Lathrop, "Politician" (December 1789), p. 444, who holds that education was to inculcate such values so that there would be "little occasion for the restraints of public law."

on its head.[150] It would be in the thought of the Romantics that the self, the very source of uniqueness, first came to be positively valued in America. This embrace of the particularity of each individual occurred as the older Christian consensus and the more recent rational ethical one began to unravel. As William Nelson explains it, by early in the 19th century it had become clear to some that "the age of moral certainty had passed and that truth could no longer be seen as a unitary set of values formulated by God and readily ascertainable by man."[151] With an elite loss of confidence in the objective character of the moral cosmos,[152] the uniqueness and particularity of the self became less objectionable; it even came to be valued.

Students of the period do not question the centrality of individualism to early 19th-century Romanticism. As Vernon Parrington saw it, Romantic thought, finally free from both the communal and the rational constraints of the 18th century, was a "glorification of the ideal of individualism." Fundamental to this movement, he argues, was "an assertion of the inalienable worth of man; theoretically it was an assertion of the immanence of divinity in instinct, the transference of supernatural attributes to the natural constitution of mankind." In particular, he found that "the master idea of the Emersonian philosophy is the divine sufficiency of the individual"; more succinctly put, "the apotheosis of individualism—such in briefest terms was the gospel of Emerson."[153]

The autonomous, free individual gained in importance as the central moral and fundamental political unit in 18th-century thought, the community, suffered a precipitous decline in legitimacy among the most progressive Americans.[154] With "the collapse of the Commonwealth conception in the middle of the nineteenth century . . . [e]ach person was [to be] the best judge of his own mode of laying out his existence."[155] A fundamental transformation in the basics of elite American political thought was thus effected, one that was far more fundamental than that which had accompanied the ratification of the Constitution in 1789. This early 19th-century transformation created an intellectual chasm between many 19th-century elites and their 18th-century ancestors.

It was indeed an incident that "presage[d] some great and interesting

[150]See D. Bell, "Resolving the Contradictions," pp. 45–46; and Lyons, *Invention of the Self*, p. 70, who contrasts the Renaissance's almost classical interest in the heroic with the Romantic concern with the unique "inner life" of each individual.

[151]W. E. Nelson, *Americanization of the Common Law*, p. 115.

[152]See Hampson, *Enlightenment*, p. 250.

[153]Parrington, *Main Currents in American Thought*, 2:x, 302, 371; see also Conkin, *Puritans and Pragmatists*, p. 165; and Curry and Goodheart, "Individualism in Trans-National Context," p. 37.

[154]The European experience is much more complicated. See Lukes, *Individualism*, pp. 20–21; and Baumer, *Modern European Thought*, p. 290, who finds that, unlike in America, "for most romantics, especially after the [French] Revolution, the nation or nation-state constituted the highest form of social organism."

[155]Handlin and Handlin, *Dimensions of Liberty*, pp. 76–77.

changes in the state of this world."[156] Unlike anything embraced in the late 18th century, the "Great God Self" became a "new theology of Selfhood," one that would develop in America and have as its "first commandment: Thou shall have no other gods before me."[157] As Henry May notes, it is "doubtful whether the Constitution could have been framed or adopted" several years later than it was. By the turn of the century, the older body of moderate thought, the fragile equilibrium that was 18th-century Whiggish thought, was beginning to be "challenged by a new kind of revolutionary ideology."[158] Early in the 19th century, the autonomous individual became for some the preeminent value to be preserved and served. Consequently, Americans became divided between the few who understood that human flourishing was best accomplished by individualistic means and the many who were still supportive of communal ones. Something like the modern division between liberals and conservatives emerged in the early 19th century from an intellectual field that in the late 18th century had been, by comparison, unified.

This new 19th-century world thus is not to be confused with the earlier birth of the new national republic, when the unconstrained self was still universally and almost unequivocally denounced. At the end of the 18th century, the autonomous modern individual, delighting in his or her uniqueness, had been at best tolerated rather than embraced by even the most progressive members of the American elite of that period.[159] This sizable divide separating the most progressive elite thought regarding the self of the early 19th century from that of the late 18th, however, is much less true of the values embraced by the agrarian majority. Even in the later period, they continued to believe that "the self stood as no accommodating channel to enhancement or perfection; it stood rather as an endlessly frustrating, dark-hued impediment." Lewis Saum finds that "insofar as their untutored jottings reveal them, the average Americans warned as insistently, if not as eloquently, as did their unrecognized spokesmen Hawthorne and Melville against the unleashing of the self."[160] The communal assumptions of the 18th century would thus long outlive that century in the norms of America's agrarian majority.[161]

---

[156]Cyprian Strong, *The Kingdom Is the Lord's* (1799 Connecticut election sermon), p. 32.

[157]Richard D. Mosier, *The American Temper: Patterns of Our Intellectual Heritage*, pp. 201–3, cited by Saum, *Popular Mood*, p. 108.

[158]May, *Enlightenment in America*, p. 99; see also Martin, "Long and the Short of It," pp. 100–101; and Lienesch, *New Order of the Ages*, p. 81.

[159]See Crowley, *This Sheba, Self*, pp. 156–57.

[160]Saum, *Popular Mood*, p. 108–9; see also Weaver, *Ideas Have Consequences*, pp. 71–72.

[161]Cf. Wood, *Radicalism of the American Revolution*; and Hatch, *Democratization of American Christianity*, p. 23, who emphasizes the changed character of this group in the decades following the Revolution. This transformation, he contends, was marked by the rise of "vulgar democracy and materialistic individualism."

Three Leading Views of the Individual, Plus One

> Now, as everyone knows, it has only been in the last two
> centuries that the majority of people in civilized countries
> have claimed the privilege of being individuals. Formerly
> they were slave, peasant, laborer, even artisan, but not
> person. It is clear that this revolution . . . has also
> introduced new kinds of grief and misery, and so far, on
> the broadest scale, it has not been altogether a success.
>
> —Saul Bellow, *Mr. Sammler's Planet*

THE DOMINANT American views of the individual and his or her standing vis-à-vis the public were in agreement with the public-centered and communal norms discussed above. Most Americans accepted that the space surrounding the individual was to be conditioned by a socially mediated ethics. This ethics valued the aggregate needs of the public over the arbitrary ones of the particular individual, and corporately defined the outlines of individual human flourishing. This was true at least until the last decade of the 18th century and the emergence among the elite of an individualistic fourth view, which nevertheless still did not challenge the status of the public good. Much of the argument presented here, therefore, should by now be familiar. Additional corroboration, however, may increase the reader's confidence in this otherwise unfamiliar and discomfiting portrait of the Revolutionary generation in which "the best and the brightest" of that century are seen as having "been steeped in thought processes akin to those of McCarthyites and John Birchers."[1]

The late 18th-century intellectual landscape was not simple. Each of the three most important traditions of political discourse helping shape American social and political thought (republicanism, reformed Protestantism, and early modern rationalism) served what it believed to be the true needs

---

[1]Rodgers, "Republicanism," p. 15 (published version); see also Wolin, *Presence of the Past,* pp. 79–80, who describes the more popular tradition, those who were the defenders of "local self-government, decentralized politics, [and] participatory democracy," as being part of the same historical culture as "religious fundamentalism, 'moralism,' and racial, religious, and ethnic prejudices." Neither, thus, depicts the stuff from which individualist legends are made.

of the individual. They all might be fairly described as fitting imperfectly with the public-dominated description of American political thought offered above. And each in a different way is capable of being misunderstood and seen as supporting the customary individualistic reading of Revolutionary political thought. Nevertheless, such a reading would be anachronistic, for it would ignore the subtle but salient differences between political theories that serve the "true" or "higher" needs of the individual and a theory such as individualism that awards an elevated standing to the express wishes and arbitrary or even irrational needs of the individual.[2]

INDIVIDUALISM AND THE PUBLIC/PRIVATE CONTINUUM

A fundamental distinction between dominant 18th-century views of the individual and the elite modern one turns on how each conceives of the individual and the area of volition that immediately surrounds him or her. In the 18th century, the concerns of the individual were delimited by various intrusive public constraints. Publicly countenanced individual freedoms, needs, and rights were necessarily informed by a substantive Christian or Christian-derived rationalist moral telos.[3] In present-day America, such restrictive limitations on the self by social forces are not generally condoned or encouraged by the national cultural and political elites who are frequently associated with individualism. Today "*everyone knows* [that] morality consists of tearing down restraints on personal autonomy, [and] of fighting *repression*."[4] The Revolutionary generation's understanding of the individual and his or her substantively constrained area of choice was not "negative" (to use a contemporary designation); quite to the contrary, their view of this individual space was "positive" and substantive. As noted by a mid-19th-century observer, the American "conception of freedom" continued to be radically "different from the purely negative notion which prevails amongst the radicals . . . of Europe. With the American, freedom is anything but a mere absence of restraint, an arbitrary, licentious indulgence."[5] It was unlike contemporary individualism, then, which is usually considered "negative" because its primary range of concerns is procedural rather than substantive.[6]

---

[2]See Laski, "Liberty," p. 444; Sartori, "Relevance of Liberalism in Retrospect," p. 10; and R. M. Smith, *Liberalism and American Constitutional Law*, p. 49, who writes in defense of modern individualism.

[3]See Dworetz, *Unvarnished Doctrine*, p. 132, who argues that the God-centered thought of John Locke with its concerns about individual salvation has nothing in common with modern individualism.

[4]Bartley, "No Guardrails," p. A14; see also Klein, "Whose Values?" pp. 19–22.

[5]Schaff, *America*, p. 370.

[6]See *The Compact Edition of the Oxford English Dictionary*, s.v. "individualism": "a self-

The theorist largely responsible for having popularized this distinction between positive and negative forms of individual freedom is Isaiah Berlin.[7] Although his position has been widely criticized for its lack of sharpness, because the gulf between 18th-century and contemporary views of the individual is so large,[8] it is adequate for the present discussion. In fact, its analytical bluntness serves my purpose well. In his most influential essay, "Two Concepts of Liberty," Berlin set forth his understanding of these two different views of the publicly mediated area surrounding an individual. In this area of individual freedom, one's actions, thoughts, aspirations, and indeed love of God and people exist.

Berlin identifies this space, which is normally associated with modern individualism, as negative.[9] He holds that this conception should answer the question "what is the area within which the subject—a person or group of persons—is or should be left to do or be what he is able to do or be, without interference by other persons?" This growing free space around an individual is that which many members of America's intellectual and cultural elite demarcate as largely inviolable, particularly when one's action is self-referential.

Educated Americans today associate the other understanding with communal intolerance and governmental coercion of the individual, and are disapproving when directly confronted by it.[10] Berlin describes this understanding as positive. He associates it with the desire "to participate in the process by which my life is to be controlled." He admits that this opportunity to participate in corporate self-direction, as a form of liberty, "may be as deep a wish as that of a free area for action, and perhaps historically older." He concludes that this " 'positive' conception of liberty" is best understood as "freedom to—to lead one prescribed form of life." When portrayed in this way, it is opposed to "freedom from" societal intrusion, which is the customary 20th-century American understanding of the space surrounding the individual.[11] Berlin further recognizes that by contempo-

---

centered feeling or conduct as a principle," or "a mode of life in which the individual pursues his own ends," or simply, the advocacy of egoism; and MacIntyre, *After Virtue*, p. 59.

[7] This was a discrimination popularized earlier in the century by the prominent German legal scholar Georg Jellinek.

[8] See Pitkin, "Are Freedom and Liberty Twins?" pp. 30–31 (draft version); MacCallum, "Negative and Positive Freedom"; Gray, "On Negative and Positive Liberty"; Parent, "Some Recent Work"; Reed, "Berlin and the Division of Liberty"; Ryan, "Freedom"; and Skinner's superb review of this literature, "Paradoxes of Political Liberty."

[9] See also C. Taylor, "What's Wrong with Negative Liberty," pp. 212–15, and Skinner, "Idea of Negative Liberty."

[10] Of late, a split has developed between more traditional liberal individualists and others more willing to defend positive and coercive varieties of freedom that serve the putative needs of oppressed populations. This is not to say, however, that most are comfortable with defending, as such, the desired limitations on the negative individual freedoms of members of the oppressor population.

[11] Berlin, "Two Concepts of Liberty," pp. 121–22, 131.

rary American standards, this earlier positive sense of liberty is discomfiting and alien.[12]

But to comprehend the 18th-century perception of the individual and his or her socially mediated space, one must recognize that the contemporary negative understanding of personal liberty was foreign to the Revolutionary generation. Most Americans would have been ill at ease with the idea that individuals should enjoy freedom from public, and even from familial, moral interference. Conversely, communal encroachment into the private space reserved for an individual's autonomous development is little countenanced today. The distance between the two perspectives becomes apparent when one considers an anonymous 18th-century source who, in writing on "personal liberty," reminded his audience that freedom was "not to be construed a liberty to do evil or detriment, even to the persons themselves."[13] In sharp contrast to contemporary sensibilities, the Revolutionary generation almost unanimously approved of some variant of positive freedom, of the freedom to lead a "prescribed form of life." As the republican martyr Algernon Sidney explained, liberty did not "place the felicity of man in an exemption from the laws of God, but in a most perfect conformity to them."[14] This positive understanding defined socially approved and communally directed (and more indirectly, divinely commanded) ethical uses to be made of choice by the individual.

Thus, when it thought of freedom, America's founding generation, shaped by reformed-Protestant principles, "did not mean negative liberty *from* authority so much as" it "meant positive liberty *toward* the goals of a dedicated Christian life."[15] Those more influenced by rationalist or classical republican streams of thought held to other mutually reinforcing "positive" understandings of individual choice. To be free in this positive sense, even a "good man [who] has *conquered* himself" had to "declare war against his inbred *unruly* inclinations, and *bind* them down in subjection and servitude."[16] Socially approved freedom was not procedural, but substantive.

Individual liberty was usually controlled by a distinct understanding of virtue that was Christian, rational, and positive. As President Clap of Yale remarked, this understanding demanded "conformity to the *moral Perfections of God*."[17] Not even the esteemed 17th-century philosopher John Locke was understood as defending "the individual's right to think as he pleases," but rather only "his right to think as he must." Locke held that one who was not controlled by reason but instead was overwhelmed by

---

[12]See also Patterson, *Freedom*, pp. 403–4, who agrees with Berlin that this form of liberty "has been the dominant conception of freedom for most of Western history," but also reminds us that 20th-century Nazi Germany may have most perfectly embodied it.

[13]"Rudiments of Law and Government" (1783), p. 575.

[14]A. Sidney, *Discourses Concerning Government* (1698), pp. 8–9.

[15]Niebuhr, "Protestant Movement and Democracy," p. 31; see also Schaff, *America*, p. 38.

[16][Serle], *Americans against Liberty* (1776), pp. 4–5.

[17]Clap, *Nature and Foundation of Moral Virtue* (1765), p. 3.

passion could "be treated as a beast of prey," for by "quitting reason," one is "liable to be destroyed by him he uses force against, as any savage ravenous beast that is dangerous."[18]

Most articulate Americans today would not describe such positive descriptions of liberty as freedom. They would be more likely to associate them with offensive political ideologies, most typically some form of fascist or Marxist totalitarianism (as does Berlin himself),[19] or other forms of communalism.[20] Conversely, the Revolutionary generation would have found the contemporary understanding of individual freedom to be a form not of liberty, but of license. Revolutionary political language that enjoyed social approval did not and could not have accepted the negative conception of individual freedom as a form of liberty. It is thus misleading to use in an unguarded fashion present-day concepts to depict the three traditions of social and political discourse dominant in Revolutionary America. Moreover, because of this problem in "translating" 18th-century into 20th-century English, and vice versa, one must avoid describing earlier views of the individual and his or her approved use of personal space as forms of individual liberty (with unavoidable 20th-century connotations).[21]

When something similar to individualism began to be embraced by a few in the early national period,[22] it continued to be a political or social theory that failed to describe most Americans' values. This was especially true of members of the agricultural majority, who were most supportive of communal and familial control over the individual self.[23] They were like the lower-middle classes of today who continue to believe that "individuals depend on the moral community to keep them on the straight and narrow path."[24]

Not surprisingly, foreign travelers to America found the majority of Americans intolerant of individual diversity. For example, it was observed early in the 19th century that there was "no country in which there is so little independence of mind and real freedom of discussion as in America." Alexis de Tocqueville even held that in America "freedom of opinion does not exist" at all. According to Michael Chevalier, American thinking on individual freedom was extraordinarily contracted; Americans did not allow one to "outrage all that is sacred on earth, to set religion at defiance, to laugh morals to scorn," or even to live "in private different from the

---

[18]Canavan, *Freedom of Expression*, p. 69; Locke, *Treatise of Civil Government* (1690), pp. 13, 123; see also R. M. Smith, "Constitution and Autonomy," p. 177; and Wolin, *Presence of the Past*, pp. 103, 110.

[19]See Berlin, "Two Concepts of Nationalism."

[20]See Holmes, "Permanent Structure of Antiliberal Thought."

[21]See Appleby, "One Good Turn Deserves Another," pp. 1327–29.

[22]See Banning, "Quid Transit?" pp. 200–201; and Murrin, "Self-Interest Conquers Patriotism," p. 226.

[23]See Saum, *Popular Mood*, p. 109.

[24]Rieder, *Canarsie*, pp. 136–37, 142, 152.

rest of" one's fellow citizens. And a German visitor, Philip Schaff, said that the kind of intellectual freedom found, for example, in German universities was "considered dangerous and impraticable [*sic*] in America." In addition, he believed that Americans allowed their young people far less individual latitude than did Germans.[25] Apparently, the widespread adherence of most Americans to the outlines of an individualistic political or social theory would only come well after the Revolutionary period.[26]

It is evident that a select population during the last years of the 18th century had begun to embrace a more tolerant and "negative" understanding of the individual and his or her realm of moral choice. This new vision of the individual served as the foundation of a second political theory that has competed with and in most instances eclipsed older communal ones. Students of modern history have shown, moreover, that the actions of the American elite were not unusual. These Americans were, according to Foucault and others, participants in a great modernizing transformation, an "epistemic dislocation," that occurred around 1800.[27] Yet in spite of the undoubted importance of such millennial transformations (as one commentator has said, possibly "the greatest [that] the world has undergone"),[28] my attention remains on the normative social and political thought of the earlier Revolutionary era. During this period, this transformatory individualist vision, to the degree it was attended to, was most often a target of derision.

THREE 18TH-CENTURY VIEWS OF THE INDIVIDUAL

In their diverse yet mutually reinforcing ways, each of the three major traditions of social and political discourse held that individuals were to be allowed a certain domain of choice. Within a larger framework of public-centered and communally directed ethical goals and behavior, republicanism, reformed Protestantism, and early modern rationalism supported varying, though limited, degrees of individual freedom. However, they did so because of their concern with developing that part of the individual's being that was eternal. Republicanism was committed to fostering the virtue of citizens and, for the most gifted, facilitating their acquisition of immortality through public fame and familial honor. Christianity attended to the transcendental souls of the saved so that they might live in bliss with God for eternity. And rationalism desired that the noumenal individual

---

[25]Tocqueville, *Democracy in America* (1835), 1:273–75; Chevalier, *Society Manners and Politics* (1839), pp. 339–40; and Schaff, *America*, p. 60.
[26]See Henretta, "Slow Triumph of Liberal Individualism," p. 98; and Kloppenberg, "Virtues of Liberalism," p. 29.
[27]See Prospo, "Paine and Sieyès," pp. 191–92.
[28]Weaver, *Ideas Have Consequences*, p. 164.

achieve his or her unique dignity and highest well-being through harmonizing with the larger cosmos.

Consider classical republicanism (and indirectly its Renaissance and Whig variants). Most noticeably, this vision of politics failed to distinguish between ethics and politics, or between the immediate needs of the polity and the ultimate needs of the individual. As Leo Strauss, an influential 20th-century student of political thought, argued, political activity in classical republican theory was only properly directed when it was "directed toward human perfection or virtue. The city has therefore ultimately no other end than the individual,"[29] or more specifically, the individual's moral development. The polity, because it provided the only means for human flourishing, was capable of demanding great sacrifices from the individual as it facilitated the living of a truly human life.[30] The individual life of virtue "thus presupposes the *polis* even as the end of the *polis* is the perfection of the citizen (*polities*) through education and training in virtue."[31] Republicanism, accordingly, must be viewed as a tradition that was concerned fundamentally with the ultimate needs of the individual citizen, but without being universalistic or maintaining a conception of rights that could legitimate the individual's opposition to that very collective's common good.

Republicanism's concern with its citizens being able to live well also allowed for considerable latitude in personal matters. Thus, the transitional role it played in the movement from communal moral and political precepts to emergent individualistic ones in the late 18th century might have been expected. In classical theory, great displays of individual-enhancing behavior among a chosen few were even encouraged, but only so long as such actions served the public good.[32] Republicanism, when embraced in the 18th century, was thus capable of helping reconceptualize individualistic, otherwise selfish or passionate, behavior into that which served the public or common good (Publius's *Federalist* immediately comes to mind).

From the republican perspective, however, the most glorious individual, whether a brilliant general, a courageous hero, or a just lawgiver, must sacrifice whatever was demanded of him in pursuit of the public's welfare. As Alasdair MacIntyre explains, republicanism in the 18th century understood virtue to be "allowing the public good to provide the standard of individual behavior."[33] Such sacrifices were made in exchange for the opportunity of gaining glory and blessed immortality in the public's collective memory. A well-lived human existence, ignoring the counsel offered by

---

[29]Strauss, *Natural Right and History*, p. 134.
[30]See Weintraub, "Virtue," pp. 45–46.
[31]Dupré and O'Neill, "Social Structures and Structural Ethics," pp. 330–31.
[32]See Pocock, *Machiavellian Moment*, p. 213.
[33]MacIntyre, *After Virtue*, p. 236.

John Calvin or later by his rationalist offspring, did not demand self-effacement, but instead that the individual seek "to be great and to be brilliant, to shine, to be *lampros:* this was the desire that animated the Greek *polis*. Long before Euripides and Democritus voiced the sentiments of their contemporaries, and even longer before Aristotle fully articulated the meaning of citizenship, Homer depicted a luminous world in which men shared in the nature of the gods and sought to shed mortality."[34] Such deeds often demanded a great Homeric personality, an Achillean *kleos,* complete with great character flaws with which to fill the heroic roles played out on the stage of public life.

Total self-abnegation as such was not expected from such larger-than-life men. With Alexander Hamilton in mind, Douglass Adair argued that "the love of fame is a noble passion because it can transform ambition and self-interest into dedicated effort for the community, because it can spur individuals to spend themselves to provide for the common defense, or to promote the general welfare."[35] Republican-inspired American political actors could view the gifted individual as living a virtuous life if it was lived in public service.[36] Without a public to serve, the individual would be without an audience for his deeds. The individual would necessarily be unable to obtain glory, honor, and everlasting memory, and a man's life would lose meaning.[37] Life would become short and brutish. A decade after the close of the Revolutionary era, with himself in mind, Hamilton cynically suggested that, above all, it was vanity that ensured that there would "be some *public fools* who sacrifice private to public interest at the certainty of ingratitude and obloquy."[38] Heroic individuals, whatever their motivation, and the larger public were therefore tied in a symbiotic relationship in which each, in its own way, served the common good.

Such logic flowed effortlessly into the modern governmental arrangements defended by Publius in *The Federalist*. There, he argued that certain human passions should be accommodated by a popular government, particularly those that encouraged the pursuit of honor and fame by leaders. He believed that the political arrangements he defended would foster public virtue without the need for self-abnegation, which was impossible to achieve. As William Livingston presciently remarked in one of his exceptional editorials in the *Independent Reflector:*

'Tis true, every Man ought to promote the Prosperity of his Country, from a sublimer Motive than his private Advantage: But it is extremely difficult, for the best of Men, to divest themselves of Self-Interest. Nor is it rational, to

[34]Rahe, "Primacy of Politics in Classical Greece," p. 282.
[35]Adair, "Fame and the Founding Fathers," pp. 11–12.
[36]See McDonald, *Novus Ordo Seclorum*, p. 189.
[37]See Selby, *Concept of Liberty*, p. 45, and Maier, *Old Revolutionaries*, p. 198, who are respectively citing to this effect Arthur Lee and Richard Henry Lee.
[38]Cited by Wood, "Interests and Disinterestedness," p. 90.

expect great Geniuses, accomplished Heroes, or any other illustrious Characters, in a Government that overlooks Merit. . . . The Ambition natural to the
Mind of Man, wants, at least, the Prospect of Fame and Honour, to keep him
in the Pursuit of Glory.[39]

In the correct framing of a popular government, as Publius later so persuasively argued, men must be taken as they are.

The classical literature that so impressed the Revolutionary elite allowed
great attention and glory to be awarded the individual. One might say that
it encouraged such efforts so that the honored one might gain the pagan
equivalent of Christian immortality.[40] In effect, republicanism offered a
secular theory of salvation as its highest end, a normative theory of the
good life that was clearly at odds with the highest ends pursued by Christians. This is a powerful difference. This divergence helps one discriminate
among various communal political theories (such as republicanism and
Christian-inspired political visions) in deciding which of them was preeminent and provided the foundation for American political thought.

The republican perspective, however, is incompatible with the claims of
individualism in which the individual possesses presocial rights that the
public cannot abrogate. Such claims were not countenanced in classical
political histories, nor in those of their Renaissance interpreters.[41] Nevertheless, 18th-century republicans' embrace and encouragement of individual fame and glory in a Christian world of spiritually sanctified individuals left their thought and aspirations vulnerable to such a transformation.
Republicanism thus helped ease the transition to individualism without
directly valuing the individual in an abstract or universal fashion.

Reformed Christianity and early modern rationalism each had its own
understanding of salvation, and thus its own normative political vision of
the good. Like republicanism, they both held that the "true" needs of the
individual were the ethical ends that the community must ultimately serve.
And from a traditional Christian perspective, glorifying God and somehow
facilitating individual salvation,[42] not assuring the collective welfare of the
group,[43] were the sacred goals that a community of Christians was committed to serving. As the celebrated German sociologist Max Weber noted,
human morality never defined the ultimate ends served by the great Reformation leaders. For them, "the salvation of the soul and that alone" was at

[39]Livingston, "Public Virtue to be Distinguished by Public Honours" (1753), in *Independent Reflector*, pp. 111–13.

[40]See Adair, "Fame and the Founding Fathers," pp. 11–12.

[41]See Weintraub, "Virtue," p. 83.

[42]For Calvinists, the theological status and utility of "facilitation," or pastoral preparation,
was a source of continual controversy.

[43]Nevertheless, 17th-century Puritans understood themselves to be the second chosen people and like the earlier Hebrews to be covenantally and corporately bound to obey God's
wishes. For both peoples, individual disobedience was met with temporal corporate as well as
eternal individual punishment.

"the center of their life and work."[44] The dominant Protestant dispensations held to this precept in spite of their keen awareness that with humankind, fallen and deformed, such an understanding surely would support a perverted and confused selfishness. Nevertheless, Luther and Calvin unequivocally insisted "that freedom of conscience, the right of personal conviction in religious matters, was something clearly inviolable."[45]

For reformed Protestants, the ability of the saved individual (saint) to live voluntarily in accordance with the laws of God was an important indication to both the individual and the community that he or she was indeed truly reborn in Christ. A certain measure of individual freedom was thus necessary. "In 1770 as in 1630 the covenant required that God's Word alone be sovereign and that God's people be at liberty to voluntarily commit themselves to its precepts."[46] Yet when added to the corporate need to glorify God, this respect for voluntarism was transformed by Americans in highly communal ways. Individual liberty became legitimately limited by communal standards that were prescribed by civil and ecclesiastical leaders.[47] God's greater glory and Adam's and his descendants' apostasy demanded as much.

Finally, for early modern rationalists, facilitating an individual's pursuit of a life of reason in an environment of freedom was of the utmost importance.[48] Only in a relatively free social setting could the noumenal part of a person's being be sufficiently free to flourish by legislating and following rational precepts that demanded obedience.[49] Society, at the most fundamental level, was a forum in which the individual was to develop quasi-divine rational capacities.[50] As noted by Hannah Arendt, "it was not just reason which Jefferson promoted to the rank of the 'higher law' which would bestow validity on both the new law of the land and the old laws of morality; it was divinely informed reason, the 'light of reason.' " Indeed, it "still was the voice of God."[51] In the rationalist conception of the individual, it was one's destiny and duty "to acquire perfected personality through the ascent to God."[52] Individuals were freed from more onerous social and political constraints so that they could voluntarily act as they must—that is, in an objectively true and moral fashion.[53]

Early modern rationalism was committed to an understanding of the

[44]M. Weber, *Protestant Ethic*, pp. 89–90.

[45]Holl, *Cultural Significance of the Reformation*, p. 31.

[46]Stout, *New England Soul*, p. 274; see also Lockridge, *New England Town*, pp. 55–56.

[47]See Haskins, *Law and Authority in Early Massachusetts*, p. 18.

[48]See Walzer, *Revolution of the Saints*, pp. 302–3.

[49]See Hampson, *Enlightenment*, p. 198.

[50]See "Dignity and Manners of Man" (June 1792), p. 275.

[51]Arendt, *On Revolution*, p. 194; see also Clap, *Nature and Foundation of Moral Virtue* (1765), p. 26, who writes that "*our reason* seems to be an Emanation from and Part of the infinite *Intelligence* and *Wisdom* of God."

[52]Troeltsch, *Protestantism and Progress*, pp. 35–36.

[53]See Wood, *Radicalism of the American Revolution*, pp. 218–19.

individual as a conscious and voluntary decision maker in a manner reminiscent of Protestantism (and different in emphasis from Judaism and Roman Catholicism).[54] The capacity to make informed rational choices concerning moral conduct was understood to be the quintessential element
that made humans truly human. Yet this ability to order one's internal
cosmos in accord with the larger one was only possible because of a divine
spark whose presence within made humans worthy of moral dignity. Cato
(John Trenchard and Thomas Gordon) had thus held that "it is not *human
Shape*, but human Reason, that places a *Man* above the *Beasts* of the Field,
and lifts him into a Resemblance with God himself. . . . And, in what Sense
can a Man be said to be *made after the image of God*, unless by possessing
that REASON, which is a *divine Particle of the GODHEAD.*"[55]

In much of his writing, William Livingston also conspicuously defended
the centrality of moral self-direction. But one must not confuse his and
Cato's position with present-day pleas for individual autonomy. Livingston's remarks, like those of others of his age, are delimited by their
concern with acting in accordance with the dictates of universal moral
truth, with only that which is right and just.[56] For example, Livingston
begins one essay by noting that "it is evident, that Man is a Being imbued
with an unalienable Right to think and act freely, according to the Dictates
of a self-determining Will," for "the Laws of his Reason, or the Will of his
Creator, which in Effect are the same Things" are capable of inhibiting
"the Practice of Evil." Livingston adds, however, that "his Will must be
allowed to have an independent Right of determining itself," but only
"upon the supposition that he will always chuse to do good."[57]

The Reverend Dr. Price, an authoritative voice in America,[58] also reflected on this notion of self-direction. Addressing his attentive American
readership, he noted that at the foundation of all varieties of liberty "there
is one general idea, that runs through them all; I mean, the idea of *Self-
direction*, or *Self-government*—Did our volitions originate not with *ourselves*, but with some cause over which we have not power?"[59] Yet human
passions and irrational motivations, the principal elements of our personalities, do not originate for Price with our true or higher selves. Thus, like
the great 17th-century rationalists (for example, Spinoza and Locke) and

[54]See Troeltsch, "Renaissance and Reformation," p. 21.

[55]Trenchard and Gordon, "Of Reason" (1720), in Jacobson, *English Libertarian Heritage*,
pp. 31–32.

[56]See H. S. Smith, *Changing Conceptions of Original Sin*, pp. 18–19; Lakoff, "Autonomy
and Liberal Democracy," p. 390; and Hutson, "Bill of Rights," pp. 92–93.

[57]Livingston, "Further Reflections on the Doctrines of PASSIVE OBEDIENCE" (1753) in Livingston et al., *Independent Reflector*, p. 331.

[58]See Peach, *Richard Price*, p. 10, who writes that after Price's "political tracts were trans-
mitted to or published in America his name became a household word," so much so that "on
April 24, 1781, he and George Washington were voted Doctors of Laws degrees by the Yale
Corporation."

[59]Price, *Observations* (1776), p. 3.

the influential Whig political theorist James Harrington,[60] Price includes these elements among those causes that rob us of "true" liberty. Only when one was capable of acting in conformity with the higher, reasonable parts of oneself could one be judged to be both truly free and fully human. Again, for the rationalist mind, once one understood "the rational necessity" of a particular act, one could not "while remaining rational, want to do otherwise."[61]

For the moral agent, then, knowledge of what was rationally prescribed created an obligation that could only be willfully denied by the abnegation of one's unique moral standing as a rational being. For people powerfully influenced by the precepts of 18th-century rationalism, to will otherwise than that which was good and right was evidence that one either was not free or was, in fact, irrational and thus almost subhuman. As the Locke scholar James Tully notes, even for the influential John Locke, "natural law freedom to perfect our nature in performing our rational duties to God runs parallel to Berlin's concept of 'positive' freedom, 'freedom to,'" rather than freedom from moral prohibitions.[62] John Gray adds that "neither Locke's nor (as Berlin acknowledges) Kant's view of liberty was negative: each saw the loss of liberty as consisting in the submission to arbitrary will, and liberty as being preserved and enlarged by conforming to rational law."[63] Berlin confirms that the early modern rational understanding of freedom "is not the 'negative' conception" of freedom, but instead a "notion of self-direction or self-control," a positive sense of individual freedom. Therefore, to behave rationally demands that "whatever I can demonstrate to myself as being necessary, as incapable of being otherwise in a rational society," I cannot, being rational, "wish to sweep out of my way."[64] The rationalist gave intrinsic value only to those beings capable of conforming to reason's dictates.

Each of the three dominant traditions of political discourse held that certain elements of an individual's life were of fundamental importance. And each in a different way encouraged government and society to provide for the individual's full human, spiritual, or moral development. It might be claimed, therefore, that late 18th-century views of the individual have much in common with modern individualism, given their common commitment to the unfolding of individual potential. Such a conclusion, however, would be in error, for the respect these three traditions awarded the individual shares little with the standards set by modern individualism.

The modern reverence for the individual is founded on a mixture of

---

[60]See Harrington, "Commonwealth of Oceana" (1656), p. 169, who writes that "whatever was passion in the contemplation of man . . . is vice and the bondage of sin"; and Canavan, *Freedom of Expression*, p. 77.

[61]Berlin, "Two Concepts of Liberty," pp. 141–42.

[62]Tully, "Locke on Liberty," p. 71.

[63]Gray, "On Negative and Positive Liberty," p. 342.

[64]Berlin, "Two Concepts of Liberty," p. 144.

secular faith in human goodness and irremediable epistemic uncertainty concerning the particular ends humans are to pursue. The three dominant 18th-century traditions of political thought instead rested their respect and concern for the individual on a soon-to-be-achieved (they believed) ontological and epistemic certainty concerning humans, God, and the cosmos.[65] The individual was soon to be guided by certain knowledge of these ends, and government and various familial and local communal institutions were to aid people in living in accord with true moral standards.

Subjectivity, uniqueness, and antinomian sensitivities had no place in this logic. Yet these attributes, radically devalued by much of 18th-century thought, are valued by defenders of modern individualism. Individual autonomy is taken as a standard that awards an absolute status to the individual who possesses God-given but not God-defined rights. Accordingly, the individual cannot justly be made to serve society against his or her will.[66] As Leo Strauss explained, this modern sense of individualism is based on a new understanding of rights, a sense that "was the ideal basis for an appeal from society to something indefinite and undefinable, to the ultimate sanctity of the individual as individual, unredeemed and unjustified."[67] Modern individualism, then, in spite of the standing that 18th-century traditions awarded the "true" or "higher" needs of the individual, does not describe Revolutionary-era Americans' atavistic views of the individual.[68]

It is in the details of the earlier epoch's view of the individual and his or her needs that it is unlike modern individualism. The conceptual language shared by the 18th and 20th centuries is incapable of readily capturing the nuanced character of these differences. Without translation, these concepts are likely only to foster confusion. Evidently, early Americans' views of individuals and their true needs, as shaped by each of the three traditions of discourse, were at odds with the more open-ended and liberal modern understanding of individual needs.

REPUBLICANISM, RATIONALISM, CHRISTIANITY, AND INDIVIDUALISM

The convoluted developmental relationship that the three prominent traditions of discourse maintained with a fourth, emergent individualism, further illuminates 18th-century views of the individual. In that period of worldwide intellectual turmoil, each of the older traditions shaped and was shaped by emergent individualism, albeit not always in expected ways. For example, republicanism's role as a link or conduit to 19th-century

[65]See E. Lewis, "Contribution of Medieval Thought," p. 470.
[66]See Wolin, *Politics and Vision*, p. 338; and Sabine, *History of Political Theory*, pp. 673ff.
[67]Strauss, *Natural Right and History*, p. 294.
[68]See Lacey and Haakonssen, "Introduction," p. 2, who write that "the basic premise for rights discourse—the existence of an objective moral order accessible to reason and amenable to formulation in terms of rights and duties—has become a highly controversial assertion."

individualism, even if still not well understood, should have been predictable, even if paradoxical. Conversely, reformed Protestantism and early modern rationalism were less able than one might have expected to serve as pathways to individualism, in spite of their later lending to individualism their significant moral ballast.

Each of the three dominant 18th-century traditions of discourse had a role in the American development of modern individualism without ever having supported the tenets of what would become individualism. The public-centered character of the older traditions, Americans' faith in a purposeful cosmos, and the dogma of original sin were unimpeachable truisms that would not allow it. At least this was true until the last decade of the 18th century, when progressive authors began publicly to question these centuries-old beliefs.

One can impose on this otherwise messy landscape a developmental scheme that places in relation to emerging individualism each of the three views of the individual. By following two intellectual dimensions, one can distinguish among the three views and delineate how each tradition, more or less discretely, viewed the individual, God, and society. First is whether these traditions of discourse supported in the 18th century anthropocentric or theocentric views of the cosmos. Second is whether the individual was seen in a unitary fashion or as radically divided between elevated and base elements, with the base ones to be repressed, or at least stringently controlled.

Regarding the first question, republicanism and rationalism were more supportive of the emerging "modern" perspective than was reformed Protestantism. That is, they generally empowered humans and were derisive, at least in the private views of their most committed adherents, of Christians' declared dependence on a distant and usually inscrutable God.[69] The supposedly debilitating role that the Christian conceptions of sin and virtue played in the secular life of a polity was a central concern of such prominent authors as Machiavelli and Rousseau in postclassical republican thought.[70] Those, then, who were most influenced by the claims of early modern rationalism or classical or Renaissance republicanism held more anthropocentric outlooks. They also were relatively confident, unlike reformed Protestants, of humans' natural virtues and the polity's ability to guide and direct its moral life without direct, constant, and active divine intervention.

Many elite Christians were also enthusiastic students of science who had rejected Calvinism's most severe beliefs regarding humans' total depen-

---

[69]See Westminster Assembly, "Westminster Confession of Faith" (1646), p. 202; Davies, *Religion and Public Spirit* (1761), p. 12; and more generally see Skinner, *Foundations of Modern Political Thought*, 1:92–93.

[70]See Machiavelli, "Discourses," book 1, chaps. xi–xiv; Rousseau, *Social Contract* (1762), book 4, chap. 8; and Skinner, *Foundations of Modern Political Thought*, 1:167.

dence on God. Their beliefs were therefore invariably a mixture of some kind of rationalism and a moderate and "reasonable" form of Christianity.[71] William Livingston assuredly had supporters among the liberal Christian ranks when he held that the more orthodox Calvinists erred in their insistence that "mankind are purely passive in their reformation from vice to virtue." From the progressive perspective, people were not wholly dependent on "a superior and irresistible agency" that reduced them "to mere machines, void of intelligence and free volition."[72]

Yet those who are usually associated with the more anthropocentric side also defy rigid characterization because they also often turned to the divine in search of objective moral standards. For example, the 17th-century English martyr to republicanism Algernon Sidney, like later 18th-century thinkers inspired by rationalist and classical republican thought, believed that there were "but three ways of distinguishing between good and evil; when God by his word reveals it to us; when by his deeds he declareth it," and finally, by that which would prove the most elusive and open to controversy, "the light of reason, which is good, in as much as it is from God."[73]

Nevertheless, differences along this first axis (anthropocentrism versus theocentrism) did exist, and reformed Protestantism in its essence denied that fallen humans were capable of self-direction or self-improvement. In fact, prominent pastors such as the 17th-century founder Joseph Cotton denied that unaided people could do anything truly good. He noted that without Christ's intercession humans can do nothing that is good, "not even a good thought much less a good desire."[74] And 130 years later, Princeton's president, Samuel Davies, continued to argue that without God first transforming the heart of the sinner, a person's effort to act righteously would have "no more real Goodness in it, than the instinctive Fondness of a Brute for its young."[75] Reformed-Protestant pastors and their flocks insisted, then, on people's total dependence on a sometimes inscrutable God, on his freely given grace, and on a local congregation's willingness to walk fraternally with each member sinner.

From a traditional reformed-Protestant perspective, it was the local congregation's liberty (albeit in service of individual soteriological ends and the greater glory of God) that was to be protected, not that of self-directed individuals.[76] Michael Walzer concludes his study of Puritanism by stating that indeed reformed Protestantism did rest on voluntaristic foundations, but that this "never led to respect for privacy. Tender conscience had its

[71]See Bonomi, *Under the Cope of Heaven*, p. 104.

[72]Cited by Milton M. Klein in Livingston et al., *Independent Reflector*, pp. 334–35 n. 2.

[73]A. Sidney, *Discourses Concerning Government* (1698), p. 38.

[74]Cotton, "Mr. Cotton's Rejoynder" (1636), pp. 144–45.

[75]Davies, *Religion and Public Spirit* (1761), p. 11.

[76]See May, *Enlightenment in America*, pp. xi–xviii, 358–62; and Heimert, *Religion and the American Mind*, p. 18.

rights, but it was protected only against the interference of worldlings and not against 'brotherly admonition.' "[77] Spiritual voluntarism, when weighed down by the constraints of communal watchfulness and brotherly admonition, was incapable of fostering modern individual liberty.[78]

According to Karl Holl, one of the great early 20th-century German sociologists, this was to have been expected, for it was in keeping with reformed-Protestant tradition. That tradition had always taught "that love of self should be replaced by love of neighbor" and "in place of the individual ego, the community became primary," for "only within it did the individual find himself and indeed find himself as a serving member."[79] Reformed Protestants therefore could readily support the communal influences of more explicitly communitarian traditions, such as Whig republicanism or agrarian communalism. But it remains something of a paradox that reformed Protestantism, with its emphasis on spiritual individualism, was so insistent on the priority of the public good.

Awarding prominence to the community's pastoral role, however, did not disparage the centrality of individual salvation (the soteriological mission) in the Christian scheme. Rather, it was a recognition of an unaided person's inability to serve God or to pursue his or her own salvation in a weakened and deformed apostate condition. To effect one's true ends, corporate and superpersonal assistance were absolutely necessary. The community, from this perspective, was no more than a tool. Yet it was a most necessary one that aided the regenerate soul in overcoming the siren calls of "execrable" arbitrary wants and egoistic passions. The community of saints was to use the collective power of its members' freely given wills to control what today would be described as the most expressive elements of each individual's autonomous self. Thus, a commentator must find himself or herself in the awkward position of arguing that a religious culture that was profoundly individualistic in its spiritual essence is, nevertheless, best described as fundamentally public-centered in its political and social outlooks. In sum, God was best served by a community of believers mutually and reciprocally ensuring that they chose his ways over the siren calls of the flesh.

Along the second basic human dimension introduced above (whether people are radically divided between elevated and base elements), the 18th-century discourses group differently. Here, we find rationalism and reformed Protestantism in agreement and in opposition to the changes associated with individualism (leaving only republicanism on both indices more or less supportive of such changes). Rationalism and Protestantism

---

[77]Walzer, *Revolution of the Saints*, p. 301.

[78]See Arieli, *Individualism and Nationalism in American Ideology*, pp. 251, 267; D. Bell, "Resolving the Contradictions," pp. 71–72; and Carden, *Puritan Christianity in America*, pp. 147–48.

[79]Holl, *Cultural Significance of the Reformation*, p. 37.

each held that people were divided creatures composed of higher selfless and Godlike aspects and lower egotistical and bestial elements. For most Americans, a good life should only be had by living in accord with the dictates of the higher divine or rational parts of one's being. That is, to live a morally worthy life, the individual had to be controlled by the rational or divine part of his or her being. This human element, in turn, reflected God's true ethical standards, and linked people to the moral universe.[80]

Not only individuals but governments as well were to be held to universal moral standards. The fiery patriot James Otis declared that "Parliaments are in all cases to *declare* what is for the good of the whole; but it is not the *declaration* of parliament that makes it so: There must be in every instance, a higher authority, viz. GOD. Should an act of parliament be against any of *his* natural laws, which are *immutably* true, *their* declaration would be contrary to eternal truth, equity and justice, and consequently void."[81] Governments were to be judged by these divine standards and also were to enforce them on their individual constituents. Government was understood to be "a combination of the whole community, against the vices of each particular member."[82] Thus, in a fashion at odds with later individualistic doctrines, governments were held responsible for placing individuals beyond their own capacity for moral debasement.[83]

Americans influenced by the tenets of early modern rationalism, in clear tension with the local particularism of their less-educated brethren, believed, "as all educated men in that era of reason did, in standards of behavior and thought that transcended temporal and national boundaries." For them, "it was not native originality, but universal and eternal truth" that was to be sought.[84] Jean Jacques Burlamaqui, an eminent natural-law theorist, declared that "man can neither answer his end, nor perfect his talents and faculties, nor acquire any solid happiness, or reconcile it with that of his fellow-creature, but by the help of reason; that it ought to be therefore his first care to improve his reason, to consult it, and follow the counsels thereof."[85] James Wilson, a Scottish immigrant to America and a true child of his native land's Enlightenment, captured this understanding of the proper role of reason in ordering human social and political life. He wrote that "the will of God" is "the supreme law," and

[80]See Fosdick, *What Is Liberty?* p. 46.

[81]Otis, "Rights of the British Colonies" (1764), in *Tracts of the American Revolution*, pp. 32–33.

[82][Lathrop], "Politician" (December 1789), p. 443.

[83]See W. H. Nelson, *American Tory*, p. 188.

[84]Wood, introduction to *Rising Glory of America*, p. 8.

[85]Burlamaqui, *Principles of Natural and Politic Law* (1763), 1:268; see also 1:55–56, where he writes that reason was "the noblest part of man, and constituting his principal essence, whatever is inconsistent with reason, cannot form his happiness"; and see White, *Philosophy of the American Revolution*, pp. 37–38, who argues that Burlamaqui was a thinker who powerfully influenced Revolutionary American thought.

that "this law, or right reason, as Cicero calls it, is thus beautifully described by that eloquent philosopher" as "a true law, conformable to nature, diffused among all men, unchangeable, eternal," which "requires no interpreter." According to Wilson and most other educated 18th-century thinkers, "it is the same eternal and immutable law, given at all times and to all nations: for God, who is its author and promulgator, is always the sole master and sovereign of mankind."[86]

There were disagreements among and within the modern rational, republican, and reformed-Protestant traditions about how coercive different levels of society or government should be in encouraging such behavior. There was none, however, concerning their view of human passions and the emotional potential of human beings, which, by contemporary standards, seems restrictive and desiccated. This central aspect of late 18th-century social and political thought was what the Romantics were so dissatisfied with, and would declare war on in the early 19th century. Yet in comparison to rationalism and reformed Protestantism, classical and Renaissance republican authors had adopted a more tolerant view of the individual. Their stance was more modern (and less Christian), and less concerned with suppressing irrational passions and bestial urges.[87]

In classical political thought, as a Latin favorite of Americans, Sallust, observed, vice and virtue were separated by surprisingly little distance. It was "a thirst for glory, and ever more glory," that described ambitious men in search of "true wealth." Moreover, it was "ambition that disturbed men's minds—a fault which after all comes nearer to being a virtue. For distinction, preferment, and power are the desire of good and bad alike."[88] Even Machiavelli had little faith in "an austere ideal of self-abnegation and service to the public good."[89] Thus, from the stricter perspective of rationalism and reformed Protestantism, republicanism's more accommodationist outlook should have appeared almost immoral.

The republican tradition demanded dedication to the public good, but without insisting on stripping away that which made an individual unique. Such individual aspects, when devoted to the public good, were even celebrated. Indeed, the republican-inspired view of fame had such broad appeal in the 18th century that even Burke had held that the "passion for fame" is a commendable "instinct of all great souls."[90] According to re-

[86]J. Wilson, *Works of James Wilson*, ed. Andrews, 1:105, 125.
[87]See Pocock, *Machiavellian Moment*, pp. 249–50.
[88]Sallust, "Conspiracy of Catiline," in *Jugurthine War and The Conspiracy of Catiline*, pp. 180–82.
[89]Pocock, "Between Gog and Magog," p. 342.
[90]Cited by Adair, "Fame and the Founding Fathers," p. 11 n. 7; see that note for further references. Anti-Federalists and Christians also found the desire for public glory to be an acceptable goal for public-spirited men. See A Farmer, "Essay VII" (1788), p. 58; and Hurt, "Love of Country" (1777), p. 154, who finds that "glory is the reward of honorable toils, and public fame is the just retribution for public service."

publican teachings, the heroic, the larger than life, was to be promoted, though without any recognition of presocial rights that could (in Ronald Dworkin's words) "trump" the will of the community. Republicanism was thus relatively accepting of the individual, even celebratory of his uniqueness, but only so long as his capacities ultimately served to further public welfare.

As the McDonalds recognize, for men like Hamilton and his immediate circle who were taken with the classical idea of heroic and immortal public fame,[91] "the term *character*" did not refer to moral qualities but rather to one's reputation, to one's public persona. One's public being thus mirrored one's fame and reputation and was to be acted "like a part in a play."[92] Like an ensemble of actors that nevertheless enjoyed a recognized star, between the great man and the public there existed a symbiotic relationship without which neither could fully realize its potential. Paul Rahe finds that in the republican tradition a public life offered individuals (with the notable exception of philosophers) the only acceptable means to achieve a fully human life, by in effect indulging one's self-love, for

the *polis* offered the ordinary citizen a participation in greatness . . . to display eloquence in council and courage in battle. Because the city constituted an audience with the prospect of permanence, it provided the citizen with the hope of achieving through his contributions to its welfare at least a shadow of the eternal fame that Hesiod gave Heracles and Homer, Achilles. . . . It was this straining after immortality that distinguished a human life . . . from mere animal existence.[93]

But one must not exaggerate the differences among the three traditions, for republicanism as understood in the 18th century also demanded that the individual exercise a large measure of self-control and self-overcoming.[94] In his hugely popular play "Cato: A Tragedy," Joseph Addison had one of his characters teach that "a Roman soul is bent on higher views," on cultivating "the wild, licentious savage," indeed, in being "severely bent against himself."[95] And by the Roman patriot Sallust, Americans were reminded:

since only a short span of life has been vouchsafed us, we must make ourselves remembered as long as may be by those who come after us. . . . many are the men who, slaves of gluttony and sloth, have gone through life ignorant and uncivilized . . . reversing, surely, the order of nature by treating their bodies as means of gratification and their souls as mere encumbrances. The truth is that no

[91]See also Adair, "Fame and the Founding Fathers," pp. 14–16; and Stourzh, *Alexander Hamilton,* pp. 99–100.

[92]McDonald and McDonald, *Requiem,* pp. 13–15.

[93]Rahe, "Primacy of Politics in Classical Greece," p. 286; see also Stourzh, *Alexander Hamilton,* p. 106; and Lienesch, *New Order of the Ages,* p. 181.

[94]See Hexter, review of *The Machiavellian Moment,* p. 321.

[95]Addison, "Cato," p. 180.

man really lives or gets any satisfaction out of life, unless he devotes all his energies to some task and seeks fame by some notable achievement.[96]

Note, in particular, the balance to be maintained between the demand for individual expression and that for self-control, in a manner subtly different from that found in Christian as well as early modern rationalist thought.

But despite the stringent communalism recommended by various classical authors, 18th-century republicanism was nevertheless strangely compatible with emergent individualism.[97] At any rate, it was more so than either of the two traditions that were more modern in origin. Unlike reformed-Protestant thought, republicanism was anthropocentric. Particularly in its Renaissance incarnation (and that of its modern imitators), it fully celebrated men qua men and allowed them corporately,[98] through public political debate and choice, to create meaning in lives that otherwise might be meaningless. In this most modern view, meaning was not to be discovered, but rather created by men in a morally empty universe.[99]

Unlike both rationalism and reformed-Protestant thought, republicanism was partly willing to accommodate the richness of the human personality. Most significantly, it accepted some of the emotions that Christianity and early modern rationalism found excessively egoistic or passionate—those that would be congenial only to individualism. This heroic view of the individual certainly proved well adapted to a world about to be buffeted by the claims of romanticism and all that it entailed (sentimentality, inwardness, and so forth).

THE TWISTED 18TH-CENTURY PATH TO INDIVIDUALISM

Republicanism's tolerance for the love of honor played a useful though largely unintended role in facilitating the slow transformation of elite American political thought from more to less communal. The broad approbation elites gave the pursuit of individual fame provided a vehicle for this change so ably defended by the fittingly pseudonymous Publius. The elites slowly came to accept that "the pursuit of fame" was an almost painless "way of transforming egotism and self-aggrandizing impulses into public service" without demanding that the individual act in a truly selfless manner.[100] By comparison, the self-abnegating demands of rationalism and reformed Protestantism must have seemed unduly restrictive from an emerging individualistic per-

[96]Sallust, "Conspiracy of Catiline," in *Jugurthine War and The Conspiracy of Catiline*, pp. 175–76.
[97]See Shalhope, "Individualism in the Early Republic," pp. 84–85.
[98]See Skinner, *Foundations of Modern Political Thought*, 1:99.
[99]I suspect that it is because of this feature that republicanism, rather than Christian communalism, has attracted so much attention from those dissatisfied with liberal historiography and political theory.
[100]Adair, "Fame and the Founding Fathers," pp. 7–8.

spective. Conversely, from the more restrictive republican perspective described by commentators such as Montesquieu, the insistence on selflessness appeared too noble and demanding for a modern people. At the end of the 18th century, this would be the lament of despondent American traditionalists beginning to confront potent popular and venal state governments.

Republicanism's confidence in the salutary power of fame thus allowed one to embrace a politics of individual accommodation. But when properly channeled, it did not necessitate that one abandon the need to serve the public good as the highest secular standard for individual behavior. The history of various republics and Revolutionary America testify that the hunger for fame and glory can be made to serve public welfare.[101] Publius seized on and innovatively developed this republican line of argument in *The Federalist*. In doing so, he was most likely influenced by the novel faculty psychology of the Scottish philosopher Thomas Reid, who had argued that self-interest, and in particular ambition, was a defensible form of rationality.[102] With that in hand, Publius could and did reject communalism and the politics of virtue and self-renunciation as unnecessary (and unobtainable).[103] Public ends could, however, still be served as long as they were kept modest and ambition and the pursuit of fame were properly channeled (as Madison argued in Federalist no. 51 and Hamilton even more emphatically in no. 72).[104]

In a celebrated passage, Madison wrote that "ambition must be made to counteract ambition. The interest of the man must be connected with the constitutional rights of the place. It may be a reflection on human nature . . . but what is government itself, but the greatest of all reflections on human nature?"[105] Although Madison at this point might still have been working within the limits of republican thought, it would be only a short step before the border was crossed and individuals' needs became defensible in their own right. Republicanism, particularly in the hands of Publius,[106] facilitated the radical alteration of American political thought from being principally communal to being divided between communal and individualistic strands.

It is more than a little ironic, however, that republicanism, and the American Patriots who embraced it, helped foster such a transformation. As Gordon Wood persuasively shows, republicanism was congenial to modern individualism in certain ways, yet "like Puritanism, of which it was a more relaxed, secularized version, republicanism was . . . a final

---

[101]See Weintraub, "Virtue," pp. 76–77.

[102]See Howe, "Political Psychology of *The Federalist*," pp. 490–91.

[103]See Hamilton, Jay, and Madison, *Federalist;* in particular, Hamilton (no. 6), p. 30; Madison (no. 10), p. 58; Hamilton (no. 15), p. 92; and Madison (no. 49), pp. 329–31.

[104]See Appleby, *Liberalism and Republicanism,* pp. 227–28; Pocock, *Machiavellian Moment,* p. 487; and Katz, "Thomas Jefferson," pp. 486–87.

[105]J. Madison, "Federalist No. 49," in Hamilton, Jay, and Madison, *Federalist,* p. 337.

[106]See Maynard Smith, "Reason, Passion, and Political Freedom," p. 531.

attempt to come to terms with the emergent individualistic society that threatened to destroy once and for all the communion and benevolence that civilized men had always considered the ideal of human behavior."[107] From various vantage points, however, it now seems inevitable that republicanism proved attractive to an elite moving away from predestinarian Christianity toward modern individualism.

This emerging world of new and old ideas was at once modern, relatively individualistic, and yet, as Publius demonstrates, still capable of respecting the public good as a higher good. When joined, these aspects make otherwise anomalous aspects of the Revolutionary period more comprehensible. For example, it is easier to understand the transformation of Massachusetts under the 1780 constitution from "a Bible commonwealth" to "a secular commonwealth in which the common good supplanted salvation as the end of civil society."[108] In effect, Massachusetts, even if only temporarily, became less individual-centered. Why had the elite of Boston (and Philadelphia, and New York), following the intellectual lead of numerous British authors, not militated directly for a modern individualistic political culture? Their transitional espousal of certain republican categories of thought suggests that Americans, even the elite, were unprepared to adopt modern individualism directly with its wholesale rejection of the preeminence of serving the public good (which they would continue to embrace for much of the next two centuries). This is what England was believed to have begun doing under Robert Walpole, and it was against such English practices that Americans were rebelling. At least Americans believed that they were doing so in opposition to the modernizing transformations that had corrupted their motherland.

For those rare Americans who continued to appreciate the importance of serving the common good but had little faith in reason, revelation, or the moral sense, Renaissance republicanism must have also provided an attractive alternative. When compared to the dominant rationalist and reformed-Protestant views, republicanism was less dependent on certain moral knowledge, yet was comparably public-centered. Was classical republicanism in Revolutionary America, then, an ill-fated body of thought that principally served as a way station between traditionalist Christianity and 19th-century individualism? Quite possibly it served as a bridge, though it also continued to help shape public discourse in public-centered ways well into the 19th century. Notwithstanding the exaggerated claims of some of its present-day apologists, republicanism might truly be emblematic of the American Revolution in unanticipated ways, particularly in its doomed effort to renew and rebuild on a more secular foundation America's communal ethos.

Reformed Protestantism and early modern rationalism suffered from

---

[107]Wood, *Creation of the American Republic*, pp. 418–19.
[108]Peters, *Massachusetts Constitution of 1780*, p. 193.

disabling flaws that prevented each from serving as a ready conduit to emergent individualism. With regard to the first question discussed above (theocentrism or anthropocentrism), rationalism, like Renaissance republicanism, accepted anthropocentrism, which clearly is a distinguishing mark of modern thought. But regarding the second question, concerning humans' supposedly divided nature, rationalism is unacceptable to modern individualism. This is because rationalism emphatically holds to objective ethical standards that render indefensible subjectivity and arbitrary individual behavior. In fact, without confidence that it is possible ultimately to arrive at moral truth, rationalism's "demand for freedom of thought and expression" would have been unsustainable in the 18th century.[109]

Moreover, rationalism's absolute moral standards, even if obtainable, were incompatible with an individualistic understanding of autonomy. Berlin is particularly concerned about how such an understanding of moral truth might have led one to respond to the question "How am I to treat recalcitrant human beings?" He answers for an imagined 18th-century rationalist: "I must, if I can, impose my will on them too, 'mould' them to my pattern," for "if my plan is fully rational, it will allow for the full development of their 'true' natures."[110] For the early modern rationalist, individual choice did not entail freedom "to do what is irrational or stupid, or wrong." And the forcing of "empirical selves into the right pattern" was not tyranny, but liberation.[111] Such a moral stance is incompatible with most understandings of individualist ethical claims.

More unexpectedly, given its long-standing defense of spiritual individuality, reformed Protestantism could not have been at ease with emerging social and political individualism. First, Protestantism was most emphatically God-centered rather than human-centered.[112] Most American Protestants must have found the pride and self-love of apostate humans inconsistent with reformed Christianity's vision of the total impotence of humans and their dependence on Christ.[113] Indeed, according to Ernst Troeltsch, Calvin had taught that the world is "never anything but the God-ordained sphere of our action," which "we must never set our affections on." "Only for God's sake and from obedience are we to desire to have to do with" the world where "pain and suffering are the essence."[114] In 1770s America, Calvin's voice remained a powerful one.

According to this intellectual map, then, republicanism played an important transitional role in Revolutionary America (though assuredly not the one sought by its Revolutionary or contemporary defenders). Early modern rationalism and reformed Protestantism, for the reasons suggested

---

[109]Canavan, *Freedom of Expression*, p. 144.
[110]Berlin, "Two Concepts of Liberty," p. 146.
[111]Ibid., p. 148.
[112]See Lindsay, "Individualism," p. 677.
[113]See Cotton, "Mr. Cotton's Rejoynder" (1636), pp. 103–4.
[114]Troeltsch, *Protestantism and Progress*, pp. 78–79.

above, were less capable of moving elite thought in the direction of individualism, at least until important foundational principles of each had been rejected or transformed.

This schematic of change also reveals that Americans during the Revolutionary era were most reluctant to surrender two beliefs that had political importance. First, Americans held that there was a cosmos, that is, a moral universe that was divinely or rationally ordered, and that moral life was linked to that heavenly order.[115] Most thoughtful Americans still had confidence in their (and sometimes even their less-intelligent fellows') ability to understand and be guided by the natural or divine ordering of the cosmos. Without this assurance in the human capacity to master moral truths, claims made on behalf of freedom would have been unsustainable. Second, Americans continued to believe that the public good must be awarded preeminence over that of the individual.

These two beliefs would each in turn come under attack in the early 19th century. Americans' belief in the absolute priority of the common or public good over the needs of particular individuals would, with the emergence of individualism, be the first to be challenged. Somewhat later, Romantics would also question whether the universe was morally ordered. It is likely that some Americans had embraced views in the 18th century that prepared for these changes that eventually culminated in the emergence of a new understanding of individual flourishing. But in regard to these two defining beliefs of the Revolutionary era, the priority of the public good and the morally ordered and purposeful nature of their universe, almost all Americans of whose thought some record exists had been unwilling to make this journey.

In the early 19th century, religious concerns slowly developed into weapons capable of defending the abandonment of the 18th century's high valuation of the public good. What for most Americans had been illegitimate claims on behalf of the heteronomous individual slowly became publicly defensible. "The centre of gravity . . . shifted" and ever-greater attention was given "to personal subjective conviction."[116] As the consensus concerning the fallen condition of humans atrophied,[117] Christianity's emphasis on the spiritual sanctity of the individual could be exploited in more secular and individualistic ways.

In some elite circles, even the 18th-century understanding of the community's need to shape and restrict the wants of the individual was abandoned. It was exchanged for one in which the newly private inner world became the primary source and standard of human truth and transcen-

---

[115]See Lutz, *Origins of American Constitutionalism*, p. 165, and *Preface to American Political Theory*, p. 132.

[116]Troeltsch, *Protestantism and Progress*, p. 194.

[117]See H. S. Smith, *Changing Conceptions of Original Sin*, p. 76.

dence.[118] This reflected the surrender in the early national period of the traditional Western "dichotomy—both Platonic and Christian—between body and soul."[119] With these changes, the foundations were laid in America for a "theory of the inviolability of the inner personal life by the State." What in the 18th century had been largely spiritual in the early 19th century became more secular.[120]

During this period, a truly revolutionary understanding of reason capable of freeing the individual emerged in opposition to the older view of individual reason that had been dominant in Western culture for much of two millennia. With this new perception of the individual, the divine reason of the cosmos, which was authoritatively to "guide us in our choices," became the subjective "property of individual men and not something eternal and unchanging that exists independently." In this new world, the individual was "freed to discover the uniqueness of his own self, to pursue his own happiness in nature, God, or the marketplace in his own way."[121] This was a brave new world that most of the Revolutionary generation would have little understood and less condoned.

Indeed, many who lived to see the turn of the 18th century were dismayed by the unsought radical changes that the American Revolution (to say nothing of the French one) had helped foster.[122] Yet with continued confidence, Joseph Lathrop, one of the most respected ministers in New England for more than sixty years, was still in 1786 pleading in a remarkably traditional fashion for a renewal of American moral resolve. He warned that America was endangered by the usual list of miscreants regularly assembled in prerevolutionary America on such occasions, "the prevalence of vice and impiety" and "increasing luxury, extravagance, selfishness and injustice."[123]

On a revealingly different and more somber note, however, Cyprian Strong, in the closing Connecticut election sermon of the century, complained in a strangely modern conservative voice. He found that "the *liberalizing* spirit of the present day (which looks with *indifferency* and *patience*, on every thing) . . . tells us, that moral and religious principles are

---

[118]Ironically, the republican tradition, although substantially transformed during the early 19th century, proved resistant to change and continued to exert a limiting influence in antebellum American social thought. See Wish, "From Yeoman Farmer to Industrious Producer," and R. M. Smith, " 'American Creed' and American Identity," for their exploration of this relationship.

[119]Lyons, *Invention of the Self*, p. 19.

[120]Troeltsch, *Protestantism and Progress*, p. 125; see also Somkin, *Unquiet Eagle*, pp. 28–29.

[121]Lyons, *Invention of the Self*, pp. 2–3; see also Sandel, *Liberalism and the Limits of Justice*, p. 175.

[122]See Greven, *Protestant Temperament*, p. 358; Maier, *Old Revolutionaries*, p. 48; Pocock, *Machiavellian Moment*, p. 517; Gillespie, "Ratification of the Constitution," p. 17; Wood, "Significance of the Early Republic," pp. 10–20, and *Radicalism of the American Revolution*, p. 365.

[123]Lathrop, "Miscellaneous Collection of Original Pieces" (1786), p. 666.

of no importance; yea, it is a discovery made by the modern *Illuminati,* that both religion and government are enemies to the happiness of mankind." With the French Revolution probably in mind (little could he have imagined the horrors of 20th-century totalitarianism), he likewise warned that "when moral feelings and religious restraints are eradicated, and God is not acknowledged and reverenced, the barriers against the most atrocious wickedness are removed, and the lusts of the human heart will be unrestrained."[124]

With more resignation than anger, Fisher Ames six years later lamented that political virtue, the love of country that demands that one "suffer much for his country," was not to be found in "the habits and passions that predominate in America." Americans, he claimed, were "wholly engrossed by the pursuit of wealth and pleasure" and dominated by "the propensities of the individual" without any social feeling.[125] America, for him and other disillusioned members of the elite, had become a land where the most cherished public-centered and communal aspirations of the Revolution were no longer discoverable.[126] But many residents of 1950s America might have claimed that some of the high value attached to the public good in the Revolutionary era still endured. Even if it was weakened as a standard, service in defense of the public good did not die with the close of the 18th century.

EMERGENT INDIVIDUALISM

At the end of the eighteenth century, in contrast to the disappointed old Revolutionaries, other members of the national elite, particularly those who have captured the American historical imagination, rejected much of that century's normative political theory. They no longer believed that it was the responsibility of government to facilitate human self-overcoming through republican public-spirited actions by citizens, restrictive and demanding rational self-control, or godly service. In their view, each person was a distinct individual with particular physical wants and passions. Without abandoning their continued deference to the public good, they accepted that individuals were to be accommodated by government in

---

[124] Cyprian Strong, *Kingdom Is the Lord's* (1799 Connecticut election sermon), p. 37; see also (from the same year) Daggett, "Sunbeams May Be Extracted from Cucumbers"; "Remarks on a Passage" (1791), p. 243, in which a defender of enlightened thought is said to be a "theological quack, who poisons their souls, and disseminates doctrines subversive to all morality"; and Lundberg and May, "Enlightened Reader in America," p. 265.

[125] Ames, "Dangers of American Liberty" (1805), p. 1327.

[126] See Jefferson, "Letter to William Smith" (2 February 1788), in *Papers of Thomas Jefferson,* 12:558; A Farmer, "Essay III" (1788), p. 30, who writes that "I see nothing in my fellow-citizens, that will permit my still fostering the delusion, that they are now capable of sustaining the weight of SELF-GOVERNMENT"; Somkin, *Unquiet Eagle,* p. 16; May, *Enlightenment in America,* pp. 272–73; Hatch, *Sacred Cause of Liberty,* pp. 167–69; and Wood, "Illusions and Disillusions," p. 360.

the fulfillment of their higher and lower wants. For example, Hamilton claimed that society "cannot without breach of faith and injustice, refuse to any individual, a single advantage which he derives under the [social] compact."[127] It is striking, Don Lutz observes, to notice "the extent to which human nature and the requirements of the human environment are taken as 'givens'" by members of this elite, and how divergent this vision was from the older intrusive communal political thinking that it was attempting to replace.[128] With this transformation, the public good in the early national period came to be seen by the most progressive thinkers as "best promoted by the exertion of each individual seeking his own good in his own way," a sentiment reportedly held by Jefferson in 1806.[129]

These farsighted founders of contemporary America prepared the way in the last decade of the 18th century for some of the individualist changes wrought in the early 19th century. Such modern men, by one rather harsh assessment, were concerned with "how men live as distinguished from how they ought to live." In effect, they had taken as their symbol "the Beast Man as opposed to God Man," and understood "man in the light of the sub-human rather than of the superhuman."[130] Yet it is probably more accurate to see them as transitional figures who "prepared the way for the individualistic, egalitarian, and democratic future of America," but "were not modern men" themselves. Only by comparison to the more reactionary agricultural majority and those one might describe as America's first conservatives can this elite be described as modern.[131] Thus, in comparison to today's well-educated Americans, 18th-century Americans were still part of "a classical world that was rapidly dying, a world so different from what followed—and from our own—that an act of imagination is required to recover it."[132]

For many, a willingness to live with the new, more hedonistic order was a mark more of resignation than of enthusiastic approval. Many of the old Revolutionaries only unhappily accepted that their fellow Americans were not made of the heroic human stuff from which traditional republics were reported to have been constructed. It was their belief that "self-interest, not virtue" was the most prevalent characteristic of their fellow citizens.[133] This group of bypassed traditional moralists did not hold, however, that it

[127]Hamilton, "Second Letter from Phocion" (1784), p. 83.

[128]Lutz, *Popular Consent and Popular Control*, p. 197; see also Boorstin, *Genius of American Politics*, pp. 18–38; Wood, *Radicalism of the American Revolution*, p. 253; and Katz, "Thomas Jefferson," p. 484.

[129]Reported by Benjamin Henry Latrobe in a letter to Philip Mazzei, 28 December 1806, in Mazzei, *Philip Mazzei*, p. 439.

[130]Strauss, *Thoughts on Machiavelli*, pp. 296–97.

[131]Wood, "Fundamentalists and the Constitution," p. 38. See also Wood, "Interests and Disinterestedness," p. 83; and Cornell, "Aristocracy Assailed."

[132]Wood, "Fundamentalists and the Constitution," p. 38; see also Hanson, *Democratic Imagination in America*, pp. 73–74.

[133]Eastland, "Use and Abuse of Liberty," p. 29.

was morally preferable to organize American political and social lives on such selfish and materialist principles. Rather, in mute acceptance they found it impossible to do otherwise with a people already corrupted by unusually high levels of affluence. A particularly ironic example of tepid acceptance of the emerging individualistic world was provided by John Adams, who had castigated Carter Braxton's precocious 1776 rejection of a politics of virtue as "too absurd to be considered twice." By 1787, however, he declaimed with a certain arrogance that

> To expect self-denial from men . . . is to disbelieve all history and universal experience. . . . There have been examples of self-denial and will be again; but such exalted virtue never yet existed in any large body of men and lasted long. . . . There is no man so blind as not to see that to talk of founding a government upon a supposition that nations and great bodies of men, left to themselves, will practice a course of self-denial is either to babble like a new-born infant or to deceive like an unprincipled imposter.[134]

One can only wonder which of these faults he believed he and his colleagues had been guilty of in the 1770s when they had held such expectations.

For many other relatively progressive members of the elite, the business of government, as Hamilton's Publius noted in his defense of the Constitution, was not to serve God or to shape and care for souls,[135] but rather, as described by Madison's future vice president, Elbridge Gerry, to protect "individuals in the absolute rights which were vested in them by the immediate laws of nature."[136] A modern observer thus finds that Publius's greatest novelty was not the institutional innovations he proposed, but rather his "assertion that the end of government was not the achievement of a particular moral quality of civic life but, rather, the guarantee of individual security" and the protection of "a commercially competitive civil society."[137]

With the Constitution's adoption, the moral level of public concern was undeniably altered at the national level. One might well describe it as "a lowering of the aims and expectations of political life, perhaps of human life generally."[138] At the national level, the ultimate end of public activity was limited to the promotion and protection of commercial activity and the securing of individual or minority rights, particularly those of property, often against the will of the majority of the political nation.[139]

---

[134]J. Adams, *Defence* (1788), 3:289; see also Hamilton, "Continentalist Papers" (1782), pp. 63–64.

[135]See Hamilton, "Federalist No. 23," in Hamilton, Jay, and Madison, *Federalist*, p. 142.

[136]Gerry, "Observations on the New Constitution" (1788), p. 8.

[137]Sullivan, *Reconstructing Public Philosophy*, p. 12; see also Kramnick, "Great National Discussion," p. 31.

[138]Diamond, "Ethics and Politics," pp. 82–83.

[139]See McWilliams, "Democracy and the Citizen," p. 86; Murrin, "Great Inversion," pp. 400–404; and Yarbrough, "Republicanism Reconsidered," p. 75.

But what immediate effect this had on the local and state governments that had the responsibility of policing American morals is more difficult to say. That era's state constitutions and declarations of rights argue that the changes were far more limited than one might believe from examining only national documents and the private correspondence of the nation's truest elite. The states continued to demonstrate a commitment to preserving their foundational Protestant cultures,[140] to shaping the moral character of their residents, and to placing individual rights in an inferior position to those of the majority. Consider then, the South Carolina Constitution, which enunciated that various forms of Christianity would be tolerated before it established "the Christian Protestant religion." It then declared that "no freeman of this State be taken or imprisoned, or disseized of his freehold, liberties, or privileges, or outlawed, exiled, or in any manner destroyed or deprived of his life, liberty, or property, but by the judgement of his peers or by the law of the land."[141] Clearly, these rights that were subject to the judgment of one's peers were far from fully inalienable and were dependent on the will of the enfranchised majority. This is not the stuff of individualism.

James Madison was the Founding period's most innovative political thinker and America's greatest early defender of a moderate form of individualism. He held in an almost religious fashion that "the first object of government" and "the principal task of modern legislation" was the protection of the "rights of property," and more generally, of those individual rights likely to be threatened by democratic majorities.[142] In private, he went further and confided to Jefferson that "a constitutional negative on the laws of the States seems equally necessary to secure individuals agst. encroachments on their rights." But because his fervent concern with individual rights was not shared by others, even by most of his fellow elite nationalists, the national veto power over police powers that he had sought was not forthcoming. It was rejected both by the Philadelphia convention and by the first session of Congress when the first ten amendments were hammered out, again over Madison's importuning for such federal power. Accordingly, the Constitution remained for him "materially defective," since it failed to make adequate "provision for private rights."[143]

Madison had not rejected the need to value the public good; this he continued to defend, if predominantly through institutional and mechani-

[140]For example, see "Maryland Declaration of Rights" (1776), in B. Schwartz, *Roots of The Bill of Rights*, p. 283, and "Vermont Declaration of Rights" (1777), in ibid., p. 322.

[141]"South Carolina Constitution" (1778), in ibid., pp. 333–35.

[142]J. Madison, "Federalist No. 10," in Hamilton, Jay, and Madison, *Federalist*, pp. 56–57; see also "Majority Governments" (1833), in Madison, *Mind of the Founder*, p. 524; and Lockridge, *Settlement and Unsettlement in Early America*, pp. 113–14.

[143]J. Madison, "Letter to Thomas Jefferson" (24 October 1787), in *Papers of James Madison*, 10:212; see also Madison, "Speech" (6 June 1787), in Farrand, *Records of the Federal Convention*, 1:134–35.

cal rather than moral and religious contrivances.[144] It was instead the propriety of communal ethical intrusiveness, with its insistence on fostering virtue in the American citizenry, that troubled him. He wrote passionately and frequently (in this instance to Jefferson) that "in our Government the real power lies in the majority of the community, and the invasion of private rights is *chiefly* to be apprehended."[145] He believed that the "great object to which" the new government must be directed was resolving this peculiarly democratic problem by securing "the public good and private rights against the danger" of majorities,[146] or through the creation of the myth of a sovereign national people (a subterfuge that recently has been both celebrated and condemned).[147]

The American republic of virtue began to be systematically abandoned only with the promulgation of the moderately individualistic political vision embedded in *The Federalist,* if not actually in the federal Constitution of 1787.[148] With this radical but gradual change in elite public philosophy, the "vision of the public good obliterating individual self-interest and desires" ceased to be one of the central metaphors of elite public discourse in America.[149] Traditional intrusive communal ends, products of an ethical unity lost during the early national period,[150] began to be replaced by a concern with a new and rather wondrous individual freedom. According to Madison, the new theory of the good that he had come to embrace, a moderate form of individualism, most importantly freed the "weaker party or an obnoxious individual" from fear of majority intrusion into his or her realm of individual choice.[151]

Madison's driving concern that the sphere of choice surrounding the individual not be intruded on by an intolerant majority, however, still lacked popular support. James Lincoln, in the South Carolina ratifying convention, voiced the sentiments of disappointed Americans. In the 1780s, they continued to view liberty as positive and communal rather than negative and individual. Lincoln therefore asked, "What does this

---

[144]See Gibson, "Commercial Republic," p. 524. One might question, however, how serious his commitment was to protecting the public good. See Pangle, "Civic Virtue," p. 133.

[145]J. Madison, "Letter to Thomas Jefferson" (17 October 1788), in Madison, *Mind of the Founder,* p. 206.

[146]J. Madison, "Federalist No. 10," in Hamilton, Jay, and Madison, *Federalist,* pp. 57–58.

[147]See E. S. Morgan, *Inventing the People,* p. 285, and "Government by Fiction," pp. 338–39; J. Miller, "Ghostly Body Politic," p. 104, and *Rise and Fall of Democracy,* p. 113; and Stourzh, *Alexander Hamilton,* pp. 52–53.

[148]See Palmer, "Liberties as Constitutional Provisions," pp. 87–88, for his persuasive case that "the United States Constitution was little concerned with individual liberties"; and Hutson, "Riddles of the Federal Constitutional Convention," p. 420, who notes that historians, unlike political scientists, have been skeptical as to how accurate a map *The Federalist* is of the Constitution.

[149]Greven, *Protestant Temperament,* p. 359.

[150]See W. E. Nelson, *Americanization of the Common Law,* pp. 109–10.

[151]J. Madison, "Federalist No. 10," in Hamilton, Jay, and Madison, *Federalist,* p. 58.

proposed Constitution do?" He answered that it changes their government from "a well-digested, well-formed democratic [one] . . . into an aristocratic government." He demanded to know "what have you been contending for these ten years past? Liberty! What is Liberty? The power of governing yourselves. If you adopt this Constitution, have you this power?" He responded emphatically, "No."[152] However, he was wrong. For much of the next century the individualistic protections sought by Madison, and feared by Lincoln, were not enforceable except possibly at the harmless and largely deserted level of the federal government.[153] The states continued for at least another century to police their citizens' morals, in effect constraining and shaping their citizens' inner selves.[154]

This incomplete transformation in America was part of a broader phenomenon; "the development of the conception of individualism" at the end of the 18th century "coincided in time with the disappearance of [active] political liberty" on a much broader European horizon.[155] But again, below the elite national level, Americans long remained hostile to many aspects of social and political individualism. Only a few decades ago there was "a wholesale extension of federal standards of tolerance into local communities, to the immense relief of suffering minorities, but not without determined resistance from local majorities." It must not be ignored, then, that until at least the middle of the 20th century, it was "local and state governments," the most democratic elements of the federal system, that were "responsible for the most grievous repression of minorities and effective denials of due process" to nonconforming individuals.[156] This alone offers testimony to the historic weakness of the individualist vision in America.

The history of democracy and individualism in America evidences two quite separate, often antagonistic, lineages. America, by the close of the 18th century, had in several ways become a divided nation: one more democratic, agrarian, rural, evangelical Protestant, local, and popular; the other more individualistic, commercial, urban, secular or refined in religiosity, national, and elite. Most late 18th-century progressive elites, however, were born and raised before this bifurcation had fully developed. Those raised in America were thus necessarily shaped by a localistic, agrar-

---

[152]Lincoln, "Speech" (18 January 1788), in Elliot, *Debates in the Several State Conventions,* 4:313.

[153]See Murrin, "Great Inversion," p. 428; Robert Nisbet, "Citizenship," p. 617; and Young, *Washington Community,* pp. 27–28, who writes that "the [national] government of Jeffersonian times was not, by any candid view, one of the important institutions in American society," for it was situated in "a society of preeminently provincial attachments."

[154]See Griffin, *Their Brothers' Keepers,* pp. 116–51, who reports that in many instances the state's moral policing of its citizens was actually increased in the early 19th century.

[155]Carlyle, *Political Liberty,* pp. 9–11.

[156]Conkin, "Freedom," p. 211.

ian, reformed-Protestant, and communal political environment.[157] More-over, they were forced to speak and write in public (regardless of what they may have thought and written in private) in the language common to all Americans, which was at once Protestant, public centered, and commu-nalistic.[158] Therefore, one must still apply the individualist label with cau-tion at the end of the century to even the most enthusiastic supporter of the new way of thinking about the individual.

Nevertheless, during the last decade of the 18th century, concern with individual rights and needs grew into the cornerstone of a new political vision that today dominates articulate social and political thought in the United States. From the older communalistic and the newer individualistic public philosophies, which Alan Heimert rigidly characterizes as "Calvin-ism and Liberalism," emerged markedly different evaluations of the just relation between public and private needs and rights.[159] They differed on a wide range of publicly determined moral issues. Among them were the preeminence to be awarded the public's needs over those of the individual, the protection of nonconforming individuals or ethnic or religious minor-ities, the best means of fostering human flourishing, and the appropriate-ness of public ethical intrusion into the self-regarding behavior of the indi-vidual.

Each of these two major patterns of thought, one communal and the other individualistic, is loosely identifiable with different groups of politi-cal, social, and religious actors who developed these ethical and political traditions during the last decade of the 18th century. Thomas Bender finds that the older one "was a localistic oral culture based upon intimate, face-to-face relations," while the newer one was "abstract, general, and based on the written word." The first "pattern of solidarity was popular," while the "other was based on a formal tradition in the custody of the elites."[160] It was the nationalist elite who spoke for and defended this second tradi-tion, an emerging secular individualist one, while the common people gen-erally continued to adhere to a changing but traditional version of Amer-ica's communal and reformed-Protestant public philosophy.

By the end of the century, then, there had occurred abrupt changes in the political thinking of some of the ex-Revolutionary elite nationalists.

---

[157]See Appleby, "Republicanism in Old and New Contexts," p. 31; and Zuckerman, *Peace-able Kingdoms*, p. 221.

[158]See Meyers, *Jacksonian Persuasion*, pp. 31–32, 121, 204–5; Wood, "Fundamentalists and the Constitution," pp. 37–38; and Pangle, *Spirit of Modern Republicanism*, p. 21, who also admits that the elite leadership "were in important respects influenced by Christianity," and "were compelled to speak and accommodate themselves to a Christian citizenry; all this is indisputable." This is what is being argued here. The private or secret concerns of a hand-ful of Americans are not addressed.

[159]See Heimert, "Towards the Republic," in Rutman, *Great Awakening*, p. 129.

[160]Bender, *Community and Social Change in America*, p. 77; see also Murrin, "Great Inver-sion," pp. 400–401.

Gordon Wood notes that their new individualist public philosophy emphasized "the protection of individual rights against all governmental encroachments" and that "the aim of republican government was no longer"
to ensure the protection of the common good, but instead "to provide for
the security of every individual, even against the will of the community."
He agrees that "these new ideas about private rights eventually came to
form the basis for the nineteenth century's conception of individualism."[161]
Wood, however, overstates the denigration by these new currents of thought
of the traditional value placed on the public good, and describes a wholesale transformation of America's communal political theory rather than
the addition to it of an important new way of viewing the individual.[162]

More accurately, when the national republic was born in 1787 it was
born politically, socially, and intellectually bifurcated, rather than simply
and uniformly transformed. America had divided along a cultural fault line
with one side more or less communal, traditional, derived from reformed-
Protestant thought and practices, "rooted in the habit and custom of local
control," and centered on "the majority and the community." The other
side of this divide, Lutz suggests, was less democratic, "more recent and
was derived from the formal and intellectual 'liberal' perspective" and
"was more attuned to progress, secularism, and individual freedom."[163]
Yet this new view of the individual as autonomous that came to be associated with the most ardent defenders of the federal Constitution began to
mature only during the early national period. Its ability to structure political thought and institutions in the late 18th century was still underde-
veloped. Nevertheless, when America emerged from the 18th century it
had two traditions of viewing the individual, his or her development, and
that space of choice around him or her; each tradition was "founded on its
own set of premises and rooted in its own historic and social context."[164]
Wood is correct, then, when he argues that "it was the formation of the
Constitution, not the Declaration of Independence, that laid the basis for
our modern conception of personal freedom."[165] Emergence of the individualistic perspective thus occurred in the early national rather than the Revolutionary (or any earlier) period in American history.

In a broader comparative perspective, these two contrasting ethical vi-

---

[161]Wood, "Freedom and the Constitution," p. 52; see also Gross, *Minutemen and Their
World*, p. 190; and Lockridge, "Social Change," p. 436.

[162]See Wood, *Radicalism of the American Revolution*, pp. 367–68, who now finds that the
changes were both radical and reactionary. He writes that America "was not progressing, but
seemed to be going backward. The people were more religious, more sectarian, and less
rational than they had been at the time of the Revolution."

[163]Lutz, *Popular Consent and Popular Control*, p. 171; see also Wolin, *Presence of the
Past*, pp. 86–87; Shalhope, *John Taylor of Caroline*, p. 192; and Martin, "Long and the
Short of It," p. 110.

[164]Roche, "American Liberty," p. 161.

[165]Wood, "Freedom and the Constitution," p. 45; see also Wolin, *Presence of the Past*, p.
128.

sions were not unique to the American experience, but instead paralleled broader trends in modern Western political thought.[166] Describing the monarchical vision that Publius was to adapt to the exigencies of popular government, Montesquieu wrote that in those modern governments unconcerned with virtue, either public or private, "art has reduced the number of movements, springs, and wheels," and "the state subsists independently of the love of our country, of the thirst of true glory, of self-denial, of the sacrifice of our dearest interests, and of all those heroic virtues which we admire in the ancients, and to us are known only by tradition. The laws supply here the place of those virtues; they are by no means wanted."[167] William Sullivan adds that "since the Enlightenment, Western political and social thought has struggled with two conflicting visions of the kind of society that ought to replace the old regime." The individualistic one "projected instrumental organization and formal contract as its ideal of social life," while the communal one insisted that social life must be "lived meaningfully for ends beyond power and the satisfaction of private desire."[168] One must be careful, however, not to exaggerate the absence of a commitment to the public good by Americans moved by the more mechanical vision.

What was rejected by some members of the American elite was not the priority of the public good, nor even the utility of virtuous leadership, but instead the necessity and propriety of communally determined individual ethical ends.[169] They reintroduced and popularized in America the largely institutionalist, heretofore monarchical, perspective. As one critical pastor observed in 1801, it was indeed the national elite, "those in the highest places of power," who had become "apostatized from the religion of their countrymen" and were the most corrupt and infatuated with new currents of individualistic and progressive thought. He believed that this was exposing the majority of Christian Americans to "the greatest danger."[170] Yet Americans from the 1790s to the early 20th century were able to sustain both traditions simultaneously at different levels of government—the ethically restrictive and demanding familial and communalist approach at the local level, and the morally more accommodating institutional and individualist one at the often vacant national level. (State governments have been a contested middle ground that have not adequately served either vision.)

By the early 19th century, though, the communal traditions of discourse of the Revolutionary era had lost much of their former legitimacy. As Daniel Rogers notes, the supporters of early 19th-century majoritarian democracy already had difficulty articulating and defending a politics of communally

---

[166]See Skinner, *Foundations of Modern Political Thought*, 1:44–45.

[167]Montesquieu, *Spirit of the Laws* (1748), 1:23.

[168]Sullivan, *Reconstructing Public Philosophy*, pp. 91–92; and see Hunter, *Culture Wars*, p. 132 for evidence of the continuation of this split.

[169]See Lutz, *Popular Consent and Popular Control*, p. 210.

[170]Emmons, *Discourse Delivered on the Annual Fast* (1801), p. 21.

shaped individual morals. As the articulate elite embraced individualism in a complex and uneven fashion (particularly in the South),[171] the needed conceptual vocabulary was increasingly lacking.[172] In America, it became the unsought responsibility of the inarticulate residents of small towns and urban ethnic neighborhoods to sustain communally based ethics and political thought.

In so doing, they continued to adhere to those views of the individual that had guided 18th-century America and much of Western civilization for the previous two millennia. As Alasdair MacIntyre has discovered, in 20th-century America, communal ethical traditions best survive in the lives of those whose ties to their historic communities remain powerful. In particular, this is true of some ethnic communities that have inherited "their moral tradition not only through their religion, but also from the structure of the peasant villages and households which their immediate ancestors inhabited on the margins of modern Europe."[173]

It is in a vitiated fashion, however, that some lower-middle-class Americans continue to adhere to communalistic views of the individual, a fashion marked by provincialism; ethnic, racial, and religious intolerance; and a lack of respect for "deviant" individuals. But in spite of such evident flaws and the dangers they represent, this "highly flourishing archaic political culture" is one that deserves attention from divergent perspectives. The scholar and activist Sheldon Wolin explains that this democratic, participatory, and localist political culture is the only available alternative to an ever-expanding statism, with its own considerable dangers.[174] Indeed, some working- and lower-middle-class Americans' sense of the good life is still compatible with an understanding of public life, both social and political, as an ethical project best fulfilled through familial, democratic, and social structuring, promoting, and limiting of each member's uniquely human telos.[175]

[171]See May, *Enlightenment in America,* p. 327.

[172]See Rodgers, *Contested Truths,* p. 223. Some commentators believe that this problem has become more acute in the 20th century, particularly because the lived patterns of American local communalism have come under attack and popular access to communal public philosophies is wanting, as noted by Bellah et al., *Habits of the Heart;* McWilliams, "Democracy and the Citizen," pp. 95–96; and Sandel, "Democrats and Community."

[173]MacIntyre, *After Virtue,* p. 252.

[174]See Wolin, *Presence of the Past,* p. 81.

[175]See Rieder, *Canarsie,* p. 167; and Marsden, "Great Divide," p. 288.

PART TWO

The Meaning of Liberty in the

Revolutionary Era

CONSISTENT with most Americans' hostility toward the emerging tenets of political individualism, liberty was understood by them to be a socially directed and, preferably, individually imposed control over the most common source of arbitrariness, the individual "self." As Moses Hemmenway, the long-serving and highly regarded pastor of Wells, Massachusetts, explained, "liberty ought not to be used for an occasion to the flesh, or a pretense for carnal and licentious indulgences." Thus, even when socially constrained, no one had "any reason to complain that he is denied the liberty of a free citizen, when he is restrained by human laws and penalties, from vice and immorality."[1] Hanna Pitkin has shown that this understanding of liberty was historically the norm. It was congruent with a traditional Western understanding of liberty that incorporated "the absence of (some particular) constraint" while also denoting "the continuation of a surrounding network of restraint and order."[2] In America, liberty and submission to a regime of righteousness, not of license, were nearly synonymous.[3] In this section, I examine that era's political theory and its understanding of the just relationships among the individual, the community, and God. I explore the meanings given to their most important political concept, liberty, particularly those meanings that add the most to our understanding of their political theory.

Rather than budding individualists, Americans were reformed-Protestant communalists who viewed the universe as an ordered cosmos. Thus, the results of an examination of their central political concept corroborate the findings of the broader-based focus of part 1.

Chapter 5 sets the stage for an examination of various 18th-century meanings of liberty. Contemporary definitions of liberty share certain features with their 18th-century antecedents. But when the substance of the 18th-century connotations is examined, it becomes apparent that the two sets of meaning are, in fact, distinct. I also present here an introductory typology of the different meanings of liberty available in 18th-century America. Eight different meanings of liberty can be teased out of Revolutionary-era texts, only one of which can be readily associated with individualism. Finally, I discuss personal independence in chapter 5 because, like liberty in general, it too has frequently been confused with more individualistic senses of liberty.

In chapter 6, I describe one of the most important 18th-century senses of liberty, spiritual liberty, and show how it defined the American essence of

---

[1] Hemmenway, *Massachusetts Election Sermon* (1784), pp. 9, 23.
[2] Pitkin, "Are Freedom and Liberty Twins?," pp. 28–29 (draft version). She offers convincing evidence that the 18th-century meaning described here did accord with its traditional one.
[3] See Kammen, *Spheres of Liberty*, p. 83.

liberty: a socially mediated, voluntary acceptance of a life of righteousness. The Protestant character and origin of American social and political thought are emphasized, along with the centrality of the Christian dogma of original sin. This important dogma continued to shape Americans' political thought even after they no longer felt so compelled to serve God corporately as they had in the 17th and early 18th centuries.

The other significant understandings of liberty, corporate ones that were descriptive of a people taken as an aggregate, are discussed in chapter 7. In particular, that chapter describes the kind of political liberty that was sought and embraced by Americans. Most Americans' understanding of political liberty was influenced but not primarily shaped by the republican sense of the concept. Americans showed little interest in direct democracy, and yet were nevertheless deeply committed to jury trials and the right to political representation. This sense of political liberty, which is most readily associated with their English political inheritance, was so important to Revolutionary-era Americans that it became one of only two rights regularly claimed as inalienable (the other being the right of religious conscience). Finally, civil liberty is examined and shown to have had a corporate focus and to have shared little with the contemporary individualistic sense of liberty. Indeed, civil liberty did not define those personal exemptions that today the individual cannot be asked to surrender, but instead described the residue of natural liberty that society allowed the individual to retain.

The last chapter addresses the concept of slavery. It defined the absence of liberty, and thus adds much to the understanding of liberty, and more generally, to the understanding of 18th-century American political thought. Slavery was a concept that described much more than chattel enslavement, for it was used broadly to characterize a state of political, private, and moral dependence. In opposition to true liberty, it defined a state of license that described the condition of one outside the coercive boundaries of community. In sum, outside the confining walls of community, whether in a condition of what is now called freedom or what is now called slavery, liberty was impossible to achieve. At least this is what late 18th-century Americans claimed. Communalism was for them, thus, not just a preferred path to liberty, but the only one.

A Delusive Similarity:
(Ordered) Liberty and Freedom

The republican concept of liberty was Christian too: *"Cui servire est regnare,"* says the prayer about God, or as the English version has it, "whom to serve is perfect freedom," and what the Christian said about God the republican says of the republic.

—Alasdair MacIntyre, *After Virtue*

RARELY ARE contemporaries, or the scholars who give voice to their long-dead thoughts and sentiments,[1] unanimous in their estimation of the importance awarded by a people to a particular concept. Yet all agree that Revolutionary-era Americans were deeply committed to the concept of liberty.[2] As the distinguished 18th-century British statesman Edmund Burke noted, "a love of freedom is the predominating feature which marks and distinguishes" Americans, for "this fierce spirit of liberty is stronger in the English colonies probably than in any other people of the earth."[3] It is difficult to examine the written record of 18th-century America without coming to such a conclusion.

Take, for example, the urgings of the Canterbury, Connecticut, pastor James Cogswell: "liberty is one of the most sacred and inviolable Privileges Mankind enjoy; without it Life itself is insipid and many Times burdensome."[4] Twenty years later, during the Revolution, comparable references were frequently made to the centrality of liberty. As a Loyalist critic remarked, Americans "have been often told that Liberty is a very great Blessing; they talk incessantly of it, they find something inchanting in the very Sound of the Word."[5]

---

[1] See Callcott, *History in the United States*, p. 187.
[2] See Reid, *Constitutional History of the American Revolution: The Authority to Tax*, p. 9.
[3] Edmund Burke, "[First] Speech on American Conciliation" (22 March 1775), in *On the American Revolution*, p. 82.
[4] Cogswell, *God the Pious Soldier's Strength and Instructor* (1757), cited by Hatch, *Sacred Cause of Liberty*, p. 21.
[5] [Boucher], *Letter From a Virginian* (1774), p. 6.

Later still, at the beginning of the early national period, the quintessen-tial defender of American liberty Patrick Henry described the American vision of an empire of liberty. It was for him "a world reshaped in truly moral order, which lay at the heart of both the revolutionary evangelical and revolutionary patriot movements."[6] He warned the delegates to the Virginia ratifying convention: "you are not to inquire how your trade may be increased," but rather "how your liberties can be secured; for liberty ought to be the direct end of your government. . . . Liberty, the greatest of all earthly blessings—give us that precious jewel, and you may take every thing else!"[7] Likewise, with some bitterness, Boston's Sam Adams looked back on his youth and remembered that liberty was the goal for which Americans had been willing to sacrifice all.[8] And a disappointed Dr. Ben-jamin Rush, questioning the intentions of his fellow Americans, recalled that "liberty is the object and life of all republican governments."[9]

An examination of English sources popular in America, such as the Brit-ish Cato, reveals few Americans who would have disagreed with his assess-ment of the worth of liberty. Unlike Cato's numerous English critics, even those Americans who took umbrage at his secular and libertarian language did not challenge the importance he awarded liberty.[10] He, for example, asked (in letter 25) how "can we ever over-rate it [liberty], or be too jealous of a Treasure which includes in it almost all Human Felicities? . . . It is the Parent of Virtue, Pleasure, Plenty, and Security."[11] Later in the century, Dr. Price, an even more respected and popular dissident author,[12] wrote of liberty that "there is not a word in the whole compass of lan-guage which expresses so much of what is important and excellent."[13] Lib-erty, whatever it meant, was clearly a blessing and the foundation of popu-lar forms of government.

Of the scholars who have written recently on the theme of liberty in the

[6]Isaac, "Preachers and Patriots," p. 154.

[7]Henry, "Speech Against the Federal Constitution," p. 8. Henry was adamant in his refusal to associate himself in any way with what he considered to be an illegitimate government, the national government, declining to serve as United States senator, secretary of state, or chief justice of the United States Supreme Court.

[8]See S. Adams, Writings of Samuel Adams, 4:342.

[9]Rush, "Thoughts Upon the Mode of Education" (1786), p. 681.

[10]According to Jacobson, English Libertarian Heritage, p. xxx, "Cato" (Trenchard and Gordon), in spite of their popularity among American and pedestrian English audiences, enjoyed no such following among the sophisticated English reading public. For example, see J. Brown, Thoughts on Civil Liberty (1765), pp. 18–19, who comments on the libertarian rhetoric found in letter 62 thus: "these Expressions are crude, inaccurate, and ambiguous; leaving the thoughtful Reader at a Loss for the Author's precise and determined Meaning."

[11]Thomas Gordon, "Cato's Letter #25" (10 June 1721), in Jacobson, English Libertarian Heritage, p. 70.

[12]See W. Morgan, Life of the Rev. Richard Price, pp. 62–63, 105, and Peach, Richard Price, pp. 9–11.

[13]Price, Observations (1776), p. 5.

Anglo-American world, none substantially disagrees with Nathan Hatch, who finds that "ministers of varying theological persuasion came to do homage at the same shrine, that of liberty." In both religion and politics, "the advance of mankind was measured by one simple gauge: the comparative success or failure of liberty."[14] Gordon Wood concurs and notes that liberty was the most commonly invoked political concept in Revolutionary America, with the public good being the next most common.[15] According to Forrest McDonald, during the twenty years between 1765 and 1785, "American political discourse was an ongoing public forum on the meaning of liberty."[16] In fact, due to the consensus regarding the importance of liberty, the debate has come to focus on minor concerns.

Joyce Appleby, for example, takes issue with Hatch's depiction of liberty as a simple gauge. Like others, she understands that "no other political ideal was invoked more often in the Anglo-American world than that of liberty, yet its meaning was far from precise."[17] Clinton Rossiter, writing in the 1950s, found that liberty was always the central motive that urged people to immigrate to America and that "liberty, in one guise or another, was the aspiration of most men and the characteristic of most currents of thought that moved westward to America."[18] Michael Kammen, writing some thirty years later, challenged this characterization and argued instead that Americans only "became obsessed by it during the course of the eighteenth" century. Yet he too recognized that during the Revolutionary period that extended from 1765 to 1785, liberty was the most frequently invoked concept.[19]

Regardless of when exactly Americans first became obsessed with it, liberty was one of the most important social, political, and ethical concerns of Revolutionary-era Americans. The central undertaking that historians have left us to accomplish, then, is to decipher its various meanings as we map out the political theory of the greater Founding era. As John Gray notes, "there is a conception of liberty at the heart of every well-developed political theory in the modern Western tradition," but it is more puzzling and more difficult to discover "what is this liberty."[20] In this case, it will be all the more trying to uncover because during the past half-century, liberty's meaning has greatly changed and the history of the concept has come to be manipulated in multiple ways.

[14]Hatch, *Sacred Cause of Liberty*, pp. 22–23, 72.
[15]See Wood, *Creation of the American Republic*, p. 55.
[16]McDonald, *Novus Ordo Seclorum*, p. 10.
[17]Appleby, *Capitalism and a New Social Order*, p. 22.
[18]Rossiter, *Seedtime of the Republic*, p. 191.
[19]See Kammen, *Spheres of Liberty*, p. 17.
[20]Gray, introduction to Pelezynski and Gray, *Conceptions of Liberty in Political Philosophy*, p. 1.

The 18th-Century Understanding of Liberty:
Substance over Form

It is widely believed that 20th-century Americans are still devoted to liberty. For example, Everett Carll Ladd reports that when asked what they were most proud of about America, more than two-thirds of Americans responded "'our freedom,' or 'liberty,' or some variant." From this he concludes that "*individual freedom* is the most insistent claim of classical liberalism—and it is the proudest claim of Americans."[21] Introductory college textbooks in political science and American history also help modern American young people feel comfortable with their past by regularly reporting that the Revolutionary period's foundational belief was that "the purpose of government was to maximize the liberty of the individual."[22] Such accounts suggest that a continuity exists between Revolutionary Americans and their 20th-century descendants in regard to their love of individual liberty. But perhaps Abraham Lincoln was correct when he remarked, "we all declare for liberty; but in using the same *word* we do not all mean the same *thing*."[23] Lincoln's cautionary note is one worth heeding, especially when moving between the 18th and 20th centuries.

The constellation of ideas attached to the contemporary understanding of liberty inevitably shapes our perception and investigation of the 18th-century concept; this pushes us toward adopting Ladd's assessment. Only with difficulty can one avoid attaching anachronistic meanings to 18th-century language that uses common 20th-century terms. Thus, a contemporary (and less obviously a comparative historical) framework of understanding is thrust upon the modern student of liberty.[24] Such linguistic and analytic obstacles must, however, not allow a lazy acceptance of an equivalence between the two centuries' understandings of liberty. Yet many scholars, especially those in political and legal studies, seem to have done as much. It is commonly asserted, for example, that "the animating idea of the American Founding was individual liberty" or that during the period preceding the Revolution, "the world view of liberal individualism was fast pushing aside older paradigms." It is further insisted that "with respect to political values, the evidence overwhelmingly suggests a high level of continuity"; that is, even if "ideals such as liberty and equality acquire different meanings through their application in new contexts, the core meaning of the value remains."[25] In sum, commentators and respected

[21]E.C. Ladd, "205 and Going Strong," p. 10.

[22]Baradat, *Understanding American Democracy,* pp. 6, 3–14; more generally, see Sheridan, "Republican Revision."

[23]Lincoln, "Address at Sanitary Fair, Baltimore" (1864), in *Collected Works of Abraham Lincoln,* 7:301.

[24]See Skinner, *Foundations of Modern Political Thought,* 1:xi.

[25]D. Himmelfarb, "Freedom, Virtue, and the Founding Fathers," p. 117; Krammick, *Republicanism and Bourgeois Radicalism,* p. 198; S. Huntington, *American Politics,* p. 23. See

scholars too readily assign 20th-century individualist meanings to the critical political vocabulary found in 18th-century documents.[26]

This willingness of students of politics to ascribe anachronistic meanings to important 18th-century moral and political terms continues even though abundant evidence has become available during the past three decades that warns against such proleptic abuses.[27] One scholar, for instance, writing for a political-science audience, warns that "there has been something of a revolution in the historiography of the founding of the American Republic," yet "many scholars have failed fully to understand either the causes of the founding of the American political system or the philosophic meaning of the critical documents."[28] Without appropriate consideration of the differences in the meanings of concepts, we are incapable of understanding, for example, Blackstone's "legal theory because the vocabulary of liberty has so changed that we read his words—'liberty,' 'freedom,' 'licentiousness'—and attach to those words our meanings, not his meanings."[29] Indeed, anachronistic readings will regularly be challenged only when it becomes still clearer that present-day normative concepts, such as liberty, are not equivalent in substantive meaning to those held by late 18th-century Americans. Given that the two centuries' different conceptions of liberty are ultimately rooted in and shaped by contrasting notions of nature and the cosmos, and (as is becoming clear) different theories of the good, little else should be expected.[30]

The assumption of unchanging meaning for the same political or moral concept used in substantially different historical periods should always be received with suspicion. Even if the concept describes the same phenomenon in different eras, it will carry connotations shaped by the surrounding ideational world. And if these worlds are different, the concept when used will be effectively changed. Quentin Skinner, in his influential work in the history of ideas, has argued that "political texts must be understood according to their author's intentions and that those intentions can only be recovered by close attention to the linguistic conventions of the time."[31] In the instance before us, the basic meaning of liberty has changed over the past two centuries, and the epistemic and ontological framing of the concept has been transformed even more. Consequently, the similarities in the formal definitions of liberty in both periods are of limited help in telling us what liberty actually signifies in each period. The observed continuity in

---

most recently E. Schwartz, "Chorus of Moral Voices," p. 10; and Whitehead, "Dan Quayle Was Right," pp. 83–84. For additional references, see the introduction.

[26]See Tucker, *Protean Shape*, p. 8, and McDonald, "Conservative Scholarship," pp. 61–63.
[27]See Skinner, "Meaning and Understanding," pp. 22ff.
[28]Matthews, "Liberalism," p. 1128.
[29]Reid, *Concept of Liberty*, pp. 116–17.
[30]See D. Miller, "Resurgence of Political Theory," pp. 425–26.
[31]As described by K. Thomas, "Politics Recaptured," p. 26; see also Handlin and Handlin, "Who Read John Locke?" p. 556.

some of the formal meanings of liberty masks fundamental differences in the substantive meanings in separate worlds of understanding.[32]

Is the substantive meaning of liberty in one century comparable to that in the other? As Ola Winslow observed of liberty at the close of the 18th century, "it was the word of the hour," yet one that even by then had changed, as "lifetime by lifetime it had appeared in new contexts and with new connotations."[33] None of the minor changes in the 18th century, however, can compare with the more fundamental ones in the elite understanding of liberty that occurred early in the next century (to say nothing of those to occur in the middle of the 20th century). The distance between the 18th-century meanings of liberty and today's "either 'individualistic' or 'permissive'" ones are too great; the concept cannot be accepted as the same across the expanse of America's past two centuries of history.[34]

When examined in a cursory fashion, some of the 18th-century formal (denotative) meanings of liberty do look familiar. For instance, early 18th-century English dictionaries (there were no American dictionaries until late in the century)[35] offer as the basic sense of liberty one that has not changed formally in at least three centuries. Writing in 1708, John Kersey defined liberty as "freedom, Leave or Free-Leave," and N. Bailey, in his *Universal Etymological English Dictionary,* printed in 1737, described liberty as "a being free from obligation, servitude, or constraint."[36] At midcentury, Thomas Dyche supplied several definitions of liberty, one of which sounds particularly modern: "liberty in *common Speech,* is freedom of doing anything that is agreeable to a person's disposition, without the controul of another."[37] The 1773 edition of the *Encyclopaedia Britannica* defines liberty simply as "a state of freedom, in contradiction to slavery."[38] The legal historian Charles Warren noted that liberty's meaning later in the century, in 1789, continued to be "freedom from physical restraint of the person."[39] And liberty understood in this latter sense as freedom from physical restraint has been preserved, as evidenced in Webster's current definition of liberty as "the quality or state of being free: freedom from usu. external restraint or compulsion."[40] This first formal meaning of liberty thus ap-

---

[32]See Lutz, *Preface to American Political Theory,* p. 36; Dworetz, *Unvarnished Doctrine,* pp. 132–33; and Andrews, *Colonial Background of the American Revolution,* p. 179, who warns that unless one exercises great care "one is almost certain to read into words and phrases of our ancestors meanings that did not exist."

[33]Winslow, *Meeting House Hill,* pp. 249–50.

[34]Reid, *Concept of Liberty,* p. 2; see also Conkin, "Freedom," pp. 208–9.

[35]The first was W. Perry, *Royal Standard English Dictionary,* published by Isaiah Thomas in Worcester in 1788.

[36]Kersey, *Dictionarium Anglo-Britannicum* (1708); Bailey, *Universal Etymological English Dictionary* (1737); see also Coles, *English Dictionary* (1713).

[37]Dyche and Pardon, *New General English Dictionary* (1752).

[38]Dilly and Dilly, *Encyclopedia Brittanica.*

[39]C. Warren, "New 'Liberty' under the Fourteenth Amendment," p. 441.

[40]*Webster's Third New International Dictionary of the English Language,* unabridged ed.,

pears to be constant across almost three centuries. Yet all is not what it appears to be.

In longer narrative descriptions, the actual substantive 18th-century meaning of this definition of liberty is distinct from modern ones. This makes sense because of the different intellectual environments within which each century's meanings are embedded. In particular, the 18th-century understanding of liberty was framed by Anglo-American presuppositions of a rationally ordered and purposeful universe in which the central antithesis to liberty was licentiousness. And license described an indifference to the obligatory dictates of the true moral order.

For Revolutionary-era Americans, "PERFECT LIBERTY is the Latitude of voluntary Conduct informed by Reason, and limited by Duty." Moreover, liberty was the "image of Divinity which GOD impressed upon man."[41] As perceived by an anonymous New Englander two decades later, liberty was a rationally limited freedom that distinguished humans "from the inferior creatures," for "*absolutely to follow their own will and pleasures,* what is it, in true sense, but to follow their own corrupt inclinations, to give the reins to their lusts. . . . Are they whose character this is at *liberty?* So far from it, that instead of being *free,* they are *very slaves.*"[42] Thus, without God and a morally ordered universe, liberty would have been impossible to achieve. Liberty would have necessarily been inseparable from license.

The strict Christian or rational boundaries that framed the 18th-century sense of liberty offered only a narrow range of permissible behavior. And only within this circumscribed band is the first definition of liberty understandable, for only when thus restrained was "doing anything that is agreeable to a person's disposition" understood as liberty rather than license. For most 18th-century Americans, the "true freedom, allotted to man, is a freedom within bounds, and these bounds are marked and prescribed by his great Creator."[43] Again, if there were no God and no universally prescribed limits, then there could be no liberty.

The second meaning of liberty offered in 18th-century dictionaries, corporate exemptions and privileges from authoritative political demands and oversight, was medieval in origin, technical, and legal. In 1708, John Kersey defined liberty as not only freedom but as "a Privilege by which Men enjoy some Benefit or Favour beyond the ordinary Subject." In 1737, liberty was defined by Nathan Bailey as "a privilege by grant or prescription to enjoy some extraordinary benefit."[44] Later in the century, in the *British*

---

s.v. "liberty"; see also *Random House Dictionary of the English Language,* unabridged ed., s.v. "liberty," where it is defined as "freedom from control, interference, obligation, restriction, hampering conditions, etc."

[41][Brooke?], *Liberty and Common-Sense* (1759–60), letter 2, p. 6.

[42]S.M., "Letter to the Printer" (6 April 1778), p. 2.

[43][Serle], *Americans against Liberty* (1776), p. 8; see also "Virtue" (16 November 1747).

[44]Kersey, *Dictionarium Anglo-Brittanicum;* and Bailey, *Universal Etymological English Dictionary.*

Liberties of 1766, widely read on both sides of the Atlantic, Edward and Charles Dilly described liberties as "franchises and privileges which the subjects have of the gift of the king."[45] And in the 1773 *Encyclopaedia Britannica,* which the Dillys also edited, liberty "in a legal sense" continued to be "some privilege that is held by charter or prescription."[46] Liberty was "the state wherein a man acts freely," as well as "privilege, immunity, leave, permission."[47]

Nor should one be surprised by the widespread 18th-century acceptance of this understanding of liberty. As C. S. Lewis has shown, in European thought as a whole, liberty below the level of the sovereign state traditionally referred "to the guaranteed freedoms or immunities (from royal or baronial interference) of a corporate entity."[48] With regard to the most famous of such guarantees, the Magna Carta, Alan Harding finds that it was the last of many such medieval negotiated relationships and not the first bill of individual rights. He writes that it was "the greatest charter of territorial immunity and communal privilege rather than a bill of rights for individuals."[49] This rich tradition of legal development that defined one of the most prominent 18th-century meanings of liberty thus did not issue in individual rights, but rather in a charter of historically grounded corporate ones.

This fundamentally medieval and early modern corporate sense of liberty has disappeared from contemporary usage.[50] Drawing an important distinction between such liberties and the contemporary understanding of liberty, Friedrich Hayek explains that such "liberties appear only when liberty is lacking: they are the special privileges and exemptions that groups and individuals may acquire while the rest are more or less unfree."[51] As Harding and Frug have noted, in English history, liberties were exemptions won by a town or some other corporate group; they did not imply that the individual was likewise free from local interference.[52] This older sense of liberty therefore played an important role only before the modern sense of individual liberty had developed; it usually did not add to an individual's freedom from corporate restrictions.

In sum, according to the two most common 18th-century formal definitions of liberty, the substance of liberty was concerned with restricting

[45]Dilly and Dilly, *British Liberties,* p. 27.

[46]Dilly and Dilly, *Encyclopaedia Brittanica.*

[47]Dyche and Pardon, *New General English Dictionary* (1752); see also Cole, *They Preached Liberty,* pp. 126–33.

[48]C.S. Lewis, *Studies in Words,* p. 124; see also Pitkin, "Are Freedom and Liberty Twins?" p. 22 (draft version); Harding, "Political Liberty in the Middle Ages," pp. 424, 430; and Laski, "Liberty," p. 442.

[49]Harding, "Political Liberty in the Middle Ages," p. 434.

[50]See Lederer, *Colonial American English,* p. 135.

[51]Hayek, *Constitution of Liberty,* p. 19.

[52]See Frug, "City as a Legal Concept," pp. 1086–87; see also Harding, "Political Liberty in the Middle Ages."

permissible human behavior to a relatively narrow range. It described voluntary submission to rules of behavior constrained by slender boundaries of corporate-serving divine or natural law, or it was a political gift to a designated corporation offering a provisional exemption from authoritative and hierarchical governmental controls that did nothing to free the individual from frequently onerous local communal controls. In both instances, it was an opportunity for individual self-regulation or corporate regulation of the individual in the service of God or the public good. Liberty as individual autonomy or self-creation was not described, or even hinted at, in these definitions.

A third common meaning contained in 18th-century dictionaries, the liberty of conscience, however, appears to be a more promising candidate for an individualistic sense of liberty. It may offer the sought-after continuity of meaning that the two definitions previously discussed fail to provide. In 1737, Bailey described "liberty [of conscience as] a right or power of making profession of any religion a man sincerely believes."[53] This new sense of liberty was an innovative exemption from the norms established under medieval Christianity. In England and on the Continent, liberty was hesitantly granted by sovereigns confronting violence and civil unrest that had been stirred by their attempt to impose confessional uniformity on recalcitrant or deeply divided populations. But by the late 18th century, as Perry Miller ungenerously described the situation, "the upper or the educated classes were tired of the religious squabbling of the seventeenth century, and turned to the more pleasing and not at all contentious generalities of eighteenth-century rationalism."[54]

This 18th-century freedom of religious conscience had not been part of the original theologies of either of the two major Protestant confessions. As Ernst Troeltsch showed, "the applicability of religious standards to the whole body, the exclusion or, at least, disenfranchisement of unbelievers and heretics, [and] the principle of intolerance and infallibility, are for it [Protestantism] also self-evident necessities."[55] Nevertheless, by the beginning of the Revolutionary era, the freedom of religious conscience, one of only two truly inalienable rights (the other being the corporate right of self-government), had become uncontested in America.

Here indeed, then, are "the roots of the old liberal theory of the inviolability of the inner personal life by the State, which was subsequently extended to more outward things." At first the idea had been religious; "later, it [became] secularized and overgrown by the rationalistic, skeptical, and utilitarian ideas of toleration."[56] In Revolutionary-era America, however, this understanding of liberty continued to be framed by re-

---

[53]Bailey, *Universal Etymological English Dictionary*, p. 1i.
[54]P. Miller, "Crisis and Americanization," p. 142.
[55]Troeltsch, *Protestantism and Progress*, p. 67.
[56]Ibid., p. 125.

formed-Protestant religiosity, and had not as yet metastasized much beyond its sacred foundations.

On inspection, however, this apparent continuity also proves illusive. The liberty of conscience no longer carries the heavy responsibilities formerly associated with the exercise of religious duties. No longer is this sense of liberty informed and defended by the search for divine moral precepts, so that one can with confidence "profess *a true faith* and . . . practice *a right mode of worship.*"[57] The modern freedom of conscience is applied to a wide range of pursuits, where any pretense of serving God or seeking moral truth would be inappropriate.[58] No longer does this understanding of liberty revolve around the most important concerns "of life, where whim and fancy have no place."[59] This richly Protestant 18th-century sense of freedom of religious conscience is no longer defended as a necessary reflection of our humanity by modern political theory.

In fact, today the liberty of religious conscience no longer even merits inclusion in dictionaries under the heading of liberty. This inalienable and absolute individual right continues, though, to provide legitimacy to other legally sanctioned individual freedoms. Such freedoms are usually described as civil liberties and defined as "inalienable liberties guaranteed to the individual by law and by custom; rights of thinking, speaking, and acting as one likes without interference or restraint."[60] But the 18th-century logic that had originally legitimated such inalienable rights is forgotten today. The question "why should the reason, conscience, or faith of the individual man be respected as inviolable?" is no longer asked. Nor is the probable answer of 18th-century Americans heard: that "the reason in man corresponds to and is part of the reason of the universe. To violate this principle in man is to transgress the universal law."[61] One should believe in a morally ordered universe to be convinced by such appeals to inalienable rights. Skeptics, doubters, atheists, and postmodernists need not apply.[62]

In short, the freedom of conscience or thought was for Americans a self-evident necessity only because of humans' spiritual essence and their "hope and intention of discovering truth" as a consequence of their freedom.[63] Yet its 20th-century descendant, freedom of expression, does not demand such an elevated moral end to legitimate it within a rationally defensible hierarchy of moral truths. Once again, then, the apparent similarity be-

---

[57] *Liberty: Civil and Religious* (1815), pp. 63–64.

[58] See Lippmann, "What Modern Liberty Means," p. 29.

[59] Canavan, *Freedom of Expression*, pp. 68–69.

[60] *Webster's New World Dictionary of the American Language*, 2d college ed., s.v. "civil liberties."

[61] Bainton, "Appeal to Reason," pp. 124–25.

[62] See Haskell, "Curious Persistence of Rights Talk."

[63] Lippmann, *Essays in the Public Philosophy*, pp. 97–98.

tween the 18th and 20th centuries' meanings of liberty dissipates when the moral emphasis of the 18th-century sense is brought to bear.

Finally, a fourth definition of liberty is found in 18th-century dictionaries: freedom from enslavement. This was another of liberty's traditional meanings,[64] but not one frequently employed early in the 18th century.[65] It became conspicuous, however, during the second half of the century and has remained so until the present.[66] With Samuel Johnson's 1766 *Dictionary of the English Language,* liberty became "freedom as opposed to slavery." Today, it still is defined as "freedom or release from slavery."[67] This sense is the one that has probably shown the greatest substantive continuity during the last two hundred years.

But slavery's meaning throughout the 18th century did not revolve solely around bondage in the sense of chattel enslavement. Its meaning reflected Americans' ethical thought, in which slavery was fundamentally a disordering of the soul in relation to God's or nature's moral structuring of a purposeful universe. If one were unable voluntarily to conform to the strictures of the divinely ordered cosmos—because of absolute bondage to another person or because of bondage to sin and Satan—one was a slave. Congruent with this traditional Western understanding, C. S. Lewis contrasts the idealized freedom of the "slave" and the ordered liberty of the "master" who leads a life of duty and responsibility where even recreation must be "deliberate, approved and allowed for."[68] The critical aspect here is the pervasive sense of self-imposed (though not defined) limits that liberty carried; these limits are absent from the traditional connotations of slavery as well as from the modern sense of liberty as personally defined autonomous freedom.

The restricted understanding of liberty so typical of the Revolutionary era is exemplified in an anonymous author's letter to a printer. He argues that "there is, without doubt such a thing as *liberty, free, and unconstrained liberty.* . . . As men are intelligent moral agents, they have no *liberty* as such, God had given them none, 'tis agreeable to their nature they should have none . . . but under the guidance and controul of *right*

[64]See Pitkin, "Are Freedom and Liberty Twins?" p. 20 (draft version).

[65]No specific mention is made of slavery in the definitions of liberty in Kersey, *Dictionarium Anglo-Britannicum* (1708); Bailey, *Universal Etymological English Dictionary* (1737); Coles, *English Dictionary* (1713); or Dyche and Pardon, *New General English Dictionary* (1752). However, in most dictionaries I consulted that were printed after 1775, it was a central meaning.

[66]See, for example, Dilly and Dilly, *Encyclopedia Brittanica* (1773), s.v. "liberty." The *Oxford English Dictionary* (1933), s.v. "liberty," has as its first definition "exemption or release from captivity, bondage, or slavery"; see also *Webster's New World Dictionary of the American Language,* s.v. "liberty."

[67]S.v. "liberty," in Samuel Johnson, *Dictionary of the English Language* (1766); *Webster's New World Dictionary of the American Language;* and Ash, *New and Complete Dictionary* (1775), who offers as his first definition "freedom as opposed to slavery."

[68]C. S. Lewis, *Studies in Words,* p. 128.

reason."[69] For Americans in 1775, "true Liberty, then is a liberty to do every thing that is right, and being restrained from doing any thing that is wrong. So far from our having a right to do every thing that we please, under a notion of liberty, liberty itself is limited and confined."[70] As later argued by the onetime president of Brown University, Union College, and the University of South Carolina, the real danger of the French Revolution was that its adherents wished "to change real liberty into licentiousness."[71] Until the end of the 18th century, this danger Americans had done well to contain.

Liberty as the antithesis of slavery was understood to be a sought-after voluntary submission to the moral ordering of the universe. In the present-day world, where confidence in such an ordered universe no longer exists among the most educated, neither liberty as freedom from slavery, nor slavery itself, can be understood in a fashion comparable to the way in which those terms were used in the 18th century. Revolutionary-era Americans' conception of an ordered and purposeful universe ensures, therefore, that there can be no continuity in the substantive meaning of liberty as the antithesis of slavery, beyond the merest shell of formal meaning. Today, slavery principally describes the organized use of chattel labor, and liberty is understood to be the freedom to do what one pleases, legitimated but unconstrained by a higher rational order.

By 18th-century lights, what is today described as liberty would have been seen as license. By those standards, contemporary meanings of liberty are devoid of defensible extrapersonal goals. Definitions not enmeshed in a broader historical context can offer only a limited understanding of 18th-century political concepts such as liberty, or more generally, of Protestant-inspired communal political theory.

EIGHTEENTH-CENTURY LIBERTY: AN INTRODUCTORY TYPOLOGY

The assured centrality of liberty in late 18th-century American political discourse, as well as the differences between the connotations attached to it, then and now, invites further consideration of the concept's full range of meaning. Surprisingly, to date only two scholars writing recently on the concept of liberty have broadly canvassed its meaning:[72] Joyce Appleby,

---

[69]S. M., "Letter to the Printer" (6 April 1778), p. 2.

[70]Boucher, "On Civil Liberty," p. 511.

[71]Maxcy, "Oration" (1799), p. 1047.

[72]Other modern scholars who have discussed the 18th-century American concept of liberty in book-length works include: Rossiter, *Seedtime of the Republic*, 1953; Handlin and Handlin, *Dimensions of Liberty*, 1966; Leder, *Liberty and Authority*, 1968; Hatch, *The Sacred Cause of Liberty*, 1977; H. T. Dickinson, *Liberty and Property*, 1977; W. P. Adams, *First American Constitutions*, 1980; Jaenicke, "American Ideas of Political Party," 1981; Gunn, *Beyond Liberty and Property*, 1983; Potter, *Liberty We Seek*, 1983; Kammen, *Spheres of*

who in nine sensitive and insightful pages explores the Anglo-American sense of the concept, and David Hackett Fischer, who offers as the central thesis of his magnum opus that "the interplay of four 'freedom ways' has created an expansive pluralism" in modern America.[73] Yet neither of these authors truly accepts the burden of exploring at length or in depth the full range of meanings that Americans in the late 18th century assigned to liberty.

This unusual scholarly lacuna accords with Lord Bryce's early 20th-century observation that "no one seems to have undertaken the task" of analyzing "the conception of liberty and the . . . various meanings which the term has borne at different times and in different countries." In the same vein, John Roche holds that "we have discovered little of what liberty has meant . . . to individual Americans or groups of Americans."[74] In this and the next two chapters, I will attempt to meet in part this challenge with regard to Americans living in the Revolutionary era.[75]

Each of these four authors has attempted to describe the American understanding of liberty and has produced contextual maps that, if not identical, nevertheless overlap. Roche describes two broad traditions of liberty that divide America into two peoples. Bryce, in a more detailed fashion, offers a fourfold division of liberty: civil, religious, political, and individual. His categories are reminiscent of John Mellen's much earlier tripartite description of natural or common liberty, political or civil liberty, and moral or religious liberty.[76] Mellen makes no mention of any form of liberty that is reserved for the autonomous individual. Appleby, however, believes that individual liberty was one of three kinds current in the late 18th century: personal or individual liberty, corporate or political liberty, and the liberties of secure possession. With one exception, her meanings of liberty are congruent with those offered by Bryce and Mellen as well as Jonathan Mayhew (discussed below) and Fischer. Unlike the others, how-

---

Liberty, 1986; Handlin and Handlin, *Liberty and Power*, 1986; Cooke, *American Tradition of Liberty*, 1986; G. B. Madison, *Logic of Liberty*, 1986; Jehlen, *American Incarnation*, 1986; J. R. Nelson, *Liberty and Property*, 1987; Nelson and Palmer, *Liberty and Community*, 1987; Reid, *Concept of Liberty*, 1988; Kramer, *Paine and Jefferson on Liberty*, 1988; Paul and Dickman, eds., *Liberty*, 1988; Webking, *American Revolution*, 1988; Kammen, *Sovereignty and Liberty*, 1988; Handlin and Handlin, *Liberty in Expansion*, 1989; Fischer, *Albion's Seed*, 1989; and Pahl, *Free Will and Political Liberty*, 1992.

[73]See Appleby, *Capitalism and a New Social Order*, and Fischer, *Albion's Seed*, p. 7. Fischer, however, devotes only twenty-eight of his nine hundred pages to developing and exploring his central thesis.

[74]Roche, "American Liberty," pp. 129–30; see also Kammen, *Spheres of Liberty*, pp. 163–69.

[75]See also Patterson, *Freedom*, who has accepted this challenge for the entire Western world across more than two thousand years of history.

[76]See Bryce, *Modern Democracies*, 1:51; and Mellen, *Great and Happy Doctrine of Liberty* (1795), pp. 11–18.

ever, she makes no mention of Christian or spiritual liberty, possibly the most fundamental American liberty.

Mayhew's and Fischer's listings have much in common with those described above, but both are more inclusive. In his 18th-century account, Mayhew includes Mellen's three senses of liberty (natural, civil, and religious) plus three additional ones, for a total of six types of liberty. The three not listed by Mellen are "Philosophical liberty, or freedom of choice & action. . . Gracious liberty, given in regeneration, and consisting in a will or disposition to do good, in opposition to the slavery of [sin]. [And] . . . Liberty, or freedom from the ceremonial [Mosaic] law."[77]

It is worth noting that philosophical liberty was rarely included in theological or political discussions of liberty because it was understood as being in the purview of philosophy. Additionally, Mayhew's gracious liberty and freedom from the ceremonial law were normally taken as twin aspects of spiritual or Christian liberty (distinct from religious liberty, which is better understood as a political exemption or a prescribed liberty). It is most significant that this theologically and politically progressive thinker, whom the young Paul Revere was reportedly whipped for having heard,[78] like Mellen thirty years later, did not bother to include personal liberty as a recognizable form of liberty. At the time, it was either not a legitimate form of civil liberty or not important enough to warrant mention. Only later historians such as Appleby (and she only grudgingly) have given it pride of place.

Fischer also has an extensive list. He suggests that Americans understood liberty through four regional subcultures, each with its own meaning of the term, with the exception of New England, where liberty was used in at "least four ways which ring strangely in a modern ear." According to Fischer, New Englanders understood liberty as public or political, Christian, individual, and civil. In Virginia, liberty took the form of "hegemonic freedom," and in the Delaware Valley, liberty primarily described something reciprocal. In the backcountry, liberty was natural or libertarian. Regarding the latter, however, Fischer notes in a perplexing fashion that this libertarian understanding "did not recognize the right of dissent or disagreement," and that within its geographical hegemony, "opposition was suppressed by force."[79] Although at times his discussion of these seven meanings of liberty is not so clear as one might wish, his impressive scholarship corroborates Bryce's and Appleby's assessments that at least three

---

[77]Mayhew, "Memorandum" (1765), p. 141.

[78]See Bailyn, "Introduction to Mayhew's *A Discourse Concerning Unlimited Submission*" (1750), in *Pamphlets of the American Revolution,* p. 205, who further reports that only two ministers could be found to attend his ordination; and Schneider, *History of American Philosophy,* p. 44, who cites the American Samuel Johnson describing him "as one of those 'loose thinkers who can scarcely be accounted better Christians than the Turks.'"

[79]Fischer, *Albion's Seed,* pp. 199, 781; see also pp. 7, 200–205, 410–18, 595–603, and 777–82.

quite different meanings of liberty were current in late 18th-century America.[80]

Building on these foundations, I find that in early Americans' writings, they assigned to liberty eight different meanings that cut across the various regions. They are: philosophical (freedom of the will), political, spiritual (or Christian), prescriptive, familial (economic independence or autonomy), natural, civil, and individualistic (modern individual autonomy). Because the length of my list is similar to Fischer's, it might be useful to begin by discussing our differences. However, because of its clarity and precision, Appleby's briefer discussion with its three well-delineated senses of liberty provides a more suitable basis of comparison.

She first draws attention to the great dissimilarity between the widely accepted senses of liberty current then and today. In particular, she argues that individual liberty, largely disparaged then, subsequently came to dominate contemporary thinking about liberty. Indeed, according to her, the "least familiar concept of liberty used then was the most common to us— that is, liberty as personal freedom." This is clearly true. With good reason she further finds that it was political liberty, the right of a corporate body (usually local) to be governed by its citizens, that dominated the secular thought of Americans, and that "before the Revolution liberty more often referred to a corporate body's right of self determination. Within countless communities the ambit of [personal] freedom might well be circumscribed, yet men would speak of sacrificing their lives for liberty—the liberty of the group to have local control."[81]

This most important American secular and corporate understanding of liberty can be reduced to two concerns: the citizen's right of political self-determination and a community's autonomy. As described by an anonymous English pamphleteer, Americans "obey no laws but their own, or in other words they obey no will but their own, and this is the summit of political freedom." For them, he held, "freedom consists in not being sub-

---

[80]One might also consider Patterson, *Freedom*, pp. 3–4, who offers his own tripartite division of personal, sovereign, and civic freedoms. Although personal and civic liberty are readily understandable in terms of the above lists (as well as mine below) as individual and political liberty, his understanding of sovereign freedom is harder to place in the early modern period—not because it is entirely absent, but rather because it seems to have been part of their understanding of spiritual and corporate (particularly, localist political) liberty, albeit only in greatly weakened forms. Moreover, I have trouble seeing the Nazi Germans, for example, as an exemplar of this form of liberty, without recourse to Christianity or some other universalistic doctrine. I wonder if either chattel slavery or the slaughter of Native Americans was ever defended by 18th-century European Americans on what Patterson might take to be purely sovereign grounds? That kind of corporate hubris and callousness, as such, seems to have been out of fashion in the early modern period. See also pp. 219–20, where Patterson notes that Jochen Bleicken has found that the Romans employed *libertas* in ten different ways.

[81]Appleby, *Capitalism and a New Social Order*, p. 16.

jected to the will and power of another [people]."[82] But Friedrich Hayek reminds us that political liberty describes "the participation of men in the choice of their government . . . a sort of collective liberty," and that "a free people in this sense is not necessarily a people of free men."[83] That is, they are not free as understood by contemporary standards of individual liberty.

For Americans, this corporate liberty was not one of existential self-definition or license, but "a freedom of acting and speaking what is right, a freedom founded in reason, happiness, and security. All licentious freedom, called by whatever specious name, is a savage principle of speaking and doing what a depraved individual thinks fit."[84] An anonymous author also held in 1776, "to be free from coercion is a privilege which no man has a right to enjoy. The wild beasts for whom it is best calculated, may perhaps have some right to such liberty, but man can have none. The truest and most complete freedom that man can enjoy, and which best becomes rational creatures who are accountable for their actions, is the liberty to do all the good in his power." In fact, he continues, "if any citizen were at liberty to do what he pleased, this would be the extinction of liberty."[85] Such views of the delimited and ordered character of liberty accord well with the generalized preference Americans awarded to the immediate needs of the public over those of the individual. And it was just such corporate political institutions that "however opposed they might be to personal liberty [had] . . . served to keep alive the love of freedom."[86]

Political liberty, even if guided by narrow standards of propriety, was not without its ambiguities. The inherently equivocal character of political liberty in the new world of nation-states allowed both sides in the first war for decolonization, the American War of Independence, to legitimate their positions. In one of the last wars against feudal particularism, the American Civil War,[87] the ambiguity continued. During the former, political liberty, understood primarily as local self-government and secondarily as an emerging sense of nationalism,[88] supported forces opposed to increased imperial and parliamentary sovereignty. Soon thereafter, the right to political liberty was invoked by each of these forces, to defend and legitimate its own position against the other.[89] In the Civil War, each side argued that it

---

[82]*Prospect of the Consequences* (1776), pp. 14–15. This argument was most prominently rehearsed in the Declaration of Independence.

[83]Hayek, *Constitution of Liberty*, p. 13.

[84][Serle], *Americans against Liberty* (1776), p. 19.

[85]*Licentiousness Unmask'd* (1776), p. 19.

[86]Tocqueville, *Democracy in America* (1835), 1:338.

[87]See Lipset, *First New Nation*, p. 2; and Moore, *Social Origins of Dictatorship and Democracy*, pp. 111–59.

[88]See Merritt, *Symbols of American Community*, on the emerging consciousness of American nationalism.

[89]See Hamilton, "Remarks and Speeches at the New York Ratifying Convention" (1788),

represented the truly legitimate majority. Southerners (like their Patriot forebears) held that the rump national state was a usurping and intrusive tyranny, whereas the North held (as had the imperial British government of the Patriots) that the South was a selfish, idiosyncratic, and particularistic political fragment. The continuous tension between local communalism and various forms of supralocalism provided a fertile ground for an American history of dispute rather than of consensus regarding the most appropriate way to understand political liberty.

This level of contention was produced without even considering the additional difficulties suggested by several competing senses of liberty. And during the imperial crisis with Britain, political liberty was only one of several kinds of liberty that Americans were fearful of losing. Another held in jeopardy was Appleby's second sense of liberty, that of secure possession, hereafter understood more expansively and described as English prescriptive liberties. She characterizes this slowly accumulated collection of historic rights as "negative, private, and limited." They were thus "unlike classical republican liberty," which held that "to have liberty was to share in the power of the state, to be actively involved in making and executing decisions." Unlike this quintessential form of political liberty, "when people talked about these [prescriptive] liberties, they referred to promises between the ruler and the ruled that carried no implications about the kind of rule that prevailed."[90] These established protections or exemptions from certain kinds of governmental activities, invariably historically established, had little to do with a people's freedom to govern itself or the rights of the individual qua individual.

One should attend carefully to Appleby's demarcation of these privileges as liberties (in the plural) rather than as liberty abstractly understood, and as promises made between "the ruler and the ruled." By depicting them as inherited and in the plural, she captures a critical distinction between them and liberty per se. Prescriptive "liberties," unlike general "liberty," usually described an inherited set of rights that were applicable to members of a particular class or a local corporation (often a town or village)[91]—rights to which, as English subjects, Americans believed themselves duly entitled. As explained by Daniel Dulany in 1765, "when the powers were conferred upon the colonies, they were conferred too as privileges and immunities . . . or, to speak more properly, the privileges belonging necessarily to them as British subjects, were solemnly declared and confirmed by their charters."[92] This collection of historic rights, privileges, and exemptions,

---

p. 219, where he argues that "the local interests of a state ought in every case to give way to the interests of the Union," for it is but "an apparent, partial interest."

[90]Appleby, *Capitalism and a New Social Order*, pp. 16–18.

[91]See J. P. Kenyon, "Rights," p. 2.

[92]Dulany, "Propriety of Imposing Taxes" (1765), pp. 103–4; see also Otis, "Rights of the British Colonies" (1764), in *Tracts of the American Revolution*, pp. 24–27, who gives his

both corporate and individual, were throughout most of the 18th century held to be an inheritance that Americans enjoyed not so much as men, but as British (English) subjects.[93]

Unlike liberty per se, which often was discussed abstractly and in the vaguest of terms, this collection of liberties was more clearly defined and generally defended as being held in fee; "it had been bequeathed to them as an inheritance."[94] Before the 1770s, these rights were rarely spoken of as being solely universal human rights. In fact, "people of different sorts had freedoms of different sorts. They enjoyed their particular freedoms as members of particular communities, inheriting them through tradition, custom, usage, and prescription."[95] The necessity of defending the Revolution did, however, force Americans to abandon the historical grounding of these rights and to "resort instead to the natural rights of man rather than those peculiar to Englishmen."[96] But that was a result unanticipated at the beginning of the Revolutionary era.

More typical, at least until the end of the period, was the claim advanced by a Massachusetts Committee of Safety that Americans were "incontestably entitled to all the rights and liberties of *Englishmen;* that, as we received them from our glorious ancestors without spot or blemish, we are determined to transmit them pure and unsullied to our posterity."[97] The words of still another Adams, the Roxbury, Massachusetts pastor, Amos, left no doubt regarding the historical foundation of this particular set of exemptions. "To God almighty we have forfeited every blessing: But of man we hold our liberties as an *hereditary* right; as the inheritance of our dear ancestors, dearly obtained with their blood and treasure. We have ever been a loyal people. . . . We have never forfeited our privileges."[98] These liberties, in effect, were understood to be a product of a contractual relationship between the central British government and the English people

---

enumeration of the rights possessed by Americans; the debate between J. Adams and J. Galloway concerning the historical or natural character of these rights, cited by Reid, *Constitutional History of the American Revolution: The Authority of Rights,* pp. 91–92; and Stourzh, *Alexander Hamilton,* p. 12.

[93]See Reid, *Constitutional History of the American Revolution: The Authority to Tax,* p. 24, and *Constitutional History of the American Revolution: The Authority of Rights,* p. 87.

[94]Reid, *Concept of Liberty,* p. 24; see also his *Constitutional History of the American Revolution: The Authority of Rights,* pp. 67–71.

[95]Countryman, *American Revolution,* p. 17.

[96]Leder, *Liberty and Authority,* pp. 145–46; see also Rodgers, *Contested Truths,* p. 52; and in disagreement, see Reid, *Constitutional History of the American Revolution: The Authority of Rights,* p. 65, who importantly distinguishes between the rights themselves, which he persuasively argues were always British, and the grounds used to legitimate them.

[97]Force, "Resolutions of Worcester County Committee" (7 June 1775), p. 924; for a more typical mixture of natural and English rights see [S. Adams?], "Rights of the Colonists" (1772), p. 239.

[98]A. Adams, *Religious Liberty an Invaluable Blessing* (1768), p. 54.

of North America, a relationship that Americans insisted they had done nothing to abrogate.

This form of liberty, then, must be first understood in its English historical context, where it defined and limited the nature of the relationship between a relatively autonomous local community and its members, and the normally distant but nevertheless sovereign central government. This sense of liberty, more than any other, described "not a right but a congeries of rights—liberties, not liberty—that were derived from civil society and ultimately from the sovereign." In fact, in England, most "liberties had been granted by the Crown (usually under duress)."[99] And local communities, as distinct from the central and sovereign government, were with the exception of the right of religious conscience not subject to this "civil rights" contract between the central government and local communities and their constituent members. Nor in England had they needed to be, for "when authority came from the king, government was palpably something other, a force against which representatives protected their constituents."[100] Thus, the corporate power of the local community was not understood to be part of the governmental other.

It was not until after their Revolution that a few forward-looking Americans began to consider how a truly free and democratic sovereign people might endanger heretofore inviolate "civil rights." (European authors had done so for decades.)[101] Even Alexander Hamilton's forward-looking Publius had argued against the need for a bill of rights on the ground that such legal barriers were only necessary to protect a people against the uncontrolled excesses of kings, not against their legitimate representatives. He explained that civil rights "are in their origin, stipulations between kings and their subjects, abridgments of prerogative in favor of privilege," before arguing that therefore "they have no application to constitutions, professedly founded upon the power of the people," and that the people "have no need of particular reservations."[102]

Even more surprising was John Leland's comparable understanding of the nature and history of such rights. Leland was the second most forceful Baptist advocate for the separation of church and state (after Isaac Backus) in the Founding era. Additionally, he was instrumental in the passage of Madison's Virginia Statute of Religious Freedom in 1786. Nevertheless, when he rhetorically asked what the value of a bill of rights is, he responded that it is valuable only when "all the power is in the monarch" and "the liberty of the people is commensurate with the bill of rights that is squeezed out of the monarch." And when all the power is in the hands

[99]McDonald, *Novus Ordo Seclorum*, pp. 36–37.
[100]E. S. Morgan, "Government by Fiction," pp. 334–35.
[101]See [S. Adams?], "Rights of the Colonists" (1772), p. 239; and Lolme, *Constitution of England* (1775), p. 112.
[102]Hamilton, "Federalist No. 84," in Hamilton, Jay, and Madison, *Federalist*, p. 558.

of the people, he wondered, "where is the propriety of having a bill of rights?"[103] English prescriptive or "civil" rights for many, even at the end of the 18th century, were legal exemptions won by a people from their monarch, not rights that could be guaranteed an individual against a legitimately sovereign people.[104] (Leland, an advocate for such rights, in particular those of religious conscience, knew better than to trust parchment barriers in a democracy.)

One should not ignore, then, that "liberty in the classical republican paradigm and liberty in the historic rights tradition are distinct and potentially contradictory concepts."[105] A democratic self-governing people may be highly concerned with protecting its corporate liberty while paying little attention to those individual safeguards previously negotiated between it and its former unelected sovereign. But some American authors, seemingly oblivious to the internal tensions between them, did jointly defend in equal measure corporate political liberty and individual prescriptive liberties. For example, an anonymous patriot had held that "true self love and social are the same; [and] that the publick good and his own are so intimately connected and interwoven together, that whatever is inconsistent with the *former,* is equally incompatible with the *latter.*" He continued, however, that "wide, infinitely wide is the difference between *social liberty,* and *savage licentiousness*—the *one,* it is our duty to estimate and cherish" while the other "we ought carefully to guard against, as the most destructive pest."[106]

But what was needed to make this equilibrium functional was that the sovereign will of the people and that of each truly free individual should be mediated by the moral truths of Christian or natural law. What was not countenanced, however, was idiosyncratic behavior on the part of the individual or the valorization of the immediate needs of the individual over those of the public. Thus, the Anti-Federalist Agrippa, while insisting that the good of the individual and that of the public were inextricably intertwined, held that individuals were first bound "to promote the welfare of the whole."[107]

Few Americans both recognized that the public's legitimate needs and those of particular individuals could be at odds, and gave preference to those of the individual. Even by the end of the War of Independence, only the most progressive and perceptive American theorists and statesmen approached such a stance.[108] No one proved more sensitive to this emerging dilemma and the immediate needs of the individual than James Madison.[109] Yet even Madison was unwilling to valorize (at least publicly) the needs of the individual over those of the public. Tom Paine, however, the sometime

[103][Leland], writing as Jack Nips, "Yankee Spy" (1794), pp. 977–78.
[104]See J. A. Smith, "Spirit of American Government," p. 9; and Patterson, *Freedom,* p. 364.
[105]Appleby, *Capitalism and a New Social Order,* p. 18.
[106]Philanthrop, in the *Boston Evening Post,* 14 January 1771.
[107]Agrippa, "Letter VII" (1787), p. 241.
[108]See Lienesch, *New Order of the Ages,* p. 78.
[109]See J. Madison, "Federalist No. 10," in Hamilton, Jay, and Madison, *Federalist,* p. 56.

American who was soon to be excoriated as a blasphemer and atheist, approached it still more closely. In 1786, he argued that the "public good is not a term opposed to the good of individuals; on the contrary, it is the good of every individual collected. It is the good of all because it is the good of everyone."[110] His remarks are atypical of Americans and about as bold an individualistic statement as one can find during the Revolutionary era.[111] Americans, even in the late 1780s, were not yet ready to privilege the needs of the individual without the assurance that the common good was simultaneously being promoted.[112]

Unlike those in America, perceptive British thinkers throughout the 18th century (frequently Tories) had rejected this too easily balanced equation between public and private needs. Most had found it naive. Some, however, such as the editor Fenning, seemed to share Americans' optimism. In his dictionary of 1775, he defined political liberty as "a power of acting agreeable to the laws which are enacted by the consent of a people, and no ways inconsistent with the natural rights of a single person, or the good of society."[113] Yet there were many others, such as the Cambridge fellow and essayist Richard Hey, who were outspoken defenders of individual rights without making any bow to public needs. Arguing against Dr. Richard Price, Hey held that "the common idea of liberty is merely negative, and is only the *absence of restraint*," and that liberty, "like every other blessing to be viewed and estimated accurately, must be considered in respect of the advantage it brings to each individual."[114] But this kind of unequivocal statement defending individual rights against those of the community cannot be found in the public writing of Revolutionary-era Americans. Instead, one finds ambiguous remarks that at best refuse to side blindly, as was the norm, with the majority against the deviant individual or the oppressed ethnic, racial, or religious minority.

In England, by contrast, Hey was not alone in his preference for individual over corporate welfare. There were others, such as Thomas Pownall,

[110]Paine, "Dissertations on Government" (1786), 2:372.

[111]One might also consider the individualistic intent of Quincy, "Observations" (1774), p. 323, who argues that "the proper object of society and civil institutions is the advancement of 'the greatest happiness of the greatest number.'" We should keep in mind, though, that John Adams took a similar position in 1776, before going on to explain in his "Thoughts on Government," in *Political Writings of John Adams*, p. 85, that following the teachings of "Confucius, Zoraster, Socrates, [and] Mahomet," the true "happiness of man, as well as his dignity, consists in virtue."

[112]See Handlin and Handlin, *Popular Sources of Political Authority*, p. 423, who report that the town of Stoughton, Massachusetts, in its instructions to its delegate to the 1780 Constitutional Convention declared for both and held that "the Great End and design of all government ought to be the Safety and Happiness of the people or for the Security and Protection of the Community as Such"; see also p. 903.

[113]Fenning, *Royal English Dictionary* (1775).

[114]Hey, *Observations* (1776), pp. 7–8, 42–43. See also the American statesman, Gouverneur Morris, "Political Enquiry" (n.d.), pp. 328–29, who in this unpublished piece gives vent to comparable individualistic sentiments.

the colonial governor of Massachusetts for three years and a friend of the colonies in Parliament, who, along with Paine, comes the closest to a public "American" proponent of individualism.[115] Another was Thomas Blacklock, who ridiculed two of the avatars of America's understanding of liberty, Price and Montesquieu, by asking whether "it is possible for political and personal freedom to take different directions." He wished to know "who invested this arrogant majority with a legitimate power, not only to supersede the volition and discretion of the minority, but to obtrude its own volition and discretion upon them? In such a conjuncture, there must be a manifest violation of personal and physical liberty."[116] Yet in America, such questions and attitudes were not aired in public before the late 1780s. Only then would exceptional men such as James Madison, William Vans Murray, and James Wilson begin to press such questions from the center-left, while Fisher Ames, John Adams, Noah Webster (and in private, G. Morris), and their associates did so from the center-right.

But prescriptive liberties were not valued only by defenders of individual autonomy. They were also cherished by those who defended local corporate autonomy. Support for these liberties, therefore, did not define a person as a proponent of one or the other. Consider, for example, the politically oriented prescriptive liberties enumerated in the federal Bill of Rights (e.g., the rights to a militia or to bear arms, to be tried by or sit on a jury, and the newly emergent popular freedoms of speech and press).[117] From the dominant late 18th-century perspective, they were not so much individual rights as local corporate ones that formed a wall of protection against the potentially intrusive practices of a tyrannous central government. Even during the ratification debate, "the concern for individual rights in the debate was not a concern for rights as such, not a concern for individuals and individualism, but for the rights vis-a-vis the federal government." Indeed, there was no similar movement to restrict the police powers of the state governments.[118]

In the eyes of many, the central government had taken on the former role of the monarch, and self-governing local communities needed to renegotiate their protection from its intrusions. As Chief Justice John Marshall observed in 1833, the history of the first amendments to the Constitution, those most concerned with such rights, is unequivocal. "They demanded security against the apprehended encroachments of the general government, not against those of the local governments."[119] Thus, these rights were not so much to guard the individual from the community's democratic excesses (as Publius had hoped, sought, and unsuccessfully argued

[115]See Pownall, *Memorial* (1783), pp. 106–7.

[116]Blacklock, *Nature and Extent of Liberty* (1776), p. 7.

[117]See C. Warren, "New 'Liberty' under the Fourteenth Amendment," p. 461.

[118]Palmer, "Liberties as Constitutional Provisions," p. 115; and see Amar, "Consent of the Governed," p. 497.

[119]Marshall, "Barron v. Baltimore" (1833), p. 310.

they should be), but rather to protect a democratic subnational corporate people from a potentially tyrannous central national government.

This collection of historic exemptions slowly took on its current association with individual rights that were to be guaranteed by a nondemocratic judiciary of a (future) national government.[120] From this newer perspective, these rights were not a defense against an intrusive central government, but a defense against a local majority's communal understanding of human flourishing and its too often coercive and intrusive efforts politically to embody it. In America, "the basic civil-liberties problem has been not the arbitrary exercise of centralized power but the despotism of the militant majority." The national government sought the job of protecting individual freedom, and as the former grew so did the range of the latter.[121] Nevertheless, the outcome of this struggle over the ultimate meanings of these historical rights remained in doubt until the 20th century, and possibly as late as 1925, when the Supreme Court finally began the process of incorporating the Bill of Rights following the *Gitlow v. New York* decision. With the application of the Bill of Rights' protections to those areas of private behavior that had previously been under the jealously guarded corporate police powers of the states, frequently in order to protect persecuted minorities from majoritarian intolerance, the individual's rights grew apace.[122]

This brings us to Appleby's third and final sense of liberty, that of individual autonomy. This emergent individualistic sense, she correctly notes, was dissimilar to other 18th-century meanings. Unlike them, it was "instrumental, utilitarian, individualistic, egalitarian, abstract, and rational." In fact, Appleby wonders how two understandings of liberty so at odds as the individualist and political understandings "could have coexisted in the same political discourse."[123] The answer is simple. During most of the 18th century, for most Americans, they did not. In Revolutionary America, a political or social theory defending individualistic liberty was a foundling few men were willing to claim publicly as their own.[124] Indeed, this sense of liberty would not be publicly defensible in America (unlike in Britain) until at least the last decade of the 18th century and even then only by a few.

[120]See Brutus, "Essays I–XVI" (1787–1788), for his careful critique of the most antidemocratic aspect of the proposed national Constitution, the federal judiciary.

[121]Roche, "Curbing of the Militant Majority," p. 36.

[122]These historic civil liberties are of great long-term historical importance, but they will not be discussed further here. They were uniformly defended; thus it is unlikely that additional analysis would yield undisclosed insights relevant to an understanding of late 18th-century American political thought. Additionally, unlike many of the other 18th-century senses of liberty, prescriptive liberties have been surveyed frequently. Recently this has been accomplished by Forrest McDonald in his discussion of the rights of Englishmen in *Novus Ordo Seclorum;* by Willi Paul Adams in *The First American Constitutions;* and by John Phillip Reid in *Constitutional History of the American Revolution: The Authority of Rights.*

[123]Appleby, *Capitalism and a New Social Order,* pp. 19–21.

[124]See Kammen, *Spheres of Liberty,* p. 3.

Daniel Rodgers, in fact, has argued that only at the end of the 19th century did Americans begin to embrace an individualist discourse of the kind described by Appleby. Using Jeremy Bentham's writings as a surrogate for such discourse, Rodgers finds that through the end of the 19th century, Americans believed, for example, that "utilitarianism was a 'repulsive' philosophy."[125] Modern autonomy was not, therefore, a sense of liberty that was of great importance in the late 18th century.

As helpful as Appleby's clear typology has shown itself to be, it can only serve as a point of departure in describing the late 18th-century American concept of liberty. Her triad of political, individual, and prescriptive liberties must be augmented because it fails to capture the full range of meanings attached to liberty in Revolutionary America. Five other senses of liberty must be considered if one is correctly to comprehend the 18th-century understanding of liberty that informed the goals of the American Revolution. These five other conceptions are philosophical liberty (freedom of the will), familial independence, spiritual (or Christian) liberty, natural liberty, and corporate civil liberty.

The first of these, freedom of the will, although of vital importance to that century's philosophers and assumed by 18th-century authors to be a necessary human attribute,[126] was nonetheless discussed by very few of them. Indeed, other than in the work of America's finest 18th-century philosopher, Jonathan Edwards,[127] little mention is made of it. Exceptions, of course, do exist. For example, consider an anonymous author describing what he takes to be Locke's meaning of liberty; he writes that "liberty is a power to act or not to act, according as the mind directs. A power to direct the operative faculties to motion or rest, in particular instances, is that which we call the will." But the author does not go on to use this sense of liberty to define or describe a particular political or social teaching.[128]

The great Scottish philosopher David Hume also argued that by liberty "we can only mean *a power of acting or not acting, according to the determination of the will*." But, he added, this understanding of liberty was so basic that it was never "the subject of dispute."[129] Surely he exaggerates here, for by his own admission the relationships among sin, free-

---

[125]Cited by Rodgers, *Contested Truths*, pp. 32, 39–41.

[126]Most particularly, this defined the core concern of that century's most famous and celebrated philosopher, Immanuel Kant.

[127]See Pahl, *Free Will and Political Liberty*, pp. 160–61; Breitenbach, "Unregenerate Doings," pp. 482–83; and Ramsay, introduction to Edwards, *Freedom of the Will*.

[128]"Locke's Definition of Liberty" (1771); see also Westminster Assembly, "Westminster Confession of Faith" (1646), p. 199; and Hobbes, *Leviathan* (1651), p. 261, who famously wrote that "LIBERTY, or FREEDOME, signifieth (properly) the absence of Opposition; (by Opposition, I mean externall Impediments of motion)," and did derive a normative political teaching from this understanding of liberty.

[129]Hume, *Enquiry Concerning Human Understanding* (1748), p. 63.

dom of the will, and God's sovereignty are a mystery "which mere natural and unassisted reason is very unfit to handle."[130] Nevertheless, his sense that this question was beyond dispute (or at least of such a complex nature that few could contemplate it) may explain why it rarely entered into the normative political discussions of the time. In fact, it was so widely accepted by all sides that it had little value in shaping popular moral and political considerations. Philosophical liberty was thus aptly named by Mayhew, because it concerned questions that were best left to formal philosophers, of which America had very few.

Another important understanding of liberty not discussed by Appleby, and one of great popular concern, was the familial independence or autonomy of a household. It describes the household's freedom to be uncontrolled economically, politically, or socially by outside individuals. This hallowed meaning of liberty has little in common with the late 20th century's ideal of individual autonomy.[131] As it had been in Attic political philosophy and history, republican Rome, and feudal England, familial independence was understood as a socially defined characteristic of self-supporting male heads of house who were the central ligaments of these largely agricultural communities. More significantly, it was accepted that their economic independence did nothing to free householders from communal oversight or communally defined familial, social, and political responsibilities.

That a community of independent citizens was expected to serve public needs is especially evident in Thomas Jefferson's often-cited remarks on the superiority of agricultural pursuits. Jefferson had claimed that the "cultivators of the earth are the most valuable citizens. They are the most vigorous, the most independent, the most virtuous, & they are tied to their country & wedded to its liberty & interests by the most lasting bonds." Two years later, in his only published book, he gave voice to the popular spirit of the time and to the importance attached to economic and political independence. He wrote that "dependence begets subservience and venality, suffocates the germ of virtue, and prepares fit tools for the design of ambition."[132] Their sense of familial or personal independence freed men and their households from dependence on other individuals, but did not free them from communal controls or the need to serve the public good.

A third sense of liberty ignored by Appleby is spiritual or Christian liberty, one found by Mayhew, Mellen, Bryce, and Fischer to have been a core 18th-century sense of liberty. This understanding of liberty defined

---

[130]Ibid., p. 69; see also H. S. Smith, *Changing Conceptions of Original Sin,* for his stimulating discussion of these matters.

[131]See Christman, "Constructing the Inner Citadel," p. 110.

[132]Jefferson, "Letter to John Jay" (23 August 1785), in *Writings,* ed. Peterson, p. 818, and *Notes on the State of Virginia* (1787), p. 217; see also A Farmer, "Essay V," pp. 270–71, who voices a frequent refrain that "they who hold the property of the soil, are alone entitled to govern it"; and Main, *Social Structure of Revolutionary America,* pp. 209–11.

the relative freedom that a Christian enjoyed through Christ from sin and from the necessity of obeying the Mosaic law (Mayhew's gracious liberty and freedom from ceremonial law). This most traditional Anglo-American understanding of liberty had been outlined in 1646 by the Westminster Confession, the still authoritative statement of Anglo-American reformed doctrine. It held that "the liberty which Christ hath purchased for believers under the gospel consists in their freedom from the guilt of sin . . . [and] bondage to Satan." In addition, "under the New Testament the liberty of Christians is further enlarged in their freedom from the yoke of the ceremonial law, to which the Jewish Church was subjected."[133]

This sense of liberty continued to captivate American social and ethical discourse until well into the 19th century. Even then, "influential members of the American community stressed that the most valuable form of freedom was a freedom from sin and a freedom to do God's will."[134] Thus, this understanding of liberty was equally at home in the America of 1635 and 1850 (if not, for many, in that of the 1990s). Considering the continual importance of spiritual liberty in the history of American social and moral thought, it is surprising that Appleby makes no mention of it.

Perhaps she ignores this sense of liberty because it was relatively eclipsed in Revolutionary America by more secular and political senses of the term. In her defense, one should take note of colonial America's bibliographer, Charles Evans, who reported "heretofore the periods of growth into a national literature had been distinctly religious," yet beginning in the 1770s, American publishing entered "a period of a complete and radical change in its character, now distinctively political."[135] This is not to say that spiritual concerns had a minor standing even then—only that they had become less dominant in an America that, at the corporate and political level, had become less religious.

But as late as 1798, pastors and other public figures continued to argue that spiritual and corporate political liberty and liberty of religious conscience were the only fully defensible forms of liberty, for with them people are "possessed of all that *liberty*, which the nature of man, and the condition of this world can well admit."[136] The secular tide itself would again shortly turn; the most popular and influential American in the early part of the 19th century was the evangelical minister and theologian Charles Finney. For him and his millions of followers, "there was no freedom for a Christian to commit sin: his liberty consisted in an ability to do God's will with a good and eager heart."[137]

The final two senses of liberty are usefully viewed as a pair. They are

[133]Westminster Assembly, "Westminster Confession of Faith" (1646), p. 215.
[134]Cooke, *American Tradition of Liberty*, p. 100.
[135]Evans, preface to vol. 3 of *American Bibliography* (1774–1778), p. vii.
[136]I. B. Woodward, *American Liberty and Independence* (1798), p. 10.
[137]Cooke, *American Tradition of Liberty*, pp. 57–60.

natural and (communal) civil liberty. The celebrated British legal theorist Sir William Blackstone explained that "civil liberty . . . is no other than natural liberty so far restrained by human laws."[138] Castigating Dr. Price for supposedly confusing the two, an anonymous British author further noted that natural liberty is "suggested by the will of an individual, accommodated by his own interest and inclination, rather than marked out and defined by the community for general use and public benefits [as is civil liberty]."[139] Nathaniel Niles left little doubt about the legitimacy of the corporate-serving limits imposed by this discrimination between natural or presocial freedom and that which is appropriate within society. He wrote that "civil Liberty consists, not in any inclinations of the members of a community; but in the being and due administration of such a system of laws, as effectually tends to the greatest felicity of a state."[140] Natural liberty, then, only fully belonged to the individual presocially, while civil liberty described what remained of this freedom after society's expansive communal needs were fully met.

This dual meaning of liberty helped frame the various 18th-century understandings of liberty that shaped American political thought, yet like the others, it was not free from ambiguity. Natural liberty described quite different human conditions depending on whether it was depicting humans before or after the Fall. Original sin thus played an important role in determining how natural liberty, and by extension its residual, civil liberty, were understood. But civil liberty, even more confusingly, could refer to any one of three kinds of liberty: political liberty, individual civil (natural) liberties, or what I call corporate communal liberty, the residual liberty that belongs to the individual after the needs of society were fulfilled.[141]

FAMILIAL INDEPENDENCE AND THE RIGHT OF PROPERTY:
A MISUNDERSTOOD TRADITION

Students of the late 18th century regularly note the centrality of personal independence in Americans' understanding of individual liberty. Clinton Rossiter found that liberty was often "defined simply and unanimously as that 'which exempts one Man from Subjection to another.'"[142] More recently, Jack Greene has written that one of the central secular goals of

---

[138]Blackstone, *Commentaries* (1765), 1:121; see also Hamilton, "The Farmer Refuted" (1775), p. 104, who finds that "Civil liberty, is only natural liberty, modified and secured by the sanctions of civil society"; and Morris, "Political Enquiries" (n.d.), p. 330.

[139]*Civil Liberty Asserted* (1776), p. 7.

[140]N. Niles, "[First of] Two Discourses on Liberty" (1774), p. 260.

[141]See Reid, *Concept of Liberty*, p. 32.

[142]Cited by Rossiter, *First American Revolution*, p. 225.

Americans was "the achievement of personal independence."[143] As Arthur Lee observed to his brother, Richard Henry Lee, in 1765, "liberty & independence [are] to me the most valuable of all blessings, since I know not a more bitter ingredient than dependence that can enter into the cup of life."[144] Revolutionary-era Americans were clearly concerned about maintaining their independence not only in a political and corporate sense but also in a familial or personal one.[145]

David Szatmary notes, however, that this feeling of independence was not equivalent to, nor did it lead to, individualism.[146] This understanding of personal liberty shared little with later senses of individual liberty as a form of "self-expression,"[147] and would have been at odds with the modern "cultural emphasis on self-fulfillment."[148] Indeed, Americans wished to avoid following "a course of life according to one's own mind," for that would have been "libertinism."[149] The most desired form of secular personal liberty was the more limited one of a man and his family enjoying independence from familial, especially economic, dependence on others.

This highly sought form of personal liberty did not belong to individual males per se, but only to those who were owners of land, usually heads of households. It was not universal and could not be possessed by women, children, or servants, or by other males without sufficient economic resources with which to support themselves.[150] This is one way in which real property was closely associated in Anglo-American thought with freedom. Those without sufficient property to support themselves and their families were believed incapable of economic and political self-direction, and thus, by default, their opinions and political actions were believed to be "owned" by other individuals.[151] They could not, therefore, be truly free.

In 1774, James Wilson noted that those "whose poverty is such, that they cannot live independent, and must therefore be subject to the undue influence of their superiors . . . have no will of their own: and it is judged improper that they should vote in the representation of a free state."[152] In

---

[143]J. P. Greene, *Pursuits of Happiness,* p. 195.

[144]Cited by Breen, *Tobacco Culture,* p. 89.

[145]See Kloppenberg, "Virtues of Liberalism," p. 23; and A. Taylor, *Liberty Men and Great Proprietors,* pp. 5–6.

[146]See Szatmary, *Shays' Rebellion,* pp. 6–7.

[147]See Conkin, "Freedom," pp. 205–7.

[148]Poponoe, "Family Decline," pp. 68–69.

[149]Ash, *New and Complete Dictionary,* (1775), vol. 1.

[150]See Clinton, "The Letters of 'Cato'" (1780), p. 270; Wood, *Radicalism of the American Revolution,* p. 56; and Maier, *Old Revolutionaries,* p. 181, who reports that Richard Henry Lee in 1778 had been willing to see the franchise extended "to adult women who held lands of their own right." See also Kerber, *Women of the Republic.*

[151]See Wood, *Radicalism of the American Revolution,* p. 178; J. P. Greene, *All Men Are Created Equal,* p. 19; and W. P. Adams, *First American Constitutions,* pp. 208–15.

[152]J. Wilson, "Considerations on the Nature and Extent of the Legislative Authority of the British Parliament," in *Works of James Wilson,* ed. McCloskey, 2:725.

the 1778 *Essex Result,* it was held that "all the members of the state are qualified to make the election, unless they have not sufficient discretion, or are so situated as to have no wills of their own." Michael Zuckerman further observes that "participation in community decisions was the prerogative of independent men, of *all* a town's independent men, but, ideally, *only* of those."[153] Throughout the 18th century, it was accepted that he "who would govern himself must own his soul." Yet to do so, he "must own property, the means of economic security."[154] An adult male's standing as free in American society, at least until the 1820s,[155] was ultimately defined by his ownership of productive property, and in most instances that meant land.

Discussions of real property in Revolutionary America rarely abstracted it from its social purposes and the benefits it brought to the owner, his family, and society as a whole. Indeed, the individual right to own property was rarely defended as an end in itself;[156] in most cases, it was seen as a socially mediated gift from God that was to be used for both private and public ends.[157] Real property was viewed as an instrumental good that made possible familial independence and the more important intrinsic goods of political self-government and religious freedom. As President Witherspoon of Princeton explained to his students, "there is not a single instance in history in which civil liberty was lost, and religious liberty preserved entire. If therefore we yield up our temporal property, we at the same time deliver the conscience into bondage."[158] In his mind, property was valuable, but principally in order to serve godly ends.

Property ownership in the 18th century, like familial independence, was not an absolute right that exempted the individual owner from corporate oversight.[159] Rather, it was a right of stewardship that the public entrusted to an individual, for both private and public benefit. It was a right the public could withdraw if necessary.[160] As Joseph Priestley noted, "the very idea of property, of right of any kind, is founded upon a regard to the

---

[153]Zuckerman, *Peaceable Kingdoms,* p. 196.

[154]Griswold, *Farming and Democracy,* pp. 35–36.

[155]See Wish, "From Yeoman Farmer to Industrious Producer," pp. 117–18.

[156]See Scheiber, "Economic Liberty and the Constitution," p. 77, who argues that American property theories served two quite different ends: one private and individualistic and the other communal and societal. Evidence of the private position in the Revolutionary era, however, is slim.

[157]See Selby, *Concept of Liberty,* pp. 131–32; and Fliegelman, *Prodigals and Pilgrims,* pp. 27–28.

[158]Witherspoon, *Dominion of Providence* (1776), p. 40; see also Selby, *Concept of Liberty,* pp. 127–28, 131.

[159]See *Civil Liberty Asserted* (1776), pp. 10–11. Pangle, *Spirit of Modern Republicanism,* p. 34, disagrees; he argues for the "primacy of individual liberty," in particular, "the individual's natural right to property."

[160]See Wood, *Radicalism of the American Revolution,* p. 423; Ditz, *Property and Kinship,* p. 170; and Scheiber, "Economic Liberty and the Constitution," p. 78.

general good of the society under whose protection it is enjoyed; and nothing is properly *a man's own*, but what general rules, which have for their object the good of the whole, give to him."[161] Even Ben Franklin, supposedly the most bourgeois of the Founding Fathers, counseled that except for the barest necessities of life, all remaining personal property belonged to "the Publick, who, by their Laws, have created it, and who may therefore by other Laws dispose of it, whenever the Welfare of the Publick shall demand such Disposition." Anyone who did not like these terms, he added, should "retire and live among the savages."[162]

Revolutionary-era Americans, then, did not value private property above public needs, for as the Vermont Declaration of Rights proclaims, "private property ought to be subservient to public use."[163] As Jefferson explained, "our Creator made the earth for the use of the living and not for the dead"; accordingly, the majority has the right to change any laws, especially those affecting property, "whenever a change of circumstances or of will calls for it. Habit alone confounds what is civil practice with natural right."[164] For 18th-century Americans, if not for their 19th-century descendants, private property was paradoxically both a valued right and a social creation that only retained its status as a right to the degree to which it served publicly endorsed social ends.

Not surprisingly, most Americans were not supporters of the novel claims then being advanced for a form of political economy in which individuals were to be unconstrained in their economic lives by the needs of the public. As Hamilton explained, "this is one of those wild speculative paradoxes, which have grown into credit among us, contrary to the uniform practice and sense of the most enlightened nations."[165] However, Revolutionary-era Americans did believe that property ownership was a right and that widespread ownership of private property, the foundation of familial or personal independence, was essential to the health of the polity and to the well-being of its citizens.[166] Productive property did make

---

[161]Priestley, "Essay" (1771), p. 26.

[162]Franklin, "Letter to Robert Morris" (1783), in *Political Thought of Benjamin Franklin*, p. 358.

[163]"Vermont Declaration of Rights" (1771), in B. Schwartz, *Roots of the Bill of Rights*, p. 322.

[164]Jefferson, "Letter to Thomas Earle" (24 September 1823), in *Writings of Thomas Jefferson*, ed. Washington, p. 311. After a century-long hiatus, this is a position to which some contemporary legal scholars, particularly those on the left, such as Cass Sunstein, are returning.

[165]Hamilton, "Continentalist Papers" (1781), p. 55; see also Crowley, "Commerce and the Philadelphia Constitution," pp. 74, 77; and Maier, *Old Revolutionaries*, p. 187, who quotes Richard Henry Lee making a similar plea against laissez-faire capitalism.

[166]They did not, however, support agrarian laws that would have legislated a more equitable distribution of private property. See Jefferson, "Letter to James Madison" (28 October 1785), in *Writings*, ed. Peterson, p. 841, in which he flirts with such ideas, but backs away; Maier, *Old Revolutionaries*, pp. 121–22, who discusses the even more serious flirtation of

independence possible, and familial economic independence made political and religious liberty feasible. Together they made almost all other good things obtainable.[167]

Revolutionary-era Americans were not alone in viewing familial independence in this elevated fashion. In England, the common law as far back as the 13th century supported and maintained a fundamental division between those who owned real property and those who did not. From the perspective of the common law, "liberty and property are one and the same thing [and that] . . . 'consists in not being obliged to do or suffer any thing, but under the direction of known laws.'"[168] In fact, a man's and his family's fullest sense of liberty, his entire constellation of rights and duties, his entire secular existence, and according to some, his sacred state as well, were defined by the degree to which he was independent—that is, in possession of land in freehold with which to farm and provide for himself and his family.

Nevertheless, in spite of the vaunted independence that a landed Englishman might possess in his extrafamilial personal relationships, individual deviance from corporate guidelines was rarely tolerated. England was a world of communities in which critical questions of everlasting spiritual life constantly abutted questions of survival. Freedom from personal dependence did not prevent communal intrusion into the life of the individual and his family, as the community pursued temporal and spiritual ends. Thus, "the free peasant was controlled by communal practice just as much as the unfree."[169] The English understanding of familial independence, like the American one, evidenced little concern with procuring individual freedom from corporate oversight.[170]

---

the Pennsylvania Declaration of Rights with such a proposal; and W. P. Adams, *First American Constitutions*, p. 213, who notes that the singular attempt in Pennsylvania, in the end, failed.

[167]See [Dickinson], "Letters of a Farmer in Pennsylvania" (1768), p. 400.

[168]Delman, "Liberty and the Common Law," p. 170.

[169]Hogue, *Origins of the Common Law*, p. 128.

[170]Arguing in opposition is Macfarlane, *Origins of English Individualism*. The author claims that English farmers were not Polish peasants because "the central feature of 'peasantry' is the absence of absolute ownership of land" (p. 80), and "'freehold' tenure . . . gave an individual complete and total rights over his land" (p. 89). Thus the English were not peasants, and furthermore, their "highly individualized ownership had severed the link between a family group and land" (p. 94). This, moreover, is believed by Macfarlane to show that the English must have been individualists and that "England back to the thirteenth century was not based on either 'Community' or 'communities'" (p. 163). The author, though, is guilty of serious lapses in both logic and evidence, and his work is generally dismissed for these reasons. See for example, the review by Appleby, p. 1047, who asks why it necessarily follows from the English not being Polish peasants (which is shown) that they were individualists? This is particularly problematic, she claims, because no evidence is adduced in support. L. Stone, in "Goodbye to Nearly All That," pp. 40–41, describes the book as totally unpersuasive and "monotonously monocausal," and the author as myopic and ignorant. Faith asks in her review "why is this such a thoroughly unsatisfactory book," and answers that "it is a

Most English and Scottish authors read in America defended familial liberty as a form of economic independence, not as a form of private autonomy from societal intrusion, and boasted of its essential importance to both individual and communal well-being.[171] Lest it appear that such authors' remarks about personal liberty had little resonance in America, consider the response of John Adams, who, when asked late in life to define liberty, answered that he could be of no service. He directed his interlocutor first to the works of Dr. Price, and then added that "I would rather refer you to other writers than to anything of my own. Sidney, Harrington, Locke, Montesquieu, and even Hobbes, are worth consulting, and many others."[172] Apparently no American was worthy of his direct recommendation.

One of the most important of these English authors undoubtedly was the late 17th-century philosopher John Locke. He defined familial or personal independence as the freedom "to follow my own will in all things, [only] where that rule prescribes not; and not to be subject to the inconsistent, uncertain, unknown, arbitrary will of another man."[173] A late 17th-century republican martyr, Algernon Sidney, had declared that personal "liberty solely consists in an independency upon the will of another, and by the name of slave we understand a man who can neither dispose of his person nor goods but enjoys all at the will of his master."[174] Neither thinker, however, understood personal liberty as freeing one from corporate oversight or warranting a disregard of communal standards or the necessity of serving the public.[175]

Even David Hume defended a traditional understanding of individual liberty similar to the American understanding of familial independence rather than the delusively comparable freedom of individual modern autonomy. Hume was an 18th-century Tory of extraordinarily modern and cosmopolitan sensibilities, who cannot be accused of having Protestant or republican sympathies.[176] Yet even for Hume, personal liberty was "the

---

very slapdash piece of work: wild statements fly about, tentative conclusions are presented as established facts, and [there are] many careless slips." Moreover, "a large part of the book, though interesting, seems quite irrelevant in presenting evidence of 'individualistic' attitudes and behaviour in the sixteenth and seventeenth centuries" (p. 388).

[171]See J. P. Greene, "Slavery or Independence," p. 207.

[172]J. Adams, *Works of John Adams*, 10:377. The correspondent was J. H. Tiffany, who at the same time (1819) had also asked Jefferson to define *liberty* and *republic*. For Jefferson's not very illuminating response, see *Political Writings of Thomas Jefferson*, p. 55.

[173]Locke, *Treatise of Civil Government* (1690), p. 16; see also p. 37.

[174]A. Sidney, *Discourses Concerning Government* (1698), p. 12.

[175]Also see Addison and Steele, *Spectator* (29 January 1712), p. 205; Addison writes that personal liberty was simply that which "exempts one Man from Subjection to another so far as the Order and Oeconomy of Government will permit."

[176]For evidence of Hume's rather distinct hostility toward the ancients in general, and in particular republicanism with its repressive form of liberty, see "Of the Populousness of Ancient Nations" (1777), in *Essays*, p. 383.

absence of arbitrary coercion . . . [and] liberty on this interpretation is not limited by constraints as such, but by arbitrary constraint, applied without due process of law."[177] Hume went on to defend a traditional differentiation between free and slave as depending on whether one person was subject to the arbitrary will of another, not whether one was subject to the legitimate will of a corporate body.

The salient difference between an Eastern-style despotism and a Western monarchy, for Hume, was that in the former, one was constantly subject to the arbitrary will of individual government officials who were not restrained by law. He believed that "a people arbitrarily governed in this way are 'slaves in the full and proper sense of the word.'. . .They are at the mercy of the wills of particular individuals."[178] It was not the potentially repressive character of corporate edicts that he most objected to, but rather a dependence on the arbitrary will of "particular individuals." Personal or familial independence, even for this truly enlightened British thinker, was not the same as individual modern autonomy.

Among those generally associated with Enlightenment thought, 18th-century British authors were not alone in defending the importance of familial independence as traditionally conceived by Americans. Important Protestant-inspired Continental authors such as Rousseau and Kant also argued for understandings of independence that eschewed individual dependence on others,[179] without comparably insisting on freedom from corporate oversight. For example, Rousseau, writing in the *Social Contract* near midcentury, had held that his understanding of human flourishing took as one of its primary goals the making of "each citizen" perfectly "independent of all the rest, and at the same time very dependent on the city."[180] And Kant, although little concerned in most of his work with the liberty of a citizen, stipulated that "to be fit to vote, a person must have an independent position among the people," and that this excludes from active citizenship apprentices, servants (except to the state), women, minors, and "all those who are obliged to depend for their living (i.e., for food and protection) on the offices of others (excluding the state)." Kant felt that women, children, and the poor had "no civil personality," and thus could "not possess civil independence."[181] Personal independence and full citizenship were not even for Kant universal rights, but rather privileges only of those possessing economic autonomy.

Additionally, Kant held that a citizen enjoyed "lawful *freedom*" when

[177]D. Miller, *Philosophy and Ideology*, pp. 148–49.
[178]Forbes, *Hume's Philosophical Politics*, pp. 156–57.
[179]See Berlin, "Two Concepts of Liberty," p. 138, who argues that the heart of liberal humanism was formed by Kant and Rousseau and that "in its *a priori* version it is a form of secularized Protestant individualism, in which the place of God is taken by the conception of the rational life."
[180]Rousseau, *Social Contract* (1762), p. 52, and even more emphatically, pp. 38–39.
[181]Kant, "The Metaphysics of Morals," p. 139.

he obeyed "no law other than that to which he has given his consent" and that he enjoyed "civil *equality*" when he recognized "no-one among the people as superior to himself, unless it be someone whom he is just as morally entitled to bind by law as the other is to bind him."[182] For Kant, then, as for Revolutionary-era Americans, personal independence demanded reciprocal dependence such that no free citizen had "rights of coercion over others which are not symmetrical with their rights over him, except where he is acting in an official capacity. . . . In their personal capacity, citizens enjoy perfectly symmetrical rights of coercion relative to each other."[183] And in contrast to the rights language often associated with individual liberty, personal independence's demand for reciprocal dependence does not offer inherent limits on the mutual coercion that a corporate body might impose on its members.

Indeed, Americans did argue for the necessity of reciprocally binding relationships between otherwise independent citizens.[184] Timothy Stone, a Congregational minister from Lebanon, Connecticut, forcefully held that reciprocal dependence on other members of the community was to be encouraged. He asserted that "a state of society necessarily implies reciprocal dependence in all its members; and rational government, is designed to realize and strengthen this dependence." He went on to claim that "the laws of a state, should equally bind every member, whether his station be the most conspicuous, or, the most obscure."[185] This position was reiterated a decade later by Governor Caleb Strong.[186] Personal or familial economic independence did not mean freedom from intrusive corporate oversight.

When Americans turned to classical sources, they discovered there a comparable understanding of personal independence.[187] Classicist Richard Mulgan argues from the *Politics* and the *Metaphysics* that for Aristotle the standard definition of personal independence was "not belonging to another or . . . being one's own person." He notes, moreover, that for Aristotle as well as for Plato, this kind of individual liberty was appropriately tempered by the legitimate obedience, even subservience, that they felt the free male (with the possible exception of the philosopher) owed his community. Mulgan shows that "to Aristotle autonomy is not a pressing problem. Free men are men who have independent interests of their own but will readily and as a

[182]Ibid.

[183]C. Taylor, "Kant's Theory of Freedom," p. 117.

[184]See Ditz, *Property and Kinship*, pp. 159–69; Lemon, "Spatial Order," p. 87; and Wood, *Radicalism of the American Revolution*, p. 57.

[185]T. Stone, "Connecticut Election Sermon" (1792), p. 842; see also Dwight, *True Means of Establishing Public Happiness* (1795), p. 17, for his sharply critical remarks on the confusion between individual liberty and license and the necessarily deleterious effects of this confusion on society.

[186]See Caleb Strong, "Speech" (1804), p. 156.

[187]See Sartori, "Liberty and Law," pp. 289–90; and Rahe, "Primacy of Politics in Classical Greece," p. 278.

matter of course submit to laws and social norms. . . . Like Plato, Aristotle countenances widespread legal and social compulsion of individual behaviour without any suggestion that compulsion, the overriding of individual choice, involves moral loss or sacrifice, so long as it prevents people from doing wrong."[188] Quentin Skinner finds that the understanding of personal independence envisioned by classical Attic thought was shared by two Roman authors highly regarded by 18th-century readers, Livy and Cicero.[189] Skinner notes that "Cicero had already laid it down in *De Officiis* (I.10.31) that individual and civic liberty can only be preserved if *communi utilitati serviatur,* if we act 'as slaves to the public interest.' And in Livy there are several echoes of the same astonishing use of the vocabulary of chattel slavery to describe the condition of political liberty."[190] For these authors, there was no inconsistency in arguing for personal or familial independence, reciprocal dependence, and the need to put the public first.

Freedom from personal dependence thus described the head of house's "absolute exemption from any degree of subordination, support, or control by any other person." But, as clarified by Thomas Tucker in 1784, "only in 'an uncivilized State' . . . did any man have an absolute 'right to consider himself or his family independent of all the world.'"[191] Regardless of economic independence, the individual male head of house was to be enmeshed in the life of his family, congregation, and polity so that he could aid others to live, and be aided in living, a life of moral righteousness. This is in keeping with the central moral teaching about liberty in the Christian and classical West. As the contemporary moral theorist Alasdair MacIntyre has written, to be a virtuous man in either of these ethical traditions was to be a bearer of rights who filled "a set of roles each of which has its own point and purpose: member of a family, citizen, soldier, philosopher, servant of God."[192] Traditionally, personal independence had compromised neither the interdependent relation that existed between the independent male and his family nor that which existed between him and the local community.[193]

In late 18th-century America, the traits that best characterized familial independence demanded "freedom from the sordid subordination of considerations of honor and dignity to calculations of interest." Yet in America too, this sense of freedom was not cultivated for individualistic ends but so that a man could undertake "important responsibilities in the com-

---

[188]Mulgan, "Liberty in Ancient Greece," pp. 17–18, 23.

[189]See Hampson, *Enlightenment,* p. 148.

[190]Skinner, "Idea of Negative Liberty," p. 214; see also Weintraub, "Virtue," pp. 75, 101, who argues that in Renaissance republicanism as well, particularly for Machiavelli, "virtue requires the union of personal autonomy with willing subordination to collective discipline."

[191]J. P. Greene, "Slavery or Independence," pp. 195–97.

[192]MacIntyre, *After Virtue,* pp. 58–59.

[193]See Nobles, "Breaking Into the Backcountry," p. 648; Berthoff, "Independence and Attachment, Virtue and Interest," p. 107; and Ford, "Ties that Bind?" p. 66.

munity at large" and elevate, through studious application to authoritative books, his mind and soul.[194] Personal or familial independence was not at variance with the obligations due to the religious, social, and political communities within which each head of household and his family lived.[195] And the immediate needs of the public were what a virtuous man of honor was obliged to serve and protect.

Moses Hemmenway reminded his auditors of this while also drawing their attention to their standing as free individuals. He noted that "we are required to be subject to our lawful superiors in *families,* in *church* and *state,* yet God requires us to yield this obedience not with a slavish, but a free and liberal spirit. . . . For we are not the servants of men, but of God alone."[196] In recognition of this balance between the demands of independence and corporate oversight, Zuckerman further explains that Americans "placed no premium on independence as such," for they "were expected to be independent but not too independent." Moreover, "any *genuine* independence . . . was denigrated if not altogether denied a place in the community."[197] Communalist patterns and norms, mixed with freedom from personal dependence, defined an ideal balance to which late 18th-century Americans were committed.

The Revolutionary cause itself was a prime opportunity for many Americans to seek familial independence while serving hallowed communal norms.[198] Their opposition efforts often allowed for a loss of self in group actions, "for self-fulfillment through self-denial, for autonomy through participation."[199] Late 18th-century Americans, not unlike their early 20th-century parochial descendants, felt that personal independence and some measure of self-renunciation before family, God, and community were perfectly compatible goals, even if difficult to achieve.

Jeremy Belknap, a historian, educator, and pastor, followed this logic and warned that "our notions of liberty, if they be not guided and limited by good education, degenerate into a savage independence."[200] Even more pointedly, Sam Adams in 1770 asked his readers, "where did you learn that in a state or society you had a right to do as you please? And that it was an infringement of that right to restrain you? This is a refinement which I dare say, the true sons of liberty despise. Be pleased to be informed that you are bound to conduct yourselves as the Society with which you are joined, are pleased to have you conduct, or if you will please, you may

[194]Isaac, *Transformation of Virginia,* p. 131; see also J. P. Greene, *Landon Carter,* pp. 25–26.

[195]See Ditz, "Ownership and Obligation," p. 256.

[196]Hemmenway, *Massachusetts Election Sermon* (1784), pp. 11–12.

[197]Zuckerman, "Social Context of Democracy in Massachusetts," p. 533.

[198]See Tillson, "Localist Roots of Backcountry Loyalism," pp. 387–88.

[199]Crowley, *This Sheba, Self,* p. 126.

[200]Belknap, *Election Sermon* (1785 New Hampshire election sermon), p. 18.

leave it."[201] Some years later, Joseph Lyman demanded legislation to reduce material consumption, a form of license. Without it, he believed citizens would "certainly [be] degraded to a state of servility and dependence." He showed no sign of uneasiness, however, in defending both intrusive sumptuary legislation and familial independence, "for nothing kills the noble spirit of freedom, like a state of dependence, which will ever attend the folly of spending more than we earn."[202]

Crèvecoeur, the "French Thoreau" and longtime United States resident, also distinguished between licentiousness and salutary familial or personal independence when he observed that when men are unnaturally independent and "remote from the power of example and check of shame, many families exhibit the most hideous parts of our society," for man, he continued, "cannot live in solitude, he must belong to some community bound by some ties, however imperfect." He found that although each family was economically independent, Americans were a people bound by community and convention. The "true American freeholders," he held, were usually "the most respectable set of people in this part of the world," with "their happy independence," a "great share of freedom," and "the good regulation of their families."[203] Liberty as private independence did not describe the absence of corporate limits, but rather liberty's fulfillment by means of such limits.

The difference between the modern understanding of independence and the traditional understanding that had been held by highly regarded classical authors, embodied in the common law, defended by early modern Europeans, and shared by Revolutionary-era Americans is admittedly elusive. The *Oxford English Dictionary*, however, offers as its second definition of liberty one that approximates the meaning of familial independence explored above: the "exemption or freedom from arbitrary, despotic, or autocratic rule or control." Moreover, this understanding of liberty is followed by different interpretations of the original language, interpretations that capture the distinct ways in which 18th-century and contemporary thinkers viewed personal or familial independence.

The first understanding delineates the older, corporate-deferring sense, while the second describes a modern, individualistic one. The first is from Locke in 1690; the second is from Mill in 1845. Each defines a different world of understanding of personal independence or (as it is called today) individual autonomy. First, following Locke: "the Liberty of Man, in Society, is to be under no other Legislative Power, but that established by Consent in the Commonwealth." A man thus was free when he was allowed to participate in the shaping of the laws that would bind him. But according to Mill, "the modern spirit of liberty is the love of individual

[201]S. Adams, "Determinatus" (8 January 1770), in *Writings of Samuel Adams*, 2:5.

[202]Lyman, *A Sermon* (1787 Massachusetts election sermon), pp. 43–44.

[203]Crèvecoeur, *Letters from an American Farmer* (1782), pp. 43, 51, 192–93.

independence,"[204] with the clear implication that all societal limitations that go beyond the similar protection of other autonomous individuals, whether tacitly consented to or not, were repressive and illegitimate.[205]

In this sense, Americans in the 18th century may have been Lockean, but this does not mean that they understood personal or familial independence in a modern individualist fashion any more than Locke likely did.[206] For classical authors, Locke, and other British writers influential in Revolutionary America, familial independence was an adult male's and his family's freedom from unequal dependence on other individuals acting in a personal capacity or in an arbitrary fashion. And although empirical reality rarely was in full accord with this ideal,[207] this vision met with wide acceptance in Revolutionary America.[208]

As one recent historian has observed, the 18th-century understanding of personal independence was one of the few senses of liberty inherited from the Revolutionary era that would not be contested in the early 19th century. Cooke notes that "Jefferson had believed that independence from the will of another and liberty of conscience and opinion were the most precious of all liberties; three decades later the latter two usages were either moribund or embattled."[209] Even into the early 20th-century, familial independence continued to be the goal of many rural Americans. For them, it meant "ow[n]ing your own farm and some good stock, being out of debt, and having money in the bank," a condition that was favorably contrasted to "the lot of city wage earners, who 'work (or slave) for others.'"[210] This long-enduring sense of personal liberty, which consistently failed to claim for its beneficiaries any freedom from societal oversight, is not to be confused with the modern sense of autonomy that exempts the individual from just such familial and societal intervention.

[204]*Oxford English Dictionary*, s.v. "liberty."

[205]See Gray, *Liberalisms*, pp. 224–25.

[206]See Dworetz, *Unvarnished Doctrine*, p. 31; and Lutz, *Preface to American Political Theory*, pp. 119–20.

[207]See Sydnor, *American Revolutionaries in the Making*, p. 116.

[208]See J. Lewis, *Pursuit of Happiness*, pp. 108–10; D. B. Smith, *Inside the Great House*, pp. 46–54; Burnaby, *Travels through the Middle Settlements* (1775), pp. 55–56; and Breen, *Tobacco Culture*, pp. 85–92.

[209]Cooke, *American Tradition of Liberty*, p. 158.

[210]West [Withers], *Plainville, U.S.A.*, p. 50.

Spiritual Liberty: The Quintessential Liberty

In early democracies, as in American democracy at the time
of its birth, all individual rights were granted because man
is God's creature. That is, freedom was given to the
individual conditionally, in the assumption of his constant
religious responsibility. Such was the heritage of the
preceding thousand years. Two hundred or even fifty years
ago, it would have seemed quite impossible, in America,
that an individual could be granted boundless freedom
simply for the satisfaction of his instincts or whims.

—Aleksandr Solzhenitsyn, "A World Split Apart"

AMERICA was a land shaped by the tenets of reformed-Protestant theology
and spiritual or Christian liberty had an important role to play in this
formation. For spiritually awakened Christians this is the liberty that frees
them from absolute servitude to sin and the necessity of adhering to the
tenets of Mosaic law.[1] But less expected than its central place in Christian
thought is the degree to which Christian liberty shared elements with
other, more secular senses of liberty. They too were characterized by an
insistence on voluntary acceptance of a life of righteousness. Spiritual liberty was Revolutionary-era Americans' most fundamental understanding
of liberty—so much so that it set the standard by which other forms of
liberty were judged.

An examination of the American understanding of spiritual liberty invites an exploration of the critical role played by original sin in Americans'
conception of liberty and, by extension, in their political thought. Its powerful presence in their thought, and the certainty it provided regarding the
innate egotistical character of human beings, circumscribed the range of
social and political possibilities they could embrace. In a putative age of

---

[1]Spiritual or Christian liberty is not to be confused with religious liberty or that of conscience, which are more accurately seen as English (and then American) prescriptive liberties
or rights.

reason, their almost unchallenged belief in original sin (or at the very least in a secular equivalent) shaped how most Americans thought about things political and social. Of particular relevance here is their expectation that they could best, though only partially, protect themselves from the siren calls of bodily lust by living together in a morally intrusive community of relative equality (women, those without property, and non-European Americans were rarely awarded equal status) and reciprocal dependency.

The 18th century in America, nevertheless, was a tortured century. Its people were pulled in one direction by the demands of a two-millennia-old ethical vision of an ordered and rational universe in which communal life was to limit the range of individual freedom and human selfishness and thereby shape the ethical existence of each individual. They were also pulled in the opposite direction by material and social forces and certain intellectual currents that demanded higher levels of unstructured personal freedom and a greater acceptance of human selfishness. There is little disagreement among students of the modern period that these powerful forces, often unplanned and uncontrolled, helped transform the economic, political, religious, and social spheres within which liberty was exercised. Collectively, these changes have come to be known as modernity.[2] They include extended legal rationalization and the massive influence of the market economy on patterns of communal social norms and the traditional moral economy.[3] Although it is widely acknowledged that ideal forces, especially the onslaught of new learning associated with empirical science, played a substantial role in this process, the exact nature of their input is not always clear.

But the power exercised by reformed Protestantism in shaping the American understanding of personal liberty need not be in question. This is especially apparent when one considers the sharp limitations placed on personal liberty in the midst of the changing social and economic climate sketched above. In fact, the persistence of such strenuous limits is only fully comprehensible if, as Georg Jellinek claims, "the idea of legally establishing inalienable, inherent and sacred rights of the individual is not of political but religious origin. What has been held to be a work of the [French] Revolution was in reality a fruit of the Reformation and its struggles."[4] Indeed, the primary inspiration for the American valuation of per-

---

[2] See S. Huntington, *Political Order in Changing Societies*, p. 32; D. Bell, "Resolving the Contradictions," pp. 43–46; and Kolakowski, "Modernity on Endless Trial," pp. 8–11.

[3] See K. Thomas, *Religion and the Decline of Magic*; Jones, *European Miracle*; Polanyi, *Great Transformation*; and Laslett, *World We Have Lost*. On the changes in the 18th-century American economy, see R. D. Brown, *Modernization*; Rezneck, "Development of Industrial Consciousness"; Henretta, *Evolution of American Society*; and McCusker and Menard, *Economy of British America*.

[4] Jellinek, *Declaration*, p. 77. Jellinek was a German historical sociologist to whom both Max Weber and Ernst Troeltsch deferred concerning knowledge of America.

sonal liberty, and Americans' understanding of it and associated rights, is recognized as having been reformed Protestant in origin.[5]

Even if Revolutionary America was a land in which the majority of the citizens may have been formally unchurched, it was still a country in which "the idiom of religion penetrated all discourse, underlay all thought, marked all observances, gave meaning to every public and private crisis." More boldly put, "Puritanism provided the moral and religious background of fully 75 percent of the people who declared their independence in 1776"; possibly "85 or 90 percent would not be an extravagant estimate."[6] As Ben Franklin reported, this was a nation in which the two most commonly owned and read books were the Bible and John Bunyan's 1684 Puritan classic, *The Pilgrim's Progress.*[7] Of the two, the Bible was undoubtedly "the most important source of meaning for eighteenth-century Americans."[8] Such a choice accords with a nation shaped by Protestant institutions rather than, as in Europe, by Catholic ones. As Philip Schaff notes, even in Protestant countries in Europe, "most of the city and village churches, the universites, and religious foundations, point to a medieval" Catholic origin. In America, however, "everything had a Protestant beginning"; thus, past "and present condition[s] are unquestionably due mainly to the influence of Protestant principles." Perhaps Louis Hartz was close to getting it right: what makes America anomalous is its lack of medieval origins. However, it is not the absence of feudalism so much as the near-absence of Catholic institutions that defines America's exceptional social and political origins.[9]

Prominent colonial historians continue to find that "no understanding of the eighteenth century is possible if we unconsciously omit, or consciously jam out, the religious themes," for in America, "the most enduring and absorbing public question from 1689 to 1777 was religion" and the major political developments of the 18th century continued to be "dis-

[5]See Lutz, *Origins of American Constitutionalism,* p. 120, and *Preface to American Political Theory,* pp. 73–74; Baldwin, *New England Clergy,* p. 172; Bloch, *Visionary Republic,* pp. 44–45; Counts, "Political Views," p. 199; Gribbin, "Republicanism," p. 26; Vetterli and Bryner, *In Search of the Republic,* p. 54; and Schaff, *America* (1855), p. 47.

[6]Bonomi, *Under the Cope of Heaven,* p. 3; and Ahlstrom, *Religious History of the American People,* p. 124; see also Haskins, *Law and Authority in Early Massachusetts,* pp. 223–24; and Fischer, *Albion's Seed,* p. 423, who reports that of approximately three thousand congregations in 1775, only five hundred, or 15 percent, were Anglican (Episcopal), with the vast remainder reformed congregations.

[7]See Franklin, *Autobiography,* pp. 21–22; and Main, *Social Structure of Revolutionary America,* p. 258.

[8]Appleby, "American Heritage," p. 225; see also Baldwin, *New England Clergy,* p. 7; and Noll, *Princeton and the Republic,* p. 144.

[9]Schaff, *America* (1855), pp. 72–73. The exception to this generalization, Maryland, in fact gives further credence to it, evidenced by the state's colonial history of extreme intolerance and state-sponsored persecution of Catholics. See Ahlstrom, *Religious History of the American People,* pp. 330–35.

cussed and understood by men of the time in terms derived from the Puritan ethic."[10] At the very least, then, "for most inhabitants of the American colonies in the eighteenth century, Calvinism was . . . in the position of laissez-faire in mid-nineteenth-century England or democracy in twentieth-century America."[11] Put differently (and possibly too strongly), "after a century and a half of colonial settlement in which the overwhelming majority of citizens were Protestant, a contemporary would in many instances have been hard put to define where Protestantism ended and secular life began."[12]

Religiosity, if not a deep commitment to Protestantism, also characterized men during the Revolutionary years who are usually considered Enlightenment figures. Take, for example, the progressive writings of the influential British "Cato," so popular in this period; one unexpectedly finds him arguing that "happiness is the chief End of Man, and the saving of his Soul is his chief Happiness," and that "religion and government, particularly, are at the Beginning and End of every Thing."[13] It is also surprising that the elitist and seemingly libertine and enlightened South Carolinians penned one of the most religiously intolerant constitutions and supported a solidly reformed-Protestant culture.[14] John Adams, looking back on the Revolutionary period, reminded his fellow Deist Thomas Jefferson that "the *general Principles,* on which the Fathers Atchieved Independence, were . . . the Principles of Christianity, in which all" were united.[15]

More surprising still, Ben Franklin, truly a man of the Enlightenment, proposed in the Constitutional Convention that "we have not hitherto once thought of humbly applying to the Father of lights to illuminate our understandings." He implored that this be done, for he noted that "the longer I live, the more convincing proofs I see of this truth—*that God*

---

[10]E. S. Morgan, "Puritan Ethic," p. 240; and Bridenbaugh, *Mitre and Sceptre,* p. xi; see also Bridenbaugh, *Myths and Realities,* pp. 180–81, and *Spirit of '76,* p. 118; McLoughlin, "Role of Religion in the Revolution," pp. 253–55; and Grasso, "Between Awakenings," pp. 89–90.

[11]May, *Enlightenment in America,* pp. 45–46; see also Katz, "Legal and Religious Context," pp. 36–37; and more generally regarding 18th-century thought, Hampson, *Enlightenment,* p. 131.

[12]T. J. Curry, *First Freedoms,* p. 218.

[13]Cato, "Letter #66" and "Letter #71" (1722), in Jacobson, *English Libertarian Heritage,* pp. 168, 190; see also Hatch, *Sacred Cause of Liberty,* pp. 92–93.

[14]See "The South Carolina Constitution" (1778), in B. Schwartz, *Roots of the Bill of Rights,* pp. 333–35, in which the Christian Protestant religion is established; and P. Miller, "From the Covenant to the Revival," pp. 332–33.

[15]J. Adams, "Letter to Thomas Jefferson" (1813), in Adams and Jefferson, *Adams-Jefferson Letters,* pp. 339–40; see also J. Adams, "Discourse XIII on Davilla" (1790), in *Works of John Adams,* 6:277, in which he described the rights that Americans went to war to protect as those of men, Christians, and subjects. This echoes the 1772 claim of his cousin Samuel, who had advanced it in "The Rights of the Colonists," which Samuel had written for the Boston Committee of Correspondence. See S. Adams, *Writings of Samuel Adams,* 2:350–59.

governs in the affairs of men."[16] Some have even claimed that those men legitimately described as Founding Fathers, the eighty-eight men who signed the Declaration and the Constitution, can with one exception all be shown to have been "religious."[17] Mark Tushnet, a Critical Legal theorist and certainly no Christian apologist, has even argued that the liberal-establishment clause of the First Amendment cannot be properly understood without recognizing that for those who ratified it, America was foremost "a Protestant nation."[18]

Even if Americans attended formal religious services as rarely as some scholars have contended,[19] they read the Bible as an authoritative guide to morality and used as their elementary school primer the Westminster "shorter Catechism" of reformed doctrine. America was a land, therefore, in which the dominant language and pattern of social and political thought was derived from reformed Protestantism.[20] This is possibly most clearly evidenced in the states' and the Continental Congresses' numerous proclamations for days of thanksgiving and days of "public humiliation, fasting, and prayer," so that Americans could "with united hearts and voices, unfeignedly confess and deplore" their "many sins."[21] On these state and

[16]Franklin, "Speech" (28 June 1787), in Farrand, *Records of the Federal Convention,* 1:451–52; see also Franklin, *Autobiography,* pp. 74–75, in which he speaks highly of the propriety and utility of public worship.

[17]See Hartnett, "Religion of the Founding Fathers," pp. 49–68; Sandoz, *Government of Laws;* Vetterli and Bryner, *In Search of the Republic,* p. 62; and Amos, *Defending the Declaration,* who ironically accuses evangelical scholars of having unduly secularized the Founding. The one exception almost always mentioned is Thomas Jefferson. I find the description "religious" too vague and slippery a term to be of much value. See also Nichols, *Democracy and the Churches,* pp. 39–40, who usefully distinguishes between the latitudinarian theology of half to two-thirds of the founding elite, on the one hand, and the army and the majority of those supporting the Revolution, who were "orthodox Puritan, whether Presbyterian, Baptist Congregationalist, or Low Anglican," on the other.

[18]Tushnet, "Supreme Court's Invitation," p. 13; see also J. Story, *Commentaries,* 2:602–9, who writes that "the right of a society or government to interfere in matters of religion will hardly be contested," for "the great doctrines of religion . . . never can be a matter of indifference in any well-ordered community." Indeed, "the real object of the First Amendment was not to countenance, much less to advance, Mahometanism, Judaism, or infidelity, by prostrating Christianity; but to exclude rivalry among Christian sects." Therefore, "the whole power over the subject of religion is left exclusively to the State governments." Also see Cord, *Separation of Church and State,* pp. 2–15. Note that Madison promoted the First Amendment without the supporting recommendations that had been advanced by the states. See Bowling, "Tub to the Whale," pp. 235–36.

[19]See Stark and Finke, "American Religion in 1776," pp. 42, 45–47, who estimate that among the white population only 12 percent of Americans were members of churches. In disagreement are Stiles, *Discourse on the Christian Union* (1761), pp. 112–13; Bonomi and Eisenstadt, "Church Adherence," pp. 275–76; Whitlock, *Parish of Amity,* pp. 189–90; Stout, *New England Soul,* p. 6; and Hackett, "Social Origins of Nationalism," p. 661, who reports that the church records of Albany, New York "show that more than 70% of the inhabitants were members of the church."

[20]See Buel, "Democracy and the American Revolution," p. 125, and D. D. Hall, "Religion and Society," pp. 322–23.

[21]Continental Congress, *Journals of the Continental Congress* (12 June 1775), 2:87; see

national days of humiliation and fasting, "two services were maintained in most communities, and these occupied the major portion of the day." Indeed, until the "breaking up of old customs" that was a consequence of "the Revolutionary war, the people usually abstained from food until after the second service." And as instructed by the New-York Committee of Safety, all citizens were to follow these guidelines and "abstain from all and every kind of servile labour, business, and employment, and attend upon Divine service in publick." In addition, no one was to be "permitted to cross the ferries, ride or walk out of town, or about the streets, for amusement or diversion; and . . . all parents and masters will be careful to restrain their children and servants from playing and straggling about this City."[22]

As Perry Miller explains, other public documents (such as the celebrated Declaration of Independence) were written to appeal to European audiences, and thus used the Enlightenment language of "social compact [and] inalienable rights." The state and national fast proclamations, however, spoke to "the ranks of the militia and citizens" who were fighting the war, and accordingly spoke of spiritual purges, sin, contrition and humiliation, and God's blessing for "His repentant children."[23] In these proclamations, as in America's first national day of thanksgiving set for 18 December 1777, soldiers at Valley Forge and citizens alike were requested to repair to their Protestant houses of worship in "penitent confession of their manifold sins" and implore "in humble and earnest supplication that it may please God, through the merits of Jesus Christ, mercifully to forgive and blot them out." They were to do so in order to spread "the means of religion for the promotion and enlargement of that kingdom which consisteth 'in righteousness, [and] peace and joy in the Holy Ghost.'" And on this day of national thanksgiving after the surrender of General Burgoyne, all citizens were to forgo "servile labour and such recreation" as "might be unbecoming the purpose of this Appointment."[24] Thus, this was clearly a Protestant country in which the language and rituals of Christianity had a highly visible governmental, even national, presence.

---

also Sandoz, *Government of Laws*, p. 136, who estimates that sixteen or more proclamations were issued. In addition, this was a tradition preserved in three of the first four presidencies. Jefferson, the exception, refused to issue a proclamation because he believed that the "power to prescribe any religious exercise, or to assume authority in religious discipline, has [not] been delegated to the general government. It must then rest with the states." See "Letter to Rev. Samuel Miller" (23 January 1808), in *Writings*, ed. Peterson, p. 1187. As a member of the Virginia House of Burgesses, Jefferson had shown no such reluctance. As noted by Kerr, "Politics and Religion," p. 378, Jefferson in 1774 supported the House of Burgesses in cooking "up a resolution . . . for a day of fasting, humiliation & prayer, to implore heaven."

[22]Love, *Fast and Thanksgiving Days*, pp. 416–17; and Force, "Resolutions of New-York Committee" (16 May 1776).

[23]P. Miller, "From the Covenant to the Revival," p. 333.

[24]Continental Congress, *Journals of the Continental Congress* (1 November 1777), 9:854–55. See also Love, *Fast and Thanksgiving Days*, pp. 339–41, 400–401. Cf. Pangle, *Spirit of Modern Republicanism*, p. 81, who in defending his view of the Revolution as secular and enlightened, claims that in public documents Americans made "no explicit reference to the Trinity or even to Jesus Christ."

LIBERTY'S ESSENCE: VOLUNTARY AND RIGHTEOUS

The liberty of a Christian, as explained centuries earlier by St. Augustine in his *Confessions,* was that "whenever God converts a sinner, and translates him into the state of grace, he freeth him from his natural bondage under sin, and by His grace alone inables him freely to will and to do that which is spiritually good."[25] Martin Luther had even claimed that the doctrine of Christian liberty "contains the whole of Christian life in a brief form, provided you grasp its meaning" (an admittedly large proviso).[26] In the modern world, the adherents of the reformed tradition are the most emphatic defenders of Augustinian Christianity (with its view of human impotence in the face of God's omnipotence and his inscrutable justice of divine predestination).[27]

Following in this tradition, Phillips Payson, a scholar in the natural sciences and a member of the American Academy of Sciences as well a Congregational minister in Chelsea, Massachusetts, explained that "next to the liberty of heaven," the chosen possess spiritual liberty "in which they are freed from the bondage of corruption, the tyranny of evil lusts and passion." This spiritual liberty was to be accounted as "the greatest happiness of man, considered in a private capacity."[28] Jonas Clark, the minister who hid John Hancock and Sam Adams on the night of Paul Revere's ride, further revealed that "the gospel of *Jesus Christ,* is the source of liberty, the soul of government and the life of a people."[29] Nathaniel Niles also defends the superior importance of spiritual liberty and differentiates between two common senses of liberty: that which "takes place in earthly communities is called domestic or civil," while that which belongs "to the kingdom of God . . . [is] termed divine or spiritual." Yet according to this popular jurist, minister, land developer, inventor, and member of Congress, only spiritual liberty is of intrinsic worth. Only through Christ's intercession can people begin to overcome the deforming effects of the Fall, which made them incapable of conforming to God's will and a life of true liberty of any kind.[30] Spiritual liberty, even for these politically active ministers during the height of the Revolution, was the personal form of liberty most sought and most highly valued.

Its importance, however, was defended by others besides orthodox Congregational pastors who were politically active. Simeon Howard, the theologically liberal successor to Jonathan Mayhew in the pulpit of Boston's

[25]Cited by P. Miller, *New England Mind,* 2:69.
[26]Luther, "Dedication: The Freedom of a Christian," in *Martin Luther,* p. 52.
[27]See Westminster Assembly, "Westminster Confession of Faith" (1646), p. 198.
[28]Payson, "Massachusetts Election Sermon" (1778), p. 524.
[29]J. Clark, *Massachusetts Election Sermon* (1781), p. 37.
[30]N. Niles, "Second Discourse" (1774), pp. 39–40; see also C. Turner, *Sermon,* (1773), p. 33. Turner was an orthodox Congregational minister, a state senator, and a member of the Connecticut convention to ratify the Constitution. See also Powers, *Jesus Christ the True King* (1778 Vermont election sermon), p. 40.

West Church, was denounced as a heretic by Congregationalists. He too, however, instructed that "there is another and more valuable kind of liberty [than political] . . . which consists in being free from the power and dominion of sin, through the assistance of the divine spirit."[31] Similarly, Stephen Johnson, argued that "we are planted in this land for God; and all our deliverances are wrought for God"; and "our forefathers left the dear delights of their native country . . . not for worldly wealth or honours, pomps or pleasures; but for the glorious cause of liberty," that is, to promote "the great and everlasting interests of his gospel and kingdom."[32] Consider as well the florid language of David Thomas, a Baptist minister in Virginia, who declared that liberty was beyond human reach without the aid of Christ. He held that "sin and Satan, and the world, and the flesh have an absolute dominion over" men, so much that no man has the "power to deliver himself out of this woeful condition. . . . The dead as soon might leave their tombs, or dry bones, awake and live, as natural men by any virtue in them, repent and turn to GOD. . . . For without faith it is impossible to please him. And that faith . . . is to be obtained but by the operation of the HOLY-GHOST."[33] Americans continued to be reminded by a well-respected cultural and intellectual elite, composed of evangelical and rationalist ministers, that spiritual liberty was the key to true liberty. And this took place during two of the most politically charged decades of the 18th century, the mid-1760s through the mid-1780s, an era of intense political upheaval and change.

These theologically and geographically diverse ministers were united in teaching that human liberty, the ability to surrender voluntarily to a life of righteousness, was beyond the limited capacities of humans. A life of liberty was, according to them, not a heroic act, but rather one of humility before God. As Princeton's president, Samuel Davies, a man with pastoral experience throughout the colonies, explained to his graduating seniors: "so deep and universal is the present innate Depravity of human Nature, that the sacred Structure of a truly great and good Man, can never be built upon" a natural human foundation. One first must be reborn in Jesus Christ.[34] For America's reformed Protestants, humans were dependent on outside mediation—God's freely given grace and the community's close supervision—to make possible a life of authentic liberty.

The late 18th-century general understanding of liberty as voluntary submission to righteousness mediated through community or congregation was not noticeably different from the more specialized meaning of spiritual liberty. In both instances, a life of liberty could only be lived when the individual was aided by extrapersonal forces such as those found in a

[31]S. Howard, "Sermon Preached in Boston" (1773), p. 208.
[32][Stephen Johnson], *Some Important Observations* (1766), pp. 56–57.
[33]D. Thomas, *Virginian Baptist* (1774), pp. 9–10.
[34]Davies, *Religion and Public Spirit* (1761), p. 13.

close-knit Protestant community. It is likely that Charles Turner in 1783 was not exaggerating when he held that the *"true* spirit of liberty" was "nothing more nor less than a spirit of true Christianity, considered as extending itself in reference to matters of civil and ecclesiastical government,"[35] for "the happiness and freedom of the sons of moral liberty consists in their voluntary subjection and obedience to" moral righteousness, and to it alone.[36] Human beings, we are repeatedly reminded had "full Liberty to do all the Good we can in our Places, to serve GOD and our Generation," but they had "no Right or Liberty to do wrong,"[37] since "the freedom wherewith Christ has made us free, has nothing of licentiousness or lawless liberty in it . . . it is a rule of obedience."[38] Liberty was defended by the clergy and laity alike as a reflection of an objective set of divine and universal ethical standards by which it and license could be carefully distinguished.

Early Americans' understanding of liberty followed that of their ministers; it "was not liberty in the modern sense, a freedom to pursue individual wishes or inclinations."[39] H. Richard Niebuhr confirms that the traditional sense of Christian liberty was unlike the contemporary "negative" sense of liberty. Instead, it was a "positive" form that carried within its meaning the specific moral ends for which it could be legitimately exercised. This sense of liberty was "the freedom from the rule of Satan, sin, and death" as well as from complete "domination by self-interest and the passions."[40] Thus, spiritual liberty, unlike contemporary senses of liberty, captures the recognizable essential features of late 18th-century American liberty: voluntary though communally mediated (and potentially coercive) obedience to true ethical standards derived from a divinely ordered cosmos.

Spiritual liberty provided the template for an understanding of liberty in which "every freedom which is freedom for something, every freedom which is justified by a reference to something higher than the individual or than man as mere man, necessarily restricts freedom or, which is the same thing, establishes a tenable distinction between freedom and license."[41] This distinction between the freedom to act in ways that might be legal though morally unacceptable (defined as license) and the freedom to act in rationally or religiously responsible ways (defined as liberty), although often implied rather than explicit, was the fundamental distinction that Americans, following their ministers' teaching, maintained between liberty and license. It was spiritual liberty writ large.

---

[35] C. Turner, *Due Glory* (1783), p. 29.
[36] Mellen, *Great and Happy Doctrine of Liberty* (1795), pp. 12–13.
[37] Lockwood, *Worth and Excellence* (1759), pp. 16–17.
[38] Tufts, *Believers Most Sure Freedom* (1757), p. 11.
[39] Haskins, *Law and Authority in Early Massachusetts*, p. 17.
[40] Niebuhr, "Protestant Movement and Democracy," pp. 31–36.
[41] Strauss, *Natural Right and History*, p. 294.

One anonymous author held in 1759 that "in the Universe there is not a greater Contrast, no two Things can differ more essentially from Each other" than liberty and licentiousness.[42] In 1776, Samuel West, one of the most learned Americans of his time, argued that "to have a liberty to do whatever is fit, reasonable, or good, is the highest degree of freedom that rational beings can possess." Moreover, it is society's role "to secure to men this rational liberty, and to promote" their happiness and welfare while "suppressing vice and immorality."[43] The overlap between spiritual liberty and general liberty is striking, and it is difficult to distinguish their descriptions. Spiritual liberty thus cannot be relegated to a distant corner of the 18th-century intellectual landscape as an obscure notion to which idiosyncratic Christian ministers adhered. To the contrary, it should be recognized as a foundational understanding of liberty that shaped the 18th-century view of liberty in its entirety.

The Reverend Dr. Price, whose works were read faithfully in the colonies by supporters of various traditions of thought, offers further evidence of the mainstream character and the power of reformed Protestantism in shaping the 18th-century understanding of liberty. Dr. Price's books, one of his many critics claimed, "go by Dozens and Scores to the different Provinces [of America], where they will be read with great Avidity, by all American Insurgents: Admiring pious Congregations will neglect their Creed and Catechism, to read and hear their political Confession of Faith."[44] This important English dissenting Protestant and rationalist maintained the same distinction between freedom as license and as liberty in his most influential essay as is found in descriptions of spiritual liberty. In the fateful year of 1776, he held that "MORAL LIBERTY is the power of following, in all circumstances, our sense of right and wrong; or acting in conformity to our reflecting and moral principles, without being controuled by any contrary principles. . . . [And] he whose perceptions of moral obligations are controuled by his passions has lost his *Moral Liberty;* and the most common language applied to him is, that he wants *Self-government.*"[45] This discrimination between freedom as liberty and freedom as license was indeed congenial to the dominant patterns of thought in late 18th-century America.

This Protestant-inspired embrace of freedom as liberty was effected with the expectation that liberty would not thereby lose its bounded and restrictive nature. This clear sense of limits is conveyed by John Zubly, a Swiss Presbyterian minister who, before resigning, was a member of the Continental Congress. In 1775, before the provincial congress of Georgia, he

---

[42][Brooke?], *Liberty and Common-Sense* (1760), letter 2, p. 5.

[43]S. West, "Right to Rebel Against Governors" (1776 Massachusetts election sermon), pp. 430–31.

[44]Stewart, *Letter to the Rev. Dr. Price* (1776), pp. 50–51.

[45]Price, *Observations* (1776), pp. 3–4.

preached that "liberty and law are perfectly consistent; liberty does not consist in living without all restraint," and that "a more unhappy situation could not easily be devised unto mankind, than that every man should have it in his power to do what is right in his own eyes."[46] Indeed, this discrimination was so basic to 18th-century American thought that even an elite nationalist like James Wilson in his law lectures argued in good faith that "without law, liberty loses its nature and its name, and becomes licentiousness."[47] Regardless of religious affiliation, virtually all Americans thought as reformed Protestants did and condemned liberty without corporately defined limits as licentiousness.

Of comparable importance in the Protestants' scheme of liberty, though, was their perplexing insistence that righteous action should preferably result from uncoerced submission. This was an essential element of traditional Christian liberty that also helped shape the 18th-century understanding of liberty. They thought the believer was "freely" bound to order himself or herself in accord with the commandments of Christ, indeed even to enslave himself or herself to Christ, for "he that was called in the Lord being a bondservant, is the Lord's freeman: likewise he that was called being free, is Christ's bondservant."[48] Or, as Martin Luther described this paradoxical relationship, "a Christian is a perfectly free lord of all, subject to none. A Christian is a perfectly dutiful servant of all, subject to all."[49]

In like fashion, John Winthrop, the founding governor and one of the leading lights of the Massachusetts Bay Colony, expanded on this curious mixture of freedom and servitude by means of an analogy that likely would be offensive to modern-day American sensibilities. He compared true liberty to marriage in which "the woman's own choice makes such a man her husband; yet being so chosen, he is her lord, and she is to be subject to him, yet in a way of liberty, not of bondage; and a true wife accounts her subjection her honor and freedom."[50] Freedom was essential—or at least the opportunity of giving oneself freely was. But one was to surrender voluntarily to a regime of effective subservience to God and his lieutenants on earth, within both the family and the polity.

Over a century later, Hugh Alison, a South Carolinian pastor writing in 1769, continued to preach this traditional reformed-Protestant understanding of liberty with its perplexing mixture of freedom and subjection. He taught that Christ's gift of spiritual liberty "frees us from the yoke of the ceremonial [Mosaic] law . . . from the dominion of lust and passion;

[46]Zubly, *Law of Liberty* (1775), p. 26.

[47]J. Wilson, "Introduction to Law," in *Works of James Wilson*, ed. Andrews, 1:6–7.

[48]Cited by Davis from 1 Corinthians 7:20–22; 12:13 in "Slavery and Sin," pp. 26–27; see also Romans 6:15–23; Troeltsch, *Protestantism and Progress*, pp. 17–18; and Fliegelman, *Prodigals and Pilgrims*, pp. 19, 174.

[49]Luther, "The Freedom of a Christian," in *Martin Luther*, p. 53.

[50]Winthrop, "Speech to the General Court" (3 July 1645), in Miller and Johnson, *Puritans*, 1:206–7; see also Kerber, "Can a Woman Be an Individual?" pp. 151–53.

and restores the soul to a religious self-government, and to the rational life of a Christian . . . [and] brings every thought into the obedience of Christ; nor does the soul ever act with greater liberty than when it acts under a divine command . . . those are the men of freest thought, whose thoughts are captivated and brought unto obedience to Christ."[51] Christian liberty, in the 17th and 18th centuries, invariably demanded not only the existence of strict and objective moral standards to which one submitted in service to God, country, and family—in that order[52]—but also the possibility of doing so voluntarily. This was a curious combination, one that, when freed from the constraints of community and revelation, would prove difficult to hold together.

A certain measure of freedom, or more exactly, the possibility of voluntarily surrendering to moral righteousness, is important to all Christians because of the special role of faith in Christian teachings. But it was essential to reformed Protestants, to their psyches if not to their theology, because for 18th-century non-Arminian reformed Protestants, neither following a set of divine commandments (Judaism) nor adhering to sacramental rituals (Catholicism) was able to inspire confidence in one's ultimate salvation.[53] Without freedom with which to obey or disobey God's demands, no such confidence in salvation could be generated, nor could one's status as one of God's chosen few be properly demonstrated to one's neighbors through constant trial.[54] It was assumed by reformed Protestants with their dark view of unaided human abilities that without justification and sanctification in Christ, a person would be unable to live a righteous life.[55] The opportunity to submit voluntarily to strict moral standards was absolutely essential in the effort to overcome the uncertainty of an eternity of bliss or perdition.[56]

Yet all people, saved or not, were to obey and live in accord with godly standards.[57] Freedom may have been essential, and voluntarism may have been the hoped-for means, but godly living by all was a necessary social standard by which to measure the public good. As David Little explains, "the true fulfillment of man, as Calvin reiterates over and again, is voluntary, wholehearted obedience to the true God." But as Calvin, like his

[51]Alison, *Spiritual Liberty* (1769), p. 19.

[52]See Sidney, "Maxims for Republics" (1787), p. 81.

[53]See Westminster Assembly, "Westminster Confession of Faith" (1646), p. 205; Cotton, "Mr. Cotton's Rejoynder" (1636), pp. 98–99; and Trinterud, "New Light Snuffed Out," p. 177.

[54]See M. Weber, *Protestant Ethic*, pp. 111–15.

[55]See Presbyterian Church, "Shorter Catechism" (1646), pp. 292–94; and Duché, "Duty of Standing Fast" (1775), p. 79.

[56]See Greven, *Protestant Temperament*, p. 103.

[57]See M. Weber, *Protestant Ethic*, pp. 104–5, who reminds us that according to orthodoxy, "the membership of the external Church included the doomed. They should belong to it and be subjected to its discipline, not in order thus to attain salvation, that is impossible, but because, for the glory of God, they too must be forced to obey His commandments."

18th-century American followers, knew full well, people rarely obeyed God, and instead usually followed their licentious passions, despite the ruin and destruction thus brought to them eternally, and more immediately to their community. In a fallen state, a man usually will be driven by natural necessity, and when that fails to lead him to righteousness, he will have to be led "by political coercion, in the direction of the genuine obedience he ought to *will* to do of his own accord."[58]

The same reformed Protestants who were so insistent on the need for freedom and voluntarism were willing to force godly living on the damned and saved alike. American reformed Protestants believed that they were individually joined to God through a covenant of grace, yet like the ancient Hebrews, they were being judged by God not just personally, but collectively because of their national or public covenant.[59] Thus, throughout the 17th and 18th centuries, they expected temporal reward and punishment (for example, bountiful harvests or plagues) for their collective actions, and in particular for their sins. Corporate control over the behavior of individuals was not effected in order to gain salvation, for most 18th-century Americans more or less accepted that individual behavior had no effect on one's chances for eternal salvation. (This would radically change in the early 19th century with the great expansion of Methodism.) But whether an individual's behavior was pleasing or displeasing to God was understood to have a significant influence on a community's temporal well-being. So throughout the last years of the colonies and the early years of the nation, when Americans were reported by all to be intoxicated by liberty, appropriate moral legislation continued to be enacted and days of fasting and humiliation continued to be proclaimed.[60]

Still, the ideal was that at least those who were saved should embrace godly living without coercion. One horn of the dilemma that reformed Protestants (if not all Americans) confronted was how to make possible voluntary submission to the path of righteousness without legitimating licentiousness. The other horn of the dilemma was, when people proved recalcitrant or simply failed, as Christians knew they must, how, without becoming tyrants, to force them to live more or less godly lives. In practice, the resolution of this dilemma often led Americans to accept that those who are unwilling to be free must be forced to be "free," as was so vividly described by that true son of Calvin's Geneva, Rousseau.[61]

[58]Little, "Max Weber Revisited," p. 422.

[59]See Grasso, "Between Awakenings," pp. 42–43.

[60]See McLoughlin, "Role of Religion in the Revolution," p. 210.

[61]See Little, "Max Weber Revisited," pp. 423–24. But Rousseau's social and political thought did not depend, as does Calvinism, on a revealed God and text. Therefore, his citizens were able collectively to prescribe moral laws for themselves without regard to their ultimate truth as revealed by God in his revelation, or according to universal reason. Additionally, political activity for Rousseau, at least in *The Social Contract*, was the preferred way to encourage human flourishing.

Notwithstanding this perverse dilemma, reformed Protestantism must be seen as one of the most important causal agents in legitimating the historically novel concept of individual liberty in America and in the modern West (and in the 20th century, in much of the rest of the world).[62] Reformed Protestantism's central role in the sustenance of the concept of personal liberty has been recognized by some of its most obdurate opponents. Even David Hume argued that "the precious spark of liberty had been kindled, and was preserved, by the puritans alone; and it was to this sect, whose principles appear so frivolous and habits so ridiculous, that the English owe the whole freedom of their constitution."[63] John Stuart Mill, a man utterly contemptuous of Calvinism, believed that it was reformed Protestants "who first broke the yoke of what called itself the Universal Church" and who were almost solely responsible for "the rights of the individual" having been asserted against society.[64] Yet in practice, reformed Protestantism in its supervision of the individual invariably was genuinely censorious and coercive, and as Mill also noted, destructive of what he considered authentic individual liberty.[65]

Individual liberty as voluntary servitude thus is a reformed-Protestant heritage that draws on the Protestant understanding of spiritual liberty, and has deeply affected social and political life in America, as it has throughout the modern Western world.[66] As Hume and Mill recognized, spiritual liberty was not to be contained in the realm of religious observance. Instead, its influence shaped many modern social and political norms, in particular those senses of liberty embraced by reformed-Protestant America, with its ever-increasing Protestant church membership and its paradoxical insistence on both voluntarism and strict personal morality.[67]

SPIRITUAL AND CORPORATE LIBERTY: JOINED BUT UNEQUAL

Along with the Christian sense of liberty and its curious insistence that people should have the opportunity to submit voluntarily to the ways of God, Americans inherited the temptation to secularize this spiritual sense of individual liberty.[68] Centuries earlier, Calvin had understood that this was to be expected, for there would be many who "under the pretext of this liberty, [would] cast off all obedience to God, and precipitate them-

[62]See Troeltsch, *Protestantism and Progress*, p. 205.

[63]Cited by E. F. Miller, "Hume on English Liberty," p. 157.

[64]Mill, "On Liberty" (1859), p. 133.

[65]See M. Weber, *Protestant Ethic*, pp. 151–52; and Mill, "On Liberty" (1859), pp. 190–91.

[66]See Walzer, *Revolution of the Saints*, p. 47; and Davis, "Slavery and Sin," pp. 5–6.

[67]See Stark and Finke, "American Religion in 1776," pp. 50–51; Benson, "Polls"; Caplow, "Religion in Middletown"; Galston, "Public Morality and Religion"; and Reichley, "Democracy and Religion."

[68]See Troeltsch, *Protestantism and Progress*, p. 57.

selves into the most unbridled licentiousness."[69] In spite of Calvin's sensitivity to this problem, Ernst Troeltsch's overall assessment seems accurate: "neither Confession [Lutheran or Calvinist] has been able to solve the problem of Protestant organization, the reconciliation of the free inwardness, regulated by conscience, of individual religious conviction with the requirements of a society based on a common cultus and administration."[70] This intractable dilemma, in the long term, has proven incapable of resolution in America and elsewhere. Like John Stuart Mill, however, many find this process to be a desirable evolutionary step on the path toward full individual autonomy.

Nevertheless, in America, from the time Anne Hutchinson and her followers were suppressed in the early 17th century until the late 18th century, such antinomian and libertarian demands had been successfully combated by reformed-Protestant public officials, pastors, and congregations.[71] Jonathan Todd served his congregation in East Guilford, Connecticut, for fifty-seven years, and like other ministers, he warned of those who "under a *Pretence* of Liberty, *falsly so called,* they would *put down all Rule, & all Authority, & Power* among Men: Pleading in Defence of their licentious Doctrine, that CHRIST *hath made all his People Kings: and they shall reign on Earth.* This, they pretend is the *Liberty where with Christ have made them free.*"[72] But according to reformed doctrine, the accepted sense of Christian liberty had little in common with such libertine principles.

The dictionaries in use at the time also described as libertine those who exceeded liberty's strict limits. Fenning, for example, in the 1775 *Royal English Dictionary,* characterized those who live outside these limits as "licentious; having no respect to the precepts of religion." Samuel Johnson defined "libertine" as "one who lives without restraint or law . . . one who pays no regard to the precepts of religion." In the 1794 edition of Thomas Dyche's dictionary, "libertine" was still defined as "one who lives without restraint, and pays no regard to the precepts of religion," and "licentious" was defined as "unrestrained, wild, ungoverned, presumptuous."[73] At least until the end of the 18th century, freedom as liberty was seen as "the acting and behaving within those reasonable bounds that the law has appointed, and being protected therein by the civil magistrate."[74] Usually, those limits were set by the dogma of reformed Protestantism.

At the end of the 18th century, even the proto-Unitarian minister John Mellen was still arguing strenuously for the same differentiation between license and liberty. He warned in 1795, on a national day of public

[69]Calvin, "Of Christian Liberty," in *Institutes of the Christian Religion,* trans. Allen, p. 63.
[70]Troeltsch, *Protestantism and Progress,* pp. 103–4.
[71]See J. Turner, *Without God, without Creed,* pp. 262–69.
[72]Todd, *Civil Rulers the Ministers of God* (1749), p. 2.
[73]Fenning, *Royal English Dictionary* (1775); Samuel Johnson, *Dictionary of the English Language* (1766); and Dyche and Pardon, *New General English Dictionary* (1794).
[74]Dyche and Pardon, *New General English Dictionary* (1752).

thanksgiving in which all Americans were requested to repair to their Protestant houses of worship, that "it must be remembered, and deserves particular attention, that no natural liberty gives men a right to be *libertines,* or renders them *lawless,* for all are under God and nature. In the most *perfect* state of nature, free from all social and domestic obligations . . . [we] are still bound by the laws of reason and everlasting righteousness. . . . There is no such thing in nature, *as a right or privilege to do wrong.*"[75] In fact, according to Max Weber, reformed Protestantism's true goal had always been to destroy "spontaneous, impulsive enjoyment," to "bring order into the conduct of its adherents," rather than autonomous freedom.[76] But in late 18th-century America, this authoritative understanding of liberty did not solely describe that of the spirit. It captured, or so Americans believed, the essential qualities of true liberty—mediated voluntarism, submission, and ordered righteousness.

For at least 150 years, then, Americans in the older colonies had been successful in combating the inherent antinomian and individualistic propensities of Protestant Christianity. But from the time of the founding of the Massachusetts Bay Colony in the early 17th century, they had readily succumbed to another excess associated with Christian liberty. They had collapsed the claims of spiritual liberty with political ones, just as they had joined in their twin covenants individual and corporate spiritual responsibilities. Americans had rejected the emphatic teachings of the medieval church and the less strenuous ones of the Protestant fathers regarding the separate swords of political and religious authority.[77] Nevertheless, Americans, from the beginning of colonization, systematically defended corporate political liberty on what they took to be orthodox Christian grounds.[78]

During the Revolutionary crisis, high-church Anglican pastors belatedly drew attention to this traditional American abuse of spiritual liberty. The most articulate among them, Jonathan Boucher of Prince Georges County, Maryland, fruitlessly reminded his flock that "every sinner is, literally, a slave . . . and the only true liberty is the liberty of being the servant of God; for *his service is perfect freedom.* The passage cannot, without infinite perversion and torture, be made to refer to any other kind of liberty . . . [for] the word *liberty,* as meaning civil [more accurately, political] liberty, does not, I believe, occur in all the Scriptures."[79] Yet the political

[75] Mellen, *Great and Happy Doctrine of Liberty* (1795), pp. 11–12.

[76] M. Weber, *Protestant Ethic,* p. 119.

[77] See Calvin, "Of Civil Government," in *Institutes of the Christian Religion,* trans. Beveridge, 2:651; and Holl, *Cultural Significance of the Reformation,* p. 72.

[78] See Bercovitch, *Puritan Origins of the American Self,* pp. 91–97.

[79] Boucher, "On Civil Liberty" (1775), pp. 504–5; and from different sides of the theological and political spectrum, see in concurrence, Mayhew, "Discourse Concerning Unlimited Submission" (1750), pp. 216–17, and Bercovitch, *Puritan Origins of the American Self,* p. 109, who recounts Roger Williams's much earlier but comparable efforts to distinguish between the two forms of liberty.

extension of Christian liberty to corporate bodies had had a long and distinguished history in America.

In one of the most celebrated speeches in this history, John Winthrop set the tone for subsequent discussions of liberty. For his auditors, he differentiated between "natural" (post-Fall) human liberty, held in common "with beasts and other creatures," and true moral liberty, natural in the classic ontological sense of being attributable to the pre-Fallen human state. Of particular interest is his apparent joining of (or at least his unwillingness to discriminate between) corporate and spiritual liberty. He instructed the General Court in 1645 that in addition to natural liberty there is a civil or federal one that:

> may also be termed moral, in reference to the covenant between God and man, in the moral law, and the politic covenants and constitutions, amongst men themselves. This liberty is the proper end and object of authority, and cannot subsist without it; and it is a liberty to that only which is good, just, and honest. . . . This liberty is maintained and exercised in a way of subjection to authority; it is the same kind of liberty wherewith Christ hath made us free.[80]

He surely is doing more than describing the differences between political and spiritual liberty when he compares them and notes that they are "the same kind of liberty."

Yet in spite of Americans' perversion of what is usually taken to be the Christian orthodoxy of separate swords, for most of the next two centuries, they successfully resisted the extension of spiritual liberty in individualistic and antinomian directions. In fact, by collapsing spiritual and political liberty, they may have augmented and sanctified corporate intrusiveness and provided increased legitimacy to the power of the public over a wayward individual. Like their spiritual ancestors, the Israelites, Christian Americans believed that because of their national or public covenant, they were corporately responsible for the behavior of their fellow citizens. At a corporate level, particularly in New England, public officials took seriously the lead question and answer of the "Shorter Catechism," which formed the core of the *New England Primer*. It asked, "What is the chief end of man?" The answer was, "to glorify God."[81] Thus, fires, wars, earthquakes, thunderstorms, plagues, and other such disasters were believed to be expressions of God's displeasure with a community for the failure of its public officials to control sinful behavior that failed to honor God.

It was incumbent on public and church officials, therefore, to demand private and public contrition (confession; state and later national days of fasting and humiliation) on a regular basis and to regulate offensive behavior. And regulate they did. Statutory legislation, constables and courts,

---

[80]Winthrop, "Speech to the General Court" (3 July 1645), in Miller and Johnson, *Puritans*, 1:206–7.

[81]Presbyterian Church, "Shorter Catechism" (1646), p. 283.

church discipline and church elders, and the moral pressure of the villages of America in which everyone knew everyone else's business (as Mill was to acknowledge, gossip is most effective at discouraging socially unapproved behavior) combined to control the wayward individual.[82] Privacy as we know it was little valued in the 18th century.[83] In these regulations, the Protestant nature of American society is apparent. As a mid-19th-century German visitor observed, "the strict observance of the Sabbath, the countless churches and religious schools, the zealous support of Bible and tract societies," as well as the strict prohibitions against "blasphemy, atheism, Sabbath-breaking, polygamy, and other gross violations of general Christian morality" are clearly indicative of the "Christian character of the people."[84]

The list of the kinds of intrusiveness that colonial society and governments were capable of effecting can be extended further. Individuals were, at times, prevented from living alone; were forced to seek public acceptance when moving to a new town and sometimes when leaving; had their choice of clothing controlled by sumptuary legislation; and could have their children removed if they raised them without benefit of a Christian education, or for simple parental poverty. In regard to purely religious questions, Americans could be prosecuted for breaking any number of Sabbatarian laws (many vestiges of which still exist): for not attending church services, for not paying taxes to support a minister they might revile, or for swearing or profaning the Lord. In addition, they faced criminal prosecution for moral breaches such as committing fornication or sodomy, being economically unproductive or idling,[85] being highly disrespectful of one's parents (at one time a capital crime), gambling or cockfighting, drinking too much in public or even at home (tippling), smoking tobacco, dancing or putting on a ball, or more generally, living in a disorderly or ungodly manner.

The English laws of libel, slander, blasphemy, censorship (of books, pamphlets and newspapers, and pictures), and treason also did much to dampen freedom of artistic expression, thought, press, and speech. (The last two of these freedoms, before the enactment of the First Amendment, were usually only applicable to legislative debate or more generally "pub-

---

[82]See West [Withers], *Plainville, U.S.A.,* p. 162, who describes the effectiveness of church and gossip in controlling behavior in an early 20th-century agricultural town and notes that, in particular, "the religious control of morals operates mainly through gossip and the fear of gossip."

[83]See Wood, *Radicalism of the American Revolution,* p. 59.

[84]Schaff, *America* (1855), pp. 76–77.

[85]This crime was particularly irksome to the English dissenter James Burgh, who was widely read in America. See Kramnick, *Republicanism and Bourgeois Radicalism,* pp. 226–27, 233–34, 248–49, who describes Burgh's and Locke's "utter disregard for private right when idleness was involved," and Burgh's willingness to proscribe great wealth and all manner of immorality. See also Bryan and McClaughry, *Vermont Papers,* p. 203, for their description of Vermont's Draconian 1797 poor laws.

lick Men in their publick Conduct.")[86] Little of what we consider private behavior, therefore, was free of control by one's brethren in church, neighborhood, society, or government.[87] It seems reasonable to infer that Americans' associating political and spiritual liberty and their fear of corporate retribution for the moral transgressions of individuals encouraged their insistence on the community's moral stewardship role.

During the Revolutionary period, ministers defended the traditional link between corporate and spiritual liberty. According to the chaplain of the Continental Congress, British "tyranny" demanded that "the citizen, the Christian . . . 'stand fast in the liberty wherewith Christ . . . hath made them free.'"[88] It was stated that "LIBERTY is the spirit and genius, not only of the gospel, but the whole of that revelation, we have first and last received from God. Every dispensation breathes the same spirit, both of moral and civil liberty,"[89] and "ministers from one end of the theological spectrum to the other came to include political liberty as a fundamental article of faith."[90] It thus appears that America's revolutionary embrace of political liberty, generously informed by classical, Whig republican, and English common-law references, nonetheless found an important legitimation in their reformed Protestantism.

Spiritual and corporate political liberty, then, were linked in America from its founding, and many during the Revolution further believed that political liberty could not be exercised without the purgative of a spiritual rebirth. This idea also has a long and rich history of support in colonial America, especially in New England. In 1774, Nathaniel Niles, speaking amid the supercharged atmosphere created by the imposition of the "Intolerable Acts," was not staking out a new or aberrant position when he argued in the second of his two discourses on liberty that "if we refuse spiritual liberty, that of the civil kind will be no otherwise agreeable than as it tends to advance our own private interests. . . . Thus, by neglecting to embrace the gospel, we convert civil liberty, which is in itself, a delicious

---

[86]Handlin and Handlin, "The Return of the Town of Boston" (1780), in *Popular Sources of Political Authority,* pp. 756, 763; and for example see "New Hampshire Bill of Rights" (1783), in B. Schwartz, *Roots of the Bill of Rights,* p. 378, in which the "freedom of deliberation, speech, and debate in either house of the legislature" was defended only in this circumscribed environment seven years before the Bill of Rights; see also Blackstone, *Commentaries,* 4:151–52; C. Warren, "New 'Liberty' under the Fourteenth Amendment," p. 461; McDonald, *Novus Ordo Seclorum,* pp. 46–47, who implicitly corrects Warren by noting that one state, Pennsylvania, did extend freedom of speech to the people at large; and Levy, "Liberty and the First Amendment," pp. 35–36.

[87]See Flaherty, *Privacy in Colonial New England.* He provides copious evidence for the conclusions drawn here without his sharing them. Although he treats a slightly later period, Griffin, *Their Brother's Keepers,* comes to conclusions similar to mine.

[88]Duché, "Duty of Standing Fast" (1775), p. 82.

[89]Mellen, *Great and Happy Doctrine of Liberty* (1795), p. 9.

[90]Hatch, *Sacred Cause of Liberty,* pp. 157–58, and see p. 53; Stout, *New England Soul,* pp. 289–90; and John 8:31–37, and Galatians 5:1.

kind of food, into a slow poison which will render our death vastly more terrible than otherwise it would have been. It had been better for us not to have been born, or, to have been born slaves."[91] From a reformed-Protestant perspective, only spiritual liberty could prepare a person to exercise corporate political liberty. This demonstrated a most nonheroic view of man that understood him to be unable to exercise freedom without divine intercession.[92] Personal liberty, unaided by divine grace and corporate oversight, would necessarily degenerate into depraved license controlled by selfish lusts.

Looking back at the expanse of American history beginning in the 1630s, Harry Stout finds that through the end of the Revolutionary era, spiritual liberty was consistently seen as necessary for the exercise of corporate political liberty. America's ministers understood that "the political language of 'freedom,' 'union,' 'liberty,' and 'deliverance' sounded very much like the old gospel message of liberation from the bondage of sin," yet they continued to emphasize that "America's political redemption from bondage and tyranny was important and necessary, but not as important as personal, eternal redemption. Without spiritual redemption, ministers insisted, political redemption meant nothing."[93] Jonathan Edwards's most devoted student, Joseph Bellamy, in a letter to his son in 1775, made clear his priorities: "my desire and prayer to God is, that my son Jonathan may be saved. And then, whatever happens to America or to you, this year or next, you will be happy forever."[94] William Gordon of Roxbury, Massachusetts, a man of intense political commitments who moved from chaplaincy of the Provincial Congress to Loyalism and exile, reminded his congregation that there were "more important purposes than the fate of kingdoms" or the "civil rights of human nature," to wit, the emancipation of humans from the "slavery of sin and Satan" and their "escape from future misery through faith in a crucified Jesus."[95]

John Witherspoon, the president of Princeton, a member of the Continental Congress, a signer of the Declaration of Independence, a bright light in the firmament of the Scottish Enlightenment, and a powerful influence on the young James Madison,[96] impressed much the same idea upon his Princeton students at their commencement in late May 1776. He warned of "the truly infinite importance of the salvation of" their souls and the

---

[91] N. Niles, "Second Discourse" (1774), pp. 56–57.

[92] See Holl, *Cultural Significance of the Reformation*, pp. 30–31.

[93] Stout, *New England Soul*, p. 297; see also Jedrey, *World of John Cleaveland*, p. 134; and Kerr, "Character of Political Sermons," pp. 31–32.

[94] Bellamy, "Letter to Jonathan Bellamy" (3 April 1775), in *Works of Joseph Bellamy*, 1:xl, and see his remarks to his daughter in which he compares her spiritual well-being to her worldly estate, p. xli.

[95] Gordon, "Discourse Preached December 15th, 1774," p. 197.

[96] See Wills, *Inventing America*, pp. 45–46, 289; and Spurlin, *Montesquieu in America*, p. 179.

lesser importance of whether or not their "children shall be rich or poor, at liberty or in bonds," or whether "this bountiful country shall increase in fruitfulness."[97] The concerns of the spirit were intimately tied to those of the corporate body, even legitimating them, yet those of the spirit were expected to dominate those of the polity. This position was defended even by theologically liberal ministers deeply involved in the politics of the period.[98]

In 1792, it was still spiritual liberty that was claimed "to be preferred to everything," for "there is no temporal blessing to be compared with it. In proportion to the value of the soul above the body, so must the liberty that respects the one, surpass the other."[99] Although these two senses of liberty were usually paired in America,[100] there was little confusion about which was of greater importance. It was that of the spirit. Without it one was not free from the deforming effects of original sin, and by necessity, then, one must remain an abysmal slave to one's lusts.[101] Like anyone controlled by outside agents, under these conditions one was insufficiently free to exercise the responsibilities and rights of political liberty.[102]

But by the end of the 18th century, this generalization was no longer true of all Americans. In particular, elite rationalists did not assign importance to spiritual liberty qua Christian liberty. Yet in their view, closely allied with spiritual liberty was a secular equivalent sometimes known today as "inner" or "metaphysical" freedom. Friedrich Hayek notes that this understanding of liberty "refers to the extent to which a person is guided in his actions by his own considered will, by his reason," and that the "opposite of 'inner freedom' is not coercion by others but the influence of temporary emotions, or moral or intellectual weakness."[103] However, in considering this caveat regarding the otherwise dominant standing of the decidedly Christian sense of liberty in shaping Americans' political attitudes, two cautions must be borne in mind.

First, 18th-century rationalists were also "religious," though usually not orthodox adherents of a variant of reformed Protestantism. As the intellectual historian Carl Becker argued with clear exaggeration, "the underlying preconceptions of eighteenth-century thought were still, allowance made

[97]Witherspoon, *Dominion of Providence* (1776), p. 30.

[98]See Champion, *Christian and Civil Liberty* (1776 Connecticut election sermon), pp. 8, 10; and Murray, *Nehemiah* (1779), p. 21, who writes that "between civil liberties and those of religion there is a near and necessary connexion; when the one expires, the other cannot long survive. When earth and hell conspire against the former, their ultimate purpose is to stab the latter."

[99][W. Taylor], *Liberty without Licentiousness* (1792), p. 29.

[100]See Baldwin, *New England Clergy*, p. 168; and Bloch, *Visionary Republic*, p. 53, and "Religion and Ideological Change," p. 50.

[101]See N. Niles, "Second Discourse," p. 41.

[102]See McWilliams, "Democracy and the Citizen," pp. 85–86, who reminds us that in its essence "democracy aims at the governance of body by soul."

[103]Hayek, *Constitution of Liberty*, p. 15.

for certain important alterations in the bias, essentially the same as those of the thirteenth century."[104] More pointedly, American rationalists' faith in reason and the ordered coherence of the universe was no more amenable to empirical verification than was the faith of Christians. As Roland Bainton argues, "the eighteenth century came to have a great confidence in man's ability to understand and plan his world. Yet this confidence alone would scarcely explain the inviolability of individual reason, had not the secularized concept trailed with it the aura of sanctity with which faith had been invested."[105]

The liberty that rationalists sought demanded the same kind of suppression of the passions as that sought by more orthodox Christians. For those strongly influenced by this body of thought, personal liberty was still a matter of voluntary surrender to the righteousness of an ordered and purposeful universe, even if it was one without an interventionist or personal God. Their conception of personal, or spiritual, liberty was as demanding in regard to the suppression of all that was unique in the individual (and soon to be so highly valued by individualists and Romanticists) as that of more orthodox adherents of reformed Protestantism.

Second, these men were often as publicly committed to "religion" and Christian liberty as any of the pastors or publicists cited below. Although certain of these men, particularly those later described as the "Founders," understood Christian liberty and religiosity in a rather instrumental fashion, this does not vitiate the power of their publicly voiced commitment to the public good and the need for Christian-based corporate oversight of the lives of individuals to effect it. Such students of the period as Perry Miller, Henry May, Leonard Levy, John Murrin, and Thomas Curry demonstrate that the Founders understood religion to be "an essential precondition of social order and a crucial prop for the novel sort of government they were creating." Mark Tushnet notes that "it was not 'religion in general' that the framers saw as the basis of secular order. Rather, it was Christianity and, more specifically, Protestant Christianity."[106]

Furthermore, to the degree that some advanced thinkers were contemptuous of Christianity, their musings were kept from the broader public. Most governmental figures refused to offer such sentiments for common consumption, and if they did come to the reading public's attention, their authors denied holding such views.[107] Consider the efforts of John Mason, the Presbyterian founder of Union Theological Seminary, the president of Dickinson College, and one of the greatest pulpit orators of his day, who hoped to expose Jefferson's unorthodox beliefs. Jefferson, he claimed, was

[104]Becker, *Heavenly City*, p. 31.

[105]Bainton, "Appeal to Reason," p. 123.

[106]Tushnet, "Origins of the Establishment Clause," p. 1515; see also Pangle, *Spirit of Modern Republicanism*, p. 81; and May, *Enlightenment in America*, p. 257.

[107]See May, *Enlightenment in America*, p. 274; Murrin, "Religion and Politics in America," p. 29; and Bloch, *Visionary Republic*, p. 195.

"a confirmed infidel."[108] But he failed to offset the success of the Jeffersonian party in keeping from the public Jefferson's extreme deistic views of Christ's divinity. As late as the early 19th century, Benjamin Hale, pastor, professor of chemistry, and the president of Hobart College, continued to look back at the Founding Fathers as deeply religious men, while holding in contempt the few, like Paine, who, after publicly announcing their deistic sympathies,[109] greatly suffered for their courageous honesty.[110]

The average American could easily have failed to recognize that the religion that prominent members of the elite actively supported was different from that which their pastors preached and to which many faithfully adhered. As counseled by J.G.A. Pocock, we must distinguish here between "the history of authorship" and that "of readership."[111] Clearly in this case, it would have been most difficult for the public to have known, as subsequent scholars would, that some members of the nationalist elite had little interest in preserving Christianity or in defending a Christian liberty concerned primarily with partial freedom from sin. To the average American, the elite's embrace of religion and liberty must have seemed to be more of the same—self-denying submission to a life of moral righteousness guided by objectively true moral constraints.

But even if the doubts of a few members of the elite concerning Christian dogma had been publicly defended, it is unlikely, given the continued power of the ministers as the most respected and learned men of their time, that their concerns would have had much effect. Sam Adams indirectly testified to this in 1802 when, thirty-five years before Benjamin Hale's criticism of Paine, he harshly rebuked Paine, writing that "when I heard you had turned your mind to a defence of infidelity, I felt myself much astonished and more grieved, that you had attempted a measure so injurious to the feelings and so repugnant to the true interest of so great a part of the citizens of the United States." He then reminded Paine that "our friend, the President of the United States, has been calumniated for his liberal sentiments by men who have attributed that liberality to a latent design to promote the cause of infidelity . . . without the least shadow of proof."[112] Those who admitted their deistic beliefs were shunned by others, affirming the continuing adherence of the wider public, whether active church members or not, to the outlines of reformed Protestantism and the social and political landscape it helped create.[113]

---

[108][Mason], *Voice of Warning* (1800), pp. 8–9; and see the anonymously authored rebuttal, *Serious Facts Opposed to "Serious Considerations"* (1800).

[109]See Hale, *Liberty and Law* (1838), p. 23; and Schaff, *America* (1855), p. 34.

[110]See E. Foner, *Tom Paine and Revolutionary America*, pp. 257–58, on Jefferson's rejection of his embarrassing former friend and fellow Deist.

[111]Pocock, introduction to Burke, *Reflections on the Revolution in France*, p. ix.

[112]S. Adams, *Writings of Samuel Adams*, 4:412–13.

[113]See D. D. Hall, "Religion and Society," p. 327; and P. Miller, "From the Covenant to the Revival," p. 342.

Harry Stout has compared the influence of ministers to that of political actors and the authors of pamphlet literature. In New England, where the pressure for the War of Independence began, he estimates that churchgoers listened to "somewhere around fifteen thousand hours" of sermons in a lifetime and that their extant handwritten notes offer persuasive evidence that they understood and retained much of what they had heard. After four years of college education, conversely, the average 20th-century student has sat through only fifteen hundred hours of lectures or "10% of the total number of hours regular churchgoers sat through sermons in the course of their lifetimes."[114] It is therefore not surprising that the reformed-Protestant understanding of Christian or spiritual liberty shaped Americans' view of liberty and their political thought.[115]

Stout also reminds us that the ministers were widely dispersed throughout New England (and the Middle colonies); they were found in almost every village. Political publicists, by contrast, were highly concentrated in the five large "urban" centers (those with ten thousand to twenty-five thousand inhabitants) with less than 3 percent of the total population of European-Americans. Thus, the general population's exposure to the pamphlet literature and its authors was, by necessity, limited. Nor did the average American farmer necessarily care, for as Charles Andrews reminds us, few were interested in "high" politics. He wrote that "the proceedings of the Stamp Act Congress itself, emblazoned as they are on the pages of history, passed almost unnoticed at the time, and there is nothing to show that the somewhat precise and finely spun reasoning of these intellectual leaders had any marked influence on the popular mind."[116]

According to one New Englander writing at the relatively late date of 1798, rural Americans like himself who sought access to the polemical literature had difficulty gaining it. This was even true of the main conduit for secular thought, the newspapers, because "unless some speedy & cheaper method is adopted to convey knowledge than by the present mode of newspapers we shall not injoy Libberty of the press long, for there is not one fift part of the common farmers & labourers that are the most interested in the measures of the times, that git any information for them."[117]

---

[114]Stout, *New England Soul,* pp. 4–5, 317.

[115]See Heimert, *Religion and the American Mind,* p. 450; and Niebuhr, *Kingdom of God in America,* p. 124.

[116]Andrews, *Colonial Background of the American Revolution,* p. 136; see also Nobles, *Divisions throughout the Whole,* pp. 156–58; Jedrey, *World of John Cleaveland,* p. 103; and in regard to the Constitutional period, see Roche, "Strange Case of the 'Revolutionary' Establishment," pp. 180–81.

[117]Manning, *Key of Libberty* (1798), pp. x–xi; see also Baldwin, *New England Clergy,* p. 125, who provides corroborating evidence from Manning's social superiors; and Main, *Social Structure of Revolutionary America,* pp. 261–62, who places the communication revolution wrought by cheap newspapers in the 1780s. R. D. Brown, *Knowledge Is Power,* p. 79, finds that much before 1790 this dearth of secular information did exist, but that after this date,

Stout confirms that in the late 18th century, "pamphlets and newspapers were growing in importance—particularly in urban centers—but for sheer public exposure and influence, neither could match the sermon."[118] In sermons, the liberty that only faith in Christ could bring was preached first, while the associated liberty of the corporate body was of secondary importance.

The difference between rural and urban demographics and the limitations of 18th-century communication technology (snow, physical obstacles, often hostile relations with Native Americans, mud and more mud) combined to support the contention that the vision of the ministers best defined the ethical standards of most late 18th-century Americans. Ministers not only collectively delivered several thousand sermons each week but also published them in unprecedented quantities that vastly outstripped the relatively limited publication of secular pamphlets.[119] Thus, their understanding of personal liberty as primarily spiritual and that of the corporate body as ancillary must be given a central place in any typology of 18th-century American liberty. When these factors are combined with those gleaned from the research of social historians, Stout becomes all the more persuasive; he holds that "unlike most pamphlets, which were composed in private for a limited, informed audience of the educated elite, printed sermons originated in speech and more accurately express Revolutionary sentiments as they were heard."[120]

Nor should one assume that Stout's account, based on his study of New England, is in its general contours descriptive of only those colonies, or that the thought and sentiments disseminated by their ministers had little impact on the other colonies.[121] As Edmund Morgan reminds us, "the intellectual center of the colonies was New England, and the intellectual leaders of New England were the clergy, who preached and wrote indefatigably of human depravity and divine perfection . . . and [that] the purpose of government was to restrain the sinfulness of man, [and] to

---

especially between 1800 and 1820, this situation would be dramatically altered by the mushrooming of newspapers, printers, and public libraries (which offered a new and broader source of reading material in addition to the minister's private library).

[118]Stout, *New England Soul*, p. 260.

[119]See ibid., p. 6.

[120]Ibid., p. 7; see also R. D. Brown, *Knowledge Is Power*, pp. 79–80, who adds that the Revolution, which the clergy had done so much to support, would end up helping "destroy their special role as authoritative intermediaries."

[121]See Stark and Finke, "American Religion in 1776," p. 44, who note that "the consensus among historians of the colonial period is that New England, and particularly Massachusetts, far surpassed other colonies in terms of churches and membership. . . . This view is *not* sustained by our data. While Massachusetts' church membership rate does surpass the rate we have estimated for the nation as a whole, it is not remarkable in comparison with others of the larger and older colonies. Indeed, Pennsylvania and New Jersey have higher rates, while several other colonies are as well-churched as Massachusetts."

prevent and punish offenses against God."[122] With confidence, then, one can argue that it was the reformed-Protestant vision of spiritual liberty, not that of the political pamphleteers sometimes read too avidly today, that best defines the late 18th-century American understanding of liberty. At the level of shared beliefs, liberty for Americans described the potential for voluntary submission to a life of righteousness that accorded with universal moral standards mediated by divine revelation and the authoritative interpretive capacity of a congregation of citizen-believers.

ORIGINAL SIN: A FORMATIVE AMERICAN INFLUENCE

According to the post-Augustinian Christian understanding of humans,[123] their apostate condition makes it impossible for them, without divine aid, to enjoy a life of ordered freedom. As observed by Princeton's Dr. Witherspoon, "nothing can be more absolutely necessary to true religion than a clear and full conviction of the sinfulness of our nature and state."[124] Two centuries later, the most famous student of American Puritanism, Perry Miller, noted that the colonies had been begun with such a "hypothesis of original sin" and the need for "a coercive state to restrain evil impulses."[125] This was because, as the most authoritative confession of reformed dogma taught,

> Our first parents, being seduced by the subtilty and temptation of Satan, sinned in eating the forbidden fruit. . . . By this sin they fell from their original righteousness and communion with God, and so became dead in sin, and wholly defiled in all the faculties and parts of soul and body. . . . From this original corruption, whereby we are utterly indisposed, disabled, and made opposite to all good, and wholly inclined to all evil, do proceed all actual transgressions. . . . Man, by his fall into a state of sin, hath wholly lost all ability of will to any spiritual good accompanying salvation; so as a natural man, being altogether averse from that good, and dead in sin, is not able, by his own strength, to convert himself, or to prepare himself thereunto.[126]

People were thus absolutely in need of divine intercession and corporate control if they were to live lives of liberty rather than of total subservience to sin.

This strong sense of limits continued in the 18th century to determine

[122]E. S. Morgan, "American Revolution," p. 29.

[123]See Pagels, "Politics of Paradise," who argues that before St. Augustine of Hippo, there was no Christian orthodoxy or consensus regarding man's putatively fallen condition.

[124]Witherspoon, *Dominion of Providence* (1776), pp. 7–8.

[125]P. Miller, "The Puritan State and Puritan Society," in *Errand into the Wilderness*, pp. 142–43.

[126]Westminster Assembly, "Westminster Confession of Faith" (1646), pp. 201, 205; see also Presbyterian Church, "Shorter Catechism," pp. 287–88; and Clap, *Nature and Foundation of Moral Virtue* (1765), p. 9.

Americans' understanding of things political, even if not quite so starkly as it had in 17th-century Virginia and Massachusetts, when "political doctrine was founded on the premise of original sin," which was a "logical consequence of a theology of depravity and enslavement of the will."[127] It was, however, in their concept of liberty that their belief in original sin played its most conspicuous political role. There was widespread agreement in America with the highly regarded Reverend Dr. Price, who wrote that "without *Moral Liberty*," that is, the divinely facilitated fortitude to withstand the promptings of passions and desires,[128] a human being is a "wicked and detestable being, subject to the tyranny of base lusts, and the sport of every vile appetite."[129] The freedom to live a life directed by lusts and passions, a selfish life, was one of sin and license rather than liberty, and was condemned by Americans of both religious and more secular perspectives.

On one side of the political and religious landscape, Isaac Backus, an influential Baptist preacher, a champion of religious freedom, and one of America's greatest defenders of religious individualism, based his understanding of liberty "more on human depravity than on rationality or inalienable rights."[130] He held that "freedom is not acting at random, but by reason and rule. Those who walk after their own lusts, are clouds without water, carried about of wind . . . while the true SONS OF LIBERTY are like streams, which run down in a clear and steady channel."[131] And the British Cato, a radical Whig author not known for his piety, also paid his respects to the dogma of original sin. Like most American authors, he too found that claims regarding natural wisdom and virtue only made sense when applied "before the Fall." But in regard to his current condition, Cato believed that people are "now degenerated." The cause was clear: "by the Sins of our first Parents, we are fallen into this unhappy and forlorn Condition."[132] For Revolutionary-era Americans, even for those as firmly committed to the concept of "rights" and the freedom of conscience as were Backus and Cato, freedom only gained approbation as liberty when it ad-

---

[127]P. Miller, "Religion and Society in the Early Literature of Virginia," in *Errand into the Wilderness,* pp. 129–32.

[128]The category of moral liberty was, however, unusual. As Stewart noted in *Letter to the Rev. Dr. Price* (1776), pp. 6–7, "as to Moral Liberty, I never heard of it!"

[129]Price, *Observations* (1776), p. 5; see also Lynd, *Intellectual Origins of American Radicalism,* p. 27, who emphasizes that the mid-18th-century English dissenters were religious men; and Hatch, *Sacred Cause of Liberty,* pp. 92–93.

[130]Hatch, "In Pursuit of Religious Freedom," p. 393.

[131]Backus, *Government and Liberty Described* (1778), p. 3; see also Heimert, *Religion and the American Mind,* p. 459.

[132][Trenchard and Gordon], "Letter #105," in Wilkins, Woodward, Walthoe, and Peele, *Cato's Letters* (1733), 3:332–35, see also "Letter #60" (1721), in Jacobson, *English Libertarian Heritage,* pp. 118–19; and A. Sidney, *Discourses Concerning Government* (1698), p. 83, who writes that "misery of man proceeds from his being separated from God: This separation is wrought by corruption."

hered to the natural order like a stream bordered on both sides by firm and certain banks of corporate control.

From the opposite end of the political and religious spectrum, New England Federalists like Jeremiah Atwater, the first president of Middlebury College, and David Daggett, United States senator and chief justice of Connecticut's supreme court, staked out comparable positions. According to the theologically liberal Atwater, "liberty, if considered as a blessing, must be taken in a qualified sense" in which "unbounded liberty" was nothing "other than the liberty of sinning, the liberty of indulging lawless passions."[133] Bill Pencak finds even in Franklin's late letters and autobiography frequent references to the world being "ruled by the minions of Satan."[134] Edmund Morgan feels that the Revolutionary leadership "steered Americans through the Revolution" with political views based on a firm "conviction of human depravity."[135] The importance and formative role of the dogma of original sin in 18th-century American thought and lives are widely accepted.[136] What has been overlooked, though, is its importance in shaping Americans' understanding of liberty and more generally, their political theory of the good.

For example, without an appreciation of its importance, one may misinterpret the libertarian-sounding praise of 18th-century pamphleteers and ministers for the beauties of natural freedom.[137] One might fail to recognize that the nature that Americans sought was not a rugged wilderness designed by God for a Romantic in search of individual autonomy, but a Newtonian one suitable for a people living within a divine order who sought to constrain corrupted souls.[138] American Revolutionary statements that explicated liberty, particularly natural liberty and the associated state of nature, are made coherent only by taking note of the centrality of the concept of original sin.

If not for the Fall, reason would have been able to guide people "unruffled by passions, unclouded by prejudice, unimpaired by disease or intemperance" just as "it was in our first parents before their transgression." But subsequent to Adam's (or in Edward's telling, all of mankind's) tragic

---

[133]Atwater, "Vermont Election Sermon" (1802), p. 1172; see also Daggett, "Sunbeams May Be Extracted from Cucumbers" (1799), pp. 41–42.

[134]Pencak, "Benjamin Franklin's *Autobiography*," p. 13; and in disagreement, see Pahl, *Free Will and Political Liberty*, p. 80.

[135]E. S. Morgan, "American Revolution," p. 36.

[136]See Wood, *Creation of the American Republic*, pp. 115–16; E. Foner, *Tom Paine and Revolutionary America*, pp. 90–91; Heimert, *Religion and the American Mind*, p. 15; Noll, *Christians in the American Revolution*, p. 150; J. P. Greene, *Landon Carter*, pp. 12, 16; Bercovitch, *Puritan Origins of the American Self*, p. 16; Selby, *Concept of Liberty*, pp. 123–24; Lienesch, *New Order of the Ages*, pp. 41–43; and Pahl, *Free Will and Political Liberty*, pp. 144–45.

[137]See Reid, *Concept of Liberty*, p. 28.

[138]See Wood, introduction to *Rising Glory of America*, p. 17.

indiscretion,[139] "every man must acknowledge" that "he is a poor, indigent, frail and helpless being; his reason corrupt, his understanding full of ignorance and error, his will and desires bent upon evil."[140] Even a rationalist Christian such as Samuel West, an active member of the convention that drew up the Massachusetts Constitution and a delegate to that state's ratifying convention for the federal Constitution, held that "the highest state of liberty subjects us to the law of nature and the government of God. The most perfect freedom consists in obeying the dictates of right reason, and submitting to natural law." He then further clarifies the legitimate boundaries of liberty by reminding his auditors of their sinful condition and that "the law of nature is a perfect standard and a measure of action for beings that persevere in a state of moral rectitude; but the case is far different with us, who are in a fallen and degenerate estate. We have a law in our members which is continually warring against the law of the mind, by which we often become enslaved to the basest lusts, and brought into bondage to the vilest passions."[141] For late 18th-century Americans, then, the joys of natural unfettered freedom were depictions of a paradise lost. Natural perfection was only partially recoverable through spiritual liberty (or for a minute fraction, through rational self-overcoming), and ultimately, through death and the loss of their worldly selves in Christ.[142]

It was widely believed that humans in the state of natural freedom were, "so far as we know," the only creatures "throughout the boundless universe who, if left to their natural liberty, would be so mischievous to one another."[143] Another author suggested that "there is no circumstance which so unfavorably proclaims the imperfections of human nature, as the necessity of transferring our natural liberty to" our fellows gathered in a republic in which they are to serve as "mutual guards upon each other's conduct."[144] Human nature after the Fall was not a standard against which Americans measured their righteousness.

The famous late 17th-century republican martyr Algernon Sidney also weighed in eloquently on the corrupt character of human nature. In a most orthodox manner he distinguished between the natural and the spiritual man and held that "the natural man is in perpetual enmity against God." This alienation, he added, cannot be overcome unless the old man, the self,

---

[139]See H. S. Smith, *Changing Conceptions of Original Sin*, pp. 33–34, who explores Jonathan Edwards's creative and fascinating effort to explain the transmission of original sin to all people from a single transgression. It is oddly reminiscent of a Jewish view of the receiving of the laws at Sinai at which all Jews, both living and those to be born, were in some manner present.

[140]*Licentiousness Unmask'd* (1776), p. 9.

[141]S. West, "Right to Rebel Against Governors" (1776 Massachusetts election sermon), p. 415.

[142]See the Westminster Assembly, "Westminster Confession of Faith" (1646), pp. 208–9.

[143]S. Howard, "Massachusetts Election Sermon" (1780), p. 383.

[144]Worcester Speculator, "Letter No. VI" (1787), pp. 699–701.

is destroyed and people are renewed and regenerated "through the spirit of grace."[145] Even for this republican theorist, people were born free but, as a result of Adam's fall from grace and the consequent sinful nature of humans, they were forced to live in the less-perfect world in which liberty was only accessible because of Christ's love, sacrifice, and freely given grace.[146]

Peter Powers, in Vermont's second election sermon, given in 1778, might be seen as defending a regime of autonomous individual freedom. He begins by describing absolute natural freedom, that is, mankind's long-lost natural liberty before the Fall. He holds that "all men, indeed, are by nature equal: and all have, most certainly, an equal right to freedom and liberty by the great law of nature. No man or number of men, *has* or *can* have a right to infringe the natural rights, liberties or privileges of others." He seems to be presenting a most liberal understanding of individual rights, yet this is not the case.

Powers returns to the theme of relative natural liberty and that which is appropriate for a fallen species. He reigns in his briefly liberated auditors by reminding them that:

> It is a very plain case that many people of the present day, have very absurd notions of Liberty, as if it consisted in a right for every one to believe, do, or act as he pleases in all things civil and religious. This is a *Libertine* principle. No man has any right, before God, to believe or practice contrary to scripture. And Liberty consists in a freedom to do that which is right. The great law of nature, the moral law, is the rule of right action. Man's fall has taken away his freedom of right action; for *whosoever committeth sin is the servant of sin.*[147]

Original sin stood between humans and their lost natural liberty.[148] As long as most Americans continued to be powerfully influenced by reformed orthodoxy, their belief in original sin would assure that the individual liberty most sought in Revolutionary America was the liberty by which Christ freed the sinner from unremitting loss of control to the sinful self.

Evidence of Americans' pervasive adherence to the Christian dogma of original sin not only makes it easier to recognize that Christian liberty was the quintessential form of personal liberty and that natural liberty was a shadow of lost innocence, but also makes more understandable other aspects of their social and political thought. For example, the anachronistic (by elite English standards) attachment of 18th-century Americans to local communalism and corporate oversight of the individual makes much

---

[145]A. Sidney, *Discourses Concerning Government* (1698), p. 123.

[146]See Bloch, *Visionary Republic*, p. 174; and E. Lewis, "Contribution of Medieval Thought," p. 468.

[147]Powers, *Jesus Christ the True King* (1778 Vermont election sermon), pp. 10, 40.

[148]See Blackstone, *Commentaries*, 1:40–41. He follows a similar logic in describing the pre-Fall unity of self-love and the good of the whole, and the corrupting consequence of the Fall.

greater sense. It becomes clearer why most Americans believed that only the local group could effectively "walk" with a fellow citizen, by necessity a sinner, and help him or her to lead a more righteous life.[149] Localism and communalism were integral parts of the American response to innate sinfulness.

The American antipathy to political and ecclesiastic hierarchy also becomes more reasonable when it is realized that no sinful human, no matter how socially elevated, could be trusted with corrupting power.[150] In 1753, William Livingston captured this particularly American (and generally reformed-Protestant) distrust of hierarchy and the empowering of sinful individuals when he wrote that "it is unreasonable to suppose, that Government which is designed chiefly to correct the Exorbitancies of human Nature, should entirely consist in the uncontroulable Dictates, of a Man of equal Imperfections with the Rest of the Community, who being invested with the Authority of the Whole, has an unlimited Power to commit whatever Exorbitancies he shall think fit."[151] Max Weber found this distrust of authority to be part and parcel of the reformed canon,[152] and part of the historical makeup of Americans.[153]

Consistent with their belief in an egalitarianism in sin, Americans were dedicated to what was for the 18th century a high degree of political and social equality. Because everyone was a sinner, no one acting alone could be trusted to behave in accord with the highest standards of righteousness regarding either personal or public matters. Calvin is instructive here. He had taught that owing "to the vices or defects of men, it is safer and more tolerable when several bear rule, that they may thus mutually assist, instruct, and admonish each other, and should anyone be disposed to go too far, the others are censors and masters to curb his excess."[154] One should not exaggerate their egalitarianism, but the dogmas of original sin and God's grace did encourage at least a broad-based aristocracy of saints, if not an all-encompassing egalitarian utopia. In this instance, the impetus for an environment of relative equality was not Enlightenment confidence in the individual to choose wisely, but quite the opposite, a uniform distrust of all fallen humans.[155]

Americans envisioned the necessity of government itself through the lens

---

[149]See Hatch, *Sacred Cause of Liberty*, p. 125; and Zuckerman, *Peaceable Kingdoms*, pp. 116–17.

[150]See Bailyn, *Ideological Origins of the American Revolution*, pp. 59–60; E. S. Morgan, *Birth of the Republic*, pp. 6–7; and Counts, "Political Views," pp. 60–61.

[151]Livingston, "Further Reflections on the Doctrines of PASSIVE OBEDIENCE and NON-RESISTANCE" (1753), in Livingston et al., *Independent Reflector*, p. 329.

[152]See M. Weber, *Protestant Ethic*, p. 225.

[153]Ibid., pp. 255–56; see also Zuckerman, *Peaceable Kingdoms*, pp. 248–49.

[154]Calvin, "Of Civil Government," in *Institutes of the Christian Religion*, trans. Beveridge, 2:657.

[155]See Merrill and Wilentz, *Key of Liberty*, pp. 55, 76.

of original sin. From the elite nationalist Alexander Hamilton to the common farmer in the field, Americans believed that people were destined always to live under the restraints of government because of their innately deformed nature.[156] In the words of the moderate and highly respected pastor Andrew Eliot, "the necessity of government arises wholly from the disadvantages, which, in the present imperfect state of human nature, would be the natural consequence of unlimited freedom."[157] An anonymous author writing under the pseudonym Republicus also held that "universal observation assures us, that mankind are more generally actuated by their passions and appetites, than by their reason . . . hence the necessity of civil government."[158] Even John Leland, the Baptist minister and activist for the separation of church and state, writing at the end of the 18th century, continued to believe that government was necessary only because of original sin. He explained that it was not until "sin had intoxicated man with the principal of self-love" that government was required.[159]

But the most important political implication of Americans' reformed-Protestant confidence in the equally sinful nature of all people might have been the Revolution itself. By passing the Declaratory Act on 18 March 1766, and demanding from Americans "unlimited submission" in "all cases whatsoever," the British Parliament had created a situation that Americans as reformed Protestants were obligated to resist.[160] As Martin Bucer, Calvin's teacher and a famed reformer, had written in his *Lectures on the Book of Judges,* "wherever absolute power is given to a prince, there the glory and the dominion of God is injured. The absolute power, which is God's alone, would be given to a man liable to sin."[161] By demanding unlimited submission, the British Parliament, an external body of sinful men, had effectively "set itself alongside God's Word as a competing sovereign."[162] The response of Americans, theologically and historically committed to submitting only to God, "and only God's word—in all aspects of life and faith," should have been predictable.[163] The members of Parliament had framed the debate in such a way that many Americans

[156]See Detweiler, "Changing Reputation," p. 568.

[157]Eliot, *Massachusetts Election Sermon* (1765), pp. 8–9.

[158]"Republicus" (1788), in *Complete Anti-Federalist,* ed. Storing, 5:161.

[159][Leland], writing as Jack Nips, "Yankee Spy" (1794), p. 972.

[160]See Baron, "Calvinist Republicanism and Its Historical Roots," p. 36; Valeri, "New Divinity and the American Revolution," pp. 765–66; Bercovitch, *Puritan Origins of the American Self,* pp. 112–13; Nichols, *Democracy and the Churches,* p. 25; J. P. Greene, *Landon Carter,* p. 70; and Bloch, *Visionary Republic,* pp. 60–61, 93.

[161]Cited by Baron, "Calvinist Republicanism and Its Historical Roots," p. 37; see also Calvin, "Of Civil Government," in *Institutes of the Christian Religion,* trans. Beveridge, 2:674–75.

[162]Stout, *New England Soul,* p. 7.

[163]Ibid., p. 259.

immediately understood their demand for "unlimited submission" as a struggle between eternal life and perpetual damnation.[164]

The members of Parliament, however, are not necessarily to be faulted. They could hardly have expected, in a putatively enlightened age like their own, that so many Americans, even well-educated elites, would view their actions largely through the filter of an atavistic Augustinian Christianity in which original sin occupied a central role. It is hard to keep in mind just how anomalous members of America's political class (with certain exceptions such as Ethan Allen, Dr. Thomas Young, Joel Barlow, and the nominally American Tom Paine) were in comparison to the influential radical deists in Britain and France.[165] Americans had rejected one of the central tenets of the 18th-century (particularly the French) Enlightenment: the innate perfectibility of humans.[166] Regarding a closely related plank of the Enlightenment program, only a few highly visible American rationalists were willing to accept that people are "capable, guided solely by the light of reason and experience, of perfecting the good life on earth."[167] For a handful, then, humans might have had more of an inner light than reformed doctrine was willing to concede, but no prominent American has been shown to have thought that people were born free of the deformed and selfish nature so aptly described by the dogma of original sin.

Americans in the 18th century had demonstrated little interest in the most optimistic tenets of the Enlightenment. They had rejected those who had labeled as absurd the doctrine of original sin,[168] as well as those who argued for infinite human progress.[169] Instead, Americans continued to adhere to various versions, some relatively secularized, of the Christian dogma of original sin. Even Louis Hartz, the most prominent defender of an understanding of the Founding era as liberal, recognized this and reported that "Americans refused to join in the great Enlightenment enterprise of shattering the Christian concept of sin, [and] replacing it with an unlimited humanism."[170]

This firm rejection, even by the nationalist elite, of Enlightenment faith in human goodness was well exemplified by Dr. Witherspoon. A product

---

[164]See Bonomi, *Under the Cope of Heaven*, pp. 199, 214; and K. Thomas, "Politics Recaptured," p. 28.

[165]See Prospo, "Paine and Sieyès," p. 196, who argues that even Paine was influenced by the Christian concept of original sin; alternatively, see Kramnick, *Republicanism and Bourgeois Radicalism*, p. 146, who reminds us that Paine was English, and that "his Englishness" saturates his written work. On Young, see Maier, *Old Revolutionaries*, p. 125.

[166]See Hampson, *Enlightenment*, pp. 102–3; and Selby, *Concept of Liberty*, p. 103.

[167]Becker, *Heavenly City*, pp. 102–3.

[168]See Hamilton, "Views on the French Revolution" (1794), pp. 414–15, for his blistering critique of the French Revolution's societal explanation of evil, and his defense of original sin, religion, and strong government; more generally, see May, *Enlightenment in America*, p. 231.

[169]See Persons, "Cyclical Theory of History," p. 158; for an example of a prominent English author defending such a notion of progress, see Priestley, "Essay" (1771), pp. 8–9.

[170]Hartz, "American Political Thought," pp. 324–26.

of the Scottish Enlightenment, a man of vast education, and the highly respected president of Princeton, he held that the truth of man's sinful nature "must be owned" even "in times of the greatest tranquillity." For "others may, if they please, treat the corruption of our nature as a chimera; for my part, I see it everywhere, and I feel it every day."[171] Judge Chipman observed that all respected political writers had agreed that "man is totally depraved, wicked, and corrupt; that the utmost perverseness in power, is inherent in his very nature."[172] Original sin, rather than Enlightenment optimism, lies at the dark heart of late 18th-century American social and political thought.[173]

James Madison and Alexander Hamilton's reiteration of this theme in *The Federalist* is well known and even celebrated. One of many examples is Madison's claim that the "latent causes of faction are thus sown in the nature of man." Another is Hamilton's claim that the moral assumptions underlying the Articles of Confederation "betrayed an ignorance of the true springs by which human conduct is actuated." He charged the earlier constitution's framers with having ignored that "the passions of men will not conform to the dictates of reason and justice, without constraint."[174] But Publius's acceptance of the portrayal of human nature as deformed is in truth rather unexceptional. In America "the idea of inevitable evil in human nature" was widely accepted. Both the Founding Fathers and the common citizens had been schooled in "the Christian doctrine of original sin and its secularized" equivalents and understood humans to be "cursed by the 'Fall.'"[175] Thus, Publius's concurrence in this assessment of people as innately imperfect and selfish (if not depraved) was in keeping with the contemporary beliefs of his time. (What was radical in his thinking was his belief that the response Americans had heretofore deemed appropriate, intrusive publicly supported efforts at controlling and ameliorating much of sinful human behavior, must be abandoned.)[176]

Ralph Ketcham holds that other national political leaders, those who

---

[171]Witherspoon, *Dominion of Providence* (1776), p. 8.

[172]Chipman, *Sketches of the Principles of Government* (1793), p. 78.

[173]See for example, "Remarks on a Passage," pp. 243–44, and Fobes, "An Election Sermon" (1795 Massachusetts election sermon), p. 1006, who describes deism as "that old harlot, lately re-baptized by the name of reason."

[174]J. Madison, "Federalist No. 10," p. 55, and Hamilton, "Federalist No. 15," p. 92, in Hamilton, Jay, and Madison, *Federalist.*

[175]Howe, "Political Psychology of *The Federalist*," p. 502; and Diggins, *Lost Soul of American Politics*, pp. 7, 67, 83. See also Wald, *Religion and Politics*, pp. 51–52; and Nichols, *Democracy and the Churches*, p. 40.

[176]See Diamond, "Ethics and Politics," p. 98, who notes that Aristotle and Madison agreed about the human condition, but disagreed "over what to do about this perennial difficulty." Madison thus had rejected the traditional Whig understanding that, in spite of the corrupt character of human beings, the polity was to fight rather than accommodate this disposition. For a spirited defense of the traditional position, see Bolingbroke, *Idea of a Patriot King* (1754), pp. 411–13.

might be expected to have held more progressive views, such as the "four ex-presidents still alive in 1826," also believed "that evil in human nature and in world affairs was indelible, and that the hardships of life spring from 'basic nature,' not from custom or 'second nature.'"[177] John Diggins writes that for most of the Founders, in particular for John Adams, "man had lost his reason through the Fall, the Christian account of alienation that stood as a lesson to the pretensions of classical politics."[178] Adams had argued that "the nature of mankind is one thing, and the reason of mankind another. . . . In the institution of government, it must be remembered, that although reason ought always to govern individuals, it certainly never did since the Fall, and never will till the Millennium."[179] Even a leading "specimen of the radical temperament" such as Dr. Benjamin Rush, a scientist and an ardent republican, was "a lifelong believer in original sin, divine grace, and the Christian millennium."[180] Thus, belief in original sin cannot be relegated only to the uneducated, the most theologically orthodox Protestants, or those now considered conservative, like John Adams.[181]

At the end of the century, when truly bold ideas of human perfectibility were being championed by apologists for the French Revolution, the moderate pillars of American provincial society continued to distance themselves from any rejection of the concept of original sin. In 1798, Israel Woodward, the popular minister of Wolcott, Connecticut, compared the worldview of the progressive French to that of the Americans still bound to the Christian dogma of original sin (or for some, a secular equivalent), and described how these different views of human ontology produced radically distinct understandings of liberty: "The *liberties* of the American and French nations, are grounded upon totally different and opposite principles. In their matters of civil government, they adopt this general maxim, that mankind are virtuous enough to need no restraint; which idea is most justly reprobated by the more enlightened inhabitants of the United States, who denominate such liberty, licentiousness; the fruit of it, corruption."[182]

---

[177]Ketcham, *Presidents above Party*, p. 144; see also Ketcham, "James Madison," p. 66.

[178]Diggins, *Lost Soul of American Politics*, pp. 84–85. Cf. Pangle, *Spirit of Modern Republicanism*, p. 21, who claims that Diggins's position is "outlandish."

[179]J. Adams, "Defense" (1788), in *Works of John Adams*, 6:114–15.

[180]May, *Enlightenment in America*, p. 211; see also p. 97, where May argues that unlike Jefferson, Madison was interested in religious questions and desirous of preserving vital religion; Hartnett, "Religion of the Founding Fathers," p. 60, who defends the reformed orthodoxy of another elite nationalist, James Wilson, including his belief in original sin; and J. P. Greene, *Landon Carter*, pp. 40–44, who describes this great 18th-century Southern planter in terms usually reserved for 17th-century Puritans. In addition, it is well accepted that other prominent Founders, such as John Jay, Patrick Henry, and Sam Adams, were believing orthodox reformed Protestants.

[181]See Spurlin, *French Enlightenment in America*, pp. 126–27.

[182]I. B. Woodward, *American Liberty and Independence* (1798), p. 8.

At this late date, sin continued to shape how liberty and things political were understood in reformed-Protestant America.

Not all of America's true elite who otherwise accepted that humans were innately flawed also adhered to the Christian dogma of this account. This is of limited importance, though, to the argument I advance here, because even these men held that the source of evil was internal, not external.[183] Thus, for Americans ill at ease with Christian dogma, people, not poorly designed social institutions, must be held responsible for human misery and suffering.[184] Eighteenth-century Americans, therefore, cannot accurately be described as adherents of the central tenet of modern and enlightened political thought.[185] And this was (and two centuries later, still is) the issue that divides opponents of and apologists for progressive or enlightened social thought.[186] If humans are innately deformed and radically selfish (even if not "evil"), the liberating social changes sought by progressive thinkers cannot rationally be sustained.

Americans were unified in their view of humans as creatures divided between two natures. One was depraved or, without the Christian connotation, simply base, animalistic, and selfish, while the other was God-given or, again in more secular language, godlike and rational. The accepted view from all perspectives was that divine reason's legitimate supremacy "had been jeopardized by the corruption of human nature in the Fall."[187] These competing Revolutionary-era "theologies" almost equally accepted the axiom that people were born of two worlds and that the rational half of the spirit, as part of the transcendent or eternal, needed to master the corporal half tied to the phenomenal world.[188]

American rationalists should not therefore be confused with 18th-century French skeptics or latter-day atheists bereft of faith in a morally or-

---

[183]See A Fellow Citizen, *Political Establishments of America Reviewed* (1784), pp. 5, 20–21. In an unusual fashion, he argues both for the inescapable reality of original sin and that the state governments should be abolished and replaced with one united national government.

[184]See Crowley, *This Sheba, Self,* p. 110; and Murrin, "Religion and Politics in America," p. 31, who questions whether any delegate to the Constitutional Convention accepted the reformed-Protestant position on original sin, but little doubts they believed that people were corrupt and selfish and the cause of their misfortune.

[185]See Chipman, *Sketches of the Principles of Government* (1793), p. 81, who comes close (but not too close) to ascribing the causes of human evil to extrapersonal forces. He writes that it is more complex than as outlined in the Fall, "and, that it is the effect of other causes; some existing in the nature of man, others arising from the nature of the power." See also Bloch, *Visionary Republic,* pp. 197–98, who draws attention to the few Americans, such as Tunis Wortman, who fully defended the environmentalist position on human sin.

[186]See H. S. Smith, *Changing Conceptions of Original Sin,* p. 208.

[187]Howe, "Political Psychology of *The Federalist,*" pp. 488–89.

[188]See Trinterud, "New Light Snuffed Out," p. 179.

dered and purposeful universe.[189] The Americans who were most power-fully influenced by rationalist thought also believed that the universe was divinely ordered.[190] But they did differ from Christians. What separated them was how each claimed spiritual (or metaphysical) liberty could be achieved or, in the language of Christianity, how the natural man could be reborn in Christ. In the extreme rationalist assessment (usually only pri-vately communicated) each person, through proper education and personal will, could overcome his or her irrational desires and passions totally un-aided by superpersonal agents.

This extreme claim was naturally rejected by Christians such as the emi-nent Great Awakening ministers Samuel Davies and Gilbert Tennent, who disagreed that righteousness was "rectitude of a reasonable creature, or conformity to rule and law." For them, "Christian morality was morality that conformed to Christian norms" and "obedience was the obedience that God enabled man to perform."[191] Whereas a consensus existed con-cerning the woeful natural state of human beings, there was a much weaker one concerning the necessary means by which to overcome innate human selfishness and deformity.

Most Americans, however, were more reformed-Protestant than ratio-nalist in their moral precepts. For them, unlike for some of their national political leaders, the wages of sin could not be eradicated through the ef-forts of individual will and appropriate moral education.[192] Through the teaching of their ministers and the norms of their culture, they implicitly followed John Calvin, who had taught: "We are not our own; therefore, neither is our own reason or will to rule our acts and counsels. We are not our own; therefore, let us not make it our end to seek what may be agree-able to our carnal nature. We are not our own; therefore, as far as possi-ble, let us forget ourselves and the things that are ours. On the other hand, we are God's; let us, therefore, live and die to him."[193] Here was where the battle lines were drawn between rationalists and Christians, to the degree that this differentiation was publicly recognized before the 1790s.[194] In the

---

[189]See Schneider, *History of American Philosophy,* p. 71; and Friedman, "Shaping of the Radical Consciousness," pp. 785–86 who argues that American nationalism "was grounded in an essentially abysmal conception of human nature," in which human nature was "locked in an eternal struggle between reason and feeling."

[190]See Beattie, introduction to Rousseau, *Creed of a Priest of Savoy,* p. v.

[191]Trinterud, *Forming of an American Tradition,* p. 192.

[192]See May, *Enlightenment in America,* pp. xv, xviii; J. P. Greene, *Landon Carter,* p. 36; and Breitenbach, "Unregenerate Doings," pp. 490–91.

[193]Calvin, *Institutes of the Christian Religion,* trans. Beveridge, 2:7.

[194]This division was much noted by the presidents of Harvard and Yale. See Langdon, "Government Corrupted by Vice" (1775 Massachusetts election sermon), in *Puritan Political Ideas,* pp. 360–61; and Clap, *Nature and Foundation of Moral Virtue* (1765), pp. 47–50. Rather precociously and more powerfully, Clap denounces the pretensions of natural law and of the limits of man's unaided reason divorced from revelation. In America, their condemna-

estimation of most Americans, purely human-centered devices were viewed as inadequate for overcoming the sinful self.

An understanding of humans as sinful and in need of undeserved grace, not just selfish and born corrupt, was thundered from pulpits and public meetings throughout America. In the South, for example, Hugh Alison, a minister in South Carolina, reminded his listeners that all people are "by nature the children of wrath and disobedience," but "believers in Christ are already freed from the condemning sentence of the law, and delivered from the guilt of sin," and that through "the operation of the blessed spirit . . . their bondage is at an end, and their obedience is a *perfect freedom*."[195] Before the provincial congress of Georgia, John Zubly warned the legislators in an often reprinted sermon that "no external enemy can so completely tyrannize over a conquered enemy as sin does over all those who yield themselves its servants . . . till the grace of GOD brings salvation, when he would do good, evil is present with him: in short, instead of being under a law of liberty, he is under the law of sin and death . . . but whenever he feels the happy influence of the grace of the gospel, then this 'law of liberty makes him free from the law of sin and death.' Rom viii. 2."[196] In the North, the same message of the human inability to fend off the wages of original sin unless aided by Christ was repeated by orthodox and liberal ministers alike.[197] The respected Congregational minister Stephen Johnson reminded his listeners in Old Lyme, Connecticut, that "sin kindles a fire in the divine anger, which (without repentance and pardon in the blood of Christ) will burn to the lowest hell."[198]

President Clap of Yale instructed his students that since the Fall, "man's Understanding is *darkened,* his Judgment is *perverted* . . . and his *Mind,* and *Conscience is defiled.*"[199] Ezra Stiles, another of Yale's presidents and a leading intellectual figure, claimed in his great synthetic work on colonial Congregationalism that even though there might be disagreement among pastors concerning various aspects of universal depravity, there could be none in regard to God's blameless nature and the truth of it. For "observation on the state of the world for 6000 years . . . shew that in fact disorder and vicious principles are predominant and reign with great strength in human nature."[200]

Even the progressive minister Simeon Howard maintained that people were incapable through individual effort of overcoming their inherent sin-

---

tion of natural religion and of reason would become commonplace after the French Revolution turned tyrannical in the early 1790s.

[195] Alison, *Spiritual Liberty* (1769), pp. 14–16.

[196] Zubly, *Law of Liberty* (1775), p. 27.

[197] See Tufts, *Believers Most Sure Freedom* (1757), pp. 5–6; Wheelock, *Liberty of Conscience* (1776), p. 16; and Duché, "Duty of Standing Fast" (1775), p. 81.

[198] [Stephen Johnson], *Some Important Observations* (1766), p. 52.

[199] Clap, *Nature and Foundation of Moral Virtue* (1765), p. 24.

[200] Stiles, *Discourse on the Christian Union* (1761), p. 10.

fulness. In 1780 he asked his audience "to reflect with shame upon the selfishness and corruption of our species, who, with all their rational and moral powers, can not otherwise [than through Christ] be kept from injuring and destroying one another."[201] And according to Stout, such a consensus is to have been expected, for "a purely natural theology was unacceptable even to the most liberal and open-minded New England ministers." The unaided man, "no matter how wise and enlightened[,] was incapable of reconciling himself to God. This reconciliation could be accomplished only through the intervention of the Holy Spirit."[202]

There were, however, a few Americans who were moved neither by the logic and appeals of Christianity nor by those of modern rationalism. They were most often influenced by the moral-sense claims of David Hume.[203] Yet for them too, something like original sin was nonetheless understood to be a permanent human condition that demanded that ordered liberty be a form of freedom with restraints on human selfishness and hedonism. This is most famously evidenced throughout *The Federalist*, in particular where Publius asks "what is government itself, but the greatest of all reflections on human nature? If men were angels, no government would be necessary."[204] Although Publius rejects both the possibility and the desirability of government-fostered virtue (rather than virtuous behavior),[205] he does so without rejecting the standard American view of human beings as innately selfish and flawed.[206]

Like Vans Murray, Publius held that those who had gone before had been wrong about the possibility of innate human character being ameliorated through communal governmental or social intervention. But happily, earlier commentators had also been wrong concerning the dependence of popular government on truly virtuous citizens or public leaders. Publius mixed a certain kind of "scientific" optimism with his evident moral pessimism. His optimism, though, did not concern man's putative innate goodness, as might have been true of a more progressive thinker like William Godwin. Instead, his optimism was that of the 17th-century Enlightenment, and thus was based on a Newtonian faith in the ability of the new science of politics to achieve relatively benign outcomes with flawed human inputs. It might be said that he saw the Framers' achievement as analogous to that produced by the Deist's caretaker God. He wrote that government, like the solar system, must be designed so that "its several constituent parts may, by their mutual relations, be the means of keeping

[201]S. Howard, "Massachusetts Election Sermon" (1780), pp. 382–83.

[202]Stout, *New England Soul*, pp. 135–36.

[203]See J. Turner, *Without God, without Creed*, p. 56; more generally, see Noll, *Princeton and the Republic*, p. 326, and the sources listed therein.

[204]J. Madison, "Federalist No. 51," in Hamilton, Jay, and Madison, *Federalist*, p. 337.

[205]See Maynard Smith, "Reason, Passion, and Political Freedom," pp. 540–41.

[206]See Howe, "Political Psychology of *The Federalist*," pp. 487–88, 502.

each other in their proper places."[207] He believed that this new science could offer a mechanism or logic by which to create stable government and moderately attractive political conditions. This new form of government would render unnecessary subsequent generations of virtuous, even godlike, men like him and his Revolutionary colleagues.[208]

Late 18th-century Americans learned from almost every public source, including the innovative Publius, that a life of liberty rather than license demanded that passions, lusts, and selfishness be at least properly channeled if not tightly controlled. In the words of an anonymous author of the early 19th century, such a life entailed the "subduing of the inordinate affections and irregular passions of a corrupt nature, and bringing the whole spirit, and soul, and body, into subjection to the law of a superior Being."[209] Even from Publius, deeply influenced by the skeptical Hume, Americans learned that they should try to follow their reason, even though Publius knew that all but a few would be unable to do so. But he was also certain that more elevated, socially useful passions such as the desire for fame or more generally enlightened self-interest could, with the proper political art, be made to displace somewhat lower passions such as carnal or monetary greed. As Hamilton's Publius had argued so memorably, one must excite "the love of fame, the ruling passion of the noblest minds" so that a man's "avarice [for public honor] might be a guard upon his avarice [for private monetary gain]."[210] Only the most limited hope was thus maintained by Publius that people in the future would be capable of rising above their passions. His proposed government would be built on the sounder republican and Newtonian foundations of the noble greed for public honor and recognition, or more broadly, what he took to be the mutual attraction and repulsion of human self-interest correctly understood.

Most of these same national figures, whether or not they were sincere believers in original sin, accommodated Americans' continued belief that their inherently sinful natures could only be overcome by surrendering themselves to Christ and seeking spiritual liberty in him.[211] American elites

---

[207]J. Madison, "Federalist No. 51," in Hamilton, Jay, and Madison, *Federalist*, p. 336; see also Madison, "Speech in the Constitutional Convention" (8 June 1787), in Farrand, *Records of the Federal Convention*, 1:165, where he describes the federal government as "the great pervading principle that must controul the centrifugal tendency of the States; which, without it, will continually fly out of their proper orbits"; for other comparisons between the Constitution and the Solar System, see Fobes, "An Election Sermon" (1795 Massachusetts election sermon), p. 1003; Davidson, *Oration* (1787), pp. 14–15; and Lienesch, *New Order of the Ages*, pp. 134–35.

[208]See Howe, "Political Psychology of *The Federalist*," p. 506.

[209]*Liberty: Civil and Religious* (1815), pp. 32–33.

[210]Hamilton, "Federalist No. 72," in Hamilton, Jay, and Madison, *Federalist*, pp. 470–71.

[211]For a relevant anecdote, see Counts, "Political Views," p. 202, who reports that one minister, Azel Backus, cited Hamilton to show that "the doctrine of human depravity can be proved by the history of every nation, without the aid of the holy scriptures."

(again with the possible exception of Jefferson) were not, like their French counterparts, openly anticlerical or at war with Christianity.[212] And not even Jefferson opposed what he took to be its ethical teachings. Thus, by the end of the Revolutionary period, even for most progressive Americans like Publius, the modern free individual was at best tolerated, rather than encouraged and celebrated. The individualistic and Romantic encouragement of the autonomous self would have to wait for another day and a less somber and catechized leadership.[213]

THE COMMUNITY AND THE BATTLE AGAINST SIN: A CHANGING RELATIONSHIP

For many in Protestant America, combating sin demanded not only the efforts of the individual but that of the Holy Spirit as well. It was anticipated that one's brethren, joined together in community (and often in congregation), were also needed to assist one in walking in the path of righteousness. However, this was to occur in an environment in which freedom of religious conscience was respected. Thus, in the late 18th century, local corporate religious and moral supervision of the individual had to be pursued without trespassing on this by then hallowed right.[214]

In addition, the end served by corporate intrusiveness was slowly but steadily transformed from primarily religious (God's glory) to largely moral (societal betterment).[215] As Thomas Curry suggests, "it would be misleading to portray the majority of eighteenth-century Americans as anything less than fervently religious by modern standards, nevertheless, for more and more of them, concern with intricacies of doctrinal belief gradually gave way to a conviction that morality counted for more than theological correctness."[216] Yet amidst these changes, it was the evil of original sin that the community continued to battle.

In the first half of the 18th century, things had been different. It was still usual then for ministers to demand that the community control the sinful individual largely for God's greater glory. The theologically liberal and highly respected first minister of Boston's Brattle Street Church, Benjamin Colman, preached that "the *Sovereign* GOD . . . calls and uses whom He will, inclines and spirits how He will, and improves to what Degree He will. They are HIS therefore, and His is the *Greatness and the Glory and*

---

[212]See Hartnett, "Religion of the Founding Fathers," pp. 67–68.

[213]See Appleby, "Jefferson's Political Philosophy," p. 299, who argues that Jefferson (again) was unusual in holding that "the purpose of government" was "to ensure the conditions for liberating man's self-actualizing capacities."

[214]See Wiebe, *Segmented Society*, p. 31; Borden, "Federalists, Antifederalists, and Religious Freedom," pp. 472–73; and Lingeman, *Small Town America*, p. 61.

[215]See Evans, preface to vol. 3 of *American Bibliography*, p. viii.

[216]T. J. Curry, *First Freedoms*, p. 92; and see Noll, *Christians in the American Revolution*, pp. 163–75.

the Majesty!"[217] Yet John Barnard, in what A. W. Plumstead describes as the sermon that was "the harbinger of the age of reason," after first invoking the then-familiar themes of corporate service for the glory of God and individual salvation, gives heightened emphasis to the need for corporate control over the sinful individual for purely secular communal ends. He held that an individual "should be under subjection not only to such laws as more especially relate his conduct, to his Maker, but such also as have a more particular reference to his fellow creatures."[218]

About a decade later, Samuel Hall began by lecturing that God's goals should be the community's goals, and that the magistrate should actively "step in to weed and pluck up and assist [God] in the Cultivation of the Field." In case that were not a sufficiently compelling reason, he then opposes those arguing for a sharper separation of church and state. He reminds his legislative audience that "human Nature won't many times be restrained from the utmost Extravagance of Ill, without the awful Vigilance and Animadversion of the civil Magistrate," who to be effective must be legitimated by religious sanction.[219] Thus, for Hall and his generation, the community's legitimate opposition to the sinful character of human beings was not in question. The widely accepted fundamental goal behind this stance, however, had begun to change.

The attitudes reflected by these preachers were not particular to New England. An anonymous editorial in the *New-York Mercury* of 27 August 1753 defends the social utility of religion by asking rhetorically, "is there any Thing so friendly to Government as Religion, or of so much Use and Importance to make Men good Citizens and useful members of Society in this World, as to plant the Fear of God in their hearts?" In a letter to Peter Zenger, the "libertarian" editor, another anonymous author takes to task any who might believe that societal control of sinful behavior was not necessary. The writer believed they deserved condemnation, for "freedom within a Rule is very desirable, yet there is scarcely any one Thing has done more mischief than this Word misunderstood, absolute *Liberty* is a jest, 'tis a visionary and romantik Priviledge . . . some People are for repealing the Laws of Morality, for throwing open the inclosure of Religion, and leaving all in common to licentiousness and violence, they are for making their Inclinations the Rule, and their Power the boundary of Actions."[220] The theocentric ends previously used to defend the need for corporate oversight of the lives of member families and individuals were slowly coming to be doubted and challenged. Was the community to shape the moral lives of its members in order to help save the souls of individ-

[217]Colman, *Government the Pillar of the Earth* (1730), p. 11.

[218]Barnard, "Throne Established" (1734 Massachusetts election sermon), pp. 223, 235.

[219]S. Hall, *Legislature's Right, Charge and Duty* (1746 Connecticut election sermon), pp. 10, 18–19.

[220]*New-York Weekly Journal*, 7 July 1740, in Nelson, *Colonial History of New Jersey*, 2:38–39.

uals, to enforce obedience to God's commandments for his glory, or to serve the temporal needs of the community itself?

By midcentury the question of whether the community should be involved in the shaping of its members' moral practices for primarily theocentric or anthropocentric ends still had made only limited inroads into the orthodoxy of the democratically chosen ministers of New England. Many pastors continued faithfully to follow Calvin, who in 1536 had attacked those "who wish magistrates to neglect all thoughts of God, and to confine themselves entirely to the administration of justice among men." Calvin, confident of people's ability to understand what was demanded of them, counseled that "all laws are preposterous which neglect the claims of God, and merely provide for the interests of men . . . as though God appointed governors in his name to decide secular controversies, and disregarded that which is of far greater importance—the pure worship of himself according to the rule of his law."[221]

The remarks of the East Guilford pastor Jonathan Todd, delivering the Connecticut election sermon of 1749, still maintained much of Calvin's strict theocentrism. He held that "GOVERNMENT is appointed to incourage & promote universal Righteousness & Goodness; that Men might live not only peaceably and honestly, but *religiously* in the World . . . the *civil Magistrate is the Keeper of both Tables of the Law. . . .* [And thus] *The Object of the Magistrate's Power, is not simply a peaceable Life . . . and external Peace of humane Societies, but also Honesty and Godliness.*"[222] Thus, at the dawn of America's Revolutionary difficulties, articulate voices continued to preach that religion and government were instituted most importantly to glorify God and to enforce his commandments on his apostate creatures, not that they were instituted to serve the worldly ends of his fallen creatures.[223]

Yet in 1765, the year the Stamp Act was passed, a shifting balance is nevertheless evident.[224] Consider Edward Dorr, who began by telling his audience that "civil rulers are to suppress all immorality and vice, and to encourage the practice of virtue and piety . . . and [they] ought to support religion." Then, however, he described the ends to be served: "the practice of religion and virtue tends, above all things, to promote the public welfare and happiness of mankind, and to secure the ends of civil government . . .

---

[221]Calvin, *Institutes of the Christian Religion*, trans. Allen, 1:641.

[222]Todd, *Civil Rulers the Ministers of God* (1749 Connecticut election sermon), pp. 11–12, 18–19.

[223]See for example *Licentiousness Unmask'd* (1776), p. 8.

[224]See Miller and Johnson, "Theory of State and Society," in *Puritans,* 1:194, who write that "with Jonathan Mayhew . . . the advantages to be derived from corporate existence are no longer salvation, but the well-being of the citizen." However, see Curry, *First Freedoms,* p. 86, who claims that even though ministers sounded as if they were on a "temperance campaign," in fact, their "references to moral reform served as a shorthand communication that the civil power was still the supporter of regeneration and the New England Way."

[and] uncleanliness, intemperance, fraud, cruelty, malice, idleness and injustice, of every kind, are directly contrary to the ends of civil government."[225] All the same ills that New England pastors had denounced for a century were there, but the ends to be served were new. Even less concerned with godliness per se was Dorr's counterpart that year in Boston, Andrew Eliot. He argued that it was the responsibility of both the ministry and the legislature to "find some more effectual method to suppress our vices, and to encourage industry, frugality and sobriety."[226] Still more direct was Stephen Johnson, who held that public officials must make "salutary provision for the protection and support of public worship, religion and vertue" because the "interests of true religion . . . must be patronized and encouraged according to its benignant influence to the good of the state."[227] Religion was still to be defended, but increasingly for reasons concerned ultimately with the welfare of society, not for godly reasons or ones solely concerned with the eternal salvation of individuals.

Original sin, though, still dominated the thoughts of late 18th-century Americans regardless of the end served, corporate or godly. Prominent, national, and very public expressions of this continuing focus on the need for Americans and their government to combat human sin were the fast proclamations of the Continental Congresses and all of the early administrations except that of Jefferson. These national jeremiads leave little doubt about the Christian character of America and the centrality of the belief in original sin. On these hallowed days, Congress asked that "Christians of all denominations" gather for public worship and that the governors set aside "a day of humiliation, fasting, and prayer; that we may, with united hearts, confess and bewail our manifold sins and transgressions, and by a sincere repentance and amendment of life, appease his righteous displeasure, and, through the merits and mediation of Jesus Christ, obtain his pardon and forgiveness."[228] Sin was still being fought, even if for new, more worldly human ends.

Another telling example is the "Proclamation of the [Massachusetts] General Court," also issued in 1776. Here too the ends served were primarily temporal rather than sacred in nature, yet it is just as certain that what was to be controlled was sinful human nature.[229] The proclamation

---

[225]Dorr, *Duty of Civil Rulers* (1765 Connecticut election sermon), pp. 9, 17–18.

[226]Eliot, *Massachusetts Election Sermon* (1765), p. 55.

[227]Stephen Johnson, *Integrity and Piety* (1770), pp. 24–25; see also Shute, "Massachusetts Election Sermon" (1768), p. 133.

[228]Continental Congress, *Journals of the Continental Congress* (March 1776), 4:209.

[229]See Handlin and Handlin, *Popular Sources of Political Authority*, pp. 65–68, who cite from the proclamation that the following should be avoided: "all Debauchery, Prophaneness, Corruption, Venality, all riotous and tumultuous Proceedings, and all Immoralities whatsoever; and that they decently and reverently attend the public Worship of God . . . all Judges, Justices, Sheriffs . . . are hereby Strictly enjoined and commanded that they contribute all in their Power, by their Advice, Exertions, and Examples, towards a general Reformation

begins by noting that "the frailty of human Nature" had made government necessary, adding that "the great and General Court have thought fit to issue this Proclamation, commanding and enjoining it upon the good People of this Colony, that they lead Sober, Religious and peaceable Lives, avoiding all Blasphemies, contempt of the holy Scriptures, and of the Lord's day and all other Crimes and Misdemeanors."[230] Regarding the ends government was to serve in suppressing vice as viewed in article 3 of the 1780 Massachusetts constitution, there is even less doubt: "the happiness of a people, and the good order and preservation of civil government, essentially depend upon piety, religion and morality."[231] Curry is, therefore, correct in charging that "the makers of the constitution of 1780 stood their Puritan ancestors on their heads" by using "religion to protect and sustain good government" (instead of government to sustain religion).[232] But in its turn to moralism, the government of Massachusetts continued to adhere to its traditional understanding of original sin and the necessity of corporately effected instruction and punitive action.

Even theologically liberal Boston, in defense of this contested third article of the Massachusetts Constitution, demonstrated its acceptance of the dogma of original sin while it maintained a generally secular rather than godly goal as its end. Thus, the town of Boston held that "human Laws were feble barriers opposed to the uninformed lusts of Passions of Mankind. But though we are not supporting the kingdom of Christ may we not be permitted to Assist civil society by an adoption, and by the teaching of the best set of Morals that were ever offered to the World."[233] From a town less liberal in theology, we learn from a 1784 memorial from the presbyter of Hanover that religion does "not require the aid of government for its support" but that "it is absolutely necessary to the existence and welfare of every political combination of men in society, to have the support of religion and its solemn institutions."[234] And in 1787, the Congress used comparable language in setting up provisions for the governance of the Northwest Territories.[235] Priorities were shifting, but the American understanding of human nature was not. People were innately flawed, and the teachings of Christianity and morality, and communal intrusion, were necessary if civilized life was to be sustained.[236]

---

of Manners, and, that they bring to condign Punishment, every Person who shall commit any of the Crimes or Misdemeanors aforesaid, or that shall be guilty of any Immoralities whatsoever."

[230]Ibid.

[231]Ibid., p. 442.

[232]T. J. Curry, *First Freedoms*, p. 165.

[233]Handlin and Handlin, *Popular Sources of Political Authority*, p. 764.

[234]Hood, "Revolution and Religious Liberty," p. 178.

[235]See E. S. Morison, "The Northwest Ordinance," in *Sources and Documents*, p. 231; and Cord, *Separation of Church and State*, p. 61.

[236]See Selby, *Concept of Liberty*, p. 123.

Such arguments were heard in the South as well. In 1788, Thomas Reese, the rationalist Presbyterian minister of Charleston, South Carolina, argued in every imaginable way for eighty-seven pages that "religion is of great importance to society." Why was it of such importance? Because it restrained "men from vice by the dread of punishment, and [by] alluring them to virtue by the hope of reward."[237] Given the uncontested nature of Americans' belief in original sin, Christianity clearly had an important communal role to play even if it was no longer primarily a godly one. In any event, the combination of a continued belief in original sin and an expanding human-centered focus did not lead initially toward individualism, but rather away from it and toward a renewed emphasis on the (more secular) needs of the community.

For the last two decades of the 18th century, speakers and authors with diverse perspectives continued to distance themselves from any association with a regime of individualism or Enlightenment optimism. Instead they hammered home the theme that every government "ought to adopt a code of regulation which tends to prevent the commission of evil. This is the most essential and benevolent part of the government."[238] Before the legislature of Massachusetts, Henry Cumings insisted that "the morals of a people are among the great objects, which claim the particular attention of the legislature and civil authority," in particular "to provide means, by law, for the suppression of vice and wickedness."[239] Around the turn of the 18th century, Lemuel Haynes continued to insist that the true end of government was "to curb the passions of men; to suppress vice and immorality; to build up society, and to establish religion in the world."[240] Secular leaders too believed that human nature was corrupt, and that "the civil power has a right . . . to prohibit and punish gross immoralities and impieties" and "professed atheism."[241] This understanding was not a minority position defended only by conservatives, but was held by "the vast majority of Americans," who agreed that the "government should enforce the sabbath and respect for the scriptures, limit office to Christians or Protestants, and generally support the Christian Protestant mores that entwined both state and society."[242] Even the Presbyterians in Virginia, while trying to prevent the reestablishment of the hated Episcopal church in 1784, insisted on as much.[243]

But during the years that witnessed the birth of the Constitution, some

---

[237]Reese, *Essay on the Influence of Religion* (1788), p. 4.

[238]Z. Adams, "Massachusetts Election Sermon" (1782), pp. 552–53.

[239]Cumings, *Massachusetts Election Sermon* (1783), p. 43.

[240]Haynes, "Nature and Importance of True Republicanism" (1801), p. 85; see also "Influence of Civil Government on Religion" (1798), p. 66, where the same theme is rehearsed.

[241][Ellsworth], "Letters of a Landholder," p. 171; see also Whitney, *Essential Requisites* (1788 Connecticut election sermon), p. 11.

[242]T. J. Curry, *First Freedoms*, p. 190; see also Botein, "Religious Dimensions," p. 319.

[243]See Hood, "Revolution and Religious Liberty," p. 175.

public figures refused to abandon the more demanding traditional re-formed-Protestant understanding of the God-centered relationship between congregation and local community that took God's glory as its primary goal.[244] In 1790, Daniel Foster held that "it is their [civil rulers'] duty to uphold the kingdom of CHRIST, which consists in 'righteousness, and peace, and joy in the HOLY GHOST.'"[245] Timothy Stone, a Congregational minister from Lebanon, Connecticut, ridiculed the idea of complete sep-aration of church and state by noting that it "appears to rest upon this absurd supposition; that men by entering into society . . . cease to be moral beings; and consequently, lose their relation and obligations to God."[246] Cyprian Strong of Chatham, Massachusetts, observed in 1799 that "CIVIL government was not instituted merely to amuse men. . . . And, although it is an institution, which is peculiar to this world, and may seem more immediately designed to protect men from injury and violence; yet, is it not certain, that . . . it is ultimately designed for and to be administered, with a view to the advancement and establishment of a spiritual and holy kingdom?"[247]

Even Joseph Story, a highly respected jurist, Harvard professor of law, and supreme court justice, in explicating the freedom of religion clause of the First Amendment in 1833, reminded his readers of the intimate rela-tionship that Americans had traditionally maintained between church and state. After describing the social benefits of a well-churched population, he notes that "it is impossible for those who believe in the truth of Chris-tianity as a divine revelation to doubt that it is the especial duty of govern-ment to foster and encourage it among all the citizens and subjects."[248] Yet, notwithstanding the continued prominence of those who defended explic-itly Christian public goals, the ends served by corporate oversight of mo-rality changed during the last half of the 18th century.

The most important 18th-century ends that had legitimated the re-formed-Protestant nature of American life and the corporate control over private morals, serving God and his greater glory, and aiding the individ-ual in the quest for certain knowledge of his or her salvation, were being abandoned. In tandem with such changes, Christianity's central mission had evolved into preventing licentious behavior from disrupting corporate social, economic, and political life.[249] Thus, by the time of the Revolution,

[244]See T. J. Curry, First Freedoms, p. 165.
[245]Foster, Massachusetts Election Sermon (1790), p. 11.
[246]T. Stone, "Connecticut Election Sermon" (1792), p. 850.
[247]Cyprian Strong, Kingdom Is the Lord's (1799 Connecticut election sermon), p. 14.
[248]J. Story, Commentaries, 2:603.
[249]See S. Kendall, "Religion" (1804), pp. 1244–45, 1247, who argues that "such is the imperfection of man, that . . . religious faith, or sentiment, must then be called in to the support of that morality, which is essential to the order and well-being of society"; and Wood, Radicalism of the American Revolution, p. 331, who draws on Chancellor James Kent's 1811 blasphemy decision in which he declared against the right to treat with contempt

sermons against the evil of dancing, such as Oliver Hart's in Charleston, were becoming less common. Especially among the American elite, claims that dancing was sinful, "because it contributed nothing to the chief end of man," were no longer fashionable.

Many of the faithful, however, continued to be persuaded that "the chief end of man is to glorify God . . . [and that] this ought to be our principal aim in every thing we do."[250] But for others, the aims of criminal law became "the preservation of order in society without reference to the saving of souls or the building of God's kingdom on earth."[251] As Joseph Lathrop, the theologically liberal pastor of West Springfield, Massachusetts, and fellow of the Academy of Arts and Sciences, observed, there is little for government legitimately to do in facilitating human salvation. But, he reminded his readers, there is another end that religion serves that does demand governmental patronage: "the present peace and happiness of mankind."[252] No mention is made of God's greater glory; the goals of the holy commonwealth had clearly changed.

Yet in America, this change took place without attacking the idea of the innate sinfulness of human beings or the need for corporate intrusiveness into the lives of individuals or their families. Although the ultimate reason that Americans sought freedom from domination by sin had changed, the means to combat it had not. The necessity of communalism for most was not in question. The self still needed restraint, and the means continued to be the community's active efforts to shape and control the selfish and benighted behavior of the fallen individual.[253] Individualism, therefore, could offer little of value in the war against sin, but for many, the most important ingredient continued to be their hoped-for rebirth in Christ.[254]

---

the Christianity of almost all Americans, because it was "to strike at the roots of moral obligation and weaken the security of the social ties."

[250]O. Hart, "Dancing Exploded" (1778), p. 241; see also Main, *Social Structure of Revolutionary America*, pp. 266–67.

[251]Flaherty, "Law and the Enforcement of Morals," p. 248.

[252][Lathrop], "Reformer III" (October 1789), pp. 269–70.

[253]See Flaherty, "Law and the Enforcement of Morals," p. 245.

[254]See Wood, *Radicalism of the American Revolution*, pp. 329–30.

Corporate Liberty: Political and Civil

Political freedom implies that all political authority is
derived from the community, the community which is
composed of men who are capable of directing and
controlling their public as well as private lives to ends
determined by themselves.

—A.J. Carlyle, *Political Liberty*

IN LATE 18TH-CENTURY America, political liberty did not describe a unitary
concept, but rather two analytically distinct yet overlapping strands of
thought, denominated here as republican and English political liberty.
Making for greater complexity and confusion, civil liberty was often used
as a synonym for political liberty as well as to describe a different corporate and communal understanding of liberty.[1] In Revolutionary America,
however, these separate voices smoothly harmonized to produce an integrated concept of liberty that was pervasive, communal, and valued corporate goals over individualistic ends.[2] This multifaceted corporate and communal understanding of liberty was of sufficient importance that it was
over this, rather than an individualistic understanding of liberty, that the
War of Independence was waged.

In its traditional Western formulation, the meaning of political liberty as
derived from classical republican sources and defined by Renaissance hu-
manists was corporate "independence and self-government—liberty in the
sense of being free from external interference as well as in the sense of
being free to take an active part in the running of the commonwealth."[3] In
late 18th-century America, the prevalent understanding of political liberty
included these two elements, plus other streams of meaning that added to
and competed with the traditional republican one. The American understanding was shaped by a tradition that was most immediately English in

---

[1] The names chosen are congruent with 18th-century usage; however, no particular language was consistently employed.

[2] See Hayek, *Constitution of Liberty*, p. 18.

[3] Skinner, *Foundations of Modern Political Thought*, 1:77, see also "Paradoxes of Political
Liberty," p. 242; Pocock, *Machiavellian Moment*, pp. 226–27; and Hexter, review of *The
Machiavellian Moment*, p. 330.

origin. As Edmund Burke observed, Americans were a people devoted to liberty and their understanding of it was based on "English ideas and on English principles."[4] And although English political liberty itself may ultimately have been derived from classical or Renaissance republican inheritances,[5] in the 18th century, it represented a stream of thought that did more than older secular inheritances to shape American political thought and culture.

English and republican liberty, as well as the commonly associated civil liberty, were primarily corporate in form. That is, they were determined by and protective of a political group's needs. As Willmoore Kendall and George Carey noted, when Revolutionary-era Americans "spoke of their rights, their 'liberties, immunities, and privileges,'" they almost always meant collective "self-government."[6] What is less evident is that these corporate forms of liberty were also actively communal—that is, supportive of a vision of human flourishing that favored communal intrusion into the individual's life rather than the protection and encouragement of his or her autonomy. However, these traditions of political liberty were insistent that the will of the majority be awarded sovereign discretion in shaping and serving both immediate corporate ends and the communal understanding of long-term individual ones. Consequently, each of the two major understandings of political liberty were little concerned with protecting the rights of particular individuals. And when individuals confronted legitimately constituted majorities, indifference was often transformed into intolerance.

The corporate nature of political liberty as it was then understood must first be examined, because the very dominance of the right of a group of Americans (defined by ethnicity, geography, language, or religion) to corporate self-determination offers indirect evidence of the communal character of their political thought. (Since tensions between the needs of the corporate body and those of particular individuals are unavoidable, giving preference to corporate rights must surely lead at times to a loss of individual ones.)[7] Indeed, the corporate consideration was of such fundamental importance to Americans that, in the 1770s, majoritarianism was defended as one of two fully inalienable rights. The will of the politically enfranchised majority had preeminence in all matters except when it stood in competition with the other 18th-century moral trump, the hallowed Protestant right of religious conscience. And this right, it should be noted, was the only Revolutionary-era *individual* right that was seen by most Ameri-

---

[4]Burke, "[First] Speech on American Conciliation" (22 March 1775), in *On the American Revolution*, p. 82.

[5]See Fink, *Classical Republicans*, pp. 183–87, who describes the propensity of the English to naturalize classical political thought and then claim it as original to them.

[6]Kendall and Carey, *Basic Symbols*, p. 58.

[7]See Berlin, "Two Concepts of Liberty," pp. 161–62; and Hayek, *Constitution of Liberty*, p. 13.

cans as truly inalienable. Thus, except when an individual's right of religious conscience was in danger, a deviant individual or small minority benefited little from possessing the valued collective right of political liberty.

The communal character of 18th-century political liberty is sometimes difficult to perceive because from the Revolution onward it was a contested term, especially regarding the appropriate size of the political unit whose autonomy was to be protected. The notion of political liberty as the freedom of local communities to be self-determining and free from external intrusion shortly came into competition with the freedom of the entire nation to control its various parts and for it to be free from foreign interference.[8] Following the end of the War of Independence, this tension was exacerbated by a few perceptive nationalists who took critical note of the intrusive and communal character of local political governance. They realized how threatening local political liberty was to divergent minority and individual concerns,[9] particularly those of individuals judged threatening or morally repugnant by local majorities. By the last decade of the century, the traditional focus of political liberty that was local, majoritarian, and communal came into competition with a new sense of it that was national, centralizing, and moderately individualistic.

It was not until well after the Civil War, however, that the balance of power between these hostile postrevolutionary American traditions of political liberty shifted decisively and permanently away from local communalism and toward nationalism and individualism.[10] The ultimate dominance of the nationalist elite perspective, therefore, must not be allowed to cloud our understanding of most 18th-century Americans' views of political and civil liberty. Their preference was for a majoritarian understanding of corporate liberty that was locally communal and at odds with centralization, nationalism, and individualism.

CORPORATE LIBERTY: MAJORITARIANISM AND THE INALIENABLE RIGHT TO REVOLT

Americans were, most immediately, fighting their War of Independence for political liberty. (The description of their violent separation from Britain as a war of independence rather than as a revolution highlights the idea that political liberty was their preeminent concern.) They stressed "the public rights of the collective people" rather than "the private rights of individuals against the general will." As described by one observant minister, this

[8]See M. L. Wilson, *Space, Time, and Freedom*, p. 20; and Shy, "American Revolution," pp. 154–55.

[9]See Berlin, "Two Concepts of Liberty," p. 165; Peters, *Massachusetts Constitution of 1780*, p. 154; and Wood, "Interests and Disinterestedness," p. 76.

[10]See Leuchtenburg, *Perils of Prosperity*, pp. 225, 272–73.

sought-after liberty was "the freedom of bodies politic, or States,"[11] for, "if Paul esteemed personal liberty a valuable inheritance, he certainly esteemed the liberty of a community a far richer inheritance."[12] As a third author explained, "true political liberty" demands that an individual not be "guided by his own will."[13] Yet even later in the century, in the contentious debates surrounding the ratification of the Constitution, corporate political liberty continued to be the accepted standard.[14]

The lure of increased political liberty, understood as the corporate right of self-government, was the central claim advanced by the Continental Congress in its effort to attract future Canadians to join it in its escalating confrontation with the British Parliament. In rehearsing the various advantages that would accrue from joining the Revolutionaries, the soon-to-be Americans emphasized benefits that were political and corporate, rather than private and individual. In particular, the Congress held that the foremost benefit to be gained would be "that of the people having a share in their own government by their representatives chosen by themselves, and, in consequence of being ruled by *laws* which they themselves approve." Indeed, of the five particular benefits discussed, only that of habeas corpus related "merely to the liberty of the person."[15] And looking back from 1802 at the early Revolutionary period, a staunch Federalist, Noah Webster, corroborated this assessment as he recalled that "the real object of the revolution was, to secure to the United States, the privilege of governing themselves . . . not to resign our country to be the sport of licentious passions."[16] Corporate political liberty, then, whether it is found ultimately to be republican in derivation (as has been contended by some historians of late) or English (as is argued here), was what Revolutionary-era Americans sought.

One should not believe, however, that this concern with preserving political liberty was characteristic only of the members of the articulate political class who have left behind their records in speech and documents. In the last several decades, social historians have convincingly demonstrated that corporate liberty was not uniquely valued by those elites whose written records have naturally attracted a disproportionate share of scholarly attention. Gregory Nobles, for example, in his examination of the largely

[11]Wood, *Creation of the American Republic*, p. 61; and Whitaker, *An Antidote Against Toryism* (1777), p. 11.

[12]N. Niles, "[First of] Two Discourses on Liberty" (1774), p. 258.

[13]*Civil Liberty Asserted* (1776), pp. 30–31.

[14]See Epstein, *Political Theory of the Federalist*, p. 147; and Palmer, "Liberties as Constitutional Provisions," p. 146, who writes that "the less republican elements [of the Constitution] were vitally necessary to prevent a national majority from overwhelming state minorities: a federal government more resistive to popular opinion was necessary for the preservation of state republican governments."

[15]Continental Congress, "Appeal to the Inhabitants of Quebec" (1774), p. 233.

[16]Webster, "Oration" (1802), p. 1237.

inarticulate farmers of a parochial and rural section of western Massachusetts (Hampshire County), has shown that the controlling secular understanding of liberty was the familiar one of corporate independence and local political self-government.[17] According to Lewis Saum, corporate political liberty even continued to inform the popular understanding of liberty throughout much of the antebellum period.[18] Clinton Rossiter extends the popular reach of political liberty even further and claims that "the political liberty of the American Revolution . . . remains the political tradition of the American people."[19]

Nevertheless, the majoritarianism so readily associated with Revolutionary-era political liberty was not a precept that had been traditionally valued in the villages of North America.[20] The preeminent goal Americans during the 17th and early 18th centuries had striven to achieve in making corporate decisions was unanimity,[21] arrived at by compromise, not by the imposition of the will of the majority on a minority. In fact, local communities initially could "no more condone a competing minority by their values than they could have constrained it by their police power."[22] By the time of the American Revolution, however, majoritarianism with its corporate focus and communal implications had become an accepted tenet of popular American values.[23] As Dr. Richard Price argued in the twenty-one editions of his *Observations,* originally published in 1776, a correct understanding of political liberty insists that "any will distinct from that of the majority of a Community, which claims a power of making laws for it" defines the distinction "between *Liberty* and *Slavery.*"[24]

For holding this position in Britain, though not in Revolutionary-era America (James Madison's hostility to what he described as factious majorities would only come later), Price attracted considerable critical attention.[25] To many educated Europeans, his hearty dedication to a majoritarian and corporate understanding of liberty was anachronistic. Democratic majoritarianism looked back to classical (Greek or Roman) or

[17]See Nobles, *Divisions throughout the Whole,* p. 155.
[18]See Saum, *Popular Mood,* p. 156.
[19]Rossiter, *Seedtime of the Republic,* p. 449.
[20]See Lockridge, *New England Town,* p. 136.
[21]See Lockridge, *Settlement and Unsettlement in Early America,* p. 23.
[22]Zuckerman, *Peaceable Kingdoms,* p. 94.
[23]Still, however, it was expected that a self-governing people would share "manners, sentiments, and interests," for "if this be not the case, there will be constant clashing of opinions; and the representatives of one part will be continually striving against those of the others." From Brutus, "Essay I" (1787), pp. 114–15. Most Americans did not see majoritarian rule as involving a clash between major blocks of interests, but between a supermajority and a recalcitrant and errant small minority.
[24]Price, *Observations* (1776), pp. 4–5.
[25]Price, however, was not without considerable support as well. For example, see the otherwise progressive Priestley, "Essay" (1771), pp. 12–13; and the still-respected voice of A. Sidney, *Discourses Concerning Government* (1698), p. 519.

Renaissance Italian republics, even to medieval particularism (in the minds of Saxon and Teutonic admirers) for models to emulate, and not to modern European monarchical states, which were centralizing. Only later would a weaker form of democracy be found compatible with the concerns of the emerging bureaucratic states and their novel commitment to protecting disfavored individuals and minorities from local majorities.[26]

John Wesley, the progressive founder of Methodism, explained in response to Price that liberty in truth was a private rather than a corporate matter and that Price's understanding of liberty "is not what all the world means by liberty and slavery; . . . he that is thus governed, not by himself, but the laws, is, in the general sense of mankind, a free man."[27] According to the progressive European sense of liberty (as a private rather than a corporate matter), liberty did not demand a particular political arrangement. It was primarily a question of private and legal justice, not collective self-government. Gunn, no apologist for Price, finds that he "blurred the relations between the situation of individuals and the organization of the polity" by calling "the freedom of a community analogous to that of the individual."[28] Yet in America, it was exactly this more traditional understanding of the corporate and majoritarian character of political liberty that was dominant and that brought Price his great popularity.

It is to be expected, then, that Americans, as uncritical supporters of Price, when formulating a defense in the 1770s of their desire to separate from England, described it as a striving for corporate rather than private liberty. They claimed for the majority of European landed males in America the right of self-government, a right they asserted to be the inalienable corporate privilege of a people—ironically and particularly, an English one.[29] "Even after 1774, when Americans began to arm themselves and to give unequivocal support to the doctrine of resistance," they continued to rest their claims on communal grounds as "they described resistance as a right exercised only by decision of the community, never on the initiative of individuals."[30] And their claimed majoritarian right clearly adhered to the community rather than to a group of individuals qua individuals. How else could they have defended and explained to themselves, and (more importantly) to interested parties in Europe, their resistance to the greatest 18th-century champion of individual freedom, the English Parliament?[31]

Not unexpectedly, then, in America's Declaration of Independence, the majoritarian right of a sovereign people to self-government and the ancillary right to revolt from an oppressive and increasingly separate people

---

[26]See W. P. Adams, "Republicanism in Political Rhetoric before 1776," p. 400; and Pekelis, *Law and Social Action*, p. 70.

[27]Wesley, "Some Observations on Liberty," p. 247.

[28]Gunn, *Beyond Liberty and Property*, p. 248.

[29]See Andrews, *Colonial Background of the American Revolution*, pp. 200–201.

[30]T. W. Tate, "Social Contract in America," pp. 377–78.

[31]See Galloway, "Candid Examination" (1775), p. 360.

was prominently claimed in the justly famous second paragraph. There it is written that "whenever any form of government becomes destructive of" the ends for which popular governments are constituted, "it is the right of the people to alter or to abolish it, and to institute a new government." Revolutionary-era Americans, therefore, were not claiming for themselves, whatever might later have been read into their Declaration of Independence, a set of new radical individual rights.[32] As Lafayette later explained, Jefferson was asserting in their behalf "only the principles of the sovereignty of the people and the right to change the form of government."[33] He was doing so, not for American Patriots who already considered this claim unexceptional, but for their European and recalcitrant Loyalist audiences.

As Jefferson claimed in the opening paragraph, Congress's intention in issuing the Declaration was primarily to show Americans' "respect to the opinions of mankind [in that chauvinistic world, Europeans]" by declaring and explaining to it "the causes which impel them to the separation."[34] As such, its principal importance at the time was as a "foreign-policy statement."[35] Nearly fifty years later, Jefferson continued to claim that Americans had not issued a bold new manifesto of individual rights. Instead, Americans had understood that

> when forced, therefore, to resort to arms for redress, an appeal to the tribunal of the world was deemed proper for our justification. This was the object of the Declaration of Independence. Not to find out new principles, or new arguments never before thought of . . . but to place before mankind the common sense of the subject, in terms so plain and firm as to command their assent, and to justify ourselves in the independent stand we are compelled to take. Neither aiming at originality of principle or sentiment, nor yet copied from any particular and previous writing, it was intended to give expression of the American mind, and to give to that expression the proper tone and spirit called for by the occasion.[36]

[32]See Wishy, "John Locke," p. 421; W. Kendall, "Equality," p. 30; and Sheldon, *Political Philosophy of Thomas Jefferson*, p. 45, who argues that "the primary right to be secured [in the Declaration] is the fundamental quality of political existence: local, autonomous control of legislation. It is the essential right of democratic sovereignty." Numerous commentators, however, argue to the contrary. For example, see Becker, *Declaration of Independence*, pp. 225, 257; C. M. Kenyon, "Republicanism and Radicalism," p. 319, and "Declaration of Independence," pp. 114–20; Roelofs, "American Political System," p. 326; J. P. Greene, *Pursuits of Happiness*, pp. 195–96; Webking, *American Revolution*, p. 107; Skidmore, *American Political Thought*, p. 46; and Kulikoff, *Agrarian Origins of American Captialism*, pp. 113–16.

[33]Cited by Jellinek, *Declaration*, p. 17. Even this claimed right was new and still more or less contested.

[34]See Becker, *Declaration of Independence*, pp. 5–7.

[35]Dull, *Diplomatic History of the American Revolution*, p. 52.

[36]Jefferson, "Letter to Henry Lee" (8 May 1825), in *Writings*, ed. Peterson, p. 1501. Note that what Jefferson, the stylist who penned the document, might have thought is not the issue here, for this is a public document, and as Lutz, in *Origins of American Constitutionalism*, p.

Thus, beyond the principal one of corporate self-governance, the rights that were claimed must be understood in the larger framework of 18th-century American political thought from which they are drawn, the document's purpose, and the enlightened sensitivities of its intended audiences. The American mind, Jefferson noted, was to be described for its target audiences in the "proper tone and spirit called for by the occasion." This meant largely Enlightenment ones, nominally Christian at best.[37]

Jefferson claimed that "all men are created equal," and that they have been "endowed by their Creator with certain inalienable rights; that among these, are life, liberty, and the pursuit of happiness."[38] First, then, in Jefferson's logical priority, was the need to convince his audience of European aristocrats, bankers, and British and American merchants that all sovereign peoples are equally endowed with the right to self-government. His stated goal was to assign to "free and independent states" those rights that often are associated with "Locke's 'free and independent' individuals."[39] But this was a language that was, by then, familiar, though in Europe still contested. For example, his friend and senior colleague, Richard Bland, had written of "the *Rights* of a people" and that a people's "*Rights* imply *Equality*," while an anonymous author had claimed that "no man will deny that the provincial Americans have an inherent, *unalienable Right* to all the Privileges of British Subjects."[40] Or as the African American pastor Lemuel Haynes explained, both in 1776 and again twenty-five years later, the true meaning of the Declaration is found in "the holy oracles, Acts 17:26," where Paul taught that God loves all nations equally and that each is of equal importance in his eyes—Jews and

---

113, suggests, it should "be read for surface meaning," as then understood. H. J. Powell, "Original Understanding of Original Intent," pp. 937–38, argues that Madison too insisted "on distinguishing the binding public intention of the state from the private opinions of any individual or group of individuals." Thus, it is how Jefferson's remarks were likely to have been understood by various audiences in 1776, particularly in Britain, Europe, and the colonies, that is significant. And in this context, Jefferson serves here simply as a reporter.

[37] See P. Miller, "From the Covenant to the Revival," p. 333, whose remarks, cited in chapter 6, bear repeating. He explains that the intended European audience "made it necessary for the official statement to be released in primarily 'political' terms—the social compact, inalienable rights, [and] the right of revolution," rather than in the reformed-Protestant language that the Congress regularly used in addressing "the ranks of militia and citizens."

[38] See Robbins, *Pursuit of Happiness*, p. 18, who writes that in the 18th century, "happiness meant public happiness—this cannot be too greatly stressed." For Jefferson, she finds, "public happiness was achieved by satisfaction of the aspirations of the majority of the people living together. It could not be attained by each consulting only self-interest, but to it all must contribute. The general sum of enjoyment was what counted."

[39] Cited by Sheldon, *Political Philosophy of Thomas Jefferson*, p. 50.

[40] Bland, "Inquiry" (1766), p. 116; see also *Considerations upon the Rights* (1766), p. 12. For additional American views on individual equality, see for example Lyman, *Sermon* (1787 Massachusetts election sermon), p. 8, who writes that "there is greater variety amongst men, than amongst several different species of animals"; and Spurlin, *French Enlightenment in America*, pp. 82–83, who describes that J. Adams and N. Webster found claims to human equality to be absurd, unreasonable, and inconsistent with facts and experience.

Greeks alike.[41] This sense of equality thus was understood to be that of "constitutional governing bodies" rather than "the social equality of persons."[42] Equality was understood to be a right of individuals that is transferred to civil society upon their entering it. And Americans happily claimed this corporate right to equality as Englishmen with "equal rights with those in Britain."[43]

Next, Jefferson listed those inalienable individual rights of which no people could deprive another. But these rights, although important, were not understood by an internal American Loyalist audience and by an intended external British and European one, as inalienable vis-à-vis the people themselves. They were only raised to the status of being fully inalienable, if then, when a sovereign people was deprived of them by another such people.[44] This itself was a bold but logically necessary claim to have made before the intended audiences. No such protection, however, was claimed by 18th-century Americans to exist in opposition to a legitimately constituted people (and for a few, at best, of the Europeans who were to be influenced by this document).

The document's logic and limitations become clearer when, as claimed by Jefferson and explained by Donald Lutz, the Declaration is read as part of an extended or assembled text. Without the aid of other 18th-century American statements of rights to complete and contextualize it, the Declaration's meaning cannot be readily grasped by 20th-century readers.[45] The state constitutions and declarations of rights add much to our understanding and make obvious the limited nature of the individual claims being advanced therein by Americans.[46] Regarding the intended British audience, the great British jurist William Blackstone's authoritative jurisprudence is

[41]Haynes, "Nature and Importance of True Republicanism" (1801), pp. 80–81, and see "Liberty Further Extended" (1776?), pp. 17–18.

[42]Berthoff and Murrin, "Feudalism, Communalism, and the Yeoman Freeholder," p. 282. See also Bradford, *Better Guide*, pp. 36–41; and J. Clark, *Massachusetts Election Sermon* (1781), p. 11.

[43]Stephen Hopkins, "Rights of Colonies Examined" (1764), in *Tracts of the American Revolution*, p. 47; see also Otis, "Rights of the British Colonies" (1764), in ibid, pp. 24–27; M. Howard, "Letter from a Gentleman" (1765), pp. 66–67; Hicks, "Nature and Extent of Parliamentary Power" (1768), pp. 170–72; Jefferson, "Summary View" (1774), pp. 264–65; and Galloway, "Candid Examination" (1775), p. 360. See also [Stephen Johnson], *Some Important Observations* (1766), pp. 34–35; Thacher, "Sentiments of a British American" (1764), pp. 490–92; Stamp Act Congress, "Declaration" (19 October 1765), p. 530; Virginia House of Burgesses, "Resolutions of 30 May 1765," pp. 47–48; Patten, *Discourse Delivered at Hallifax* (1766), pp. 13–14; Reid, *Constitutional History of the American Revolution: The Authority to Tax*, pp. 18–19; McDonald, *Novus Ordo Seclorum*, pp. 53–55; J. P. Greene, *All Men Are Created Equal*, p. 34; D. S. Lovejoy, "Rights Imply Equality"; and W. P. Adams, *First American Constitutions*, pp. 169–74.

[44]See Kendall and Carey, *Basic Symbols*, pp. 69–70, 121–22; W. P. Adams, *First American Constitutions*, pp. 169, 174; and Lutz, *Origins of American Constitutionalism*, p. 80.

[45]See Lutz, *Preface to American Political Theory*, pp. 32–48, 62–71.

[46]See Palmer, "Liberties as Constitutional Provisions," pp. 65–66; Peters, *Massachusetts Constitution of 1780*, pp. 79, 155–56; W. P. Adams, *First American Constitutions*, pp. 137–38; and Lutz, *Origins of American Constitutionalism*, pp. 98–99.

dispositive in demonstrating that the cherished rights of life, liberty, and property were not individual trumps that could ever be exercised against one's legitimately constituted and sovereign people.

Consider first Blackstone's words in his *Commentaries on the Laws of England,* which were highly valued on both sides of the Atlantic.[47] Rights, or as he describes them in the most relevant passage, private immunities, are either the residual of natural liberty, which society allows the individual to retain, "or else those civil privileges, which society hath engaged to provide, in lieu of the natural liberties so given up by individuals."[48] These, he suggests, "may be reduced to three principal or primary articles; the right of personal security, the right of personal liberty; and the right of private property." The protection of these rights to life, liberty, and property, he believes, equals "the preservation of our civil immunities in their largest and most extensive sense."[49] But these traditional English rights, familiar to both Americans and Britons, were not absolute or fully inalienable, for they were always limited by the superior right of a majority of the people to its sovereignty.

He makes clear their limited natures as he further defines each of them. The right of personal security, he writes, is a "person's legal and uninterrupted enjoyment of his life, his limbs, his body, his health, and his reputation." That of personal liberty "consists in the power of loco-motion, of changing situation, or removing one's person." And "the third absolute right, inherent in every Englishman, is that of property." Yet all of these rights are subject to "control or diminution . . . by the laws of the land."[50] These rights were thus important and necessary protections of the individual from the arbitrary actions of the monarch, but they could not provide the individual with a protective hedge against the legitimate will of the majority expressed in Parliament.[51]

The language and logic used in the state declaration of rights and constitutions makes much the same argument. Consider, then, one state from

---

[47]He enjoyed great prestige in America during the 18th and 19th centuries. See Williamson, "American Suffrage and Sir William Blackstone," p. 555. For example, see [S. Adams?], "Rights of the Colonists" (1772), p. 239, who follows Blackstone and writes that "the *absolute Rights* of Englishmen, and all freemen in or out of Civil society, are principally, *personal security, personal liberty and private property*"; Handlin and Handlin, "The 1778 Return of Lenox [Massachusetts]," in *Popular Sources of Political Authority,* p. 254, in which Blackstone's language is again closely followed; and Hutson, "Bill of Rights," pp. 78–79, who describes how George Mason, in writing the earlier Virginia Declaration of Rights, had borrowed his sense of protected rights from Blackstone. The same rights also "appeared in five of the seven remaining state bills of rights." See also Glendon, *Rights Talk,* pp. 22–24.

[48]See my discussion at the end of this chapter on the 18th-century corporate, rather than individualistic, understanding of the relationship between natural and civil liberty.

[49]Blackstone, *Commentaries,* 1:125.

[50]Ibid., 1:125–34; see also 1:135–39, for his discussion of lesser rights that serve "to protect and maintain inviolate the three great and primary rights."

[51]See Roche, "Curbing of the Militant Majority," pp. 35–36.

each of the three large geographical divisions and, as representative of a national view, the Northwest Territories. North Carolina, for example, after describing in a most acceptable fashion that one right was truly inalienable, that of religious conscience, implicitly argues that all other rights are subject to the will of the majority. It does so by urging that "no freeman ought to be taken, imprisoned, disseized of his freehold, liberties or privileges, or outlawed, or exiled, or in any manner destroyed, or deprived of his life, liberty, or property, but by the law of the land."[52] These suggested rights were all subject to majority oversight and limitation, assuming (as one should) that the government was to be democratic. These nonetheless valuable rights were not then individual trumps that could be used against the sovereign majority.[53]

In the New York Constitution, its citizens again describe the unique status held by the right of religious conscience. But they too declared "that no member of this State shall be disenfranchised, or deprived of any of the rights or privileges secured to the subjects of this State by the constitution, unless by the laws of the land, or the judgment of his peers."[54] Here, not only could statutory law acting directly control the putative rights of individuals, but the potentially more arbitrary majority will of a jury could as well. No individual right was truly inalienable in the sense that only religious conscience was. That is, no other individual right, no matter how highly valued, was protected from being legitimately alienated or taken from an individual.

The state of Connecticut in its Declaration of Rights found individual rights to be privileges that accrue to "every Man in his Place and Proportion" as "Humanity, Civility and Christianity call for." It then lists numerous privileges, such as: "No Man's Life shall be taken away; No Man's Honor or good Name shall be stained; No Man's Person shall be arrested, restrained, banished, dismembered, nor any Ways punished; [and] No Man shall be deprived of his Wife or Children." But these cherished individual rights were not universal, absolute, or inalienable. Nor were they even applicable to women, for it is clear that here "man" refers to male citizens. Rather, a male citizen of Connecticut held these rights conditionally. These were important rights, but not so important that they took precedence over those of the majority to be self-governing and to safeguard its corporate welfare. Thus an individual could be deprived of these privileges whenever it was "clearly warranted by the Laws of this State."[55]

It was the majority that made such determinations in Connecticut and

---

[52]"The North Carolina Declaration of Rights" (1776), in B. Schwartz, *Roots of the Bill of Rights*, pp. 286–87.

[53]See Lutz, *Preface to American Political Theory*, pp. 75–82.

[54]"The New York Constitution" (1777), in B. Schwartz, *Roots of the Bill of Rights*, pp. 306, 312.

[55]"The Connecticut Declaration of Rights" (1776), in ibid., pp. 289–90.

each of the other American states. Indeed, as the Congress demanded, the majority would also rule in the Northwest Territories, for it stipulated that for the residents of those territories, "no man shall be deprived of his liberty or property, but by the judgment of his peers or the law of the land."[56] The individual's ultimate right was to be judged by the unchecked will of the majority, a condition not usually associated with individualism or the protection of individual rights, but rather with democratic sovereignty. And America's Declaration of Independence was one of the most important 18th-century documents that defended the right of a people to make such determinations. Thus, when understood as a part of an extended 18th-century document that incorporates and is made comprehensible by the language and texts of the state constitutions and Declarations of Rights, as well as the authoritative understanding of the common law offered by Blackstone, the Declaration is correctly seen to defend the right of a people to self-government and to certain other important individual rights that no other people could legitimately deny them.[57] But it does not defend, as some modern commentators have suggested, that individual rights are such that "by definition [they] *cannot* be given up by individuals in the name of some transcendent public good or in the name of anything else."[58] Everything that is known about the political thought of 18th-century Americans argues to the contrary.

If textual exegesis alone is not convincing, commonsense contextualism follows suit and argues that such a highly controversial declaration of fully inalienable individual rights that could be used as trumps against a sovereign majority would have little served the needs of a divided people in rebellion or the propagandistic purposes of the authentic public document. As Jefferson explained, his intention was not to claim for Americans anything theoretically new in this war-declaring document; rather, it was to set forth the emerging American understanding of their legal rights as a sovereign people vis-à-vis their former ruler.[59] Above all else, the true authors, the signatories of this document, "the representative of the United States of America, in general Congress assembled," wished to convince their friends in Britain (of which they still had some) of the propriety and

---

[56]Morison, "The Northwest Ordinance" (initially approved in 1787), in *Sources and Documents,* p. 230.

[57]See Reid, "Irrelevance of the Declaration," p. 58, and *Constitutional History of the American Revolution: The Authority of Rights,* p. 5; Lutz, *Origins of American Constitutionalism,* p. 113; Detweiler, "Changing Reputation," p. 557; and Amar, "Consent of the Governed," pp. 477, 480–83.

[58]Schmitt and Webking, "Revolutionaries, Antifederalists, and Federalists," p. 198.

[59]One of the most truly explosive aspects of the document has had nothing to do with it being misunderstood in individualistic ways. Rather, it derives from a correct (if mildly exaggerated) reading. Its claimed existence of a right of a people to self-determination has proved most appealing to oppressed peoples throughout the former colonial territories during the 19th and 20th centuries. In America, however, this logic would initially be perversely exploited by the white Southerners, not their African slaves, when the Confederacy claimed this corporate right and seceded from the national union.

necessity of their declaration, and their bankers in Holland and France of their resolve and sovereignty.[60] Bankers and merchants, then and now, are usually little interested in revolutionary statements of philosophical principles. And the Declaration was not understood to be a revolutionary statement by its 18th-century American and European audiences.[61]

Well after the issuance of the Declaration, and even after the cessation of hostilities following the Treaty of Paris, Moses Hemmenway, delivering that year's Massachusetts election sermon, continued to claim for the majority this by then vaunted right to self-rule. He held that "the Supreme civil authority remains always in the community at large," and that the people always "have a right to alter and reform their laws," all other laws or compacts "to the contrary notwithstanding."[62] It was the majority's right to self-determination, not that of the individual to stand in defiance of a legitimately constituted people, that Americans regularly defended and believed was at stake in their violent separation from England.[63] The centrality of this concern to their most important secular goals and aspirations speaks directly to their higher valuation of corporate rather than individual autonomous liberty.

Still later, during the Virginia ratification debate, Patrick Henry referred his auditors to the third section of the Virginia Declaration of Rights (cited below) and charged that it, unlike the federal Constitution they were considering, contains the true "language of democracy; [in] that a majority of the community have a right to alter their Government when found to be oppressive."[64] Sam Adams, a fellow "Old Revolutionary," corrected his cousin John for having written that "the people should have an essential share in sovereignty" by teasingly questioning, "is not the *whole* sovereignty, my friend, essentially in the People?" Pressing his point, he asked, "is it not the uncontrollable essential right of the People to amend, and alter, or annul their Constitution, and frame a new one, whenever they shall think it will better promote their own welfare, and happiness to do it?"[65]

In the early 19th century, a French visitor observed that "the system of government in this country is, therefore, not so much a system of absolute liberty and free will, as a system of equality . . . [that] takes the charac-

---

[60]Bemis, *Diplomacy of the American Revolution*, pp. 31–32, 43.

[61]See Nicgorski, "Significance of the Non-Lockean Heritage," p. 177.

[62]Hemmenway, *Massachusetts Election Sermon* (1784), p. 20.

[63]See Bailyn, *Ideological Origins of the American Revolution*, p. 19; Wood, *Creation of the American Republic*, p. 61; Roche, "Curbing of the Militant Majority," p. 35; and Palmer, "Liberties as Constitutional Provisions," p. 62.

[64]Henry, "Speeches in the Virginia State Ratifying Convention" (1788), p. 302.

[65]S. Adams, "Letter to John Adams" (25 November 1790), in *Writings of Samuel Adams*, 4:344. He had earlier quoted John from his letter of 18 October 1790. See also J. Adams, "Letter to Dr. Rush" (1 August 1812), in Adams and Rush, *Spur of Fame*, p. 235. Here John would flesh out the meaning of liberty for his cousin; it "was like that of Parson Burr . . . the liberty of a man chained hand and foot in a dungeon: that is, a perfect liberty to stay there."

ter of a strong rule by the majority."[66] Majoritarianism, with its inherent corporate focus, implicit communalism, and potential endangerment of minorities or individuals who stood in opposition to it, must be understood to have been a well-accepted feature of late colonial and early national American life.

Although its corporate nature is evident, majoritarianism's communalism and its limited concern with the demands of individuals, particularly those out of favor, are not.[67] In this light, consider Landon Carter's claim that if the public good demanded it, "the suppression of the individual liberty of the minority" was "'a Thing absolutely necessary to be done' and 'therefore just in itself.'"[68] Benjamin Hichborn's commemoration of the Boston Massacre dead leaves little room for doubt concerning the near-absolute power a sovereign democratic people was to hold in governing itself. He urges that political liberty is a natural right and "power existing in the people at large, at any time, for any cause, or for no cause, but their own sovereign pleasure, to alter or annihilate both the mode and essence of any former government."[69] This is as it should be, for "where God does not immediately indicate his will . . . the voice of the people in cases of this nature, is *the voice of God*."[70] Although the foundation of these claimed corporate and divine rights is not perfectly clear, by what alternative right or power could an individual, considered dangerous or repugnant by a legally organized majority, stand in security against such a force?

Other than the right of religious conscience, disfavored minorities had no rights that could protect them from the will of an opposed majority. As the Federal Farmer noted, only a very few rights "are natural and unalienable, of which even the people cannot deprive individuals." Many others are constitutional or fundamental and can only be altered or abolished by the people in express acts. Among these are "the trial by jury, the benefits of the writ of habeas corpus, etc." Still other laws, he explained, "are common or mere legal rights, that is, such as individuals claim under law."[71] In the New Hampshire Bill of Rights much the same was posited. It was explained that upon entering society people surrender certain rights "to insure the protection of others." Among these rights only a few are "unalienable, because no equivalent can be given or received for them. Of this kind are the rights of conscience."[72] Other than the right of conscience,

---

[66]Chevalier, *Society Manners and Politics*, pp. 336–37.

[67]See Handlin and Handlin, *Dimensions of Liberty*, p. 21.

[68]Cited by J. P. Greene, *Landon Carter*, p. 44.

[69]Hichborn, "Oration, March 5th, 1777," in H. Niles, *Principles and Acts of the Revolution*, p. 47.

[70]J. Huntington, *Discourse* (1781), p. 9.

[71]Federal Farmer, "Letter VI" (25 December 1787), p. 70.

[72]"New Hampshire Bill of Rights" (1783), in B. Schwartz, *Roots of the Bill of Rights*, p. 375. This was a position outlined in most of the state declarations of rights; for another example, see the "North Carolina Declaration of Rights" (1776), in ibid., pp. 286–87.

little else that protected the individual from majoritarian demands was considered inalienable.

Without a powerful set of individual rights capable of trumping majoritarian ones, those that do exist "are not absolute, and they are circumscribed directly and formally by the rights of the people to self-government." Thus, even if majoritarian political liberty does not necessitate that the rights of minorities or individuals be sacrificed to popular will, at the very minimum, it provides no internal obstacles to a people with intolerant ethical or religious intentions.[73] By implication, people as concerned with the protection of corporate rights and as willing to cede control over personal ones to the majority as Americans were are unlikely to value those of an individual standing in defiance of that corporate will.

It was well known, as the Loyalists reminded their fellow Americans, that if the colonists had been primarily concerned with securing personal rather than corporate liberty, they would never have sought independence from Britain. One of the most articulate Loyalists, in fact, wrote that England was "by the Confession of the wisest Men in Europe, the freest and the noblest Government, of the Records of History."[74] What he had in mind was the unusual range of private rights enjoyed only by British subjects. The actions of the American Patriots, therefore, are only understandable if it is recognized that they were driven by a quest for a kind of freedom different from that offered by the centralizing imperial ministries of Britain, one that was corporate and communal rather than private and individual.[75]

Again, political liberty was not only understood to be a right exercised by a majority of the political community, but was of sufficient importance in the estimation of Revolutionary-era Americans that it was usually described as one of only two fully inalienable rights.[76] Unlike in modern America, only a few select freedoms were then believed to be "gifts of God" and so vital to living a full human life that their absence would render that life not worth living, thus deserving the status of inalienability.[77] In particular, only the liberty of religious conscience claimed "an entire Exemption from all human Jurisdiction: because its Ends, Offices, and Interests, are superior to all the Ends of Civil Association; and subjecting it

[73]Peters, *Massachusetts Constitution of 1780*, p. 51; see also Berlin, "Two Concepts of Liberty," pp. 129–30; Patterson, *Freedom*, pp. 404–5; and Lutz, *Preface to American Political Theory*, p. 120.

[74][Boucher], *Letter From a Virginian* (1774), p. 25; see also Wesley, "Calm Address to Our American Colonies" (1775), p. 417; Troeltsch, *Protestantism and Progress*, p. 118; and Breen, "Persistent Localism," p. 20.

[75]See [J. Allen], *American Alarm* (1773), essay 3, pp. 2, 7; and in agreement regarding the nature of the conflict, though from the opposite (Loyalist) political perspective, see M. Howard, "Letter from a Gentleman" (1765), pp. 66–67.

[76]See Lynd, *Intellectual Origins of American Radicalism*, pp. 23–24.

[77]*Civil Liberty Asserted* (1776), pp. 44–45; see also Canavan, "Relevance of the Burke-Paine Controversy," p. 166.

to the Power of Man, is inconsistent with the very Being of Religion."[78] No other individual right was consistently held in such esteem.[79] Even comprehensive religious liberty was still contested and far from being fully countenanced. As Abraham Williams explained, "the rights of Conscience, are unalienable; inseparable from our Nature;—they ought not—they cannot possibly be given up to Society. . . . Yet civil Societies have a right, it is their Duty, to encourage and maintain social public Worship of the Deity, and Instructions in Righteousness."[80] The only right besides that of religious conscience that Revolutionary-era Americans held to be inalienable, then, was the corporate right of a people to be self-governing.

This valuation of private and corporate claims to rights was clearly enunciated during the struggle in 1778 over the proposed Massachusetts constitution. Here, in their returns, the citizens of the villages and towns of the western part of the state ardently defended the inalienability only of an individual's right to religious conscience and of a people's corporate right to form or abolish their government. The citizens of Berkshire County affirmed this common understanding of late 18th-century Americans when they wrote that "the people at large are endowed with alienable and unalienable Rights. Those which are unalienable, are those which belong to Conscience respecting the worship of God and the practice of the Christian Religion, and that of being determined or governed by the Majority in the Institution or formation of Government. The alienable are those which may be delegated for the Common good, or those which are for the Common good to be parted with."[81] From this widely shared 18th-century perspective, then, the individual was fully free in serving God and family, and in surrendering himself to the majoritarian will of his community, but in precious little else.[82]

One might object that these remarks were not common sentiments, except among rural radicals in the most politicized colony in America, Massachusetts. Yet the historical record indicates that such a view was not unique to them. It shows that in both Northern and Southern colonies

---

[78]Smith, *The Occasional Reverberator*, 5 October 1753, cited by Leder, *Liberty and Authority*, pp. 73–74; see also Stiles, *Discourse on the Christian Union* (1761), p. 28; Dorr, *Duty of Civil Rulers* (1765 Connecticut election sermon), p. 13; Patten, *Discourse Delivered at Hallifax* (1766), pp. 13–14; and Stillman, *Massachusetts Election Sermon* (1779), pp. 8–9. Stillman was a minister deeply influenced by Locke, politically active, and at that time uniquely honored as a Baptist in being asked to give the prestigious annual election sermon. Nevertheless, he too limited his accounting of inalienable rights to one. See also Cord, *Separation of Church and State*, p. 70.

[79]Other rights, some individual, were also occasionally and inconsistently claimed to be natural or inalienable. For a comprehensive listing of those declared thus by New England ministers, see Baldwin, *New England Clergy*, p. 82.

[80]Williams, "Massachusetts Election Sermon" (1762), p. 10.

[81]Handlin and Handlin, *Popular Sources of Political Authority*, pp. 374–75; see also pp. 410–11, 423, 436; and Federal Farmer, "Letter VI" (1787), p. 70.

[82]See Palmer, "Liberties as Constitutional Provisions," pp. 65–66.

public voices defended comparable opinions regarding the fully inalienable right of a majority of citizens to govern themselves as they saw fit. To the east in Lexington, for example, the politically active Reverend Jonas Clark held that the right of political self-determination resides "in the people, whether emerging from a state of nature, or the yoke of oppression, [and] is *an unalienable right.*"[83] In Rhode Island, the lawyer and activist Silas Downer claimed that the "essence of the *British* constitution [was] that the people shall not be governed by laws, in the making of which they had no hand, or have their monies taken away without their own consent." This, he claimed, was both an inherited right and one that is also "a natural right which no creature can *give,* or hath a right to take away."[84] And in the South, the protection of corporate rather than individual rights was the leading concern of George Mason's seminal Revolutionary document, the 1776 Virginia Declaration of Rights. In it, Virginia held that "a majority of the community hath an indubitable, inalienable, and indefeasible right to reform, alter, or abolish" the government, "in such a manner as shall be judged most conducive to the public weal."[85] And as usual, no limits were placed on the majority's power to do so.

George Washington also recognized the uncontested character of the people's right to be corporately self-governing, yet in so doing he presciently drew attention to the potential elasticity of such appeals. He assured his audience that "the basis of our political system is the right of the people to make and alter their constitutions of government." He then warned that "the constitution which at anytime exists, until changed by an explicit and authentic act of the whole people, is sacredly obligatory upon all. The very idea of the power and the right of the people to establish government, presupposes the duty of every individual to obey the established government."[86] Here, Washington highlighted a fear that by the end of the 18th century many among the more conservative elite shared. They worried not so much about the power of the majority, but about the language of freedom and the right to self-government that they had employed so successfully in defending their conduct in the war and how it might prove difficult to control.[87] They rightfully feared that these corporate

[83]J. Clark, *Massachusetts Election Sermon* (1781), pp. 8–9.
[84][Downer], "Discourse" (1768), p. 100.
[85]Poore, *Federal and State Constitutions,* 2:1908.
[86]Washington, "Washington's Farewell Address" (17 September 1796), pp. 143–44; see also Rush, "Address to the Freemen of America" (1787), p. 9, who declares that "'all power is derived *from* the people.' They possess it only on the days of their elections. After this, it is the property of their rulers."
[87]See Reid, *Concept of Liberty,* p. 121; Szatmary, *Shays' Rebellion,* pp. 97–98; Hatch, *Democratization of American Christianity,* p. 76; and Rodgers, *Contested Truths,* p. 13. See also Burke, *Reflections on the Revolution in France* (1790), pp. 12–31, who also tried to vitiate the revolutionary implications of the majoritarian claims advanced by British Whigs in defense of the Glorious Revolution. This is a problem that the British would again confront after both world wars in their relationships with their later colonies.

claims would be exploited by all manners of disaffected people and minorities, to say nothing of great regional majorities. Others, such as Madison, however, were more worried by the probable coerciveness of the majority than by its potential weaknesses.

But Washington's fears were not unfounded, and even before the outbreak of the Revolutionary War, newly expansive corporate appeals had already begun to be insistently voiced. Witness the radical British-born John Allen's 1773 argument on behalf of his fellow Massachusetts Baptists against ecclesiastic taxes. Or consider the even more radical claim for fully universal free male suffrage made by the people of Northfield in their "return" regarding the proposed 1780 Massachusetts constitution. In it, they reminded the Massachusetts Convention that anything less than universal suffrage was "materially defective," as it was "rescinding the natural, essential, and unalienable rights of many persons, inhabitants of this Commonwealth, to vote in the choice of a Representative." They continued by asking if we shall "treat these polls precisely as Britain intended and resolved to treat all the sons of America?"[88] Curiously, however, except for a large minority of Loyalists, those concerned about the potential elasticity of the newly inalienable right to self-government were either unwilling or unable to speak out against it during the Revolution.

ENGLISH POLITICAL LIBERTY: REPRESENTATIVE AND COMMUNAL

It is apparent that most Americans supported the right of a people (whether Anglo-Americans, residents of New York, or whomever) to govern themselves. What is less certain is how they understood self-government. But if one attends to their language, their sense of it becomes clear. They sought to govern themselves following the logic and customs of English political liberty. This usually was identified as a people's right to political representation, to the nearly indistinguishable right of majoritarian consent to laws (especially with regard to taxation), and the right to trial by a jury of one's peers.[89] In comparison with classical or Renaissance republicanism (a frequently suggested alternative understanding), it was less a political vision that was an end in itself and more an instrumental one. In particular, English liberty served corporately defined Protestant moral and religious ends as well as a rule-governed or a liberal theory of government controlling the possession and alienation of private property. (English liberty is of special interest because its dominance in the period challenges those who find the republican understanding of political liberty to have been preeminent.)

Americans believed themselves to have inherited English liberty as sub-

[88]See [J. Allen], *American Alarm* (1773), essay 4, p. 8; and Handlin and Handlin, *Popular Sources of Political Authority*, pp. 577, 584.

[89]See Reid, *Constitutional History of the American Revolution: The Authority of Rights*, pp. 18–19; and Dworetz, *Unvarnished Doctrine*, pp. 89–90.

jects of the British Crown, and not to have forfeited it with their removal to his North American colonies.[90] This is to be expected, for "the colonists' attitude to the whole world of politics and government was fundamentally shaped by the root assumption that they," as Englishmen, possessed a unique inheritance of liberties and rights.[91] Part of what English liberty described was captured by Abraham Cowley, who defined it as a people "being govern'd by laws which they have made themselves, under whatsoever form it be of government."[92] One might also begin with the early 18th-century definition of a pamphleteer in the 1735 *Daily Gazetteer* (of London). The author rhetorically asked what liberty truly was and then answered, is it not "being governed by just and equal laws of the People's making? Is not this the highest liberty? Is not this the perfection of liberty?" Turning to an editorial two years later in *Common Sense,* the English understanding of corporate liberty is again defined as "that liberty [which] involves giving one's consent, personally or by representative, to the laws which one is obliged to obey."[93]

Later, Americans held that they possessed true political liberty because they were governed only by laws "to which [they] themselves have some way consented."[94] The Virginia House of Burgesses on 30 May 1765 resolved that "the Taxation of the People by themselves, or by Persons chosen by themselves . . . is the distinguishing Characteristick of *British* Freedom . . . the inestimable Right of being governed by such Laws, respecting their internal Polity and Taxation, as are derived from their own Consent."[95] It was the active consent of the majority, usually by representation, then, rather than its active participation in the actual debating and crafting of laws, that was an essential part of the Anglo-American understanding of English political liberty.

An anonymous author writing in 1759 declared that English liberty rested on an additional cornerstone. He wrote that "the First of these great Fundamentals is our TRIAL BY JURIES. The Second of them is our REPRESENTATION BY PARLIAMENT."[96] What he adds to the requisites of English political liberty is the importance of jury trial. In the American understanding of English liberty, the common-law jury was an integral element. John Philip Reid reports that "to London's Common Council, jury trial was

[90]See Winslow, *Meeting House Hill,* pp. 250–51.

[91]Bailyn, *Origins of American Politics,* pp. 66–67; see also Delman, "Liberty and the Common Law," pp. 16–17; Reid, *Constitutional History of the American Revolution: The Authority of Rights,* p. 25; Pennsylvanecus in the *Pennsylvania Journal,* 28 September 1758; and Otis, "Rights of the British Colonies," in *Tracts of the American Revolution,* pp. 24, 27, who writes that "the colonists, black and white, born here, are free born British subjects, and entitled to all the essential civil rights of such."

[92]Cited by Gunn, *Beyond Liberty and Property,* p. 231.

[93]Cited by Forbes, *Hume's Philosophical Politics,* p. 148.

[94]Stephen Hopkins, "Rights of Colonies Examined" (1764), in *American Political Writing,* p. 46.

[95]Virginia House of Burgesses, "Resolutions of 30 May 1765," p. 48.

[96][Brooke?], *Liberty and Common-Sense* (1760), letter 1, pp. 2–3.

'that sacred Bulwark of *English* Liberty,' and to the New York grand jury as well it was 'the foundation of *British* liberty.'" To the Massachusetts General Court the right of jury trial was "that inestimable privilege and characteristic of English liberty."[97] And to Stephen Johnson of Lyme, Connecticut, trial by one's peers was one of the "most important civil liberties." In fact, he held that "if any in the Magna Charta [are] secure and sacred to the subject, it is this right of trial by our own peers."[98]

The importance of the jury trial is of special interest because of the role it played in enforcing communal standards. In fact, the jury with its trial and ancillary administrative responsibilities was not so much an individual source of protection as it was a communal one.[99] The institution was predicated on the understanding that "it is the quality of being a good neighbor that makes a man a good citizen, or better a citizen at all, [and] that gives him his political status and his personal liberty."[100] Full individual citizenship status was not a presocial attribute, therefore, but a corporately endowed privilege that could be withheld or withdrawn as a result of political or social ostracism. And the English common-law jury, until the end of the 18th century, when it was weakened by modernizing forces in England,[101] had traditionally been a powerful communal institution.[102]

Thus, English liberty describes a political situation in which a majority of the people consent to the laws that would govern them, they are represented in the crafting of these laws, and when they break them they are tried by juries of their peers. As explained by the Stamp Act Congress, "Englishmen have ever considered as their birthrights, that of being free from all taxes but such as they have consented to in person, or by their representatives, and of trial by their peers."[103] Years later John Adams still held that "the foundation of English liberty," was the "right in the people to participate in their legislative council . . . and more especially to the great and inestimable privilege of being tried by your peers of the vicinage."[104] These elements, then, were emphasized in early as well as later characterizations of the English understanding of political liberty. And

---

[97]Reid, *Constitutional History of the American Revolution: The Authority of Rights*, p. 49; see also W. E. Nelson, *Americanization of the Common Law*, p. 31.

[98]Stephen Johnson, "To the Freemen of the Colony of Connecticut," *New London Gazette*, September 1765, reprinted in Bailyn, "Religion and Revolution," pp. 146–48.

[99]See Leder, *Liberty and Authority*, p. 118; McDonald, *Novus Ordo Seclorum*, p. 40; W. E. Nelson, *Americanization of the Common Law*, p. 36; Palmer, "Liberties as Constitutional Provisions," pp. 100–101; and Maier, *Old Revolutionaries*, pp. 222–23, who describes the greater fear that Maryland Catholics had of the "hostilities and prejudices of juries" than they had of even the popular branch of the legislature.

[100]Pekelis, *Law and Social Action*, pp. 61–62.

[101]See W. E. Nelson, *Americanization of the Common Law*, pp. 165–71.

[102]See McDonald, *Novus Ordo Seclorum*, pp. 290–91; W. E. Nelson, "Eighteenth Century Constitution," p. 20; and Canavan, *Freedom of Expression*, pp. 149–51.

[103]Stamp Act Congress, "Petition" (23 October 1765), pp. 89–90.

[104]J. Adams, "Discourse XIII on Davila" (1790), in *Works of John Adams*, 6:278.

throughout the Revolutionary era, these components of English liberty continued to enjoy the complete support of all sectors of the American political nation, and were touted by them as their most cherished inheritance as British subjects.[105]

Oxenbridge Thacher argued early in the conflict that essential British rights were consent to taxation, active participation or representation, and trial by jury.[106] Then, in October 1765, the Stamp Act Congress in its resolution reiterated such claims to British liberty and held that "it is inseparably essential to the Freedom of a People, and the undoubted Right of *Englishmen,* that no Taxes be imposed on them, but with their own Consent, given personally, or by their Representative . . . [and] that trials by jury are the inherent and invaluable rights of every British Subject in these Colonies."[107] In 1787, "the essential parts of a free and good government" continued to be "a full and equal representation of the people in the legislature, and the jury trial of the vicinage in the administration of justice."[108] But it was not only to taxation that the right of consent was extended. As William Hicks argued in 1768, it applied to general issues of governance as well. "The very spirit of the English constitution requires, that general regulations framed for the governing of society, must have the sanction of *general approbation*" and that such principles are "the foundation of English liberty."[109] Indeed, these refrains were a constant in the political discourse of Revolutionary-era Americans.

This understanding of English liberty, which emphasized the role of active consent rather than either citizens' passive acquiescence or their still more direct political participation in the crafting of laws, was shared by even those who eventually opposed the Revolution. For example, the clear need for active consent, yet little more, was defended by both the insightful and outspoken future Loyalist Joseph Galloway and the precocious revolutionary Alexander Hamilton. Galloway, writing in defense of his plan of union, one similar to that promoted some twelve years later by Hamilton, notes that "under it [his plan of union], no law can be binding on America, to which the people, by their representatives, have not previously given their consent: This is the essence of liberty, and what more would her people desire?"[110] Majoritarian consent, then, was a common political goal for both Loyalist and Patriot.

Missing, however, in Revolutionary America were the voices of radical European republicans, who insisted on a more active role for each citizen

---

[105]Other examples include *Prospect of the Consequences* (1776), pp. 92–93; and Patten, *Discourse Delivered at Hallifax* (1766), pp. 13–14.

[106]See Thacher, "Sentiments of a British American" (1764), pp. 490–92.

[107]Dickinson, "Resolution of the Stamp Act Congress" (19 October 1765), pp. 184–85.

[108]Federal Farmer, "Letter II" (9 October 1787), p. 39.

[109]Hicks, "Nature and Extent of Parliamentary Power" (1768), p. 183.

[110]Galloway, "Candid Examination" (1775), p. 393; see also Hamilton, "Full Vindication" (1774), p. 47.

in the crafting of legislation—in essence, classical or Renaissance republican political liberty. Adherents of the republican idea of political liberty such as Rousseau were most often bereft of faith in an active and concerned deity. Thus, for them, a life of moral liberty was only possible when citizens were capable of actively shaping their own lives through political debate and the direct crafting of general legislation.[111] But Americans were different; they were a Christian people.

Although committed to a communal and ordered understanding of liberty, they did not believe political activity to be the most efficacious means of achieving the most elevated human ends. Aside from an exceptional few during the Revolutionary years, Americans would have rejected any notion that political debate and self-governance or the new claims in defense of individualism represented the true path to human development. Ultimately, most believed that people had only a limited role in making possible human flourishing and a life of liberty. Americans, as reformed Protestants or adherents of early modern rationalism, believed that true liberty, a moral liberty that accorded with the dictates of God or the laws of nature, was only achievable because of God's gift of grace or of reason. And for many Americans, without grace and the intercession of the Holy Spirit, no amount of individual reason, corporate political effort, or republican heroics could remove the stain of original sin.

Opinions concerning the proper (English) character of political liberty stayed within a narrow range during the entire Revolutionary period. But there were differences over the proper interpretation of these generally agreed-upon norms. For example, Loyalists argued for the right of consent by local political elites within an imperial British framework. The Patriots instead demanded that consent required something more than an elite's negotiated acceptance of imperial decrees. They therefore rejected the "plans for an imperial union, such as that outlined by Galloway and the moderates in the first Continental Congress," for they held that political liberty meant "complete control of their own government, free from intervention of any external body whatever."[112] But even this more radical position did not insist on direct citizen participation in the framing of laws. Instead, it emphasized national rather than imperial representation.

During the crisis, however, perceptions evolved somewhat and new grounds were established for a still more active and more majoritarian view than had formerly been embraced of consent and of English political liberty. Yet it is important not to overreact, as one Progressive-era historian did, suggesting that during the Revolution "we see a tendency . . . to reject the old passive view of state interference as limited by the consent of the governed and take the view that real liberty implies . . . the power to

---

[111]See Rosenfeld, "Rousseau's Unanimous Contract," pp. 101–2; and Ackerman, *We the People,* p. 206, who claims that this describes 18th-century American political culture.

[112]Andrews, *Colonial Background of the American Revolution,* p. 167.

actively control and direct the policy of the state.[113] Few American spokesmen, elite or popular, argued for direct democratic participation in governance beyond the most immediate local level (the writer known as "A Farmer," at the end of the period, was the most demanding). Not even a sometime utopian like Jefferson strayed far beyond the acceptable limits of English-style consent-based representative government.[114] During the next forty years he never seriously proposed that the nation actively try to embrace a classical or Renaissance republican form of government with full participatory and direct democratic institutions.[115] Revolutionary-era Americans were a communal people with deep reformed-Protestant roots who gave every appearance of being perfectly content with English political liberty as embodied in active consent, legislation by representation, and trial by a jury of one's peers.

There was widespread insistence, though, that the need for representation in the crafting of legislation and in judicial and executive appointments was a necessary element of English political liberty. For example, in an oration to commemorate the Boston Massacre, one of the probable leaders of the Boston Tea Party and a future British agent, Benjamin Church, did not differentiate between personal active consent and that of representatives. Holding them to be of comparable value, he argued that "we must be careful to maintain that inestimable blessing liberty. By liberty I would be understood, the happiness of living under laws of our own making, by our personal consent, or that of our representative."[116] Donald Lutz, in fact, contends that it was representation that was the principle structural plank in Americans' understanding of corporate liberty, along with devotion "to radical Protestant theology," to the public good "over private avarice, and the fundamental rights derived from English common law."[117]

Even relatively emphatic 18th-century defenders of classical republican perspectives on political liberty, those we might least expect to offer their approbation to representative government, defended political liberty in its English sense. Consider, for example, the remarks of Dr. Benjamin Rush, the author of the celebrated apologia for forming young men into selfless republican machines, who nevertheless held that liberty consisted "in a man being governed by men chosen by himself." Seven years later, Rush continued to hold that the true definition of liberty was "being governed by laws made by ourselves, or by rulers chosen by ourselves."[118] Again, no hesitation is visible on his part in accepting the legitimacy of representation.

[113]J. A. Smith, "Spirit of American Government," p. 15.

[114]Cf. Matthews, *Radical Politics of Thomas Jefferson,* pp. 79–85; and Sheldon, *Political Philosophy of Thomas Jefferson,* pp. 54–55.

[115]See Zuckert, "Republicanism and American Identity"; and Matthews, *Radical Politics of Thomas Jefferson,* for an opposing view.

[116]Church, "Oration" (1773), p. 35.

[117]Lutz, *Popular Consent and Popular Control,* p. 60.

[118]Rush, *Selected Writings,* p. 72, and *Considerations Upon the Present Test Law of Pennsylvania,* cited by Countryman, "Very Spirit of Liberty," p. 21 (draft version).

Most authors discoverable in the historical record demonstrate an absence of concern with differentiating among various types of consent, representation, and direct participation in the crafting of laws. In 1780, Simeon Howard spoke to this concern and equated political liberty with the right to choose one's representatives. He notes that "as every people have a right to be free, they must have a right of choosing their own rulers, and appointing such as they think most proper; because this right is so essential to liberty, that the moment a people are deprived of it they cease to be free."[119] Even later, toward the end of the 1780s, most Anti-Federalists and Federalists continued to adhere to this traditional English understanding of political liberty.

The soon-to-be Federalist Alexander Hamilton, for example, in 1784 wrote that "a share in the sovereignty of the state, which is exercised by the citizens at large, in voting at elections is one of the most important rights of the subject." It is, he added, "their *liberty;* or in other words, their *right* to *share* in the government." During the debates over ratification, another high Federalist, Noah Webster, also held that the "principal bulwark of freedom is the *right of election.*"[120] On the other side of the debate, Brutus, one of the most articulate Anti-Federalists, also did not distinguish between representation and more direct political participation when he held that "in every free government, the people must give their assent to the laws by which they are governed. This is the true criterion between a free government and an arbitrary one. The former are ruled by the will of the whole, expressed in any manner they may agree upon; the latter by the will of one, or a few." Defending the core elements of English political liberty, another Anti-Federalist argued that "the essential parts of a free and good government are a full and equal representation of the people in the legislature, and the jury trial of the vicinage in the administration of justice."[121] Again and again, what Americans demanded in their legal maneuvers with the Crown was neither an increase in individual liberty nor more direct control over the creation and execution of the nation's laws, but rather the relatively modest English sense of corporate or political liberty.

In the 18th century, then, English political liberty enjoyed nearly universal support. Even the future Loyalist Joseph Galloway, for example, held without demurral that "this power of legislation in the people" is "the essence of the English government . . . and the main support of the freedom and liberty of the English subjects." With it, he held, "we have a perfect idea of civil liberty, and free government."[122] Writing in the *Massa-*

[119]S. Howard, "Massachusetts Election Sermon" (1780), pp. 364–65.

[120]Hamilton, "Second Letter from Phocion" (April 1784), p. 78; and [Webster], "Examination" (1787), p. 58.

[121]Brutus, "Essay I" (18 October 1787), p. 114; and Federal Farmer, "Letter II" (9 October 1787), p. 39.

[122]Galloway, "Candid Examination" (1775), p. 381.

chusetts Gazette and Boston Newsletter in 1766, a precocious but anonymous patriot, Aequus, found that *"English Liberty* is a propriety attached to the individuals of the community," one that he defined as "the primitive right that every freeholder had of *consenting* to those laws by which the community was to be obliged." Moreover, he concluded that this right of consenting to the laws that one would be governed by was paid for by the "price of individual subjection."[123] Again, communal intrusiveness was not inimical to corporate liberty, in this instance English liberty, and the associated constitutional demands for popular consent, legislative representation, and trial by a jury of one's peers.[124]

When one looks overseas at Britain in the 1770s, ironically, one finds considerably less consensus than was found in America regarding the meaning of political liberty, and even some dissatisfaction with the contours of what Americans took to be English political liberty. Instead, diverse perspectives on liberty had emerged that foreshadowed America's future at the end of the century. Consider the aggressively individualistic remarks of Cato. He claimed (though this claim is in clear tension with other of his remarks) that liberty is the power of doing whatever one likes "as far as by it he hurts not the Society, or any Members of it" and that "every Man is sole Lord and Arbiter of his own private Actions and Property." He added that "it is a mistaken Notion in Government, that the interest of the Majority is only to be consulted."[125] Majoritarianism was a political principle that Cato recognized as not being neutral in its impact, one that had to be contested because of its close association with communalism and moral intrusiveness.

In a similar vein, Richard Hey challenged Price to explain why the will of the majority should be given preference over that of opposed minorities. An anonymous author also suggested that Price was in error concerning liberty, because for Price's critic, liberty was not directly related to matters such as representation. Instead, it was the ability to enjoy one's rights as a free man without any necessary concern with who in fact frames "the laws by which he is governed."[126] It is clear that some 18th-century British authors were willing to attack the propriety of majoritarianism and the hallowed English standards of political liberty. In so doing, they often defended a novel individualistic understanding of liberty.

America, as a new country in revolt against England, showed little interest in and could ill afford to embrace such doctrines. It especially needed

---

[123]Aequus, "From the Craftsmen" (1766), p. 63.

[124]See G. Himmelfarb, *On Liberty and Liberalism,* p. 327, who writes that "the older Whig tradition had no compunctions about the intervention of society and government whether in the sphere of economics or morals." She then notes that "at a later period a distinction was made. . . . the moral part . . . was deemed to be too important to be left to the unguided impulses."

[125]Cato, "Letter #62" (1721), in Jacobson, *English Libertarian Heritage,* pp. 127–29.

[126]Hey, *Observations* (1776), p. 61; and *Civil Liberty Asserted* (1776), pp. 16–17.

the legitimacy offered by a communal understanding of liberty to defend its separation from what was reputedly the most benign government in Europe, one celebrated for its dedication to the protection of individual liberties. Those voices raised in defense of liberty during the Revolutionary years, therefore, argued for a corporate and majoritarian understanding, though usually not a demanding republican conception of it. Indeed, it is difficult to avoid perceiving American thinking on liberty as paradoxically but understandably (given their tenuous situation) reactionary. Samuel Huntington suggests that "in the constitutional debates before the American Revolution, the colonists in effect argued the case of the old English constitution against the merits of the new British constitution."[127] One might claim, then, as indeed the colonists did, that Americans were only defending their "traditional" rights as Englishmen when they adhered to an "English" understanding of political liberty that already had begun to be challenged in Britain.[128]

On the Continent there were prominent authors who were even more forceful in their denunciation of the corporate or communal features of liberty. Taking an extreme position was the Swiss jurist J. L. de Lolme, who in his rejection of the centrality and importance of political liberty denied that corporate or political liberty was truly a form of liberty. He argued instead that it was a form of power. According to him and other progressive thinkers (often defining themselves in opposition to Price and thus indirectly to his American adherents), liberty described a realm of privacy. The political mechanisms by which this might be achieved were not directly concerned with liberty. Lolme wrote that "to concur by one's suffrage in enacting laws, is to enjoy a share, whatever it may be, of Power. To live in a state where the laws are equal for all, and sure to be executed, (whatever are the means by which these advantages are attained) is to be free. Be it so: we grant, that to give one's suffrage is not liberty itself, but only a means of procuring it."[129] Corporate life for him had already become thoroughly instrumental in the service of the private realm. His position is thus at odds with the stance taken by proponents of republican political liberty, as well as the more nuanced position taken by American adherents of their English understanding of political liberty.

Yet by the late 1780s in America, some of the most articulate voices had begun to make room for new interpretations of liberty, rivaling the here-

---

[127]S. Huntington, "Political Modernization: America vs. Europe," in *Political Order in Changing Societies*, p. 97.

[128]See Thacher, "Sentiments of a British American" (1764), pp. 490–92; Dickinson, "Resolution of the Stamp Act Congress" (19 October 1765), pp. 184–85; Continental Congress, "Petition" (23 October 1765), pp. 89–90; and still later see Federal Farmer, "Letter VI" (1787), pp. 69–70. For more recent commentators, see Delman, "Liberty and the Common Law," p. 201; and Reid, *Constitutional History of the American Revolution: The Authority of Rights*, p. 237.

[129]Lolme, *Constitution of England* (1775), p. 226.

tofore largely uncontested corporate understanding. Included among these voices were the classical liberal interpretations that had been defended for decades by European thinkers such as Hey and Lolme. Even then, though, the greatest American defender of individual rights, James Madison, was as yet unwilling to challenge majoritarianism directly. Majoritarianism and the preeminent corporate rights of a people to self-determination, at least before the court of public opinion, still had to be paid their due.

Instead, Madison turned to reeducation as he sought to redefine the accepted American understanding of English political liberty. To do so, he innovatively linked the accepted rights of the majority to self-direction with the detested quality of selfishness. In effect, he redefined and transformed majoritarianism into self-serving factionalism. Conversely, he tried to protect the rights of the minority and "obnoxious individuals" by arguing that their good was necessarily linked to securing the common or public good. Their good, he suggested, could not be put at risk without also endangering that of the public.

His clever indirection in argument, however, demonstrates that majoritarianism and corporate liberty, like the priority of the public good, were not yet publicly contestable. If he wanted to reshape the thinking of his audience (both contemporary and future), which seems to have been his goal, he was obliged to associate behavior he wished to condemn with behavior that was broadly despised (ironically, selfishness). And he was forced to associate behavior he wished to encourage with values and actions that were usually applauded. Hence, his association of minority rights with the public good and majoritarianism with selfish factionalism becomes understandable.[130]

Again, Madison's strategy suggests that a frontal attack on majoritarianism or a direct advocacy of minority rights was still not advisable even in the 1780s. Consider, then, the more orthodox and contrasting sentiments on majoritarian liberty of Rev. Zabdiel Adams, John's first cousin. He held that "the *majority can,* and *does always govern.* . . . Individuals having a different interest may be disposed to resist and even to call others into their vortex; but their feeble efforts may be easily overcome by the contrary exertions of the more numerous, the more virtuous and more rational part of their fellow citizens."[131] Here, in opposition to Madison's unorthodox view of the individual's moral status,[132] majoritarianism is defended, as was the norm, by associating it with reason and virtue.[133] The

---

[130]See Plato, *Republic* 561a, who predicts that such manipulation of moral language where anarchy is called freedom is the necessary outcome of a democratic ethos.

[131]Z. Adams, "Massachusetts Election Sermon" (1782), pp. 544–45; and see J. Madison, in Hamilton, Jay, and Madison, *Federalist,* pp. 54–59.

[132]See Lutz, *Popular Consent and Popular Control,* p. 127.

[133]See E. Lewis, "Contribution of Medieval Thought," pp. 471–72; Federal Farmer, "Letter XVII" (1788), p. 95; and Ohmori, "Artillery of Mr. Locke," p. 23.

corrupt passions of minorities and individuals were conversely linked to degeneracy and selfishness (the usual marks of original sin).

It was perceptions like those of Zabdiel Adams rather than those of James Madison that had led Americans to embrace as their Revolutionary goal a corporate understanding of liberty, their sense of English political liberty.[134] In fact, it must have been a corporate and communal sense of liberty rather than the proto-individualist one of Madison's that had guided Americans into the War of Independence. To make sense of the American Revolution, fought against the greatest 18th-century defender of individual rights, their most valued secular understanding of liberty would have had to have been corporate and political, not individual and private.[135]

REPUBLICAN LIBERTY: HEARD AND FELT, BUT NOT LIVED

Turning to that strand of the American understanding of political liberty that had a well-established Western pedigree, the republican one, we find it to have been understood historically as a people's "right to be free from any outside control of their political life—an assertion of sovereignty," as well as "their corresponding right to govern themselves as they thought fit."[136] A. J. Carlyle further portrayed it as having developed from deep roots in the Hellenistic Mediterranean basin with its principal instantiation having been in classical and Italian Renaissance republics. He describes it as a political community that "lived by its own laws, and under the terms of the supremacy of the community itself, not only in its law, but in its control over all matters which concerned its life."[137]

Republican liberty, however, does not simply articulate the collected aspirations of an aggregation of disparate individuals, but something more: the normative aspirations of a community committed to a common moral agenda. Central to this meaning of political liberty "*is* the notion of a public good which is prior to and characterizable independently of the summing of individual desires and interests."[138] Yet, in this respect, republican liberty's powerful insistence on corporate autonomy and communal ends did not differ from Americans' understanding of English political liberty.

But there was a difference. Republicanism's communalism, unlike that of English political liberty, was not a byproduct of majoritarianism, nor was it contingent on Americans having embraced a Protestant moral theory. Instead, republican liberty's highly intrusive communalism is an in-

---

[134]See Countryman, "Very Spirit of Liberty," p. 27 (draft version).

[135]See M. Cohen, "Berlin and the Liberal Tradition," p. 217.

[136]Skinner, *Foundations of Modern Political Thought*, 1:6–7, 155–57.

[137]Carlyle, *Political Liberty*, p. 21.

[138]MacIntyre, *After Virtue*, p. 236.

trinsic and necessary aspect of it. Its essence is found in its being a moral end rather than a means (as is the case with English political liberty), and it is the nature of that end which necessitated its communalism. One perspicacious Loyalist, in dismay, reflected on these features of republican liberty. Fearing that Americans were to embrace it, he asked if there ever had been a people "so disaffected to government, so uniformly intolerant towards all who differ from them . . . in short, so impatient under every proper legal restraint not imposed by themselves."[139] He drew attention to republican liberty for its being even more intrusive and more intolerant than the majoritarianism and communalism of English political liberty (with which he and his readers were intimately familiar).

This theme is reiterated by the founder of Methodism, John Wesley, who asked in an essay reprinted in the 1 February 1776 edition of the *Massachusetts Gazette*, whether "republican government[s] give more liberty, either religious or civil?" He answered no, for "no governments under heaven are so despotic as the Republican." Another critic reminded literate Americans that with the advent of a republican government "there would be no peace in the colonies, till we all submitted to the republican zealots" who were described as being ever "cruel, towards all that presumed to differ from them in matters either of religion or government."[140] The history of the English Civil War and Interregnum suggested as much. Still, the difference between English and republican political liberty regarding the intrusiveness of the community into the private life of its members is slim. There has not yet been found a sharp demarcation between these two corporate and communal senses (republicanism by its internal logic and English liberty in its reformed-Protestant American instantiation) of liberty.

To differentiate between the two, we must go beyond republicanism's clear antipathy toward monarchy and join it to that institution, practice, or normative precept that it uniquely defended.[141] Luckily there is such a trait, for republican liberty was (and continues to be) frequently associated with direct citizen participation in the debate over and framing of laws.[142] As Thomas Jefferson explained, the essence of republicanism was "a government by its citizens in mass, acting directly and personally, according to

---

[139]Boucher, "Dispute" (1775), p. 474.

[140][M. Cooper], *Friendly Address* (1774), p. 182.

[141]When republicanism is understood simply as a rejection of monarchy, there can be no question regarding its ascendancy in Revolutionary-era America. See W. P. Adams, "Republicanism in Political Rhetoric before 1776," pp. 420–21. In the 1790s, when it came to be identified with representative government, which was anathema to the older tradition of republican liberty, and seen as distinct from democracy, again its success cannot be questioned. But the richer aspects of republicanism as a fully developed political theory, which are of interest here, are not captured by either of these two more restricted senses.

[142]See Pocock, *Politics, Language, and Time*, pp. 85–86, and *Machiavellian Moment*, p. 518; Rahe, "Primacy of Politics in Classical Greece," pp. 275–76; and Harpham, "Liberalism," p. 766.

rules established by the majority; and that every other government is more or less republican, in proportion as it has in its composition more or less of this ingredient of the direct action of the citizens."[143] Here is the marker, for English political liberty was largely indifferent to this concern.

Most Americans, though, neither questioned the legitimacy of representation nor were troubled by their instrumentalist view of politics. Indeed, Americans were products of a reformed-Protestant culture in which it was widely held that human betterment ultimately depended on grace rather than on secular self-determination. Americans who were active Christians could not have fully endorsed the republican valuation of politics and its humanistic sensibilities. They were influenced by, but could not have embraced, a vision of the good that emphasized active citizenship and gave centrality of place to an anthropomorphic quest for meaning.[144] Evidence of a powerful classical or Renaissance republican presence in the thought or actions of Revolutionary-era Americans should therefore be hard to discover. And it is.[145]

All but missing in America, and among the English authors read avidly by Americans, were spokesmen denigrating representation from the demanding republican perspective voiced by 18th-century theorists such as Mably or Rousseau. Rousseau, for example, had argued that "the moment a people allows itself to be represented, it is no longer free, it no longer exists."[146] Instead, Dr. Price had written without any hint of derision that "*civil liberty* [political liberty], in its most perfect degree, can be enjoyed only in small states." There are, however, "methods by which such near approaches may be made to perfect Liberty" as "by the appointment of *Substitutes* or *Representatives*."[147] With one possible exception, the secular and existential developmental concerns of European adherents of Renaissance republican political thought, people who lived in a world already bereft of faith, were absent in Christian America.

The lone exception I have been able to uncover is A Farmer, an anonymous Anti-Federalist author whose essays appeared in Baltimore's *Mary-*

---

[143]Jefferson, "Letter to John Taylor" (28 May 1816), in *Writings*, ed. Peterson, p. 1392; but see Wood, *Radicalism of the American Revolution*, p. 95, who cites both Hamilton and Adams, indicating that they had little idea what the word actually meant. See also, however, J. Adams, *Defence* (1788), 3:157–59, who first notes that "of all the words, in all languages, perhaps there has been none so much abused" as republic, but then describes it in terms similar to Madison's new understanding of it as representative government.

[144]See E. S. Morgan, "American Revolution," p. 37; and J. J. Ellis, review of *The Lost Soul of American Politics*, p. 134.

[145]See Kerber, "Republican Ideology of the Revolutionary Generation," pp. 480–81; Appleby, "Jefferson's Political Philosophy," pp. 311–12; and Pangle, *Spirit of Modern Republicanism*, pp. 28–39, who acidly writes (p. 29) that "in attempting to assess the merits of this contemporary infatuation with 'classical republicanism,' one cannot avoid being struck by the ignorance its proponents display as regards the original texts."

[146]Rousseau, *Social Contract* (1762), p. 96.

[147]Price, *Observations* (1776), p. 7.

land Gazette.[148] He contends that "throughout the world government by representation, seems only to have been established to disgrace itself." For "where representation has been admitted as a component part of government, it has always proved defective, if not destructive." He then asks that we contrast "this scene with one, where the people *personally* exercise the powers of government," such as Switzerland where "every Swiss farmer is by birth a legislator."[149] Such a republican political environment is what he would recommend to his readers—that is, if they were not already debased (which he believes they were).

Yet in spite of his conditional hostility to representation and his infatuation with Machiavelli,[150] he is rather unrepublican in his Enlightenment concern with "the *rights* of *individuals,* the primary object of every good and free government."[151] Richard Sinopoli thus goes too far when he concludes that A Farmer's account of the benefits of an active and directly democratic life of politics is comparable to those of more celebrated republican theorists.[152] A Farmer's description of and commitment to the moral character of republican corporate institutions and their intrusiveness are equivocal at best. When his singularity, his belief that Americans are too corrupt for republican institutions, his overall equivocation, and his seeming lack of influence are taken into consideration, there seems little reason to alter the overall impression regarding the absence of a committed republican theorist in Revolutionary-era America.[153] The appearance of an internally consistent republican theorist in America would have to await the embrace of classical republicanism by desperate defenders of slavery in the mid-19th century.[154]

Americans accepted the legitimacy of representation on civil matters of the most fundamental nature; therefore, in their valuation of political life they were at odds with the priorities of classical republicanism. Few Americans could honestly have said of themselves, as Pericles did of Athenians, that "even those who are mostly occupied with their own business are

[148]See Storing, "Introduction to A Farmer," in *Complete Anti-Federalist,* 5:5–9, who suggests that the author may have been the nonsigning member of the Constitutional Convention and leading Maryland Anti-Federalist John Francis Mercer; see also Sinopoli, *Foundations of American Citizenship,* pp. 151–55, for his thoughtful discussion.

[149]A Farmer, "Essay V," pp. 263–64, 267.

[150]See ibid., p. 270, where the author claims that "the greatest human discernment, ever concentrated in the mind of one man, was the portion of the celebrated Nicolas Machiavelli."

[151]A Farmer, "Essay VI," p. 51; see also "Essay VII," p. 63; Storing, "Introduction to A Farmer," in *Complete Anti-Federalist,* p. 6; and Sinopoli, *Foundations of American Citizenship,* p. 153.

[152]See Sinopoli, *Foundations of American Citizenship,* p. 153.

[153]One other author who bordered, though even more equivocally, on the cusp of rejecting representation as an unalloyed good was the anonymous author of "The People the Best Governors" (1776), p. 655.

[154]See Shalhope, "Race, Class, Slavery," pp. 564–70; and Shklar, "Gone with the Wind," p. 41.

extremely well-informed on general politics." Nor could they truthfully have opined that "we do not say that a man who takes no interest in politics is a man who minds his own business; we say that he has no business here at all."[155] American corporate life was intrusive into the private life of the individual, and the good of the public did enjoy an indisputable preeminence. Yet political life per se was not privileged.

In Revolutionary America, only for an exceptional few did political liberty carry the intrinsic importance awarded it by classical Greek and Roman authors, or by Renaissance citizens of the cities of northern Italy.[156] As a largely Christian and overwhelmingly rural people, Americans instead understood politics as instrumental in the service of higher religious and other publicly defined goals. For most of them, politics could only indirectly serve human development and righteous living. Instead, such goals were to be pursued through allegiance to family, local communal oversight, and God's love and his freely given grace.[157] The republican tradition of political liberty, however, insisted that full human development was only achievable through direct political participation.[158] It also demanded a deeper communalism, a broader intrusiveness and inclusiveness, and a more absolute subordination or surrender of the individual to the demands of a common culture than did the English tradition of liberty, although the difference was one more of degree than of substance.

Consider the 18th-century republican aspirations of Rousseau in the *Social Contract*. He claimed that the "individual is nothing, the citizen is everything,"[159] and that the proper goal of a republican polity is "transforming each individual, who is by himself a complete and solitary whole, into part of a greater whole from which he in a manner receives his life and being." Each citizen was to become nothing alone and was to be able to "do nothing without the rest."[160] It was Rousseau, after all, who provided the still haunting apologia for corporate intrusion into the ethical and political life of the individual in service of the common good and the individual's higher freedom. That is, "whoever refuses to obey the general will shall be compelled to do so by the whole body. This means nothing

---

[155]Thucydides, *History of the Peloponnesian War*, pp. 118–19.

[156]See Dworetz, *Unvarnished Doctrine*, p. 52; Pangle, "Civic Virtue," p. 110; Howe, "Political Psychology of *The Federalist*," pp. 506–7; and in fanciful disagreement, see Ackerman, *We the People*, p. 206.

[157]In regard to the tension between them, see P. Miller, *New England Mind*, 2:408, who describes "a charter government by saints" being transformed into "a charter expounded in the name of property rights." Yet Hatch, *Sacred Cause of Liberty*, p. 9, writes that "for the New England clergy, as for John and Samuel Adams, the quest for personal accumulation was the antithesis of a spirit of liberty."

[158]See Rahe, "Primacy of Politics in Classical Greece," p. 286; and Diamond, "Ethics and Politics," pp. 93–94.

[159]Vallete cited by Rosenfeld, "Rousseau's Unanimous Contract," p. 100.

[160]Rousseau, *Social Contract* (1762), p. 38.

less than that he will be forced to be free."[161] And Rousseau's project in *The Social Contract* was not atypical of 18th-century republican-inspired communal aspirations.[162]

The themes captured in Rousseau's thought (as found in *The Social Contract*) are partially embraced by the communalism of English political liberty in America, but the emphasis in each is different. Although Americans' understanding of political liberty was also corporate and communal, it was clearly not predominantly shaped by a classical or Renaissance republican understanding. Instead, one finds ubiquitous mention in America of the value of representative democracy and the absolute necessity of grace and of surrendering to God for full human development.[163] Absent are institutionalized efforts to foster direct citizen participation beyond the local level (mostly by fining citizens for their frequent poor attendance at town meetings). The lack of such institutional efforts demonstrates that republicanism did not enjoy a pervasive power in the shaping of late 18th-century America. The telltale footprints of republican institutions are simply not to be found.[164]

But evidence abounds of Americans' Christocentric culture and of late 18th-century institutions in which politics were newly emphasized, but still secondary to their reformed-Protestant concerns.[165] An instrumental politics, therefore, must not be equated with a politics of individualism with which it is also compatible. One must, therefore, avoid assuming "if not republicanism, then individualism."[166] For in America, a political regime in which the rule of law dominated and the central government was constitutionally bound to respect the rights of individuals and communities was conjoined to a normative vision of the good that demanded that local intermediate institutions intrusively mold the recalcitrant clay of a fallen humanity. In effect, Americans enjoyed what has since come to be called a liberal theory of (central) governmental institutions while also profiting from a local and communal, largely Protestant-derived, theory of the human good. Mixing and matching between regime types and theories of the good are obviously possible, even if not in the long term necessarily stable.

---

[161]Ibid., p. 18. This language, as noted in chapter 6, is as much Calvinist as it is republican. In this case, however, Rousseau's vehicle, an active political life of corporate self-direction, is more appropriately identified with his republican side.

[162]See Wood, *Creation of the American Republic*, p. 59; and Hampson, *Enlightenment*, pp. 212–13.

[163]See Banning, "Quid Transit?" pp. 201–3.

[164]See Diggins, *Lost Soul of American Politics;* Appleby, "Liberalism and the American Revolution"; Kloppenberg, "Virtues of Liberalism"; Herzog, "Some Questions for Republicans"; R. M. Smith, "'American Creed' and American Identity," p. 247; and Kramnick, "Republican Revisionism Revisited," p. 633.

[165]See Bonomi, *Under the Cope of Heaven*, p. 216; and Hatch, *Sacred Cause of Liberty*, p. 157.

[166]See Pangle, *Spirit of Modern Republicanism*, pp. 28–39, who offers us the paradigm case of such fallacious reasoning.

Republican themes, nevertheless, had in the 18th century entered the American educated consciousness. They came in directly through frequently read works of classical political thought, rhetoric, and history, and indirectly through these works' influence on aristocratic Renaissance writers, 17th-century English Christian republicans, and popular novelists and dramatists.[167] Yet ironically, it was in the largely popular and ad hoc political arrangements of Revolutionary committees and in the inarticulate politics of local communities that republicanism most fully found life in America. In both instances, the most affected populations were often men not deeply versed in the thought of classical or Renaissance republican authors, as was generally true of their social "betters." Republicanism was, nonetheless, an important part of the late 18th-century political mix, if for no other reason than that it offered elite inspiration and thus secular ballast to the otherwise reformed-Protestant-inspired communal features of American political thought.

Yet some of those most familiar with and impressed by republican thought also questioned its applicability in America. For example, Alexander Hamilton declaimed that "the ancient democracies, in which the people themselves deliberated, never possessed one feature of good government."[168] Jefferson added that republican governments could only be implemented when "restrained to very narrow limits of space and population. I doubt if it would be practicable beyond the extent of a New England township."[169] Active republican government, then, as Hamilton and Jefferson observed,[170] was only suitable for small New England towns or possibly Virginian counties, not state or national politics. Republican political liberty thus paradoxically had a limited appeal to some who were most assuredly students of this literature and often taken to be its most staunch advocates.

I am not arguing that republican ideas about liberty did not influence American thought. Rather, I believe that the classical and Renaissance republican sources of inspiration currently in vogue were mediated by more immediate and more powerful inheritances from English political norms, the common law, Scottish moral-sense philosophy, and agrarian practices, and reformed-Protestant cultural, religious, and political patterns of thought and behavior. As Harry Stout has concluded, "the Revolutionary generation had more in common with their theocratic and aristocratic

---

[167]See Sabine, *History of Political Theory*, pp. 475–76; and McDonald, *Novus Ordo Seclorum*, pp. 68–69.

[168]Hamilton, "Remarks and Speeches at the New York Ratifying Convention" (1788), p. 207.

[169]Jefferson, "Letter to John Taylor" (28 May 1816), in *Writings*, ed. Peterson, p. 1392.

[170]See also Hamilton, "Federalist No. 9," in Hamilton, Jay, and Madison, *Federalist*, p. 50; and Jefferson, "Letter to Samuel Kercheval" (12 July 1816), in *Portable Thomas Jefferson*, p. 555.

Puritan forebears than with pagan 'republicans' of ancient Greece and Rome."[171]

In addition, political statements made by those most likely to have been strongly influenced by republican thought rarely went beyond the more moderate corporate claims made by outspoken advocates of English political liberty. The absence of direct textual evidence and the paucity of political institutions uniquely shaped by a republican understanding of liberty suggest that it had a limited influence on Revolutionary-era politics.[172] Rhys Isaac has written of even the relatively irreligious 18th-century Virginians that "the language and terms of Classical republicanism . . . could not readily arouse a populace whose limited experience of higher culture was of the Bible rather than of the Classics. More effective than the imagery of Roman republicanism was the Anglo-Virginian sense of identity as a Protestant people."[173] Ironically, then, classical or Renaissance republicanism's 19th-century influence on American politics and thought, with a decline in the hegemony of Protestant communalism, may have been greater than its immediate ability to define Revolutionary-era institutions, practices, and norms.[174]

Conversely, English political liberty was practical and uniformly supported at the time of the Revolution by an array of defenders of different social, religious, and political outlooks. Included among likely supporters were constitutional monarchists, reformed-Protestant localists, and future centralizing nationalists and liberal individualists. English political liberty emphasized the instrumental rather than the intrinsic value of political life. Therefore, different political visions of the good, with their distinct moral goals, could be served by a politics of English political liberty.

What could not be accepted, then, by many Americans dissatisfied with republicanism was its insistence on the primacy of politics and corporate self-creation, not its corporate or even communal character. Republicanism's secularism found few dedicated American adherents. Those who supported an intrusive form of politics, but one based instead on divine or natural moral truths, almost certainly would have found English political liberty more congenial; they did not understand political life as having intrinsic worth or as defining the sole path toward full human develop-

---

[171]Stout, *New England Soul*, p. 310.

[172]See W. P. Adams, *First American Constitutions*, p. 104; and Shalhope, *John Taylor of Caroline*, pp. 67–68. However, see Jefferson, "Letter to Samuel Kercheval" (12 July 1816), in *Portable Thomas Jefferson*, p. 555, who asks "where then is our republicanism to be found? Not in our Constitution certainly, but merely in the spirit of the people."

[173]Isaac, *Transformation of Virginia*, pp. 246–47; see also Hatch, *Sacred Cause of Liberty*, pp. 14, 109.

[174]See for example, Wish, "From Yeoman Farmer to Industrious Producer," pp. 152–53; Meyers, *Jacksonian Persuasion*, p. 12; and R. M. Smith, "'American Creed' and American Identity," p. 247.

ment. Indeed, English political liberty in its instrumentalism was compatible with a range of political visions, including fully communal ones.

In sum, English political liberty could encompass those who understood human development as best pursued through private channels as well as those who believed that such efforts must be corporately assisted and communally determined (but not through secular politics). American citizens' embrace of English political liberty, with its lack of intrinsic purposefulness, in the main reflected their continuing confidence in the Protestant path of human development marked out by faith, dependence on God and brotherly oversight, and respect for God's commandments. The Protestant, rural, and communal character of late 18th-century American political culture demands that theoretical narratives consistent with their own real lived experiences be sought, rather than turning to those better suited for a different people living in a different time.

CIVIL LIBERTY: A CORPORATE LIBERTY IN TRANSITION

In the 18th century there were no conventions strictly adhered to regarding the classification of political liberty or its component elements. Often, as noted above, political and civil liberty were used interchangeably to describe various kinds of corporate liberty.[175] For example, the most famous British jurist of the age, William Blackstone, used these terms interchangeably,[176] as had Montesquieu, another author highly regarded by Americans. And Dr. Richard Price defined civil liberty as "the power of *Civil Society* or *State* to govern itself by its own discretion; or by laws of its own making, without being subject to any foreign discretion, or to impositions of any extraneous will or power . . . there is one general idea . . . the idea of Self-direction, or *Self-government*."[177] Here, then, he described civil liberty in a manner that would be reserved for political liberty in the 19th century.

For having confused what in late 18th-century Britain were becoming distinct senses of liberty and, more importantly, for having emphasized corporate rather than individual liberty, Price was widely taken to task (although again not in America). "One of the more sophisticated replies came in 1776 from John Lind, with the assistance of Jeremy Bentham," who accused Price of having confused civil and political liberty. More particularly, like Richard Hey, Lind "stressed the negative quality of liberty and the inappropriateness of applying the term to powers of self-government."[178] Nevertheless, such distinctions were new. Gunn claims that the

[175]See Banning, "Jefferson Ideology Revisited," p. 18.
[176]See Blackstone, *Commentaries*, 1:119–23; Forbes, *Hume's Philosophical Politics*, p. 149; and Gunn, *Beyond Liberty and Property*, pp. 237–38.
[177]Price, *Observations* (1776), p. 3.
[178]Cited by Gunn, *Beyond Liberty and Property*, pp. 245–46.

first person in the Anglo-American world to have differentiated systematically between them was the English radical religious dissenter, celebrated chemist, man of letters, and future American, Joseph Priestley.[179]

Earlier in the 18th century, however, civil liberty had been used to describe the corporate power of collective self-government. In fact, civil liberty was the accepted English description of such political claims. Political liberty as a distinct concept in English did not enjoy currency until it was first popularized in French by the Baron de Montesquieu at midcentury. But his "initial effect on ordinary vocabulary may perhaps be reflected in certain sermons where conventional references to civil liberty were broadened to read 'political or civil Liberty.'"[180] Political liberty as a separate sense of liberty in English was thus carved out of a less differentiated corporate understanding of liberty that had been known as civil liberty. Yet by the end of the 18th century, civil liberty had already begun to be used to describe two senses of liberty that were distinct from political liberty and different from each other. First, it defined a traditional Anglo-American corporate and communal understanding of liberty. Second, it described a newer private-regarding sense of liberty that was planted in the soil of emerging individualism.

By the 19th century, at least some of the confusion surrounding the meaning of civil liberty had been resolved, as civil and political liberty were no longer readily confused. Noah Webster explained that "*political liberty* is sometimes used as synonymous with *civil liberty*. But it more properly designates the *liberty of a nation*." Civil liberty properly described "the liberty of men in a state of society, or natural liberty, so far only abridged and restrained, as is necessary and expedient for the safety and interests of the society, state, or nation."[181] And regarding the two meanings of civil liberty that were distinct from political liberty, Webster continued in the middle of the 19th century to use the communal understanding of civil liberty. This is evident because he defined civil liberty as the residue of the individual's natural liberty that remained after the society's needs were met as determined by the political community. This is the traditional sense of the term. The more modern alternative held that civil liberty defined a set of individual privileges and exemptions (radicalized prescriptive liberties) from corporate intrusion—in effect, a private space into which the corporate body could not legitimately intrude.

In the 18th century, as one might expect, the corporate understanding of civil liberty was dominant. It was regularly portrayed as that portion of natural liberty that the polity allowed the individual to continue possessing, after removing those elements of natural personal independence that might have interfered with peaceful social existence, service to God, or the

---

[179]See ibid., pp. 243–44.
[180]Ibid., pp. 238–39.
[181]Webster, *American Dictionary of the English Language* (1829).

amelioration of the public good. As the radical Thomas Paine explained, "a *natural* right is an animal right," whereas "*civil* rights are derived from the assistance or agency of other persons; they form a sort of common stock, which, by the consent of all, may be occasionally used for the benefit of any."[182] And the more moderate Jean Jacques Burlamaqui, an 18th-century Swiss legal theorist taken as authoritative by James Wilson, similarly drew attention to the corporate character of civil liberty. He declared that "civil liberty is therefore, in the main, nothing more than natural liberty, divested of that part of it which formed the independence of individuals."[183]

But decades later, after a change in outlook, Wilson looked back on his earlier Revolutionary-era understanding of civil liberty and critically observed that such a perspective had meant that "the right of individuals to their private property, to their personal liberty, to their health, to their reputation, and to their life, flow from a human establishment, and can be traced to no higher source. The connexion between man and his natural rights is intercepted by the institution of civil society . . . [and] he can claim nothing but what the society provides."[184] To Wilson's dismay, civil liberty, as traditionally understood, had freed the individual from a debased natural liberty and offered him in its stead a more restricted social one, which was claimed to be more elevated. As Noah Webster reminded him in 1802, "civil liberty . . . instead of being derived from *natural freedom* and *independence,* is the creature of society and government."[185] But by the end of the 18th century, some Americans, like the immigrant Wilson educated and raised in Scotland, found this exchange to be highly disadvantageous to the individual's newly sought autonomy.

More generally, it is easy to understand why those drawn to the ideas of the later Enlightenment would have found the corporate sense of civil liberty, with its close affinity to the Protestant concept of original sin, so unacceptable. Most Americans, however, were likely attracted to it for that reason, for its embrace of the general outlines of original sin. As one anonymous author explained, it was "when dark and stormy Passions obscured the Light of *Reason*" that "the fair Realm of LIBERTY [was] laid waste, and LICENTIOUSNESS usurped both her Title and Dominion." It was a common understanding, then, that man's deformation had made natural liberty unsustainable and societal intervention, with its attendant civil liberty, necessary. Years later, another author noted that "whatever be the

---

[182]Paine, "Candid and Critical Remarks," 2:274.

[183]Burlamaqui, *Principles of Natural and Politic Law* (1763), 2:18–19; see also J. Wilson, "Considerations on the Nature and Extent of the Legislative Authority" (1774), in *Works of James Wilson,* ed. McCloskey, 2:723.

[184]Wilson, "Of the Natural Rights of Individuals" (1790–92), in *Works of James Wilson,* ed. McCloskey, 2:589. He is here comparing Blackstone to Burke and finding them both wanting.

[185]Webster, "Oration" (1802), p. 1229.

case in a state of innocence, no sooner did sin enter into the world, but subjection and inequality entered likewise." In fact, he argued that the loss "of perfect liberty must be dated from the loss of innocence; and must be continued till that can be regained."[186] Natural individual liberty, a perfect liberty, should have been available for all to enjoy for an eternity. The Fall, however, made that impossible.

Given humanity's apostate condition, then, civil liberty was the socially acceptable residue of natural liberty allowed the fallen individual by the community (of similarly fallen individuals). "LICENTIOUSNESS accompanied the Depravity of Man and immediately succeeded to the Loss of natural Liberty" only to be regained to the degree that society might "suppress or controul LICENTIOUSNESS."[187] Samuel Chase, chief justice of the Maryland Supreme Court, associate justice of the United State Supreme Court, and a signer of the Declaration of Independence, had famously instructed his grand jury that "liberty and rights, (and also property) must spring out of civil society, and must be forever subject to the modifications of particular governments."[188]

During the 18th century, such orthodox but constrained views "of the relationship between natural and civil liberty displayed remarkable tenacity." According to Michael Kammen, almost "no one had much to say of an approving character about natural liberty. It was invariably and pejoratively associated with the lifestyle of 'savages,'"[189] that is, fallen individuals who were bereft of the benefits of God's grace and the restraint of society. For most Americans, then, people could be allowed some measure of natural liberty, but only as mediated by local intermediate social and political institutions rather than as comprehended by the untrustworthy individual. And although critical stances toward the traditional understanding of civil liberty did arise in America, such as Wilson's 1804 remarks above, they are normally found after the close of the Revolutionary period. They would develop as a few members of the national elite came to question the dogma of original sin (or its secular equivalent) and the spiritually dependent condition of human beings.

Even in far more progressive Britain, this new sense of civil liberty as individualistic had not yet emerged by the mid-18th century, and was, at best, only "implicit in Hume's thought."[190] Instead, civil liberty still was understood as a communally defined sense of liberty (#1 below) or confused with corporate or political liberty (#2 below). Both senses of liberty valued the autonomy of the collective over that of the individual. Duncan Forbes writes that "the best and fullest contemporary treatment . . . seems

[186][Brooke?], *Liberty and Common-Sense* (1760), letter 1, p. 13; and *Boston Gazette and Country Journal*, 10 May 1756.

[187]*Liberty: Civil and Religious* (1815), p. 20.

[188]Chase, "Charge to Grand Jury" (1803), p. 194.

[189]Kammen, *Spheres of Liberty*, pp. 21–22.

[190]Forbes, *Hume's Philosophical Politics*, p. 160.

to be that of Thomas Rutherford in his *Institutes of Natural Law* (1754)
. . . [and] Rutherford distinguished two kinds of civil liberty established by
the social contract: (1) of the parts [individuals] and (2) of the whole collectively. (1) implies a freedom from all except civil subjection, and (2) a
freedom from all subjection whatever [for the body politic]."[191] Thus, in
this midcentury understanding, the possession of civil liberty assured that
an individual would not be oppressed by another equally sinful individual.
It did nothing to protect him or her from the intrusiveness of civil association. Only communal bodies could be trusted to possess full freedom from
intrusion, that is, corporate or political liberty.

In the Colonies, an anonymous author writing in Peter Zenger's *New-
York Weekly Journal* explained that authentic civil liberty must be limited
by society and its conventions, for "liberty against Virtue and Laws, is
only a Privilege to be unhappy, a License for a Man to Murder himself."[192]
About the same time, the progressive American journalist and lawyer William Livingston discussed civil liberty in a traditional communalist fashion
in the *Independent Reflector*. He wrote that "civil Liberty is talked of by
many, and understood by few"; in fact, it is "built upon a Surrender of so
much of our natural Liberty, as is necessary for the Good Ends of Government." Until this point, he had set forth a traditional definition of (communal) civil liberty. With the addition of one more sentence, however, the
impression Livingston creates in modern readers is changed. He continued,
"the Design of entering into a State of Society, is to promote and secure
the Happiness of its Individuals."[193] Varying understandings of individual
happiness can sustain different normative goals and the limits to be legitimately imposed upon individuals under the auspices of civil liberty.

Depending on how these constituent elements are understood, civil liberty can thus be exploited by those holding radically different understandings of the individual and his or her proper relationship to the community.
As George Washington explained, "the magnitude of the sacrifice" that
"individuals entering society" must make necessarily depends "on the situation and circumstances." Thus, "it is at all times difficult to draw with
precision the line between those rights which must be surrendered, and
those which may be reserved."[194] The critical determinant was how
broadly or narrowly the legitimate aims of society and the goal of individual happiness were defined, and by whom. The Revolutionary-era's understanding of civil liberty was essentially a Rorschach test of one's foundational social, political, and (through one's stance on original sin) religious
beliefs. But it was not usually an interesting issue for Americans. For most,

[191]Ibid., p. 162.

[192]*New-York Weekly Journal*, 7 July 1740.

[193]Livingston, "Of the Use, Abuse, and Liberty of the Press" (1753), in Livingston et al.,
Independent Reflector, p. 339.

[194]Washington, "Letter to Congress" (17 September 1787), 2:666–67. For a progressive
view of this demarcation, see Morris, "Letter" (1774), p. 319.

local communal intervention was absolutely necessary for human happiness. Humans' innate deformities demanded that their souls be constrained and shaped if personal and social happiness were to be achieved.

A latent ambiguity in the common understanding of civil liberty, however, did exist, and it would be exploited by those defending more progressive senses of individual liberty. This tension is visible in a 1763 written debate in which the two competing visions of civil liberty are defended. As is often the case, the participants did not directly articulate their views of the good; instead, they are embedded in a discussion of political institutions, something that Americans were more comfortable directly examining. Their political theory must be teased out of the discussion—here, out of their remarks on the "separation of powers." Although the exchange on the separation of powers lacks originality (as also was the norm), these remarks are of interest because of what they reveal regarding the beginnings of a new ideational division in the American mind.

At the center of this division are two different understandings of civil liberty (here confusingly denominated as political liberty, but it is evident that the authors are describing two contrasting senses of what came to be called civil liberty). Each staked out his position by citing the most respected source in America after the Bible on social and political matters,[195] "the justly celebrated author of *The Spirit of the Laws*," the Baron de Montesquieu. (His understanding of liberty, however, was also equivocal at best.)[196] Each opponent used Montesquieu to defend his view of civil liberty: either the new sense of civil liberty just beginning to emerge or the conventional 18th-century corporate understanding.[197]

One of the authors, T.Q., writing in the progressive *Boston Gazette and Country Journal* of 18 April 1763, opened the exchange by arguing that "political liberty, as it is defined by a great writer is 'a tranquility of mind arising from the opinion each man has of his own safety.'"[198] The selection of this passage from Montesquieu suggests, as does the rest of the letter, that T.Q. was outlining civil liberty in its emerging individualistic sense. He was answered in the *Boston Evening Post* of 23 May 1763 by a more learned adversary writing under the pseudonym "J," who responded that Montesquieu cannot be accurately understood based on one line, and asked

> leave to add what the same inimitable author says, a little before, upon this subject: "Political liberty does not consist in an unrestrained freedom. In governments, that is in societies directed by laws, liberty can consist only in the

[195]See Spurlin, *Montesquieu in America*, pp. 260–61.

[196]See Baumer, *Modern European Thought*, pp. 226–27; and May, *Enlightenment in America*, pp. 40–41.

[197]See Forbes, *Hume's Philosophical Politics*, p. 161; and Gunn, *Beyond Liberty and Property*, pp. 243–44.

[198]T. Q. and J., "Exchange of Letters" (1763), p. 19.

power of doing what we ought to will, and in not being constrained to do what we ought not to will. We must have continually present to our minds the difference between independence and liberty. Liberty is a right of doing whatever the laws permit." The whole of this taken together forms, in my opinion, the just idea of *political liberty* . . . any other, than this complex idea of *political liberty,* is partial and will lead to endless error.[199]

Certainly it is difficult to impeach J's more inclusive reading of Montesquieu, but note the different tone (borne out by the remainder of the letter) that he brings to bear on this question. At its essence, his understanding of civil liberty was that it demanded that fallen humans be restrained and shaped by corporately determined limits.

The debate was rejoined by T.Q. in the 6 June 1763 issue of the *Boston Gazette*. There he argued that the citation he previously had employed "needs not any thing that goes before or follows after it to give us a just idea of what the author would define by it, it being by itself a full definition of political liberty." Still later in his rebuttal to J, he added that "I have nothing against Mr. J's taking into his idea of liberty what the author . . . says of it in another distinct chapter. . . . But I cannot see why he needs to insist upon it, for it does not appear to me to be necessary to form an adequate idea of liberty."[200] Here, in their disparate perspectives, we have encapsulated the divergent interpretations to which "civil liberty" would be subject by the end of the 18th century.

Yet the more expansive understanding of civil liberty hinted at by the anonymous T.Q. is rarely found fully developed in extant American materials written before the last decade of the century. Not even the theologically and politically radical Jonathan Mayhew, writing two years after this exchange, understood civil liberty in a sense different from the traditional one defended by J. Civil liberty, for Mayhew, was still a residue that society allowed the individual who had given up his natural liberty "for the sake of the common good, and mutual security." And civil liberty continued to be that situation in which an individual is prevented from doing "what is right in his own eyes," rather than being viewed as a hallowed private area into which the corporate body could not intrude. Such a condition of privacy, assuredly for Mayhew one of licentiousness, he describes most traditionally as "a state of anarchy & confusion."[201] Positions embodying a mildly individualistic understanding of civil liberty, like T.Q.'s, almost invariably appear as shadow images under attack by orthodox opponents.

British defenders of the more expansive sense of individual civil liberty, however, were not so rare. As Joseph Priestley understood civil liberty, it was "that power over their own actions, which the members of the state

[199]Ibid., p. 23.
[200]Ibid., pp. 28–29.
[201]Mayhew, "Memorandum" (1765), p. 141.

reserve to themselves, and which their officers must not infringe."[202] Yet, even in Britain, such modern views did not dominate. As an anonymous British critic of Dr. Price (this time a conservative one) explained in 1776, the limits that civil liberty was to impose on individuals continued to be decided by how one answered a "single question." It was "whether one in a state of nature has not a right to depart from it to join with a civil state, to relinquish the guidance of one's self by one's own will, [and] to be guided by the law of a civil state by which one expects to be benefitted." He answered that "the practice of every part of the civilised world answers in the affirmative."[203] The transition from natural to civil liberty that he defended stipulated that the individual must relinquish the prerogative of drawing the line where socially acceptable individual liberty begins and ends. Even in Britain, civil liberty was still to be corporately defined. In America, the fallen nature of humanity would demand no less.

For Price's anonymous critic (and in truth, for Price himself); for J and according to him, for Montesquieu; and for most recorded pronouncements of late 18th-century American authors, civil liberty was a matter of corporately limiting the freedom of the individual. The individual must not be at liberty to follow his or her unique and sinful understanding of individual good. Thus in 1765, John Brown, in a pamphlet frequently cited by his contemporaries, defined civil liberty as the salutary restraint of "every natural Desire which might in any Respect be inconsistent with the general Weal [which] is given up as a voluntary Tax, paid for the higher, more lasting, and more important *Benefits,* which we reap from *social life.*"[204] This understanding of civil liberty reflected most authors' sense that an authoritative public must be in a position to decide what limits were to be imposed on individual members, with little concern for the unusual wants of particular individuals and none for deviant or licentious ones.

Nathaniel Whitaker powerfully argued for the corporate and communal character of civil liberty, in a sermon entitled *An Antidote Against Toryism.* Given the title of his sermon, the author's zealous Whig sympathies, and his persecution of Tories after the war, he obviously was no political reactionary. Yet by later individualistic standards, his thinking is insensitive to the needs of the autonomous individual. He begins, as did many others, by discussing natural liberty and by referring to the thought of Locke. He argues, however, in a fashion not characteristic of Locke, but nevertheless common in American sermons and political pamphlets.[205] Natural liberty, he reports (in a fashion reminiscent of Peter Powers's previ-

---

[202]Priestley, "Essay" (1771), 22:11.

[203]*Civil Liberty Asserted* (1776), pp. 38–39.

[204]J. Brown, *Thoughts on Civil Liberty* (1765), p. 13.

[205]See Strauss, *Natural Right and History,* pp. 202–51, who questions Locke's motivation for not following the conventional early modern analysis of liberty, which begins with pre-fallen nature and then moves to humanity's subsequent alienation from God and righteousness.

ously discussed 1778 Vermont election sermon), is of little interest to fallen humanity "since the corruption of nature by sin, the lusts and passions of men so blind their minds, and harden their hearts, that this perfect law of love is little considered." He continues, noting in a style as much Hobbesian as Calvinist, that the fallen state of nature is truly "a state of war, rapine and murder."[206] For this respected American public figure, original sin was the implacable foe of human beings, and it alone prevented them from enjoying the absolute freedom of natural liberty consistent with the state of nature before the Fall. What stood between natural individual liberty and corporately determined communal civil liberty was original sin.

Whitaker then discussed the central determinant that shaped how civil liberty was to be interpreted. He described how the critical boundary between corporate needs and the individual's legitimate residual freedom was to be set. More to the point, in a fashion that most Americans approved of in both written statements and in lived testimony, he argued that it is the public rather than the individual that must determine how much personal liberty is to be surrendered by the sinful individual for the benefit of corporate needs. This is the smoking gun. He recounted that

> perfect civil Liberty differs from natural, only in this, that in a natural state our actions, persons and possessions, are under the direction, judgment and controul of none but ourselves; but in a civil state, under the directions of others. . . . In the first case, private judgment; in the second, the public judgment of the sense of the law of nature is to be the rule of conduct. When this is the case, civil Liberty is perfect, and every one enjoys all that freedom which God designed for his rational creatures in a social state. All Liberty beyond this is mere licentiousness, a liberty to sin, which is the worst of slavery.

He leaves no doubt that in society, it is the public's right to determine the inherently ambiguous outlines of civil liberty, not the right of individuals blessed by an assortment of inalienable natural rights yet to be discovered.

He sought, however, to protect himself against a charge of supporting tyranny (positive human statutes that are imposed and incompatible with divine or natural law). He remarked that "when any laws are enacted, which cross the law of nature, there civil Liberty is invaded, and God and man justly offended."[207] Note, however, that even in a situation marked by what he found to be tyrannical, this good American pastor held that it was the legitimately constituted public that must decide on the boundary between appropriate and inappropriate restraints on the individual. If the community's actions are judged by God to be unjust, individuals and God simply are left affronted. The latter, though, was understood to have powerful means of redressing his displeasure at such injustice. Civil liberty, in

[206]Whitaker, *Antidote Against Toryism* (1777), pp. 10–11.
[207]Ibid., pp. 11–12.

the mind of this respected minister and most other 18th-century Americans whose views can be known, was to be corporately, not individually, determined and sharply delimited. Thus, it was usually the immediate interests of the community, not those of the individual, that were to be served first.

When Whitaker turns to discuss the other important corporate liberty, that of the polity, he argues that the "rights" of the individual cannot be defended against the prerogatives of social needs. He insists that "no power on earth" was free to intervene against the corporate will other than the people themselves. He argues that "the freedom of a society or State consists in acting according to their own choice, within the bounds of the law of nature, in governing themselves, independent of all other States. This is the Liberty wherewith God hath made every State free, and which no power on earth may lawfully abridge, but by their own consent."[208] A properly constituted sovereign people, therefore, even when acting inconsistently with a divine or natural law higher than its own positive law, could not legitimately be brought to the bar of justice by any power on earth.

Aggrieved individuals had little recourse other than Locke's famous appeal to heaven. But as Joseph Clark explained a few years later, "EQUALITY and INDEPENDENCE are the just claim, the indefeasible birth-right of men: In a state of nature, as individuals; in society, as states or nations."[209] These were "natural rights" that individuals surrendered upon acceptance into a political body. Corporate liberty, political and civil, was the direct product of people coming to live together in society, the indirect product of the Fall, and the ground of secular liberty correctly understood. Americans distinguished sharply between the natural state of individual liberty, an absolute state of liberty that existed before the Fall, and the severe limitations that people must endure in their post-Fall deformity. Americans' almost universal acceptance of the general outlines of original sin shaped their understanding of civil liberty and its corporate rather than individualistic character.

By the late 1780s, civil liberty began to be described more regularly in what appears to be an individualistic fashion, but this cannot be argued with certainty. Few of the equivocal remarks on this subject penned or spoken by America's part-time essayists, planters, and statesmen are of sufficient length or depth to allow one to say with confidence that they have captured their meaning. This is a concern when working with the occasional pieces of political actors who, unlike pastors, rarely had the time or inclination to pursue normative questions in depth. Their posi-

---

[208]Ibid., p. 12. See also Haynes, "Influence of Civil Government on Religion" (1798), p. 75. Haynes also holds that it cannot be an "infringement of our liberties to [be] subject to the decision of the majority." He reminded his audience that "true freedom does not consist in every man's doing as he thinks fit, or following the dictates of unruly passions."

[209]J. Clark, *Massachusetts Election Sermon* (1781), p. 11.

tions, therefore, are usually less clearly developed (and often less rigorous and morally interesting) than the work of more scholarly ministers. In treating the essayists' brief remarks, one must be "cautious in applying modern labels" anachronistically. In particular, because of "the verbal baggage that they carry,"[210] one must hesitate before describing 18th-century language or norms as individualistic. (This is particularly apt because individualism was a concept and ideology that would not be born for another thirty years.)

With these caveats in mind, consider the statement attributed to Sam Adams that appeared in the *Boston Gazette* of 2 April 1781. Here he berated his fellow citizens for not having voted in their then recent state election (less than 25 percent voted!). He then reminded his readers, in language seemingly adaptable to 20th-century liberal patterns of thought, that "the Framers of our [Massachusetts] Constitution, while they gave due Attention to *Political* were not forgetful of *Civil* Liberty—that personal Freedom and those Rights of Property, which the meanest Citizen is intitled to, and the Security of which is the great End of political Society." One must exercise particular caution, though, in interpreting his putative remarks regarding these highly valued English prescriptive liberties, partly because in a letter written the next day, he boldly notes that "a Citizen owes everything to the Commonwealth. And after he has made his utmost Exertions for its Prosperity, has he done no more than his duty?"[211] The balance between private and corporate rights in his earlier defense of prescriptive liberties, therefore, was assuredly not so individualistic as it appears today.

Consider as well one of the "Letters of Agrippa" and its probable author, James Winthrop, whom economic historian John Crowley describes as "exceedingly idiosyncratic both intellectually and ideologically," in particular regarding his extraordinarily liberal economic views.[212] He held that when public power "is pushed beyond the degree necessary for rendering justice between man and man, it debases the character of individuals, and renders them less secure in their persons and property." He then suggests that civil liberty is truly an intrinsic good to be protected by an instrumentally valuable political liberty. He writes in a fashion reminiscent of T.Q. (and of Montesquieu) that "civil liberty consists in the consciousness of the

[210]Rotunda, *Politics of Language*, p. 9.

[211][S. Adams], "Unsigned Article in the *Boston Gazette*" (2 April 1781), and "Letter to Caleb Davis" (3 April 1781), in *Writings of Samuel Adams* 4:252, 255; see also J. Adams, "Letter to Dr. Rush" (1 August 1812), in Adams and Rush, *Spur of Fame*, p. 235, in which he describes his cousin's vision of liberty as that of being chained hand and foot; and Pencak, "Samuel Adams and Shays's Rebellion," pp. 69–70, who cites Adams in 1786 defending majoritarianism, be it "ever so much in the wrong," for to "say the majority shall not govern, is saying, either that we will reduce ourselves to a State of Nature, or reject the ideas of civil liberty."

[212]Crowley, "Commerce and the Philadelphia Constitution," p. 95.

security, and is best guarded by political liberty, which is the share that every citizen has in the government."[213] The existence of his (and G. Morris's, noted immediately above) almost unique set of concerns evidences that the anti-Federalists and the Federalists are not divisible in any simple fashion on this matter. What can be said with confidence, however, is that out of the debates over the Constitution a new understanding of civil liberty emerged that was committed to protecting the rights of the individual against many forms of local corporate intrusion.[214]

Many Americans, articulate and not, did not embrace this changing perception of the right balance between the individual good and the public good and, like Webster in the mid-19th century, continued to adhere to the corporate and communal understanding of civil liberty. Thus, the Congregational minister from Lebanon, Connecticut, Timothy Stone, continued to preach that

> civil liberty is one of the most important blessings which men possess of a temporal nature . . . [but to believe] That liberty consists in freedom from restraint, leaving each one to act as seemeth right to himself, is a most unwise mistaken apprehension. Civil liberty, consists in the being and administration of such a system of laws, as doth bind all classes of men, rulers and subjects, to unite their exertions for the promotion of virtue and public happiness.[215]

At this relatively late date (1792), then, it was the public crafting of souls rather than the protection of individual rights that Stone had set before the legislature as its most important goal. Moreover, Kammen and others show that this corporate understanding of liberty continued to dominate the intellectual landscape of 19th-century America as well.[216]

Nevertheless, Agrippa's language does indeed sound remarkably like that of Benjamin Constant, who, thirty years later in France, would frame this quintessentially individualist vision of civil liberty as he wrote that "individual liberty, I repeat, is the true modern liberty. Political liberty is its guarantee, consequently political liberty is indispensable. But to ask the peoples of our day to sacrifice, like those of the past, the whole of their individual liberty to political liberty, is the surest means of detaching them from [both]." Yet even Constant, the man Isaiah Berlin believes to be the likely father of modern liberal individualism,[217] besought his audience at the end of his celebrated speech in a language that was not only corporate but fully republican in spirit. He asked them to recall that "it is not to

---

[213][Winthrop?], "Letter VIII of Agrippa" (1787), p. 243. For a comparable Federalist position, see Morris, "Political Enquiries" (n.d.), p. 331.

[214]See Wood, "Freedom and the Constitution," p. 52.

[215]T. Stone, "Connecticut Election Sermon" (1792), p. 842.

[216]See Kammen, *Spheres of Liberty*, pp. 69, 102; Bender, *Community and Social Change in America*, p. 81; Cooke, *American Tradition of Liberty*, pp. 57, 157–58; Rodgers, *Contested Truths*, p. 117; and P. Miller, *Life of the Mind in America*, pp. 3–98.

[217]Berlin, "Two Concepts of Liberty," pp. 126, 161.

happiness alone, it is to self-development that our destiny calls us; and political liberty is the most powerful, the most effective means of self-development that heaven has given us."[218] Apparently, even this early 19th-century statesman and liberal theorist continued to be powerfully pulled by the seductive appeals of republican discourse and its defense of the centrality and necessity for human development of corporate self-direction and an active political life.

Shortly after Constant spoke, a fellow Frenchman visiting America observed that the local community continued to have the responsibility and the legitimate power to restrain its individual members within corporately defined moral boundaries. Alexis de Tocqueville wrote that Americans' "diverse municipal laws appeared to me so many means of restraining the restless ambition of the citizens within a narrow sphere and of turning those same passions which might have worked havoc in the state to the good of the township or parish."[219] And this was during the putative reign of extreme individualism in Jacksonian America. Thus, if Tocqueville is to be trusted here, the corporate and communal understanding of civil liberty shaped by the reformed-Protestant concept of original sin was not vanquished by the modern individualist understanding of civil liberty until a date well beyond the end of the 18th century.[220]

[218]Constant, "Liberty of the Ancients" (1819), pp. 323, 327.
[219]Tocqueville, *Democracy in America* (1835), 1:337.
[220]See Jaenicke, "American Ideas of Political Party," pp. 441–42.

The Concept of Slavery: Liberty's Antithesis

> "Slavery" was a central concept in eighteenth-century
> political discourse. As the absolute political evil, it appears
> in every statement of political principle, in every discussion
> of constitutionalism or legal rights, in every exhortation
> to resistance.
>
> —Bernard Bailyn, *The Ideological Origins of*
> *the American Revolution*

SLAVERY was another important concept in the American political lexicon, a concept that had a broad range of meaning well beyond that of chattel enslavement. It is of special interest here because, when used in political pamphlets and sermons, slavery was posited as liberty's antithesis,[1] and thus a formative influence in shaping the meaning of liberty.[2] Indeed, John Phillip Reid finds that "the contrast that eighteenth-century legal and political theorists drew between liberty and slavery is today truly startling. Recall that everything good in the world, even religion, was credited to liberty. By the same reasoning, everything bad was due to slavery."[3] A correct understanding of slavery, then, helps complete the understanding of liberty and is a critical component in a still incomplete reconstruction of late 18th-century American political thought.

Most notably, Revolutionary-era Americans, in spite of their frequently voiced fears of enslavement, did not actually believe that their impasse with Britain would lead to their being sold into domestic slavery, if only because of the absence of a legal market in Caucasians in Western Europe. Therefore, American references to their enslavement could not have been made with chattel slavery in mind. Neither were these references pompous rhetoric because for Americans, slavery "was not hyperbole

---

[1] See Crowley, *This Sheba, Self,* p. 130; and Finley, "Between Slavery and Freedom," pp. 236–37.

[2] See Davis, *Slavery and Human Progress,* p. 20; and Patterson, *Slavery and Social Death,* pp. 341–42.

[3] Reid, *Concept of Liberty,* p. 52.

to be snickered at, but a term that was charged with normative meaning."[4]

As Jonathan Mayhew, the celebrated and controversial pastor of Boston's liberal West Church, explained, the Parliament's program of taxation threatened Americans "with perpetual bondage and slavery," for those from whom the fruit of their "labor and industry may be lawfully taken" without their consent, are "to all intents and purposes . . . really slaves."[5] What concerned Americans in their imperial relations was the possibility of British-sponsored enslavement with slavery understood as the absence of political liberty for a corporate body and loss of economic independence for the individual. But underlying these more political senses of slavery was another, more fundamental one, the inability or unwillingness to be self-governing, or more specifically, the inability to control bodily lusts and passions, above all selfishness.[6]

When properly conceived, then, cries of impending slavery are not to be seen as "bombastic and overwrought" or having "little or no objective reality" as "the dean of Progressive historians," Arthur Schlesinger, Sr., wrote.[7] Rather, the concept of slavery must be understood as having played a critical role in 18th-century political and social thought, not only in America, but in Britain as well. And there is no evidence that residents there were apprehensive of being enslaved.[8] Consider the all-encompassing remarks of an anonymous Irish author who covered the gamut of private, public, and spiritual meanings then assigned to the concept of slavery without specifically referring to the chattel enslavement of Africans or evidencing that he was using the word in a hyperbolic fashion. He wrote:

> The first and gentlest Degree of natural Slavery is the *Subjection* of a Man, against his *Will*, to the Appointments of a *reasonable* and *conscientious* Master. The first and gentlest Degree of political Slavery is the *Subjection* of a People, without *Consent*, to *wise Laws* and a *just Magistracy*. The second Degree of natural Slavery is the *Subjection* of a Man, against his *Will*, to the *unreasonable* Appointments of a *wicked* Master . . . [or of a People] to the *arbitrary Laws* of an *iniquitous Magistracy*. But, the last and deepest Degree of Slavery in any Man or any People is where, *Reason* being depraved and *Conscience* debauched, the *Will* itself concurs with the Suggestions of Guilt and the Measures of the Unrighteousness . . . in the last Case, no Remedy can be applied, no Recovery expected [when] . . . *Reason, Will,* and *Conscience* become the Servants of Sin, the Universe can afford no further Recourse, no Principles or Ingredients whereof *Liberty* may be compounded. A sound Body

---

[4] Ibid., pp. 42, 119–20.
[5] Mayhew, "Snare Broken" (1766), p. 245.
[6] See Davis, *Problem of Slavery in Western Culture*, pp. 292–95.
[7] Wood, "Rhetoric and Reality," pp. 48–49.
[8] See Reid, *Concept of Liberty*, p. 42; and Davis, *Problem of Slavery in Western Culture*, p. 438.

can never consist of rotten Members. A free People can never consist of private Slaves.[9]

For him, as for most of his Anglo-American audience, that which most distinguished among varying degrees of slavery was not whether one was actually bought and sold (or so he claimed), but whether one voluntarily sought to live righteously in accord with the divine and rational ordering of the universe.

With the imperial crisis in mind, another anonymous British author gives further evidence that it was common to use *slavery* to describe various political and economic conditions unassociated with chattel slavery. He critically notes that "if Great Britain doth make war against the Americans because they will not resign their Liberty, then Great Britain doth make war against Americans because they will not consent to become her slaves."[10] Nearly a century earlier, Algernon Sidney had noted in a most traditional fashion that "liberty consists only in being subject to no man's will, and nothing denotes a slave but a dependence upon the will of another [individual]."[11] The American patriot and lawyer John Dickinson, attempting to detail how Americans were being enslaved, refers his readers to Mr. Pitt's speech in the House of Commons. Dickinson reports that Pitt had argued that without the right of "GIVING AND GRANTING THEIR OWN MONEY," Americans "would have been slaves."[12] Thus, readers in both Britain and America were accustomed to seeing in print the concept of slavery describing political, economic, and moral conditions unassociated with chattel slavery. Surely, then, it was not chattel slavery that Americans and the British had in mind when they described Americans' potential enslavement by Britain.[13]

Unfortunately, in regard to chattel enslavement itself, "John Jay recalled, 'the great majority' of Northerners accepted slavery as a matter of course, and 'very few among them doubted the propriety and rectitude of it.'"[14] This is reflected in their writings, for American authors, especially before the Revolution, were generally unconcerned about the plight of African slaves in their midst.[15] Even after the commencement of the war, their primary focus continued to be their economic and political relationship

[9][Brooke?], *Liberty and Common-Sense* (1760), letter 2, p. 11.

[10]*Prospect of the Consequences* (1776), pp. 94–95.

[11]A. Sidney, *Discourses Concerning Government* (1698), pp. 402–3. See also Houston, *Algernon Sidney,* pp. 114–22.

[12][J. Dickinson], "Letter VII" (1768), in "Letters of a Farmer in Pennsylvania," pp. 356–57.

[13]See Maier, *Old Revolutionaries,* p. 188, who writes that slavery "in Whig political thought . . . was a technical" term.

[14]Cited by Freehling, "Founding Fathers and Slavery," p. 86.

[15]See Tise, *Proslavery,* pp. 15–16; and Jordan, *White over Black,* p. 195, for their enumeration of the probably dozen or so pre-Revolutionary pamphlets published on each side of the debate over African slavery.

with Britain and their spiritual well-being.[16] What the war produced, how-ever, was a far greater consciousness of the possible inconsistency of their arguing for corporate liberty and equality while simultaneously enslaving members of other potentially sovereign peoples.[17] But only by first recog-nizing that slavery was a concept with political, economic, and moral meanings independent of its application to chattel slavery can one place in perspective the opening round of a debate that eventually would tear the not-yet-born country apart. In addition, by so doing, one gains a better purchase on the then-dominant strains of political thought.

Conversely, by collapsing the 18th-century concept of slavery and the chattel enslavement of sub-Saharan Africans, one unnecessarily imposes modern values on that century's still rather distant political and moral precepts. One thereby needlessly deforms and burdens the logic of the so-cial and political thought of the time.[18] Doing this decontextualizes the early debates concerning the propriety of chattel slavery and in the process loses much of the concept's rich and possibly alien texture. Most critically, it fails to recognize that before and during the Revolutionary period, slav-ery was an important concept with political, economic, and religious sig-nificance, and that it is within this context that chattel bondage must be seen as having exemplified the absolute embodiment of these various senses of slavery.[19] Also, one might fail to realize the degree to which their understanding of slavery further evidences Americans' belief that liberty's boundaries were shaped by a divine and rational order, or the extent to which their understanding of the broader concept of slavery emphasized

[16]See W. P. Adams, *First American Constitutions*, p. 182, who reports that only Delaware in 1776 prohibited the importation of slaves in its constitution, and that when Virginia fol-lowed suit in 1778 its intention was "to have better control over the slave market." See also MacLeod, *Slavery, Race, and the American Revolution*, p. 32, who contends (following Du-Bois) that the most powerful forces pushing for Northern abolition and American cessation of the slave trade were, in fact, also economic. He writes that "the motivation which resulted in the resolution of the Continental Congress in 1774 putting a stop to the trade was essen-tially political and economic"; and Finkelman, "Slavery and the Constitutional Convention," pp. 222–24, who also contends that even as late as the Constitutional Convention, "few delegates had expressed moral qualms over slavery. . . . most of the criticism had been politi-cal and economic."

[17]See MacLeod, *Slavery, Race, and the American Revolution*, p. 65; and Towner, "Sew-all-Saffin Dialogue on Slavery," p. 52. Cf. Jordan, *White over Black*, pp. 269–314, who claims that the Revolution produced a broad public opposition to domestic slavery; and Bailyn, *Ideological Origins of the American Revolution*, p. 239, who also argues that "by 1774 this cry [against slavery] had become commonplace in the [secular] pamphlet literature of the northern and middle colonies." A few years later, in "Central Themes of the American Revolution," p. 28, Bailyn went further and advanced the highly questionable claim that to believe that the principles defended in the Declaration of Independence were meant "to apply only to whites" is "to fundamentally misread the history of the time." My sense instead is that secular opposition to slavery was still far from broadly based, as is reflected in the fact that not one of the state constitutions ratified between 1776 and 1783 prohibited slavery.

[18]See Reid, *Concept of Liberty*, p. 42; and Patterson, *Slavery and Social Death*, p. ix.

[19]See MacLeod, *Slavery, Race, and the American Revolution*, pp. 16–17.

their belief that humans can truly only flourish within the confining and restrictive walls of a community that prevents the little-trusted individual from enjoying autonomous freedom.

Nevertheless, there were important American authors during the Revolutionary period, particularly highly motivated Quakers, and later, Baptist, Congregational, and Methodist ministers and assorted millennialists,[20] who were deeply concerned about the continuing evil of enslaving human beings. Consider, for example, the precocious remarks of the citizens of Hardwick, Massachusetts. After objecting to the proposed state constitution for its insufficiently restrictive clause concerning the religious affiliation of the governor (they wanted it to read "Christian Protestant" rather than just "Christian"), they turned their attention to slavery. Here, these religiously intolerant citizens demanded that the line in the state constitution that read "all men are born free and equal" be changed to read "all men, whites and blacks, are born free and equal." Their fear was that the passage might otherwise "be misconstrued hereafter, in such a manner as to exclude blacks."[21]

Even more insistent, and doubtlessly more influential, were the remarks of the leading New Divinity pastor, Samuel Hopkins, and those of Princeton's vice president, Jacob Green.[22] Hopkins repeatedly drew attention to

[20]See Davis, *Problem of Slavery in Western Culture*, pp. 291–332 and 488–89; Jordan, *White over Black*, pp. 271–75; Robinson, *Slavery*, pp. 54–97; Bloch, *Visionary Republic*, pp. 100–109; and Hatch, *Democratization of American Christianity*. The most important Quaker authors writing in prerevolutionary and Revolutionary America were Benzet, *Observations* (1759) and *Some Historical Accounts of Guinea* (1771); [D. Cooper], *Mite Cast into the Treasury* (1772) and *Serious Address* (1783); and Woolman, *Some Considerations* (1754). For a "respectable" dissenting voice, see Stillman, *Massachusetts Election Sermon* (1779), p. 34, who writes that "in order to compleat a system of government, and to be consistent with ourselves, it appears to me that we ought to banish from among us that cruel practice, which has long prevailed, of reducing to a state of slavery for life, the free-born Africans." Samuel Stillman was the minister of the First Baptist Church in Boston and the first Baptist minister to deliver a Massachusetts election sermon. In addition, see the sermons of the Baptist activist John Allen, for example, *Watchman's Alarm to Lord N——h* (1774), pp. 24–28. For early orthodox Presbyterian voices, see Cooke, "A Sermon" (1770 Massachusetts election sermon), in *Pulpit of the American Revolution;* and [Rush], "Address to the Inhabitants" (1773), pp. 217–30. His essay, however, was immediately met by Richard Nisbet's *Slavery Not Forbidden by Scripture* (1773), arguing in slavery's defense. The earliest 18th-century Congregational voice raised in opposition to slavery was that of Judge Samuel Sewall in 1700, *The Selling of Joseph: A Memorial*, which was met in 1703 by Samuel Willard's defense of slavery as part of God's order. Among the more secular Revolutionary voices raised in condemnation, see Otis, "Rights of the British Colonies" (1764), in *Pamphlets of the American Revolution*, p. 439, and [Lee], *Essay in Vindication* (1764), pp. 42–43.

[21]Handlin and Handlin, "The 1780 Return of Hardwick," in *Popular Sources of Political Authority*, p. 830.

[22]For a full listing of other Congregational opponents of slavery, including Jonathan Edwards, Jr., Jeremy Belknap, David Avery, Nathaniel Emmons, Andrew Eliot, and Ezra Stiles, see Baldwin, *New England Clergy*, p. 128.

the inconsistency of America's claiming for itself the right of corporate liberty while enslaving other peoples, both in Africa and in America. He compared the American concerns regarding possible British enslavement to the real condition of African slaves in America, noting the wide, almost ridiculous, discrepancy between their two conditions. The Africans, he wrote, "see the slavery the *Americans* dread as worse than death is lighter than a feather, compared to their heavy doom."[23] But even though he drew attention to what must have been obvious to all, his voice was a relatively uncommon one.

In a powerful sermon, the influential Jacob Green attacked slavery along similar lines. He declared that "supporting and encouraging slavery, is one of the greatest and crying evils among us." He then asked "if liberty is one of the natural and unalienable rights of all men." Answering that it is, he charged that it is therefore unjust and inhuman for "Americans, not only to attempt, but actually to violate this right."[24] Americans, in their plea for external help and outside recognition, had argued before the world in their Declaration of Independence that one people cannot legitimately deprive another people of its rights and liberties. Yet even these morally awakened authors and religiously motivated citizens who vehemently opposed the continuation of this egregious stain on America accepted the claims of the Patriots regarding their potential British and actual moral enslavement as meaningful assessments of their condition. Thus, they often addressed the horrendous problem of African chattel slavery as but a special case of a more general economic, political, or moral problem.[25]

However, Americans inhabited a world in which that form of enslavement which is most hideous to us, chattel slavery, was being imposed on increasing numbers of sub-Saharan Africans. It is clear, then, that the 18th-century abstract understanding of slavery can never be fully separated from chattel slavery. Quite to the contrary: Africans were usually portrayed as natural slaves, an idea to which their putative acceptance of their bondage bore witness, and thus their enslavement was recognized as an absolute embodiment of public and private dependence, dishonor, and sinfulness.[26] (By following this logic, the inconsistency of the American position can be reduced.)[27]

---

[23][Samuel Hopkins], *Dialogue Concerning the Slavery of Africans* (1776), pp. 30, 50.

[24]Green, *Sermon Delivered at Hanover* (1778), pp. 12–13.

[25]See for example, L. Hart, "Liberty Described and Recommended" (1775), p. 312; Duché, "Duty of Standing Fast" (1775), p. 84; and J. Parsons, *Freedom from Civil and Ecclesiastical Slavery* (1774), p. 12.

[26]See Patterson, *Slavery and Social Death*, p. 78.

[27]See J. P. Greene, *All Men Are Created Equal*, pp. 30–31, who writes that "far, therefore, from being 'perfectly clear that the principles for which Americans fought required the complete abolition of slavery,'" it can be argued that their "principles actually served to sustain an institution that merely functioned to preserve in an unfree status peoples who lacked the independence and virtue requisite for freedom."

But 18th-century Americans' fuller conception of slavery was not engulfed by the all-too-real horrors of chattel slavery. Thus, the fundamental understanding of slavery is of interest here, because of the light it casts on Americans' understanding of liberty, and more broadly, their conception of the good. It is an understanding that speaks powerfully of their belief that a fully human life is only possible when an individual has the capacity and ability to order his or her being in accord with the unbending and eternally valid laws of God and nature.

Moreover, by focusing on this larger understanding of slavery, one can better comprehend why a sufficient number of Americans believed or could be convinced that a separation from Britain was necessary. Fearing that they would become corporately and personally dependent, slaves in the greater sense of the word, they demonstrated their commitment to living full human lives of political and economic self-governance and virtue, not simply of material comfort and safety. Unfortunately, their sensitivity usually did not extend to the African slaves in their midst, who long continued to be cruelly exploited.[28] Indeed, their racial animus applied in varying degrees to all people who were not of Anglo-Saxon descent. Even the most enlightened and cosmopolitan American, Ben Franklin, was opposed to the continued importation of Africans as well as the immigration of Europeans who were of "a swarthy Complexion" because of their race or color. Why, he asked, should we "increase the Sons of Africa, by Planting them in America, where we have so fair an Opportunity, by excluding all Blacks and Tawneys, of increasing the lovely White and Red" (with "White and Red" referring to the rosy cheeks of the English, not native Americans, who were "Tawneys").[29]

Nonetheless, the various political, social, and intellectual changes that the Revolution unleashed led to a rejection by some Americans of the propriety of chattel slavery and even occasionally to a lessening of racism.[30] Such a development, however, would not have emerged after the Revolutionary period with the force that it did if "it had not been preceded by a revolutionary shift in attitudes toward sin, human nature, and progress," away from the very social and political thought that had dominated the late 18th century and had led to the Revolution itself.[31] To a certain extent,

---

[28]Not even James Madison, America's great defender of individual rights, was particularly concerned about the plight of sub-Saharan Africans in America. See Shalhope, *John Taylor of Caroline,* p. 198, who reports that Madison staunchly opposed those who tried to interpret the Constitution as prohibiting either the movement of slaves in the country or their entry into the territories.

[29]Franklin, "Observations Concerning the Increase of Mankind" (1755), in *Political Thought of Benjamin Franklin,* p. 71.

[30]For example, see Rush, "Letter to Dr. Price" (15 October 1785), p. 126, who notes that "the slaves who have been emancipated among us [in Pennsylvania] are in general more industrious and orderly than the lowest class of white people."

[31]Davis, *Problem of Slavery in Western Culture,* p. 363.

then, the changes in attitudes toward chattel slavery wrought by the Revolution, like so much else that it altered, were unintended and even sometimes perverse consequences of the modernization that followed in its wake. Perverse, that is, because the new more secular ways of viewing humanity and its universe facilitated more enlightened (rather than biblically derived) theories of slavery and theories of racial inferiority.[32] Such views would be long appealed to even by men of goodwill like Thomas Jefferson.

SLAVERY: THE ABSENCE OF POLITICAL AND PERSONAL INDEPENDENCE

During the period surrounding the Revolution, Americans were particularly sensitive to any loss of corporate political power, a loss that they described as a form of enslavement. But this understanding of slavery was not one that they had to invent; rather, it was one they had inherited. Their interpretation was consistent with the use of the term in classical political thought, where what made one free rather than a slave was being "entitled to take part in the political life of his city and to affect the workings of its legislative institutions." In this hallowed Western intellectual lineage, liberty, unlike slavery, "is none other than obedience to laws which one prescribes to himself."[33] And it was within this tradition, which held that "WHERE ANNUAL ELECTIONS END, SLAVERY BEGINS," that Americans continued to think and write about liberty and slavery.[34]

When Americans rebelled against their putative enslavement by the British, it was not, therefore, public intrusiveness that they were concerned with preventing. Rather, it was the possibility that citizens might have no future say in shaping that intrusiveness—in other words, they feared the absence of political liberty. Exemplifying American worries about a potential loss of self-governing powers, Governor Stephen Hopkins in 1765 followed the republican martyr Algernon Sidney and held that "those who are governed at the will of another, or of others, and whose property may be taken . . . without their consent, and against their will, are in the miserable condition of slaves."[35]

Almost ten years later, Alexander Hamilton, in one of his early pamphlets, stated that the only "distinction between freedom and slavery" was that in "the former state, a man is governed by the laws to which he has

[32]See ibid., p. 446; Jordan, *White over Black*, pp. 454–57, 481; Schmidt and Wilhelm, "Early Proslavery Petitions in Virginia," p. 136; MacLeod, *Slavery, Race, and the American Revolution*, pp. 8, 12; and Frey, "Liberty, Equality, and Slavery," p. 238.

[33]Gray, "On Negative and Positive Liberty," p. 327.

[34]Demophilus [Bryan?], "Genuine Principles of the Ancient Saxon" (1776), p. 354; see also McWilliams, "Democracy and the Citizen," p. 82.

[35]Stephen Hopkins, "Rights of Colonies Examined" (1764), in *Tracts of the American Revolution*, p. 43.

given consent. . . . In the latter, he is governed by the will of another."[36] As Tom Paine, who was more radical, argued in 1791, "there is *one* general principle that distinguishes freedom from slavery, which is, that *all hereditary Government over a people is to them a species of slavery, and representative Government is freedom.*"[37] For Paine, as for Hamilton, the critical difference between monarchy and representative government, between liberty and slavery, was whether the collective citizenry could shape the laws that would govern it.

Invariably, then, in sermons and pamphlets where (political) slavery was described, it was referred to as a state where an individual was politically impotent and lived "at the mere mercy and caprice of another."[38] For Americans, it made "no alteration in the nature of the case; for one who is bound to obey the will of another, is as really a slave, though he may have a good master, as if he had a bad one."[39] Precocious individualists such as Thomas Hobbes in the 17th century and J. L. de Lolme in the 18th found such thinking perverse.[40] But most of the British authors avidly read in America held that "liberty of any sort in civil society is impossible unless all the people share in the making of the laws and give their consent freely." Otherwise, they are "the subjects of absolute government [and] are 'slaves.'"[41]

Even David Hume (who was neither a rationalist, a Christian, nor a republican) had argued that a people at the mercy of a sole individual were truly "slaves in the full and proper sense of the word; and it is impossible they can ever aspire to any refinements of taste or reason."[42] As Dr. Price observed, "in every free state every man is his own Legislator," yet "if the laws are made by one man, or a junto of men in a state, and not by COMMON CONSENT, a government by them does not differ from Slavery."[43] But even as self-government was thought crucial if slavery were to be avoided, most American essayists and ministers showed a marked lack of interest in the unavoidable tension between corporate and individual liberty.[44]

It is common to find such late 18th-century statements attesting to the

---

[36]Hamilton, "Full Vindication" (15 December 1774), 1:47; see also McDonald, *Novus Ordo Seclorum*, p. 160.

[37]Paine, "Rights of Man, Part Second" (1792), p. 390.

[38]Alison, *Spiritual Liberty* (1769), p. 4.

[39]Stephen Hopkins, "Rights of Colonies Examined" (1764), in *Tracts of the American Revolution*, p. 54. One can readily see that such a perspective is ill suited for an industrial society.

[40]See Hobbes, *Leviathan* (1651), p. 264; and Lolme, *Constitution of England* (1775), pp. 225–27.

[41]Forbes, *Hume's Philosophical Politics*, p. 142.

[42]Hume, "On the Rise and Progress of the Arts and Sciences," in *Essays*, p. 117.

[43]Price, *Observations* (1776), pp. 4–7; see also *Prospect of the Consequences* (1776), pp. 92–93.

[44]See McDonald, *Novus Ordo Seclorum*, pp. 159–60.

importance of political self-government and the difference between liberty and slavery. It is rare, however, to find ones that explain the theoretical grounds on which such observations rested. But an anonymous author on 14 November 1774 did this in his "Political Observations, Without Order; Addressed to the People of America." He wrote that "a freeman in honouring and obeying the Congress, honours and obeys *himself*. The man who refuses to do both, is a slave. He knows nothing of the dignity of his nature. He cannot govern himself. Expose him for sale at publick vendue. Send him to plant Sugar with his fellow slaves in *Jamaica*."[45] Those who were "inwardly the Servants of *Sin*, must be outwardly the Servants of *Influence*," and were incapable of enjoying political liberty and unworthy of it.[46] It was only when there was a conjunction of individual self-government (broadly understood) and hard-won political liberty that a person was considered a fit repository of human dignity and freedom rather than debasement and slavery.

Americans continued throughout the Revolutionary era to describe slavery as the absence of political self-government. Zabdiel Adams, a Congregational minister, argued this position with great flair, holding that "to be deprived of the power of chusing our rulers, is to be deprived of self determination. If *they* are appointed over us, by those over whom we have no controul, we are in a state of slavery. There is no difference, in this respect, between such a people, and the horses they ride on; neither are governed by their own will, in which the essence of all freedoms consists."[47] Yet slavery was not simply the loss of political liberty; it was also the loss of the ability or opportunity to govern oneself on a private or familial economic and spiritual level.

What might be categorized as a form of personal slavery described an adult male head of house's economic dependence on another individual, which, according to Jefferson, fosters "subservience and venality, suffocates the germ of virtue, and prepares fit tools for the design of ambition."[48] Nor is this association between economic dependence and slavery surprising when it is remembered that "the concept of labor as a salable commodity, apart from the person of the seller, is relatively recent in the history of civilization."[49] Thus, in preindustrial America, economic dependence and the necessity of obeying the arbitrary demands of another were believed to be similar in significant ways to actual chattel enslavement. Among slavery's now lost meanings, these especially stand out, for they meant that one was "obliged to act, or not to act, according to the arbi-

[45]"Political Observations," pp. 135–36.

[46][Brooke?], *Liberty and Common-Sense* (1760), letter 2, p. 11.

[47]Z. Adams, "Massachusetts Election Sermon" (1782), p. 544.

[48]Jefferson, *Notes on the State of Virginia* (1787), p. 157; see also Scott, *In Pursuit of Happiness*, p. 36.

[49]Finley, "Slavery," p. 308; see also Patterson, *Slavery and Social Death*, p. 34.

trary will and Pleasure of another."[50] Twenty years later, Jonathan Mayhew's description of slavery emphasized the same repugnance of dependence and of being forced to follow the arbitrary wishes of another. He too found that "the essence of slavery consists in being subjected to the arbitrary pleasure of others."[51] Thus, what was described as most objectionable about economic dependence was the loss of sovereignty to another individual who would force one to act in arbitrary, rather than rationally defensible, ways.

Almost certainly exacerbating European Americans' sensitivity regarding threats to their independence was the actual presence in America of chattel slavery.[52] Indeed, one of the best of the early historians of the Revolution, Dr. David Ramsay, argued that fear of personal slavery or dependence had powerfully motivated Americans to separate from Britain. Moreover, he held that planters in the Southern colonies, where men were most likely to be masters of chattel slaves, were the most sensitive to a loss of their own familial independence to another.[53] Ramsay, a transplanted Pennsylvanian, found in the proud white Southerners that "the haughtiness of domination, combines with the spirit of liberty. Nothing could more effectually animate the opposition of a planter to the claims of Great Britain, than a conviction that those claims in their extent, degraded him to a degree of dependence on his fellow subjects, equally humiliating with that which existed between his slaves and himself."[54] He thus found that Americans' particular love of liberty and hatred of personal dependence and slavery were not only truly compatible, as the ancients had held, but that those who actually owned slaves had proved in Revolutionary America to be the most concerned about a threatened loss to public as well as personal liberty.[55]

A trenchant critic of Americans' claims to their "right" of self-government, David Hume, found that those most protective of their political liberty were most willing "really" to enslave others. He insisted, for example, that "some passionate admirers of the ancients, and zealous partisans of civil liberty . . . brand all submission to the government of a single person with the harsh denomination of slavery, [and yet] they would gladly re-

[50]"Virtue" (16 November 1747).

[51]Mayhew, "Memorandum" (1765), p. 142.

[52]See Breen, *Tobacco Culture,* p. 132, who describes how Arthur Lee took the unusual position of opposing black slavery because of the indebtedness created by the purchase of slaves from British factors. For Lee, familial independence demanded not additional slaves, but an end to their continued importation.

[53]For additional authors holding this position, see MacLeod, *Slavery, Race, and the American Revolution,* p. 94.

[54]D. Ramsay, "Selections" (1789), p. 723.

[55]See J. P. Greene, *All Men Are Created Equal,* p. 32, who writes that "the philosophy of civil rights championed by the American Revolutionaries was thus not, as so many have charged, betrayed but fulfilled by their failures to abolish slavery and adopt a more inclusive definition of citizenship."

duce the greater part of mankind to real slavery and subjection."[56] An observer friendly to America, Edmund Burke, effectively agreed with both Ramsay and Hume; he found that it was the free residents of Virginia and South Carolina, with "their vast multitude of slaves," who were "by far the most proud and jealous of their freedom."[57] Edmund Morgan has recently redrawn attention to this possibility and has written that "Virginians may have had a special appreciation of the freedom dear to republicans, because they saw every day what life without it could be like."[58]

Whatever the psychological or sociological merits of this thesis might be, Morgan's voguish emphasis on republicanism is misplaced. Oddly enough, especially given their exposure to classical histories and philosophies, 18th-century Americans never developed a republican defense of slavery in which "the free man was understood in the context of slavery and one of the characteristics of the free man was to have slaves in his control."[59] There were authors, even in the 18th century, who approached such a position. For example, Rousseau argued in the *Social Contract* that "there are some unhappy circumstances in which we can only keep our liberty at others' expense, and where the citizen can be perfectly free only when the slave is most a slave. Such was the case with Sparta."[60] Whether it was the compassionate concerns of Christianity or the humanizing effects of rationalism that prevented them from doing so, Southern apologists would begin only in the early 19th century to embrace a republican defense of slavery. Only then was chattel slavery finally seen in a fully republican light, wherein it was understood to be a potentially necessary institution that would allow slaveholding Americans to "cultivate some of the higher and more ennobling traits of humanity."[61]

Ramsay's (and by extension, Morgan's) widely accepted understanding of the positive relationship between the ownership of chattel slaves and one's attachment to liberty, however, was contested by Ramsay's contemporaries. Arguing to the contrary, for example, was Massachusetts's most influential Revolutionary, James Otis, who found that this "most shocking violation of the law of nature [chattel enslavement of Africans], has a di-

[56]Hume, "Of the Populousness of Ancient Nations," in *Essays*, p. 383.

[57]Burke, "[First] Speech on American Conciliation" (22 March 1775), in *On the American Revolution*, p. 85.

[58]E. S. Morgan, *American Slavery, American Freedom*, pp. 376, 380–82; see also Morgan, "Slavery and Freedom," pp. 5–10; and Patterson, *Slavery and Social Death*, p. 94.

[59]Mulgan, "Liberty in Ancient Greece," p. 10; see also Finley, "Between Slavery and Freedom," pp. 245–46, and "Slavery," pp. 307–8; and Patterson, *Slavery and Social Death*, pp. 341–42.

[60]Rousseau, *Social Contract* (1762), p. 96.

[61]Shalhope, "Race, Class, Slavery," pp. 564–66; see also Shalhope, *John Taylor of Caroline*, pp. 143–44, 150, in which he writes that "Taylor's perception of the good society [in 1813] rested upon an amalgam of slavery, republicanism, and racism"; A. Tate, "Remarks on the Southern Religion," pp. 155–75; Tise, *Proslavery*, pp. 97–123; and cf. Frey, "Liberty, Equality, and Slavery," pp. 232, 243.

rect tendency to diminish the idea of the inestimable value of liberty. . . . It is a clear truth that those who every day barter away other men's liberty will soon care little for their own."[62] As the English-educated Arthur Lee noted, slavery depraves "the minds of freemen; steeling their hearts against the laudable feelings of virtue and humanity."[63] Contemporary critics of American enslavement of Africans thus could not agree whether proximity to it made Americans more or less sensitive to a potential loss of political liberty and independence. Nevertheless, there was a consensus among these same Americans regarding the dangers of slavery, with slavery understood as a loss of personal economic independence or public "enslavement" to a tyrannical government.

SLAVERY TO THE PASSIONS

For 18th-century Americans, economic dependence was also feared because the capacity to give oneself freely to Christ and to set Christian or rational goals defined for many a critical component of full humanity. It was not solely a question of material well-being, therefore, that made Revolutionary-era Americans so opposed to dependence. For many, if not most, Americans, their abhorrence stemmed from the spiritual consequences they associated with the loss of independence. If one were to be fully human and a reformed Protestant, one could never allow oneself to become politically, economically, or religiously dependent on another sinful and corrupt individual. The importance of one's salvation would not allow it.

Slavery was a condition that described enslaved Africans and, to varying degrees, politically voiceless and economically dependent male heads of households. But more fundamentally, it was an embodiment of the dominion of passions and lusts over the divinely rational will of man.[64] Historically, "the notion of slavery to the passions is—for those who think in these terms—more than a metaphor." For such men to be released from bondage to the passions and irrational volitions was an "experience as real as that of liberation from a human tyrant or slave owner."[65] In 18th-century America, the understanding of an individual as torn between two different aspects of himself or herself, each "natural" in its own 18th-century way (the way of the physical "beast" or teleologically in the way of spirit

---

[62]Otis, "Rights of the British Colonies" (1764), in *Pamphlets of the American Revolution,* p. 439.

[63][Lee], *Essay in Vindication* (1764), pp. 42–43; see also Jefferson, *Notes on the State of Virginia* (1787), pp. 155–56. Lee, as noted above, also opposed slavery because of the economic debt that accompanied it.

[64]See J. P. Greene, *All Men Are Created Equal,* pp. 23–25, and *Landon Carter,* p. 25.

[65]Berlin, "Two Concepts of Liberty," p. 138.

or of Christ), was held almost universally. Congruent with it, slavery was understood to be a pathology or deformation of the human soul in which the animal part of humanity completely dominated the higher or more divine aspects.

Indeed, Reid finds that in both England and America, "fear of arbitrariness, licentiousness, and slavery dominated eighteenth-century thoughts about human freedom."[66] Each of these terms, regularly placed in opposition to liberty, lacked an essential element that defined it as antithetical to liberty. That is, they described an inability or unwillingness to order one's being freely with the laws of God and nature. It was commonly held that "he that will sacrifice his Liberty to his Palate . . . is a slave of his own making, and deserves to be used accordingly."[67] Humanity's reasonable character made liberty possible, and its enslavement to the unruly and passionate side of human beings negated that potential.[68] William Emerson continued to remind his audience in 1802 that their heroic Revolutionary forebears felt that "slavery in any of its forms is an execrable monster," and that they "neither sought nor wished the freedom of an irrational, but that of a rational being, not the freedom of savages."[69] The question of rational control over the passions (which was, for most Christians, dependent on prior intercession of the Holy Spirit),[70] in fact provided a theoretical center that unified American thoughts about chattel, political, and economic slavery.

As understood by an anonymous author in 1773, reason reflected "the harmony and order of our faculties . . . [that] represents things to us, not only as they are at present, but as they are in their whole nature and tendency."[71] Conversely, passion was considered "so dangerous because it divested man of both his freedom and morality. It disordered his mind," and thus all "behavior guided by passion upset the order of the universe."[72] The politically active liberal minister of Billerica, Massachusetts, Henry Cumings, delivered a thanksgiving sermon and besought God that they might be able "to subdue each irregular appetite and passion, to disengage ourselves from the enslaving power of vicious habit, and to acquire the *glorious* internal *liberty of the son of God,* which will make us *free indeed.*"[73] A life of liberty rather than of slavery most importantly demanded that

[66]Reid, *Concept of Liberty,* pp. 109–10.

[67]*New-York Weekly Journal,* 7 July 1740, in W. Nelson, *Colonial History of New Jersey* (1895), 12:36–37.

[68]See Patterson, *Freedom,* p. 195.

[69]W. Emerson, "Fourth of July Oration, 1802," 6:186.

[70]See, for example, Stiles, *Discourse on the Christian Union* (1761), p. 18.

[71]"Of True Happiness" (25 January 1773).

[72]Potter, *Liberty We Seek,* pp. 44–45. For a dissenting perspective, see Howe, "Political Psychology of *The Federalist,*" pp. 490–91.

[73]Cumings, *Thanksgiving Sermon Preached in Billerica* (1784), pp. 35–36.

one's passions be strictly controlled and that one voluntarily commit one-self to the universal higher law of God and nature.[74]

After all, for people of the 18th century, slavery did "not consist in being restrained from doing wrong, but in being obliged against our will to endure it."[75] Even the great Quaker critic of African slavery Anthony Benzet, in annotating Thomas Thompson's 1772 defense of it, had written that "*absolute freedom can only* consist in *restraining Evil Doers* . . . for all men ought to be *absolutely free to do good* according to their abilities; & if they are *not free to do evil*, it is not to be account'd a restraint upon *liberty;* but a restraint *only upon Tyranny*."[76] The Congregational minister of Hanover, Massachusetts, late in the century, concurred and noted that "the true notion of liberty consists rather in the privilege or license to do *right* . . . [and] the happiness and freedom of the sons of moral liberty consists in their voluntary subjection and obedience to it."[77] This theme that freedom was only defensible as liberty when it led to behavior consistent with higher universal standards was repeated over and over again in 18th-century America (as well as in England and on the Continent) by men from every walk of life and intellectual outlook.[78]

One must remember as well that for them, a life of ordered and rational liberty was only possible within a community of reciprocally and mutually dependent but individually independent heads of household. For them, both individual subjection to communal standards and mutuality were necessary for liberty. Each side of this equation was necessary: reciprocal dependence on the community and freedom from unequal personal dependence. For example, Henry Cumings in 1783 argued that all men ought "to be *subject to one another*" and that "when any one fulfills the obligations resulting from his particular condition and station in life . . . he does, on his part, conform to the great law of mutual subjection, and renders himself a good and useful member of society."[79]

Moreover, for most Americans, this was only conceivable in an environment in which the laws of God and nature could be known and followed. Their world was one in which the "end of the natural is the moral world" and "all the *events* which take place, and all God's appointments and institutions are to be viewed, as so many means to advance the moral and spiritual good, or the holiness and happiness of the intelligent beings."[80] For such a people, to be alienated from God's (or nature's) influence and

[74]See Wiebe, *Segmented Society,* pp. 14–15.
[75]*Civil Liberty Asserted* (1776), pp. 40–41.
[76]Cited by Tise, *Proslavery,* p. 27.
[77]Mellen, *Great and Happy Doctrine of Liberty* (1795), pp. 12–13; see also p. 31.
[78]See Pitkin, "Are Freedom and Liberty Twins?" p. 28 (draft version), who reminds us that traditionally liberty has been understood to be "something more formal, rational, and limited than freedom; it concerns rules, and exceptions within a system of rules."
[79]Cumings, *Massachusetts Election Sermon* (1783), pp. 6–7.
[80]Cyprian Strong, *Kingdom Is the Lord's* (1799 Connecticut election sermon), pp. 10–11.

rational self-direction and liberty, to be enslaved to one's base passions, was understandably unbearable.

John Dickinson, the sophisticated lawyer and highly popular author of the "Farmer's Letters," did not appear to be unreasonable when he threatened in 1765 that there was a fate "worse than Death—it is SLAVERY!"[81] Neither did an anonymous author writing under the pseudonym "Andrew Marvel," who warned that "it is slavery that hath made them [post-Hellenistic Greeks] barbarous, and the same cause will have the same effect upon us. . . . slavery has spread ignorance, barbarism and misery over those once delightful regions, where the people are sunk into a stupid insensibility. . . . It is better to die in defence of our rights, than to leave such a state as this to the generations that succeed us."[82] Patrick Henry was, therefore, not at all exceptional when he ended his speech before the Virginia Convention meeting in St. John's Church in Richmond with those still famous words, "is life so dear, or peace so sweet, as to be purchased at the price of chains and slavery? Forbid it, Almighty God!—I know not what course others may take; but as for me . . . give me liberty, or give me death!"[83] The polarity between liberty and slavery was analogous if not identical to that between the capacity to sustain an ordered versus a disordered soul, salvation versus eternal damnation, and ultimately for a Christian, Christ versus Satan. Slavery in its various dimensions and Americans' abhorrence of it thus cuts to the essential core of their social and political thought.[84]

When a cosmopolitan figure such as Alexander Hamilton, not known for religious zeal, compared liberty and slavery, he too used language that suggested his awareness of a deep metaphysical if not religious dualism existing between them. He noted that "no person, that has enjoyed the sweets of liberty, can be insensible of its infinite value, or can reflect on its reverse, without horror and detestation. . . . Were not the disadvantages of slavery too obvious . . . I might shew that it is fatal to religion and morality; that it tends to debase the mind, and corrupt its noblest springs of action . . . and introduces misery and indigence in every shape."[85] His comments are comparable to those of the liberal pastor Judah Champion

---

[81][J. Dickinson], "Friends and Countrymen" (1765), broadside.

[82][Goddard?], "Constitutional Courant" (1765), p. 89.

[83]Wirt, "Life or Liberty Speech" (1775), p. 141. According to Hubbell, *South in American Literature*, p. 120, Henry's speech as recorded by Wirt may actually represent Wirt's "own very considerable oratorical powers rather than Henry's." It is, however, only in this critical closing paragraph that Wirt has Henry speak in the first person. But here, either Wirt or Henry was likely influenced in his choice of words by Addison. In his "Cato," p. 187, a most unsavory character, Sempronius, holds forth and disingenuously asks "can a Roman senate long debate which of the two to choose, slavery or death!" Later, though, the noble Cato added that "it is not now a time to talk of aught / But chains or conquest, liberty or death."

[84]See Jordan, *White over Black*, p. 491; and Yazawa, *From Colonies to Commonwealth*, p. 17.

[85]Hamilton, "Full Vindication" (15 December 1774), p. 53.

of Litchfield, Connecticut. Champion instructed his audience that slavery "debases the mind—clogs the finest movements of the soul; discourages industry, frugality, and every thing praise-worthy; introduces ignorance and poverty, with the most sordid vices, and universal misery."[86] The Massachusetts pastor Simeon Howard found that "once more, from a regard to religion, men are obliged to defend their liberty against encroachments. . . . Slavery exposes too many temptations to vice, and by debasing and weakening the mind, destroying its fortitude and magnanimity renders it less capable of resisting them."[87] These frequently voiced sentiments suggest a meaning of slavery that extends well beyond the status of unfree labor. And their recovery enhances one's ability to understand more fully the richness of late 18th-century American social and political thought.

As recognized by prominent historians of American slavery, Revolutionary-era Americans also understood all forms of slavery to have been impossible before the Fall, for "man fell into spiritual slavery because of his original sin," with Christ providing the only means of deliverance from it.[88] From a more pointedly religious perspective all men who were not free in Jesus were totally debased sinners and thus slaves to Satan. In delivering a thanksgiving sermon in 1766, Joseph Emerson, a Congregational minister from Pepperell, Massachusetts, made clear just how ubiquitous the problem of spiritual slavery was. Accordingly, he asked that "sinners, of every denomination, bethink themselves. Consider your state: You are grievously afraid of slavery; why, you are slaves already, some of the worst of slaves. A drunkard is a slave.—A thief is a slave.—A liar is a slave.—An unclean sinner is a slave.—All open profane sinners are slaves.—Every unconverted person is a slave." He then exhorts them to exchange their slavery to sin for one to Christ and "be persuaded, now to break the shackles, now call away these chains, leave your sins, cast away all your idols; return unto the Lord; embrace the Lord Jesus Christ as your savior, bind yourselves to be his servants forever, then will you be truly free."[89] Nathaniel Niles preached that "human nature shrinks at the thought of the partial oppression of an earthly tyrant, [while] we quietly remain in a state of the most abject slavery to the worst of tyrants the devil himself."[90] Here, Emerson and Niles are comparing Americans' well-developed fear of political and economic enslavement to the greater one that they argued Americans should have maintained for the more grievous form of eternal slavery, that to sin and Satan.

From a Southern and Baptist perspective as well, it was argued that "all mankind according to their natural birth . . . are reduced to the vilest

[86]Champion, *Christian and Civil Liberty* (1776 Connecticut election sermon), p. 14.

[87]S. Howard, "Sermon Preached in Boston" (1773), p. 203.

[88]Jordan, *White over Black*, pp. 41–42, 54–56; see also Patterson, *Slavery and Social Death*, pp. 70–71; and Davis, *Problem of Slavery in Western Culture*, p. 199.

[89]J. Emerson, *Thanksgiving Sermon* (1766), pp. 35–36.

[90]N. Niles, "Second Discourse" (1774), pp. 54–55.

slavery; and are in perfect bondage to their spiritual enemies. Sin and Satan, and the world, and the flesh have an absolute dominion over them."[91] Hugh Alison of South Carolina also found enslavement to sin both more serious and more common than political slavery. He warned: "He that maketh provision for the flesh to fulfil the lusts thereof; he that yieldeth his members instruments of unrighteousness unto sin . . . is emphatically a *slave*. . . . Though you enjoy all the external rights of freemen and British subjects, which is a doubtful case at present, yet you are naturally in spiritual bondage; slave to corruption; and to be insensible of it is a more shocking symptom of degeneracy."[92] For most 18th-century Americans, humans were born carrying the stain of original sin and, as described here, an unredeemed life of sin was a life of slavery.[93] Thus, consistent with the reformed-Protestant ordering of moral precepts, slavery to sin was the slavery that should be fought most vigorously because it was the most virulent, deforming, and frightening form of slavery.

Yet this reformed-Protestant understanding of the deformity fostered by slavery to one's passion was not unique to Protestants. In fact, the secular concerns of early-modern rationalist authors reinforced and paralleled the Christian understanding of liberty and slavery. Rationalist authors regularly depicted slavery as the wrongful subservience of human reason to human passions, with consequent deformation of the soul and estrangement from nature's God. This was the natural theological equivalent of sin. And as Isaiah Berlin reminds us, early-modern rationalism was secularized Protestantism "in which the place of God is taken by the conception of the rational life, and the place of the individual soul which strains toward union with Him is replaced by a conception of the individual, endowed with reason, straining to be governed by reason and reason alone."[94] Thus, those American authors who embraced this rationalistic view of the geography of the soul were no more likely to liberate the individual from rational restraint than were their Christian counterparts. The rationalists were at one with the orthodox Christian understanding of enslavement to sin, even if they employed a different descriptive language. Even in this more secular understanding, slavery described one's being engulfed and controlled by irrational passions.

According to a Northern pastor writing near the end of the century, a man at ease with the language of 18th-century rationalism, "of all *slaves* he is the greatest and most *infamous*, who is enslaved to his lusts. He that committeth sin habitually is of the devil—Sin and Satan are his masters. . . . he is the man of freedom, in the most noble sense, who has the command of himself, who can rule his own spirit, command his own passions

[91]D. Thomas, *Virginian Baptist* (1774), p. 9.
[92]Alison, *Spiritual Liberty* (1769), pp. 11–12.
[93]See Davis, "Slavery and Sin," p. 25.
[94]Berlin, "Two Concepts of Liberty," p. 138.

and appetites, keep under his body, and make reason the rule of his conduct—who fears God and walks uprightly."[95] Samuel West, who was comparably theologically liberal, describes the relation between the irrational passions and slavery:

> the highest state of liberty subjects us to the law of nature and the government of God. The most perfect freedom consists in obeying the dictates of right reason, and submitting to natural law. When a man goes beyond or contrary to the law of nature and reason, he becomes the slave of base passions and vile lusts; he introduces confusion and disorder into society, and brings misery and destruction upon himself. This, therefore, cannot be called a state of freedom, but a state of the vilest slavery and the most dreadful bondage.[96]

One is hard-pressed to discern anything particularly Christian in these remarks, yet the rationalist understanding of slavery as humans disobeying the laws of nature and acting in accord with their irrational lusts nicely preserves the fundamentals of the Christian view of spiritual slavery as enslavement to one's licentious passions.

In articulating this Christian and early modern rationalist perspective on enslavement to the passions, American ministers and essayists were not original. Rather, they were the inheritors of a two-thousand-year-old tradition.[97] As C. S. Lewis explains, Aristotle had held that "the free life is to the servile as the life of the gods (the living stars) is to that of the terrestrial creatures. This is so not because the truly free man 'does what he likes', but because he imitates, so far as a mortal can, the flawless and patterned regularity of the heavenly beings, like them not doing what he likes but being what he is."[98] Another author likely read by well-educated Americans, the Stoic Epictetus, is said to have written that unless "you . . . eradicate desire utterly . . . you are a slave, you are subject, you have become liable to hindrance and to compulsion, you are entirely under the control of others."[99] John Gray finds that the Stoics contrasted freedom "with the heteronomous condition of a man whose choices go against the universal rational order and are accordingly immoral."[100] It was this understanding of liberty and its antithesis, slavery, with its long and rich pedigree, that 18th-century Americans and some of the ablest European minds of the early modern period defended.

---

[95]Mellen, *Great and Happy Doctrine of Liberty* (1795), p. 33.

[96]S. West, "Right to Rebel Against Governors" (1776 Massachusetts election sermon), p. 415.

[97]See Gray, introduction to Pelczynski and Gray, *Conceptions of Liberty in Political Philosophy*, pp. 5–6.

[98]C. S. Lewis, *Studies in Words*, p. 129; see also MacIntyre, *After Virtue*, pp. 158–59; Rahe, "Primacy of Politics in Classical Greece," p. 273; and Reed, "Berlin and the Division of Liberty," pp. 373–74.

[99]Cited by Fosdick, *What Is Liberty?* p. 20.

[100]Gray, "On Negative and Positive Liberty," p. 327; see also Patterson, *Freedom*, p. 267.

For example, Baruch de Spinoza argued in 1670 that some men had confused liberty and slavery by holding that "slaves obey commands and free men live as they like; but this idea is based on a misconception, for the true slave is he who is led away by his pleasures and can neither see what is good for him nor act accordingly: he alone is free who lives with free consent under the entire guidance of reason."[101] A few decades later, John Locke held that "to be determined by *de facto* desire is 'misery and slavery.'"[102] And in the middle of the 18th century, Rousseau declared that it was only while living "in the civil state" that man acquires "moral liberty, which alone makes him truly master of himself; for the mere impulse of appetite is slavery, while obedience to a law which we prescribe to ourselves is liberty."[103] For these more or less secular thinkers and their frequently less eloquent (and usually more Christian) American counterparts, liberty continued to be achievable only when an individual voluntarily surrendered irrational lusts to the way of reason. Anything else resulted in enslavement, whether through subservience to another man or to one's own passions.

Moreover, the perception of slavery as a disorder of the soul was an 18th-century ideal that was held by others besides ascetic rationalists and zealous reformed Protestants. Two other 18th-century men, Edmund Burke and the Baron de Montesquieu, known for their moderation and respect for cultural traditions rather than Christian dogma or abstract reason, described slavery in comparable ways. Near midcentury, Montesquieu had written that people who live in a city whose citizens are no longer controlled by virtue "were free while under the restraint of laws, but they would fain now be free to act against law; and as each citizen is like a slave who has run away from his master, that which was a maxim of equity he calls rigour; that which was a rule of action he styles constraint."[104] Burke, later in the century, appealed to a logic that must have been immediately familiar to Americans when he noted that for humans, "the worst of all Slavery" was "the despotism of their own blind and brutal passions."[105]

But only by living in an intrusive community was a life of slavery, of enslavement to the passions, to be successfully combated. The emerging views of individualists, who would later in the 19th century argue that the individual could only know true liberty by first being freed from societal oversight, were little countenanced by Americans and those they most respected.

Well into the antebellum period, Americans continued to uphold this

[101]Spinoza, *A Theologico-Political Treatise*, p. 206.

[102]Cited by Tully, "Locke on Liberty," p. 70.

[103]Rousseau, *Social Contract* (1762), p. 19.

[104]Montesquieu, *Spirit of the Laws* (1748), 1:21.

[105]Burke, "Letter to Depont" (November 1789), in *Correspondence of Edmund Burke*, p. 41.

traditional classical (particularly Stoic), Christian, and early modern rationalist perspective on slavery to the passions and sin. They even employed it in defense of America's continued enslavement of Africans,[106] those judged most at risk from such losses of control and thus most enslaved and unable to profit from even limited individual liberty.[107] Cooke notes that for many of the 19th-century Christian apologists for slavery, such as the South Carolinian divine, Dr. Thornwell, "the only really significant bondage was bondage to sin; that was 'true Slavery.' External conditions did not make a man free or unfree; true liberty was a state of mind or character, a 'domination of rectitude, in the emancipation of the will from the power of sin, [and] the release of the affections from the attractions of earth.'"[108] One must observe, however, that it is one thing for the Cynic Diogenes, impoverished and living in a barrel, to take such a position, and quite another for a wealthy, Southern planter served by African slaves to do so.

Late 18th-century critics of slavery and 19th-century abolitionists did hold that enslavement of Africans reflected and gave vent to the unruly passions of the slaveholders, rather than those of their slaves. In particular, they believed that the slaveowners' passionate desire to tyrannize others was allowed to run rampant.[109] For the abolitionists, as for their 18th-century forebears, freedom "was defined as self-mastery; the individual mastered and overcame his natural passions."[110] Indeed, Lewis Saum has argued that "even more than the enslavement of blacks, the license and self-indulgence of whites aroused the Northerners' misgivings about the South."[111] Both sides of the postrevolutionary debate over the enslavement of African Americans, then, importantly continued to describe slavery in terms of a loss of control over one's own passions. What they disagreed about was who was most truly a slave: the brutalizing master or his brutalized human "property."

TYRANNY, LICENSE, AND SLAVERY

Late 18th-century Americans' understanding of license and slavery, and indirectly of liberty, was mediated by a third concept with the most direct relevance to politics—tyranny.[112] For them, a tyrant was a man whose

[106]See Schmidt and Wilhelm, "Early Proslavery Petitions in Virginia," p. 139.

[107]See Turnbull, *Apology for Negro Slavery* (1786), pp. 7–8; and J. P. Greene, *All Men Are Created Equal*, pp. 30–31.

[108]Cited by Cooke, *American Tradition of Liberty*, p. 67.

[109]See [Samuel Hopkins], *Dialogue Concerning the Slavery of Africans* (1776), p. 52; J. Parsons, *Freedom from Civil and Ecclesiastical Slavery* (1774), p. 10; MacLeod, *Slavery, Race, and the American Revolution*, pp. 24–25; and Jaenicke, "American Ideas of Political Party," p. 446.

[110]Jaenicke, "American Ideas of Political Party," pp. 449–50.

[111]See Saum, *Popular Mood*, pp. 157, 170–71.

[112]See Reid, *Concept of Liberty*, pp. 47–48.

"savage passions are not bounded by the laws of reason, religion, honor, or a regard to his subjects, and the point to which all his movements center, is the gratification of a brutal appetite."[113] Because of his licentiousness, he was in a modern sense free,[114] and yet in the 18th-century sense, he was incapable of enjoying liberty, for he was truly a slave to his passions. True liberty demanded that one live within a community of near-equals capable of mutually restraining themselves. A tyrant by definition was without such a community and, thus, could not know liberty.[115]

Slavery defined, therefore, the boundaries of a political golden mean of local communal control over individuals, reciprocal dependence between heads of house, and ordered liberty for all capable of living a life of independence. On either side of this norm, one found only slavery. On one side was the apparently "free" tyrant, a self-indulgent man enslaved to his own licentious lusts and passions. On the other side was the more apparent slavery of absolute dependence. In such a condition, a man (and by extension his family) was subject to the arbitrary (by definition nonrational) will of another individual. He was therefore unable to be politically, economically, and spiritually self-governing. Thus, in defending the Revolution, George Washington believed that it was above all the arbitrary character of tyrannical rule that was to be feared. He noted that resistance to Britain was called for if Americans wished to avoid becoming "tame and abject slaves," like the African slaves they (and he) ruled "over with such arbitrary sway."[116] To the 18th-century American mind, various forms of slavery were avoidable only within the confines of a properly ordered corporate life wherein arbitrary rule and behavior could be limited.

The onetime president of Brown University, Union College in New York, and the University of South Carolina, Jonathan Maxcy, neatly emphasized the close relationship that existed between liberty and a structured community. He asked his audience, "what liberty has man in the unsocial, uncivilized state? I conceive he has none, which properly comes under the idea of liberty. . . . He consults no will, and no power but his own. Every man, therefore, in an uncivilized state, is either a tyrant or a slave."[117] His logic is not exceptional; for most Americans, liberty demanded an intrusive and restrictive community.

---

[113][T. Parsons], "Essex Result" (1778), p. 484. See also A. Sidney, *Discourses Concerning Government* (1698), pp. 464–65, who also describes a tyrant as one who is "a slave to his lusts and vices"; and Houston, *Algernon Sidney,* pp. 130–36.

[114]See Graebner, introduction to *Freedom in America,* p. 1, who writes that "only the tyrant, living in a secure environment and operating above the law, is, at least in theory, free to do as he chooses."

[115]See Montesquieu, *Spirit of the Laws* (1748), 2:76–77, who writes that "princes who live not among themselves under civil laws are not free."

[116]Washington, "Letter to Bryan Fairfax" (24 August 1774), in *George Washington,* p. 39; see also Wolin, *Presence of the Past,* p. 108.

[117]Maxcy, "Oration" (1799), p. 1050.

Outside the bounds of such a properly ordered community, individuals who consulted no will but their own were not truly free. In fact, they were little different from tyrants who, because of their unequal relationship with all other men, became enslaved to their own licentious whims and passions as if they too were living outside of the walls of community. Both groups, because of their individual freedom (necessarily licentious for fallen humanity), were incapable of living a life of liberty. Thus, in studying the 18th-century understanding of tyranny and slavery, one is forced to recognize how little of the modern conception of individualism, with its understanding of human flourishing, was countenanced.

As Maxcy indicated, the socially unchecked capacity of a tyrant to exercise his arbitrary will with freedom ensured that those living under his sovereignty were slaves of a different sort, either in the political or private sense of dependence, for "the unrestrained LICENTIOUSNESS of any one Person, in any one Nation, infers the universal Slavery of that Nation."[118] As an anonymous author observed, "all men are equally entitled to it [liberty]. He who assumes more than his just share of *liberty* becomes a tyrant in proportion to what he assumes; and he who loses it, becomes so many degrees a slave."[119] According to James Cogswell, a minister from Canterbury, Connecticut, Americans were becoming slaves because they were "at the Disposal of a despotic and arbitrary Tyrant, who has no other law but his Will."[120] For most Americans, then, both a certain measure of independence and an intrusive communal life were necessary if tyranny, license, and slavery were to be avoided, rather than encouraged.

The proto-Unitarian pastor of Boston's West Church, Simeon Howard, urged his congregation to oppose such tyrannous men because "yielding to the unjust demands of bad men, not only lessens our power of doing good, but encourages them to repeat their injuries. . . . It enables them to give fuller scope to their lusts. . . . It is therefore an act of benevolence to oppose and destroy that power which is employed in injuring others, and as much, when it is that of a tyrant, as of a wild beast."[121] Like his contemporaries, even the theologically liberal Howard believed the unbounded rule of one or a few, necessarily a product of their sinful passions, was the result of license instead of liberty. Tyranny, the unbounded rule of one, like anarchy, the irrational rule of the mob, was necessarily unjust, licentious, and wicked.

In America, a tyrant's licentiousness stemmed from his effectively standing outside the controlling confines of community and the natural order that it was meant to reflect. The community ensured through reciprocal

---

[118][Brooke?], *Liberty and Common-Sense* (1760), letter 2, p. 6.

[119]*Boston Gazette and Country Journal*, 22 February 1768.

[120]Cogswell, *God the Pious Soldier's Strength and Instructor*, cited by Hatch, *Sacred Cause of Liberty*, p. 21.

[121]S. Howard, "Sermon Preached in Boston" (1773), p. 202.

dependence that each member observed the collective understanding of the higher law. As the pastor Samuel Sherwood explained, all people are corrupt by nature and therefore they are equally in need of societal constraint. Without it, rulers must "degenerate into tyrants . . . unless there be some way to keep them in awe," that is, "keep them within their proper sphere."[122] For Americans, then, with their reformed-Protestant political foundation, the tyrant, just like the mob or anyone living outside communal boundaries (of family, congregation, or town), without benefit of their needed restraint, was necessarily incapable of living a life of liberty.

In this 18th-century understanding of those who lived beyond the bounds of society, there remained residues of early English law in which the "'autonomous' stranger who had no family or clan to protect him was automatically regarded as a slave."[123] Orlando Patterson, a close student of slavery, finds that in diverse cultures a slave is fundamentally "a socially dead person" living without the benefit of family, clan, or community. "Indeed, it was Moses Finley, drawing on the Greco-Roman experience, who was among the first to emphasize what he called the 'outsider' status of the slave as a critical attribute of his condition."[124] By standing outside the protective yet restrictive mutuality of a well-ordered community, people are left to be either irrational beasts, licentious tyrants, or their dependent slaves.

Americans did assume that anyone outside the bounds of community, particularly (but not only) those in positions of power over others, would necessarily act unjustly in opposition to the binding laws of God and nature. Even ministers such as Howard who had rejected Calvinism's core pessimistic theology were nevertheless still certain that the inherent sinfulness of humanity must come to the fore in a situation of individual freedom not communally controlled.[125] The optimistic evaluations of some 19th-century thinkers, with their apparent confidence in individualism and the curative and liberating power of liberty free from social censure, were (with the likely exception of Jefferson) absent in late 18th-century America.[126]

The specific reasons Americans were so opposed to tyranny are, however, less clear. Was it because individual citizens and communicants were prevented from being politically and personally self-governing? Was it primarily because of fears over the loss of their property? Or was it because the socially unbounded tyrant necessarily acted in contradiction to the

---

[122]Sherwood, "Scriptural Instructions to Civil Rulers" (1774), p. 393.

[123]Davis, *Slavery and Human Progress*, pp. 15–16.

[124]Patterson, *Slavery and Social Death*, p. 7.

[125]See Stout, *New England Soul*, pp. 224–25.

[126]See May, *Enlightenment in America*, p. 294; and Appleby, "Jefferson's Political Philosophy," p. 299, who suggests that Jefferson might have been one of the exceptions. She argues that Jefferson "ascribed the lowly state of man to repressive institutions." In disagreement, see W. P. Adams, *First American Constitutions*, pp. 25–26.

laws of justice and nature? Tyrants were capable of exciting all these concerns, for they were commonly understood to be men "who know no Justice . . . [and] set no bounds to Lust of Empire, but let it rove in all the Licence of their own Fancy."[127] American authors were prone to conflate these possibilities, unlike classical Greek authors, who had treated these questions as distinct. It is impossible, therefore, to say with certainty whether it was fear of dependence, fear of material loss, or the repugnance of the rule of injustice and irrational passions that made tyranny so contemptible in their eyes.[128] What is clear, though, is that Revolutionary-era Americans uniformly condemned the slavery of personal dependence, particularly when it was combined with the uncontrolled rule of a necessarily sinful, selfish, and unjust man.[129]

However, Americans were likely to disagree about the respective dangers of two forms of slavery, popular and elite license (anarchy and tyranny). Nevertheless, those who likely differed, Loyalists and Patriots, both eschewed the extremes of each.[130] As argued by Dr. Price, "licentiousness and despotism are more nearly allied than is commonly imagined. They are both alike inconsistent with liberty, and the true end of government," for the "one is the licentiousness of *great* men, and the other the licentiousness of *little* men."[131] The fiery patriot James Otis also held that "the laws, customs, and usages of our ancestors" could be counted on to defend them against "the whims of political and religious enthusiasts, the extremes of which are libertinism and despotism, anarchy and tyranny, spiritual and temporal, from all which God ever preserve us."[132] The outspoken Loyalist minister Jonathan Boucher, citing Bishop Butler, held that "licentiousness is, in truth, such an excess of liberty as is of the same nature with tyranny . . . one is lawless power exercised under pretence of authority . . . the other, lawless power exercised under pretence of liberty. . . . A people, then, must always be less free in proportion as they are licentious; licentiousness being not only different from liberty, but directly contrary to it."[133] Across a wide ideological spectrum, license or slavery to one's passions was condemned. It took on two different forms, however, one more appropriate to the people, moral degeneracy and anarchy, and the other more appropriate to governing elites, despotism and tyranny. Both were seen as antithetical to the preferred median of ordered liberty.

---

[127]Bradbury, "Ass" (1774), p. 247.

[128]For an example of someone who did respond to this question, see Witherspoon, *Dominion of Providence* (1776), p. 41.

[129]See Bloch, *Visionary Republic*, p. 4.

[130]See Potter, *Liberty We Seek*, p. 59.

[131]Price, *Observations* (1776), p. 13.

[132]Otis, "Vindication of the British Colonies" (1765), pp. 578–79.

[133]Boucher, "On Civil Liberty" (1775), p. 511. He is citing from Butler's sermon before the House of Lords, 30 January 1740.

The disagreement that formed an ideological division between Loyalists and Patriots thus concerned whether the license of one (tyranny) was preferable to the license of many (anarchy). The more "conservative" spokesmen represented what had been the dominant position in the colonies since their founding. They held that tyranny, although certainly repugnant, was nevertheless relatively less dangerous than anarchy, where each became a licentious tyrant enslaved to his or her passions within a multitude of such people.[134] An author in 1770 put it rather traditionally: "I own I had rather be a slave under one master; for if I know who he is, I may perhaps, be able to please him, than a slave to an hundred or more, who I don't know where to find, nor what they will expect of me."[135] Surprisingly, however, Samuel Langdon, Harvard's president, a close friend of Sam Adams, and an active Patriot, agreed. He held that "a state of absolute anarchy is dreadful. Submission to the tyranny of hundreds of imperious masters . . . is the vilest slavery, and worse than death."[136] Yet other "progressive" voices that came to the fore immediately preceding and during the Revolution generally argued for the opposite position. Patriots, such as Josiah Quincy, Jr., believed that it was "much easier to restrain liberty from running into licentiousness than power from swelling into tyranny and oppression."[137] In spite of this political division, Americans continued to agree on the more fundamental issue of a sinful individual's need for a communal life if he or she were to escape enslavement to the passions. The individual living outside community, whether a tyrant or a dependent, a member of a mob or an isolated individual, was given no chance of living in liberty.

The more "conservative" position was most consistent, then, with America's long-held reformed-Protestant understanding of humanity's sinful and deformed character and the need for communal oversight. Before the Revolution, Americans had commonly held that humanity's innate depravity and "proud Appetites and injurious Passions, has made Government necessary," in fact, "so necessary, that the most tyrannical Government that ever was in the World, is more Eligible than Anarchy, or no Government . . . [where] every one is a Tyrant."[138] That position was defended by such preeminent authorities as William Blackstone, who regarded anarchy as "a worse state than tyranny itself, as any government is

---

[134]For example, see Ames, "Dangers of American Liberty" (1805), p. 1304, who writes that "the known propensity of a democracy is to licentiousness, which the ambitious call and the ignorant believe to be liberty," and then recalls that the goal "of political wisdom in framing our Constitution, was to guard against licentiousness."

[135]Theophilus Lillie, *Boston Chronicle*, 15 January 1770.

[136]Langdon, "Government Corrupted by Vice" (1775 Massachusetts election sermon), in *Pulpit of the American Revolution*, p. 250.

[137]Quincy, "Observations" (1774), p. 304; see also Paine, "Common Sense" (1776), p. 403.

[138]S. Hall, *Legislature's Right* (1746 Connecticut election sermon), pp. 12–13.

better than none at all."[139] He also claimed that, if not for the transgression of our first ancestor, our reason would be clear and perfect and the laws of eternal justice would coincide with the happiness of each individual. But this is not the dispensation under which we live, for "every man now finds the contrary in his own experience; that his reason is corrupt, and his understanding full of ignorance and error."[140] Clearly the assumption of original sin had penetrated deeply into the recesses of Anglo-American political thought and jurisprudence.

During the Revolutionary period, it was primarily the Loyalists who continued to argue "that anarchy and popular tyranny were more imminent threats to America than was the arbitrary power of British or colonial governments."[141] Yet because they published such sentiments in a relatively popular forum, the newspaper editorial, it seems reasonable to assume that they believed they could influence their neighbors. This, along with the thoughts of Patriots such as Harvard's Samuel Langdon, suggests that a consensus had not yet been achieved regarding which was the more dangerous of the two. In 1775, the Loyalist author Isaac Wilkins held that "liberty and licentiousness are nearly allied to each other" and that "there is but a thin partition between them; and licentiousness invariably leads to slavery."[142] In 1776, another Loyalist, Ambrose Serle, invoked Locke to recall to the minds of Americans that "as tyranny, or the abuse of this public authority for private ends which oppose the general good, would be opposite to the law of God and nature: so the uncontrouled liberty of depraved and licentious individuals is equally so. I am warranted in this reasoning by Mr. *Locke* himself, whom the Americans have appointed their political apostle."[143] In short, it was various forms of license, the surrender of humanity to individual wants and desires, that was most feared and deplored by both Loyalists and Patriots.

Late 18th-century Americans were intolerant of any form of license. Included under this umbrella of contempt were licentious anarchical governments, under which individuals were free to follow their idiosyncratic passions, and licentious tyrants, whose will knew no bounds. What most Loyalists, Patriots, and the majority caught in between agreed on, then, was that the only liberty "worth contending for . . . lies equally remote from licentiousness and tyranny."[144] Nor was this high regard for a balanced and ordered liberty peculiar to the Revolutionary period.

Twenty years after the Revolution, Alexander Wilson was still lecturing that to define liberty properly, one must first differentiate it from slavery,

[139]Blackstone, *Commentaries*, 1:123.
[140]Ibid., 1:40–41.
[141]Potter, *Liberty We Seek*, p. 54.
[142]Wilkins, "Speech," in *Rivington's New-York Gazetteer*, 6 April 1775.
[143][Serle], *Americans against Liberty* (1776), p. 26; see also Otis, "Vindication of the British Colonies" (1765), p. 565.
[144]Davidson, *Oration* (4 July 1787), p. 15; see also Baldwin, *New England Clergy*, p. 36.

license, and tyranny. He warned against the ruinous character of anarchy when he noted that "there have been people in the world, weak or wicked enough to believe, that liberty was the right and privilege of doing just whatever they pleased. This so far from being liberty, is the most complete tyranny; and would, if adopted, introduce universal anarchy, and the total subversion of all society."[145] The continuation of such an outlook into the 19th century supports the idea that late 18th-century Americans were unwilling to countenance either their enslavement to the passions of the one (tyranny) or to those of the many (anarchy). They sought both a way of life and a form of government that avoided such extremes. The most visible and logical path to achieve this was through a communal life, with its intrusive intermediate institutions of family, congregation, neighborhoods, local government, and (in some instances) schools and fraternal organizations. These necessary institutions allowed for local corporate supervision of the individual, and thus potentially a life of ordered liberty.

In answer "to the political question par excellence, of how to reconcile order which is not oppression with freedom which is not license,"[146] Americans held that it was a life of ordered liberty that was necessarily communal, selectively democratic, and for most, reformed Protestant. Unlike later individualists, most Americans did not have confidence in the unaided ability of humans to live a life of rational liberty without the intervention of concerned brethren (and usually the Holy Spirit as well). They did not hold a heroic view of the individual and his or her ability to live a life of reason, as did later theorists like John Stuart Mill.[147] Americans were much more likely to believe, as explained by the nevertheless highly progressive minister Simeon Howard, that "the most desirable liberty, which we should be ready to defend, is that of a well governed society, which is as essentially different from the licentiousness, which is without law or government, as it is from absolute subjection to the arbitrary will of another. This is the liberty wherewith Christ has made us free; to which he had given us a right."[148] No individual, whether commoner or tyrant, could be trusted with unbounded liberty. The stain of original sin would not allow it. Slavery to one's passions was thus only escapable within the narrow confines of a reciprocally binding local community.

Americans were not alone in understanding liberty to be a communally maintained median between two licentious enslaving extremes. This view was also held widely by prominent spokesmen for intellectual traditions that had provided Americans with the concepts with which to express themselves and frame their thoughts, most importantly the social thought

---

[145]A. Wilson, *Oration* (1801), pp. 5–6.

[146]Asked by Strauss, *Persecution and the Art of Writing*, p. 37.

[147]See Mill, "On Liberty" (1859), p. 129; and C. Taylor, "What's Wrong with Negative Liberty," 211–15.

[148]S. Howard, "Sermon Preached in Boston" (1773), p. 208.

of reformed Protestantism. Unequivocally, John Calvin had written that humanity's sinful nature made it impossible for an individual to enjoy liberty except within a community of like-minded brethren. In the *Institutes* he taught that "it very rarely happens that kings regulate themselves so that their will is never at variance with justice and rectitude. . . . The vice or imperfection of men therefore renders it safer and more tolerable for the government to be in the hands of many, that they may afford each other mutual assistance and admonition, and that if any one arrogate to himself more than is right, the many may act as censors and masters to restrain his ambition."[149] This was a reformed-Protestant perspective that would be adhered to in the 18th century not only in America, but in Britain as well.

From across the political spectrum of British thought, whether the original source was indigenous, republican, or Protestant, Americans had learned that "the Government of One for the Sake of One, is Tyranny. . . . But Government executed for the Good of All, and with the Consent of All, is Liberty."[150] Lord Bolingbroke explained that without sufficient popular liberty, "government will degenerate into tyranny," and with too much it "will degenerate into license."[151] For Joseph Addison, liberty was a balance poised between "two formidable enemies"—tyranny and licentiousness.[152] And from Edmund Burke, a most sober source writing late in the 18th century, they also learned that "true liberty must be 'social freedom,' a condition which required restriction on raw will and prevented anyone from exercising arbitrary power."[153] Liberty was not an extreme, but a median difficult to maintain between licentious extremes on either side.

Although those Americans more influenced by classical or Renaissance republican thought may have disagreed with reformed Protestants concerning the need for divine intervention and how restrained the passions should be, they most surely agreed with them regarding the need for corporate oversight if an individual were to live a life of authentic liberty. The early modern rationalists were as resolute as the Protestants in their differentiation between true liberty and licentious enslavement to the passions. Their collective voice was as opposed as that of any people to tyranny or license, with both understood to be enslavement to the passions.

On the Continent, a contemporary theorist, Burlamaqui, described the common 18th-century understanding of liberty as a balance between two forms of enslavement when he noted that "the best governments are those which are so tempered, as to secure the happiness of the subjects, by

---

[149]Calvin, *Institutes of the Christian Religion,* trans. Allen, 2:640.
[150][Trenchard and Gordon], "Cato's Letters #24" (1721), in Jacobson, *English Libertarian Heritage,* p. 63.
[151]Bolingbroke, "Idea of a Patriot King" (1754), 2:390.
[152]Cited by D. Greene, "Sweet Land of Liberty," pp. 133–34.
[153]Cited by Stanlis, *Edmund Burke and the Natural Law,* p. 67.

avoiding tyranny and licentiousness."[154] The great 18th-century German philosopher Immanuel Kant was also committed to these goals; he captured with his usual perspicacity the fundamental tension between the need for liberty and the need to prevent its abuse for either tyrannical or licentious ends. He wrote:

> man is *an animal who needs a master.* . . . he is still misled by his self-seeking animal inclinations into exempting himself from the law where he can. He thus requires a *master* to break his self-will and force him to obey a universal valid will under which every man can be free. But where is he to find such a master? Nowhere else but in the human species. But this master will also be an animal who needs a master. . . . [he] will always misuse his freedom if he does not have anyone above him to apply force to him as the laws should require it. Yet the highest authority has to be just *in itself* and yet also a *man.* This is therefore the most difficult of all tasks, and a perfect solution is impossible. Nothing straight can be constructed from such warped wood as that which man is made of.[155]

Although this fundamental quandary certainly admits of different solutions,[156] Americans traditionally resolved it by turning to the intrusive grasp of a reciprocally bonded community as the most viable means of containing the sinful nature of humanity.

Liberty was only possible, then, within the confines of a community where men and women could mutually and reciprocally bind themselves to follow collectively the rational laws of God and nature—in effect, collectively to forge their own chains (to borrow from Rousseau).[157] For according to an anonymous author writing in 1771, "human Nature is so constituted, that without a restraint from many things, we can enjoy nothing; we cannot support an unlimited indulgence . . . nor do we properly value what we have, but by being denied in a great measure what we wish. Felicity will not blossom on the boughs of unbridled freedom; on the contrary the soul unrestrained runs wild, and like a vine unpruned, shoots into fruitless branches and leaves, and becomes sterile."[158] Thus, outside such a

---

[154]Burlamaqui, *Principles of Natural and Politic Law* (1763), 2.92, see also 2.86.

[155]Kant, "Idea for a Universal History" (1784), p. 46.

[156]See Kant, "Perpetual Peace" (1795)," pp. 112–13, for his remarkably Madisonian solution.

[157]The major disagreement between 18th-century Americans and Rousseau in *The Social Contract* was not over the necessarily communal character of the good life, but over the central vehicle to be used for human flourishing, political or religious life, and whether the chains that necessarily must bind each are to be collectively invented or imitative of a higher and more excellent standard.

[158]"Lelius," *Massachusetts Gazette and Boston Weekly News-Letter*, 6 June 1771, p. 3. Compare this to the more Germanic and tension-ridden but nevertheless similar thinking of Kant, "Idea for a Universal History" (1784), p. 46, who writes that men's "inclinations make it impossible for them to exist side by side for long in a state of wild freedom. . . . In the same way, trees in a forest, by seeking to deprive each other of air and sunlight, compel each other

community, humans are incapable of a life of liberty. They are either licentious beasts enslaved to their passions or the enslaved prey of a tyrant. They could only escape their deforming sin within society, not without its intrusiveness, as was later suggested by 19th-century individualists.[159] In either instance, slavery, not liberty, was the only form of life found beyond the necessarily confining walls of a local community.

---

to find these by upward growth, so that they grow beautiful and straight—whereas those which put out branches at will, in freedom and in isolation from others, grow stunted, bent and twisted."

[159]See Mill, "On Liberty" (1859), pp. 189–94; and Demos, *Past, Present, and Personal*, p. 86.

I have said enough to put the character of Anglo-American
civilization in its true light. It is the result . . . of two
distinct elements, which in other places have been in
frequent disagreement, but which the Americans have
succeeded in incorporating . . . and combining admirably. I
allude to the *spirit of religion* and the *spirit of liberty*.

—Alexis de Tocqueville, *Democracy in America*

WHEN MOST Revolutionary-era sermons, pamphlets, public documents,
and orations are read within the intellectual conventions of their own time
rather than those of the late 20th century, the language encountered—even
their understanding of liberty as "doing anything that is agreeable to a
person's disposition"—does not describe an individualistic disposition.[1]
Rather, it reflects a Protestant communal world of ideas in which only a
narrow range of behavior could be described as liberty rather than license,
and only within this permitted band of activity was "doing anything that is
agreeable" to be understood as liberty.

Simply because late 18th-century Americans were not precocious individualists, one must not jump to the conclusion that they were dedicated
adherents either in thought or practice of classical or Renaissance republicanism. Indeed, scant evidence exists that they were. Most Americans'
understanding of human fulfillment was not intrinsically linked to political
life. Most who concerned themselves with such questions held instead that
politics was of instrumental importance, and that human fulfillment could
only be achieved through surrender to Christ and the intercession of God's
grace. Thus, the influence of classical and Renaissance republican authors
on the political thought and institutions of late 18th-century Americans,
although important, surely was more muted than has been claimed.

But if Revolutionary-era Americans were not deeply committed to classical republicanism or incipient individualism, what then provided the foundations on which their political and ethical thought rested? The answer is
clear. Americans had available to them, aside from these two political visions, alternative ways of viewing political and social life. Most importantly, their political institutions and their understanding of collective hu-

---

[1]Dyche and Pardon, *New General English Dictionary* (1752), s.v. "liberty."

man flourishing were shaped by reformed Protestantism. In addition, Americans were close students of Scottish commonsense philosophy and were the inheritors of a rich body of English law and localist agrarian traditions. Without dismissing the importance of these other influences, my attention has been focused on that which was predominant, the reformed-Protestant character of their political thought, with particular emphasis placed on the strong sense of personal and political limits derived from the Christian dogma of original sin.

The concept of original sin helps explicate much of Revolutionary-era American political thought. Without it, for instance, one would certainly misinterpret the often libertarian-sounding praise given by late 18th-century pamphleteers and ministers to the beauties of natural, unbounded freedom. Yet with the concept in mind, one more readily understands that for most late 18th century Americans, descriptions of the joy of natural, unfettered freedom were depictions of a paradise lost that could be only partially recovered through spiritual liberty, and ultimately, through death and the loss of their worldly selves in Christ.

One should also note the vital though unintended role in Revolutionary America that Protestant religiosity played in creating and nurturing a truly radical idea: that a specific presocial right or privilege might be so integral to the accepted goals of organized human social life or so essential to being fully human that it could be neither traded nor relinquished without nullifying those ends. Thus, the first and most important inalienable right in America, the right of religious conscience, enjoyed its unimpeachable standing because of the enormous importance attached to salvation, the goal it putatively served.

But desperate apologists for the American war effort, because of the inconvenient historical ties of English political and legal rights to parliamentary sovereignty, turned to the natural and fully inalienable individual right of religious conscience to help justify their difficult-to-defend revolution. It was thus under the pressures of a constitutional crisis and war that the historical and traditional political and legal rights of Englishmen, prized for decades by Americans as such, were replanted in the fertile soil of natural-law theory.[2] By skillfully exploiting the Protestant-inspired right of religious conscience, Revolutionary-era leaders made possible a class of rights that were elastic, secular, and capable of being counterpoised to the corporate political claims of a people or the state. The future of these rights would be long, tumultuous, and even epoch forming.[3]

By the close of the Revolutionary era, therefore, significant changes and

---

[2] See E. Lewis, "Contribution of Medieval Thought," p. 466, who writes that "one will look in vain in medieval writings for any codification of the principles of the natural law to which civilists, canonists, theologians constantly appealed. Aquinas's justly celebrated analysis is only a suggestive outline—and it was by no means generally accepted." Thus, natural law was the perfect vehicle, for it was both highly flexible and respected.

[3] See Lacey and Haakonssen, "Introduction," p. 2.

innovations in American political thought had taken hold, even though many were unintended and others proved transitory, particularly in the Southern states. Yet these and many of the still more epochal 19th-century changes had been preceded by material and cultural ones occurring in the 18th century. Even before the Revolution, by the 1760s, Americans in both the North and the South were being torn between changing demographic, economic, religious, and social forces on the one hand and static communal social and political norms on the other. The overall picture that emerges, however, is not of a progressive and purposeful people moving steadily and deliberately toward political individualism and secular materialism; rather, it is of a confused and largely reactionary people trying to integrate these disruptive forces into their unyielding localist, communalist, and reformed-Protestant public philosophy.

Revolutionary-era Americans were an uncertain people cast adrift on an unknown sea of material change with an anachronistic intellectual map and a moral compass ill suited for changing times. Even the war itself proved to be an ill-conceived reactionary effort to resolve the intractable dilemmas confronting 18th-century Americans. Many went into the war hoping to halt the little-understood changes then occurring in American cultural, economic, religious, and political life. Their efforts, however, would fail. Thus the true revolution, which consisted of the war's unsought individualistic and materialistic consequences that began emerging in the 1790s, was less the product of new thinking and novel experiments in political science (Publius's hubristic claims to the contrary notwithstanding) than the result of the failure of traditional Western communal ideals and patterns of political organization. Americans backed into modernity and the 19th century; the movement toward a moderate form of political individualism was the outcome of a century of concerted American failure to control the tides of material and intellectual forces pushing toward disruptive societal changes.

In the last decade of the 18th century, limited secular individual rights and liberties had begun to be articulated by a handful of American national elites. A new, moderately individualistic political vision that "acted on the knowledge of what men actually are, not what they ought to be,"[4] which today dominates self-conscious social and political thought in the United States, had been born. It came to life not in isolation, however, but in confrontation with a communal vision of human flourishing defended by a reformed-Protestant and parochial agricultural people. And according to their not always articulate understanding, the individual was optimally to be shaped and nurtured within a circle composed of family, congregation, and local community. Yet, with the advent of constitutional government in 1789, America as a polity had been transformed—at least at the level of elite pronouncements and governmental institutions—and a two-

---

[4] Ames, "Dangers of American Liberty" (1805), p. 1330.

century experiment in popularly controlled local communal government began to be eclipsed by a bold new experiment in individualism and representative national government. Thus, by the beginning of the 19th century, there were at least two political visions defining America, each with its own level of government, mores, political economy, and political language: one of traditional American reformed-Protestant communalism and the other of nationalist individualism.[5]

Something like these divisions persisted into the 20th century.[6] Yet during the second half of the century, the sometimes salutary equilibrium that had existed between the increasingly lived communalism of small-town America and the articulate national individualism that was learned by all, and that at times guided elite behavior,[7] was transformed. America's traditional organization as a federal republic with powerful regional cultures impeding the transmission of a unitary national culture was largely replaced by a new, more confident national government, an elite with control over powerful communication tools that made possible national dissemination of their norms, and a concomitant dedication to a new, demanding form of individualism. William Galston, among others, thus contends that it was "during the past generation" that this "longstanding balance between juridical liberal principles and a complex of traditional moral beliefs" was lost.[8]

This 20th-century disruption of the traditional federal balance, however, was a long time in the making. Its roots reach back to the rift the Constitution institutionalized between certain of the elite, with their new national institutions and moderately individualistic political philosophy, and most of the people, who continued to support local political, social, and religious institutions and to understand virtue as being publicly fostered.[9] Nevertheless, it was not until aggressive nationalist public policies were adopted, after both America's entry into World War II and later the imple-

[5]See Wishy, "John Locke," p. 421, who describes the communalistic one as the "rhetoric of populism."

[6]See D. Warren, *Radical Center;* K. Phillips, *Post-Conservative America,* pp. 180–204; Lasch, *True and Only Heaven,* pp. 476–532; and Hunter, *Culture Wars,* p. 63.

[7]The ubiquitous presence of nativism, sexism, racism, and all manner of intolerance at the elite (and the mass) level makes clear just how infrequently individualism actually guided behavior. But the individualist language was available, and throughout American history it has often been used by the oppressed to advance their goals.

[8]Galston, "Public Morality and Religion," p. 807; see also Ceaser, "Alexis de Tocqueville on Political Science," p. 671, who finds that the historic balance between the national elite (those who "spoke for individuals") and the communal rural people (those who "lived for communities") has been lost.

[9]See McWilliams, "Democracy and the Citizen," pp. 95–96; and Lutz, *Popular Consent and Popular Control,* pp. 201–2, who writes that the Revolutionary period (1776–1787) "divides our political history into two bicentennials, each lived under a different political theory . . . [with] two competing political cultures that together constitute the definition of American political thought."

mentation of prominent Supreme Court decisions of the 1950s through the 1970s, that the individualist ethical vision and its adherents finally succeeded in supplanting the popular but often intolerant communalist ethical tradition. The great victory of moving to end, for example, the de facto exclusion of African Americans from full membership in the national polity enhanced the power of nationalists, both morally and legally, to the point where they were finally able to contain the sovereignty of local communities that had often exercised their rights of self-government in such morally repugnant ways. In effect, though, the historic constitutional balance was overthrown along with the welcomed end to lynching, de jure racism and intolerance, and the oppression of millions of Americans.[10]

It is against the background of this transformation that revisionist scholarship appears. But, in this instance, by making articulate the Protestant origins of American political thought and the communalism that for most of the last two centuries was lived but not given voice,[11] and in other instances by drawing attention to the republican character of American thought, this body of scholarship unavoidably alters the terms of the debate concerning America's historical essence. Most importantly, it demonstrates that Americans have more than one tradition of political thought from which to draw; this provides renewed access to authentic alternatives to the language of liberal individualism,[12] such as that of Protestant com-

[10]See Galston, "Public Morality and Religion," p. 813, who argues that "popular culture faithfully represented the white Anglo-Saxon Protestant ethos. And most important, a traditional morality was dominant and effective. Today, this cultural consensus is gone, replaced by pitched battles on numerous fronts. While many forces contributed to the breakdown of consensus, the critical event was, I believe, the civil rights movement. . . . it represented a clear collision between the juridical liberal principles of our polity and the concrete practices of our society"; and Berns, "Government by Lawyers and Judges," p. 19, who finds that "black Americans remained politically isolated, unrepresented" until "the Supreme Court intervened. Unfortunately, the instruments available to and employed by the Court were not well adapted," with the result being that "their use contributed to the deformation of the Constitution."

[11]See W. H. Nelson, *American Tory*, p. 190, who argues that if there was any serious consequence to the silencing and expulsion of the loyalists, it was the loss of "the Tories' organic conservatism [which] represented a current of thought that failed to reappear in America after the Revolution. A substantial part of the whole spectrum of European social and political philosophy seemed to slip outside the American [articulate] perspective."

[12]See Sullivan, *Reconstructing Public Philosophy*, pp. 16–17, who holds that "liberalism can find no way out of the present difficulties except more 'progress'—even when that seems to entail a further breakdown of social solidarity. . . . [Accordingly] the recent 'rediscovery' that the critical period of the American founding was strongly shaped by the tradition of civic republicanism is potentially of great importance." See also Wood, "Hellfire Politics," p. 29, who notes that "the often implicit political message of these discoveries that America was *not* always liberal (in the sense of favoring equal personal rights) or capitalistic or individualistic was that maybe we're not destined to remain what we had become"; and Horton, "African Traditional Thought and Western Science," p. 181, who writes that with "the consciousness that one's own people believed other things at other times we have the germ of a sense of alternatives." See also Bellah et al., *Habits of the Heart*, p. 303.

munalism. All social and political alternatives to liberal individualism can no longer be readily dismissed as "un-American."

But whether, for example, increased recognition of America's Protestant communal origins would effect any change in elite cultural or political norms is hard to judge. Given the complexity of American society and the multilayered insulation that guards cherished myths, it is highly doubtful. And even if revisionist scholarship were able to modify how Americans characterize their founding moment, it is far from evident that an alteration of foundational myths should be welcomed.[13] For although widespread recognition of America's communal foundations might add to a climate of greater political choice,[14] it should also be viewed as potentially divisive in a country that for the past fifty years has prospered in an intellectually monolithic environment. Indeed, the noted economist Joseph Schumpeter found in America that in spite of the vast dislocations wrought by the economic crises of the 1930s, not only "business people but a very large part of the workmen and farmers thought and felt in the terms of the bourgeois order," for, he conceded, they "did not really have a clear conception of any alternative."[15]

Additionally, it is most unclear how, in this case, the communal vision of a rural, Protestant, relatively homogeneous slaveholding people can be usefully adapted to the needs of an increasingly urban and ethnically, racially, and religiously diverse people living in a postindustrial world. Indeed, James Tully's perspective on Locke seems especially apposite here: "the only faithful attitude we can take to the original contribution [of Locke or to the predominant thought of the Revolutionary generation] as a whole is one of nostalgia (unless and until rechristianization succeeds secularization). We can, however, study it as a whole to understand how much of the fragmented ruins of liberty, once held together as a coherent structure, we cling to in desperation today."[16] It may be that the political vision of the late 18th-century Americans is available to be investigated

---

[13]See Lutz, *Preface to American Political Theory*, pp. 156–57, who writes that political theory "threatens to undermine the political myth upon which the political system is built; this is part of the age-old conflict between the polis and political philosophy"; and Strauss, *What Is Political Philosophy*, pp. 221–22, who warns that philosophy dissolves the most basic elements of society, "and thus it endangers society. Hence philosophy or science must remain the preserve of a small minority, and philosophers or scientists must respect the opinions on which society rests." See also McNeill, "Care and Repair of Public Myth," pp. 1, 4; and Burnham, "1980 Earthquake," p. 119.

[14]See Berlin, "Two Concepts of Liberty," p. 120, who argues that "what is certain is that these [political] forces, unless they clothe themselves in ideas, remain blind and undirected"; Appleby, "Republicanism in Old and New Contexts," pp. 30–31, who writes that "it is not uncommon now to read in scholarly works that a group—usually a subordinate one—did not embark on a particular program because its members did not have a language for discussing new goals"; and Rodgers, *Contested Truths*, pp. 10–11.

[15]Schumpeter, *Capitalism, Socialism, and Democracy*, p. 225.

[16]Tully, "Locke on Liberty," p. 78.

and learned from, but because of the changed nature of the contemporary world, it cannot with honesty be made to serve any particular modern political vision. Attempts to provide foundational legitimacy for contemporary political visions may necessarily be quests after useful and pleasing illusions.

It is also far from certain that most Americans, when apprised of the communal nature of their foundational inheritance, would seek to return to something like the communalism of their past. This is especially true of those minority groups who have benefited from the demise of local communalism and a more aggressive national government. It is hard to imagine that their members would look forward to newly legitimated intrusive local communities. John Roche notes that urbanization and the loss of small-town communal life "has been a major factor in the growth of liberty in the United States by bringing about the collapse of that 'natural community' which brings nostalgic tears to the eyes of sociological critics of contemporary culture."[17] African Americans, most importantly, were able to free themselves of onerous political, social, and economic burdens (to say nothing of slavery in the 19th century) only when the national government finally coerced local communities to comply with federal civil rights guarantees. The same could be said for non-Protestant Americans, who might well prefer that America's foundational Protestantism be ignored and that the Revolutionary era continue to be portrayed as secular and enlightened rather than Protestant. Local Protestant communalism, bolstered by a new sense of historical legitimacy, conceivably could again threaten the hard-won gains of various minorities.

Some members of minority racial, ethnic, or religious communities as well as members of the white Christian majority, however, might welcome an America with a more tolerant attitude toward local communal differences,[18] because along with costs, important benefits might result from a renewed balance between localist and national forces, with their often separate visions of human flourishing.[19] And if, as some contend, the quest for and the achievement of a truly human end is by necessity a corporate rather than an individual enterprise, there may be no alternative other than to welcome some variant of a renewed balance between communal and

---

[17]Roche, "Curbing of the Militant Majority," p. 34.

[18]Irving Kristol immediately comes to mind. I mention this prominent man of letters and spokesperson for many American Jews because he has been particularly articulate in defending the benefits of a renewed religiosity in America—in effect, a more Christian America. He apparently has come to the conclusion that the costs of increasing secularization are far higher than those associated with a more Christian country in which Jews may be at some disadvantage. See also Hunter, *Culture Wars*, pp. 16–17.

[19]Some of the benefits often associated with communal life are: the provision of a clear sense of personal limits; integration into a tradition of social solidarity and fraternity; encouragement in embracing charitable alternatives to selfishness, self-indulgence, and crass materialism; and ready access to concrete extrapersonal moral direction.

individualist aspirations. Indeed, some theorists have argued that the deformations of the ethical human being associated with modern size and organization are so deeply antithetical to morality that if human development is to be facilitated, if spiritual desiccation is to be avoided, local communalism must be encouraged and its risks accepted.[20] The record of America's communal past, although unable to decide or even shape these increasingly contentious debates,[21] does add to them by making communalism an authentically American vision of human flourishing.

Whatever the unpredictable political and cultural costs and benefits that could accrue from Americans coming to terms with the communal (either republican or Protestant) origins of their political thought, there are certain immediate intellectual benefits to be gained from doing so. In particular, broadening political scientists' and historians' understanding of American political thought and practices in the 19th and 20th centuries will have heuristic value. Freed from the perspective of an enduring and ubiquitous individualism, they will be relieved from having to describe so much of American history as pathological or mysteriously anomalous.[22] A theory such as that of a uniquely individualistic America, which explains so little history, from chattel slavery to patriotism, stands greatly in need of augmentation. The Protestant communalism of the Revolutionary era, especially when shown to have survived in later centuries,[23] will be able to go a long way toward effecting such repairs.

Let me close, however, by noting that the value of what I have shown in the preceding chapters is not dependent on its intellectual, social, or political utility. Americans in the Revolutionary era embraced a theory of the good that is best described as reformed Protestant and communal. Whether this theory was one of several dominant theories or, as argued here, was the primary soil in which American political thought grew should be revealed by scholarly debate during the next few decades. That many Americans wrote and spoke as if they thought in communal ways and were shaped by reformed-Protestant norms, though, must now be be-

[20]See Walzer, "Liberalism and Art of Separation," p. 328, who recognizes, with some equivocation, that with democracy comes the "unavoidable risk" of minority or individual oppression. Less equivocal on the need for communal structures to facilitate human flourishing are C. Taylor, "What's Wrong with Negative Liberty," p. 193; MacIntyre, "Is Patriotism a Virtue?"; Yankelovich, *New Rules*, pp. 53–54, 59; Lasch, *True and Only Heaven*, pp. 13–17; and the most widely acclaimed, Bellah et al., *Habits of the Heart*, pp. 8, 21, 81.

[21]Contemporary communitarians and their critics have debated the known and likely benefits and costs of increased American communalism. For critical reviews of the literature, see Kymlicka, *Liberalism, Community, and Culture;* and K. P. Phillips, *Looking Backward;* and for their collected essays, see Reynolds and Norman, *Community in America;* and Avineri and de-Shalit, *Communitarianism and Individualism.*

[22]The literature here is voluminous, but for an introduction, see Lipset and Raab, *Politics of Unreason;* and Hofstadter, *Paranoid Style in American Politics;* cf. Lasch, *True and Only Heaven,* pp. 460–68.

[23]See R. M. Smith, "Beyond Tocqueville, Myrdal, and Hartz," p. 550.

yond debate. This finding may be a cause for a distanced appreciation of what was and no longer is, or for celebration of renewed possibilities of what might be. In this instance, however, understanding does not demand agreement. Scholarly recognition of America's communal past does not demand or preclude a normative commitment to it.

• B I B L I O G R A P H Y •

Primary Sources

The following collections have been listed by their short titles in the bibliography below:

Bailyn, Bernard, and Jane N. Garrett, eds. *Pamphlets of the American Revolution, 1750–1765.* Vol. 1. Cambridge: Harvard Univ. Press, 1965. Fourteen pamphlets are included. Cited as *Pamphlets of the American Revolution.*

Ford, Paul L., ed. *Pamphlets on the Constitution of the United States Published during Its Discussion by the People, 1787–1788.* 1888. Reprint, New York: Burt Franklin, 1971. Fourteen pamphlets are included. Cited as *Pamphlets on the Constitution.*

———. *Essays on the Constitution of the United States Published during Its Discussion by the People, 1787–1788.* 1892. Reprint, New York: Burt Franklin, 1970. Seventeen series of essays are included. Cited as *Essays on the Constitution.*

Hyneman, Charles S., and Donald S. Lutz, eds. *American Political Writing during the Founding Era, 1760–1805.* 2 vols. Indianapolis: Liberty Press, 1983. Seventy-six pamphlets, essays, and sermons are included. Cited as *American Political Writing.*

Jensen, Merrill, ed. *Tracts of the American Revolution: 1763–1776.* Indianapolis: Bobbs-Merrill, 1967. Seventeen pamphlets are included. Cited as *Tracts of the American Revolution.*

Moore, Frank, ed. *The Patriot Preachers of the American Revolution, 1776–1783.* New York: n.p., 1860. Thirteen sermons are included. Cited as *Patriot Preachers.*

Sandoz, Ellis, ed. *Political Sermons of the American Founding Era, 1730–1805.* Indianapolis: Liberty Press, 1991. Fifty-five sermons are included. Cited as *Political Sermons.*

Storing, Herbert J., ed. *The Anti-Federalist.* Selected by Murray Dry. Chicago: Univ. of Chicago Press, 1985. Nine sets of essays are included. Cited as *Anti-Federalist.*

Thornton, John Wingate, ed. *The Pulpit of the American Revolution; or, The Political Sermons of the Period of 1776.* Boston: Gould and Lincoln, 1860. Nine sermons are included. Cited as *Pulpit of the American Revolution.*

Books and Articles

Adams, Amos. *Religious Liberty an Invaluable Blessing.* Boston: Kneeland and Adams, 1768.

Adams, John. *A Defence of the Constitutions of Government of the United States of America.* 3 vols. 1788. Reprint, New York: Da Capo Press, 1971.

———. *Works of John Adams, Second President of the United States.* Ed. Charles Francis Adams. Boston: Charles Little and James Brown, 1851–1865.

———. *The Political Writings of John Adams: Representative Selections.* Ed. George A. Peek, Jr. Indianapolis: Bobbs-Merrill, 1954.

Adams, John, and Abigail Adams. *Adams Family Correspondence.* Ed. L. H. Butterfield. 2 vols. Cambridge: Harvard Univ. Press, 1963.

Adams, John, and Benjamin Rush. *The Spur of Fame: Dialogues of John Adams and Benjamin Rush, 1805–1813.* Ed. John A. Schutz and Douglass Adair. San Marino, Calif.: Huntington Library, 1980.

Adams, John, Samuel Adams, and James Warren. *Warren-Adams Letters.* Ed. W. C. Ford. 2 vols. Boston: Massachusetts Historical Society, 1917.

Adams, John, and Thomas Jefferson. *The Adams-Jefferson Letters: The Complete Correspondence between Thomas Jefferson and Abigail and John Adams.* Ed. Lester J. Cappon. 2 vols. 1959. Reprint (2 vols. in 1), Chapel Hill: Univ. of North Carolina Press, 1987.

Adams, Samuel. *Boston Gazette and Country Journal,* 19 December 1768.

———. *Writings of Samuel Adams.* Ed. Harry A. Cushing. 4 vols. 1906. Reprint, New York: Octagon Books, 1968.

[Adams, Samuel?]. "A State of the Rights of the Colonists." In *Tracts of the American Revolution,* pp. 233–55.

Adams, Zabdiel. "Massachusetts Election Sermon." In *American Political Writing,* pp. 539–64.

Addison, Joseph. "Cato: A Tragedy." In *The Works of Joseph Addison,* ed. Richard Hurd, pp. 172–227. London: George Bell and Sons, 1903.

Addison, Joseph, and Richard Steele. *The Spectator.* London: S. Buckley, 1712.

Aequus. "From the Craftsmen." In *American Political Writing,* pp. 62–67.

Agrippa. "Letters of Agrippa, I–XI." In *Anti-Federalist,* pp. 227–53.

Alison, Hugh. *Spiritual Liberty: A Sermon.* Charleston, S.C.: Hugh Alison, 1769.

[Allen, John]. *The American Alarm . . . for the Rights, and Liberties, of the People.* Boston: D. Kneeland and N. Davis, 1773.

———. *An Oration, Upon the Beauties of Liberty; or, The Essential Rights of the Americans.* 3d ed. New London: Timothy Green, 1773.

———. *The Watchman's Alarm to Lord N——h.* Salem, [Mass.?]: E. Russell, 1774.

Ames, Fisher. "The Dangers of American Liberty." In *American Political Writing,* pp. 1299–1348.

Ancient and Modern Liberty Stated and Compar'd. London: J. Roberts, 1734.

Aristotle. *The Politics.* Ed. and trans. Ernest Barker. New York: Oxford Univ. Press, 1962.

Ash, John, ed. *New and Complete Dictionary of the English Language.* 2 vols. London: E. and C. Dilly, 1775.

Atwater, Jeremiah. "Vermont Election Sermon." In *American Political Writing,* pp. 1170–88.

Backus, Isaac. *Government and Liberty Described.* Boston: Powars and Willis, 1778.

Bailey, Nathan, ed. *Universal Etymological English Dictionary.* 3d ed. London: Thomas Cox, 1737.

Bancroft, Aaron. *Massachusetts Election Sermon.* Boston: Young and Minns, 1801.

Barnard, John. "The Throne Established." In *The Wall and the Garden: Selected Massachusetts Election Sermons, 1670–1775,* ed. A. W. Plumstead, pp. 223–82. Minneapolis: Univ. of Minnesota Press, 1968.

Belknap, Jeremy. *An Election Sermon Preached before the General Court of New-Hampshire.* Portsmouth, N.H.: Melcher and Osborne, 1785.

Bell, Robert, comp. *Illuminations for Legislators, and for Sentimentalists.* London: Robert Bell, 1784.

Bellamy, Joseph. *The Works of Joseph Bellamy.* Ed. Tyron Edwards. 2 vols. Boston: Doctrinal Tract and Book Society, 1853.

Benzet, Anthony. *Observations on the Inslaving, Importing, and Purchasing of Negroes.* Germantown, Penn.: Christopher Sowen, 1759.

———. *Some Historical Accounts of Guinea. With An Inquiry into the Rise and Progress of the Slave Trade.* Philadelphia: Joseph Crukshank, 1771.

Berkshire County Representatives. "Statement." In *The Popular Sources of Political Authority: Documents on the Massachusetts Constitution of 1780,* ed. Oscar Handlin and Mary Handlin, pp. 374–79. Cambridge: Harvard Univ. Press, 1966.

Blacklock, Thomas. *Remarks on the Nature and Extent of Liberty, as Compatible with the Genius of Civil Societies.* Edinburgh: W. Creech and T. Cadell, 1776.

Blackstone, William. *Commentaries on the Laws of England: A Facsimile of the First Edition of 1765–1769.* 4 vols. Chicago: Univ. of Chicago Press, 1979.

Bland, Richard. "An Inquiry into the Rights of the British Colonies." In *Tracts of the American Revolution,* pp. 108–26.

Bolingbroke, Lord. "The Idea of a Patriot King." In *The Works of Lord Bolingbroke in Four Volumes,* 2:372–429. Philadelphia: Carey and Hart, 1841.

———. *Viscount Bolingbroke: Political Writings.* Ed. Isaac Kramnick. New York: Appleton-Century-Crofts, 1970.

Boucher, Jonathan. "On Civil Liberty, Passive Obedience, and Non-resistance." In *A View of the Causes and Consequences of the American Revolution: In Thirteen Discourses, 1763–1775,* pp. 495–560. 1797. Reprint, New York: Russell and Russell, 1967.

———. "The Dispute Between the Israelites and the Two Tribes and An Half." In *A View of the Causes and Consequences of the American Revolution: In Thirteen Disourses, 1763–1775,* pp. 450–94. Reprint, New York: Russell and Russell, 1967.

[Boucher, Jonathan]. *A Letter From a Virginian to the Members of the Congress.* Boston: Mills and Hicks, 1774.

Bradbury, Thomas. "The Ass, or, The Serpent: A Comparison Between the Tribes of Issachar and Dan, in Their Regard for Civil Liberty." In *American Political Writing,* pp. 240–56.

[Braxton, Carter]. "An Address to the Convention of the Colony and Ancient Dominion of Virginia." In *American Political Writing,* pp. 328–39.

[Brooke, Henry?]. *Liberty and Common-Sense to the People of Ireland, Greeting.* 1759. Reprint, London: J. William, 1760.

Brown, John. *Thoughts on Civil Liberty, on Licentiousness, and Faction.* London: J. White and T. Saint, 1765.

Brutus. "Essays I–XVI." In *Anti-Federalist,* pp. 103–98.

Bulkeley, Peter and John Cotton. "On Union with Christ." In *The Antinomian Controversy, 1636–1638: A Documentary History,* ed. David D. Hall, pp. 34–42. 2d ed. Durham, N.C.: Duke Univ. Press, 1990.

Burke, Edmund. *On the American Revolution: Selected Speeches and Letters.* Ed. Elliott R. Barkan. New York: Harper and Row, 1966.

———. *The Correspondence of Edmund Burke.* Ed. Alfred Cobban and Robert A. Smith. Chicago: Univ. of Chicago Press, 1967.

———. *Reflections on the Revolution in France.* Ed. J. G. A. Pocock. Indianapolis: Hackett, 1987.

332 • *BIBLIOGRAPHY* •

Burlamaqui, Jean Jacques. *The Principles of Natural and Politic Law in Two Volumes.* Trans. Mr. Nugent. 2d ed. London: J. Nourse, 1763.

Burnaby, Andrew. *Travels Through the Middle Settlements in North America in the Years 1759 and 1760.* 1775. Reprint, New York: Augustus M. Kelley, 1970.

Calvin, John. *Institutes of the Christian Religion.* Trans. John Allen. 2 vols. 6th American ed. Philadelphia: Presbyterian Board of Publication, 1813.

———. *Institutes of the Christian Religion.* Trans. Henry Beveridge. 1845. 2 vols. Reprint, Grand Rapids: Wm. B. Eerdmans, 1983.

Care, Henry. *English Liberties; or, The Free-Born Subject's Inheritance.* 6th ed. Providence, R.I.: J. Carter, 1774.

Carey, Mathew, ed. *The American Museum; or, Repository of Ancient and Modern Fugitive Pieces, Prose and Poetical.* 12 vols. Philadelphia: Carey, Stewart, 1787–1792.

Champion, Judah. *Christian and Civil Liberty and Freedom Considered and Recommended.* Hartford: E. Watson, 1776.

Chase, Samuel. "Charge to Grand Jury." In *Documents of American Constitutional and Legal History,* ed. Melvin I. Urofsky, 1:192–94. New York: Knopf, 1989.

Chevalier, Michael. *Society Manners and Politics in the United States.* 1839. Reprint, New York: Augustus M. Kelley, 1966.

Chew, Samuel. *The Speech of Samuel Chew, Esq. . . . Delivered from the Bench to the Grand Jury of the County of New-Castle.* Philadelphia: Ben Franklin, 1742.

Chipman, Nathaniel. *Sketches of the Principles of Government.* Rutland, Vt.: J. Lyon, 1793.

Church, Benjamin. "An Oration Delivered March Fifth, 1773." In *Principles and Acts of the Revolution in America,* ed. Hezekiah Niles, pp. 34–37. Baltimore: William Ogden Niles, 1822.

Civil Liberty Asserted and the Rights of the Subject Defended Against the Anarchical Principles of the Reverend Dr. Price. London: J. Wilkie, 1776.

Clap, Thomas. *An Essay on the Nature and Foundation of Moral Virtue and Obligation: Being a Short Introduction to the Study of Ethics; For the Use of the Students of Yale-College.* New Haven: B. Mecom, 1765.

Clark, Jonas. *Massachusetts Election Sermon.* Boston: J. Gill and S. Edes, 1781.

Clinton, George. "The Letters of 'Cato.'" In *Essays on the Constitution,* pp. 241–78.

Cole, Franklin P., ed. *They Preached Liberty.* 1941. Reprint, Indianapolis: Liberty Press, n.d.

Coles, C., ed. *English Dictionary.* London: F. Collins, 1713.

Colman, Benjamin. *Government the Pillar of the Earth.* Boston: T. Hancock, 1730.

Congress, Continental. *Journals of the Continental Congress, 1774–1789.* Washington, D.C.: Government Printing Office, 1905.

———. "Appeal to the Inhabitants of Quebec." In *American Political Writing,* pp. 231–39.

Congress, Stamp Act. "Declaration of the Rights of the Colonists of America." *American Museum* 3 (1788): 580–81.

———. "Petition to the British House of Commons." *American Museum* 4 (July 1788): 89–91.

Considerations upon the Rights of the Colonists to the Privileges of British

Subjects. New York: John Holt, 1766.

Constant, Benjamin. "The Liberty of the Ancients Compared with that of the Moderns." In *Political Writings*, trans. and ed. Biancamaria Fontana, pp. 307–28. Cambridge Univ. Press, 1988.

[Cooper, David]. *A Mite Cast into the Treasury; or, Observations on Slave-Keeping*. Philadelphia, 1772.

———. *A Serious Address to the Rulers of America, on the Inconsistency of Their Conduct Respecting Slavery: Forming a Contrast Between the Encroachment of England on American Liberty, And, American Injustice in Tolerating Slavery*. Trenton: Isaac Collins, 1783.

Cooper, Myles. *A Friendly Address to All Reasonable Americans, on the Subject of Our Political Confusions*. New York: [J. Rivington], 1774.

Cooper, Samuel. *A Sermon Preached Before His Excellency John Hancock, Esq.* Boston: T. and J. Fleet and J. Gill, 1780.

Cotton, John. "Mr. Cotton's Rejoynder." In *The Antinomian Controversy, 1636–1638: A Documentary History*, ed. David D. Hall, pp. 78–151. 2d ed. Durham, N.C.: Duke Univ. Press, 1990.

Crèvecoeur, J. Hector St. John de. *Letters from an American Farmer*. 1782. Reprint, New York: E. P. Dutton, 1957.

Cumings, Henry. *Massachusetts Election Sermon*. Boston: T. and J. Fleet, 1783.

———. *A Thanksgiving Sermon Preached in Billerica*. Boston: T. and J. Fleet, 1784.

Daggett, David. "Sunbeams May Be Extracted from Cucumbers, But the Process Is Tedious: An Oration Pronounced on the Fourth of July, 1799." In *American Forum: Speeches on Historic Issues, 1788–1900*, ed. Ernest J. Wrage and Barnet Baskerville, pp. 37–49. New York: Harper and Brothers, 1960.

Davidson, Robert. *An Oration on the Independence of the United States of America Delivered on the 4th of July, 1787*. Carlisle, Pa.: Kline and Reynolds, [1787].

Davies, Samuel. *Religion and Public Spirit: A Valedictory Address to the Senior Class*. New York: James Parker, 1761.

Demophilus [George Bryan?]. "The Genuine Principles of the Ancient Saxon, or English Constitution." In *American Political Writing*, pp. 340–67.

Dickinson, John. "Resolutions of Stamp Act Congress." In *Political Writings of John Dickinson, 1764–1774*, ed. Paul L. Ford, pp. 183–87. 1895. Reprint, New York: Da Capo Press, 1970.

[Dickinson, John]. "Friends and Countrymen." Broadside. Philadelphia: n.p., 1765.

———. "Letters of Fabius on the Federal Constitution." In *Pamphlets on the Constitution*, pp. 163–216.

———. "Letters of a Farmer in Pennsylvania." In *The Political Writings of John Dickinson, 1764–1774*, ed. Paul L. Ford, pp. 277–406. 1895. Reprint, New York: Da Capo Press, 1970.

"The Dignity and Manners of Man." *American Museum* 11 (June 1792): 274–75.

Dilly, Edward, and Charles Dilly, comps. *British Liberties; or, The Free-Born Subject's Inheritance . . . Also An Introductory Essay on Political Liberty*. London: H. Woodfall and W. Straham, 1766.

———, eds. *Encyclopedia Britannica: or, A Dictionary of Arts and Sciences*. 3 vols. London: E. and C. Dilly, 1773.

Dorr, Edward. *The Duty of Civil Rulers*. Hartford: Thomas Green, [1765].

[Downer, Silas]. "A Discourse at the Dedication of the Tree of Liberty." In *American Political Writing*, pp. 97–108.

Duché, Jacob. "The Duty of Standing Fast in Our Spiritual and Temporal Liberties." In *Patriot Preachers*, pp. 74–89.

Dulany, Daniel. "Considerations on the Propriety of Imposing Taxes in the British Colonies." In *Tracts of the American Revolution*, pp. 94–107.

Dwight, Timothy. *The True Means of Establishing Public Happiness*. New Haven: T. and S. Green, 1795.

Dyche, Thomas, and William Pardon, eds. *A New General English Dictionary*. 7th ed. London: Richard Ware, 1752; 17th ed. London: T. Longman: 1794.

Eliot, Andrew. *Massachusetts Election Sermon*. Boston: Green and Russell, 1765.

Elliot, Jonathan, ed. *The Debates in the Several State Conventions, on the Adoption of the Federal Constitution*. 5 vols. 2d ed. 1836. Reprint, Philadelphia: J. B. Lippincott, 1941.

[Ellsworth, Oliver]. "The Letters of a Landholder." In *Essays on the Constitution*, pp. 135–201.

Emerson, Joseph. *A Thanksgiving Sermon Preached at Pepperrell*. Boston: Edes and Gill, 1766.

Emerson, William. "Fourth of July Oration, 1802." In *Old South Leaflets*, 6:185–200. Boston: Directors of the Old South Work.

Emmons, Nathaniel. *A Discourse Delivered on the Annual Fast in Massachusetts*. Reprint, Hartford: Hudson and Goodwin, 1801.

Evans, Charles. *American Bibliography: A Chronological Dictionary of All Books, Pamphlets, and Periodical Publications Printed in the United States of America, 1639–1800*. 14 vols. Chicago: C. Evans, 1903–1959.

Everett, Edward. "The History of Liberty." In *Orations and Speeches on Various Occasions*, 1:150–72. Boston: Charles Little and James Brown, 1850.

Farmer. "Essays by A Farmer, I–VII." In *The Complete Anti-Federalist*, ed. Herbert J. Storing, 5:9–73. Chicago: Univ. of Chicago Press, 1981.

———. "Essay V." In *Anti-Federalist*, pp. 257–72.

Farrand, Max, ed. *The Records of the Federal Convention of 1787*. 4 vols. Revised ed. New Haven: Yale Univ. Press, 1937.

Federal Farmer. "Letters I–VII and XVI–XVII." In *Anti-Federalist*, pp. 23–102.

Fellow Citizen. *The Political Establishment of the United States of America. In a Candid Review of Their Deficiencies*. Philadelphia: Robert Bell, 1784.

Fenning, D., ed. *The Royal English Dictionary; or, A Treasury of the English Language*. London: L. Hawes et al., 1775.

Fobes, Peres [Perez]. "An Election Sermon." In *American Political Writing*, pp. 990–1013.

Foner, Philip S., ed. *The Life and Major Writings of Thomas Paine*. Secaucus, N.J.: Citadel Press, 1948.

Force, Peter, ed. "Resolutions of New-York Committee [of Safety] on 16 May 1776." In *American Archives*, 4th ser., 6:478–79. Washington, D.C.: M. St. Clair Clarke and Peter Force, 1839.

———. "Resolutions of Worcester County Committee on 7 June 1775." In *American Archives*, 4th ser., 2:924. Washington, D.C.: M. St. Clair Clarke and Peter Force, 1839.

Foster, Daniel. *Massachusetts Election Sermon*. Boston: Thomas Adams, 1790.

Franklin, Benjamin. *The Political Thought of Benjamin Franklin.* Ed. Ralph Ketcham. Indianapolis: Bobbs-Merrill, 1965.

———. *The Autobiography and Other Writings.* Ed. Peter Shaw. New York: Bantam Books, 1982.

Galloway, Joseph. "A Candid Examination of the Mutual Claims of Great Britain, And the Colonies: With a Plan of Accommodation on Constitutional Principles." In *Tracts of the American Revolution,* pp. 350–99.

Gerry, Elbridge. "Observations on the New Constitution, and on the Federal and State Conventions." In *Pamphlets on the Constitution,* pp. 1–24.

[Goddard, William?]. "The Constitutional Courant: Containing Matters Interesting to Liberty, and No Wise Repugnant to Loyalty." In *Tracts of the American Revolution,* pp. 79–93.

Gordon, William. "A Discourse Preached December 15th, 1774." In *Pulpit of the American Revolution,* pp. 187–226.

Green, Jacob. *A Sermon Delivered at Hanover, (in New-Jersey) April 22d, 1778.* Chatham, N.J.: Shepard Kollock, 1779.

Grund, Francis J. *The Americans in Their Moral, Social, and Political Relations.* 2 vols. 1837. Reprint (2 vols. in 1), New York: Johnson Reprint, 1968.

Hale, Benjamin. *Liberty and Law: A Lecture.* Geneva, N.Y.: Ira Merrell, 1838.

Hall, Samuel. *The Legislature's Right, Charge and Duty in respect of Religion.* New London: Timothy Green, 1746.

Hamden. "On Patriotism." *South Carolina Gazette,* 29 November 1773.

Hamilton, Alexander. "The Farmer Refuted." In *The Papers of Alexander Hamilton,* ed. Harold C. Syrett, 1:81–165. New York: Columbia Univ. Press, 1961.

———. "A Full Vindication of the Measures of the Congress." In *The Papers of Alexander Hamilton,* ed. Harold C. Syrett, 1:45–79. New York: Columbia Univ. Press, 1961.

———. "The Continentalist Papers." In *Selected Writings and Speeches of Alexander Hamilton,* ed. Morton J. Frisch, pp. 40–65. Washington, D.C.: American Enterprise Institute, 1985.

———. "Remarks and Speeches at the New York Ratifying Convention." In *Selected Writings and Speeches of Alexander Hamilton,* ed. Morton J. Frisch, pp. 196–245. Washington, D.C.: American Enterprise Institute, 1985.

———. "Second Letter from Phocion." In *Selected Writings and Speeches of Alexander Hamilton,* ed. Morton J. Frisch, pp. 66–88. Washington, D.C.: American Enterprise Institute, 1985.

———. "Views on the French Revolution." In *Selected Writings and Speeches of Alexander Hamilton,* ed. Morton J. Frisch, pp. 413–16. Washington, D.C.: American Enterprise Institute, 1985.

Hamilton, Alexander, John Jay, and James Madison. *The Federalist: A Commentary on the Constitution of the United States.* Ed. Edward Mead Earle. Indianapolis: Modern Library, 1937.

Handlin, Oscar, and Mary Handlin, eds. *The Popular Sources of Political Authority: Documents on the Massachusetts Constitution of 1780.* Cambridge: Harvard Univ. Press, 1966.

Harrington, James. "The Commonwealth of Oceana." In *The Political Works of James Harrington,* ed. J. G. A. Pocock. Cambridge: Cambridge Univ. Press, 1977.

Hart, Levi. "Liberty Described and Recommended." In *American Political Writing,* pp. 305–17.

Hart, Oliver. "Dancing Exploded." In *Patriot Preachers*, pp. 232–57.

Haynes, Lemuel. "The Influence of Civil Government on Religion." In *Black Preacher to White America: The Collected Writings of Lemuel Haynes, 1774–1833*, ed. Richard Newman, pp. 65–76. Brooklyn: Carlson Publishing, 1990.

———. "Liberty Further Extended." In *Black Preacher to White America: The Collected Writings of Lemuel Haynes, 1774–1833*, ed. Richard Newman, pp. 17–30. Brooklyn: Carlson Publishing, 1990.

———. "The Nature and Importance of True Republicanism." In *Black Preacher to White America: The Collected Writings of Lemuel Haynes, 1774–1833*, ed. Richard Newman, pp. 77–88. Brooklyn: Carlson Publishing, 1990.

Hemmenway, Moses. *Massachusetts Election Sermon*. Boston: Benjamin Edes and Sons, 1784.

Henry, Patrick. "Speech Against the Federal Constitution." In *American Forum: Speeches on Historic Issues, 1788–1900*, ed. Ernest J. Wrage and Barnet Baskerville, pp. 7–22. New York: Harper and Brothers, 1960.

———. "Speeches in the Virginia State Ratifying Convention." In *Anti-Federalist*, pp. 293–328.

[Hervey, John]. *Ancient and Modern Liberty Stated and Compared*. London: J. Roberts, 1734.

Hey, Richard. *Observations on the Nature of Civil Liberty and the Principles of Government*. London: T. Cadell, 1776.

Hichborn, Benjamin. "Oration, March 5th, 1777." In *Principles and Acts of the Revolution in America*, ed. Hezekiah Niles, pp. 46–51. Baltimore: William Ogden Niles, 1822.

Hicks, William. "The Nature and Extent of Parliamentary Power Considered." In *Tracts of the American Revolution*, pp. 164–84.

Hieronymous. *Boston Gazette*, 18 January 1779.

Hobbes, Thomas. *Leviathan*. Ed. C. B. MacPherson. Baltimore: Penguin Books, 1968.

[Hopkins, Samuel]. *A Dialogue Concerning the Slavery of Africans*. Norwich, Conn.: Judah P. Spooner, 1776.

Hopkins, Stephen. "The Rights of Colonies Examined." In *Tracts of the American Revolution*, pp. 41–62. Also reprinted in *American Political Writing*, pp. 45–61.

Howard, Martin, Jr. "A Letter from a Gentleman at Halifax to His Friend in Rhode Island." In *Tracts of the American Revolution*, pp. 63–78.

Howard, Simeon. "Massachusetts Election Sermon." In *Pulpit of the American Revolution*, pp. 355–98.

———. "A Sermon Preached to the Ancient and Honorable Artillery Company in Boston." In *American Political Writing*, pp. 195–208.

Hume, David. *The Letters of David Hume*. Ed. J. Y. T. Greig. 2 vols. Oxford: Oxford Univ. Press. 1932.

———. *An Enquiry Concerning Human Understanding*. Indianapolis: Hackett, 1977.

———. *Essays: Moral, Political, and Literary*. Ed. Eugene F. Miller. Indianapolis: Liberty Press, 1985.

Huntington, Joseph. *A Discourse, Adapted to the Present Day, On The Health and Happiness or Misery and Ruin, of the Body Politic*. Hartford: Hudson and Goodwin, 1781.

Hurt, John. "The Love of Country." In *Patriot Preachers*, pp. 143–57.

Jacobson, David L., ed. *The English Libertarian Heritage*. Indianapolis: Bobbs-Merrill, 1965.

Jefferson, Thomas. *The Writings of Thomas Jefferson*. Ed. H. A. Washington. 9 vols. Washington, D.C.: Taylor and Maury, 1854.

———. *The Writings of Thomas Jefferson*. Ed. Paul L. Ford. 10 vols. New York: G. P. Putnam's Sons, 1892–1896.

———. *The Papers of Thomas Jefferson*. Ed. Julian P. Boyd, C. Cullen, and J. Catanzariti. 25 vols. to date. Princeton: Princeton Univ. Press, 1950–.

———. *The Political Writings of Thomas Jefferson: Representative Selections*. Ed. E. Dumbauld. New York: Liberal Arts Press, 1955.

———. *Notes on the State of Virginia*. New York: Harper and Row, 1964.

———. "A Summary View of the Rights of British America." In *Tracts of the American Revolution*, pp. 256–76.

———. *The Portable Thomas Jefferson*. Ed. Merrill D. Peterson. New York: Penguin Books, 1975.

———. *Writings*. Ed. Merrill D. Peterson. New York: Library of America, 1984.

Johnson, Samuel, ed. *A Dictionary of the English Language*. 3d ed. London: A. Millar, 1766.

Johnson, Stephen. *Integrity and Piety the Best Principles of a Good Administration of Government*. New London: Timothy Green, 1770.

———. "*New London Gazette* Articles, 1765." Appended to "Religion and Revolution: Three Biographical Studies," by Bernard Bailyn. *Perspectives in American History* 4 (1970): 173–98.

[Johnson, Stephen]. *Some Important Observations, Occasioned by . . . the Public Fast*. Newport, RI: Samuel Hall, 1766.

Kant, Immanuel. *The Metaphysical Elements of Justice: Part I of the Metaphysics of Morals*. Trans. John Ladd. New York: Macmillan, 1965.

———. "Idea for a Universal History with a Cosmopolitan Purpose." In *Kant's Political Writings*, ed. Hans Reiss, pp. 41–53. Cambridge: Cambridge Univ. Press, 1970.

———. "The Metaphysics of Morals." In *Kant's Political Writings*, ed. Hans Reiss, pp. 131–75. Cambridge: Cambridge Univ. Press, 1970.

———. "Perpetual Peace: A Philosophical Sketch." In *Kant's Political Writings*, ed. Hans Reiss, pp. 93–130. Cambridge: Cambridge Univ. Press, 1970.

Kendall, Samuel. "Religion the Only Sure Basis of Free Government." In *American Political Writing*, pp. 1241–63.

Kersey, John, ed. *Dictionarium Anglo-Britannicum; or, A General English Dictionary*. London: J. Wilde, 1708.

Kramer, Lloyd S., ed. *Paine and Jefferson on Liberty*. New York: Continuum, 1988.

Langdon, Samuel. "Government Corrupted by Vice, and Recovered by Righteousness: A Sermon." In *Pulpit of the American Revolution*, pp. 227–58. Also reprinted in *Puritan Political Ideas, 1558–1794*, ed. Edmund Morgan. Indianapolis: Bobbs-Merrill, 1965.

Lathrop, Joseph. "A Miscellaneous Collection of Original Pieces." In *American Political Writing*, pp. 658–74.

[Lathrop, Joseph]. "The Reformer: Numbers I–III." *American Museum* 6 (July 1789): 54–55; 6 (October 1789): 269–71.

———. "The Politician: Numbers I–IV." *American Museum* 6 (December 1789): 442–50.

[Lee, Arthur]. *An Essay in Vindication of the Continental Colonies of America.* London: T. Becket and P. A. DeHowdt, 1764.

———. *Liberty: Civil and Religious.* London: J. Hatchard, 1815.

Licentiousness Unmask'd: or, Liberty Explained. [In Answer to Dr. Price's Pamphlet Upon the Nature of Civil Liberty]. London: J. Bew, [1776].

Lincoln, Abraham. *The Collected Works of Abraham Lincoln.* Ed. Roy P. Basler. New Brunswick, N.J.: Rutgers Univ. Press, 1953.

Livingston, William, et al. *The Independent Reflector: or, Weekly Essays on Sundry Important Subjects More Particularly Adapted to the Province of New York.* Ed. Milton M. Klein. Cambridge: Harvard Univ. Press, 1963.

Locke, John. *Treatise of Civil Government and A Letter Concerning Toleration.* 1937. Reprint, New York: Irvington, 1979.

"Locke's Definition of Liberty." *Pennsylvania Chronicle and Universal Advertiser,* 26 August–2 September 1771.

Lockwood, James. *The Worth and Excellence of Civil Freedom and Liberty Illustrated, and a Public Spirit and the Love of Our Country Recommended.* New London: Timothy Green, 1759.

Lolme, J. L. de. *The Constitution of England; or, An Account of the English Government.* London: T. Spilsbury, 1775.

Luther, Martin. *Martin Luther: Selections from His Writings.* Ed. John Dillenberger. Garden City, N.Y.: Doubleday, 1961.

Lyman, Joseph. *A Sermon.* Boston: Adams and Nourse, 1787.

Machiavelli, Niccolo. "The Discourses." In *The Portable Machiavelli,* trans. and ed. Peter Bondanella and Mark Musa, pp. 167–418. New York: Penguin Books, 1979.

Madison, James. "Speech before the Virginia Ratifying Convention." In *American Forum: Speeches on Historic Issues, 1788–1900,* ed. Ernest J. Wrage and Barnet Baskerville, pp. 23–32. New York: Harper and Brothers, 1960.

———. *The Papers of James Madison.* Ed. Robert A. Rutland et al. 14 vols. to date. Chicago: Univ. of Chicago Press, 1962–.

———. *The Mind of the Founder: Sources of the Political Thought of James Madison.* Ed. Marvin Meyers. New York: Irvington, 1973.

Manning, William. *The Key of Libberty.* Ed. Samuel Eliot Morison. Billerica, Mass.: Manning Association, 1922.

Marshall, John. "Barron v. Baltimore." In *Major Opinions and Other Writings,* ed. John P. Roche, pp. 305–11. Indianapolis: Bobbs-Merrill, 1967.

Martin, Thomas S. "The Long and the Short of It: A Newspaper Exchange on the Massachusetts Charters, 1772." *William and Mary Quarterly* 43 (January 1986): 99–110.

[Mason, John Mitchell]. *The Voice of Warning, to Christians, on the Ensuing Election of a President of the United States.* New York: G. F. Hopkins, 1800.

Maxcy, Jonathan. "An Oration." In *American Political Writing,* pp. 1042–54.

Mayhew, Jonathan. "A Discourse Concerning Unlimited Submission and Non-Resistance to Higher Powers." In *Pamphlets of the American Revolution,* pp. 204–47.

———. "Memorandum on 25 August 1765 Sermon." Appended to "Religion and Revolution: Three Biographical Studies," by Bernard Bailyn. *Perspectives in American History* 4 (1970): 140–43.

———. "The Snare Broken." In *Political Sermons,* pp. 231–64.

Mazzei, Philip. *Philip Mazzei: Selected Writings and Correspondence*. Ed. Margherita Marchione. Prato: Edizioni Del Palazzo, 1983.

Mellen, John. *The Great and Happy Doctrine of Liberty*. Boston: Samuel Hall, 1795.

Mill, John Stuart. "On Liberty." In *Utilitarianism and Other Writings*, pp. 126–250. New York: New American Library, 1974.

Miller, Perry, and Thomas H. Johnson, eds. *The Puritans: A Sourcebook of Their Writings*. 2 vols. Revised ed. New York: Harper and Row, 1963.

Minority of the Pennsylvania Ratifying Convention. "The Address and Reasons of Dissent." In *Anti-Federalist*, pp. 201–24.

Monitor. "On Good Nature." *Virginia Gazette*, 28 January 1736.

Montesquieu, Baron de. *The Spirit of the Laws*. Trans. Thomas Nugent, with an introduction by Franz Neumann. 2 vols. in 1. New York: Hafner Press, 1949.

Morgan, Edmund S., ed. *Prologue to Revolution: Sources and Documents on the Stamp Act Crisis, 1764–1766*. New York: W. W. Norton, 1959.

Morgan, William. *Memoirs of the Life of the Rev. Richard Price*. London: R. Hunter, 1815.

Morison, Samuel Eliot, ed. *Sources and Documents Illustrating the American Revolution, 1764–1788*. 2d ed. Oxford: Oxford Univ. Press, 1929.

Morris, Gouverneur. "Political Enquiries. Liberty: Several Essays on the Nature of Liberty—Natural, Civil, [and] Political." Appended to " 'The Spirit of Commerce Requires that Property Be Sacred': Gouverneur Morris and the American Revolution," by Willi Paul Adams. *Amerikastudien* 21 (1976): 327–31.

———. "Letter to Mr. Penn, May 1774." Appended to " 'The Spirit of Commerce Requires that Property Be Sacred': Gouverneur Morris and the American Revolution," by Willi Paul Adams. *Amerikastudien* 21 (1976): 318–20.

Munford, Robert. "The Candidates; or, The Humours of a Virginia Election." Ed. Jay B. Hubbell and Douglass Adair. *William and Mary Quarterly* 5 (April 1948): 215–57.

Murray, John. *Nehemiah; or, The Struggle for Liberty Never in Vain, When Managed with Virtue and Perseverance*. Newburyport, Mass: John Mycall, 1779.

Murray, William Vans. "Political Sketches." *American Museum* 2 (September 1787): 228–37.

Nelson, William, ed. *Documents Relating to the Colonial History of New Jersey*. Paterson, N.J.: Press Printing and Publishing, 1895.

Niles, Hezekiah, ed. *Principles and Acts of the Revolution in America*. Baltimore: William Ogden Niles, 1822.

Niles, Nathaniel. "Second Discourse." In *Two Discourses on Liberty*. Newburyport, Mass.: I. Thomas and H. W. Tinges, 1774.

———. "[First of] Two Discourses on Liberty." In *American Political Writing*, pp. 257–76.

Nips, Jack [John Leland]. "The Yankee Spy." In *American Political Writing*, pp. 971–89.

[Nisbet, Richard]. *Slavery Not Forbidden by Scripture; or, A Defence of the West-India Planters*. Philadelphia: n.p., 1773.

"Of True Happiness and How to Attain It." *Massachusetts Gazette, and the Boston Post-Boy And Advertiser*, 25 January 1773.

"Oration." *American Museum* 2 (November 1787): 421.

Otis, James. "Speech of 1761." Appended to *Works of John Adams, Second President of the United States,* ed. Charles Francis Adams, 2:523–25. Boston: Charles Little and James Brown, 1865.

———. "The Rights of the British Colonies Asserted and Proved." In *Pamphlets of the American Revolution,* pp. 419–82. Cambridge: Harvard Univ. Press, 1965. An abridged version is found in *Tracts of the American Revolution,* pp. 19–40.

———. "A Vindication of the British Colonies, against the Aspersions of the Halifax Gentleman. . . ." In *Pamphlets of the American Revolution,* pp. 545–79.

Paine, Thomas. "Candid and Critical Remarks on a Letter signed Ludlow." In *Complete Writings of Thomas Paine,* ed. Philip S. Foner, 2:272–77. New York: Citadel Press, 1945.

———. "Dissertations on Government." In *Complete Writings of Thomas Paine,* ed. Philip S. Foner, 2:367–414. New York: Citadel Press, 1945.

———. "Rights of Man, Part Second." In *The Life and Major Writings of Thomas Paine,* ed. Philip S. Foner, pp. 345–462. Secaucus, N.J.: Citadel Press, 1948.

———. "Common Sense Addressed to the Inhabitants of America." In *Tracts of the American Revolution,* pp. 400–446.

———. *Common Sense and the Crisis.* New York: Anchor Books, 1973.

Parsons, Jonathan. *Freedom from Civil and Ecclesiastical Slavery.* Newburyport, Mass.: I. Thomas and H. W. Tinges, 1774.

[Parsons, Theophilus]. "The Essex Result." In *American Political Writing,* pp. 480–522.

Patten, William. *A Discourse Delivered at Hallifax.* Boston: D. Kneeland for Thomas Leverett, 1766.

Payson, Phillips. "Massachusetts Election Sermon." In *American Political Writing,* pp. 523–38.

Peach, Bernard, ed. *Richard Price and the Ethical Foundations of the American Revolution: Selections from His Pamphlets, with Appendices.* Durham, N.C.: Duke Univ. Press, 1979.

Pennsylvanecus. *Pennsylvania Journal,* 28 September 1758.

"The People the Best Governors." Appended to *A History of Dartmouth College and the Town of Hanover,* by Frederick Chase, ed. John K. Lord, pp. 654–63. 2d ed. Brattleboro: Vermont Printing, 1928.

Perry, William, ed. *The Royal Standard English Dictionary.* 1st American ed. Worcester, Mass.: Isaiah Thomas, 1788.

Philo Patrie. "Letter to the Editor." *Constitutional Courant,* 21 September 1765.

Plato. *The Republic.* Trans. Allan Bloom. New York: Basic Books, 1968.

Plumstead, A. W., ed. *The Wall and the Garden: Selected Massachusetts Election Sermons, 1670–1775.* Minneapolis: Univ. of Minnesota Press, 1968.

"Political Observations, Without Order; Addressed to the People of America." In *200th Anniversary of the First Continental Congress, 1774–1974.* 93d Cong., 2d sess., H. Doc., pp. 135–37.

Poore, Benjamin Perley, comp. *The Federal and State Constitutions, Colonial Charters, and Other Organic Laws of the United States.* 2d ed. 2 vols. Reprint, New York: Burt Franklin, 1972.

Powers, Peter. *Jesus Christ the True King and Head of the Government.* Newburyport, Mass.: John Mycall, 1778.

Pownall, Thomas. *Memorial Addressed to the Sovereigns of America.* London: J. Derrett, 1783.

Preceptor. "Vol. II. Social Duties of the Political Kind." In *American Political Writing,* pp. 172–80.

Presbyterian Church. "The Shorter Catechism." In *The Constitution of the Presbyterian Church in the United States of America.* Philadelphia: General Assembly of the Presbyterian Church, 1947.

Price, Richard. "Observations on the Nature of Civil Liberty." *New-York Gazette and Weekly Mercury,* 22 July 1776.

———. *Observations on the Nature of Civil Liberty, the Principles of Government, and the Justice and Policy of the War with America.* London: T. Cadell, 1776.

Priestley, Joseph. "An Essay on the First Principles of Government; and on the Nature of Political, Civil, and Religious Liberty." In *The Theological and Miscellaneous Works of Joseph Priestley, with Notes by the Editor,* ed. J. Rutt, vol. 22. Hackney, England: G. Smallfield, 1823.

A Prospect of the Consequences of the Present Conduct of Great Britain Towards America. London: J. Almon, 1776.

Quincy, Josiah. "Observations on the Act of Parliament Commonly Called the Boston Port Bill." In *Memoir of the Life of Josiah Quincy, Junior, of Massachusetts: 1744–1775.* 2d ed. Boston: Press of John Wilson and Son, 1874.

Ramsay, David. "The Oration of 1778." *Transactions of the American Philosophical Society,* ed. Robert L. Brunhouse, 55 (August 1965): 182–90.

———. "The Oration of 1794." *Transactions of the American Philosophical Society,* ed. Robert L. Brunhouse, 55 (August 1965): 190–96.

———. "Selections from *The History of the American Revolution.*" In *American Political Writing,* pp. 719–55.

Reese, Thomas. *An Essay on the Influence of Religion, in Civil Society.* Charleston, S.C.: Markland and M'Iver, 1788.

"Remarks on a Passage in Doctor Price's Observations on the American Revolution." Parts 1 and 2. *American Museum* 9 (April 1791): 182–86; 9 (May 1791): 242–44.

Rousseau, Jean-Jacques. *The Social Contract and Discourses.* Trans. G. D. H. Cole. New York: E. P. Dutton, 1950.

———. *The Creed of a Priest of Savoy.* Trans. Arthur H. Beattie. New York: Ungar, 1956.

"Rudiments of Law and Government Deduced from the Law of Nature in an Address to the People of South-Carolina." In *American Political Writing,* pp. 565–605.

Rush, Benjamin. "Address to the Freemen of America on the Defects of the Confederation." *American Museum* 1 (1787): 8–11.

———. "Letter to Dr. Price." *American Museum* 1 (February 1787): 126.

———. *The Selected Writings of Benjamin Rush.* Ed. Dagobert D. Runes. New York: Philosophical Library, 1947.

———. "Thoughts upon the Mode of Education Proper in a Republic." In *American Political Writing,* pp. 675–92.

[Rush, Benjamin]. "An Address to the Inhabitants of the British Settlements in America Upon Slave-Keeping." In *American Political Writings,* pp. 217–30.

Sallust. *The Jugurthine War and The Conspiracy of Catiline.* Trans. S. A. Handford. London: Penguin Books, 1963.

Schmidt, Fredrika Teute, and Barbara Ripel Wilhelm, eds. "Early Proslavery Petitions in Virginia." *William and Mary Quarterly* 30 (January 1973): 133–46.

Schwartz, Bernard, ed. *The Roots of the Bill of Rights: An Illustrated Source Book of American Freedom,* 2:231–382. New York: Chelsea House, 1980.

Serious Facts Opposed to "Serious Considerations"; or, The Voice of Warning to Religious Republicans. 1800.

[Serle, Ambrose]. *Americans against Liberty; or, An Essay on the Nature and Principles of True Freedom.* 2d ed. London: James Mathews, 1776.

Sewall, Samuel. *The Selling of Joseph: A Memorial.* Boston: Bartholomew Green and John Allen, 1700.

Sherwood, Samuel. "A Sermon Containing Scriptural Instructions to Civil Rulers and All Free-born Subjects." In *Political Sermons,* pp. 373–408.

Shute, Daniel. "Massachusetts Election Sermon." In *American Political Writing,* pp. 109–36.

Sidney, Algernon. *Discourses Concerning Government.* 1698. Reprint, Indianapolis: Liberty Press, 1990.

Sidney. "Maxims for Republics." *American Museum* 2 (July 1787): 80–82.

S. M. "Letter to the Printer." *Boston Gazette, and Country Journal,* 6 April 1778.

Smith, Adam. *The Theory of Moral Sentiments.* Introduction by E. G. West. Indianapolis: Liberty Press, 1976.

Smith, Melancton. "Speeches before the New York Ratifying Convention." In *Anti-Federalist,* pp. 331–59.

Smith, W. M. "On the Fall of Empire." *Pennsylvania Packet,* 28 May 1775.

[Sneyd, Ralph?]. *Liberty and Equality: Treated of in a Short History Addressed from a Poor Man to His Equals.* 3d ed. London: Hookham and Carpenter, 1792.

Some Fugitive Thoughts on a Letter Signed Freeman. South Carolina, n.p., 1774.

Some Observations of Consequence, in Three Parts. Philadephia: [Holland Sellers?], 1768.

Spinoza, Benedict. *A Theologico-Political Treatise.* Trans. R. H. M. Elwes. New York: Dover, 1951.

Stamp Act Congress. "The Declarations of the Stamp Act Congress." In *Prologue to Revolution: Sources and Documents on the Stamp Act Crisis, 1764–1766,* ed. Edmund S. Morgan, pp. 62–63. New York: W. W. Norton, 1959.

Stewart, James. *A Letter to the Rev. Dr. Price . . . His Principles Refuted . . . Also the True Principles of Liberty.* London: J. Bew, 1776.

Stiles, Ezra. *A Discourse on the Christian Union.* Boston: Edes and Gill, 1761.

Stillman, Samuel. *Massachusetts Election Sermon.* Boston: T. and J. Fleet and J. Gill, 1779

Stone, Timothy. "Connecticut Election Sermon." In *American Political Writing,* pp. 839–57.

Storing, Herbert J., ed. *The Complete Anti-Federalist.* Chicago: Univ. of Chicago Press, 1981.

Story, Isaac. *The Love of Our Country Recommended and Enforced.* Boston: John Boyle, 1775.

Story, Joseph. *Commentaries on the Constitution of the United States.* Ed. Thomas Cooley. 2 vols. 4th ed. Boston: Little, Brown, 1873.

Strong, Caleb. "Speech." In *Patriotism and Piety: The Speeches of His Excellency, Caleb Strong.* Newburyport, Mass.: Edmund M. Blunt, 1806.

Strong, Cyprian. *The Kingdom Is the Lord's.* Hartford: Hudson and Goodwin, 1799.

Tappan, David. *A Discourse Delivered at the Third Parish in Newbury*. Salem, Mass.: Samuel Hall, 1783.

[Taylor, William]. *Liberty without Licentiousness in Two Letters to a Friend*. Paisley, Scotland: John Neilson, 1792.

Thacher, Oxenbridge. "The Sentiments of a British American." In *Pamphlets of the American Revolution*, pp. 483–98.

Thomas, David. *The Virginian Baptist; or, A View and Defence of the Christian Religion as It Is Professed by the Baptists of Virginia*. Baltimore: Enoch Story, 1774.

Thucydides. *History of the Peloponnesian War*. Trans. Rex Warner. Middlesex: Penguin Books, 1954.

Tocqueville, Alexis de. *Democracy in America*. Ed. Phillips Bradley. 2 vols. New York: Vintage Books, 1954.

Todd, Jonathan. *Civil Rulers the Ministers of God*. New London: Timothy Green, 1749.

T. Q. and J. "An Exchange of Letters in *The Boston Gazette and Country Journal* and *The Boston Evening Post*." In *American Political Writing*, pp. 19–32.

[Trenchard, John, and Thomas Gordon]. *Cato's Letters; or, Essays on Liberty, Civil and Religious*. 4 vols. 3d ed. London: W. Wilkins, T. Woodward, J. Walthoe, and J. Peele, 1733.

Tufts, Joshua. *The Believers Most Sure Freedom Purchased by Jesus Christ*. Portsmouth, N.H.: Daniel Fowle, 1757.

Turnbull, Gordon. *An Apology for Negro Slavery; or The West-Indian Planters Vindicated from the Charge of Inhumanity*. 2d ed. London: J. Stevenson, 1786.

Turner, Charles. *A Sermon, Preached Before His Excellency Thomas Hutchinson, Esq*. Boston: Richard Draper, 1773.

———. *A Sermon, Preached at Plymouth, December 22d, 1773*. Boston: Greenleaf's Printing Office, 1774.

———. *Due Glory Is to Be Given to God*. Boston: T. and J. Fleet, 1783.

Virginia House of Burgesses. "Resolutions of 30 May 1765." In *Prologue to Revolution: Sources and Documents on the Stamp Act Crisis, 1764–1766*, ed. Edmund S. Morgan, pp. 44–50. New York: W. W. Norton, 1959.

"Virtue." *New-York Evening Post*, 16 November 1747.

Washington, George. "Letter to Congress." In *The Records of the Federal Convention of 1787*, ed. Max Farrand, 2:666–67. New Haven: Yale Univ. Press, 1937.

———. *George Washington: A Collection*. Ed. W. B. Allen. Indianapolis: Liberty Press, 1988.

———. "Washington's Farewell Address." In *One Hundred Years of a Nation's Life*, pp. 137–53. New York: Hurst, n.d.

Webster, Noah. "An Oration on the Anniversary of the Declaration of Independence." In *American Political Writing*, pp. 1220–40.

———, ed. *An American Dictionary of the English Language*. New York: S. Converse, 1829.

[Webster, Noah]. "An Examination into the Leading Principles of the Federal Constitution." In *Pamphlets on the Constitution*, pp. 25–66.

Wesley, John. "A Calm Address to the American Colonies." *Massachusetts Gazette*, 1 February 1776.

———. "Some Observations on Liberty Occasioned by a Late Tract." In *Richard Price and the Ethical Foundation of the American Revolution: Selections from*

His Pamphlets, with Appendices, ed. Bernard Peach, pp. 245–52. Durham, N.C.: Duke Univ. Press, 1979.

———. "A Calm Address to Our American Colonies." In *Political Sermons,* pp. 409–20.

West, Samuel. "On the Right to Rebel Against Governors." In *American Political Writing,* pp. 410–48.

Westminster Assembly. "The Westminster Confession of Faith." In *Creeds of the Churches: A Reader in Christine Doctrine,* ed. John H. Leith, pp. 192–230. Chicago: Aldine, 1963.

Wheelock, Eleazar. *Liberty of Conscience; or, No King But Christ, in His Church.* Hartford: Eben. Watson, 1776.

Whitaker, Nathaniel. *An Antidote Against Toryism.* Newburyport, Mass.: John Mycall, 1777.

Whitney, Josiah. *The Essential Requisites to Form the Good Ruler's Character.* Hartford: Elisha Babcock, 1788.

Williams, Abraham. "Massachusetts Election Sermon." In *American Political Writing,* pp. 3–19.

Wilson, Alexander. *Oration on the Power and Value of National Liberty.* Philadelphia: H. Maxwell, 1801.

Wilson, James. *Considerations on the Nature and Extent of the Legislative Authority of the British Parliament.* Philadelphia: William and Thomas Bradford, 1774.

———. *The Works of James Wilson.* Ed. James DeWitt Andrews. 2 vols. Chicago: Callaghan, 1896.

———. *The Works of James Wilson.* Ed. Robert Green McCloskey. 2 vols. Cambridge: Harvard Univ. Press, 1967.

[Winthrop, James?]. "Letters of Agrippa, I–XI." In *Anti-Federalist,* pp. 225–54.

Wirt, William. "Life or Liberty Speech, by Patrick Henry." In *Sketches of the Life and Character of Patrick Henry,* pp. 133–47. New York: McElrath, Bangs, 1834.

Witherspoon, John. *The Dominion of Providence over the Passions of Men.* Philadelphia: R. Aitken, 1776.

———. "Thoughts on American Liberty." In *The Works of the Rev. John Witherspoon,* 4:213–17. Philadelphia: William Woodward, 1801.

Woodward, Israel B. *American Liberty and Independence: A Discourse.* Litchfield, Conn.: T. Collier, 1798.

Woolman, John. *Some Considerations on the Keeping of Negroes.* Philadelphia: James Chattin, 1754.

Worcester Speculator. "Letter No. VI." In *American Political Writing,* pp. 699–701.

Wrage, Ernest J., and Barnet Baskerville, eds. *American Forum: Speeches on Historic Issues, 1788–1900.* New York: Harper and Brothers, 1960.

Zubly, John Joachim. *The Law of Liberty . . . Preached at the Opening of the Provincial Congress of Georgia.* Philadelphia: J. Almon, 1775.

Newspaper Editorials

American Chronicle (New York), 19 April 1762.

American Magazine and Historical Chronicle, September 1744.

American Minerva, 8 February 1796.

American Weekly Mercury, 5–12 March 1733/4; 21–28 March and 18–25 April 1734.

Boston Chronicle, 10 April 1769.
Boston Evening Post, 14 January 1771.
Boston Gazette, and Country Journal, 10 May 1756; 4 January 1762; 22 February 1768; 6 April 1778.
Boston Post Boy, 12 December 1768.
Continental Journal (Boston), 9 April 1778.
Independent Advertiser, 8 August 1748.
Independent Chronicle (Boston), 29 January 1778; 3 June 1779.
Independent Reflector, 2 August 1753.
Maryland Gazette, 11 and 25 November and 30 December 1790.
Massachusetts Gazette, and the Boston Post-Boy and Advertiser, 25 January 1773; 19 September 1774.
Massachusetts Gazette: and the Boston Weekly News-Letter, 6 June 1771.
New-Jersey Gazette, 8 November 1780; 10 January and 14 February 1781.
Newport Mercury, 22 August 1763.
New-York Evening Post, 16 November 1747.
New-York Gazette, 28 January–4 February 1773/4.
New-York Gazette Revived in the Weekly Post Boy, 27 January 1752.
New-York Journal, 29 November and 27 December 1780; 17, 24, and 31 January and 7 and 28 February 1781.
New-York Mercury, 27 August and 10 and 17 September 1753; 27 January 1755.
New-York Weekly Journal, 16 June 1735; 7 July 1740.
Pennsylvania Gazette, 1–7 and 8–15 April 1736.
Pennsylvania Journal, 31 January and 5 and 21 February 1781.
Pennsylvania Journal and Weekly Advertiser, 2 and 23 February and 17 August 1758.
Political and Commercial Register (Philadelphia), 6 and 13 July 1804.
Rivington's New-York Gazetteer, 6 April 1775.
South-Carolina Gazette (Charles-Town), 19 December 1774; 26 September 1775; 14–21 August 1776.
Virginia Gazette, 28 January 1736.

SECONDARY SOURCES

Abbott, Philip. *Political Thought in America: Conversations and Debates.* Itasca, Ill.: F. E. Peacock, 1991.
———. Review of *A Preface to American Political Theory,* by Donald Lutz. *Journal of Politics* 55 (November 1993): 1188–91.
Ackerman, Bruce A. *Social Justice in the Liberal State.* New Haven: Yale Univ. Press, 1980.
———. *We the People: Foundations.* Cambridge: Harvard Univ. Press, 1991.
Adair, Douglass. "Fame and the Founding Fathers." In *Fame and the Founding Fathers: Essays,* ed. Trevor Colbourn, pp. 3–26. New York: W. W. Norton, 1974.
Adams, Willi Paul. "Republicanism in Political Rhetoric before 1776." *Political Science Quarterly* 85 (September 1970): 397–421.
———. *The First American Constitutions.* Chapel Hill: Univ. of North Carolina Press, 1980.
Ahlstrom, Sydney E. *A Religious History of the American People.* New Haven: Yale Univ. Press, 1972.

"*Albion's Seed: Four British Folkways in America*—A Symposium." *William and Mary Quarterly* 48 (April 1991): 224–308.

Allen, David Grayson. "The Zuckerman Thesis and the Process of Legal Rationalization in Provincial Massachusetts." *William and Mary Quarterly* 29 (July 1972): 443–68.

———. *In English Ways: The Movement of Societies and the Transferal of English Local Law and Custom to Massachusetts Bay in the Seventeenth Century.* Chapel Hill: Univ. of North Carolina Press, 1981.

Amar, Akhil Reed. "The Consent of the Governed: Constitutional Amendment Outside Article V." *Columbia Law Review* 94 (March 1994): 457–508.

———. "Republican Government, Majority Rule, and the Problem of the Denominator." Draft. Forthcoming in *Colorado Law Review.*

Amos, Gary T. *Defending the Declaration: How the Bible and Christianity Influenced the Writing of the Declaration of Independence.* Brentwood, Tenn.: Wolgemuth and Hyatt, 1989.

Anderson, Fred. *A People's Army: Massachusetts Soldiers and Society in the Seven Years' War.* 1984. Reprint, New York: W. W. Norton, 1985.

Anderson, Perry. *Lineages of the Absolutist State.* London: Verso Editions, 1979.

Andrews, Charles M. *The Colonial Background of the American Revolution: Four Essays in American Colonial History.* Revised ed. New Haven: Yale Univ. Press, 1931.

Appleby, Joyce. "Liberalism and the American Revolution." *New England Quarterly* 49 (March 1976): 3–26.

———. Review of *The Origins of English Individualism,* by Alan Macfarlane. *American Historical Review* 84 (October 1979): 1046–47.

———. *Capitalism and a New Social Order: The Republican Vision of the 1790s.* New York: New York Univ. Press, 1984.

———. "Value and Society." In *Colonial British America: Essays in the New History of the Early Modern Era,* ed. Jack P. Greene and J. R. Pole, pp. 290–316. Baltimore: Johns Hopkins Univ. Press, 1984.

———. "Introduction: Republicanism and Ideology." *American Quarterly* 37 (Fall 1985): 461–73.

———. "Republicanism in Old and New Contexts." *William and Mary Quarterly* 43 (January 1986): 20–34.

———. "One Good Turn Deserves Another: Moving beyond the Linguistic—A Response to David Harlan." *American Historical Review* 94 (December 1989): 1326–32.

———. "The American Heritage—The Heirs and the Disinherited." In *Liberalism and Republicanism in the Historical Imagination,* pp. 210–31. Cambridge: Harvard Univ. Press, 1992.

———. *Liberalism and Republicanism in the Historical Imagination.* Cambridge: Harvard Univ. Press, 1992.

———. "Modernization Theory and Anglo-American Social Theories." In *Liberalism and Republicanism in the Historical Imagination,* pp. 90–123. Cambridge: Harvard Univ. Press, 1992.

———. "What is Still American in Jefferson's Political Philosophy?" In *Liberalism and Republicanism in the Historical Imagination,* pp. 291–319. Cambridge: Harvard Univ. Press, 1992.

Arendt, Hannah. *On Revolution.* Middlesex: Penguin Books, 1963.

Arensberg, Conrad M. "American Communities." *American Anthropologist* 57 (December 1955): 1143–62.

Arieli, Yehoshua. *Individualism and Nationalism in American Ideology*. 1964. Reprint, Baltimore: Penguin Books, 1966.

Avineri, Shlomo, and Avner de-Shalit, eds. *Communitarianism and Individualism*. New York: Oxford Univ. Press, 1992.

Bailyn, Bernard. *The Ideological Origins of the American Revolution*. Cambridge: Harvard Univ. Press, 1967.

———. *The Origins of American Politics*. New York: Random House, 1967.

———. "Political Experience and Enlightenment Ideas in Eighteenth-Century America." In *Essays on the American Revolution*, ed. David L. Jacobson, pp. 15–26. New York: Holt, Rinehart, and Winston, 1970.

———. "Religion and Revolution: Three Biographical Studies." In *Perspectives in American History* 4 (1970): 83–169.

———. "Central Themes of the American Revolution: An Interpretation." In *Essays on the American Revolution*, ed. Stephen G. Kurtz and James H. Hutson, pp. 3–31. Chapel Hill: Univ. of North Carolina Press, 1973.

Bainton, Roland. "The Appeal to Reason and the American Constitution." In *The Constitution Reconsidered*, ed. Conyers Read, pp. 121–30. New York: Columbia Univ. Press, 1938.

Baldwin, Alice M. *The New England Clergy and the American Revolution*. Durham, N.C.: Duke Univ. Press, 1928.

Banning, Lance. *The Jeffersonian Persuasion: Evolution of a Party Ideology*. Ithaca, N.Y.: Cornell Univ. Press, 1978.

———. "Jeffersonian Ideology Revisited: Liberal and Classical Ideas in the New American Republic." *William and Mary Quarterly* 43 (January 1986): 3–19.

———. "Quid Transit? Paradigms and Process in the Transformation of Republican Ideas." Review of *New Order of the Ages: Time, the Constitution, and the Making of Modern American Political Thought*, by Michael Lienesch. *Reviews in American History* 17 (June 1989): 199–204.

Baradat, Leon P. *Understanding American Democracy*. New York: Harper Collins, 1992.

Barber, Benjamin R. "Where We Learn Democracy." Review of *Free Spaces*, by S. M. Evans and H. C. Boyte. *New York Times Book Review*, 9 March 1986.

Baron, Hans. "Calvinist Republicanism and Its Historical Roots." *Church History* 8 (March 1939): 30–42.

Barron, Hal S. *Those Who Stayed Behind: Rural Society in Nineteenth-Century New England*. Cambridge: Cambridge Univ. Press, 1984.

Bartley, Robert L. " 'No Guardrails': Values Debate a Tectonic Clash." *Wall Street Journal*, 15 April 1993.

Baumer, Franklin L. *Modern European Thought: Continuity and Change in Ideas, 1600–1950*. New York: Macmillan, 1977.

Becker, Carl L. *The Declaration of Independence: A Study in the History of Political Ideas*. 1922. Reprint, New York: Random House, 1958.

———. *The Heavenly City of the Eighteenth-Century Philosophers*. New Haven: Yale Univ. Press, 1932.

———. "What Are Historical Facts?" *Western Political Quarterly* 8 (September 1955): 327–40.

Beeman, Richard R. "The New Social History and the Search for 'Community' in Colonial America." *American Quarterly* 29 (Fall 1977): 422–43.

Bell, Daniel. "Resolving the Contradictions of Modernity and Modernism." Parts 1 and 2. *Society* (March–April 1990): 43–50; (May–June 1990): 66–75.

Bellah, Robert N. et al. *Habits of the Heart: Individualism and Commitment in American Life.* Berkeley and Los Angeles: Univ. of California Press, 1985.

Bellow, Saul. *Mr. Sammler's Planet.* New York: Viking Press, 1969.

Bemis, Samuel Flagg. *The Diplomacy of the American Revolution.* 2d ed. 1957. Reprint, Bloomington: Indiana Univ. Press, 1967.

Bender, Thomas. *Community and Social Change in America.* New Brunswick, N.J.: Rutgers Univ. Press, 1978.

Bendix, Reinhard. *Nation-Building and Citizenship: Studies of our Changing Social Order.* Enlarged ed. Berkeley and Los Angeles: Univ. of California Press, 1977.

Benson, John M. "The Polls: A Rebirth of Religion." *Public Opinion Quarterly* 45 (Winter 1981).

Bercovitch, Sacvan. *The Puritan Origins of the American Self.* New Haven: Yale Univ. Press, 1975.

Berkowitz, Peter. Review of *We The People,* by Bruce Ackerman. *Eighteenth-Century Studies* 26 (Summer 1993): 692–97.

Berlin, Isaiah. "Two Concepts of Liberty." In *Four Essays on Liberty,* pp. 118–72. New York: Oxford Univ. Press, 1969.

———. "Two Concepts of Nationalism: An Interview with Isaiah Berlin." By Nathan Gardels. *New York Review of Books,* 21 November 1991, pp. 19–23.

Berns, Walter. "Government by Lawyers and Judges." *Commentary,* June 1987, pp. 17–24.

Berthoff, Rowland. "Independence and Attachment, Virtue and Interest: From Republican Citizen to Free Enterpriser, 1787–1837." In *Uprooted Americans: Essays to Honor Oscar Handlin,* ed. R. Bushman et al., pp. 97–124. Boston: Little, Brown, 1979.

———. "Peasants and Artisans, Puritans and Republicans: Personal Liberty and Communal Equality in American History." *Journal of American History* 69 (December 1982): 579–98.

Berthoff, Rowland, and John M. Murrin. "Feudalism, Communalism, and the Yeoman Freeholder: The American Revolution Considered as a Social Accident." In *Essays on the American Revolution,* ed. Stephen G. Kurtz and James H. Hutson, pp. 256–88. Chapel Hill: Univ. of North Carolina Press, 1973.

Bloch, Ruth H. *Visionary Republic: Millennial Themes in American Thought, 1756–1800.* New York: Cambridge Univ. Press, 1985.

———. "Religion and Ideological Change in the American Revolution." In *Religion and American Politics,* ed. Mark A. Noll, pp. 44–61. New York: Oxford Univ. Press, 1990.

Bockelman, Wayne L. "Local Government in Colonial Pennsylvania." In *Town and County: Essays on the Structure of Local Government in the American Colonies,* ed. Bruce C. Daniels, pp. 216–37. Middletown, Conn.: Wesleyan Univ. Press, 1978.

Bonomi, Patricia U. "Local Government in Colonial New York: A Base for Republicanism." In *Aspects of Early New York Society and Politics,* ed. Jacob Judd and Irwin H. Polishook, pp. 29–50. Tarrytown, N.Y.: Sleepy Hollow Restorations, 1974.

———. *Under the Cope of Heaven: Religion, Society, and Politics in Colonial America*. New York: Oxford Univ. Press, 1986.

Bonomi, Patricia U., and Peter R. Eisenstadt. "Church Adherence in the Eighteenth-Century British American Colonies." *William and Mary Quarterly* 39 (April 1982): 245–86.

Boorstin, Daniel J. *The Genius of American Politics*. Chicago: Univ. of Chicago Press, 1953.

Borden, Morton. "Federalists, Antifederalists, and Religious Freedom." *Journal of Church and State* 21 (Autumn 1979): 469–82.

Botein, Stephen. "Religious Dimensions of the Early American State." In *Beyond Confederation: Origins of the Constitution and American National Identity*, ed. Richard Beeman, Stephen Botein, and Edward C. Carter II, pp. 315–30. Chapel Hill: Univ. of North Carolina Press, 1987.

Bowling, Kenneth R. "'A Tub to the Whale': The Founding Fathers and the Adoption of the Federal Bill of Rights." *Journal of the Early Republic* 8 (Fall 1988): 223–51.

Bradford, M. E. *A Better Guide Than Reason: Studies in the American Revolution*. La Salle, Ill.: Sherwood Sugden, 1979.

Breen, Timothy H. "Persistent Localism: English Social Change and the Shaping of New England Institutions." *William and Mary Quarterly* 32 (January 1975): 3–28.

———. *Tobacco Culture: The Mentality of the Great Tidewater Planters on the Eve of Revolution*. Princeton: Princeton Univ. Press, 1985.

Breitenbach, William. "Unregenerate Doings: Selflessness and Selfishness in New Divinity Theology." *American Quarterly* 34 (Winter 1982): 479–502.

Bridenbaugh, Carl. *Mitre and Sceptre: Transatlantic Faiths, Ideas, Personalities, and Politics, 1689–1775*. New York: Oxford Univ. Press, 1962.

———. *Myths and Realities: Societies of the Colonial South*. New York: Atheneum, 1963.

———. *The Spirit of '76: The Growth of Patriotism before Independence, 1607–1776*. London: Oxford Univ. Press, 1975.

Brinton, Crane. *The Shaping of the Modern Mind*. Part 2 of *Ideas and Men*. New York: Mentor Books, 1953.

Bromwich, David. "The Un-American Mind." Review of *Giants and Dwarfs: Essays, 1960–1990*, by Allan Bloom. *New Republic,* 28 January 1991, pp. 26–30.

Brown, Anne S. "Visions of Community in Eighteenth-Century Essex County: Chebaco Parish and the Great Awakening." *Essex Institute Historical Collections* 125 (July 1989): 239–62.

Brown, Richard D. *Modernization: The Transformation of American Life, 1600–1865*. New York: Hill and Wang, 1976.

———. *Knowledge Is Power: The Diffusion of Information in Early America, 1700–1865*. New York: Oxford Univ. Press, 1989.

Brown, Wallace. *The Good Americans: The Loyalists in the American Revolution*. New York: William Morrow, 1969.

Bryan, Frank, and John McClaughry. *The Vermont Papers: Recreating Democracy on a Human Scale*. Post Mills, Vermont: Chelsea Green, 1989.

Bryce, James. *Modern Democracies*. 2 vols. New York: Macmillan, 1921.

Buel, Richard, Jr. "Democracy and the American Revolution: A Frame of Reference." In *The Reinterpretation of the American Revolution, 1763–1789*, ed. Jack P. Greene, pp. 122–47. New York: Harper and Row, 1968.

Burnham, Walter Dean. "The 1980 Earthquake." In *The Hidden Election,* ed T. Ferguson and J. Rogers, pp. 118–40. New York: Parthenon Books, 1981.

Burtt, Shelley. "The Good Citizen's Psyche: On the Psychology of Civic Virtue." *Polity* 23 (Fall 1990): 23–38.

Bushman, Richard. *From Puritan to Yankee: Character and Social Order in Connecticut, 1690–1765.* Cambridge: Harvard Univ. Press, 1967.

Butler, Jon. "Enthusiasm Described and Decried: The Great Awakening as Interpretive Fiction." *Journal of American History* 69 (September 1982): 305–25.

———. *Awash in a Sea of Faith: Christianizing the American People.* Cambridge: Harvard Univ. Press, 1990.

Butterfield, Herbert. *The Whig Interpretation of History.* 1931. Reprint, New York: W. W. Norton, 1965.

Byers, Edward. *"The Nation of Nantucket": Society and Politics in an Early American Commercial Center, 1660–1820.* Boston: Northeastern Univ. Press, 1987.

Calhoon, Robert M. "Religion and Individualism in Early America." In *American Chameleon: Individualism in Trans-National Context,* ed. Richard O. Curry and Laurence B. Goodheart, pp. 44–65. Kent, Ohio: Kent State Univ. Press, 1991.

Callcott, George H. *History in the United States, 1800–1860: Its Practice and Purpose.* Baltimore: Johns Hopkins Univ. Press, 1970.

Canavan, Francis. *Freedom of Expression: Purpose as Limit.* Durham, N.C.: Carolina Academic Press and the Claremont Institute for the Study of Statesmanship and Political Philosophy, 1984.

———. "The Relevance of the Burke-Paine Controversy to American Political Thought." *Review of Politics* 49 (Spring 1987): 163–76.

Caplow, Theodore. "Religion in Middletown." *Public Interest* 68 (Summer 1982): 78–87.

Carden, Allen. *Puritan Christianity in America: Religion and Life in Seventeenth-Century Massachusetts.* Grand Rapids, Mich.: Baker Book House, 1990.

Carlyle, A. J. *Political Liberty: A History of the Conception in the Middle Ages and Modern Times.* Oxford: Clarendon Press, 1941.

Carr, Lois Green. "The Foundations of Social Order: Local Government in Colonial Maryland." In *Town and County: Essays on the Structure of Local Government in the American Colonies,* ed. Bruce C. Daniels, pp. 72–110. Middletown, Conn.: Wesleyan Univ. Press, 1978.

Ceaser, James. "Alexis de Tocqueville on Political Science, Political Culture, and the Role of the Intellectual." *American Political Science Review* 79 (September 1985): 656–72.

Chandler, A. D., Jr. *The Visible Hand: The Managerial Revolution in American Business.* Cambridge: Harvard Univ. Press, 1977.

Chapman, John W. "Voluntary Association and the Political Theory of Pluralism." In *Nomos XI: Voluntary Associations,* ed. J. Roland Pennock and John W. Chapman, pp. 87–118. New York: Atherton Press, 1969.

Christman, John. "Constructing the Inner Citadel: Recent Work on the Concept of Autonomy." *Ethics* 99 (October 1988): 109–24.

Clark, Christopher. "Household Economy, Market Exchange, and the Rise of Capitalism in the Connecticut Valley, 1800–1860." *Journal of Social History* 13 (Winter 1979): 169–90.

Cohen, Charles L. "The 'Liberty or Death' Speech: A Note on Religion and Revolutionary Rhetoric." *William and Mary Quarterly* 38 (October 1981): 702–17.

Cohen, Marshall. "Berlin and the Liberal Tradition." *Philosophical Quarterly* 10 (July 1960): 216–27.

Conkin, Paul K. *Puritans and Pragmatists: Eight Eminent American Thinkers.* Bloomington: Indiana Univ. Press, 1976.

———. "Freedom: Past Meanings and Present Prospects." In *Freedom in America,* ed. Norman A. Graebner, pp. 205–22. University Park: Pennsylvania State Univ. Press, 1977.

Cook, Edward M., Jr. *The Fathers of the Towns: Leadership and Community Structure in Eighteenth-Century New England.* Baltimore: Johns Hopkins Univ. Press, 1976.

Cooke, J. W. *The American Tradition of Liberty, 1800–1860: From Jefferson to Lincoln.* Lewiston, N.Y.: Edwin Mellen Press, 1986.

Cord, Robert L. *Separation of Church and State: Historical Fact and Current Fiction.* Grand Rapids, Mich.: Baker Book House, 1988.

Cornell, Saul. "Aristocracy Assailed: The Ideology of Backcountry Anti-Federalism." *Journal of American History* 76 (March 1990): 1148–72.

Coulanges, Numa Denis Fustel de. *The Ancient City: A Study on the Religion, Laws, and Institutions of Greece and Rome.* 1864. Reprint, Baltimore: Johns Hopkins Univ. Press, 1980.

Countryman, Edward. *The American Revolution.* New York: Hill and Wang, 1985.

———. " 'The Very Spirit of Liberty': Language, Conflict and the Larger Consequences of the American Revolution." Manuscript. Draft version of " 'To Secure the Blessings of Liberty': Language, the Revolution, and American Capitalism," in *Beyond the American Revolution: Explorations in the History of American Radicalism,* ed. Alfred F. Young, pp. 123–48 (DeKalb, Ill.: Northern Illinois Univ. Press, 1993).

Counts, Martha Louise. "The Political Views of the Eighteenth Century New England Clergy as Expressed in Their Election Sermons." Ph.D. diss., Columbia Univ., 1956.

"*The Creation of the American Republic:* A Symposium of Views and Reviews." *William and Mary Quarterly* 44 (July 1987): 549–640.

Croly, Herbert. *The Promise of American Life.* 1909. Reprint, Indianapolis: Bobbs-Merrill, 1965.

Crowley, John E. *This Sheba, Self: The Conceptualization of Economic Life in Eighteenth-Century America.* Baltimore: Johns Hopkins Univ. Press, 1974.

———. "Commerce and the Philadelphia Constitution: Neo-Mercantilism in Federalist and Anti-Federalist Political Economy." *History of Political Thought* 13 (Spring 1992): 73–97.

Curry, Richard O., and Lawrence B. Goodheart. "Individualism in Trans-National Context." In *American Chameleon: Individualism in Trans-National Context,* ed. Richard O. Curry and Lawrence B. Goodheart, pp. 1–19. Kent, Ohio: Kent State Univ. Press, 1991.

———, eds. *American Chameleon: Individualism in Trans-National Context.* Kent, Ohio: Kent State Univ. Press, 1991.

Curry, Richard O., and Karl E. Valois. "The Emergence of an Individualistic Ethos in American Society." In *American Chameleon: Individualism in Trans-National Context,* ed. Richard O. Curry and Lawrence B. Goodheart, pp. 20–43. Kent, Ohio: Kent State Univ. Press, 1991.

Curry, Thomas J. *The First Freedoms: Church and State in America to the Passage of the First Amendment.* New York: Oxford Univ. Press, 1986.

Damico, A. J. "Is the Problem with Liberalism How It Thinks?" *Polity* 16 (Summer 1984): 547–66.

Daniels, Bruce C. "The Political Structure of Local Government in Colonial Connecticut." In *Town and County: Essays on the Structure of Local Government in the American Colonies,* ed. Bruce C. Daniels, pp. 44–71. Middletown, Conn.: Wesleyan Univ. Press, 1978.

———. *The Connecticut Town: Growth and Development, 1635–1790.* Middletown, Conn.: Wesleyan Univ. Press, 1979.

———, ed. *Town and County: Essays on the Structure of Local Government in the American Colonies.* Middletown, Conn.: Wesleyan Univ. Press, 1978.

Davis, David Brion. "Slavery and Sin: The Cultural Background." In *The Antislavery Vanguard: New Essays on the Abolitionists,* ed. Martin Duberman, pp. 3–31. Princeton: Princeton Univ. Press, 1965.

———. *The Problem of Slavery in Western Culture.* 1966. Reprint, New York: Oxford Univ. Press, 1988.

———. *Slavery and Human Progress.* New York: Oxford Univ. Press, 1984.

Dees, Richard, H. "Liberalism in Context." *Polity* 25 (Summer 1993): 565–82.

Delman, Barbara Munz. "Liberty and the Common Law in Eighteenth-Century England." Ph.D. diss., Columbia Univ., 1969.

Demos, John. *A Little Commonwealth: Family Life in Plymouth Colony.* New York: Oxford Univ. Press, 1970.

———. *Past, Present, and Personal: The Family and the Life Course in American History.* New York: Oxford Univ. Press, 1986.

Detweiler, Philip F. "The Changing Reputation of the Declaration of Independence: The First Fifty Years." *William and Mary Quarterly* 19 (October 1962): 557–74.

Dewey, John. *Liberalism and Social Action.* New York: G. P. Putnam's Sons, 1935.

———. *Reconstruction in Philosophy.* Enlarged ed. Boston: Beacon Press, 1948.

Diamond, Martin. "Ethics and Politics: The American Way." In *The Moral Foundations of the American Republic,* ed. Robert H. Horowitz, pp. 75–108. 3d ed. Charlottesville: Univ. Press of Virginia, 1986.

Diamondstone, Judith M. "The Government of Eighteenth-Century Philadelphia." In *Town and County: Essays on the Structure of Local Government in the American Colonies,* ed. Bruce C. Daniels, pp. 238–63. Middletown, Conn.: Wesleyan Univ. Press, 1978.

Dickinson, H. T. *Liberty and Property: Political Ideology in Eighteenth-Century Britain.* London: Weidenfeld and Nicolson, 1977.

Diggins, J. P. *The Lost Soul of American Politics: Virtue, Self-Interest, and the Foundations of Liberalism.* New York: Basic Books, 1984.

Ditz, Toby L. *Property and Kinship: Inheritance in Early Connecticut, 1750–1820.* Princeton: Princeton Univ. Press, 1986.

———. "Ownership and Obligation: Inheritance and Patriarchal Households in Connecticut, 1750–1820." *William and Mary Quarterly* 47 (April 1990): 235–65.

Dolbeare, Kenneth M. *American Political Thought.* Revised ed. Chatham, N.J.: Chatham House, 1984.

Douglas, Justice William. "Dissent from *Wisconsin v. Yoder*." In *Individual Rights in Constitutional Law*, ed. Gerald Gunther, pp. 1122–23. 2d ed. Mineola, N.Y.: Foundation Press, 1976.

Drengson, Alan R. "Toward a Philosophy of Community." *Philosophy Forum* 16 (1979): 101–25.

Dull, Jonathan R. *A Diplomatic History of the American Revolution*. New Haven: Yale Univ. Press, 1985.

Dumont, Louis. *Homo Hierarchicus: The Caste System and Its Implications*. Trans. Mark Sainsbury, Louis Dumont, and Basia Gulati. Revised ed. Chicago: Univ. of Chicago Press, 1980.

Dunn, Richard S. "The Social History of Early New England." *American Quarterly* 24 (December 1972): 661–79.

Dupré, Louis, and William O'Neill. "Social Structures and Structural Ethics." *Review of Politics* 51 (Summer 1989): 327–44.

Dworetz, Steven M. *The Unvarnished Doctrine: Locke, Liberalism, and the American Revolution*. Durham, N.C.: Duke Univ. Press, 1990.

Eastland, Terry. "The Use and Abuse of Liberty." *Christianity Today*, 10 July 1987, pp. 28–30.

———. "Attorney General and Social Worker." *Wall Street Journal*, 10 March 1993.

Elazar, Daniel J. *American Federalism: A View from the States*. New York: Thomas Y. Crowell, 1966.

Elkins, Stanley, and Eric McKitrick. "The Founding Fathers: Young Men of the Revolution." In *The Reinterpretation of the American Revolution, 1763–1789*, ed. Jack P. Greene, pp. 378–95. New York: Harper and Row, 1968.

Ellis, Joseph J. Review of *The Lost Soul of American Politics*, by John P. Diggins. *William and Mary Quarterly* 43 (January 1986): 133–36.

Ellis, Richard E. "The Persistence of Antifederalism after 1789." In *Beyond Confederation: Origins of the Constitution and American National Identity*, ed. Richard Beeman, Stephen Botein, and Edward C. Carter II, pp. 295–314. Chapel Hill: Univ. of North Carolina Press, 1987.

Epstein, David F. *The Political Theory of the Federalist*. Chicago: Univ. of Chicago Press, 1984.

Etzioni, Amitai. *The Spirit of Community: Rights, Responsibilities, and the Communitarian Agenda*. New York: Crown, 1993.

Evans, Charles. Preface to 1751–1764, vol. 3 of *American Bibliography: A Chronological Dictionary of All Books, Pamphlets, and Periodical Publications Printed in the United States of America, 1639–1800*, ed. Charles Evans, pp. vii–xiii. Chicago: Blakely Press, 1905.

Faith, Rosamond. Review of *The Origins of English Individualism*, by Alan Macfarlane. *Journal of Peasant Studies* 7 (April 1980): 384–89.

Fink, Z. S. *The Classical Republicans: An Essay in the Recovery of a Pattern of Thought in Seventeenth-Century England*. Evanston, Ill.: Northwestern Univ., 1945.

Finkelman, Paul. "Slavery and the Constitutional Convention: Making a Covenant with Death." In *Beyond Confederation: Origins of the Constitution and American National Identity*, ed. Richard Beeman, Stephen Botein, and Edward C. Carter II, pp. 188–225. Chapel Hill: Univ. of North Carolina Press, 1987.

Finley, Moses I. "Slavery." In *Encyclopedia of the Social Sciences*, ed. E. R. A. Seligman, 14:307–13. New York: Macmillan, 1933.

———. "Between Slavery and Freedom." *Comparative Studies in Society and History* 6 (1963–1964): 233–49.

Fischer, David Hackett. *Albion's Seed: Four British Folkways in America.* Vol. 1. New York: Oxford Univ. Press, 1989.

Flaherty, David H. "Law and the Enforcement of Morals in Early America." *Perspectives in American History* 5 (1971): 203–53.

———. *Privacy in Colonial New England.* Charlottesville: Univ. Press of Virginia, 1972.

Fliegelman, Jay. *Prodigals and Pilgrims: The American Revolution against Patriarchal Authority, 1750–1800.* New York: Cambridge Univ. Press, 1984.

Foner, Eric. *Tom Paine and Revolutionary America.* New York: Oxford Univ. Press, 1976.

Forbes, Duncan. *Hume's Philosophical Politics.* Cambridge: Cambridge Univ. Press, 1975.

Ford, Lacy K., Jr. "Ties that Bind?" *Reviews in American History* 17 (March 1989): 64–72.

Fosdick, Dorothy. *What Is Liberty? A Study in Political Theory.* New York: Harper and Brothers, 1939.

Foucault, Michel. *The Order of Things: An Archaeology of the Human Sciences.* New York: Vintage Books, 1970.

Freehling, William W. "The Founding Fathers and Slavery." *American Historical Review* 77 (February 1972): 81–93.

Frey, Sylvia. "Liberty, Equality, and Slavery: The Paradox of the American Revolution." In *The American Revolution: Its Character and Its Limits,* ed. Jack P. Greene, pp. 230–52. New York: New York Univ. Press, 1987.

Friedman, Bernard. "The Shaping of the Radical Consciousness in Provincial New York." *Journal of American History* 56 (March 1970): 781–801.

Frug, Gerald E. "The City as a Legal Concept." *Harvard Law Review* 93 (April 1980): 1062–1154.

Fuentes, Carlos. "History out of Chaos." Review of *Revolutionary Mexico,* by John Mason Hart. *New York Times Book Review,* 13 March 1988.

Galston, William A. "Public Morality and Religion in the Liberal State." *PS* 19 (Fall 1986): 807–25.

———. *Liberal Purposes: Goods, Virtues, and Diversity in the Liberal State.* New York: Cambridge Univ. Press, 1991.

Gibson, Alan. "The Commercial Republic and the Pluralist Critique of Marxism: An Analysis of Martin Diamond's Interpretation of *Federalist* 10." *Polity* 25 (Summer 1993): 497–528.

Gillespie, Michael Allen. "The Ratification of the Constitution in Massachusetts: The Old Revolutionaries and the Constitution." Paper presented at the annual meeting of the American Political Science Association, Chicago, Ill., 3–6 September 1987.

Glendon, Mary Ann. *Rights Talk: The Impoverishment of Political Discourse.* New York: Free Press, 1991.

Goldsmith, M. M. "Regulating Anew the Moral and Political Sentiments of Mankind: Bernard Mandeville and the Scottish Enlightenment." *Journal of the History of Ideas* 49 (October–December 1988): 587–606.

Graebner, Norman A. Introduction to *Freedom in America,* ed. Norman A. Graebner, pp. 1–22. University Park: Pennsylvania State Univ. Press, 1977.

Grant, Charles S. *Democracy in the Connecticut Frontier Town of Kent.* 1961. Reprint, New York: AMS Press, 1979.

Grasso, Christopher Daniel. "Between Awakenings: Learned Men and the Transformations of Public Discourse in Connecticut, 1740–1800." Ph.D. diss., Yale Univ., 1992.

Gray, John. Introduction to *Conceptions of Liberty in Political Philosophy,* ed. Zbigniew Pelczynski and John Gray, pp. 1–6. New York: St. Martin's Press, 1984.

————. "On Negative and Positive Liberty." In *Conceptions of Liberty in Political Philosophy,* ed. Zbigniew Pelczynski and John Gray, pp. 321–48. New York: St. Martin's Press, 1984.

————. *Liberalism.* Minneapolis: Univ. of Minnesota Press, 1986.

————. *Liberalisms: Essays in Political Philosphy.* London: Routledge, 1989.

Greene, Donald. "'Sweet Land of Liberty': Libertarian Rhetoric and Practice in Eighteenth-Century Britain." In *The American Revolution and Eighteenth-Century Culture,* ed. Paul J. Korshin, pp. 127–56. New York: AMS Press, 1986.

Greene, Jack P. Introduction to *The Diary of Colonel Landon Carter of Sabine Hall, 1752–1778,* ed. Jack P. Greene. Vol. 1. Charlottesville: University Press of Virginia, 1965.

————. *Landon Carter: An Inquiry into the Personal Values and Social Imperatives of the Eighteenth-Century Virginia Gentry.* Charlottesville: University Press of Virginia, 1967.

————. "An Uneasy Connection: An Analysis of the Preconditions of the American Revolution." In *Essays on the American Revolution,* ed. Stephen G. Kurtz and James H. Hutson, pp. 32–80. Chapel Hill: Univ. of North Carolina Press, 1973.

————. *All Men Are Created Equal: Some Reflections on the Character of the American Revolution.* New York: Oxford Univ. Press, 1976.

————. "'Slavery or Independence': Some Reflections on the Relationship among Liberty, Black Bondage, and Equality in Revolutionary South Carolina." *South Carolina Historical Magazine* 80 (July 1979): 193–214.

————. *Pursuits of Happiness: The Social Development of Early Modern British Colonies and the Formation of American Culture.* Chapel Hill: Univ. of North Carolina Press, 1988.

Greenstone, J. David. "Political Culture and American Political Development: Liberty, Union, and the Liberal Bipolarity." In *Studies in American Political Development,* ed. Steven Skowrownek, 1:1–49. New Haven: Yale Univ. Press, 1987.

————. *The Lincoln Persuasion: Remaking American Liberalism.* Princeton: Princeton University Press, 1993.

Greven, Philip. *Four Generations: Population, Land, and Family in Colonial Andover, Massachusetts.* Ithaca, N.Y.: Cornell Univ. Press, 1970.

————. *The Protestant Temperament: Patterns of Child-Rearing, Religious Experience, and the Self in Early America.* New York: New American Library, 1977.

Gribbin, William. "Republicanism, Reform, and the Sense of Sin in Ante-Bellum America." *Cithara* 14 (December 1974): 25–41.

Griffin, Clifford S. *Their Brothers' Keepers: Moral Stewardship in the United States, 1800–1865.* New Brunswick, N.J.: Rutgers Univ. Press, 1960.

Griswold, A. Whitney. *Farming and Democracy.* New Haven: Yale Univ. Press, 1952.

Gross, Robert A. *The Minutemen and Their World*. New York: Hill and Wang, 1976.

Gummere, Richard M. "The Heritage of the Classics in Colonial North America: An Essay on the Greco-Roman Tradition." *American Philosophical Society* 99 (April 1955): 68–78.

Gunn, J. A. W. *Beyond Liberty and Property: The Process of Self-Recognition in Eighteenth-Century Political Thought*. Kingston and Montreal: McGill-Queen's Univ. Press, 1983.

Gutmann, Amy. *Democratic Education*. Princeton: Princeton Univ. Press, 1987.

Haakonssen, Knud. "From Natural Law to the Rights of Man: A European Perspective on American Debates." In *A Culture of Rights: The Bill of Rights in Philosophy, Politics, and Law—1791 and 1991*, ed. Michael J. Lacey and Knud Haakonssen, pp. 19–61. New York: Cambridge Univ. Press, 1991.

Hackett, David G. "The Social Origins of Nationalism: Albany, New York, 1754–1835." *Journal of Social History* 21 (Summer 1988): 659–81.

Hahn, Steven. "The 'Unmaking' of the Southern Yeomanry." In *The Countryside in the Age of Capitalist Transformation: Essays in the Social History of Rural America*, ed. Steven Hahn and Jonathan Prude, pp. 179–204. Chapel Hill: Univ. of North Carolina Press, 1985.

Hahn, Steven, and Jonathan Prude. Introduction to *The Countryside in the Age of Capitalist Transformation: Essays in the Social History of Rural America*, ed. Steven Hahn and Jonathan Prude, pp. 3–25. Chapel Hill: Univ. of North Carolina Press, 1985.

Hall, David D. "Religion and Society: Problems and Reconsiderations." In *Colonial British America: Essays in the New History of the Early Modern Era*, ed. Jack P. Greene and J. R. Pole, pp. 317–44. Baltimore: Johns Hopkins Univ. Press, 1984.

Hampson, Norman. *The Enlightenment: An Evaluation of its Assumptions, Attitudes, and Values*. 1968. Reprint, New York: Penguin Books, 1986.

Handlin, Oscar, and Lilian Handlin. *Liberty and Power, 1600–1760*. New York: Harper and Row, 1986.

———. *Liberty in Expansion: 1760–1850*. New York: Harper and Row, 1989.

———. "Who Read John Locke? Words and Acts in the American Revolution." *American Scholar* 58 (Autumn 1989): 545–56.

Handlin, Oscar, and Mary Handlin. *The Dimensions of Liberty*. 1961. Reprint, New York: Atheneum, 1966.

———. "James Burgh and American Revolutionary Theory." *Proceedings of the Massachusetts Historical Society* 72 (1961): 38–57.

Hanson, Russell L. *The Democratic Imagination in America: Conversations with Our Past*. Princeton: Princeton Univ. Press, 1985.

Harding, Alan. "Political Liberty in the Middle Ages." *Speculum* 55 (July 1980): 424–43.

Hareven, Tamara K. "Divorce, Chinese Style." *Atlantic Monthly*, April 1987, pp. 70–76.

Harpham, E. J. "Liberalism, Civic Humanism, and the Case of Adam Smith." *American Political Science Review* 78 (September 1984): 764–74.

Hartnett, Robert C. "The Religion of the Founding Fathers." In *Wellsprings of the American Spirit*, ed. F. E. Johnson, pp. 49–68. New York: Harper and Brothers, 1948.

Hartz, Louis. "American Political Thought and the American Revolution." *American Political Science Review* 46 (June 1952): 321–42.

———. *The Liberal Tradition in America: An Interpretation of American Political Thought since the Revolution.* New York: Harcourt, Brace, and World, 1955.

Haskell, Thomas L. "The Curious Persistence of Rights Talk in the 'Age of Interpretation.'" *Journal of American History* 74 (December 1987): 984–1012.

Haskins, George Lee. *Law and Authority in Early Massachusetts: A Study in Tradition and Design.* Lanham, Md.: University Press of America, 1960.

Hatch, Nathan O. *The Sacred Cause of Liberty: Republican Thought and the Millennium in Revolutionary New England.* New Haven: Yale Univ. Press, 1977.

———. "In Pursuit of Religious Freedom: Church, State, and People in the New Republic." In *The American Revolution: Its Character and Limits,* ed. Jack P. Greene, pp. 388–411. New York: New York Univ. Press, 1987.

———. *The Democratization of American Christianity.* New Haven: Yale Univ. Press, 1989.

Hayek, Friedrich A. *The Constitution of Liberty.* Chicago: Univ. of Chicago Press, 1960.

Hays, Samuel P. "Theoretical Implications of Recent Work in the History of American Society and Politics." *History and Theory* 26 (1987): 15–31.

Heimert, Alan. *Religion and the American Mind: From the Great Awakening to the Revolution.* Cambridge: Harvard Univ. Press, 1966.

Henretta, James A. "The Morphology of New England Society in the Colonial Period." *Journal of Interdisciplinary History* 2 (Autumn 1971): 379–99.

———. *The Evolution of American Society, 1700–1815.* Lexington, Mass.: Heath, 1973.

———. "Families and Farms: Mentalité in Pre-Industrial America." *William and Mary Quarterly* 35 (January 1978): 3–32.

———. "The Slow Triumph of Liberal Individualism: Law and Politics in New York, 1780–1860." In *American Chameleon: Individualism in Trans-National Context,* ed. Richard O. Curry and Lawrence B. Goodheart, pp. 87–106. Kent, Ohio: Kent State Univ. Press, 1991.

Herzog, Don. "Some Questions for Republicans." *Political Theory* 14 (August 1986): 473–93.

———. *Happy Slaves: A Critique of Consent Theory.* Chicago: Univ. of Chicago Press, 1989.

———. Review of *Transforming Political Discourse: Political Theory and Critical Conceptual History,* by T. Ball. *Political Theory* 19 (February 1991): 141–43.

Hexter, J. H. Review of *The Machiavellian Moment,* by J. G. A. Pocock. *History and Theory* 16 (1977): 306–37.

Heyrman, Christine Leigh. *Commerce and Culture: The Maritime Communities of Colonial Massachusetts, 1690–1750.* New York: W. W. Norton, 1984.

Higonnet, Patrice. *Sister Republics: The Origins of French and American Republicanism.* Cambridge: Harvard Univ. Press, 1988.

Hillery, George A., Jr. "Definitions of Community: Areas of Agreement." *Rural Sociology* 20 (June 1955): 111–23.

Himmelfarb, Dan. "Freedom, Virtue, and the Founding Fathers: A Review Essay." *Public Interest* 90 (Winter 1988): 115–20.

Himmelfarb, Gertrude. *On Liberty and Liberalism: The Case of John Stuart Mill.* New York: Knopf, 1974.

Hine, Robert V. *Community on the American Frontier: Separate But Not Alone.* Norman: Univ. of Oklahoma Press, 1980.

Hofstadter, Richard. *The Paranoid Style in American Politics and Other Essays.* New York: Random House, 1967.

———. *The Progressive Historians: Turner, Beard, and Parrington.* Chicago: Univ. of Chicago Press, 1968.

———. *America at 1750: A Social Portrait.* New York: Vintage Books, 1971.

Hogue, Arthur R. *Origins of the Common Law.* 1966. Reprint, Indianapolis: Liberty Press, 1974.

Holl, Karl. *The Cultural Significance of the Reformation.* 1911. Reprint, New York: Meridian Books, 1959.

Holmes, Stephen. "The Permanent Structure of Antiliberal Thought." In *Liberalism and the Moral Life,* ed. Nancy L. Rosenblum, pp. 227–53. Cambridge: Harvard Univ. Press, 1989.

Holt, Wythe. Review of *We the People: Foundations,* by Bruce Ackerman. *Journal of the Early Republic* 13 (Spring 1993): 89–90.

Hood, Fred J. "Revolution and Religious Liberty: The Conservation of the Theocratic Concept in Virginia." *Church History* 40 (June 1971): 170–81.

Horton, Robert. "African Traditional Thought and Western Science: Part II." *Africa* 37 (1967): 157–87.

Houston, Alan Craig. *Algernon Sidney and the Republican Heritage in England and America.* Princeton: Princeton Univ. Press, 1991.

Howe, Daniel Walker. "The Political Psychology of *The Federalist.*" *William and Mary Quarterly* 44 (July 1987): 485–509.

Hubbell, Jay B. *The South in American Literature, 1607–1900.* Durham, N.C.: Duke Univ. Press, 1954.

Hudson, Winthrop S. "William Penn's *English Liberties:* Tract for Several Times." *William and Mary Quarterly* 26 (October 1969): 578–85.

Hunt, Agnes. *The Provincial Committees of Safety of the American Revolution.* 1904. Reprint, New York: Haskell House, 1968.

Hunter, James Davison. *Culture Wars: The Struggle to Define America.* New York: Basic Books, 1991.

Huntington, Samuel. *Political Order in Changing Societies.* New Haven: Yale Univ. Press, 1968.

———. *American Politics: The Promise of Disharmony.* Cambridge: Harvard Univ. Press, 1981.

Hutson, James H. "The Creation of the Constitution: The Integrity of the Documentary Record." *Texas Law Review* 65 (November 1986): 1–39.

———. "Riddles of the Federal Constitutional Convention." *William and Mary Quarterly* 44 (July 1987): 411–23.

———. "The Bill of Rights and the American Revolutionary Experience." In *A Culture of Rights: The Bill of Rights in Philosophy, Politics, and Law—1791 and 1991,* ed. Michael J. Lacey and Knud Haakonssen, pp. 62–97. New York: Cambridge Univ. Press, 1991.

Ignatieff, Michael. *The Needs of Strangers: An Essay on Privacy, Solidarity, and the Politics of Being Human.* New York: Penguin Books, 1984.

———. "Strange Attachments." *New Republic,* 29 March 1993, pp. 42–46.

Innes, Stephen. *Labor in a New Land: Economy and Society in Seventeenth-Century Springfield.* Princeton: Princeton Univ. Press, 1983.

Ireland, Owen S. "The Crux of Politics: Religion and Party in Pennsylvania, 1778–1789." *William and Mary Quarterly* 42 (October 1985): 453–75.

Isaac, Rhys. "Evangelical Revolt: The Nature of the Baptists' Challenge to the Traditional Order in Virginia, 1765 to 1775." *William and Mary Quarterly* 31 (July 1974): 345–68.

———. "Preachers and Patriots: Popular Culture and the Revolution in Virginia." In *The American Revolution: Explorations in the History of American Radicalism,* ed. Alfred F. Young, pp. 125–56. DeKalb, Ill.: Northern Illinois Univ. Press, 1976.

———. *The Transformation of Virginia, 1740–1790.* Chapel Hill: Univ. of North Carolina Press, 1982.

Jaenicke, Douglas Walter. "American Ideas of Political Party as Theories of Politics: Competing Ideas of Liberty and Community." Ph.D. diss., Cornell Univ., 1981.

James, Sydney V. *A People among Peoples: Quaker Benevolence in Eighteenth-Century America.* Cambridge: Harvard Univ. Press, 1963.

Jedrey, Christopher M. *The World of John Cleaveland: Family and Community in Eighteenth-Century New England.* New York: W. W. Norton, 1979.

Jehlen, Myra. *American Incarnation: The Individual, the Nation, and the Continent.* Cambridge: Harvard Univ. Press, 1986.

Jellinek, Georg. *The Declaration of the Rights of Man and of Citizens: A Contribution to Modern Constitutional History.* Trans. Max Farrand. 1901. Reprint, Westport, Conn.: Hyperion Press, 1979.

Jenson, Robert W. *America's Theologian: A Recommendation of Jonathan Edwards.* New York: Oxford Univ. Press, 1987.

Jones, E. L. *The European Miracle: Environments, Economies, and Geopolitics in the History of Europe and Asia.* Cambridge: Cambridge Univ. Press, 1981.

Jordan, Winthrop D. *White over Black: American Attitudes toward the Negro, 1550–1812.* Chapel Hill: Univ. of North Carolina Press, 1968.

Kamenka, Eugene. Introduction to *Community as a Social Ideal,* ed. Eugene Kamenka, pp. vii–ix. London: Edward Arnold, 1982.

Kammen, Michael G. *Spheres of Liberty: Changing Perceptions of Liberty in American Culture.* Madison: Univ. of Wisconsin Press, 1986.

———. *Sovereignty and Liberty: Constitutional Discourse in American Culture.* Madison: Univ. of Wisconsin Press, 1988.

Kateb, George. "Democratic Individuality and the Meaning of Rights." In *Liberalism and the Moral Life,* ed. Nancy L. Rosenblum, pp. 183–206. Cambridge: Harvard Univ. Press, 1989.

Katz, Stanley N. "Thomas Jefferson and the Right to Property in Revolutionary America." *Journal of Law and Economics* 19 (October 1976): 467–88.

———. "The Legal and Religious Context of Natural Rights Theory: A Comment." In *Party and Political Opposition in Revolutionary America,* ed. Patricia U. Bonomi, pp. 35–42. Tarrytown, N.Y.: Sleepy Hollow Press, 1980.

Kendall, Willmoore. "Equality: Commitment or Ideal?" *Intercollegiate Review* 24 (Spring 1989): 25–34.

Kendall, Willmoore, and George Carey. *The Basic Symbols of the American Political Tradition.* Baton Rouge: Louisiana State Univ. Press, 1970.

Kenyon, Cecelia M. "Alexander Hamilton: Rousseau of the Right." *Political Science Quarterly* 73 (June 1958): 161–78.

———. "Republicanism and Radicalism in the American Revolution: An Old-Fashioned Interpretation." In *The Reinterpretation of the American Revolution, 1763–1789,* ed. Jack P. Greene, pp. 291–320. New York: Harper and Row, 1968.

———. "The Declaration of Independence: Philosophy of Government in a Free Society." In *Aspects of American Liberty: Philosophical, Historical, and Political,* ed. George W. Corner, pp. 114–25. Philadelphia: American Philosophical Society, 1977.

Kenyon, John P. "Rights: Where Did the Concept of Rights Come From?" Paper presented at George Mason University, Fairfax, Va., May 1990.

Kerber, Linda K. *Women of the Republic: Intellect and Ideology in Revolutionary America.* Chapel Hill: Univ. of North Carolina Press, 1980.

———. "The Republican Ideology of the Revolutionary Generation." *American Quarterly* 37 (Fall 1985): 474–95.

———. "Can a Woman Be an Individual? The Discourse of Self-Reliance." In *American Chameleon: Individualism in Trans-National Context,* ed. Richard O. Curry and Lawrence B. Goodheart, pp. 151–66. Kent, Ohio: Kent State Univ. Press, 1991.

Kerr, Harry Price. "Politics and Religion in Colonial Fast and Thanksgiving Sermons, 1763–1783." *Quarterly Journal of Speech* 46 (December 1960): 372–82.

———. "The Character of Political Sermons Preached at the Time of the American Revolution." Ph.D. diss., Cornell Univ., 1962.

Kessler, Sanford. "Tocqueville's Puritans: Christianity and the American Founding." *Journal of Politics* 54 (August 1992): 776–92.

Ketcham, Ralph. "James Madison and the Nature of Man." *Journal of the History of Ideas* 19 (January 1958): 62–76.

———. *Presidents above Party: The First American Presidency, 1789–1829.* Chapel Hill: Univ. of North Carolina Press, 1984.

Kirby, John B. "Early American Politics—The Search for Ideology: An Historiographical Analysis and Critique of the Concept of 'Deference.'" *Journal of Politics* 32 (November 1970): 808–38.

Klein, Joe. "Whose Values?" *Newsweek,* 8 June 1992, pp. 19–22.

Kloppenberg, James T. "The Virtues of Liberalism: Christianity, Republicanism, and Ethics in Early American Political Discourse." *Journal of American History* 74 (June 1987): 9–33.

———. Review of *Sister Republics,* by Patrice Higonnet. *Journal of Interdisciplinary History* 23 (Summer 1992): 194–95.

Kolakowski, Leszek. "Modernity on Endless Trial." *Encounter,* March 1986, pp. 8–12.

Konig, David Thomas. "English Legal Change and the Origins of Local Government in Northern Massachusetts." In *Town and County: Essays on the Structure of Local Government in the American Colonies,* ed. Bruce C. Daniels, pp. 12–43. Middletown, Conn.: Wesleyan Univ. Press, 1978.

Konvitz, Milton R., and Clinton Rossiter, eds. *Aspects of Liberty.* Ithaca, N.Y.: Cornell Univ. Press, 1958.

Kramnick, Isaac. "Republican Revisionism Revisited." *American Historical Review* 87 (June 1982): 629–64.

―――. "The 'Great National Discussion': The Discourse of Politics in 1787." *William and Mary Quarterly* 45 (January 1988): 3–32.

―――. *Republicanism and Bourgeois Radicalism: Political Ideology in Late Eighteenth-Century England and America.* Ithaca, N.Y.: Cornell Univ. Press, 1990.

Krieger, Leonard. *Kings and Philosophers, 1689–1789.* New York: W\ W. Norton, 1970.

Kross, Jessica. *The Evolution of an American Town: Newtown, New York, 1642–1775.* Philadelphia: Temple Univ. Press, 1983.

Kuklick, Bruce. "Self and Selflessness in Franklin and Edwards." Paper presented at the National Conference on Benjamin Franklin and Jonathan Edwards, Yale University, New Haven, Conn., February 1990.

Kulikoff, Allan. *The Agrarian Origins of American Capitalism.* Charlottesville: Univ. Press of Virginia, 1992.

Kupperman, Karen O. "Definitions of Liberty on the Eve of Civil War: Lord Saye and Sele, Lord Brooke, and the American Puritan Colonies." *Historical Journal* 32 (1989): 17–34.

Kurtz, Stephen G., and James H. Hutson, eds. *Essays on the American Revolution.* Chapel Hill: Univ. of North Carolina Press, 1973.

Kymlicka, Will. *Liberalism, Community, and Culture.* Oxford: Oxford Univ. Press, 1989.

Lacey, Michael J., and Knud Haakonssen. "Introduction: History, Historicism, and the Culture of Rights." In *A Culture of Rights: The Bill of Rights in Philosophy, Politics, and Law—1791 and 1991,* ed. Michael J. Lacey and Knud Haakonssen, pp. 1–18. New York: Cambridge Univ. Press, 1991.

Ladd, E. C. "205 and Going Strong." *Public Opinion* 4 (June–July 1981): 7–12.

Ladd, John. "The Idea of Community." *New England Journal of Planners* 1 (August 1972): 6–43.

Lakoff, Sanford. "Autonomy and Liberal Democracy." *Review of Politics* 52 (Summer 1990): 378–96.

Larmore, Charles. "Political Liberalism." *Political Theory* 18 (August 1990): 339–60.

Lasch, Christopher. *The Culture of Narcissism: American Life in an Age of Diminishing Expectations.* New York: W. W. Norton, 1978.

―――. *The True and Only Heaven: Progress and Its Critics.* New York: W. W. Norton, 1991.

Laski, Harold J. "Liberty." In *Encyclopedia of the Social Sciences,* ed. E. R. A. Seligman, 9:442–47. New York: Macmillan, 1933.

Laslett, Peter. *The World We Have Lost: England before the Industrial Age—Further Explored.* 3d ed. New York: Charles Scribner's Sons, 1984.

Leder, Lawrence H. *Liberty and Authority: Early American Political Ideology, 1689–1763.* Chicago: Quadrangle Books, 1968.

Lederer, Richard M., Jr., comp. *Colonial American English, a Glossary: Words and Phrases Found in Colonial Writing, Now Archaic, Obscure, or Whose Meanings Have Changed.* Essex, Conn.: Verbatim Books, 1985.

Lemisch, Jesse. "Bailyn Besieged in His Bunker." *Radical History Review* 3 (1976): 72–83.

Lemon, James. *The Best Poor Man's Country: A Geographical Study of Early Southeastern Pennsylvania.* Baltimore: Johns Hopkins Univ. Press, 1972.

―――. "Spatial Order: Households in Local Communities and Regions." In *Colonial British America: Essays in the New History of the Early Modern Era,* ed.

Jack P. Greene and J. R. Pole, pp. 86–122. Baltimore: Johns Hopkins Univ. Press, 1984.

Lerner, Max. *America as a Civilization: Life and Thought in the United States Today*. New York: Simon and Schuster, 1957.

Leuchtenburg, William E. *The Perils of Prosperity, 1914–1932*. Chicago: Univ. of Chicago Press, 1958.

Levy, Leonard W. "Liberty and the First Amendment." *American Historical Review* 68 (October 1962): 22–37.

Lewis, C. S. *Studies in Words*. Cambridge: Cambridge Univ. Press, 1960.

Lewis, Ewart. "The Contribution of Medieval Thought to the American Political Tradition." *American Political Science Review* 50 (June 1956): 462–74.

Lewis, Jan. *The Pursuit of Happiness: Family and Values in Jefferson's Virginia*. Cambridge: Cambridge Univ. Press, 1983.

Liddle, William D. " 'Virtue and Liberty': An Inquiry into the Role of the Agrarian Myth in the Rhetoric of the American Revolutionary Era." *South Atlantic Quarterly* 77 (Winter 1978): 15–38.

Lienesch, Michael. *New Order of the Ages: Time, the Constitution, and the Making of Modern American Political Thought*. Princeton: Princeton Univ. Press, 1988.

Lindsay, A. D. "Individualism." In *Encyclopedia of the Social Sciences*, ed. E. R. A. Seligman, 7:674–80. New York: Macmillan, 1933.

Lingeman, Richard. *Small Town America: A Narrative History, 1620 to the Present*. New York: G. P. Putnam's Sons, 1980.

Lippmann, Walter. "What Modern Liberty Means." In *Liberty and the News*, pp. 19–68. New York: Harcourt, Brace, and Howe, 1920.

———. *Essays in the Public Philosophy: On the Decline and Revival of the Western Society*. Boston: Little, Brown, 1955.

Lipset, Seymour Martin. *The First New Nation: The United States in Historical and Comparative Perspective*. 1963. Reprint, with a new introduction, New York: W. W. Norton, 1979.

Lipset, Seymour Martin, and Earl Raab. *The Politics of Unreason: Right-Wing Extremism in America, 1790–1970*. New York: Harper and Row, 1970.

Little, David. "Max Weber Revisited: The 'Protestant Ethic' and the Puritan Experience of Order." *Harvard Theological Review* 59 (1966): 415–28.

Lockridge, Kenneth A. "Land, Population, and the Evolution of New England Society, 1630–1790." *Past and Present* 39 (April 1968): 62–80.

———. "Social Change and the Meaning of the American Revolution." *Journal of Social History* 6 (Summer 1973): 403–39.

———. *Settlement and Unsettlement in Early America: The Crisis of Political Legitimacy before the Revolution*. Cambridge: Cambridge Univ. Press, 1981.

———. *A New England Town: The First Hundred Years—Dedham, Massachusetts, 1636–1736*. Enlarged ed. New York: W. W. Norton, 1985.

Lockridge, Kenneth A., and Alan Kreider. "The Evolution of Massachusetts Town Government, 1640 to 1740." *William and Mary Quarterly* 23 (October 1966): 549–74.

Love, William DeLoss, Jr. *The Fast and Thanksgiving Days of New England*. Boston: Houghton Mifflin, 1895.

Lovejoy, Arthur O. *The Great Chain of Being: A Study of the History of an Idea*. Cambridge: Harvard Univ. Press, 1936.

Lovejoy, David S. "Rights Imply Equality: The Case against Admiralty Jurisdiction in America, 1764–1776." *William and Mary Quarterly* 16 (October 1959): 459–84.

Lukes, Steven. "The Meanings of 'Individualism.'" *Journal of the History of Ideas* 32 (January–March 1971): 45–66.

———. *Individualism.* Oxford: Basil Blackwell, 1973.

———. "Types of Individualism." In *Dictionary of the History of Ideas,* ed. Philip P. Wiener, 2:594–604. New York: Charles Scribner's Sons, 1973.

Lundberg, David, and Henry F. May. "The Enlightened Reader in America." *American Quarterly* 28 (Summer 1976): 262–93.

Lutz, Donald S. *Popular Consent and Popular Control: Whig Political Theory in the Early State Constitutions.* Baton Rouge: Louisiana State Univ. Press, 1980.

———. "The Relative Influence of European Writers on Late Eighteenth-Century American Political Thought." *American Political Science Review* 78 (March 1984): 189–97.

———. *The Origins of American Constitutionalism.* Baton Rouge: Louisiana State Univ. Press, 1988.

———. *A Preface to American Political Theory.* Lawrence: University Press of Kansas, 1992.

Lynd, Staughton. *Intellectual Origins of American Radicalism.* New York: Random House, 1968.

Lyons, John O. *The Invention of the Self: The Hinge of Consciousness in the Eighteenth Century.* Carbondale: Southern Illinois Univ. Press, 1978.

MacCallum, Gerald C., Jr. "Negative and Positive Freedom." In *Politics, Philosophy, and Society,* ed. Peter Laslett, W. G. Runciman, and Quentin Skinner, pp. 174–93. New York: Barnes and Noble, 1972.

McCoy, Drew R. *The Elusive Republic: Political Economy in Jeffersonian America.* 1980. Reprint, New York: W. W. Norton, 1982.

McCusker, John J., and Russell R. Menard. *The Economy of British America, 1607–1789.* Chapel Hill: Univ. of North Carolina Press, 1985.

McDonald, Forrest. *E Pluribus Unum: The Formation of the American Republic, 1776–1790.* 1965. Reprint, Indianapolis: Liberty Press, 1979.

———. *Alexander Hamilton.* New York: W. W. Norton, 1982.

———. "Conservative Scholarship and the Problem of Myth." *Continuity* 4–5 (Spring–Fall 1982): 51–69.

———. *Novus Ordo Seclorum: The Intellectual Origins of the Constitution.* Lawrence: Univ. Press of Kansas, 1985.

McDonald, Forrest, and Ellen McDonald. *Requiem: Variations on Eighteenth-Century Themes.* Lawrence: Univ. Press of Kansas, 1988.

McDonald, Forrest, and Grady McWhiney. "The South from Self-Sufficiency to Peonage: An Interpretation." *American Historical Review* 85 (December 1980): 1095–1118.

Macedo, Stephen. *Liberal Virtues: Citizenship, Virtue, and Community in Liberal Constitutionalism.* New York: Oxford Univ. Press, 1990.

Macfarlane, Alan. *The Origins of English Individualism: The Family, Property, and Social Transition.* Oxford: Basil Blackwell, 1978.

MacIntyre, Alasdair. *After Virtue: A Study in Moral Theory.* 2d ed. Notre Dame, Ind.: Univ. of Notre Dame Press, 1984.

———. "Is Patriotism a Virtue?" Lindley Lecture, Univ. of Kansas, 26 March 1984.

———. "The Privatization of Good: An Inaugural Lecture." *Review of Politics* 52 (Summer 1990): 344–77.

MacLeod, Duncan J. *Slavery, Race, and the American Revolution.* New York: Cambridge Univ. Press, 1974.

McLoughlin, William G. "The Role of Religion in the Revolution: Liberty of Conscience and Cultural Cohesion in the New Nation." In *Essays on the American Revolution,* ed. Stephen G. Kurtz and James H. Hutson, pp. 197–255. Chapel Hill: Univ. of North Carolina Press, 1973.

McNeill, William. "The Care and Repair of Public Myth." *Foreign Affairs* 61 (1982): 1–13.

McWilliams, Wilson Carey. *The Idea of Fraternity in America.* Berkeley and Los Angeles: Univ. of California Press, 1973.

———. "Democracy and the Citizen: Community, Dignity, and the Crisis of Contemporary Politics in America." In *How Democratic Is the Constitution?* ed. R. Goldwin and W. Schambra, pp. 79–101. Washington, D.C.: American Enterprise Institute Press, 1980.

Madison, Gary Brent. *The Logic of Liberty.* Westport, Conn.: Greenwood Press, 1986.

Maier, Pauline. *The Old Revolutionaries: Political Lives in the Age of Samuel Adams.* New York: Random House, 1982.

———. "Good Show: George Washington Plays George Washington." *Reviews in American History* 17 (June 1989): 187–98.

Main, Jackson Turner. *The Anti-federalists: Critics of the Constitution, 1781– 1788.* Chapel Hill: Univ. of North Carolina Press, 1961.

———. *The Social Structure of Revolutionary America.* Princeton: Princeton Univ. Press, 1965.

———. "An Agenda for Research on the Origins and Nature of the Constitution of 1787–1788." *William and Mary Quarterly* 44 (July 1987): 591–97.

Mann, Bruce H. *Neighbors and Strangers: Law and Community in Early Connecticut.* Chapel Hill: Univ. of North Carolina Press, 1987.

Manuel, Frank E., and Fritzie P. Manuel. *Utopian Thought in the Western World.* Cambridge: Harvard Univ. Press, 1979.

Marsden, George M. *Fundamentalism and American Culture: The Shaping of Twentieth-Century Evangelicalism, 1870–1925.* New York: Oxford Univ. Press, 1980.

———. "The Great Divide." *Reviews in American History* 17 (June 1989): 284–88.

Masur, Louis P. "'Age of the First Person Singular': The Vocabulary of the Self in New England, 1780–1850." *Journal of American Studies* 25 (1991): 189–211.

Matthews, Richard K. *The Radical Politics of Thomas Jefferson: A Revisionist View.* Lawrence: Univ. Press of Kansas, 1984.

———. "Liberalism, Civic Humanism, and the American Political Tradition: Understanding Genesis." *Journal of Politics* 49 (November 1987): 1127–53.

May, Henry F. *The Enlightenment in America.* New York: Oxford Univ. Press, 1976.

Menard, Russell R. "Yankee Puritans." Review of *Profits in the Wilderness: Entrepreneurship and the Founding of New England Towns in the Seventeenth Century,* by John Frederick Martin; and of *John Nelson, Merchant Adventurer,* by Richard R. Johnson. *Reviews in American History* 21 (September 1993): 385–89.

Merrill, Michael. "Cash Is Good to Eat: Self-Sufficiency and Exchange in the Rural Economy of the United States." *Radical History Review* 4 (1977): 42–71.

Merrill, Michael, and Sean Wilentz, eds. *The Key of Liberty: The Life and Democratic Writings of William Manning, "A Laborer," 1747–1814*. Manuscript.

Merritt, Richard L. *Symbols of American Community, 1735–1775*. New Haven: Yale Univ. Press, 1966.

Meyers, Marvin. *The Jacksonian Persuasion: Politics and Belief*. 1957. Reprint, Stanford: Stanford Univ. Press, 1960.

Miller, David. *Philosophy and Ideology in Hume's Political Thought*. Oxford: Oxford Univ. Press, 1981.

———. "The Resurgence of Political Theory." *Political Studies* 38 (Fall 1990): 421–37.

Miller, Eugene F. "Hume on English Liberty." *Political Science Reviewer* 16 (Fall 1986): 127–84.

Miller, Joshua. "The Ghostly Body Politic: *The Federalist* Papers and Popular Sovereignty." *Political Theory* 16 (February 1988): 99–119.

———. *The Rise and Fall of Democracy in Early America, 1630–1789: The Legacy for Contemporary Politics*. University Park: Pennsylvania State Univ. Press, 1991.

Miller, Perry. *The New England Mind*. Vol. 1, *The Seventeenth Century*. Cambridge: Harvard Univ. Press, 1939.

———. *The New England Mind*. Vol. 2, *From Colony to Province*. Cambridge: Harvard Univ. Press, 1953.

———. *Errand into the Wilderness*. Cambridge: Harvard Univ. Press, 1956.

———. "From the Covenant to the Revival." In *The Shaping of American Religion*, ed. J. W. Smith and A. L. Jamison, pp. 322–68. Princeton: Princeton Univ. Press, 1961.

———. *The Life of the Mind in America: From the Revolution to the Civil War*. New York: Harcourt Brace Jovanovich, 1965.

———. "Crisis and Americanization." In *The Great Awakening: Event and Exegesis*, ed. D. B. Rutman, pp. 139–56. 1970. Reprint, Huntington, N.Y.: Krieger, 1977.

Mitchell, Joshua. *Not By Reason Alone: Religion, History, and Identity in Early Modern Political Thought*. Chicago: Univ. of Chicago Press, 1993.

Moeller, Bernd. *Imperial Cities and the Reformation: Three Essays*. Trans. and ed. H. C. Erik Middleford and Mark V. Edwards, Jr. Philadelphia: Fortress Press, 1972.

Moore, Barrington, Jr. *Social Origins of Dictatorship and Democracy: Lord and Peasant in the Making of the Modern World*. Boston: Beacon Press, 1966.

Morgan, Edmund S. *The Puritan Family: Religious and Domestic Relations in Seventeenth-Century New England*. 1944. Reprint, New York: Harper and Row, 1966.

———. *The Birth of the Republic, 1763–1789*. Chicago: Univ. of Chicago Press, 1956.

———. "The Puritan Ethic and the Coming of the American Revolution." In *The Reinterpretation of the American Revolution, 1763–1789*, ed. Jack P. Greene, pp. 235–51. New York: Harper and Row, 1968.

———. "The American Revolution Considered as an Intellectual Movement." In *Essays on the American Revolution*, ed. David L. Jacobson, pp. 27–42. New York: Holt, Rinehart and Winston, 1970.

———. "Slavery and Freedom: The American Paradox." *Journal of American History* 59 (June 1972): 5–29.

———. *American Slavery, American Freedom: The Ordeal of Colonial Virginia.* New York: W. W. Norton, 1975.

———. "Government by Fiction: The Idea of Representation." *Yale Review* 72 (Spring 1983): 321–39.

———. "Popular Fiction." *New Republic,* 29 June 1987, pp. 25–36.

———. *Inventing the People: The Rise of Popular Sovereignty in England and America.* New York: W. W. Norton, 1988.

———. "Power to the People?" Review of *The Debate on the Constitution: Federalist and Antifederalist Speeches, Articles, and Letters during the Struggle over Ratification,* ed. Bernard Bailyn. *New York Review of Books,* 2 December 1993, pp. 27–29.

Morgan, William. *Memoirs of the Life of the Rev. Richard Price.* London: R. Hunter, 1815.

Morison, Samuel Eliot. *The Oxford History of the American People.* New York: Oxford Univ. Press, 1965.

———, ed. "William Manning's *The Key of Libberty.*" *William and Mary Quarterly* 13 (April 1956): 202–8.

Moulin, Leo. "On the Evolution of the Meaning of the Word 'Individualism.'" *International Social Science Bulletin* 7 (1955): 181–85.

Mulgan, Richard. "Liberty in Ancient Greece." In *Conceptions of Liberty in Political Philosophy,* ed. Zbigniew Pelczynski and John Gray, pp. 7–26. London: Athlone Press, 1984.

Murrin, John M. "The Myths of Colonial Democracy and Royal Decline in Eighteenth-Century America: A Review Essay." *Cithara* 5 (November 1965): 53–69.

———. "Review Essay." *History and Theory* 11 (1972): 226–75.

———. "The Great Inversion, or Court versus Country: A Comparison of the Revolutionary Settlements in England (1688–1721) and America (1776–1816)." In *Three British Revolutions: 1641, 1688, 1776,* ed. J. G. A. Pocock, pp. 368–453. Princeton: Princeton Univ. Press, 1980.

———. "A Roof without Walls: The Dilemma of American National Identity." In *Beyond Confederation: Origins of the Constitution and American National Identity,* ed. Richard Beeman, Stephen Botein, and Edward C. Carter II, pp. 333–48. Chapel Hill: Univ. of North Carolina Press, 1987.

———. "Self-Interest Conquers Patriotism: Republicans, Liberals, and Indians Reshape the Nation." In *The American Revolution: Its Character and Limits,* ed. Jack P. Greene, pp. 224–29. New York: New York Univ. Press, 1987.

———. "Religion and Politics in America from the First Settlements to the Civil War." In *Religion and American Politics,* ed. Mark A. Noll, pp. 19–43. New York: Oxford Univ. Press, 1990.

Mutch, Robert. "Yeoman and Merchant in Pre-Industrial America: Eighteenth-Century Massachusetts as a Case Study." *Societas* 7 (Autumn 1977): 279–302.

Neal, Patrick, and David Paris. "Liberalism and the Communitarian Critique: A Guide for the Perplexed." *Canadian Journal of Political Science* 23 (September 1990): 419–39.

Nelson, John R., Jr. *Liberty and Property: Political Economy and Policymaking in the New Nation, 1789–1812.* Baltimore: Johns Hopkins Univ. Press, 1987.

Nelson, W. H. *The American Tory.* Oxford: Oxford Univ. Press, 1961.

Nelson, William E. *Americanization of the Common Law: The Impact of Legal Change upon Massachusetts Society, 1760–1830.* Cambridge: Harvard Univ. Press, 1975.

———. "The Eighteenth Century Constitution as a Basis for Protecting Personal Liberty." In Nelson and Palmer, *Liberty and Community: Constitution and Rights in the Early American Republic,* pp. 15–53. New York: Oceana, 1987.

Nelson, William E., and Robert C. Palmer. *Liberty and Community: Constitution and Rights in the Early American Republic.* New York: Oceana, 1987.

Nicgorski, Walter. "The Significance of the Non-Lockean Heritage of the Declaration of Independence." *American Journal of Jurisprudence* 21 (1976): 156–77.

Nichols, James Hastings. *Democracy and the Churches.* Philadelphia: Westminster Press, 1951.

Niebuhr, H. R. *The Kingdom of God in America.* New York: Harper and Row, 1937.

———. "The Protestant Movement and Democracy in the United States." In *The Shaping of American Religion,* ed. J. W. Smith and A. L. Jamison, pp. 20–71. Princeton: Princeton Univ. Press, 1961.

Nisbet, Robert A. *The Quest for Community: A Study in the Ethics of Order and Freedom.* Oxford: Oxford Univ. Press, 1953; reprint, San Francisco: ICS Press, 1990.

———. "Citizenship: Two Traditions." *Social Research* 41 (Winter 1974): 612–37.

———. Review of *Conservatism: A Contribution to the Sociology of Knowledge,* by Karl Mannheim. *Society* (November–December 1987): 102–4.

Nobles, Gregory H. *Divisions throughout the Whole: Politics and Society in Hampshire County, Massachusetts, 1740–1775.* New York: Cambridge Univ. Press, 1983.

———. "Breaking Into the Backcountry: New Approaches to the Early American Frontier." *William and Mary Quarterly* 46 (October 1989): 641–70.

Noll, Mark A. *Christians in the American Revolution.* Grand Rapids, Mich.: Christian Univ. Press, 1977.

———. *Princeton and the Republic, 1768–1822: The Search for a Christian Enlightenment in the Era of Samuel Stanhope Smith.* Princeton: Princeton Univ. Press, 1989.

———. "The American Revolution and Protestant Evangelicalism." *Journal of Interdisciplinary History* 23 (Winter 1993): 615–38.

Ohmori, Yuhtaro. "'The Artillery of Mr. Locke': The Use of Locke's *Second Treatise* in Pre-Revolutionary America, 1764–1776." Ph.D. diss., Johns Hopkins Univ., 1988.

Okin, Susan Moller. *Justice, Gender, and the Family.* New York: Basic Books, 1989.

Onuf, Peter S. "Historians and the Bicentennial." *Organization of American Historians Newsletter* (May 1988): 20.

Pagels, Elaine. "The Politics of Paradise." *New York Review of Books,* 12 June 1988, pp. 28–37.

Pahl, Jon. *Free Will and Political Liberty in American Culture, 1630–1760: Paradox Lost.* Baltimore: Johns Hopkins Univ. Press, 1992.

Palmer, Robert C. "Liberties as Constitutional Provisions: 1776–1791." In Nelson and Palmer, *Liberty and Community: Constitution and Rights in the Early American Republic,* pp. 55–148. New York: Oceana, 1987.

Pangle, Thomas. "Civic Virtue: The Founders' Conception and the Traditional Concept." In *Constitutionalism and Rights,* ed. G. Bryner and N. Reynolds, pp. 105–40. Provo, Utah: Brigham Young Univ., 1987.

———. *The Spirit of Modern Republicanism: The Moral Vision of the American Founders and the Philosophy of Locke.* Chicago: Univ. of Chicago Press, 1988.

Parent, William A. "Some Recent Work on the Concept of Liberty." *American Philosophical Quarterly* 11 (July 1974): 149 67.

Parrington, Vernon. *Main Currents in American Thought.* 2 vols. New York: Harcourt, Brace, 1927.

Patterson, Orlando. *Slavery and Social Death: A Comparative Study.* Cambridge: Harvard Univ. Press, 1982.

———. *Freedom.* Vol. 1, *Freedom in the Making of Western Culture.* New York: Basic Books, 1991.

Paul, Ellen, and Howard Dickman, eds. *Liberty, Property, and the Foundations of the American Constitution.* Albany: State Univ. of New York Press, 1988.

Pekelis, Alexander H. *Law and Social Action: Selected Essays.* Ithaca, N.Y.: Cornell Univ. Press, 1950.

Pencak, William. "Benjamin Franklin's *Autobiography,* Cotton Mather, and a Puritan God." *Pennsylvania History* 53 (January 1986): 1–25.

———. "Samuel Adams and Shays's Rebellion." *New England Quarterly* 62 (March 1989): 63–74.

Perry, Ralph Barton. *Puritanism and Democracy.* New York: Vanguard Press, 1944.

Persons, Stow. "The Cyclical Theory of History in Eighteenth-Century America." *American Quarterly* 6 (Summer 1954): 147–63.

Peters, Ronald M., Jr. *The Massachusetts Constitution of 1780: A Social Compact.* Amherst: Univ. of Massachusetts Press, 1978.

Phillips, Derek L. *Looking Backward: A Critical Appraisal of Communitarian Thought.* Princeton: Princeton Univ. Press, 1993.

Phillips, Kevin P. *Post-Conservative America: People, Politics, and Ideology in a Time of Crisis.* New York: Vintage Books, 1983.

Pitkin, Hanna Fenichel. "Are Freedom and Liberty Twins?" Paper presented at the Yale Legal Theory Workshop. Published in *Political Theory* 16 (November 1988): 523–52.

Pocock, J. G. A. "Virtue and Commerce in the Eighteenth Century." *Journal of Interdisciplinary History* 3 (Summer 1972): 119–34.

———. *Politics, Language, and Time: Essays on Political Thought and History.* New York: Atheneum, 1973.

———. *The Machiavellian Moment: Florentine Political Thought and the Atlantic Republican Tradition.* Princeton: Princeton Univ. Press, 1975.

———. "Virtues, Rights, and Manners: A Model for Historians of Political Thought." *Political Theory* 9 (August 1981): 353–68.

———. *Virtue, Commerce, and History: Essays on Political Thought and History, Chiefly in the Eighteenth Century.* Cambridge: Cambridge Univ. Press, 1985.

———. "Between Gog and Magog: The Republican Thesis and the *Ideologia Americana.*" *Journal of the History of Ideas* 48 (April–June 1987): 325–46.

———, ed. *Three British Revolutions: 1641, 1688, 1776.* Princeton: Princeton Univ. Press, 1980.

Polanyi, Karl. *The Great Transformation.* 1944. Reprint, Boston: Beacon Press, 1957.

Pole, J. R. *Political Representation in England and the Origins of the American Republic.* 1966. Reprint, Berkeley and Los Angeles: Univ. of California Press, 1971.

Poponoe, David. "Family Decline in the Swedish Welfare State." *Public Interest* 102 (Winter 1991): 65–77.

Potter, Janice. *The Liberty We Seek: Loyalist Ideology in Colonial New York and Massachusetts.* Cambridge: Harvard Univ. Press, 1983.

Powell, H. Jefferson. "The Original Understanding of Original Intent." *Harvard Law Review* 98 (March 1985): 885–948.

Powell, Sumner Chilton. *Puritan Village: The Formation of a New England Town.* Middletown, Conn.: Wesleyan Univ. Press, 1963.

Prospo, R. C. De. "Paine and Sieyès." *Thought* 65 (June 1990): 191–202.

Pruitt, Bettye Hobbs. "Self-Sufficiency and the Agricultural Economy of Eighteenth-Century Massachusetts." *William and Mary Quarterly* 41 (July 1984): 333–64.

Rahe, Paul A. "The Primacy of Politics in Classical Greece." *American Historical Review* 89 (April 1984): 265–93.

———. *Republics Ancient and Modern: Classical Republicanism and the American Revolution.* Chapel Hill: Univ. of North Carolina Press, 1992.

Ramsay, Paul. Editor's introduction to *Freedom of the Will,* by Jonathan Edwards. New Haven: Yale Univ. Press, 1957.

Redfield, Robert. *The Little Community and Peasant Society and Culture.* Chicago: Univ. of Chicago Press, 1960.

Reed, Gary F. "Berlin and the Division of Liberty." *Political Theory* 8 (August 1980): 365–80.

Reichley, A. James. "Democracy and Religion." *PS* 19 (Fall 1986): 801–6.

Reid, John Phillip. "The Irrelevance of the Declaration." In *Law in the American Revolution,* ed. Hendrik Hartog, pp. 46–89. New York: New York Univ. Press, 1981.

———. *Constitutional History of the American Revolution: The Authority of Rights.* Madison: Univ. of Wisconsin Press, 1986.

———. *Constitutional History of the American Revolution: The Authority to Tax.* Madison: Univ. of Wisconsin Press, 1987.

———. *The Concept of Liberty in the Age of the American Revolution.* Chicago: Univ. of Chicago Press, 1988.

Reynolds, Charles H., and Ralph V. Norman, eds. *Community in America: The Challenge of Habits of the Heart.* Berkeley and Los Angeles: Univ. of California Press, 1988.

Rezneck, Samuel. "The Rise and Early Development of Industrial Consciousness in the United States, 1760–1830." *Journal of Economic and Business History* 4 (1932): 784–811.

Rieder, Jonathan. *Canarsie: The Jews and Italians of Brooklyn against Liberalism.* Cambridge: Harvard Univ. Press, 1985.

Rischin, Moses. "When the New York Savants Go Marching In." *Reviews in American History* 17 (June 1989): 289–300.

Robbins, Caroline. *The Eighteenth-Century Commonwealthman: Studies in the Transmission, Development, and Circumstance of English Liberal Thought from the Restoration of Charles II until the War with the Thirteen Colonies.* Cambridge: Harvard Univ. Press, 1961.

———. *The Pursuit of Happiness.* Washington, D.C.: American Enterprise Institute, 1974.

Robinson, Donald L. *Slavery in the Structure of American Politics, 1765–1820.* New York: Harcourt Brace Jovanovich, 1971.

Roche, John P. "American Liberty: An Examination of the 'Tradition' of Freedom." In *Aspects of Liberty,* ed. Milton R. Konvitz and Clinton Rossiter, pp. 129–62. Ithaca, N.Y.: Cornell Univ. Press, 1958.

———. "The Curbing of the Militant Majority: A Dissent from the Classic Liberal Interpretation of Civil Liberties in America." *Reporter,* 18 July 1963, pp. 34–38.

———. "The Founding Fathers: A Reform Caucus in Action." In *The Reinterpretation of the American Revolution, 1763–1789,* ed. Jack P. Greene, pp. 436–69. New York: Harper and Row, 1968.

———. "The Strange Case of the 'Revolutionary' Establishment." In *Sentenced to Life,* pp. 167–81. New York: Macmillan, 1974.

Rodgers, Daniel T. *Contested Truths: Keywords in American Politics since Independence.* New York: Basic Books, 1987.

———. "Republicanism: The Career of a Concept." Paper presented at the Conference on Political Identity in American Thought, Yale University, 21 April 1991. Published in *Journal of American History* 79 (June 1992): 12–38.

Roelofs, H. Mark. "The American Political System: A Systematic Ambiguity." *Review of Politics* 48 (Summer 1986): 323–48.

Rosenfeld, David. "Rousseau's Unanimous Contract and the Doctrine of Popular Sovereignty." *History of Political Thought* 8 (Spring 1987): 83–110.

Rossiter, Clinton. *Seedtime of the Republic: The Origin of the American Tradition of Political Liberty.* New York: Harcourt, Brace, and World, 1953.

———. *The First American Revolution: The American Colonies on the Eve of Independence.* Part 1 of *Seedtime of the Republic: The Origin of the American Tradition of Political Liberty.* Revised ed. New York: Harcourt Brace Jovanovich, 1956.

Rotunda, Ronald D. *The Politics of Language: Liberalism as Word and Symbol.* Iowa City: Univ. of Iowa Press, 1986.

Rutman, D. B., ed. *The Great Awakening: Event and Exegesis.* 1970. Reprint, Huntington, N.Y.: Krieger, 1977.

Rutman, D. B., and A. H. Rutman. *A Place in Time: Middlesex County, Virginia, 1650–1760.* New York: W. W. Norton, 1984.

Ryan, Alan. "Freedom." *Philosophy* 40 (April 1965): 93–112.

Sabine, George H. *A History of Political Theory.* 4th ed., rev. T. H. Thorson. Hinsdale, Ill.: Dryden Press, 1973.

Sandel, Michael J. *Liberalism and the Limits of Justice.* Cambridge: Cambridge Univ. Press, 1982.

———. "Democrats and Community: A Public Philosophy for American Liberalism." *New Republic,* 22 February 1988, pp. 20–23.

Sandoz, Ellis. *A Government of Laws: Political Theory, Religion, and the American Founding.* Baton Rouge: Louisiana State Univ. Press, 1990.

Sartori, Giovanni. "The Relevance of Liberalism in Retrospect." In *The Relevance of Liberalism,* ed. Research Institute on International Change, pp. 1–31. Boulder, Colo.: Westview Press, 1978.

———. "Liberty and Law." In *The Politicization of Society,* ed. Kenneth S. Templeton, Jr., pp. 249–312. Indianapolis: Liberty Press, 1979.

Saum, Lewis O. *The Popular Mood of Pre–Civil War America.* Westport, Conn.: Greenwood Press, 1980.

Schaff, Philip. *America: A Sketch of the Political, Social, and Religious Character of the United States of North America, in Two Lectures.* New York: C. Scribner, 1855.

Schapiro, J. Salwyn. *Liberalism: Its Meaning and History.* Princeton: Van Nostrand, 1958.

Scheiber, Harry N. "Economic Liberty and the Constitution." In *Essays on the History of Liberty,* pp. 75–99. San Marino, Calif.: Huntington Library, 1988.

Schmitt, Gary J., and Robert K. Webking. "Revolutionaries, Antifederalists, and Federalists: Comments on Gordon Wood's Understanding of the American Founding." *Political Science Reviewer* 9 (1979): 195–229.

Schneider, Herbert W. *A History of American Philosophy.* New York: Columbia Univ. Press, 1946.

Schumpeter, Joseph. *Capitalism, Socialism, and Democracy.* New York: Harper Brothers, 1942.

Schwartz, Edward. "A Chorus of Moral Voices." Review of *The Spirit of Community,* by Amitai Etzioni. *New York Times Book Review,* 11 April 1993.

Scott, William B. *In Pursuit of Happiness: American Conceptions of Property from the Seventeenth to the Twentieth Century.* Bloomington: Indiana Univ. Press, 1977.

Seiler, William H. "The Anglican Church: A Basic Institution of Local Government in Colonial Virginia." In *Town and County: Essays on the Structure of Local Government in the American Colonies,* ed. Bruce C. Daniels, pp. 134–59. Middletown, Conn.: Wesleyan Univ. Press, 1978.

Selby, John Edward. *A Concept of Liberty.* Ph.D. diss., Brown Univ., 1955.

Shaffer, Arthur H. *The Politics of History: Writing the History of the American Revolution, 1783–1815.* Chicago: Precedent, 1975.

Shalhope, Robert E. "Race, Class, Slavery, and the Antebellum Southern Mind." *Journal of Southern History* 37 (November 1971): 557–74.

———. *John Taylor of Caroline: Pastoral Republican.* Columbia: Univ. of South Carolina Press, 1980.

———. "Republicanism and Early American Historiography." *William and Mary Quarterly* 39 (April 1982): 334–56.

———. "Individualism in the Early Republic." In *American Chameleon: Individualism in Trans-National Context,* ed. Richard O. Curry and Lawrence B. Goodheart, pp. 66–86. Kent, Ohio: Kent State Univ. Press, 1991.

Sheldon, Garrett Ward. *The Political Philosophy of Thomas Jefferson.* Baltimore: Johns Hopkins Univ. Press, 1991.

Sheridan, Earl. "The 'Republican Revision' and the Teaching of American Government." *PS* 20 (Summer 1987): 689–91.

Shklar, Judith. "Gone with the Wind." Review of *The Great Triumvirate,* by Merrill D. Peterson. *New Republic,* 21 March 1988, pp. 39–41.

Shy, John. "The American Revolution: The Military Conflict Considered as a Revolutionary War." In *Essays on the American Revolution,* ed. Stephen G. Kurtz and James H. Hutson, pp. 121–56. Chapel Hill: Univ. of North Carolina Press, 1973.

Simler, Lucy. "The Township: The Community of the Rural Pennsylvanian." *Pennsylvania Magazine of History and Biography* 100 (1982): 41–68.

Simmons, R. C. *The American Colonies: From Settlement to Independence.* New York: W. W. Norton, 1976.

Singleton, Gregory H. "Protestant Voluntary Organizations and the Shaping of Victorian America." *American Quarterly* 27 (December 1975): 549–60.

Sinopoli, Richard. "Liberalism, Republicanism, and the Constitution." *Polity* 19 (Spring 1987): 331–52.

———. *The Foundations of American Citizenship: Liberalism, the Constitution, and Civic Virtue.* New York: Oxford Univ. Press, 1992.

———. "Liberalism and Contested Conceptions of the Good: The Limits of Neutrality." *Journal of Politics* 55 (August 1993): 644 63.

Skerry, Peter. "Individualist America and Today's Immigrants." *Public Interest* 102 (Winter 1991): 104–18.

Skidmore, Max J. *American Political Thought.* New York: St. Martin's Press, 1978.

Skinner, Quentin. "Meaning and Understanding in the History of Ideas." *History and Theory* 8 (1969): 3–53.

———. "The Context of Hobbes's Theory of Political Obligation." In *Hobbes and Rousseau: A Collection of Critical Essays,* ed. M. Cranston and R. Peters, pp. 109–42. New York: Anchor Books, 1972.

———. *The Foundations of Modern Political Thought.* 2 vols. Cambridge: Cambridge Univ. Press, 1978.

———. "The Idea of Negative Liberty: Philosophical and Historical Perspectives." In *Philosophy in History: Essays on the Historiography of Philosophy,* ed. R. Rorty, J. B. Schneewind, and Q. Skinner, pp. 193–224. Cambridge: Cambridge Univ. Press, 1984.

———. "The Paradoxes of Political Liberty." In *The Tanner Lectures on Human Values,* pp. 227–50. Cambridge: Cambridge Univ. Press, 1986.

Slaughter, Thomas P. *The Whiskey Rebellion: Frontier Epilogue to the American Revolution.* New York: Oxford Univ. Press, 1986.

Sly, John Fairfield. *Town Government in Massachusetts (1620–1930).* 1930. Reprint, Hamden, Conn.: Archon Books, 1967.

Smith, Daniel Blake. *Inside the Great House: Planter Family Life in Eighteenth-Century Chesapeake Society.* Ithaca, N.Y.: Cornell Univ. Press, 1980.

Smith, H. Shelton. *Changing Conceptions of Original Sin: A Study in American Theology since 1750.* New York: Charles Scribner's Sons, 1955.

Smith, J. Allen. "The Spirit of American Government." In *The Case against the Constitution: From the Antifederalists to the Present,* ed. J. F. Manley and K. M. Dolbeare, pp. 3–30. Armonk, N. Y.: M. E. Sharpe, 1987.

Smith, Maynard. "Reason, Passion and Political Freedom in *The Federalist.*" *Journal of Politics* 22 (August 1960): 525–44.

Smith, Rogers M. "The Constitution and Autonomy." *Texas Law Review* 60 (February 1982): 175–205.

———. *Liberalism and American Constitutional Law.* Cambridge: Harvard Univ. Press, 1985.

———. "The 'American Creed' and American Identity: The Limits of Liberal Citizenship in the United States." *Western Political Quarterly* 41 (June 1988): 225–51.

———. "Embedded Oligarchies: Democracy in America Reconsidered." Manuscript, December 1991.

———. "Beyond Tocqueville, Myrdal, and Hartz: The Multiple Traditions in America." *American Political Science Review* 87 (September 1993): 549–65.

Snydacker, Daniel. "Kinship and Community in Rural Pennsylvania, 1749–1820." *Journal of Interdisciplinary History* 13 (Summer 1982): 41–61.

Solzhenitsyn, Aleksandr. "A World Split Apart." In *Solzhenitsyn at Harvard,* ed. Ronald Berman, pp. 3–20. Washington, D.C.: Ethics and Public Policy Center, 1980.

Somkin, Fred. *Unquiet Eagle: Memory and Desire in the Idea of American Freedom, 1815–1860.* Ithaca, N.Y.: Cornell Univ. Press, 1967.

Sowell, Thomas. *Ethnic America: A History.* New York: Basic Books, 1981.

Spurlin, Paul Merrill. *Montesquieu in America, 1760–1801.* Baton Rouge: Louisiana State Univ. Press, 1940.

———. *The French Enlightenment in America: Essays on the Times of the Founding Fathers.* Athens: Univ. of Georgia Press, 1984.

Stanlis, Peter. *Edmund Burke and the Natural Law.* Ann Arbor: Univ. of Michigan Press, 1958.

Stark, Rodney, and Roger Finke. "American Religion in 1776: A Statistical Portrait." *Sociological Analysis* 49 (1988): 39–51.

Stone, Lawrence. "Goodbye to Nearly All That." Review of *The Origins of English Individualism,* by Alan Macfarlane. *New York Review of Books,* 19 April 1979, pp. 40–41.

Storing, Herbert J. *What the Anti-Federalists Were For.* Chicago: Univ. of Chicago Press, 1981.

Stourzh, Gerald. *Alexander Hamilton and the Idea of Republican Government.* Stanford: Stanford Univ. Press, 1970.

Stout, Harry S. *The New England Soul: Preaching and Religious Culture in Colonial New England.* New York: Oxford Univ. Press, 1986.

Strauss, Leo. *Persecution and the Art of Writing.* 1952. Reprint, Westport, Conn.: Greenwood Press, 1973.

———. *Natural Right and History.* Chicago: Univ. of Chicago Press, 1953.

———. *Thoughts on Machiavelli.* Seattle: Univ. of Washington Press, 1958.

———. *What Is Political Philosophy, and Other Studies.* Glencoe, Ill.: Free Press, 1959.

Sullivan, William M. *Reconstructing Public Philosophy.* Berkeley and Los Angeles: Univ. of California Press, 1982.

Swart, Koenraad E. "'Individualism' in the Mid-Nineteenth Century (1826–1860)." *Journal of the History of Ideas* 23 (January 1962): 77–90.

Sydnor, Charles S. *American Revolutionaries in the Making: Political Practices in Washington's Virginia.* New York: Free Press, 1952.

Szatmary, David P. *Shays' Rebellion: The Making of an Agrarian Insurrection.* Amherst: Univ. of Massachusetts Press, 1980.

Tate, Allen. "Remarks on the Southern Religion." In *I'll Take My Stand: The South and the Agrarian Tradition,* pp. 155–75. 1930. Reprint, Baton Rouge: Louisiana State Univ. Press, 1983.

Tate, Thad W. "The Social Contract in America, 1774–1787: Revolutionary Theory as a Conservative Instrument." *William and Mary Quarterly* 22 (July 1965): 375–91.

Taylor, Alan. *Liberty Men and Great Proprietors: The Revolutionary Settlement on the Maine Frontier, 1760–1820.* Chapel Hill: Univ. of North Carolina Press, 1990.

Taylor, Charles. "Kant's Theory of Freedom." In *Conceptions of Liberty in Political Philosophy,* ed. Zbigniew Pelczynski and John Gray, pp. 100–122. New York: St. Martin's Press, 1984.

———. "What's Wrong with Negative Liberty." In *Philosophy and the Human Sciences: Philosophical Papers,* 2:211–29. Cambridge: Cambridge Univ. Press, 1985.

Thomas, Keith. *Religion and the Decline of Magic.* New York: Charles Scribner's Sons, 1971.

————. "Politics Recaptured." Review of *The Foundations of Modern Political Thought,* by Quentin Skinner. *New York Review of Books,* 17 May 1979, pp. 26–29.

————. "Politics as Language." Review of *Virtue, Commerce, and History,* by J. G. A. Pocock. *New York Review of Books,* 27 February 1986, pp. 36–39.

Tillson, Albert H., Jr. "The Localist Roots of Backcountry Loyalism: An Examination of Popular Political Culture in Virginia's New River Valley." *Journal of Southern History* 54 (August 1988): 387–404.

Tise, Larry E. *Proslavery: A History of the Defense of Slavery in America, 1701–1840.* Athens: Univ. of Georgia Press, 1987.

"Toward a History of the Standard of Living in British North America." *William and Mary Quarterly* 45 (January 1988): 116–70.

Towner, Lawrence W. "The Sewall-Saffin Dialogue on Slavery." *William and Mary Quarterly* 21 (January 1964): 40–52.

Tracy, Patricia J. *Jonathan Edwards, Pastor: Religion and Society in Eighteenth-Century Northampton.* New York: Hill and Wang, 1980.

Trinterud, Leonard J. *The Forming of an American Tradition: A Re-examination of Colonial Presbyterianism.* Philadelphia: Westminster Press, 1949.

————. "The New Light Snuffed Out." In *The Great Awakening: Event and Exegesis,* ed. D. B. Rutman, pp. 176–80. 1970. Reprint, Huntington, N.Y.: Krieger, 1977.

Troeltsch, Ernst. *Protestantism and Progress: A Historical Study of the Relation of Protestantism to the Modern World.* Trans. W. Montgomery. 1912. Reprint, Boston: Beacon Hill Press, 1958.

————. "Renaissance and Reformation." In *The Reformation: Material or Spiritual?* ed. L. W. Spitz, pp. 17–27. Boston: D. C. Heath, 1962.

Tucker, Susie I. *Protean Shape: A Study in Eighteenth-Century Vocabulary and Usage.* London: Univ. of London Press, 1967.

Tully, James. "Locke on Liberty." In *Conceptions of Liberty in Political Philosophy,* ed. Zbigniew Pelczynski and John Gray, pp. 57–82. New York: St. Martin's Press, 1984.

Turner, James. *Without God, without Creed: The Origins of Unbelief in America.* Baltimore: Johns Hopkins Univ. Press, 1985.

Tushnet, Mark. "The Origins of the Establishment Clause." *Georgetown Law Journal* 75 (April 1987): 1509–17.

————. "Should Historians Accept the Supreme Court's Invitation?" *Organization of American Historians Newsletter* (November 1987): 12–13.

Valeri, Mark. "The New Divinity and the American Revolution." *William and Mary Quarterly* 46 (October 1989): 741–69.

Van Tyne, Claude H. *The Loyalists in the American Revolution.* 1902. Reprint, Gloucester, Mass.: Peter Smith, 1959.

Varga, Nicholas. "The Development and Structure of Local Government in Colonial New York." In *Town and County: Essays on the Structure of Local Government in the American Colonies,* ed. Bruce C. Daniels, pp. 186–215. Middletown, Conn.: Wesleyan Univ. Press, 1978.

Vetterli, Richard, and Gary Bryner. *In Search of the Republic: Public Virtue and the Roots of American Government.* Savage, Md.: Rowman and Littlefield, 1987.

Vickers, Daniel. "Competency and Competition: Economic Culture in Early America." *William and Mary Quarterly* 47 (January 1990): 3–29.

Vickers, Daniel, James Lemon, and Bettye Hobbs Pruitt. "Communication." *William and Mary Quarterly* 42 (October 1985): 553–62.

Vitz, Paul C. "Secular Personality Theories: A Critical Analysis." In *Man and Mind: A Christian Theory of Personality,* ed. T. J. Burke, pp. 65–94. Hillsdale, Mich.: Hillsdale College Press, 1987.

Wald, Kenneth D. *Religion and Politics in the United States.* 2d ed. Washington, D.C.: Congressional Quarterly Press, 1992.

Wall, Helena M. *Fierce Communion: Family and Community in Early America.* Cambridge: Harvard Univ. Press, 1990.

Walzer, Michael. *The Revolution of the Saints: A Study in the Origins of Radical Politics.* Cambridge: Harvard Univ. Press, 1965.

———. "Liberalism and the Art of Separation." *Political Theory* 12 (August 1984): 315–30.

Ward, John William. *Red, White, and Blue: Men, Books, and Ideas in American Culture.* New York: Oxford Univ. Press, 1969.

Warren, Charles. *The Supreme Court in United States History.* Vol. 1, *1789–1821.* Boston: Little, Brown, 1922.

———. "The New 'Liberty' under the Fourteenth Amendment." *Harvard Law Review* 39 (January 1926): 431–65.

Warren, Donald I. *The Radical Center: Middle Americans and the Politics of Alienation.* Notre Dame: Univ. of Notre Dame Press, 1976.

Waterhouse, Richard. "The Responsible Gentry of Colonial South Carolina: A Study in Local Government, 1670–1770." In *Town and County: Essays on the Structure of Local Government in the American Colonies,* ed. Bruce C. Daniels, pp. 160–85. Middletown, Conn.: Wesleyan Univ. Press, 1978.

Waters, John J. "From Democracy to Demography: Recent Historiography on the New England Town." In *Perspectives on Early American History,* ed. Alden T. Vaughan and George Billias, pp. 222–49. New York: Harper and Row, 1973.

———. "The Traditional World of the New England Peasants: A View from Seventeenth-Century Barnstable." *New England Historical and Genealogical Register* 130 (January 1976): 3–21.

Watts, Steven. *The Republic Reborn: War and the Making of Liberal America, 1790–1820.* Baltimore: Johns Hopkins Univ. Press, 1987.

Weaver, Richard M. *Ideas Have Consequences.* Chicago: Univ. of Chicago Press, 1948.

Weber, Eugen. "Renaissance Real Estate." Review of *The French Peasantry, 1450–1660,* by Emmanuel Le Roy Ladurie. *New Republic,* 27 July 1987, pp. 38–41.

Weber, Max. *The Methodology of the Social Sciences.* New York: Free Press, 1949.

———. *The Protestant Ethic and the Spirit of Capitalism.* Trans. Talcott Parsons. New York: Charles Scribner's Sons, 1958.

Webking, Robert H. *The American Revolution and the Politics of Liberty.* Baton Rouge: Louisiana State Univ. Press, 1988.

Weintraub, Jeff Alan. "Virtue, Community, and the Sociology of Liberty: The Notion of Republican Virtue and Its Impact on Modern Western Social Thought." Ph.D. diss., Univ. of California at Berkeley, 1979.

West, James [Carl Withers]. *Plainville, U.S.A.* New York: Columbia Univ. Press, 1945.

Westermann, William Linn. "Between Slavery and Freedom." *American Historical Review* 50 (January 1945): 213–27.

Wheeler, Robert. "The County Court in Colonial Virginia." In *Town and County: Essays on the Structure of Local Government in the American Colonies,* ed. Bruce C. Daniels, pp. 111–33. Middletown, Conn.: Wesleyan Univ. Press, 1978.

White, Morton. *The Philosophy of the American Revolution.* New York: Oxford Univ. Press, 1978.

Whitehead, Barbara Dafoe. "Dan Quayle Was Right." *Atlantic Monthly,* April 1993, pp. 47–84.

Whitlock, Reverdy. *The Parish of Amity: A History of the First Church of Christ Woodbridge, 1738–1904.* Woodbridge, Conn.: First Church of Christ, 1982.

Wiebe, Robert H. *The Segmented Society: An Introduction to the Meaning of America.* New York: Oxford Univ. Press, 1975.

——. *The Opening of American Society: From the Adoption of the Constitution to the Eve of Disunion.* New York: Knopf, 1984.

Will, George F. *Statecraft as Soulcraft: What Government Does.* New York: Simon and Schuster, 1983.

Williamson, Chilton. "American Suffrage and Sir William Blackstone." *Political Science Quarterly* 68 (December 1953): 552–57.

Wills, Gary. *Inventing America: Jefferson's Declaration of Independence.* Garden City, N.Y.: Doubleday, 1978.

Wilson, James Q. "Is Social Science a God that Failed?" *Public Opinion* 4 (October–November 1981): 11–15.

Wilson, Major L. *Space, Time, and Freedom: The Quest for Nationality and the Irrepressible Conflict, 1815–1861.* Westport, Conn.: Greenwood Press, 1974.

Winslow, Ola E. *Meeting House Hill: 1630–1783.* 1952. Reprint, New York: W. W. Norton, 1972.

Wish, Judith Barry. "From Yeoman Farmer to Industrious Producer: The Relationship between Classical Republicanism and the Development of Manufacturing in America from the Revolution to 1850." Ph.D. diss., Washington Univ., 1976.

Wishy, Bernard. "John Locke and the Spirit of '76." *Political Science Quarterly* 73 (September 1958): 413–25.

Wolf, Stephanie Grauman. *Urban Village: Population, Community, and Family Structure in Germantown, Pennsylvania, 1683–1800.* Princeton: Princeton Univ. Press, 1976.

Wolin, Sheldon S. *Politics and Vision: Continuity and Innovation in Western Political Thought.* Boston: Little, Brown, 1960.

——. *The Presence of the Past: Essays on the State and the Constitution.* Baltimore: Johns Hopkins Univ. Press, 1989.

Wood, Gordon S. *The Creation of the American Republic, 1776–1787.* Chapel Hill: Univ. of North Carolina Press, 1969.

——. "Rhetoric and Reality in the American Revolution." In *Essays on the American Revolution,* ed. David L. Jacobson, pp. 43–66. New York: Holt, Rinehart, and Winston, 1970.

——. Introduction to *The Rising Glory of America, 1760–1820,* ed. Gordon S. Wood, pp. 1–24. New York: George Braziller, 1971.

——. "Freedom and the Constitution." In *Freedom in America,* ed. Norman A. Graebner, pp. 44–53. University Park: Pennsylvania State Univ. Press, 1977.

————. "Hellfire Politics." Review of *The Lost Soul of American Politics,* by J. P. Diggins. *New York Review of Books,* 28 February 1985, pp. 29–32.

————. "Illusions and Disillusions in the American Revolution." In *The American Revolution: Its Character and Limits,* ed. Jack P. Greene, pp. 355–61. New York: New York Univ. Press, 1987.

————. "Interests and Disinterestedness in the Making of the Constitution." In *Beyond Confederation: Origins of the Constitution and American National Identity,* ed. Richard Beeman, Stephen Botein, and Edward C. Carter II, pp. 69–109. Chapel Hill: Univ. of North Carolina Press, 1987.

————. "The Fundamentalists and the Constitution." *New York Review of Books,* 18 February 1988, pp. 33–40.

————. "The Significance of the Early Republic." *Journal of the Early Republic* 8 (Spring 1988): 1–20.

————. "The Virtues and the Interests." Review of *Republicanism and Bourgeois Radicalism,* by Isaac Kramnick. *New Republic,* 11 February 1991, pp. 32–35.

————. *The Radicalism of the American Revolution.* New York: Knopf, 1992.

Woodward, Kenneth L. "The Elite, and How to Avoid It." *Newsweek,* 20 July 1992, p. 55.

Yankelovich, Daniel. *New Rules: Searching for Self-Fulfillment in a World Turned Upside Down.* New York: Random House, 1981.

Yarbrough, J. "Republicanism Reconsidered: Some Thoughts on the Foundation and Preservation of the American Republic." *Review of Politics* 41 (January 1979): 61–95.

Yazawa, Melvin. *From Colonies to Commonwealth: Familial Ideology and the Beginnings of the American Republic.* Baltimore: Johns Hopkins Univ. Press, 1985.

Young, James Sterling. *The Washington Community: 1800–1828.* New York: Columbia Univ. Press, 1966.

Zuckerman, Michael. "The Social Context of Democracy in Massachusetts." *William and Mary Quarterly* 25 (October 1968): 523–44.

————. *Peaceable Kingdoms: New England Towns in the Eighteenth Century.* New York: Knopf, 1970.

————. "The Fabrication of Identity in Early America." *William and Mary Quarterly* 34 (April 1977): 183–214.

————. "Introduction: Puritans, Cavaliers, and the Motley Middle." In *Friends and Neighbors,* ed. Michael Zuckerman, pp. 3–25. Philadelphia: Temple Univ. Press, 1982.

Zuckert, Michael P. "Republicanism and American Identity: Thomas Jefferson's Natural Rights Republic." Paper presented at the Conference on Political Identity in American Thought, Yale University, New Haven, Conn., 19–21 April 1991.

Zvesper, John. "The American Founders and Classical Political Thought." *History of Political Thought* 10 (Winter 1989): 701–18.